I0817786

The Essential Classics

An Anthology of Greco-Roman Literature

Edited by Catherine Lecomte Lapp
Foreword by Anya Elizabeth Leonard
Introduction by Van Bryan
Commentaries translated from the French by Eric C. Lapp

Les Belles Lettres

95, Boulevard Raspail
75006 Paris

Front and back cover by Santiago Alvira

First edition 2005
Second edition 2025

ISBN 978-0-9861084-7-1

Printed in the United States of America
Contributing Editor: Ken Dantz

TABLE OF CONTENTS

INTRODUCTION

Classical Wisdom Weekly is thrilled to be working with Les Belles Lettres, the prestigious publishing house based in Paris, on the re-printing of The Essential Classics.

We initially started discussions over a year ago when Classical Wisdom Weekly first came to be. Les Belles Lettres was then, and continues to be, a source of inspiration and support for our budding project. Their extensive knowledge and resources of the classics has been irreplaceable, as well as the good work they continue to do in the preservation and translation of Ancient Greek and Latin literature. When all others have ceased the work, Les Belles Lettres remains and perseveres, the last bastion of true and critical classical translation and publication.

We have always been in awe of their work and will continue to find ways to help support and promote their mission.

For this reason, we are very excited to re-publish The Essential Classics, an extensive and beautiful collection of over 2000 years worth of classical text, thoughtfully gathered by Les Belles Lettres for the modern reader. It contains the most exciting, influential and inspiring extracts from the classics.

Alongside helpful insights into both the authors and the excerpts, you can find the original texts from Homer, the great tragedians, as well as descriptions of the battle of Marathon and the speeches of Pericles. Readers will find the most important selections from Plato, detailing the Philosopher King, the Analogy of the Cave, and Atlantis.

But that's not all. It continues through the ages with Lucretius' definition of the Atom, Virgil's poetry from the Aeneid, and Livy's origins of Rome and Hannibal crossing the Alps. Finally there is Cicero, Caesar, and Nero murdering his mother and enduring the Great fire of Rome, all concluding with Marcus Aurelius' Meditations. And this is but an abridged list of all it entails.

It can now be the perfect addition to your collection as a reference, an inspiration, or a way to spend a few minutes with something more meaningful than just, say, browsing on the net.

It is truly a beautiful, comprehensive introduction, a window to a whole world of classical education in one book; One, we hope, everyone will enjoy.

Sincerely,

Anya Leonard

Co-Founder and Project Director
Classical Wisdom Weekly
Classicalwisdom.com

Our society is founded upon the intellectual, political, and philosophical traditions of the ancient world; that from the ancient Greek and Roman cultures, our ideas of Western society took shape.

We, as readers, can indeed see further by standing on the shoulders of giants. But how to do justice to those gargantuan presences? How to properly introduce the most significant, most monumental, and the most influential texts of the Western World? When faced with a thousand years of brilliance, the overflowing collection that is The Essential Classics can appear quite intimidating.

If you have read Classical Wisdom Weekly, then you know that we are individuals who appreciate the sheer magnitude and storied grandeur of the classics, those deep and dark waters whence much of our society was crafted. We endeavor to share these illuminating texts, and no matter the difficulty, we persevere. So with hands trembling and hearts racing, we plunge into these waters; diving toward whatever depths we may uncover.

The Essential Classics is a collection of the most enlightening Greek and Latin texts written over a thousand-year period. As such, it is an anthology that can start nowhere else than with Homer and his two epics, The Iliad and The Odyssey.

These two epics are often considered, and rightfully so, the first two masterpieces of the Western World. In the time of Ancient Greece, the stories of The Iliad and The Odyssey would have been as familiar to Greek citizens as the stories of The Bible are to us now. Through Homer, men began their pursuit of knowledge and children became acquainted with the gods and heroes of legend. So it is only fitting that we begin the same way our ancient ancestors did, with this mysterious poet, Homer.

The Iliad opens on the final year of the Trojan War. The story of wrathful Achilles and noble prince Hector is intertwined with numerous themes. Among them are the pursuit of glory, the need for vengeance, the miseries of war, and the nobility of the gods.

However, as is the case with The Iliad, the excitement of warfare is often hastened by the lengthy dialogues between characters. The Odyssey, on the other hand, is a non-stop adventure. It seems to have a never ending supply of tales concerning monsters, witches, and a literal trip to hell.

From the ancient, semi-mythical settings of Homer we travel to Athens during the 5th century.

It was during this "Golden Age of Athens" that the three most accomplished Greek tragedians (Sophocles, Aeschylus, Euripides) lived and worked. These men put ink to parchment, and from this union we have such classics as Oedipus Rex, The Oresteia, and Prometheus Bound.

Through these tragedies we become acquainted with some of the most intriguing characters of ancient legend. First there is the pitiful king Oedipus, who blinds himself out of anger and sorrow when he is unable to escape his tragic fate. Then there is Orestes, a man faced with the impossible task of murdering his mother to avenge the death of his father, Agamemnon. Finally there is the first benefactor of mankind, the Titan Prometheus, who suffers eternally for the sake of human advancement.

Of course, no anthology of the ancient world would be complete without the addition of the philosophers, the men who described the immortality of the soul and revealed to us the secrets of the examined life.

We start with the writings of Plato where we unravel the ideas that he put forth on knowledge, love, politics, and the human soul. However, in a sense we get two for the price of one. Through Plato's writings, we are also lucky enough to get a glimpse at the life of Socrates, a man who was described as being "...wisest and justest and best."

Next in this line of impressive writers are the historians Herodotus and Thucydides. These men are primarily remembered for their works The Histories and The History of The Peloponnesian War respectively. And it is in no small part because of them that we appreciate the ancient struggles that gave rise to an empire and brought one of Greece's most prominent civilizations to its knees.

And from 5th century Athens, where do we go next? We whisk forward at breakneck speed to the days of the Roman Empire. Here we are met by the great orators and poets. Among their ranks are Ovid,

Cicero, Virgil, and Plutarch; each one's contribution to the development of mankind is beyond compare.

Now we are faced with a curious question. We have traveled from the early days of Homer to the height of the Athenian empire, only so that we may venture a bit further and find ourselves in the days of Ancient Rome. A ponderous notion arises. Where does it conclude? When does the ancient world end and the modern one begin?

The answer is far from simple. Did the end of the classical world coincide with the separation of the Roman Empire in 395 AD, when the empire was split between the two capitals, Rome and Constantinople? Or was it the removal of the last Western Roman emperor, Romulus Augustulus, in 476 AD that marked the end of antiquity?

These are both worthy considerations. Even if there may be no consensus on the date when the classical world ceased to be, our examination of the ancient texts must conclude eventually. After all, a book can only have so many chapters.

So The Essential Classics, perhaps arbitrarily, concludes with Marcus Aurelius and his reflective philosophical musings on the purpose of life and the meaning of happiness, The Meditations.

The emperor wrote this journal of sorts as he neared the end of his life, most assuredly never intending it to be published. He simply wrote for the sake of introspection and self-improvement, as a man might do as he reaches the autumn of his days. Nevertheless, it is through the preservation of The Meditations that Marcus Aurelius enjoys his sparkling legacy as the man who came closest to the realization of Plato's "Philosopher King."

So there we have a brief synopsis of the contents of this sprawling anthology. We began in the age of Homer, a time when the realms of gods and men blurred and became hopelessly entangled. We briefly stopped in 5th century Athens, a period that gave rise to philosophy, democracy, and theater. From there we saw the days of Ancient Rome, a time when one of the greatest empires in history rose to prominence.

But why should we care? Why does any of this matter? Could we not abandon the classics and still live happily? That is the question that we at Classical Wisdom Weekly hear most often. And we always answer it the same way.

The pursuit of knowledge cannot, must not, be a cursory interest. It must not be something we just do on the side, or whenever we finish watching television. The pursuit of knowledge is a quest, one that leads us to the ends of the earth and back. Along the way there may be obstacles, treacherous terrain, but we press on. We must.

The brilliance and the accomplishments of the individuals described within this book are beyond compare. They are the giants upon whose shoulders we stand as we look toward new horizons. It is from their thoughts, their writings, and their deeds that our society has grown. It is from them that we have come to be the way we are today. While the men themselves have long been dead and buried, we pursue their knowledge with steeled determination.

For those of you who eagerly await such an endeavor, we wish you the best of luck as you push on. You hold the essential collection of the most important texts of the classical world. You need only turn the page.

Very Sincerely,

Van Bryan

Associate Editor
Classical Wisdom Weekly
Classicalwisdom.com

EDITOR'S NOTE

The spelling of the ancient names occurring in the commentaries may vary from that in the Greek and Latin texts. This diversity can be explained by the fact that the texts were translated by classicists educated in different scholarly traditions (i.e., American English versus British English; Greek "k" transcribed as "k" or "c").

The works of each ancient author are organized in the following manner: the passage's subject heading (e.g., "Defeat at Salamis"); the ancient author, the title of his work, and the book, paragraph or lines (e.g., "Aeschylus, The Persians 140¬514"); an introduction to the passage (e.g., "It is 480 BC and the Second Persian War rages."); the characters (e.g., "Atossa, widow of Darius and mother of Xerxes."); a brief quotation from the text (e.g., "Atossa: Yet one more word-— say, in what realm do the Athenians dwell? Chorus: Far hence, even where, in evening land, goes down our Lord the Sun."); and the select text. The quotation is included to provide the reader a flavor as to the idea, style, tone, and content of the following text.

Map Of The Mediterranean

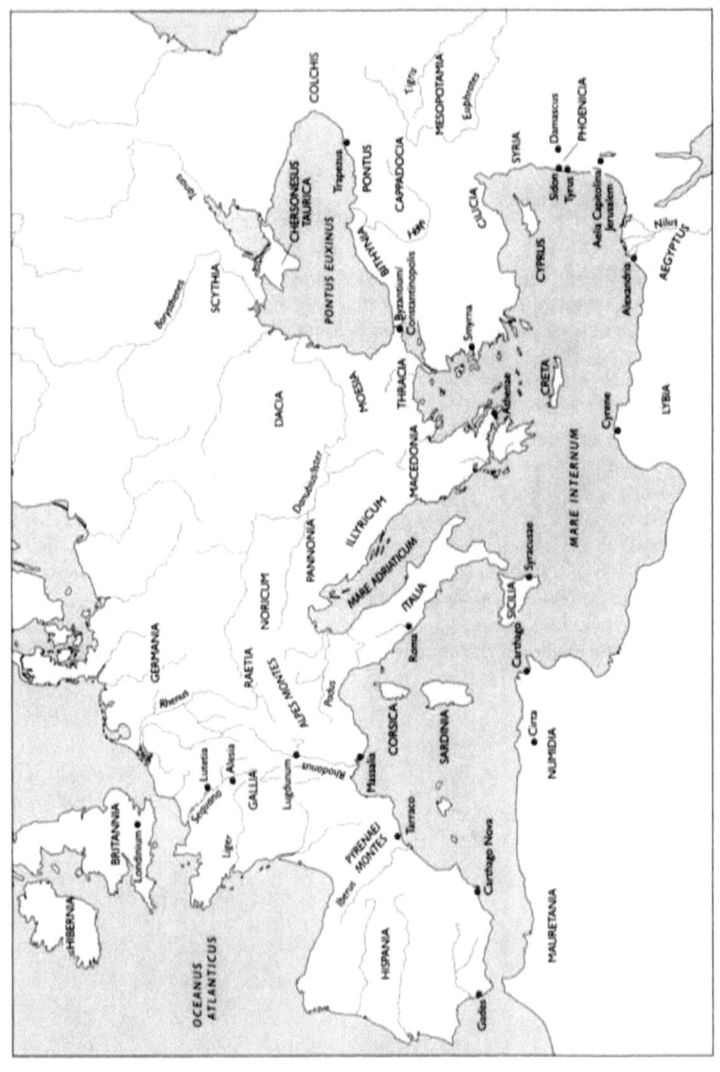

Map Of Greece and The Aegean

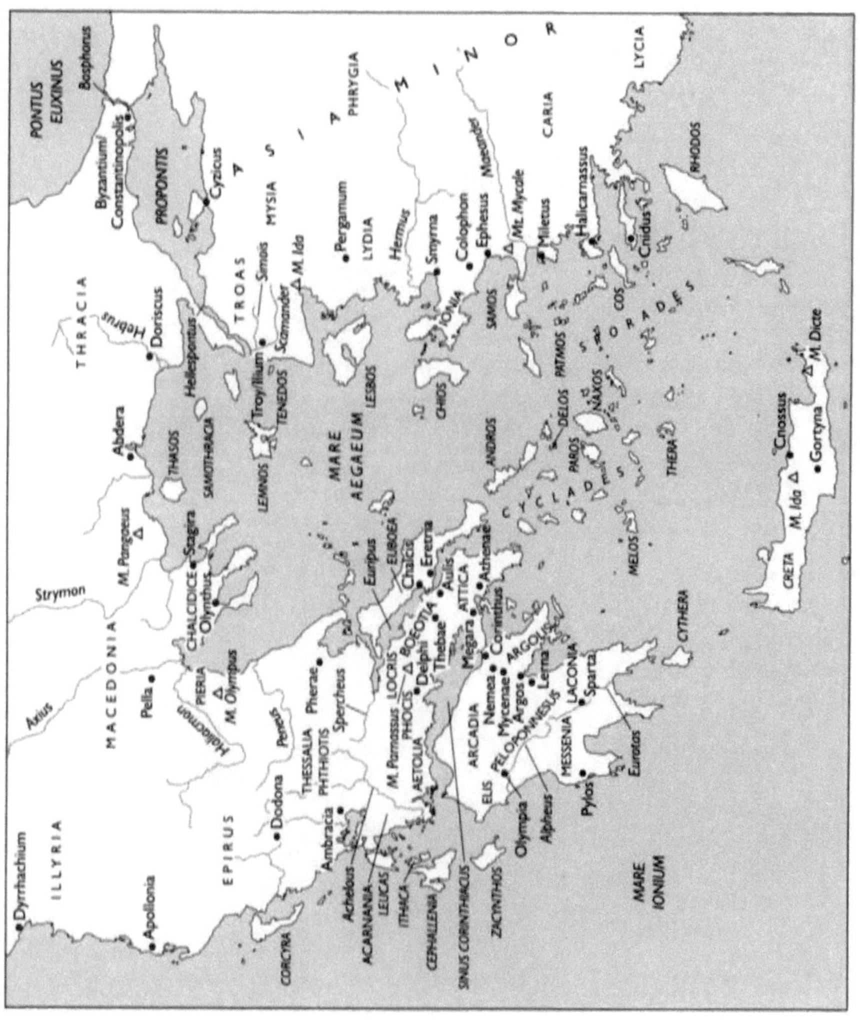

Map Of Italy

ALPES MONTES
GALLIA CISALPINA
Mediolanum
Cremona
Padus
Parma
Verona
Patavium
Mantua
Aquileia
APENNINUS MONS
Felsina/
Bononia
Ravenna
Rubico
Ariminum
Pisaurum
Ancona
ILLYRICUM
Pisae
Arnus
Florentia
Arretium
ETRURIA
PICENUM
UMBRIA
Asculum
MARE
ADRIATICUM
CORSICA
Tiberis
Tarquinii
Corfinium
Sulmo
Roma
Tibur
Praeneste
Arpinum
Ostia
Lavinium
Tusculum
Venafrum
Cannae
APULIA
LATIUM
Tarracina
Beneventum
Capua
Brundisium
CAMPANIA
Cumae
Pompeii
Capreae
Misenum
Neapolis
LUCANIA
Tarentum
Poseidonia/
Paestum
SARDINIA
Thurii
Sybaris
MARE
TYRRHENUM
Croton
BRUTTIUM
Messana
Rhegium
M. Aetna
SICILIA
Acragas/Agrigentum
Gela
Syracusae
Utica
Carthago
AFRICA

HOMER

Eighth century BC

The Iliad *and the* Odyssey *date from the middle of the eighth century BC and are considered the oldest works of Western literature. Almost nothing is known about the author except that he lived on the Aegean coast of modern Turkey and his name was Homer (which could be a nickname). Similar to their ancient counterparts, modern scholars continue to struggle with controversial issues regarding the poet, such as his actual existence, his name, and the period in which he composed his epics.*

In the courts of the aristocrats, the bards sung the epic verses that recount the exploits of the heroes of times past. The Iliad *consists of an impressive 16,000 verses and the* Odyssey *of more than 12,000. The* Iliad *is a poem about war and also a drama about the tragedy of Achilles, who, not to fail the heroic ideal, ultimately sacrifices his life. The* Odyssey *is a travel tale and a marvelous fable that sings about the wanderings of Ulysses and the endurance of a man.*

Since earliest antiquity, Homer's immense epics have been praised. Generations of fervent readers and scholars have treasured them. The ancient world regarded the Homeric poems as the founding text and source of all culture.

Achilles' Anger. Patroclus' Death. Making of Achilles' Shield.

Homer, *Iliad* 18

It is the last year of the Trojan War. The Greeks (also known as the "Achaeans") battle the Trojans. Achilles secludes himself in his tent, having refused to fight ever since Agamemnon abducted his concubine Briseis. This represents a heavy loss for the Greek army, because Achilles is its most valiant warrior. As the situation for the Greeks worsens, Achilles allows his best friend, Patroclus, to suit up with his very own helmet, breastplate, and shield. The strategy is to trick the Trojans into believing that Achilles has returned to fight and thereby to strike fear into their hearts. Patroclus fights valiantly but ultimately falls under the sword of the Trojan Hector. With reluctance, a messenger approaches Achilles and informs him of the tragic news.

"Jove does not give all men their heart's desire."

Thus then did they fight as it were a flaming fire. Meanwhile the fleet runner Antilochus, who had been sent as messenger, reached Achilles, and found him sitting by his tall ships and boding that which was indeed too surely true. "Alas," said he to himself in the heaviness of his heart, "why are the Achaeans again scouring the plain and flocking towards the ships? Heaven grant the gods be not now bringing that sorrow upon me of which my mother Thetis spoke, saying that while I was yet alive the bravest of the Myrmidons[1] should fall before the Trojans, and see the light of the sun no longer. I fear the brave son of Menoetius has fallen through his own daring and yet I bade him return to the ships as soon as he had driven back those that were bringing fire against them, and not join battle with Hector."

As he was thus pondering, the son of Nestor came up to him and told his sad tale, weeping bitterly the while. "Alas," he cried, "son of noble Peleus, I bring you bad tidings, would indeed that they were untrue. Patroclus has fallen, and a fight is raging about his naked body—for Hector holds his armour."

A dark cloud of grief fell upon Achilles as he listened. He filled both hands with dust from off the ground, and poured it over his head, disfiguring his comely face, and letting the refuse settle over his shirt so fair and new. He flung himself down all huge and hugely at full length, and tore his hair with his hands. The bondswomen whom Achilles and Patroclus had taken captive screamed aloud for grief, beating their breasts, and with their limbs failing them for sorrow. Antilochus bent over him the while, weeping and holding both his hands as he lay groaning for he feared that he might plunge a knife into his own throat. Then Achilles gave a loud cry and his mother heard him as she was sitting in the depths of the sea by the old man her father, whereon she screamed, and all the goddesses daughters of Nereus that dwelt at the bottom of the sea, came gathering round her. There were Glauce, Thalia and Cymodoce, Nesaia, Speo, Thoe and dark-eyed Halie, Cymothoe, Actaea and Limnorea, Melite, Iaera, Amphithoe and Agave, Doto and Proto, Pherusa and Dynamene, Dexamene, Amphinome and Callianeira, Doris, Panope, and the famous sea-nymph Galatea, Nemertes, Apseudes and Callianassa. There were also Clymene, Ianeira and Ianassa, Maera, Oreithuia and Amatheia of the lovely locks, with other Nereids who dwell in the depths of the sea. The crystal cave was filled with their multitude and they all beat their breasts while Thetis led them in their lament.

"Listen," she cried, "sisters, daughters of Nereus, that you may hear the burden of my sorrows. Alas, woe is me, woe in that I have borne the most glorious of offspring. I bore him fair and strong, hero among heroes, and he shot up as a sapling; I tended him as a plant in a goodly garden, and sent him with his ships to Ilius to fight the Trojans, but never shall I welcome him back to the house of Peleus. So long as he lives to look upon the light of the sun he is in heaviness, and though I go to him I cannot help him. Nevertheless I will go, that I may see my dear son and learn what sorrow has befallen him though he is still holding aloof from battle."

She left the cave as she spoke, while the others followed weeping after, and the waves opened a path before them. When they reached the rich plain of Troy, they came up out of the sea in a long line on to the sands, at the place where the ships of the Myrmidons were drawn up in close order round the tents of Achilles. His mother went up to him as he lay groaning; she laid her hand upon his head and spoke piteously, saying, "My son, why are you thus weeping? What sorrow has now befallen you? Tell me; hide it not from me. Surely Jove has granted you the prayer you made him, when you lifted up your hands and besought him that the Achaeans might all of them be pent up at their ships, and rue it bitterly in that you were no longer with them."

Achilles groaned and answered, "Mother, Olympian Jove has indeed vouchsafed me the fulfilment of my prayer, but what boots it to me, seeing that my dear comrade Patroclus has fallen—he whom I valued more than all others, and loved as dearly as my own life? I have lost him; aye, and Hector when he had killed him stripped the wondrous armour, so glorious to behold, which the gods gave to Peleus when they laid you in the couch of a mortal man. Would that you were still dwelling among the immortal sea-nymphs, and that Peleus had taken to himself some mortal bride. For now you shall have grief infinite by reason of the death of that son whom you can never welcome home—nay, I will not live nor go about among mankind unless Hector fall by my spear, and thus pay me for having slain Patroclus son of Menoetius."

Thetis wept and answered, "Then, my son, is your end near at hand—for your own death awaits you full soon after that of Hector."

Then said Achilles in his great grief, "I would die here and now, in that I could not save my comrade. He has fallen far from home, and in his hour of need my hand was not there to help him. What is there for me? Return to my own land I shall not, and I have brought no saving neither to Patroclus nor to my other comrades of whom so many have been slain by mighty Hector; I stay here by my ships a bootless burden upon the earth, I, who in fight have no peer among the Achaeans, though in council there are better than I. Therefore, perish strife both from among gods and men, and anger, wherein even a righteous man will harden his heart—which rises up in the soul of a man like smoke, and the taste thereof is sweeter than drops of honey. Even so has Agamemnon angered me. And yet—so be it, for it is over; I will force my soul into subjection as I needs must; I will go; I will pursue Hector who has slain him whom I loved so dearly, and will then abide my doom when it may please Jove and the other gods to send it. Even Hercules, the best beloved of Jove—even he could not escape the hand of death, but fate and Juno's fierce anger laid him low, as I too shall lie when I am dead if a like doom awaits me. Till then I will win fame, and will bid Trojan and Dardanian women wring tears from their tender cheeks with both their hands in the grievousness of their great sorrow; thus shall they know that he who has held aloof so long will hold aloof no longer. Hold me not back, therefore, in the love you bear me, for you shall not move me."

Then silver-footed Thetis answered, "My son, what you have said is true. It is well to save your comrades from destruction, but your armour is in the hands of the Trojans; Hector bears it in triumph upon his own shoulders. Full well I know that his vaunt shall not be lasting, for his end is close at hand; go not, however, into the press of battle till you see me return hither; to-morrow at break of day I shall be here, and will bring you goodly armour from King Vulcan."

On this she left her brave son, and as she turned away she said to the sea-nymphs her sisters, "Dive into the bosom of the sea and go to the house of the old sea-god my father. Tell him everything; as for me, I will go to the cunning workman Vulcan on high Olympus, and ask him to provide my son with a suit of splendid armour."

When she had so said, they dived forthwith beneath the waves, while silver-footed

Thetis went her way that she might bring the armour for her son.

Thus, then, did her feet bear the goddess to Olympus, and meanwhile the Achaeans were flying with loud cries before murderous Hector till they reached the ships and the Hellespont, and they could not draw the body of Mars's servant Patroclus out of reach of the weapons that were showered upon him, for Hector son of Priam with his host and horsemen had again caught up to him like the flame of a fiery furnace; thrice did brave Hector seize him by the feet, striving with might and main to draw him away and calling loudly on the Trojans, and thrice did the two Ajaxes, clothed in valour as with a garment, beat him from off the body; but all undaunted he would now charge into the thick of the fight, and now again he would stand still and cry aloud, but he would give no ground. As upland shepherds that cannot chase some famished lion from a carcase, even so could not the two Ajaxes scare Hector son of Priam from the body of Patroclus.

And now he would even have dragged it off and have won imperishable glory, had not Iris fleet as the wind, winged her way as messenger from Olympus to the son of Peleus and bidden him arm. She came secretly without the knowledge of Jove and of the other gods, for Juno sent her, and when she had got close to him she said, "Up, son of Peleus, mightiest of all mankind; rescue Patroclus about whom this fearful fight is now raging by the ships. Men are killing one another, the Danaans in defence of the dead body, while the Trojans are trying to hale it away, and take it to windy Ilius: Hector is the most furious of them all; he is for cutting the head from the body and fixing it on the stakes of the wall. Up, then, and bide here no longer; shrink from the thought that Patroclus may become meat for the dogs of Troy. Shame on you, should his body suffer any kind of outrage."

And Achilles said, "Iris, which of the gods was it that sent you to me?"

Iris answered, "It was Juno the royal spouse of Jove, but the son of Saturn does not know of my coming, nor yet does any other of the immortals who dwell on the snowy summits of Olympus."

Then fleet Achilles answered her saying, "How can I go up into the battle? They have my armour. My mother forbade me to arm till I should see her come, for she promised to bring me goodly armour from Vulcan; I know no man whose arms I can put on, save only the shield of Ajax son of Telamon, and he surely must be fighting in the front rank and wielding his spear about the body of dead Patroclus."

Iris said, "We know that your armour has been taken, but go as you are; go to the deep trench and show yourself before the Trojans, that they may fear you and cease fighting. Thus will the fainting sons of the Achaeans gain some brief breathing-time, which in battle may hardly be."

Iris left him when she had so spoken. But Achilles dear to Jove arose, and Minerva flung her tasselled aegis round his strong shoulders; she crowned his head with a halo of golden cloud from which she kindled a glow of gleaming fire. As the smoke that goes up into heaven from some city that is being beleaguered on an island far out at sea—all day long do men sally from the city and fight their hardest, and at the going down of the sun the line of beacon-fires blazes forth, flaring high for those that dwell near them to behold, if so be that they may come with their ships and succour them—even so did the light flare from the head of Achilles, as he stood by the trench, going beyond the wall—but he aid not join the Achaeans for he heeded the charge which his mother laid upon him.

There did he stand and shout aloud. Minerva also raised her voice from afar, and spread terror unspeakable among the Trojans. Ringing as the note of a trumpet that sounds alarm then the foe is at the gates of a city, even so brazen was the voice of the son of Aeacus, and when the Trojans heard its clarion tones they were dismayed; the horses turned back with their chariots for they boded mischief, and their drivers were awe-struck by the steady flame which the grey-eyed goddess had kindled above the head of the great son of Peleus.

Thrice did Achilles raise his loud cry as he stood by the trench, and thrice were the Trojans and their brave allies thrown into confusion; whereon twelve of their noblest champions fell beneath the wheels of their chariots and perished by their own spears. The Achaeans to their great joy then drew Patroclus out of reach of the weapons, and laid him on a litter: his comrades stood mourning round him, and among them fleet Achilles who wept bitterly as he saw his true comrade lying dead upon his bier. He had sent him out with horses and chariots into battle, but his return he was not to welcome.

Then Juno sent the busy sun, loth though he was, into the waters of Oceanus; so he set, and the Achaeans had rest from the tug and turmoil of war.

Now the Trojans when they had come out of the fight, unyoked their horses and gathered in assembly before preparing their supper. They kept their feet, nor would any dare to sit down, for fear had fallen upon them all because Achilles had shown himself after having held aloof so long from battle. Polydamas son of Panthous was first to speak, a man of judgement, who alone among them could look both before and after. He was comrade to Hector, and they had been born upon the same night; with all sincerity and goodwill, therefore, he addressed them thus:

"Look to it well, my friends; I would urge you to go back now to your city and not wait here by the ships till morning, for we are far from our walls. So long as this man was at enmity with Agamemnon the Achaeans were easier to deal with, and I would have gladly camped by the ships in the hope of taking them; but now I go in great fear of the fleet son of Peleus; he is so daring that he will never bide here on the plain whereon the Trojans and Achaeans fight with equal valour, but he will try to storm our city and carry off our women. Do then as I say, and let us retreat. For this is what will happen. The darkness of night will for a time stay the son of Peleus, but if he find us here in the morning when he sallies forth in full armour, we shall have knowledge of him in good earnest. Glad indeed will he be who can escape and get back to Ilius, and many a Trojan will become meat for dogs and vultures may I never live to hear it. If we do as I say, little though we may like it, we shall have strength in counsel during the night, and the great gates with the doors that close them will protect the city. At dawn we can arm and take our stand on the walls; he will then rue it if he sallies from the ships to fight us. He will go back when he has given his horses their fill of being driven all whithers under our walls, and will be in no mind to try and force his way into the city. Neither will he ever sack it, dogs shall devour him ere he do so."

Hector looked fiercely at him and answered, "Polydamas, your words are not to my liking in that you bid us go back and be pent within the city. Have you not had enough of being cooped up behind walls? In the old-days the city of Priam was famous the whole world over for its wealth of gold and bronze, but our treasures are wasted out of our houses, and much goods have been sold away to Phrygia and fair Meonia, for the hand of Jove has been laid heavily upon us. Now, therefore, that the son of scheming Saturn has vouchsafed me to win glory here and to hem the Achaeans in at their ships, prate no more in this fool's wise among the people. You will have no man with you; it shall not be; do all of you as I now say;—take your suppers in your companies throughout the host, and keep your watches and be wakeful every man of you. If any Trojan is uneasy about his possessions, let him gather them and give them out among the people. Better let these, rather than the Achaeans, have them. At daybreak we will arm and fight about the ships; granted that Achilles has again come forward to defend them, let it be as he will, but it shall go hard with him. I shall not shun him, but will fight him, to fall or conquer. The god of war deals out like measure to all, and the slayer may yet be slain."

Thus spoke Hector; and the Trojans, fools that they were, shouted in applause, for Pallas Minerva had robbed them of their understanding. They gave ear to Hector with his evil counsel, but the wise words of Polydamas no man would heed. They took their supper throughout the host, and meanwhile through the whole night the Achaeans mourned Patroclus, and the son of Peleus led them in their lament. He laid his murderous hands upon the breast of his comrade, groaning again and again as a bearded lion when a man who was chasing deer has robbed him of his young in some dense forest; when the lion comes back he is furious, and searches dingle and dell to track the hunter if he can find him, for he is mad with rage—even so with many a sigh did Achilles speak among the Myrmidons saying, "Alas! vain were the words with which I cheered the hero Menoetius in his own house; I said that I would bring his brave son back again to Opoeis after he had sacked Ilius and taken his share of the spoils—but Jove does not give all men their heart's desire. The same soil shall be reddened here at Troy by the blood of us both, for I too shall never be welcomed home by the old knight Peleus, nor by my mother Thetis, but even in this place shall the earth cover me. Nevertheless, O Patroclus, now that I am left behind you, I will not bury you, till I have brought hither the head and armour of mighty Hector who has slain you. Twelve noble sons of Trojans will I behead before your bier to avenge you; till I have done so you shall lie as you are by the ships, and fair women of Troy and Dardanus, whom we have taken with spear and strength of arm when we sacked men's goodly cities, shall weep over you both night and day."

Then Achilles told his men to set a large tripod upon the fire that they might wash the clotted gore from off Patroclus. Thereon they set a tripod full of bath water on to a clear fire: they threw sticks on to it to make it blaze, and the water became hot as the flame played about the belly of the tripod. When the water in the cauldron was boiling they washed the body, anointed it with oil, and closed its wounds with ointment that had been kept nine years. Then they laid it on a bier and covered it with a linen cloth from head to foot, and over this they laid a fair white robe. Thus all night long did the Myrmidons gather round Achilles to mourn Patroclus.

Then Jove said to Juno his sister-wife, "So, Queen Juno, you have gained your end, and have roused fleet Achilles. One would think that the Achaeans were of your own flesh and blood."

And Juno answered, "Dread son of Saturn, why should you say this thing? May not a man though he be only mortal and knows less than we do, do what he can for another person? And shall not I—foremost of all goddesses both by descent and as wife to you who reign in heaven—devise evil for the Trojans if I am angry with them?"

Thus did they converse. Meanwhile Thetis came to the house of Vulcan, imperishable, star-bespangled, fairest of the abodes in heaven, a house of bronze wrought by the lame god's own hands. She found him busy with his bellows, sweating and hard at work, for he was making twenty tripods that were to stand by the wall of his house, and he set wheels of gold under them all that they might go of their own selves to the assemblies of the gods, and come back again—marvels indeed to see. They were finished all but the ears of cunning workmanship which yet remained to be fixed to them: these he was now fixing, and he was hammering at the rivets. While he was thus at work silver-footed Thetis came to the house. Charis, of graceful head-dress, wife to the far-famed lame god, came towards her as soon as she saw her, and took her hand in her own, saying, "Why have you come to our house, Thetis, honoured and ever welcome—for you do not visit us often? Come inside and let me set refreshment before you."

The goddess led the way as she spoke, and bade Thetis sit on a richly decorated seat inlaid with silver; there was a footstool also under her feet. Then she called Vulcan and said, "Vulcan, come here, Thetis wants you"; and the far-famed lame god answered, "Then it is indeed an august and honoured goddess who has come here; she it was that took care of me when I was suffering from the heavy fall which I had through my cruel mother's anger—for she would have got rid of me because I was lame. It would have gone hardly with me had not Eurynome, daughter of the ever-encircling waters of Oceanus, and Thetis, taken me to their bosom. Nine years did I stay with them, and many beautiful works in bronze, brooches, spiral armlets, cups, and chains, did I make for them in their cave, with the roaring waters of Oceanus foaming as they rushed ever past it; and no one knew, neither of gods nor men, save only Thetis and Eurynome who took care of me. If, then, Thetis has come to my house I must make her due requital for having saved me; entertain her, therefore, with all hospitality, while I put by my bellows and all my tools."

On this the mighty monster hobbled off from his anvil, his thin legs plying lustily under him. He set the bellows away from the fire, and gathered his tools into a silver chest. Then he took a sponge and washed his face and hands, his shaggy chest and brawny neck; he donned his shirt, grasped his strong staff, and limped towards the door. There were golden handmaids also who worked for him, and were like real young women, with sense and reason, voice also and strength, and all the learning of the immortals; these busied themselves as the king bade them, while he drew near to Thetis, seated her upon a goodly seat, and took her hand in his own, saying, "Why have you come to our house, Thetis honoured and ever welcome—for you do not visit us often? Say what you want, and I will do it for you at once if I can, and if it can be done at all."

Thetis wept and answered, "Vulcan, is there another goddess in Olympus whom the son of Saturn has been pleased to try with so much affliction as he has me? Me alone of the marine goddesses did he make subject to a mortal husband, Peleus son of Aeacus, and sorely against my will did I submit to the embraces of one who was but mortal, and who now stays at home worn out with age. Neither is this all.

Heaven vouchsafed me a son, hero among heroes, and he shot up as a sapling. I tended him as a plant in a goodly garden and sent him with his ships to Ilius to fight the Trojans, but never shall I welcome him back to the house of Peleus. So long as he lives to look upon the light of the sun, he is in heaviness, and though I go to him I cannot help him; King Agamemnon has made him give up the maiden whom the sons of the Achaeans had awarded him, and he wastes with sorrow for her sake. Then the Trojans hemmed the Achaeans in at their ships' sterns and would not let them come forth; the elders, therefore, of the Argives besought Achilles and offered him great treasure, whereon he refused to bring deliverance to them himself, but put his own armour on Patroclus and sent him into the fight with much people after him. All day long they fought by the Scaean gates and would have taken the city there and then, had not Apollo vouchsafed glory to Hector and slain the valiant son of Menoetius after he had done the Trojans much evil. Therefore I am suppliant at your knees if haply you may be pleased to provide my son, whose end is near at hand, with helmet and shield, with goodly greaves fitted with ancle-clasps, and with a breastplate, for he lost his own when his true comrade fell at the hands of the Trojans, and he now lies stretched on earth in the bitterness of his soul."

And Vulcan answered, "Take heart, and be no more disquieted about this matter; would that I could hide him from death's sight when his hour is come, so surely as I can find him armour that shall amaze the eyes of all who behold it."

When he had so said he left her and went to his bellows, turning them towards the fire and bidding them do their office. Twenty bellows blew upon the melting-pots, and they blew blasts of every kind, some fierce to help him when he had need of them, and others less strong as Vulcan willed it in the course of his work. He threw tough copper into the fire, and tin, with silver and gold; he set his great anvil on its block, and with one hand grasped his mighty hammer while he took the tongs in the other.

First he shaped the shield so great and strong, adorning it all over and binding it round with a gleaming circuit in three layers; and the baldric was made of silver. He made the shield in five thicknesses, and with many a wonder did his cunning hand enrich it.

He wrought the earth, the heavens, and the sea; the moon also at her full and the untiring sun, with all the signs that glorify the face of heaven—the Pleiads, the Hyads, huge Orion, and the Bear, which men also call the Wain and which turns round ever in one place, facing Orion, and alone never dips into the stream of Oceanus.

He wrought also two cities, fair to see and busy with the hum of men. In the one were weddings and wedding-feasts, and they were going about the city with brides whom they were escorting by torchlight from their chambers. Loud rose the cry of Hymen, and the youths danced to the music of flute and lyre, while the women stood each at her house door to see them.

Meanwhile the people were gathered in assembly, for there was a quarrel, and two men were wrangling about the blood-money for a man who had been killed, the one saying before the people that he had paid damages in full, and the other that he had not been paid. Each was trying to make his own case good, and the people took sides, each man backing the side that he had taken; but the heralds kept them back, and the elders sate on their seats of stone in a solemn circle, holding the staves which the heralds had put into their hands. Then they rose and each in his turn gave judgement, and there were two talents laid down, to be given to him whose judgement should be deemed the fairest.

About the other city there lay encamped two hosts in gleaming armour, and they were divided whether to sack it, or to spare it and accept the half of what it contained. But the men of the city would not yet consent, and armed themselves for a surprise; their wives and little children kept guard upon the walls, and with them were the men who were past fighting through age; but the others sallied forth with Mars and Pallas Minerva at their head—both of them wrought in gold and clad in golden raiment, great and fair with their armour as befitting gods, while they that followed were smaller. When they reached the place where they would lay their ambush, it was on a riverbed to which live stock of all kinds would come from far and near to water; here, then, they lay concealed, clad in full armour. Some way off them there were two scouts who were on the look-out for the coming of sheep or cattle, which presently came, followed by two shepherds who were playing on their pipes, and had not so much as a thought of danger. When those who were in ambush saw this, they cut off the flocks and herds and killed the shepherds. Meanwhile the besiegers, when they heard much noise among the cattle as they sat in council, sprang to their horses, and made with all speed towards them; when they reached them they set battle in array by the banks of the river, and the hosts aimed their bronze-shod spears at one another. With them were Strife and Riot, and fell Fate who was dragging three men after her, one with a fresh wound, and the other unwounded, while the third was dead, and she was dragging him along by his heel: and her robe was bedrabbled in men's blood. They went in and out with one another and fought as though they were living people haling away one another's dead.

He wrought also a fair fallow field, large and thrice ploughed already. Many men were working at the plough within it, turning their oxen to and fro, furrow after furrow. Each time that they turned on reaching the headland a man would come up to them and give them a cup of wine, and they would go back to their furrows looking forward to the time when they should again reach the headland. The part that they had ploughed was dark behind them, so that the field, though it was of gold, still looked as if it were being ploughed—very curious to behold.

He wrought also a field of harvest corn, and the reapers were reaping with sharp sickles in their hands. Swathe after swathe fell to the ground in a straight line behind them, and the binders bound them in bands of twisted straw. There were three binders, and behind them there were boys who gathered the cut corn in armfuls and kept on bringing them to be bound: among them all the owner of the land stood by in silence and was glad. The servants were getting a meal ready under an oak, for they had sacrificed a great ox, and were busy cutting him up, while the women were making a porridge of much white barley for the labourers' dinner.

He wrought also a vineyard, golden and fair to see, and the vines were loaded with grapes. The bunches overhead were black, but the vines were trained on poles of silver. He ran a ditch of dark metal all round it, and fenced it with a fence of tin; there was only one path to it, and by this the vintagers went when they would gather the vintage. Youths and maidens all blithe and full of glee, carried the luscious fruit in plaited baskets; and with them there went a boy who made sweet music with his lyre, and sang the Linos-song with his clear boyish voice.

He wrought also a herd of horned cattle. He made the cows of gold and tin, and they lowed as they came full speed out of the yards to go and feed among the waving reeds that grow by the banks of the river. Along with the cattle there went four shepherds, all of them in gold, and their nine fleet dogs went with them. Two terrible lions had fastened on a bellowing bull that was with the foremost cows, and bellow as he might they haled him, while the dogs and men gave chase: the lions tore through the bull's thick hide and were gorging on his blood and bowels, but the herdsmen were afraid to do anything, and only hounded on their dogs; the dogs dared not fasten on the lions but stood by barking and keeping out of harm's way.

The god wrought also a pasture in a fair mountain dell, and a large flock of sheep, with a homestead and huts, and sheltered sheepfolds.

Furthermore he wrought a green, like that which Daedalus once made in Cnossus for lovely Ariadne. Hereon there danced youths and maidens whom all would woo, with their hands on one another's wrists. The maidens wore robes of light linen, and the youths well woven shirts that were slightly oiled. The girls were crowned with garlands, while the young men had daggers of gold that hung by silver baldrics;

sometimes they would dance deftly in a ring with merry twinkling feet, as it were a potter sitting at his work and making trial of his wheel to see whether it will run, and sometimes they would go all in line with one another, and much people was gathered joyously about the green. There was a bard also to sing to them and play his lyre, while two tumblers went about performing in the midst of them when the man struck up with his tune.

All round the outermost rim of the shield he set the mighty stream of the river Oceanus.

Then when he had fashioned the shield so great and strong, he made a breastplate also that shone brighter than fire. He made a helmet, close fitting to the brow, and richly worked, with a golden plume overhanging it; and he made greaves also of beaten tin.

Lastly, when the famed lame god had made all the armour, he took it and set it before the mother of Achilles; whereon she darted like a falcon from the snowy summits of Olympus and bore away the gleaming armour from the house of Vulcan.

Translated by Samuel Butler.

The Cyclopes

Homer, *Odyssey* 9.1-560

After spending many years on the island of the goddess Calypso, Ulysses journeys to the land of a mythical people called the Phaeacians. Their king, Alcinous, welcomes him with great hospitality and requests his bard, Demodocus, to entertain the guests by singing the feats of the Trojan War. Ulysses cries with emotion, for it was he who had envisioned the horse idea that enabled the Greeks to conquer the Trojans, and he who had wandered miserably from sea to sea for the past ten years trying to return to his beloved homeland, the island of Ithaca. Alcinous orders his bard to stop his chant. He asks Ulysses to introduce himself and to explain why he was so overcome with emotion during the recitation. Ulysses recounts his adventures with the Cicones, the Lotus-eaters, and the Cyclopes.

"We Cyclopes do not care about Jove or any of your blessed gods, for we are ever so much stronger than they."

And Ulysses answered, "King Alcinous, it is a good thing to hear a bard with such a divine voice as this man has. There is nothing better or more delightful than when a whole people make merry together, with the guests sitting orderly to listen, while the table is loaded with bread and meats, and the cup-bearer draws wine and fills his cup for every man. This is indeed as fair a sight as a man can see. Now, however, since you are inclined to ask the story of my sorrows, and rekindle my own sad memories in respect of them, I do not know how to begin, nor yet how to continue and conclude my tale, for the hand of heaven has been laid heavily upon me.

"Firstly, then, I will tell you my name that you too may know it, and one day, if I outlive this time of sorrow, may become my guests though I live so far away from all of you. I am Ulysses son of Laertes, renowned among mankind for all manner of subtlety, so that my fame ascends to heaven. I live in Ithaca, where there is a high mountain called Neritum, covered with forests; and not far from it there is a group of islands very near to one another-Dulichium, Same, and the wooded island of Zacynthus. It lies squat on the horizon, all highest up in the sea towards the sunset, while the others lie away from it towards dawn. It is a rugged island, but it breeds brave men, and my eyes know none that they better love to look upon. The goddess Calypso kept me with her in her cave, and wanted me to marry her, as did also the cunning Aeaean goddess Circe; but they could neither of them persuade me, for there is nothing dearer to a man than his own country and his parents, and however splendid a home he may have in a foreign country, if it be far from father or mother, he does not care about it. Now, however, I will tell you of the many hazardous adventures which by Jove's will I met with on my return from Troy.

"When I had set sail thence the wind took me first to Ismarus, which is the city of the Cicons. There I sacked the town and put the people to the sword. We took their wives and also much booty, which we divided equitably amongst us, so that none might have reason to complain. I then said that we had better make off at once, but my men very foolishly would not obey me, so they staid there drinking much wine and killing great numbers of sheep and oxen on the sea shore. Meanwhile the Cicons cried out for help to other Cicons who lived inland. These were more in number, and stronger, and they were more skilled in the art of war, for they could fight, either from chariots or on foot as the occasion served; in the morning, therefore, they came as thick as leaves and bloom in summer, and the hand of heaven was against us, so that we were hard pressed. They set the battle in array near the ships, and the hosts aimed their bronze-shod spears at one another. So long as the day waxed and it was still morning, we held our own against them, though they were more in number than we; but as the sun went down, towards the time when men loose their oxen, the Cicons got the better of us, and we lost half a dozen men from every ship we had; so we got away with those that were left.

"Thence we sailed onward with sorrow in our hearts, but glad to have escaped death though we had lost our comrades, nor did we leave till we had thrice invoked each one of the poor fellows who had perished by the hands of the Cicons. Then Jove raised the North wind against us till it blew a hurricane, so that land and sky were hidden in thick clouds, and night sprang forth out of the heavens. We let the ships run before the gale, but the force of the wind tore our sails to tatters, so we took them down for fear of shipwreck, and rowed our hardest towards the land. There we lay two days and two nights suffering much alike from toil and distress of mind, but on the morning of the third day we again raised our masts, set sail, and took our places, letting the wind and steersmen direct our ship. I should have got home at that time unharmed had not the North wind and the currents been against me as I was doubling Cape Malea, and set me off my course hard by the island of Cythera.

"I was driven thence by foul winds for a space of nine days upon the sea, but on the tenth day we reached the land of the Lotus-eaters, who live on a food that comes from a kind of flower. Here we landed to take in fresh water, and our crews got their mid-day meal on the shore near the ships. When they had eaten and drunk I sent two of my company to see what manner of men the people of the place might be, and they had a third man under them. They started at once, and went about among the

Lotus-eaters, who did them no hurt, but gave them to eat of the lotus, which was so delicious that those who ate of it left off caring about home, and did not even want to go back and say what had happened to them, but were for staying and munching lotus with the Lotus-eaters without thinking further of their return; nevertheless, though they wept bitterly I forced them back to the ships and made them fast under the benches. Then I told the rest to go on board at once, lest any of them should taste of the lotus and leave off wanting to get home, so they took their places and smote the grey sea with their oars.

"We sailed hence, always in much distress, till we came to the land of the lawless and inhuman Cyclopes. Now the Cyclopes neither plant nor plough, but trust in providence, and live on such wheat, barley, and grapes as grow wild without any kind of tillage, and their wild grapes yield them wine as the sun and the rain may grow them. They have no laws nor assemblies of the people, but live in caves on the tops of high mountains; each is lord and master in his family, and they take no account of their neighbours.

"Now off their harbour there lies a wooded and fertile island not quite close to the land of the Cyclopes, but still not far. It is over-run with wild goats, that breed there in great numbers and are never disturbed by foot of man; for sportsmen—who as a rule will suffer so much hardship in forest or among mountain precipices—do not go there, nor yet again is it ever ploughed or fed down, but it lies a wilderness untilled and unsown from year to year, and has no living thing upon it but only goats. For the Cyclopes have no ships, nor yet shipwrights who could make ships for them; they cannot therefore go from city to city, or sail over the sea to one another's country as people who have ships can do; if they had had these they would have colonised the island, for it is a very good one, and would yield everything in due season. There are meadows that in some places come right down to the sea shore, well watered and full of luscious grass; grapes would do there excellently; there is level land for ploughing, and it would always yield heavily at harvest time, for the soil is deep. There is a good harbour where no cables are wanted, nor yet anchors, nor need a ship be moored, but all one has to do is to beach one's vessel and stay there till the wind becomes fair for putting out to sea again. At the head of the harbour there is a spring of clear water coming out of a cave, and there are poplars growing all round it.

"Here we entered, but so dark was the night that some god must have brought us in, for there was nothing whatever to be seen. A thick mist hung all round our ships; the moon was hidden behind a mass of clouds so that no one could have seen the island if he had looked for it, nor were there any breakers to tell us we were close in shore before we found ourselves upon the land itself; when, however, we had beached the ships, we took down the sails, went ashore and camped upon the beach till daybreak.

"When the child of morning, rosy-fingered Dawn appeared, we admired the island and wandered all over it, while the nymphs Jove's daughters roused the wild goats that we might get some meat for our dinner. On this we fetched our spears and bows and arrows from the ships, and dividing ourselves into three bands began to shoot the goats. Heaven sent us excellent sport; I had twelve ships with me, and each ship got nine goats, while my own ship had ten; thus through the livelong day to the going down of the sun we ate and drank our fill, and we had plenty of wine left, for each one of us had taken many jars full when we sacked the city of the Cicons, and this had not yet run out. While we were feasting we kept turning our eyes towards the land of the Cyclopes, which was hard by, and saw the smoke of their stubble fires. We could almost fancy we heard their voices and the bleating of their sheep and goats, but when the sun went down and it came on dark, we camped down upon the beach, and next morning I called a council.

"'Stay here, my brave fellows,' said I, 'all the rest of you, while I go with my ship and exploit these people myself: I want to see if they are uncivilised savages, or a hospitable and humane race.'

"I went on board, bidding my men to do so also and loose the hawsers; so they took their places and smote the grey sea with their oars. When we got to the land, which was not far, there, on the face of a cliff near the sea, we saw a great cave overhung with laurels. It was a station for a great many sheep and goats, and outside there was a large yard, with a high wall round it made of stones built into the ground and of trees both pine and oak. This was the abode of a huge monster who was then away from home shepherding his flocks. He would have nothing to do with other people, but led the life of an outlaw. He was a horrid creature, not like a human being at all, but resembling rather some crag that stands out boldly against the sky on the top of a high mountain.

"I told my men to draw the ship ashore, and stay where they were, all but the twelve best among them, who were to go along with myself. I also took a goatskin of sweet black wine which had been given me by Maron, son of Euanthes, who was priest of Apollo the patron god of Ismarus, and lived within the wooded precincts of the temple. When we were sacking the city we respected him, and spared his life, as also his wife and child; so he made me some presents of great value—seven talents of fine gold,[2] and a bowl of silver, with twelve jars of sweet wine, unblended, and of the most exquisite flavour. Not a man nor maid in the house knew about it, but only himself, his wife, and one housekeeper: when he drank it he mixed twenty parts of water to one of wine, and yet the fragrance from the mixing-bowl was so exquisite that it was impossible to refrain from drinking. I filled a large skin with this wine, and took a wallet full of provisions with me, for my mind misgave me that I might have to deal with some savage who would be of great strength, and would respect neither right nor law.

"We soon reached his cave, but he was out shepherding, so we went inside and took stock of all that we could see. His cheese-racks were loaded with cheeses, and he had more lambs and kids than his pens could hold. They were kept in separate flocks; first there were the hoggets, then the oldest of the younger lambs and lastly the very young ones all kept apart from one another; as for his dairy, all the vessels, bowls, and milk pails into which he milked, were swimming with whey. When they saw all this, my men begged me to let them first steal some cheeses, and make off with them to the ship; they would then return, drive down the lambs and kids, put them on board and sail away with them. It would have been indeed better if we had done so but I would not listen to them, for I wanted to see the owner himself, in the hope that he might give me a present. When, however, we saw him my poor men found him ill to deal with.

"We lit a fire, offered some of the cheeses in sacrifice, ate others of them, and then sat waiting till the Cyclops should come in with his sheep. When he came, he brought in with him a huge load of dry firewood to light the fire for his supper, and this he flung with such a noise on to the floor of his cave that we hid ourselves for fear at the far end of the cavern. Meanwhile he drove all the ewes inside, as well as the she-goats that he was going to milk, leaving the males, both rams and he-goats, outside in the yards. Then he rolled a huge stone to the mouth of the cave—so huge that two and twenty strong four-wheeled waggons would not be enough to draw it from its place against the doorway. When he had so done he sat down and milked his ewes and goats, all in due course, and then let each of them have her own young. He curdled half the milk and set it aside in wicker strainers, but the other half he poured into bowls that he might drink it for his supper. When he had got through with all his work, he lit the fire, and then caught sight of us, whereon he said:

"'Strangers, who are you? Where do sail from? Are you traders, or do you sail the sea as rovers, with your hands against every man, and every man's hand against you?'

"We were frightened out of our senses by his loud voice and monstrous form, but I managed to say, 'We are Achaeans on our way home from Troy, but by the will of Jove, and stress of weather, we have been driven far out of our course. We are the people of Agamemnon, son of Atreus, who has won infinite renown throughout the whole world, by sacking so great a city and killing so many people. We therefore humbly pray you to show us some hospitality, and otherwise make us such presents as visitors may reasonably expect. May your excellency fear the wrath of heaven, for we are your suppliants, and Jove takes all respectable travellers under his protection, for he is the avenger of all suppliants and foreigners in distress.'

"To this he gave me but a pitiless answer, 'Stranger,' said he, 'you are a fool, or else you know nothing of this country. Talk to me, indeed, about fearing the gods or shunning their anger? We Cyclopes do not care about Jove or any of your blessed gods, for we are ever so much stronger than they. I shall not spare either yourself or your companions out of any regard for Jove, unless I am in the humour for doing so. And now tell me where you made your ship fast when you came on shore. Was it round the point, or is she lying straight off the land?'

"He said this to draw me out, but I was too cunning to be caught in that way, so I answered with a lie; 'Neptune,' said I, 'sent my ship on to the rocks at the far end of your country, and wrecked it. We were driven on to them from the open sea, but I and those who are with me escaped the jaws of death.'

"The cruel wretch vouchsafed me not one word of answer, but with a sudden clutch he gripped up two of my men at once and dashed them down upon the ground as though they had been puppies. Their brains were shed upon the ground, and the earth was wet with their blood. Then he tore them limb from limb and supped upon them. He gobbled them up like a lion in the wilderness, flesh, bones, marrow, and entrails, without leaving anything uneaten. As for us, we wept and lifted up our hands to heaven on seeing such a horrid sight, for we did not know what else to do; but when the Cyclops had filled his huge paunch, and had washed down his meal of human flesh with a drink of neat milk, he stretched himself full length upon the ground among his sheep, and went to sleep. I was at first inclined to seize my sword, draw it, and drive it into his vitals, but I reflected that if I did we should all certainly be lost, for we should never be able to shift the stone which the monster had put in front of the door. So we stayed sobbing and sighing where we were till morning came.

"When the child of morning, rosy-fingered dawn, appeared, he again lit his fire, milked his goats and ewes, all quite rightly, and then let each have her own young one; as soon as he had got through with all his work, he clutched up two more of my men, and began eating them for his morning's meal. Presently, with the utmost ease, he rolled the stone away from the door and drove out his sheep, but he at once put it back again—as easily as though he were merely clapping the lid on to a quiver full of arrows. As soon as he had done so he shouted, and cried 'Shoo, shoo,' after his sheep to drive them on to the mountain; so I was left to scheme some way of taking my revenge and covering myself with glory.

"In the end I deemed it would be the best plan to do as follows: The Cyclops had a great club which was lying near one of the sheep pens; it was of green olive wood, and he had cut it intending to use it for a staff as soon as it should be dry. It was so huge that we could only compare it to the mast of a twenty-oared merchant vessel of large burden, and able to venture out into open sea. I went up to this club and cut off about six feet of it; I then gave this piece to the men and told them to fine it evenly off at one end, which they proceeded to do, and lastly I brought it to a point myself, charring the end in the fire to make it harder. When I had done this I hid it under dung, which was lying about all over the cave, and told the men to cast lots which of them should venture along with myself to lift it and bore it into the monster's eye while he was asleep. The lot fell upon the very four whom I should have chosen, and I myself made five. In the evening the wretch came back from shepherding, and drove his flocks into the cave—this time driving them all inside, and not leaving any in the yards; I suppose some fancy must have taken him, or a god must have prompted him to do so. As soon as he had put the stone back to its place against the door, he sat down, milked his ewes and his goats all quite rightly, and then let each have her own young one; when he had got through with all this work, he gripped up two more of my men, and made his supper off them. So I went up to him with an ivy-wood bowl of black wine in my hands:

"'Look here, Cyclops,' said I, you have been eating a great deal of man's flesh, so take this and drink some wine, that you may see what kind of liquor we had on board my ship. I was bringing it to you as a drink-offering, in the hope that you would take compassion upon me and further me on my way home, whereas all you do is to go on ramping and raving most intolerably. You ought to be ashamed of yourself; how can you expect people to come see you any more if you treat them in this way?'

"He then took the cup and drank. He was so delighted with the taste of the wine that he begged me for another bowl full. 'Be so kind,' he said, 'as to give me some more, and tell me your name at once. I want to make you a present that you will be glad to have. We have wine even in this country, for our soil grows grapes and the sun ripens them, but this drinks like Nectar and Ambrosia all in one.'

"I then gave him some more; three times did I fill the bowl for him, and three times did he drain it without thought or heed; then, when I saw that the wine had got into his head, I said to him as plausibly as I could: 'Cyclops, you ask my name and I will tell it you; give me, therefore, the present you promised me; my name is

Noman; this is what my father and mother and my friends have always called me.'

"But the cruel wretch said, 'Then I will eat all Noman's comrades before Noman himself, and will keep Noman for the last. This is the present that I will make him.'

"As he spoke he reeled, and fell sprawling face upwards on the ground. His great neck hung heavily backwards and a deep sleep took hold upon him. Presently he turned sick, and threw up both wine and the gobbets of human flesh on which he had been gorging, for he was very drunk. Then I thrust the beam of wood far into the embers to heat it, and encouraged my men lest any of them should turn faint-hearted. When the wood, green though it was, was about to blaze, I drew it out of the fire glowing with heat, and my men gathered round me, for heaven had filled their hearts with courage. We drove the sharp end of the beam into the monster's eye, and bearing upon it with all my weight I kept turning it round and round as though I were boring a hole in a ship's plank with an auger, which two men with a wheel and strap can keep on turning as long as they choose. Even thus did we bore the red hot beam into his eye, till the boiling blood bubbled all over it as we worked it round and round, so that the steam from the burning eyeball scalded his eyelids and eyebrows, and the roots of the eye sputtered in the fire. As a blacksmith plunges an axe or hatchet into cold water to temper it—for it is this that gives strength to the iron—and it makes a great hiss as he does so, even thus did the Cyclops' eye hiss round the beam of olive wood, and his hideous yells made the cave ring again. We ran away in a fright, but he plucked the beam all besmirched with gore from his eye, and hurled it from him in a frenzy of rage and pain, shouting as he did so to the other Cyclopes who lived on the bleak headlands near him; so they gathered from all quarters round his cave when they heard him crying, and asked what was the matter with him.

"'What ails you, Polyphemus,' said they, 'that you make such a noise, breaking the stillness of the night, and preventing us from being able to sleep? Surely no man is carrying off your sheep? Surely no man is trying to kill you either by fraud or by force?'

"But Polyphemus shouted to them from inside the cave, 'Noman is killing me by fraud; no man is killing me by force.'

"'Then,' said they, 'if no man is attacking you, you must be ill; when Jove makes people ill, there is no help for it, and you had better pray to your father Neptune.'

"Then they went away, and I laughed inwardly at the success of my clever stratagem, but the Cyclops, groaning and in an agony of pain, felt about with his hands till he found the stone and took it from the door; then he sat in the doorway and stretched his hands in front of it to catch anyone going out with the sheep, for he thought I might be foolish enough to attempt this.

"As for myself I kept on puzzling to think how I could best save my own life and those of my companions; I schemed and schemed, as one who knows that his life depends upon it, for the danger was very great. In the end I deemed that this plan would be the best; the male sheep were well grown, and carried a heavy black fleece, so I bound them noiselessly in threes together, with some of the withies on which the wicked monster used to sleep. There was to be a man under the middle sheep, and the two on either side were to cover him, so that there were three sheep to each man. As for myself there was a ram finer than any of the others, so I caught hold of him by the back, esconced myself in the thick wool under his belly, and hung on patiently to his fleece, face upwards, keeping a firm hold on it all the time.

"Thus, then, did we wait in great fear of mind till morning came, but when the child of morning, rosy-fingered Dawn, appeared, the male sheep hurried out to feed, while the ewes remained bleating about the pens waiting to be milked, for their udders were full to bursting; but their master in spite of all his pain felt the backs of all the sheep as they stood upright, without being sharp enough to find out that the men were underneath their bellies. As the ram was going out, last of all, heavy with its fleece and with the weight of my crafty self, Polyphemus laid hold of it and said:

"'My good ram, what is it that makes you the last to leave my cave this morning? You are not wont to let the ewes go before you, but lead the mob with a run whether to flowery mead or bubbling fountain, and are the first to come home again at night; but now you lag last of all. Is it because you know your master has lost his eye, and are sorry because that wicked Noman and his horrid crew has got him down in his drink and blinded him? But I will have his life yet. If you could understand and talk, you would tell me where the wretch is hiding, and I would dash his brains upon the ground till they flew all over the cave. I should thus have some satisfaction for the harm this no-good Noman has done me.'

"As he spoke he drove the ram outside, but when we were a little way out from the cave and yards, I first got from under the ram's belly, and then freed my comrades; as for the sheep, which were very fat, by constantly heading them in the right direction we managed to drive them down to the ship. The crew rejoiced greatly at seeing those of us who had escaped death, but wept for the others whom the Cyclops had killed. However, I made signs to them by nodding and frowning that they were to hush their crying, and told them to get all the sheep on board at once and put out to sea; so they went aboard, took their places, and smote the grey sea with their oars. Then, when I had got as far out as my voice would reach, I began to jeer at the Cyclops.

"'Cyclops,' said I, 'you should have taken better measure of your man before eating up his comrades in your cave. You wretch, eat up your visitors in your own house? You might have known that your sin would find you out, and now Jove and the other gods have punished you.'

"He got more and more furious as he heard me, so he tore the top from off a high mountain, and flung it just in front of my ship so that it was within a little of hitting the end of the rudder. The sea quaked as the rock fell into it, and the wash of the wave it raised carried us back towards the mainland, and forced us towards the shore. But I snatched up a long pole and kept the ship off, making signs to my men by nodding my head, that they must row for their lives, whereon they laid out with a will. When we had got twice as far as we were before, I was for jeering at the Cyclops again, but the men begged and prayed of me to hold my tongue.

"'Do not,' they exclaimed, 'be mad enough to provoke this savage creature further; he has thrown one rock at us already which drove us back again to the mainland, and we made sure it had been the death of us; if he had then heard any further sound of voices he would have pounded our heads and our ship's timbers into a jelly with the rugged rocks he would have heaved at us, for he can throw them a long way.'

"But I would not listen to them, and shouted out to him in my rage, 'Cyclops, if any one asks you who it was that put your eye out and spoiled your beauty, say it was the valiant warrior Ulysses, son of Laertes, who lives in Ithaca.'

"On this he groaned, and cried out, 'Alas, alas, then the old prophecy about me is coming true. There was a prophet here, at one time, a man both brave and of great stature, Telemus son of Eurymus, who was an excellent seer, and did all the prophesying for the Cyclopes till he grew old; he told me that all this would happen to me some day, and said I should lose my sight by the hand of Ulysses. I have been all along expecting some one of imposing presence and superhuman strength, whereas he turns out to be a little insignificant weakling, who has managed to blind my eye by taking advantage of me in my drink; come here, then, Ulysses, that I may make you presents to show my hospitality, and urge Neptune to help you forward on your journey—for Neptune and I are father and son. He, if he so will, shall heal me, which no one else neither god nor man can do.'

"Then I said, 'I wish I could be as sure of killing you outright and sending you down to the house of Hades, as I am that it will take more than Neptune to cure that eye of yours.'

"On this he lifted up his hands to the firmament of heaven and prayed, saying, 'Hear me, great Neptune; if I am indeed your own true begotten son, grant that Ulysses may never reach his home alive; or if he must get back to his friends at last, let him do so late and in sore plight after losing all his men, let him reach his home in another man's ship and find trouble in his house.'

"Thus did he pray, and Neptune heard his prayer. Then he picked up a rock much larger than the first, swung it aloft and hurled it with prodigious force. It fell just short of the ship, but was within a little of hitting the end of the rudder. The sea quaked as the rock fell into it, and the wash of the wave it raised drove us onwards on our way towards the shore of the island.

"When at last we got to the island where we had left the rest of our ships, we found our comrades lamenting us, and anxiously awaiting our return. We ran our vessel upon the sands and got out of her on to the sea shore; we also landed the Cyclops' sheep, and divided them equitably amongst us so that none might have reason to complain. As for the ram, my companions agreed that I should have it as an extra share; so I sacrificed it on the sea shore, and burned its thigh bones to Jove, who is the lord of all. But he heeded not my sacrifice, and only thought how he might destroy both my ships and my comrades.

"Thus through the livelong day to the going down of the sun we feasted our fill on meat and drink, but when the sun went down and it came on dark, we camped upon the beach. When the child of morning rosy-fingered Dawn appeared, I bade my men on board and loose the hawsers. Then they took their places and smote the grey sea with their oars; so we sailed on with sorrow in our hearts, but glad to have escaped death though we had lost our comrades.

Translated by Samuel Butler.

Revenge of Ulysses. Trial of the Bow.

Homer, *Odyssey* 21

Ulysses finally arrives at Ithaca after ten years of fighting in Troy followed by ten more at sea. Only four people know that he has returned: his son, Telemachus; his elderly nanny, Eurykleia; and his loyal servants, Eumaeus and Philoetius. Since his departure to Troy, the nobles of Ithaca callously moved into his palace, drank and dined at his expense each day all day, and, worst of all, unabashedly courted his faithful wife, Penelope. She eventually promises to marry the suitor who succeeds in drawing Ulysses' bow and shooting an arrow through a line of axes planted in the ground. Disguised as a beggar, Ulysses stands in a corner of the palace's grand courtyard, watches the suitors' escapades, and prepares his vengeance.

"But Ulysses, when he had taken up the bow and examined it all over, strung it as easily as a skilled bard strings a new peg of his lyre and makes the twisted gut fast at both ends. Then he took it in his right hand to prove the string, and it sang sweetly under his touch like the twittering of a swallow. The suitors were dismayed, and turned colour as they heard it; at that moment, moreover, Jove thundered loudly as a sign, and the heart of Ulysses rejoiced as he heard the omen that the son of scheming Saturn had sent him."

Minerva now put it in Penelope's mind to make the suitors try their skill with the bow and with the iron axes, in contest among themselves, as a means of bringing about their destruction. She went upstairs and got the store-room key, which was made of bronze and had a handle of ivory; she then went with her maidens into the store-room at the end of the house, where her husband's treasures of gold, bronze, and wrought iron were kept, and where was also his bow, and the quiver full of deadly arrows that had been given him by a friend whom he had met in Lacedaemon—Iphitus the son of Eurytus. The two fell in with one another in Messene at the house of Ortilochus, where Ulysses was staying in order to recover a debt that was owing from the whole people; for the Messenians had carried off three hundred sheep from Ithaca, and had sailed away with them and with their shepherds. In quest of these Ulysses took a long journey while still quite young, for his father and the other chieftains sent him on a mission to recover them. Iphitus had gone there also to try and get back twelve brood mares that he had lost, and the mule foals that were running with them. These mares were the death of him in the end, for when he went to the house of Jove's son, mighty Hercules, who performed such prodigies of valour, Hercules to his shame killed him, though he was his guest, for he feared not heaven's vengeance, nor yet respected his own table which he had set before Iphitus, but killed him in spite of everything, and kept the mares himself. It was when claiming these that Iphitus met Ulysses, and gave him the bow which mighty Eurytus had been used to carry, and which on his death had been left by him to his son. Ulysses gave him in return a sword and a spear, and this was the beginning of a fast friendship, although they never visited at one another's houses, for Jove's son Hercules killed Iphitus ere they could do so. This bow, then, given him by Iphitus, had not been taken with him by Ulysses when he sailed for Troy; he had used it so long as he had been at home, but had left it behind as having been a keepsake from a valued friend.

Penelope presently reached the oak threshold of the store-room; the carpenter had planed this duly, and had drawn a line on it so as to get it quite straight; he had then set the door posts into it and hung the doors. She loosed the strap from the handle of the door, put in the key, and drove it straight home to shoot back the bolts that held the doors; these flew open with a noise like a bull bellowing in a meadow, and Penelope stepped upon the raised platform, where the chests stood in which the fair linen and clothes were laid by along with fragrant herbs: reaching thence, she took down the bow with its bow case from the peg on which it hung. She sat down with it on her knees, weeping bitterly as she took the bow out of its case, and when her tears had relieved her, she went to the cloister where the suitors were, carrying the bow and the quiver, with the many deadly arrows that were inside it. Along with her came her maidens, bearing a chest that contained much iron and bronze which her husband had won as prizes. When she reached the suitors, she stood by one of the bearing-posts supporting the roof of the cloister, holding a veil before her face, and with a maid on either side of her. Then she said:

"Listen to me you suitors, who persist in abusing the hospitality of this house because its owner has been long absent, and without other pretext than that you want to marry me; this, then, being the prize that you are contending for, I will bring out the mighty bow of Ulysses, and whomsoever of you shall string it most easily and send his arrow through each one of twelve axes, him will I follow and quit this house of my lawful husband, so goodly, and so abounding in wealth. But even so I doubt not that I shall remember it in my dreams."

As she spoke, she told Eumaeus to set the bow and the pieces of iron before the suitors, and Eumaeus wept as he took them to do as she had bidden him. Hard by, the stockman wept also when he saw his master's bow, but Antinous scolded them. "You country louts," said he, "silly simpletons; why should you add to the sorrows of your mistress by crying in this way? She has enough to grieve her in the loss of her husband; sit still, therefore, and eat your dinners in silence, or go outside if you want to cry, and leave the bow behind you. We suitors shall have to contend for it with might and main, for we shall find it no light matter to string such a bow as this is. There is not a man of us all who is such another as Ulysses; for I have seen him and remember him, though I was then only a child."

This was what he said, but all the time he was expecting to be able to string the bow and shoot through the iron, whereas in fact he was to be the first that should taste of the arrows from the hands of Ulysses, whom he was dishonouring in his own house—egging the others on to do so also.

Then Telemachus spoke. "Great heavens!" he exclaimed, "Jove must have robbed me of my senses. Here is my dear and excellent mother saying she will quit this house and marry again, yet I am laughing and enjoying myself as though there were nothing happening. But, suitors, as the contest has been agreed upon, let it go forward. It is for a woman whose peer is not to be found in Pylos, Argos, or Mycene, nor yet in Ithaca nor on the mainland. You know this as well as I do; what need have I to speak in praise of my mother? Come on, then, make no excuses for delay, but let us see whether you can string the bow or no. I too will make trial of it, for if I can string it and shoot through the iron, I shall not suffer my mother to quit this house with a stranger, not if I can win the prizes which my father won before me."

As he spoke he sprang from his seat, threw his crimson cloak from him, and took his sword from his shoulder. First he set the axes in a row, in a long groove which he had dug for them, and had made straight by line. Then he stamped the earth tight round them, and everyone was surprised when they saw him set them up so orderly, though he had never seen anything of the kind before. This done, he went on to the pavement to make trial of the bow; thrice did he tug at it, trying with all his might to draw the string, and thrice he had to leave off, though he had hoped to string the bow and shoot through the iron. He was trying for the fourth time, and would have strung it had not Ulysses made a sign to check him in spite of all his eagerness. So he said:

"Alas! I shall either be always feeble and of no prowess, or I am too young, and have not yet reached my full strength so as to be able to hold my own if any one attacks me. You others, therefore, who are stronger than I, make trial of the bow and get this contest settled."

On this he put the bow down, letting it lean against the door that led into the house with the arrow standing against the top of the bow. Then he sat down on the seat from which he had risen, and Antinous said:

"Come on each of you in his turn, going towards the right from the place at which the cupbearer begins when he is handing round the wine."

The rest agreed, and Leiodes son of Oenops was the first to rise. He was sacrificial priest to the suitors, and sat in the corner near the mixing-bowl. He was the only man who hated their evil deeds and was indignant with the others. He was now the first to take the bow and arrow, so he went on to the pavement to make his trial, but he could not string the bow, for his hands were weak and unused to hard work, they therefore soon grew tired, and he said to the suitors, "My friends, I cannot string it; let another have it, this bow shall take the life and soul out of many a chief among us, for it is better to die than to live after having missed the prize that we have so long striven for, and which has brought us so long together. Some one of us is even now hoping and praying that he may marry Penelope, but when he has seen this bow and tried it, let him woo and make bridal offerings to some other woman, and let Penelope marry whoever makes her the best offer and whose lot it is to win her."

On this he put the bow down, letting it lean against the door, with the arrow standing against the tip of the bow. Then he took his seat again on the seat from which he had risen; and Antinous rebuked him saying:

"Leiodes, what are you talking about? Your words are monstrous and intolerable; it makes me angry to listen to you. Shall, then, this bow take the life of many a chief among us, merely because you cannot bend it yourself? True, you were not born to be an archer, but there are others who will soon string it."

Then he said to Melanthius the goatherd, "Look sharp, light a fire in the court, and set a seat hard by with a sheep skin on it; bring us also a large ball of lard, from what they have in the house. Let us warm the bow and grease it—we will then make trial of it again, and bring the contest to an end."

Melanthius lit the fire, and set a seat covered with sheep skins beside it. He also brought a great ball of lard from what they had in the house, and the suitors warmed the bow and again made trial of it, but they were none of them nearly strong enough to string it. Nevertheless there still remained Antinous and Eurymachus, who were the ringleaders among the suitors and much the foremost among them all.

Then the swineherd and the stockman left the cloisters together, and Ulysses followed them. When they had got outside the gates and the outer yard, Ulysses said to them quietly:

"Stockman, and you swineherd, I have something in my mind which I am in doubt whether to say or no; but I think I will say it. What manner of men would you be to stand by Ulysses, if some god should bring him back here all of a sudden? Say which you are disposed to do—to side with the suitors, or with Ulysses?"

"Father Jove," answered the stockman, "would indeed that you might so ordain it. If some god were but to bring Ulysses back, you should see with what might and main I would fight for him."

In like words Eumaeus prayed to all the gods that Ulysses might return; when, therefore, he saw for certain what mind they were of, Ulysses said, "It is I, Ulysses, who am here. I have suffered much, but at last, in the twentieth year, I am come back to my own country. I find that you two alone of all my servants are glad that I should do so, for I have not heard any of the others praying for my return. To you two, therefore, will I unfold the truth as it shall be. If heaven shall deliver the suitors into my hands, I will find wives for both of you, will give you house and holding close to my own, and you shall be to me as though you were brothers and friends of Telemachus. I will now give you convincing proofs that you may know me and be assured. See, here is the scar from the boar's tooth that ripped me when I was out hunting on Mt. Parnassus with the sons of Autolycus."

As he spoke he drew his rags aside from the great scar, and when they had examined it thoroughly, they both of them wept about Ulysses, threw their arms round him, and kissed his head and shoulders, while Ulysses kissed their hands and faces in return. The sun would have gone down upon their mourning if Ulysses had not checked them and said:

"Cease your weeping, lest some one should come outside and see us, and tell those who are within. When you go in, do so separately, not both together; I will go first, and do you follow afterwards; let this moreover be the token between us; the suitors will all of them try to prevent me from getting hold of the bow and quiver; do you, therefore, Eumaeus, place it in my hands when you are carrying it about, and tell the women to close the doors of their apartment. If they hear any groaning or uproar as of men fighting about the house, they must not come out; they must keep quiet, and stay where they are at their work. And I charge you, Philoetius, to make fast the doors of the outer court, and to bind them securely at once."

When he had thus spoken, he went back to the house and took the seat that he had left. Presently, his two servants followed him inside.

At this moment the bow was in the hands of Eurymachus, who was warming it by the fire, but even so he could not string it, and he was greatly grieved. He heaved a deep sigh and said, "I grieve for myself and for us all; I grieve that I shall have to forgo the marriage, but I do not care nearly so much about this, for there are plenty of other women in Ithaca and elsewhere; what I feel most is the fact of our being so inferior to Ulysses in strength that we cannot string his bow. This will disgrace us in the eyes of those who are yet unborn."

"It shall not be so, Eurymachus," said Antinous, "and you know it yourself. Today is the feast of Apollo throughout all the land; who can string a bow on such a day as this? Put it on one side—as for the axes they can stay where they are, for no one is likely to come to the house and take them away: let the cupbearer go round with his cups, that we may make our drink-offerings and drop this matter of the bow; we will tell Melanthius to bring us in some goats tomorrow—the best he has; we can then offer thigh bones to Apollo the mighty archer, and again make trial of the bow, so as to bring the contest to an end."

The rest approved his words, and thereon men servants poured water over the hands of the guests, while pages filled the mixing-bowls with wine and water and handed it round after giving every man his drink-offering. Then, when they had made their offerings and had drunk each as much as he desired, Ulysses craftily said:

"Suitors of the illustrious queen, listen that I may speak even as I am minded. I appeal more especially to Eurymachus, and to Antinous who has just spoken with so much reason. Cease shooting for the present and leave the matter to the gods, but in the morning let heaven give victory to whom it will. For the moment, however, give me the bow that I may prove the power of my hands among you all, and see whether I still have as much strength as I used to have, or whether travel and neglect have made an end of it."

This made them all very angry, for they feared he might string the bow, Antinous therefore rebuked him fiercely saying, "Wretched creature, you have not so much as a grain of sense in your whole body; you ought to think yourself lucky in being allowed to dine unharmed among your betters, without having any smaller portion served you than we others have had, and in being allowed to hear our conversation. No other beggar or stranger has been allowed to hear what we say among ourselves; the wine must have been doing you a mischief, as it does with all those who drink immoderately. It was wine that inflamed the Centaur Eurytion when he was staying with Peirithous among the Lapithae. When the wine had got into his head, he went mad and did ill deeds about the house of Peirithous; this angered the heroes who were there assembled, so they rushed at him and cut off his ears and nostrils; then they dragged him through the doorway out of the house, so he went away crazed, and bore the burden of his crime, bereft of understanding. Henceforth, therefore, there was war between mankind and the centaurs, but he brought it upon himself through his own drunkenness. In like manner I can tell you that it will go hardly with you if you string the bow: you will find no mercy from any one here, for we shall at once ship you off to king Echetus, who kills every one that comes near him:[3] you will never get away alive, so drink and keep quiet without getting into a quarrel with men younger than yourself." Penelope then spoke to him. "Antinous," said she, "it is not right that you should ill-treat any guest of Telemachus who comes to this house. If the stranger should prove strong enough to string the mighty bow of Ulysses, can you suppose that he would take me home with him and make me his wife? Even the man himself can have no such idea in his mind: none of you need let that disturb his feasting; it would be out of all reason."

"Queen Penelope," answered Eurymachus, "we do not suppose that this man will take you away with him; it is impossible; but we are afraid lest some of the baser sort, men or women among the Achaeans, should go gossiping about and say, 'These suitors are a feeble folk; they are paying court to the wife of a brave man whose bow not one of them was able to string, and yet a beggarly tramp who came to the house strung it at once and sent an arrow through the iron.' This is what will be said, and it will be a scandal against us."

"Eurymachus," Penelope answered, "people who persist in eating up the estate of a great chieftain and dishonouring his house must not expect others to think well of them. Why then should you mind if men talk as you think they will? This stranger is strong and well-built, he says moreover that he is of noble birth. Give him the bow, and let us see whether he can string it or no. I say—and it shall surely be—that if Apollo vouchsafes him the glory of stringing it, I will give him a cloak and shirt of good wear, with a javelin to keep off dogs and robbers, and a sharp sword. I will also give him sandals, and will see him sent safely wherever he wants to go."

Then Telemachus said, "Mother, I am the only man either in Ithaca or in the islands that are over against Elis who has the right to let any one have the bow or to refuse it. No one shall force me one way or the other, not even though I choose to make the stranger a present of the bow outright, and let him take it away with him. Go, then, within the house and busy yourself with your daily duties, your loom, your distaff, and the ordering of your servants. This bow is a man's matter, and mine above all others, for it is I who am master here."

She went wondering back into the house, and laid her son's saying in her heart. Then going upstairs with her handmaids into her room, she mourned her dear husband till Minerva sent sweet sleep over her eyelids.

The swineherd now took up the bow and was for taking it to Ulysses, but the suitors clamoured at him from all parts of the cloisters, and one of them said, "You idiot, where are you taking the bow to? Are you out of your wits? If Apollo and the other gods will grant our prayer, your own boarhounds shall get you into some quiet little place, and worry you to death."

Eumaeus was frightened at the outcry they all raised, so he put the bow down then and there, but Telemachus shouted out at him from the other side of the cloisters, and threatened him saying, "Father Eumaeus, bring the bow on in spite of them, or young as I am I will pelt you with stones back to the country, for I am the better man of the two. I wish I was as much stronger than all the other suitors in the house as I am than you, I would soon send some of them off sick and sorry, for they mean mischief."

Thus did he speak, and they all of them laughed heartily, which put them in a better humour with Telemachus; so Eumaeus brought the bow on and placed it in the hands of Ulysses. When he had done this, he called Euryclea apart and said to her, "Euryclea, Telemachus says you are to close the doors of the women's apartments. If they hear any groaning or uproar as of men fighting about the house, they are not to come out, but are to keep quiet and stay where they are at their work."

Euryclea did as she was told and closed the doors of the women's apartments.

Meanwhile Philoetius slipped quietly out and made fast the gates of the outer court. There was a ship's cable of byblus fibre lying in the gatehouse, so he made the gates fast with it and then came in again, resuming the seat that he had left, and keeping an eye on Ulysses, who had now got the bow in his hands, and was turning it every way about, and proving it all over to see whether the worms had been eating into its two horns during his absence. Then would one turn towards his neighbour saying, "This is some tricky old bow-fancier; either he has got one like it at home, or he wants to make one, in such workmanlike style does the old vagabond handle it."

Another said, "I hope he may be no more successful in other things than he is likely to be in stringing this bow."

But Ulysses, when he had taken it up and examined it all over, strung it as easily as a skilled bard strings a new peg of his lyre and makes the twisted gut fast at both ends. Then he took it in his right hand to prove the string, and it sang sweetly under his touch like the twittering of a swallow. The suitors were dismayed, and turned colour as they heard it; at that moment, moreover, Jove thundered loudly as a sign, and the heart of Ulysses rejoiced as he heard the omen that the son of scheming Saturn had sent him.

He took an arrow that was lying upon the table—for those which the Achaeans were so shortly about to taste were all inside the quiver—he laid it on the centre-piece of the bow, and drew the notch of the arrow and the string toward him, still seated on his seat. When he had taken aim he let fly, and his arrow pierced every one of the handle-holes of the axes from the first onwards till it had gone right through them, and into the outer courtyard. Then he said to Telemachus:

"Your guest has not disgraced you, Telemachus. I did not miss what I aimed at, and I was not long in stringing my bow. I am still strong, and not as the suitors twit me with being. Now, however, it is time for the Achaeans to prepare supper while there is still daylight, and then otherwise to disport themselves with song and dance which are the crowning ornaments of a banquet."

As he spoke he made a sign with his eyebrows, and Telemachus girded on his sword, grasped his spear, and stood armed beside his father's seat.

Translated by Samuel Butler.

HESIOD
c. 700 BC

All knowledge concerning this poet can be found in his writings, the Theogony *and the* Works and Days. *Fleeing famine in ravaged Cyme in Aeolis (Western Asia Minor), his family settled at Ascra in Boeotia. Together with Homer, Hesiod is the oldest Greek poet whose works have managed to survive. Ancient and modern scholars alike have bitterly argued over who was the earliest. In general, most agree that Homer predates Hesiod.*

In the Theogony, *Hesiod proposes a synthesis of Greek religious thought. The poet describes the birth of the universe as well as the gods, the battles fought before Zeus took power, and the victory of Harmony over Chaos. He also provides ethical advice. In the eyes of Hesiod, the order of the city must imitate the Divine Order and politics must be the art of taking just measures.*

The tone of the Works and Days *is very different. In this didactic poem, Hesiod addresses men and their daily tasks: a life defined by hard work. In the first part, he presents the myths of the Five Ages of Man and of Pandora. The second part is devoted to the "works" (i.e., agriculture and navigation) and their relationship to the seasons.*

Hesiod's poetry continues to fascinate, as it discusses the origin of all things and the separation between mortals and immortals.

Battle of the Titans and the Olympians

Hesiod, *Theogony* 617-735

Zeus was not always the king of the gods. He actually belonged to the third generation of Greek gods. The first were Ouranos (the "Sky") and Gaia (the "Earth"), the primordial couple overthrown by their own children, the Titans. Kronos, the youngest of the children, took a particularly active role among them and became king of the gods. He was in turn supplanted by his son, Zeus, who himself fears being overthrown someday by one of his children.

In our selected verses of the Theogony, *we witness the battle between the gods of Kronos' generation, the Titans, and those of Zeus' generation, the Olympians. The battle has been raging for ten years and remains indecisive until Zeus learns that he will win only with the help of the Hundred-Arms. These are creatures of prodigious strength whom their father, Uranus, holds as prisoners in the underworld. They are named Obriareus, Cottus, and Gyes. Zeus frees them, defeats the Titans, dethrones his father Kronos, and becomes the first of the gods.*

"Then Zeus no longer held back his might; but straight his heart was filled with fury and he showed forth all his strength. From Heaven and from Olympus he came forthwith, hurling his lightning: the bold flew thick and fast from his strong hand together with thunder and lightning, whirling an awesome flame. The life-giving earth crashed around in burning, and the vast wood crackled loud with fire all about. All the land seethed, and Ocean's streams and the unfruitful sea."

But when first their father was vexed in his heart with Obriareus and Cottus and Gyes, he bound them in cruel bonds, because he was jealous of their exceeding manhood and comeliness and great size; and he made them live beneath the wide-pathed earth, where they were afflicted, being set to dwell under the ground, at the end of the earth, at its great borders, in bitter anguish for a long time and with great grief at heart. But the son of Cronos and the other deathless gods whom rich-haired Rhea bare from union with Cronos, brought them up again to the light at Earth's advising. For she herself recounted all things to the gods fully, how that with these they would gain victory and a glorious cause to vaunt themselves. For the Titan gods and as many as sprang from Cronos had long been fighting together in stubborn war with heart-grieving toil, the lordly Titans from high Othyrs, but the gods, givers of good, whom rich-haired Rhea bare in union with Cronos, from Olympus. So they, with bitter wrath, were fighting continually with one another at that time for ten full years, and the hard strife had no close or end for either side, and the issue of the war hung evenly balanced. But when he had provided those three with all things fitting, nectar and ambrosia which the gods themselves eat, and when their proud spirit revived within them all after they had fed on nectar and delicious ambrosia, then it was that the father of men and gods spoke amongst them:

`Hear me, bright children of Earth and Heaven, that I may say what my heart within me bids. A long while now have we, who are sprung from Cronos and the Titan gods, fought with each other every day to get victory and to prevail. But do you show your great might and unconquerable strength, and face the Titans in bitter strife; for remember our friendly kindness, and from what sufferings you are come back to the light from your cruel bondage under misty gloom through our counsels.'

So he said. And blameless Cottus answered him again: `Divine one, you speak that which we know well: nay, even of ourselves we know that your wisdom and understanding is exceeding, and that you became a defender of the deathless ones from chill doom. And through your devising we are come back again from the murky gloom and from our merciless bonds, enjoying what we looked not for, O lord, son of Cronos. And so now with fixed purpose and deliberate counsel we will aid your power in dreadful strife and will fight against the Titans in hard battle.'

So he said. And the gods, givers of good things, applauded when they heard his word, and their spirit longed for war even more than before, and they all, both male and female, stirred up hated battle that day, the Titan gods, and all that were born of Cronos together with those dread, mighty ones of overwhelming strength whom Zeus brought up to the light from Erebus beneath the earth. An hundred arms sprang from the shoulders of all alike, and each had fifty heads growing upon his shoulders upon stout limbs. These, then, stood against the Titans in grim strife, holding huge rocks in their strong hands. And on the other part the Titans eagerly strengthened their ranks, and both sides at one time showed the work of their hands and their might. The boundless sea rang terribly around, and the earth crashed loudly: wide Heaven was shaken and groaned, and high Olympus reeled from its foundation under the charge of the undying gods, and a heavy quaking reached dim Tartarus and the deep sound of their feet in the fearful onset and of their hard missiles. So, then, they launched their grievous shafts upon one another, and the cry of both armies as they shouted reached to starry heaven; and they met together with a great battle-cry.

Then Zeus no longer held back his might; but straight his heart was filled with fury and he showed forth all his strength. From Heaven and from Olympus he came forthwith, hurling his lightning: the bold flew thick and fast from his strong hand together with thunder and lightning, whirling an awesome flame. The life-giving earth crashed around in burning, and the vast wood crackled loud with fire all about. All the land seethed, and Ocean's streams and the unfruitful sea. The hot vapour lapped round the earthborn Titans. Flame unspeakable rose to the bright upper air; the flashing glare of the thunderstone and lightning blinded their eyes for all that there were strong. Astounding heat seized Chaos: and to see with eyes and to hear the sound with ears it seemed even as if Earth and wide Heaven above came together; for such a mighty crash would have arisen if Earth were being hurled to ruin, and Heaven from on high were hurling her down; so great a crash was there while the gods were meeting together in strife. Also the winds brought rumbling earthquake and duststorm, thunder and lightning and the lurid thunderbolt, which are the shafts of great Zeus, and carried the clangour and the warcry into the midst of the two hosts. An horrible uproar of terrible strife arose: mighty deeds were shown and the battle inclined. But until then, they kept at one another and fought continually in cruel war.

And amongst the foremost Cottus and Briareos and Gyes insatiate for war raised fierce fighting: three hundred rocks, one upon another, they launched from their strong hands and overshadowed the Titans with their missiles, and buried them beneath the wide-pathed earth, and bound them in bitter chains when they had conquered them by their strength for all their great spirit, as far beneath the earth to Tartarus. For a brazen anvil falling down from heaven nine nights and days would reach the earth upon the tenth: and again, a brazen anvil falling from earth nine nights and days would reach Tartarus upon the tenth. Round it runs a fence of bronze, and night spreads in triple line all about it like a neck-circlet, while above grow the roots of the earth and unfruitful sea. There by the counsel of Zeus who drives the clouds the Titan gods are hidden under misty gloom, in a dank place where are the ends of the huge earth. And they may not go out; for Poseidon fixed gates of bronze upon it, and a wall runs all round it on every side. There Gyes and Cottus and great-souled Obriareus live, trusty warders of Zeus who holds the aegis.

Translated by Hugh G. Evelyn-White.

Theft of the Fire. Creation of Pandora. Myth of the Five Ages of Man.

Hesiod, *Works and Days* 1-382

Hesiod's brother, Perses, deprived the poet of his rightful share of his inheritance. In the opening of the Works and Days, *which is mostly devoted to farm labor, Hesiod advises his brother on wisdom and justice. He encourages him to make a living by working the land. The theme of justice and integrity also creates the opportunity to evoke two myths explaining the human condition: the myth of the Creation of Woman and that of the Five Ages of Man.*

"More hands mean more work and more increase.
If your heart within you desires wealth,
do these things and work with work upon work."

Muses of Pieria[1] who give glory through song, come hither, tell of Zeus your father and chant his praise. Through him mortal men are famed or un-famed, sung or unsung alike, as great Zeus wills. For easily he makes strong, and easily he brings the strong man low; easily he humbles the proud and raises the obscure, and easily he straightens the crooked and blasts the proud,—Zeus who thunders aloft and has his dwelling most high. Attend thou with eye and ear, and make judgements straight with righteousness. And I, Perses, would tell of true things.

So, after all, there was not one kind of Strife alone, but all over the earth there are two. As for the one, a man would praise her when he came to understand her; but the other is blameworthy: and they are wholly different in nature. For one fosters evil war and battle, being cruel: her no man loves; but perforce, through the will of the deathless gods, men pay harsh Strife her honour due. But the other is the elder daughter of dark Night, and the son of Cronos who sits above and dwells in the aether, set her in the roots of the earth: and she is far kinder to men. She stirs up even the shiftless to toil; for a man grows eager to work when he considers his neighbour, a rich man who hastens to plough and plant and put his house in good order; and neighbour vies with is neighbour as he hurries after wealth. This Strife is wholesome for men. And potter is angry with potter, and craftsman with craftsman, and beggar is jealous of beggar, and minstrel of minstrel.

Perses, lay up these things in your heart, and do not let that Strife who delights in mischief hold your heart back from work, while you peep and peer and listen to the wrangles of the court-house. Little concern has he with quarrels and courts who has not a year's victuals laid up betimes, even that which the earth bears, Demeter's grain. When you have got plenty of that, you can raise disputes and strive to get another's goods. But you shall have no second chance to deal so again: nay, let us settle our dispute here with true judgement divided our inheritance, but you seized the greater share and carried it off, greatly swelling the glory of our bribe-swallowing lords who love to judge such a cause as this. Fools! They know not how much more the half is than the whole, nor what great advantage there is in mallow and asphodel.

For the gods keep hidden from men the means of life. Else you would easily do work enough in a day to supply you for a full year even without working; soon would you put away your rudder over the smoke, and the fields worked by ox and sturdy mule would run to waste. But Zeus in the anger of his heart hid it, because Prometheus the crafty deceived him; therefore he planned sorrow and mischief against men. He hid fire; but that the noble son of Iapetus stole again for men from Zeus the counsellor in a hollow fennel-stalk, so that Zeus who delights in thunder did not see it. But afterwards Zeus who gathers the clouds said to him in anger:

'Son of Iapetus, surpassing all in cunning, you are glad that you have outwitted me and stolen fire—a great plague to you yourself and to men that shall be. But I will give men as the price for fire an evil thing in which they may all be glad of heart while they embrace their own destruction.'

So said the father of men and gods, and laughed aloud. And he bade famous Hephaestus make haste and mix earth with water and to put in it the voice and strength of human kind, and fashion a sweet, lovely maiden-shape, like to the immortal goddesses in face; and Athene to teach her needlework and the weaving of the varied web; and golden Aphrodite to shed grace upon her head and cruel longing and cares that weary the limbs. And he charged Hermes the guide, the Slayer of Argus, to put in her a shameless mind and a deceitful nature.

So he ordered. And they obeyed the lord Zeus the son of Cronos. Forthwith the famous Lame God moulded clay in the likeness of a modest maid, as the son of Cronos purposed. And the goddess bright-eyed Athene girded and clothed her, and the divine Graces and queenly Persuasion put necklaces of gold upon her, and the rich-haired Hours crowned her head with spring flowers. And Pallas Athene bedecked her form with all manners of finery. Also the Guide, the Slayer of Argus, contrived within her lies and crafty words and a deceitful nature at the will of loud thundering Zeus, and the Herald of the gods put speech in her. And he called this woman Pandora, because all they who dwelt on Olympus gave each a gift, a plague to men who eat bread.

But when he had finished the sheer, hopeless snare, the Father sent glorious Argus-Slayer, the swift messenger of the gods, to take it to Epimetheus as a gift. And Epimetheus did not think on what Prometheus had said to him, bidding him never take a gift of Olympian Zeus, but to send it back for fear it might prove to be something harmful to men. But he took the gift, and afterwards, when the evil thing was already his, he understood.

For ere this the tribes of men lived on earth remote and free from ills and hard toil and heavy sickness which bring the Fates upon men; for in misery men grow old quickly. But the woman took off the great lid of the jar with her hands and scattered all these and her thought caused sorrow and mischief to men. Only Hope remained there in an unbreakable home within under the rim of the great jar, and did not fly out at the door; for ere that, the lid of the jar stopped her, by the will of Aegis-holding Zeus who gathers the clouds. But the rest, countless plagues, wander amongst men; for earth is full of evils and the sea is full. Of themselves diseases come upon men continually by day and by night, bringing mischief to mortals silently; for wise Zeus took away speech from them. So is there no way to escape the will of Zeus.

Or if you will, I will sum you up another tale well and skilfully—and do you lay it up in your heart,—how the gods and mortal men sprang from one source.

First of all the deathless gods who dwell on Olympus made a golden race of mortal men who lived in the time of Cronos when he was reigning in heaven. And they lived like gods without sorrow of heart, remote and free from toil and grief: miserable age rested not on them; but with legs and arms never failing they made merry with feasting beyond the reach of all evils. When they died, it was as though they were overcome with sleep, and they had all good things; for the fruitful earth unforced bare them fruit abundantly and without stint. They dwelt in ease and peace upon their lands with many good things, rich in flocks and loved by the blessed gods.

But after earth had covered this generation—they are called pure spirits dwelling on the earth, and are kindly, delivering from harm, and guardians of mortal men; for they roam everywhere over the earth, clothed in mist and keep watch on judgements and cruel deeds, givers of wealth; for this royal right also they received;—then they who dwell on Olympus made a second generation which was of silver and less noble by far. It was like the golden race neither in body nor in spirit. A child was brought up at his good mother's side an hundred years, an utter simpleton, playing childishly in his own home. But when they were full grown and were come to the full measure of their prime, they lived only a little time in sorrow because of their foolishness, for they could not keep from sinning and from wronging one another, nor would they serve the immortals, nor sacrifice on the holy altars of the blessed ones as it is right for men to do wherever they dwell. Then Zeus the son of Cronos was angry and put them away, because they would not give honour to the blessed gods who live on Olympus.

But when earth had covered this generation also—they are called blessed spirits of the underworld by men, and, though they are of second order, yet honour attends them also—Zeus the Father made a third generation of mortal men, a brazen race, sprung from ash-trees; and it was in no way equal to the silver age, but was terrible and strong. They loved the lamentable works of Ares and deeds of violence; they ate no bread, but were hard of heart like adamant, fearful men. Great was their strength and unconquerable the arms which grew from their shoulders on their strong limbs. Their armour was of bronze, and their houses of bronze, and of bronze were their implements: there was no black iron. These were destroyed by their own hands and passed to the dank house of chill Hades, and left no name: terrible though they were, black Death seized them, and they left the bright light of the sun.

But when earth had covered this generation also, Zeus the son of Cronos made yet another, the fourth, upon the fruitful earth, which was nobler and more righteous, a god-like race of hero-men who are called demi-gods, the race before our own, throughout the boundless earth. Grim war and dread battle destroyed a part of them, some in the land of Cadmus at seven-gated Thebe when they fought for the flocks of Oedipus, and some, when it had brought them in ships over the great sea gulf to Troy for rich-haired Helen's sake: there death's end enshrouded a part of them. But to the others father Zeus the son of Cronos gave a living and an abode apart from men, and made them dwell at the ends of earth. And they live untouched by sorrow in the islands of the blessed along the shore of deep swirling Ocean, happy heroes for whom the grain-giving earth bears honey-sweet fruit flourishing thrice a year, far from the deathless gods, and Cronos rules over them; for the father of men and gods released him from his bonds. And these last equally have honour and glory.

And again far-seeing Zeus made yet another generation, the fifth, of men who are upon the bounteous earth.

Thereafter, would that I were not among the men of the fifth generation, but either had died before or been born afterwards. For now truly is a race of iron, and men never rest from labour and sorrow by day, and from perishing by night; and the gods shall lay sore trouble upon them. But, notwithstanding, even these shall have some good mingled with their evils. And Zeus will destroy this race of mortal men also when they come to have grey hair on the temples at their birth. The father will not agree with his children, nor the children with their father, nor guest with his host, nor comrade with comrade; nor will brother be dear to brother as aforetime. Men will dishonour their parents as they grow quickly old, and will carp at them, chiding them with bitter words, hard-hearted they, not knowing the fear of the gods. They will not repay their aged parents the cost their nurture, for might shall be their right: and one man will sack another's city. There will be no favour for the man who keeps his oath or for the just or for the good; but rather men will praise the evil-doer and his violent dealing. Strength will be right and reverence will cease to be; and the wicked will hurt the worthy man, speaking false words against him, and will swear an oath upon them. Envy, foul-mouthed, delighting in evil, with scowling face, will go along with wretched men one and all. And then Aidos and Nemesis, with their sweet forms wrapped in white robes, will go from the wide-pathed earth and forsake mankind to join the company of the deathless gods: and bitter sorrows will be left for mortal men, and there will be no help against evil.

And now I will tell a fable for princes who themselves understand. Thus said the hawk to the nightingale with speckled neck, while he carried her high up among the clouds, gripped fast in his talons, and she, pierced by his crooked talons, cried pitifully. To her he spoke disdainfully: "Miserable thing, why do you cry out? One far stronger than you now holds you fast, and you must go wherever I take you, songstress as you are. And if I please I will make my meal of you, or let you go. He is a fool who tries to withstand the stronger, for he does not get the mastery and suffers pain besides his shame." So said the swiftly flying hawk, the long-winged bird.

But you, Perses, listen to right and do not foster violence; for violence is bad for a poor man. Even the prosperous cannot easily bear its burden, but is weighed down under it when he has fallen into delusion. The better path is to go by on the other side towards justice; for Justice beats Outrage when she comes at length to the end of the race. But only when he has suffered does the fool learn this. For Oath keeps pace with wrong judgements. There is a noise when Justice is being dragged in the way where those who devour bribes and give sentence with crooked judgements, take her. And she, wrapped in mist, follows to the city and haunts of the people, weeping, and bringing mischief to men, even to such as have driven her forth in that they did not deal straightly with her.

But they who give straight judgements to strangers and to the men of the land, and go not aside from what is just, their city flourishes, and the people prosper in it: Peace, the nurse of children, is abroad in their land, and all-seeing Zeus never decrees cruel war against them. Neither famine nor disaster ever haunt men who do true justice; but light-heartedly they tend the fields which are all their care. The earth bears them victual in plenty, and on the mountains the oak bears acorns upon the top and bees in the midst. Their woolly sheep are laden with fleeces; their women bear children like their parents. They flourish continually with good things, and do not travel on ships, for the grain-giving earth bears them fruit.

But for those who practise violence and cruel deeds far-seeing Zeus, the son of Cronos, ordains a punishment. Often even a whole city suffers for a bad man who sins and devises presumptuous deeds, and the son of Cronos lays great trouble upon the people, famine and plague together, so that the men perish away, and their women do not bear children, and their houses become few, through the contriving of Olympian Zeus. And again, at another time, the son of Cronos either destroys their wide army, or their walls, or else makes an end of their ships on the sea.

You princes, mark well this punishment you also; for the deathless gods are near among men and mark all those who oppress their fellows with crooked judgements, and reck not the anger of the gods. For upon the bounteous earth Zeus has thrice ten thousand spirits, watchers of mortal men, and these keep watch on judgements and deeds of wrong as they roam, clothed in mist, all over the earth. And there is virgin Justice, the daughter of Zeus, who is honoured and reverenced among the gods who dwell on Olympus, and whenever anyone hurts her with lying slander, she sits beside her father, Zeus the son of Cronos, and tells him of men's wicked heart, until the people pay for the mad folly of their princes who, evilly minded, pervert judgement and give sentence crookedly. Keep watch against this, you princes, and make straight your judgements, you who devour bribes; put crooked judgements altogether from your thoughts.

He does mischief to himself who does mischief to another, and evil planned harms the plotter most.

The eye of Zeus, seeing all and understanding all, beholds these things too, if so he will, and fails not to mark what sort of justice is this that the city keeps within it. Now, therefore, may neither I myself be righteous among men, nor my son—for then it is a bad thing to be righteous—if indeed the unrighteous shall have the greater right. But I think that all-wise Zeus will not yet bring that to pass.

But you, Perses, lay up these things within you heart and listen now to right, ceasing altogether to think of violence. For the son of Cronos has ordained this law for men, that fishes and beasts and winged fowls should devour one another, for right is not in them; but to mankind he gave right which proves far the best. For whoever knows the right and is ready to speak it, far-seeing Zeus gives him prosperity; but whoever deliberately lies in his witness and forswears himself, and so hurts Justice and sins beyond repair, that man's generation is left obscure thereafter. But the generation of the man who swears truly is better thenceforward.

To you, foolish Perses, I will speak good sense. Badness can be got easily and in shoals: the road to her is smooth, and she lives very near us. But between us and Goodness the gods have placed the sweat of our brows: long and steep is the path that leads to her, and it is rough at the first; but when a man has reached the top, then is she easy to reach, though before that she was hard.

That man is altogether best who considers all things himself and marks what will be better afterwards and at the end; and he, again, is good who listens to a good adviser; but whoever neither thinks for himself nor keeps in mind what another tells him, he is an unprofitable man. But do you at any rate, always remembering my charge, work, high-born Perses, that Hunger may hate you, and venerable Demeter richly crowned may love you and fill your barn with food; for Hunger is altogether a meet comrade for the sluggard. Both gods and men are angry with a man who lives idle, for in nature he is like the stingless drones who waste the labour of the bees, eating without working; but let it be your care to order your work properly, that in the right season your barns may be full of victual. Through work men grow rich in flocks and substance, and working they are much better loved by the immortals. Work is no disgrace: it is idleness which is a disgrace. But if you work, the idle will soon envy you as you grow rich, for fame and renown attend on wealth. And whatever be your lot, work is best for you, if you turn your misguided mind away from other men's property to your work and attend to your livelihood as I bid you. An evil shame is the needy man's companion, shame which both greatly harms and prospers men: shame is with poverty, but confidence with wealth.

Wealth should not be seized: god-given wealth is much better; for it a man take great wealth violently and perforce, or if he steal it through his tongue, as often happens when gain deceives men's sense and dishonour tramples down honour, the gods soon blot him out and make that man's house low, and wealth attends him only for a little time. Alike with him who does wrong to a suppliant or a guest, or who goes up to his brother's bed and commits unnatural sin in lying with his wife, or who infatuately offends against fatherless children, or who abuses his old father at the cheerless threshold of old age and attacks him with harsh words, truly Zeus himself is angry, and at the last lays on him a heavy requittal for his evil doing. But do you turn your foolish heart altogether away from these things, and, as far as you are able, sacrifice to the deathless gods purely and cleanly, and burn rich meats also, and at other times propitiate them with libations and incense, both when you go to bed and when the holy light has come back, that they may be gracious to you in heart and spirit, and so you may buy another's holding and not another yours.

Call your friend to a feast; but leave your enemy alone; and especially call him who lives near you: for if any mischief happen in the place, neighbours come ungirt, but kinsmen stay to gird themselves. A bad neighbour is as great a plague as a good one is a great blessing; he who enjoys a good neighbour has a precious possession. Not even an ox would die but for a bad neighbour. Take fair measure from your neighbour and pay him back fairly with the same measure, or better, if you can; so that if you are in need afterwards, you may find him sure.

Do not get base gain: base gain is as bad as ruin. Be friends with the friendly, and visit him who visits you. Give to one who gives, but do not give to one who does not give. A man gives to the free-handed, but no one gives to the close-fisted. Give is a good girl, but Take is bad and she brings death. For the man who gives willingly, even though he gives a great thing, rejoices in his gift and is glad in heart; but whoever gives way to shamelessness and takes something himself, even though it be a small thing, it freezes his heart. He who adds to what he has, will keep off bright-eyed hunger; for if you add only a little to a little and do this often, soon that little will become great. What a man has by him at home does not trouble him: it is better to have your stuff at home, for whatever is abroad may mean loss. It is a good thing to draw on what you have; but it grieves your heart to need something and not to have it, and I bid you mark this. Take your fill when the cask is first opened and when it is nearly spent, but midways be sparing: it is poor saving when you come to the lees.

Let the wage promised to a friend be fixed; Even with your brother smile—and get a witness; for trust and mistrust, alike ruin men. Do not let a flaunting woman coax and cozen and deceive you: she is after your barn. The man who trusts womankind trust deceivers. There should be an only son, to feed his father's house, for so wealth will increase in the home; but if you leave a second son you should die old. Yet Zeus can easily give great wealth to a greater number. More hands mean more work and more increase. If your heart within you desires wealth, do these things and work with work upon work.

Translated by Hugh G. Evelyn-White.

AESOP

Sixth century BC

Not much is known about Aesop to whom the ancients attributed a great number of fables. In essence, his life quickly became a myth. Herodotus introduces him as the slave of a wealthy Samian whose descendents traveled to Delphi to receive a ransom after Aesop's murder. Various versions of this event exist. In some of them, while he journeyed to Delphi to collect the offerings sent by King Croesus, Aesop stole a gold cup from the god, and this action alone justified his execution. Others maintain that he poked fun at the Delphians because, while not having land to cultivate, they lived off the offerings the pilgrims made to Apollo.

Aesop's fables had a significant influence on playwrights and other writers throughout antiquity. Aristophanes (see Lysistrata *in this volume) and the other comic poets allude to his short tales, whose characters are often animals (though sometimes humans and at other times gods, plants, or inanimate objects) that serve to illustrate a universal truth and transmit a moral teaching. If Aristophanes is to be believed, these excerpts were accepted not only in banquets for their light and amusing tone but also, more surprisingly, in civic institutions for their popular wisdom.*

Transmitted orally, the fables were codified for the first time around the fourth century BC. In Hellenistic times, when interest in this genre blossomed, it is possible that the collection of Aesop's fables was expanded. The success of the fables was confirmed in Rome when Phaedrus adapted Aesop's prose into verse in the first century AD. In the 17th century, the celebrated French poet Jean de la Fontaine drew most of his Fables *from Aesop.*

The Sick Lion
Aesop, *Fables* 196

A lion, unable from old age and infirmities to provide himself with food by force, resolved to do so by artifice. He returned to his den, and lying down there, pretended to be sick, taking care that his sickness should be publicly known. The beasts expressed their sorrow, and came one by one to his den, where the Lion devoured them. After many of the beasts had thus disappeared, the Fox discovered the trick and presenting himself to the Lion, stood on the outside of the cave, at a respectful distance, and asked him how he was. "I am very middling," replied the Lion, "but why do you stand without? Pray enter within to talk with me." "No, thank you," said the Fox. "I notice that there are many prints of feet entering your cave, but I see no trace of any returning."

He is wise who is warned by the misfortunes of others.

Mercury and the Workmen
Aesop, *Fables* 253

A workman, felling wood by the side of a river, let his axe drop by accident into a deep pool. Being thus deprived of the means of his livelihood, he sat down on the bank and lamented his hard fate. Mercury appeared and demanded the cause of his tears. After he told him his misfortune, Mercury plunged into the stream, and, bringing up a golden axe, inquired if that were the one he had lost. On his saying that it was not his, Mercury disappeared beneath the water a second time, returned with a silver axe in his hand, and again asked the Workman if it were his. When the Workman said it was not, he dived into the pool for the third time and brought up the axe that had been lost. The Workman claimed it and expressed his joy at its recovery. Mercury, pleased with his honesty, gave him the golden and silver axes in addition to his own. The Workman, on his return to his house, related to his companions all that had happened. One of them at once resolved to try and secure the same good fortune for himself. He ran to the river and threw his axe on purpose into the pool at the same place, and sat down on the bank to weep. Mercury appeared to him just as he hoped he would; and having learned the cause of his grief, plunged into the stream and brought up a golden axe, inquiring if he had lost it. The Workman seized it greedily, and declared that truly it was the very same axe that he had lost. Mercury, displeased at his knavery, not only took away the golden axe, but refused to recover for him the axe he had thrown into the pool.

This fable shows that the divinity is as favorable to honest people as it is hostile to the dishonest.

The Bear and the Two Travelers

Aesop, *Fables* 254

Two men were traveling together, when a Bear suddenly met them on their path. One of them climbed up quickly into a tree and concealed himself in the branches. The other, seeing that he must be attacked, fell flat on the ground, and when the Bear came up and felt him with his snout, and smelt him all over, he held his breath, and feigned the appearance of death as much as he could. The Bear soon left him, for it is said he will not touch a dead body. When he was quite gone, the other Traveler descended from the tree, and jocularly inquired of his friend what it was the Bear had whispered in his ear. "He gave me this advice," his companion replied. "Never travel with a friend who deserts you at the approach of danger."

Misfortune tests the sincerity of friends.

The Miser

Aesop, *Fables* 344

A miser sold all that he had and bought a lump of gold, which he buried in a hole in the ground by the side of an old wall and went to look at daily. One of his workmen observed his frequent visits to the spot and decided to watch his movements. He soon discovered the secret of the hidden treasure, and digging down, came to the lump of gold, and stole it. The Miser, on his next visit, found the hole empty and began to tear his hair and to make loud lamentations. A neighbor, seeing him overcome with grief and learning the cause, said, "Pray do not grieve so; but go and take a stone, and place it in the hole, and fancy that the gold is still lying there. It will do you quite the same service; for when the gold was there, you had it not, as you did not make the slightest use of it."

This fable demonstrates that ownership amounts to nothing if one does not enjoy that which one owns.

The Brazier and His Dog

Aesop, *Fables* 345

A brazier had a little dog, which was a great favorite with his master, and his constant companion. While he hammered away at his metals the Dog slept; but when, on the other hand, he went to dinner and began to eat, the Dog woke up and wagged his tail, as if he would ask for a share of his meal. His master one day, pretending to be angry and shaking his stick at him, said, "You wretched little sluggard! what shall I do to you? While I am hammering on the anvil, you sleep on the mat; and when I begin to eat after my toil, you wake up and wag your tail for food. Do you not know that labor is the source of every blessing, and that none but those who work are entitled to eat?'

Lazy people who live off others' hard work will recognize themselves in this fable.

Translated by George Fyler Townsend. Revised by Catherine Lapp.

AESCHYLUS

c. 525 - 456 BC

Aeschylus was born at Eleusis. In his youth, he fought the battles at Marathon and at Salamis near Athens. (He recounted the latter in his tragedy The Persians.*) He was also an actor and one of the great tragic poets of ancient Greece. He contributed many innovations to the dramatic arts. In the tragedies of his time, it was customary that only one actor carried out dialogue with the chorus while on stage. Aeschylus, however, introduced a second actor, and by doing so, heightened the intrigue, making the exchanges between characters more complex. His theatre is spectacular: Aeschylus likes flamboyant costumes and stunning verbal images. His grandiose works emphasize the disarray of men linked to their destiny, a destiny that is often conditioned by their ancestors' mistakes.*

Aeschylus composed 73 to 90 plays. Only seven survive. The Persians *is the earliest among his tragedies to be preserved. It was first staged in 472 BC.* Prometheus Bound *forms the first part of a trilogy (a group of three plays that were traditionally staged during the Festival of Dionysus at Athens) in which Zeus and Prometheus, the rebellious Titan, move toward reconciliation.*

Defeat at Salamis

Aeschylus, *The Persians* 140-514

It is 480 BC and the Second Persian War rages. Ten years after their defeat at Marathon, the Persians attempt to conquer Greece once again. The Persian and Greek fleets are poised for attack, and meet at Salamis off the shore of Attica. The Persian fleet suffers heavy losses and is decisively defeated.

In this play, Aeschylus introduces two new elements to tragedy: (1) the subject is not mythological but historical and (2) his perspective is not Greek but Persian. Instead of celebrating the victory of the Greeks, he underscores the despair of the Persians.

The play unfolds in the court of the Persian king Darius at Susa (modern Iraq). Queen Atossa awaits news from the frontlines. Her anxiety is great. She is about to learn the debacle concerning her son Xerxes and the Persian army: King Xerxes failed to avenge his father's defeat at Marathon. All Persian ambitions are crushed. Henceforth, the women are left alone to mourn the loss of their husbands in distant Greece. The messenger provides a dramatic recitation of the Battle of Salamis, the sea stained red with the blood of the vanquished.

Characters

ATOSSA, widow of Darius and mother of Xerxes
LEADER of the Chorus
CHORUS of Persian elders
MESSENGER

"ATOSSA: Yet one more word—say, in what realm do the Athenians dwell?
CHORUS: Far hence, even where, in evening land, goes down our Lord the Sun."

CHORUS
But now, ye warders of the state,
Here, in this hall of old renown,
Behoves that we deliberate
In counsel deep and wise debate,
For need is surely shown!
How fareth he, Darius' child,
The Persian king, from Perseus styled?

Comes triumph to the eastern bow,
Or hath the lance-point conquered now?

[*Atossa enters with her retinue. The Elders do their obeisance to her.*]

See, yonder comes the mother-queen,
Light of our eyes, in godlike sheen,
The royal mother of the king!
Fall we before her! well it were
That, all as one, we sue to her,
And round her footsteps cling!

Queen, among deep-girded Persian dames thou highest and most royal,
Hoary mother, thou, of Xerxes, and Darius' wife of old!
To godlike sire, and godlike son, we bow us and are loyal—
Unless, on us, an adverse tide of destiny has rolled!

ATOSSA
Therefore come I forth to you, from chambers decked and golden,
Where long ago Darius laid his head, with me beside,
And my heart is torn with anguish, and with terror am I holden,
And I plead unto your friendship and I bid you to my side.

Darius, in the old time, by aid of some Immortal,
Raised up the stately fabric, our wealth of long-ago:
But I tremble lest it totter down, and ruin porch and portal,
And the whirling dust of downfall rise above its overthrow!

Therefore a dread unspeakable within me never slumbers, Saying,
Honour not the gauds of wealth if men have ceased to grow,
Nor deem that men, apart from wealth,
can find their strength in numbers—
We shudder for our light and king, though we have gold enow!

No light there is, in any house, save presence of the master—
So runs the saw, ye aged men! and truth it says indeed—
On you I call, the wise and true, to ward us from disaster,
For all my hope is fixed on you, to prop us in our need!

CHORUS
Queen-Mother of the Persian land, to thy commandment bowing,

Whate'er thou wilt, in word or deed, we follow to fulfil—
Not twice we need thine high behest, our faith and duty knowing,
In council and in act alike, thy loyal servants still!

ATOSSA
Long while by various visions of the night
Am I beset, since to Ionian lands
With marshalled host my son went forth to war.
Yet never saw I presage so distinct
As in the night now passed.—Attend my tale!—
A dream I had: two women nobly clad
Came to my sight, one robed in Persian dress,
The other vested in the Dorian garb,
And both right stately and more tall by far
Than women of to-day, and beautiful
Beyond disparagement, and sisters sprung
Both of one race, but, by their natal lot,
One born in Hellas, one in Eastern land.
These, as it seemed unto my watching eyes,
Roused each the other to a mutual feud:
The which my son perceiving set himself
To check and soothe their struggle, and anon
Yoked them and set the collars on their necks;
And one, the Ionian, proud in this array,
Paced in high quietude, and lent her mouth,
Obedient, to the guidance of the rein.
But restively the other strove, and broke
The fittings of the car, and plunged away
With mouth un-bitted: o'er the broken yoke
My son was hurled, and lo! Darius stood
In lamentation o'er his fallen child.
Him Xerxes saw, and rent his robe in grief.

Such was my vision of the night now past;
But when, arising, I had dipped my hand
In the fair lustral stream, I drew towards
The altar, in the act of sacrifice,
Having in mind to offer, as their due,
The sacred meal-cake to the averting powers,
Lords of the rite that banisheth ill dreams.
When lo! I saw an eagle fleeing fast

To Phoebus' shrine—O friends, I stayed my steps,
Too scared to speak! for, close upon his flight,
A little falcon dashed in winged pursuit,
Plucking with claws the eagle's head, while he
Could only crouch and cower and yield himself.
Scared was I by that sight, and eke to you
No less a terror must it be to hear!
For mark this well—if Xerxes have prevailed,
He shall come back the wonder of the world:
If not, still none can call him to account—
So he but live, he liveth Persia's King!

CHORUS
Queen, it stands not with my purpose to abet these fears of thine,
Nor to speak with glazing comfort! nay, betake thee to the shrine!
If thy dream foretold disaster, sue to gods to bar its way,
And, for thyself, son, state, and friends, to bring fair fate to-day.
Next, unto Earth and to the Dead be due libation poured,
And by thee let Darius' soul be wistfully implored—
I saw thee, lord, in last night's dream, a phantom from the grave,
I pray thee, lord, from earth beneath come forth to help and save!
To me and to thy son send up the bliss of triumph now,
And hold the gloomy fates of ill, dim in the dark below!
Such be thy words! my inner heart good tidings doth foretell,
And that fair fate will spring thereof, if wisdom guide us well.

ATOSSA
Loyal thou that first hast read this dream, this vision of the night,
With loyalty to me, the queen—be then thy presage right!
And therefore, as thy bidding is, what time I pass within
To dedicate these offerings, new prayers I will begin,
Alike to gods and the great dead who loved our lineage well.
Yet one more word—say, in what realm do the Athenians dwell?

CHORUS
Far hence, even where, in evening land, goes down our Lord the Sun.

ATOSSA
Say, had my son so keen desire, that region to o'errun?

CHORUS
Yea—if she fell, the rest of Greece were subject to our sway!

ATOSSA
Hath she so great predominance, such legions in array?

CHORUS
Ay—such a host as smote us sore upon an earlier day.

ATOSSA
And what hath she, besides her men? enow of wealth in store?

CHORUS
A mine of treasure in the earth, a fount of silver ore!

ATOSSA
Is it in skill of bow and shaft that Athens' men excel?

CHORUS
Nay, they bear bucklers in the fight, and thrust the spear-point well.

ATOSSA
And who is shepherd of their host and holds them in command?

CHORUS
To no man do they bow as slaves, nor own a master's hand.

ATOSSA
How should they bide our brunt of war, the East upon the West?

CHORUS
That could Darius' valiant horde in days of yore attest!

ATOSSA
A boding word, to us who bore the men now far away!

CHORUS
Nay—as I deem, the very truth will dawn on us to-day.
A Persian by his garb and speed, a courier draws anear—
He bringeth news, of good or ill, for Persia's land to hear.
[*A messenger enters.*]

MESSENGER
O walls and towers of all the Asian realm,
O Persian land, O treasure-house of gold!
How, by one stroke, down to destruction, down,
Hath sunk our pride, and all the flower of war
That once was Persia's, lieth in the dust!
Woe on the man who first announceth woe—
Yet must I all the tale of death unroll!
Hark to me, Persians! Persia's host lies low.

CHORUS
O ruin manifold, and woe, and fear!
Let the wild tears run down, for the great doom is here!

MESSENGER
This blow hath fallen, to the utterance,
And I, past hope, behold my safe return!

CHORUS
Too long, alack, too long this life of mine,
That in mine age I see this sudden woe condign!

MESSENGER
As one who saw, by no loose rumour led,
Lords, I would tell what doom was dealt to us.

CHORUS
Alack, how vainly have they striven!
Our myriad hordes with shaft and bow
Went from the Eastland, to lay low
Hellas, beloved of Heaven!

MESSENGER
Piled with men dead, yea, miserably slain,
Is every beach, each reef of Salamis!

CHORUS
Thou sayest sooth—ah well-a-day!
Battered amid the waves, and torn,
On surges hither, thither, borne,

Dead bodies, bloodstained and forlorn,
In their long cloaks they toss and stray!

MESSENGER
Their bows availed not! all have perished, all,
By charging galleys crushed and whelmed in death.

CHORUS
Shriek out your sorrow's wistful wail!
To their untimely doom they went;
Ill strove they, and to no avail,
And minished is their armament!

MESSENGER
Out on thee, hateful name of Salamis,
Out upon Athens, mournful memory!

CHORUS
Woe upon this day's evil fame!
Thou, Athens, art our murderess;
Alack, full many a Persian dame
Is left forlorn and husbandless!

ATOSSA
Mute have I been awhile, and overwrought
At this great sorrow, for it passeth speech,
And passeth all desire to ask of it.
Yet if the gods send evils, men must bear.

[*To the messenger*]

Unroll the record! stand composed and tell,
Although thy heart be groaning inwardly,
Who hath escaped, and, of our leaders, whom
Have we to weep? what chieftains in the van
Stood, sank, and died and left us leaderless?

MESSENGER
Xerxes himself survives and sees the day.

ATOSSA
Then to my line thy word renews the dawn
And golden dayspring after gloom of night!

MESSENGER
But the brave marshal of ten thousand horse,
Artembares, is tossed and flung in death
Along the rugged rocks Silenian.
And Dadaces no longer leads his troop,
But, smitten by the spear, from off the prow
Hath lightly leaped to death; and Tenagon,
In true descent a Bactrian nobly born,
Drifts by the sea-lashed reefs of Salamis,
The isle of Ajax. Gone Lilaeus too,
Gone are Arsames and Argestes! all,
Around the islet where the sea-doves breed,
Dashed their defeated heads on iron rocks;
Arcteus, who dwelt beside the founts of Nile,
Adeues, Pheresseues, and with them
Pharnuchus, from one galley's deck went down.
Matallus, too, of Chrysa, lord and king
Of myriad hordes, who led unto the fight
Three times ten thousand swarthy cavaliers,
Fell, with his swarthy and abundant beard
Incarnadined to red, a crimson stain
Outrivalling the purple of the sea!
There Magian Arabus and Artames
Of Bactra perished—taking up, alike,
In yonder stony land their long sojourn.
Amistris too, and he whose strenuous spear
Was foremost in the fight, Amphistreus fell,
And gallant Ariomardus, by whose death
Broods sorrow upon Sardis: Mysia mourns
For Seisames, and Tharubis lies low—
Commander, he, of five times fifty ships,
Born in Lyrnessus: his heroic form
Is low in death, ungraced with sepulchre.
Dead too is he, the lord of courage high,
Cilicia's marshal, brave Syennesis,
Than whom none dealt more carnage on the foe,
Nor perished by a more heroic end.

So fell the brave: so speak I of their doom,
Summing in brief the fate of myriads!

ATOSSA
Ah well-a-day! these crowning woes I hear,
The shame of Persia and her shrieks of dole!
But yet renew the tale, repeat thy words,
Tell o'er the count of those Hellenic ships,
And how they ventured with their beaked prows
To charge upon the Persian armament.

MESSENGER
Know, if mere count of ships could win the day,
The Persians had prevailed. The Greeks, in sooth,
Had but three hundred galleys at the most,
And other ten, select and separate.
But—I am witness—Xerxes held command
Of full a thousand keels, and, those apart,
Two hundred more, and seven, for speed renowned!
So stands the reckoning, and who shall dare
To say we Persians had the lesser host?

ATOSSA
Nay, we were worsted by an unseen power
Who swayed the balance downward to our doom!

MESSENGER
In ward of heaven doth Pallas' city stand.

ATOSSA
How then? is Athens yet inviolate?

MESSENGER
While her men live, her bulwark standeth firm!

ATOSSA
Say, how began the struggle of the ships?
Who first joined issue? did the Greeks attack,
Or Xerxes, in his numbers confident?

MESSENGER
O queen, our whole disaster thus befell,
Through intervention of some fiend or fate—
I know not what—that had ill will to us.
From the Athenian host some Greek came o'er,
To thy son Xerxes whispering this tale—
Once let the gloom of night have gathered in,
The Greeks will tarry not, but swiftly spring
Each to his galley-bench, in furtive flight,
Softly contriving safety for their life.
Thy son believed the word and missed the craft
Of that Greek foeman, and the spite of Heaven,
And straight to all his captains gave this charge—
As soon as sunlight warms the ground no more,
And gloom enwraps the sanctuary of sky,
Range we our fleet in triple serried lines
To bar the passage from the seething strait,
This way and that: let other ships surround
The isle of Ajax, with this warning word—
That if the Greeks their jeopardy should scape
By wary craft, and win their ships a road.
Each Persian captain shall his failure pay
By forfeit of his head. So spake the king,
Inspired at heart with over-confidence,
Unwitting of the gods' predestined will.
Thereon our crews, with no disordered haste,
Did service to his bidding and purveyed
The meal of afternoon: each rower then
Over the fitted rowlock looped his oar.
Then, when the splendour of the sun had set,
And night drew on, each master of the oar
And each armed warrior straightway went aboard.
Forward the long ships moved, rank cheering rank,
Each forward set upon its ordered course.
And all night long the captains of the fleet
Kept their crews moving up and down the strait.
So the night waned, and not one Grecian ship
Made effort to elude and slip away.
But as dawn came and with her coursers white
Shone in fair radiance over all the earth,
First from the Grecian fleet rang out a cry,

A song of onset! and the island crags
Re-echoed to the shrill exulting sound.
Then on us Eastern men amazement fell
And fear in place of hope; for what we heard
Was not a call to flight! the Greeks rang out
Their holy, resolute, exulting chant,
Like men come forth to dare and do and die
Their trumpets pealed, and fire was in that sound,
And with the dash of simultaneous oars
Replying to the war-chant, on they came,
Smiting the swirling brine, and in a trice
They flashed upon the vision of the foe!
The right wing first in orderly advance
Came on, a steady column; following then,
The rest of their array moved out and on,
And to our ears there came a burst of sound,
A clamour manifold.—On, sons of Greece!
On, for your country's freedom! strike to save
Wives, children, temples of ancestral gods,
Graves of your fathers! now is all at stake.
Then from our side swelled up the mingled din
Of Persian tongues, and time brooked no delay—
Ship into ship drave hard its brazen beak
With speed of thought, a shattering blow! and first
One Grecian bark plunged straight, and sheared away
Bowsprit and stem of a Phoenician ship.
And then each galley on some other's prow
Came crashing in. Awhile our stream of ships
Held onward, till within the narrowing creek
Our jostling vessels were together driven,
And none could aid another: each on each
Drave hard their brazen beaks, or brake away
The oar-banks of each other, stem to stern,
While the Greek galleys, with no lack of skill,
Hemmed them and battered in their sides, and soon
The hulls rolled over, and the sea was hid,
Crowded with wrecks and butchery of men.
No beach nor reef but was with corpses strewn,
And every keel of our barbarian host
Hurried to flee, in utter disarray.
Thereon the foe closed in upon the wrecks

And hacked and hewed, with oars and splintered planks,
As fishermen hack tunnies or a cast
Of netted dolphins, and the briny sea
Rang with the screams and shrieks of dying men,
Until the night's dark aspect hid the scene.
Had I a ten days' time to sum that count
Of carnage, 'twere too little! know this well—
One day ne'er saw such myriad forms of death!

ATOSSA
Woe on us, woe! disaster's mighty sea
Hath burst on us and all the Persian realm!

MESSENGER
Be well assured, the tale is but begun—
The further agony that on us fell
Doth twice outweigh the sufferings I have told!

ATOSSA
Nay, what disaster could be worse than this?
Say on! what woe upon the army came,
Swaying the scale to a yet further fall?

MESSENGER
The very flower and crown of Persia's race,
Gallant of soul and glorious in descent,
And highest held in trust before the king,
Lies shamefully and miserably slain.

ATOSSA
Alas for me and for this ruin, friends!
Dead, sayest thou? by what fate overthrown?

MESSENGER
An islet is there, fronting Salamis—
Strait, and with evil anchorage: thereon
Pan treads the measure of the dance he loves
Along the sea-beach. Thither the king sent
His noblest, that, whene'er the Grecian foe
Should 'scape, with shattered ships, unto the isle,
We might make easy prey of fugitives

And slay them there, and from the washing tides
Rescue our friends. It fell out otherwise
Than he divined, for when, by aid of Heaven,
The Hellenes held the victory on the sea,
Their sailors then and there begirt themselves
With brazen mail and bounded from their ships,
And then enringed the islet, point by point,
So that our Persians in bewilderment
Knew not which way to turn. On every side,
Battered with stones, they fell, while arrows flew
From many a string, and smote them to the death.
Then, at the last, with simultaneous rush
The foe came bursting on us, hacked and hewed
To fragments all that miserable band,
Till not a soul of them was left alive.
Then Xerxes saw disaster's depth, and shrieked,
From where he sat on high, surveying all—
A lofty eminence, beside the brine,
Whence all his armament lay clear in view.
His robe he rent, with loud and bitter wail,
And to his land-force swiftly gave command
And fled, with shame beside him! Now, lament
That second woe, upon the first imposed!

ATOSSA
Out on thee, Fortune! thou hast foiled the hope
And power of Persia: to this bitter end
My son went forth to wreak his great revenge
On famous Athens! all too few they seemed,
Our men who died upon the Fennel-field!
Vengeance for them my son had mind to take,
And drew on his own head these whelming woes.
But thou, say on! the ships that 'scaped from wreck—
Where didst thou leave them? make thy story clear.

MESSENGER
The captains of the ships that still survived
Fled in disorder, scudding down the wind,
The while our land-force on Boeotian soil
Fell into ruin, some beside the springs
Dropping before they drank, and some outworn,

Pursued, and panting all their life away.
The rest of us our way to Phocis won,
And thence to Doris and the Melian gulf,
Where with soft stream Spercheus laves the soil.
Thence to the northward did Phthiotis' plain,
And some Thessalian fortress, lend us aid,
For famine-pinched we were, and many died
Of drought and hunger's twofold present scourge.
Thence to Magnesia came we, and the land
Where Macedonians dwell, and crossed the ford
Of Axius, and Bolbe's reedy fen,
And mount Pangaeus, in Edonian land.
There, in the very night we came, the god
Brought winter ere its time, from bank to bank
Freezing the holy Strymon's tide. Each man
Who heretofore held lightly of the gods,
Now crouched and proffered prayer to Earth and Heaven!
Then, after many orisons performed,
The army ventured on the frozen ford:
Yet only those who crossed before the sun
Shed its warm rays, won to the farther side.
For soon the fervour of the glowing orb
Did with its keen rays pierce the ice-bound stream,
And men sank through and thrust each other down—
Best was his lot whose breath was stifled first!
But all who struggled through and gained the bank,
Toilfully wending through the land of Thrace
Have made their way, a sorry, scanted few,
Unto this homeland. Let the city now
Lament and yearn for all the loved and lost.
My tale is truth, yet much untold remains
Of ills that Heaven hath hurled upon our land.

[*The messenger withdraws.*]

Translated by E.D.A. Morshead.

Prometheus' Punishment for Supplying Fire

Aeschylus, *Prometheus Bound* 90-397

As punishment for giving fire to man, Zeus enchains Prometheus to a rocky outcrop on the shore of Scythia at the northern extremity of the world. The Titan laments his lot and attracts the visit of the Oceanides. Their father, too, comes to cheer him up. Prometheus further receives a visit from Io, the reluctant lover of Zeus. Hera's anger earlier transformed her into a heifer. Now she wanders the earth in a desperate effort to avoid the gadfly that pursues her. Prometheus sympathizes with her, for he sees in her yet another victim of injustice at the hands of the gods. Hermes arrives next with a message: Zeus will free Prometheus if he reveals his secret. Prometheus knows that the king of the gods will be dethroned, but he refuses to speak. Zeus strikes the rock with a bolt of lightning where he is enchained. Entombed beneath the fallen rocks, Prometheus will dwell there, forever rebellious against Zeus' injustice.

Characters

PROMETHEUS, Titan, cousin of Zeus
CHORUS of the Oceanides
OCEANUS

"PROMETHEUS: Ay, man thro' me ceased to foreknow his death.
CHORUS: What cure couldst thou discover for this curse?
PROMETHEUS: Blind hopes I sent to nestle in man's heart."

PROMETHEUS
O Sky divine, O Winds of pinions swift,
O fountain-heads of Rivers, and O thou,
Illimitable laughter of the Sea!
O Earth, the Mighty Mother, and thou Sun,
Whose orbed light surveyeth all—attest,
What ills I suffer from the gods, a god!
Behold me, who must here sustain
The marring agonies of pain,
Wrestling with torture, doomed to bear
Eternal ages, year on year!
Such and so shameful is the chain
Which Heaven's new tyrant doth ordain

To bind me helpless here.
Woe! for the ruthless present doom!
Woe! for the Future's teeming womb!
On what far dawn, in what dim skies,
Shall star of my deliverance rise?

Truce to this utterance! to its dimmest verge
I do foreknow the future, hour by hour,
Nor can whatever pang may smite me now
Smite with surprise. The destiny ordained
I must endure to the best, for well I wot
That none may challenge with Necessity.
Yet is it past my patience, to reveal,
Or to conceal, these issues of my doom.
Since I to mortals brought prerogatives,
Unto this durance dismal am I bound:
Yea, I am he who in a fennel-stalk,
By stealthy sleight, purveyed the fount of fire,
The teacher, proven thus, and arch-resource
Of every art that aideth mortal men.
Such was my sin: I earn its recompense,
Rock-riveted, and chained in height and cold.

[*A pause*]

Listen! what breath of sound,
what fragrance soft hath risen
Upward to me? is it some godlike essence,
Or being half-divine, or mortal presence?
Who to the world's end comes, unto my craggy prison?
Craves he the sight of pain, or what would he behold?
Gaze on a god in tortures manifold,
Heinous to Zeus, and scorned by all
Whose footsteps tread the heavenly hall,
Because too deeply, from on high,
I pitied man's mortality!
Hark, and again! that fluttering sound
Of wings that whirr and circle round,
And their light rustle thrills the air—
How all things that unseen draw near
Are to me Fear!

[*Enter the Chorus of Oceanides in winged cars.*]

CHORUS
Ah, fear us not! as friends, with rivalry
Of swiftly-vying wings, we came together
Unto this rock and thee!
With our sea-sire we pleaded hard, until
We won him to our will,
And swift the wafting breezes bore us hither.
The heavy hammer's steely blow
Thrilled to our ocean-cavern from afar,
Banished soft shyness from our maiden brow,
And with unsandalled feet we come, in winged car!

PROMETHEUS
Ah well-a-day! ye come, ye come
From the Sea-Mother's teeming home—
Children of Tethys and the sire
Who around Earth rolls, gyre on gyre,
His sleepless ocean-tide!
Look on me—shackled with what chain,
Upon this chasm's beetling side
I must my dismal watch sustain!

CHORUS
Yea, I behold, Prometheus! and my fears
Draw swiftly o'er mine eyes a mist fulfilled of tears,
When I behold thy frame
Bound, wasting on the rock, and put to shame
By adamantine chains!
The rudder and the rule of Heaven
Are to strange pilots given:
Zeus with new laws and strong caprice holds sway,
Unkings the ancient Powers, their might constrains,
And thrusts their pride away!

PROMETHEUS
Had he but hurled me, far beneath
The vast and ghostly halls of Death,
Down to the limitless profound Of Tartarus,
in fetters bound, fixed by his unrelenting hand!

So had no man, nor God on high,
Exulted o'er mine agony—
But now, a sport to wind and sky,
Mocked by my foes, I stand!

CHORUS
What God can wear such ruthless heart
As to delight in ill?
Who in thy sorrow bears not part?
Zeus, Zeus alone! for he, with wrathful will,
Clenched and inflexible,
Bears down Heaven's race—nor end shall be, till hate
His soul shall satiate,
Or till, by some device, some other hand
Shall wrest from him his sternly-clasped command!

PROMETHEUS
Yet,—though in shackles close and strong
I lie in wasting torments long,—
Yet the new tyrant, 'neath whose nod
Cowers down each blest subservient god,
One day, far hence, my help shall need,
The destined stratagem to read,
Whereby, in some yet distant day,
Zeus shall be reaved of pride and sway:
And no persuasion's honied spell
Shall lure me on, the tale to tell;
And no stern threat shall make me cower
And yield the secret to his power,
Until his purpose be foregone,
And shackles yield, and he atone
The deep despite that he hath done!

CHORUS
O strong in hardihood, thou striv'st amain
Against the stress of pain!
But yet too free, too resolute thy tongue
In challenging thy wrong!
Ah, shuddering dread doth make my spirit quiver,
And o'er thy fate sits Fear!
I see not to what shore of safety ever

Thy bark can steer—
In depths unreached the will of Zeus doth dwell,
Hidden, implacable!

PROMETHEUS
Ay, stern is Zeus, and Justice stands,
Wrenched to his purpose, in his hands—
Yet shall he learn, perforce, to know
A milder mood, when falls the blow—
His ruthless wrath he shall lay still,
And he and I with mutual will
In concord's bond shall go.

CHORUS
Unveil, say forth to us the tale entire,
Under what imputation Zeus laid hands
On thee, to rack thee thus with shameful pangs?
Tell us—unless the telling pain thee—all!

PROMETHEUS
Grievous alike are these things for my tongue,
Grievous for silence—rueful everyway.
Know that, when first the gods began their strife,
And heaven was all astir with mutual feud—
Some willing to fling Cronos from his throne,
And set, forsooth, their Zeus on high as king,
And other some in contrariety
Striving to bar him from heaven's throne for aye—
Thereon I sought to counsel for the best
The Titan brood of Ouranos and Earth;
Yet I prevailed not, for they held in scorn
My glozing wiles, and, in their hardy pride,
Deemed that sans effort they could grasp the sway.
But, for my sake, my mother Themis oft,
And Earth, one symbol of names manifold,
Had held me warned, how in futurity
It stood ordained that not by force or power,
But by some wile, the victors must prevail.
In such wise I interpreted; but they
Deigned not to cast their heed thereon at all.
Then, of things possible, I deemed it best,

Joining my mother's wisdom to mine own,
To range myself with Zeus, two wills in one.
Thus, by device of mine, the murky depth
Of Tartarus enfoldeth Cronos old
And those who strove beside him. Such the aid
I gave the lord of heaven—my meed for which
He paid me thus, a penal recompense!
For 'tis the inward vice of tyranny,
To deem of friends as being secret foes.
Now, to your question—hear me clearly show
On what imputed fault he tortures me.
Scarce was he seated on his father's throne,
When he began his doles of privilege
Among the lesser gods, allotting power
In trim division; while of mortal men
Nothing he recked, nor of their misery
Nay, even willed to blast their race entire
To nothingness, and breed another brood;
And none but I was found to cross his will.
I dared it, I alone; I rescued men
From crushing ruin and th' abyss of hell—
Therefore am I constrained in chastisement
Grievous to bear and piteous to behold,—
Yea, firm to feel compassion for mankind,
Myself was held unworthy of the same—
Ay, beyond pity am I ranged and ruled
To sufferance—a sight that shames his sway!

CHORUS
A heart of steel, a mould of stone were he,
Who could complacently behold thy pains
I came not here as craving for this sight,
And, seeing it, I stand heart-wrung with pain.

PROMETHEUS
Yea truly, kindly eyes must pity me!

CHORUS
Say, didst thou push transgression further still?

PROMETHEUS
Ay, man thro' me ceased to foreknow his death.

CHORUS
What cure couldst thou discover for this curse?

PROMETHEUS
Blind hopes I sent to nestle in man's heart.

CHORUS
This was a goodly gift thou gavest them.

PROMETHEUS
Yet more I gave them, even the boon of fire.

CHORUS
What? radiant fire, to things ephemeral?

PROMETHEUS
Yea—many an art too shall they learn thereby!

CHORUS
Then, upon imputation of such guilt,
Doth Zeus without surcease torment thee thus?
Is there no limit to thy course of pain?

PROMETHEUS
None, till his own will shall decree an end.

CHORUS
And how shall he decree it? say, what hope?
Seest thou not thy sin? yet of that sin
It irks me sore to speak, as thee to hear.
Nay, no more words hereof; bethink thee now,
From this ordeal how to find release.

PROMETHEUS
Easy it is, for one whose foot is set
Outside the slough of pain, to lesson well
With admonitions him who lies therein.
With perfect knowledge did I all I did,

I willed to sin, and sinned, I own it all—
I championed men, unto my proper pain.
Yet scarce I deemed that, in such cruel doom,
Withering upon this skyey precipice,
I should inherit lonely mountain crags,
Here, in a vast tin-neighboured solitude.
Yet list not to lament my present pains,
But, stepping from your cars unto the ground,
Listen, the while I tell the future fates
Now drawing near, until ye know the whole.
Grant ye, O grant my prayer, be pitiful
To one now racked with woe! the doom of pain
Wanders, but settles, soon or late, on all.

CHORUS
To willing hearts, and schooled to feel,
Prometheus, came thy tongue's appeal;
Therefore we leave, with lightsome tread,
The flying cars in which we sped—
We leave the stainless virgin air
Where winged creatures float and fare,
And by thy side, on rocky land,
Thus gently we alight and stand,
Willing, from end to end, to know
Thine history of woe.

[*The Chorus alight from their winged cars. Enter Oceanus, mounted on a griffin.*]

OCEANUS
Thus, over leagues and leagues of space
I come, Prometheus, to thy place—
By will alone, not rein, I guide
The winged thing on which I ride;
And much, be sure, I mourn thy case—
Kinship is Pity's bond, I trow;
And, wert thou not akin, I vow
None other should have more than thou
Of my compassion's grace!
'Tis said, and shall be proved; no skill
Have I to gloze and feign goodwill!
Name but some mode of helpfulness,

And thou wilt in a trice confess
That I, Oceanus, am best
Of all thy friends, and trustiest.

PROMETHEUS
Ho, what a sight of marvel! what, thou too
Comest to contemplate my pains, and darest—
(Yet how, I wot not!) leaving far behind
The circling tide, thy namefellow, and those
Rock-arched, self-hollowed caverns—thus to come
Unto this land, whose womb bears iron ore?
Art come to see my lot, resent with me
The ills I bear? Well, gaze thy fill! behold
Me, friend of Zeus, part-author of his power—
Mark, in what ruthlessness he bows me down!

OCEANUS
Yea, I behold, Prometheus! and would warn
Thee, spite of all thy wisdom, for thy weal!
Learn now thyself to know, and to renew
A rightful spirit within thee, for, made new
With pride of place, sits Zeus among the gods!
Now, if thou choosest to fling forth on him
Words rough with anger thus and edged with scorn,
Zeus, though he sit aloof, afar, on high,
May hear thine utterance, and make thee deem
His present wrath a mere pretence of pain.
Banish, poor wretch! the passion of thy soul,
And seek, instead, acquittance from thy pangs!
Belike my words seem ancientry to thee—
Such, natheless, O Prometheus, is the meed
That doth await the overweening tongue!
Meek wert thou never, wilt not crouch to pain,
But, set amid misfortunes, cravest more!
Now—if thou let thyself be schooled by me—
Thou must not kick against the goad. Thou knowest,
A despot rules, harsh, resolute, supreme,
Whose law is will. Yet shall I go to him,
With all endeavour to relieve thy plight—
So thou wilt curb the tempest of thy tongue!
Surely thou knowest, in thy wisdom deep,

The saw—Who vaunts amiss, quick pain is his.

PROMETHEUS
O enviable thou, and unaccused—
Thou who wast art and part in all I dared!
And now, let be! make this no care of thine,
For Zeus is past persuasion—urge him not!
Look to thyself, lest thine emprise thou rue.

OCEANUS
Thou hast more skill to school thy neighbour's fault
Than to amend thine own: 'tis proved and plain,
By fact, not hearsay, that I read this well.
Yet am I fixed to go—withhold me not—
Assured I am, assured, that Zeus will grant
The boon I crave, the loosening of thy bonds.

PROMETHEUS
In part I praise thee, to the end will praise;
Goodwill thou lackest not, but yet forbear
Thy further trouble! If thy heart be fain,
Bethink thee that thy toil avails me not.
Nay, rest thee well, aloof from danger's brink!
I will not ease my woe by base relief
In knowing others too involved therein.
Away the thought! for deeply do I rue
My brother Atlas' doom. Far off he stands
In sunset land, and on his shoulder bears
The pillar'd mountain-mass whose base is earth,
Whose top is heaven, and its ponderous load
Too great for any grasp. With pity too
I saw Earth's child, the monstrous thing of war,
That in Cilicia's hollow places dwelt—
Typho;[1] I saw his hundred-headed form
Crushed and constrained; yet once his stride was fierce,
His jaws gaped horror and their hiss was death,
And all heaven's host he challenged to the fray,
While, as one vowed to storm the power of Zeus,
Forth from his eyes he shot a demon glare.
It skilled not: the unsleeping bolt of Zeus,
The downward levin with its rush of flame,

Smote on him, and made dumb for evermore
The clamour of his vaunting: to the heart
Stricken he lay, and all that mould of strength
Sank thunder-shattered to a smouldering ash;
And helpless now and laid in ruin huge
He lieth by the narrow strait of sea,
Crushed at the root of Etna's mountain-pile.
High on the pinnacles whereof there sits
Hephaestus, sweltering at the forge; and thence
On some hereafter day shall burst and stream
The lava-floods, that shall with ravening fangs
Gnaw thy smooth lowlands, fertile Sicily!
Such ire shall Typho from his living grave
Send seething up, such jets of fiery surge,
Hot and unslaked, altho' himself be laid
In quaking ashes by Zeus' thunderbolt.
But thou dost know hereof, nor needest me
To school thy sense: thou knowest safety's road—
Walk then thereon! I to the dregs will drain,
Till Zeus relent from wrath, my present woe.

OCEANUS
Nay, but, Prometheus, know'st thou not the saw—
Words can appease the angry soul's disease?

PROMETHEUS
Ay—if in season one apply their salve,
Not scorching wrath's proud flesh with caustic tongue.

OCEANUS
But in wise thought and venturous essay
Perceivest thou a danger? prithee tell!

PROMETHEUS
I see a fool's good nature, useless toil.

OCEANUS
Let me be sick of that disease; I know,
Loyalty, masked as folly, wins the way.

PROMETHEUS
But of thy blunder I shall bear the blame.

OCEANUS
Clearly, thy word would send me home again.

PROMETHEUS
Lest thy lament for me should bring thee hate.

OCEANUS
Hate from the newly-throned Omnipotence?

PROMETHEUS
Be heedful—lest his will be wroth with thee!

OCEANUS
Thy doom, Prometheus, cries to me "Beware"!

PROMETHEUS
Mount, make away, discretion at thy side!

OCEANUS
Thy word is said to me in act to go:
For lo, my hippogriff with waving wings
Fans the smooth course of air, and fain is he
To rest his limbs within his ocean stall.

[*Exit Oceanus.*]

Translated by E.D.A. Morshead.

PINDAR

c. 518 - 438 BC

Pindar is considered the most significant Greek choral poet. He was born into an aristocratic family at Cynoscephalae in Boeotia. From the beginning of his career, he mingled closely with the prominent families and the courts of continental Greece and the islands. The ancients collected his poems in 17 books, of which four survive: the Olympian, Pythian, Isthmian, and Nemean triumphal odes. He excelled in the art of epinicia, *the composing of victory songs honoring the winners of athletic competitions. In his odes, Pindar compares the victors to the heroes, the sons of the gods, and lauds their cities of origin.*

His poems helped spread his fame throughout the ancient world. Despite his success as a poet, however, Pindar had a formidable rival, Bacchylides, who frequented the same courts and who was commissioned by Hieron of Syracuse to sing his victory in 468 BC. Pindar, too, quickly found a new patron, the king of Cyrene (modern Libya) in North Africa, for whom he composed Pythian Odes *4 and 5 between 462 BC and 461 BC.*

Pindar demonstrates his poetic genius in full measure in his triumphal odes. They would represent the last echoes of the aristocratic way of life. Yet, although he had admirers, Pindar did not have immediate followers. The exploits to sing were no longer those of the games but those of political life.

Founding of the Olympic Games
Pindar, *Olympian Odes* 6

This ode celebrates the victory of Agesias, the son of Sostratos, in the chariot race at the Olympic games of 472 BC. As he often does in his poems, Pindar praises the winner by lauding his prestigious ancestors and his family's achievements. Agesias was a descendent of Iamos, the hero of Olympia and the son of Apollo. The myth claims that Pitane, the daughter of the River Eurotas, bore Poseidon a daughter, Evadne, who was raised by her human "father," Aepytos. Evadne was seduced by Apollo and gave birth to a son whom she abandoned. The infant survived and received the name Iamos ("the child of the violets") because his mother found him again by chance among the blooming violets. As an adult, Iamos journeyed to Olympia where Heracles would establish the games. He became the father of a long line of priests and seers.

Pindar celebrates this in his sixth Olympian Ode, *and also recounts that the descendents of Iamos were among the first settlers of Syracuse. Pindar observes that the winner, Agesias, belonged to two places: he was both a citizen of Syracuse and of Stymphalus in Arcadia where the ode was sung.*

"Deeds of no risk are honourless."

Golden pillars will we set up in the porch of the house of our song, as in a stately palace-hall; for it beseemeth that in the fore-front of the work the entablature shoot far its splendour.

Now if one be an Olympian conqueror and treasurer to the prophetic altar of Zeus at Pisa,[1] and joint founder of glorious Syracuse, shall such an one hide him from hymns of praise, if his lot be among citizens who hear without envy the desired sounds of song? For in a sandal of such sort let the son of Sostratos know that his fortunate foot is set. Deeds of no risk are honourless whether done among men or among hollow ships; but if a noble deed be wrought with labour, many make mention thereof.

For thee, Agesias, is that praise prepared which justly and openly Adrastos spake of old concerning the seer Amphiaraos the son of Oikleus, when the earth had swallowed him and his shining steeds.[2] For afterward, when on seven pyres dead men were burnt, the son of Talaos spake on this wise: 'I seek the eye of my host, him who was alike a good seer and a good fighter with the spear.'

This praise also belongeth to the Syracusan who is lord of this triumphal song. I who am no friend of strife or wrongful quarrel will bear him this witness even with a solemn oath, and the sweet voice of the Muses shall not say me nay.

O Phintis[3] yoke me now with all speed the strength of thy mules that on the clear highway we may set our car, that I may go up to the far beginning of this race. For those mules know well to lead the way in this course as in others, who at Olympia have won crowns: it behoveth them that we throw open to them the gates of song, for to Pitane by Eurotas' stream must I begone betimes to-day.

Now Pitane, they say, lay with Poseidon the son of Kronos and bare the child Euadne with tresses iris-dark. The fruit of her body unwedded she hid by her robe's folds, and in the month of her delivery she sent her handmaids and bade them give the child to the hero son of Elatos to rear, who was lord of the men of Arcady who dwelt at Phaisane, and had for his lot Alpheos to dwell beside.

There was the child Euadne nurtured, and by Apollo's side she first knew the joys of Aphrodite.

But she might not always hide from Aipytos the seed of the god within her; and he in his heart struggling with bitter strain against a grief too great for speech betook him to Pytho that he might ask of the oracle concerning the intolerable woe.

But she beneath a thicket's shade put from her silver pitcher and her girdle of scarlet web, and she brought forth a boy in whom was the spirit of God. By her side the gold-haired god set kindly Eleutho and the Fates, and from her womb in easy travail came forth Iamos to the light. Him in her anguish she left upon the ground, but by the counsel of gods two bright-eyed serpents nursed and fed him with the harmless venom of the bee.

But when the king came back from rocky Delphi in his chariot he asked all who were in the house concerning the child whom Euadne had born; for he said that the sire whereof he was begotten was Phoibos, and that he should be a prophet unto the people of the land excelling all mortal men, and that his seed should be for ever.

Such was his tale, but they answered that they had neither seen nor heard of him, though he was now born five days. For he was hidden among rushes in an impenetrable brake, his tender body all suffused with golden and deep purple gleams of iris flowers; wherefore his mother prophesied saying that by this holy name of immortality he should be called throughout all time.

But when he had come to the ripeness of golden-crowned sweet youth, he went down into the middle of Alpheos and called on wide-ruling Poseidon his grandsire, and on the guardian of god-built Delos, the bearer of the bow, praying that honour might be upon his head for the rearing of a people; and he stood beneath the heavens, and it was night.

Then the infallible Voice of his father answered and said unto him: Arise, my son, and come hither, following my voice, into a place where all men shall meet together.

So they came to the steep rock of lofty Kronion; there the god gave him a twofold treasure of prophecy, that for the time then being he should hearken to his voice that cannot lie; but when Herakles of valorous counsels, the sacred scion of the Alkeidai, should have come, and should have founded a multitudinous feast and the chief ordinance of games, then again on the summit of the altar of Zeus he bade him establish yet another oracle, that thenceforth the race of Iamidai should be glorious among Hellenes.

Good luck abode with them; for that they know the worth of valour they are entered on a glorious road.

The matter proveth the man, but from the envious calumny ever threateneth them on whom, as they drive foremost in the twelfth round of the course, Charis sheddeth blushing beauty to win them fame more fair.

Now if in very truth, Agesias, thy mother's ancestors dwelling by the borders of Kyllene did piously and oft offer up prayer and sacrifice to Hermes, herald of the gods, who hath to his keeping the strife and appointment of games, and doeth honour to Arcadia the nurse of goodly men,—then surely he, O son of Sostratos, with his loud-thundering sire, is the accomplisher of this thy bliss.

Methinks I have upon my tongue a whetstone of loud sounding speech, which to harmonious breath constraineth me nothing loth. Mother of my mother was Stymphalian Metope of fair flowers, for she bare Thebe the charioteer, whose pleasant fountain I will drink, while I weave for warriors the changes of my song.

Now rouse thy fellows, Ainëas, first to proclaim the name of maiden Hera, and next to know for sure whether we are escaped from the ancient reproach that spake truly of Boeotian swine. For thou art a true messenger, a writing-tally of the Muses goodly-haired, a bowl wherein to mix high-sounding songs.

And bid them make mention of Syracuse and of Ortygia, which Hieron ruleth with righteous sceptre devising true counsels, and doth honour to Demeter whose footsteps make red the corn, and to the feast of her daughter with white steeds, and to the might of Aetnaean Zeus. Also he is well known of the sweet voices of the song and lute. Let not the on-coming time break his good fortune. And with joyful welcome may he receive this triumphal song, which travelleth from home to home, leaving Stymphalos' walls, the mother-city of Arcadia, rich in flocks.

Good in a stormy night are two anchors let fall from a swift ship. May friendly gods grant to both peoples an illustrious lot: and thou O lord and ruler of the sea, husband of Amphitrite of the golden distaff, grant this my friend straight voyage and unharmed, and bless the joyous flower of my song.

Translated by Ernest Myers.

Birth of Rhodes, the Island of the Sun

Pindar, *Olympian Odes* 7

The Olympian winner celebrated in this poem heralds from Rhodes, and, for this reason, Pindar explains the mythical origins of the island. Legend has it that the island was colonized by Tlepolemos, a son of Heracles who first settled at Argos but later exiled himself after killing his great uncle, Likymnios, with a club. Pindar further explains how the gods forgot Helios when they divided the world among themselves. Rhodes then emerged from the sea and was allotted to the sun god. Plato mentions a similar partitioning of the earth between the gods, whereby Poseidon receives the mythical island of Atlantis.

"Now round the minds of men hang follies unnumbered—this is the unachievable thing, to find what shall be best hap for a man both presently and also at the last."

As when from a wealthy hand one lifting a cup, made glad within with the dew of the vine, maketh gift thereof to a youth his daughter's spouse, a largess of the feast from home to home, an all-golden choicest treasure, that the banquet may have grace, and that he may glorify his kin; and therewith he maketh him envied in the eyes of the friends around him for a wedlock wherein hearts are wedded—

So also I, my liquid nectar sending, the Muses' gift, the sweet fruit of my soul, to men that are winners in the games at Pytho or Olympia make holy offering. Happy is he whom good report encompasseth; now on one man, now on another doth the Grace that quickeneth look favourably, and tune for him the lyre and the pipe's stops of music manifold.

Thus to the sound of the twain am I come with Diagoras sailing home, to sing the sea-girt Rhodes, child of Aphrodite and bride of Helios, that to a mighty and fair-fighting man, who by Alpheos' stream and by Kastalia's hath won him crowns,[4] I may for his boxing make award of glory, and to his father Demegetos in whom Justice hath her delight, dwellers in the isle of three cities with an Argive host, nigh to a promontory of spacious Asia.

Fain would I truly tell from the beginning from Tlepolemos the message of my word, the common right of this puissant seed of Herakles. For on the father's side they claim from Zeus, and on the mother's from Astydameia, sons of Amyntor.

Now round the minds of men hang follies unnumbered—this is the unachievable thing, to find what shall be best hap for a man both presently and also at the last. Yea for the very founder of this country once on a time struck with his staff of tough wild-olive-wood Alkmene's bastard brother Likymnios in Tiryns as he came forth from Midea's chamber, and slew him in the kindling of his wrath. So even the wise man's feet are turned astray by tumult of the soul.

Then he came to enquire of the oracle of God. And he of the golden hair from his sweet-incensed shrine spake unto him of a sailing of ships that should be from the shore of Lerna unto a pasture ringed with sea, where sometime the great king of gods rained on the city golden snow, what time by Hephaistos' handicraft beneath the bronze-wrought axe from the crown of her father's head Athene leapt to light and cried aloud with an exceeding cry; and Heaven trembled at her coming, and Earth, the Mother.

Then also the god who giveth light to men, Hyperion, bade his beloved sons see that they guard the payment of the debt, that they should build first for the goddess an altar in the sight of all men, and laying thereon a holy offering they should make glad the hearts of the father and of his daughter of the sounding spear. Now Reverence, Forethought's child, putteth valour and the joy of battle into the hearts of men; yet withal there cometh upon them bafflingly the cloud of forgetfulness and maketh the mind to swerve from the straight path of action. For they though they had brands burning yet kindled not the seed of flame, but with fireless rites they made a grove on the hill of the citadel. For them Zeus brought a yellow cloud into the sky and rained much gold upon the land; and Glaukopis[5] herself gave them to excel the dwellers upon earth in every art of handicraft. For on their roads ran the semblances of beasts and creeping things: whereof they have great glory, for to him that hath knowledge the subtlety that is without deceit is the greater altogether.

Now the ancient story of men saith that when Zeus and the other gods made division of the earth among them, not yet was island Rhodes apparent in the open sea, but in the briny depths lay hid. And for that Helios was otherwhere, none drew a lot for him; so they left him portionless of land, that holy god. And when he spake thereof Zeus would cast lots afresh; but he suffered him not, for that he said that beneath the hoary sea he saw a certain land waxing from its root in earth, that should bring forth food for many men, and rejoice in flocks. And straightway he bade her of the golden fillet, Lachesis,[6] to stretch her hands on high, nor violate the gods' great oath, but with the son of Kronos promise him that the isle sent up to the light of heaven should be thenceforth a title of himself alone.

And in the end of the matter his speech had fulfilment; there sprang up from the watery main an island, and the father who begetteth the keen rays of day hath the dominion thereof, even the lord of fire-breathing steeds. There sometime having lain with Rhodos he begat seven sons, who had of him minds wiser than any among the men of old; and one begat Kameiros, and Ialysos his eldest, and Lindos: and they held each apart their shares of cities, making threefold division of their father's land, and these men call their dwelling-places. There is a sweet amends for his piteous ill-hap ordained for Tlepolemos leader of the Tirynthians at the beginning, as for a god, even the leading thither of sheep for a savoury burnt-offering, and the award of honour in games.

Of garlands from these games hath Diagoras twice won him crowns, and four times he had good luck at famous Isthmos and twice following at Nemea, and twice at rocky Athens. And at Argos the bronze shield knoweth him, and the deeds of Arcadia and of Thebes and the yearly games Boeotian, and Pellene and Aigina where six times he won; and the pillar of stone at Megara hath the same tale to tell.

But do thou, O Father Zeus, who holdest sway on the mountain-ridges of Atabyrios[7] glorify the accustomed Olympian winner's hymn, and the man who hath done valiantly with his fists: give him honour at the hands of citizens and of strangers; for he walketh in the straight way that abhorreth insolence, having learnt well the lessons his true soul hath taught him, which hath come to him from his noble sires. Darken not thou the light of one who springeth from the same stock of Kallianax. Surely with the joys of Eratidai the whole city maketh mirth. But the varying breezes even at the same point of time speed each upon their various ways.

Translated by Ernest Myers.

Expedition of the Argonauts. Founding of Cyrene.

Pindar, *Pythian Odes* 4

The winner of the chariot race at the games held at Delphi in 462 BC was from the Libyan city of Cyrene. In his usual manner, Pindar retraces the history of the city's founding, which, according to him, dates back to the expedition of the Argonauts. The story is as follows: When Jason reclaims the power due him, his uncle, Pelias, makes it conditional that he return the golden fleece. The coveted fleece is located in Colchis at the extremity of the Black Sea. Jason launches the expedition of the Argonauts, retrieves the golden fleece with Medea's help, and returns to Greece. On his journey back to the homeland, the Argonaut Euphemus throws a clod of earth into the sea and thereby causes the island of Thera to spring from the waters. One of his descendents, Battus, founds the colony of Cyrene. Why does Pindar express so much interest in this myth? It happens that Arkesilas, the Pythian winner, is also the king of Cyrene and descends from the eighth generation of Battus. The buckle is buckled.

Pindar further writes the ode for his friend, Demophilos, who was banished from Cyrene and was traveling in Thebes during the victory of Arkesilas. In the last part of the poem, Pindar addresses the king of Cyrene and asks him to exercise leniency toward Demophilos and allow him back into the country.

"Too ready are the minds of mortal men to choose a guileful gain rather than righteousness, howbeit they travel ever to a stern reckoning."

This day O Muse must thou tarry in a friend's house, the house of the king of Kyrene of goodly horses, that with Arkesilas at his triumph thou mayst swell the favourable gale of song, the due of Leto's children, and of Pytho. For at Pytho of old she who sitteth beside the eagles of Zeus—nor was Apollo absent then—the priestess, spake this oracle, that Battos should found a power in fruitful Libya, that straightway departing from the holy isle he might lay the foundations of a city of goodly chariots upon a white breast of the swelling earth, and might fulfil in the seventeenth generation the word of Medea spoken at Thera, which of old the passionate child of Aietes, queen of Colchians, breathed from immortal lips. For on this wise spake she to the warrior Jason's god-begotten crew: 'Hearken O sons of high-hearted mortals and of gods. Lo I say unto you that from this sea-lashed land the daughter of Epaphos[8] shall sometime be planted with a root to bring forth cities that shall possess the minds of men, where Zeus Ammon's shrine is builded.

And instead of short-finned dolphins they shall take to them fleet mares, and reins instead of oars shall they ply, and speed the whirlwind-footed car.

By that augury shall it come to pass that Thera shall be mother-city of mighty commonwealths, even the augury that once at the outpourings of the Tritonian lake Euphemos leaping from the prow took at the hands of a god who in the likeness of man tendered this present to the stranger of a clod of earth; and the Father Kronian Zeus confirmed it with a peal of thunder.

What time he came suddenly upon them as they were hanging against the ship the bronze-fluked anchor, fleet Argo's bridle; for now for twelve days had we borne from Ocean over long backs of desert-land our sea-ship, after that by my counsel we drew it up upon the shore.

Then came to us the solitary god, having put on the splendid semblance of a noble man; and he began friendly speech, such as well-doers use when they bid new-comers to the feast.

But the plea of the sweet hope of home suffered us not to stay. Then he said that he was Eurypylos son of the earth-embracer, immortal Ennosides; and for that he was aware that we hasted to be gone, he straightway caught up of the chance earth at his feet a gift that he would fain bestow. Nor was the hero unheeding, but leaping on the shore and striking hand in hand he took to him the fateful clod.

But now I hear that it was washed down from the ship and departed into the sea with the salt spray of evening, following the watery deep. Yet verily often did I charge the labour-lightening servants that they should keep it safe, but they forgat: and now upon this island is the imperishable seed of spacious Libya strown before the time appointed; for if the royal son of Poseidon, lord of horses, whom Europa Tityos' child bare him on Kephisos' banks, had in his own home thrown it down beside the mouth of Hades' gulf, then in the fourth generation of his sons his seed would have taken that wide continent of Libya, for then they would have gone forth from mighty Lakedaimon, and from the Argive gulf, and from Mykenai.

But now he shall in wedlock with a stranger-wife raise up a chosen seed, who coming to this island with worship of their gods shall beget one to be lord of the misty plains. Him sometime shall Phoibos in his golden house admonish by oracles, when in the latter days he shall go down into the inner shrine at Pytho, to bring a host in ships to the rich Nile-garden of the son of Kronos.'

So ran Medea's rhythmic utterance, and motionless in silence the godlike heroes bowed their heads as they hearkened to the counsels of wisdom.

Thee, happy son of Polymnestos, did the oracle of the Delphian bee approve with call unasked to be the man whereof the word was spoken, for thrice she bid thee hail and declared thee by decree of fate Kyrene's king, what time thou enquiredst what help should be from heaven for thy labouring speech.[9] And verily even now long afterward, as in the bloom of rosy-blossomed spring, in the eighth descent from Battos the leaf of Arkesilas is green. To him Apollo and Pytho have given glory in the chariot-race at the hands of the Amphiktyons: him will I commend to the Muses, and withal the tale of the all-golden fleece; for this it was the Minyai sailed to seek when the god-given glories of their race began.[10]

What power first drave them in the beginning to the quest? What perilous enterprise clenched them with strong nails of adamant?

There was an oracle of God which said that Pelias should die by force or by stern counsels of the proud sons of Aiolos, and there had come to him a prophecy that froze his cunning heart, spoken at the central stone of tree-clad mother Earth, that by every means he should keep safe guard against the man of one sandal, whensoever from a homestead on the hills he shall have come to the sunny land of glorious Iolkos, whether a stranger or a citizen he be.

So in the fullness of time he came, wielding two spears, a wondrous man; and the vesture that was upon him was twofold, the garb of the Magnetes' country close fitting to his splendid limbs, but above he wore a leopard-skin to turn the hissing showers; nor were the bright locks of his hair shorn from him but over all his back ran rippling down. Swiftly he went straight on, and took his stand, making trial of his dauntless soul, in the marketplace when the multitude was full.

Him they knew not; howbeit some one looking reverently on him would speak on this wise: 'Not Apollo surely is this, nor yet Aphrodite's lord of the brazen car; yea and in glistening Naxos died ere now, they say, the children of Iphimedeia, Otos and thou, bold king Ephialtes: moreover Tityos was the quarry of Artemis' swift arrow sped from her invincible quiver, warning men to touch only the loves within their power.'

They answering each to each thus talked; but thereon with headlong haste of mules and polished car came Pelias; and he was astonied when he gazed on the plain sign of the single sandal on the right foot. But he dissembled his fear within his heart and said unto him, 'What land, O stranger, dost thou claim to be thy country, and who of earth-born mortals bare thee of her womb out of due time? Tell me thy race and shame it not by hateful lies.'

And him with gentle words the other answered undismayed, 'I say to thee that I bear with me the wisdom of Cheiron, for from Chariklo and Philyra I come, from the cave where the Centaur's pure daughters reared me up, and now have I fulfilled twenty years among them without deceitful word or deed, and I am come home to seek the ancient honour of my father, held now in rule unlawful, which of old Zeus gave to the chief Aiolos and his children. For I hear that Pelias yielding lawlessly to evil thoughts hath robbed it from my fathers whose right it was from the beginning; for they, when first I looked upon the light, fearing the violence of an injurious lord, made counterfeit of a dark funeral in the house as though I were dead, and amid the wailing of women sent me forth secretly in purple swathing-bands, when none but Night might know the way we went, and gave me to Cheiron the son of Kronos to be reared.

But of these things the chief ye know. Now therefore kind citizens show me plainly the house of my fathers who drave white horses; for it shall hardly be said that a son of Aison, born in the land, is come hither to a strange and alien soil. And Jason was the name whereby the divine Beast[11] spake to me.'

Thus he said, and when he had entered in, the eyes of his father knew him; and from his aged eyelids gushed forth tears, for his soul was glad within him when he beheld his son, fairest of men and goodliest altogether.

Then came to him both brothers, when they heard that Jason was come home, Pheres from hard by, leaving the fountain Hypereis, and out of Messena Amythaon, and quickly came Admetos and Melampos to welcome home their cousin. And at a common feast with gracious words Jason received them and made them friendly cheer, culling for five long nights and days the sacred flower of joyous life.

But on the sixth day he began grave speech, and set the whole matter before his kinsmen from the beginning, and they were of one mind with him.

Then quickly he rose up with them from their couches, and they came to Pelias' hall, and they made haste and entered and stood within.

And when he heard them the king himself came forth to them, even the son of Tyro of the lovely hair. Then Jason with gentle voice opened on him the stream of his soft speech, and laid foundation of wise words: 'Son of Poseidon of the Rock, too ready are the minds of mortal men to choose a guileful gain rather than righteousness, howbeit they travel ever to a stern reckoning. But thee and me it behoveth to give law to our desires, and to devise weal for the time to come. Though thou knowest it yet will I tell thee, how that the same mother bare Kretheus and rash Salmoneus, and in the third generation we again were begotten and look upon the strength of the golden sun. Now if there be enmity between kin, the Fates stand aloof and would fain hide the shame. Not with bronze-edged swords nor with javelins doth it beseem us twain to divide our forefathers' great honour, nor needeth it, for lo! all sheep and tawny herds of kine I yield, and all the lands whereon thou feedest them, the spoil of my sires wherewith thou makest fat thy wealth. That these things furnish forth thy house moveth me not greatly; but for the kingly sceptre and throne whereon the son of Kretheus sate of old and dealt justice to his chivalry, these without wrath between us yield to me, lest some new evil arise up therefrom.'

Thus he spake, and mildly also did Pelias make reply: 'I will be even as thou wilt, but now the sere of life alone remaineth to me, whereas the flower of thy youth is but just burgeoning; thou art able to take away the sin that maketh the powers beneath the earth wroth with us: for Phrixos biddeth us lay his ghost, and that we go to the house of Aietes, and bring thence the thick-fleeced hide of the ram, whereby of old he was delivered from the deep and from the impious weapons of his step-mother.[12] This message cometh to me in the voice of a strange dream: also I have sent to ask of the oracle at Kastalia whether it be worth the quest, and the oracle chargeth me straightway to send a ship on the sacred mission. This deed do thou offer me to do, and I swear to give thee up the sway and kingly rule. Let Zeus the ancestral god of thee and me be witness of my oath and stablish it surely in thine eyes.'

So they made this covenant and parted; but Jason straightway bade heralds to make known everywhere that a sailing was toward. And quickly came three sons of Zeus, men unwearied in battle, whose mothers were Alkmene and Leto of the glancing eyes,[13] and two tall-crested men of valour, children of the Earth-shaker, whose honour was perfect as their might, from Pylos and from farthest Tainaros: hereby was the excellence of their fame established—even Euphemos' fame, and thine, wide-ruling Periklymenos. And at Apollo's bidding came the minstrel father of song, Orpheus of fair renown.

And Hermes of the golden staff sent two sons to the toilsome task, Echion and Eurytos in the joy of their youth; swiftly they came, even from their dwelling at the foot of Pangaios: and willingly and with glad heart their father Boreas, king of winds, harnessed Zetes and Kalaïs, men both with bright wings shooting from their backs. For Hera kindled within those sons of gods the all-persuading sweet desire for the ship Argo, that none should be left behind and stay by his mother's side in savourless and riskless life, but each, even were death the price, achieve in company with his peers a magic potency of his valour.

Now when that goodly crew were come to Iolkos, Jason mustered them with thanks to each, and the seer Mopsos prophesied by omens and by sacred lots, and with good will sped the host on board.

And when they had hung the anchors over the prow, then their chief taking in his hands a golden goblet stood up upon the stern and called on Zeus whose spear is the lightning, and on the rush of waves and winds and the nights and paths of the deep, to speed them quickly over, and for days of cheer and friendly fortune of return. And from the clouds a favourable voice of thunder pealed in answer; and there came bright lightning flashes bursting through.

Then the heroes took heart in obedience to the heavenly signs; and the seer bade them strike into the water with their oars, while he spake to them of happy hopes; and in their rapid hands the rowing sped untiringly.

And with breezes of the South they came wafted to the mouth of the Axine sea; there they founded a shrine and sacred close of Poseidon, god of seas, where was a red herd of Thracian bulls, and a new-built altar of stone with hollow top.

Then as they set forth toward an exceeding peril they prayed the lord of ships that they might shun the terrible shock of the clashing rocks: for they were twain that had life, and plunged along more swiftly than the legions of the bellowing winds; but that travel of the seed of gods made end of them at last.

After that they came to the Phasis; there they fought with dark-faced Kolchians even in the presence of Aietes. And there the queen of keenest darts, the Cyprus-born, first brought to men from Olympus the frenzied bird, the speckled wry-neck, binding it to a four-spoked wheel without deliverance, and taught the son of Aison to be wise in prayers and charms, that he might make Medea take no thought to honour her parents, and longing for Hellas might drive her by persuasion's lash, her heart afire with love.

Then speedily she showed him the accomplishment of the tasks her father set, and mixing drugs with oil gave him for his anointment antidotes of cruel pain, and they vowed to be joined together in sweet wedlock.

But when Aietes had set in the midst a plough of adamant, and oxen that from tawny jaws breathed flame of blazing fire, and with bronze hoofs smote the earth in alternate steps, and had led them and yoked them single-handed, he marked out in a line straight furrows, and for a fathom's length clave the back of the loamy earth; then he spake thus: 'This work let your king, whosoever he be that hath command of the ship, accomplish me, and then let him bear away with him the imperishable coverlet, the fleece glittering with tufts of gold.'

He said, and Jason flung off from him his saffron mantle, and putting his trust in God betook himself to the work; and the fire made him not to shrink, for that he had had heed to the bidding of the stranger maiden skilled in all pharmacy. So he drew to him the plough and made fast by force the bulls' necks in the harness, and plunged the wounding goad into the bulk of their huge sides, and with manful strain fulfilled the measure of his work. And a cry without speech came from Aietes in his agony, at the marvel of the power he beheld.

Then to the strong man his comrades stretched forth their hands, and crowned him with green wreaths, and greeted him with gracious words. And thereupon the wondrous son of Helios told him in what place the knife of Phrixos had stretched the shining fell; yet he trusted that this labour at least should never be accomplished by him. For it lay in a thick wood and grasped by a terrible dragon's jaws, and he in length and thickness was larger than their ship of fifty oars, which the iron's blows had welded.

Long were it for me to go by the beaten track, for the time is nigh out, and I know a certain short path, and many others look to me for skill. The glaring speckled dragon, O Arkesilas, he slew by subtlety, and by her own aid he stole away Medea, the murderess of Pelias. And they went down into the deep of Ocean and into the Red Sea, and to the Lemnian race of husbandslaying wives;[14] there also they had games and wrestled for a prize of vesture, and lay with the women of the land.

And then it was that in a stranger womb, by night or day, the fateful seed was sown of the bright fortune of thy race. For there began the generations of Euphemos, which should be thenceforth without end. And in time mingling among the homes of Lakedaimonian men they made their dwelling in the isle that once was Kalliste:[15] and thence the son of Leto gave thy race the Libyan plain to till it and to do honour therein to your gods, and to rule the divine city of golden-throned Kyrene with devising of the counsels of truth.

Now hearken to a wise saying even as the wisdom of Oedipus. If one with sharp axe lop the boughs of a great oak and mar the glorious form, even in the perishing of the fruit thereof it yet giveth token of that it was; whether at the last it come even to the winter fire, or whether with upright pillars in a master's house it stand, to serve drear service within alien walls, and the place thereof knoweth it no more.

But thou art a physician most timely, and the god of healing maketh thy light burn brightly. A gentle hand must thou set to a festering wound. It is a small thing even for a slight man to shake a city, but to set it firm again in its place this is hard struggle indeed, unless with sudden aid God guide the ruler's hand. For thee are prepared the thanks which these deeds win. Be strong to serve with all thy might Kyrene's goodly destiny.

And of Homer's words take this to ponder in thy heart: "Of a good messenger," he saith, "cometh great honour to every deed." Even to the Muse is right messengership a gain. Now good cause have Kyrene and the glorious house of Battos to know the righteous mind of Demophilos. For he was a boy with boys, yet in counsels an old man of a hundred years: and the evil tongue he robbeth of its loud voice, and hath learnt to abhor the insolent, neither will he make strife against the good, nor tarry when he hath a deed in hand. For a brief span hath opportunity for men, but of him it is known surely when it cometh, and he waiteth thereon a servant but no slave.

Now this they say is of all griefs the sorest, that one knowing good should of necessity abide without lot therein. Yea thus doth Atlas struggle now against the burden of the firmament, far from his native land and his possessions. Yet the Titans were set free by immortal Zeus. As time runneth on the breeze abateth and there are shiftings of the sails. And he hath hope that when he shall have endured to the end his grievous plague he shall see once more his home, and at Apollo's fountain joining in the feast give his soul to rejoice in her youth, and amid citizens who love his art, playing on his carven lute, shall enter upon peace, hurting and hurt of none. Then shall he tell how fair a fountain of immortal verse he made to flow for Arkesilas, when of late he was the guest of Thebes.

Translated by Ernest Myers.

SOPHOCLES

c. 497 - *c.* 405 BC

Sophocles was born at Colonos, a suburb of Athens. After studying music, he devoted himself to theater and achieved his first victory in drama against Aeschylus in 468 BC. He played an important role in Athenian politics and trained several magistracies. He was, among others, a general with Pericles in 441-440 BC. Extremely pious, Sophocles developed a keen interest in healing divinities like Amynos and Alcon for whom he served as priest. He introduced the cult of Asclepius at Athens around 420 BC. He never left Athens, and he died, at a ripe old age, about 405 BC, several months after the death of Euripides and shortly before the staging of Aristophanes' play The Frogs.

The ancients attributed 123 tragedies to Sophocles. It is probable that he won the grand prize 26 times. Seven plays are preserved, three of which treat the tragedy of Oedipus: Antigone, Oedipus at Colonos, *and* Oedipus the King.

Scholars often commend his succinct style and his superb effectiveness in developing his characters. He introduced numerous innovations to the staging and to the structure of tragedy. For example, he was the first to use painted scenery and to expand the number of chorists from 12 to 15. Above all, he introduced a third actor that enhanced the play's intrigue while adding flexibility to the scenic game.

While treating universal problems, Sophocles often stresses the position of man in the city, more specifically man's difficulty in adapting himself to the constraints of civilized life and of law.

Oedipus in Search of Himself

Sophocles, *Oedipus the King* 216-462

Oedipus is the king of Thebes. He is loved and respected by his subjects whom he liberated from the Sphinx. However, the plague strikes Thebes and leaves women and cattle sterile. The city is slowly dying. Oedipus consults the Oracle of Delphi. It responds by insisting that he must free the city from contamination by avenging the assassination of King Laius carried out by brigands years ago. Oedipus promises his people clarification on the murder and launches an investigation.

The drama centers on Oedipus, who is unaware that he is the murderer of the previous king, who also happened to be his father. Abandoned at birth by Laius because an oracle had predicted that the child would kill his father and marry his mother, Oedipus was raised by the king of Corinth and is ignorant of his true origin. When an oracle tells him that his destiny is to kill his father, he flees Corinth, meets Laius on the way, and kills him following a quarrel. By doing so, Oedipus carries out the inescapable will of the god Apollo. Next, he travels to Thebes, marries Jocasta, the widowed queen who is also his mother, and becomes the sovereign of the city. It is thus he himself whom Oedipus looks for without realizing it, whereas the spectators and the seer Teiresias know the story and understand its tragic ambiguity line by line.

Characters
OEDIPUS, king of Thebes
CHORUS of Theban elders
TEIRESIAS, seer

"Alas, alas, what misery to be wise
When wisdom profits nothing!"

OEDIPUS
Ye pray; 'tis well, but would ye hear my words
And heed them and apply the remedy,
Ye might perchance find comfort and relief.
Mind you, I speak as one who comes a stranger
To this report, no less than to the crime;
For how unaided could I track it far
Without a clue? Which lacking (for too late

Was I enrolled a citizen of Thebes)
This proclamation I address to all:—
Thebans, if any knows the man by whom
Laius, son of Labdacus, was slain,
I summon him to make clean shrift to me.
And if he shrinks, let him reflect that thus
Confessing he shall 'scape the capital charge;
For the worst penalty that shall befall him
Is banishment—unscathed he shall depart.
But if an alien from a foreign land
Be known to any as the murderer,
Let him who knows speak out, and he shall have
Due recompense from me and thanks to boot.
But if ye still keep silence, if through fear
For self or friends ye disregard my hest,
Hear what I then resolve; I lay my ban
On the assassin whosoe'er he be.
Let no man in this land, whereof I hold
The sovereign rule, harbor or speak to him;
Give him no part in prayer or sacrifice
Or lustral rites, but hound him from your homes.
For this is our defilement, so the god
Hath lately shown to me by oracles.
Thus as their champion I maintain the cause
Both of the god and of the murdered King.
And on the murderer this curse I lay
(On him and all the partners in his guilt):—
Wretch, may he pine in utter wretchedness!
And for myself, if with my privity
He gain admittance to my hearth, I pray
The curse I laid on others fall on me.
See that ye give effect to all my hest,
For my sake and the god's and for our land,
A desert blasted by the wrath of heaven.
For, let alone the god's express command,
It were a scandal ye should leave unpurged
The murder of a great man and your king,
Nor track it home. And now that I am lord,
Successor to his throne, his bed, his wife,
(And had he not been frustrate in the hope
Of issue, common children of one womb

Had forced a closer bond twixt him and me,
But Fate swooped down upon him), therefore I
His blood-avenger will maintain his cause
As though he were my sire, and leave no stone
Unturned to track the assassin or avenge
The son of Labdacus, of Polydore,[1]
Of Cadmus, and Agenor first of the race.
And for the disobedient thus I pray:
May the gods send them neither timely fruits
Of earth, nor teeming increase of the womb,
But may they waste and pine, as now they waste,
Aye and worse stricken; but to all of you,
My loyal subjects who approve my acts,
May Justice, our ally, and all the gods
Be gracious and attend you evermore.

CHORUS
The oath thou profferest, sire, I take and swear.
I slew him not myself, nor can I name
The slayer. For the quest, 'twere well, methinks
That Phoebus, who proposed the riddle, himself
Should give the answer—who the murderer was.

OEDIPUS
Well argued; but no living man can hope
To force the gods to speak against their will.

CHORUS
May I then say what seems next best to me?

OEDIPUS
Aye, if there be a third best, tell it too.

CHORUS
My liege, if any man sees eye to eye
With our lord Phoebus, 'tis our prophet, lord
Teiresias; he of all men best might guide
A searcher of this matter to the light.

OEDIPUS
Here too my zeal has nothing lagged, for twice

At Creon's instance have I sent to fetch him,
And long I marvel why he is not here.

CHORUS
I mind me too of rumors long ago—
Mere gossip.

OEDIPUS
Tell them, I would fain know all.

CHORUS
'Twas said he fell by travelers.

OEDIPUS
So I heard,
But none has seen the man who saw him fall.

CHORUS
Well, if he knows what fear is, he will quail
And flee before the terror of thy curse.

OEDIPUS
Words scare not him who blenches not at deeds.

CHORUS
But here is one to arraign him. Lo, at length
They bring the god-inspired seer in whom
Above all other men is truth inborn.

[*Enter Teiresias, led by a boy.*]

OEDIPUS
Teiresias, seer who comprehendest all,
Lore of the wise and hidden mysteries,
High things of heaven and low things of the earth,
Thou knowest, though thy blinded eyes see naught,
What plague infects our city; and we turn
To thee, O seer, our one defense and shield.
The purport of the answer that the God
Returned to us who sought his oracle,
The messengers have doubtless told thee—how
One course alone could rid us of the pest,

To find the murderers of Laius,
And slay them or expel them from the land.
Therefore begrudging neither augury
Nor other divination that is thine,
O save thyself, thy country, and thy king,
Save all from this defilement of blood shed.
On thee we rest. This is man's highest end,
To others' service all his powers to lend.

TEIRESIAS
Alas, alas, what misery to be wise
When wisdom profits nothing! This old lore
I had forgotten; else I were not here.

OEDIPUS
What ails thee? Why this melancholy mood?

TEIRESIAS
Let me go home; prevent me not; 'twere best
That thou shouldst bear thy burden and I mine.

OEDIPUS
For shame! no true-born Theban patriot
Would thus withhold the word of prophecy.

TEIRESIAS
Thy words, O king, are wide of the mark, and I
For fear lest I too trip like thee...

OEDIPUS
Oh speak,
Withhold not, I adjure thee, if thou know'st,
Thy knowledge. We are all thy suppliants.

TEIRESIAS
Aye, for ye all are witless, but my voice
Will ne'er reveal my miseries—or thine.

OEDIPUS
What then, thou knowest, and yet willst not speak!
Wouldst thou betray us and destroy the State?

TEIRESIAS
I will not vex myself nor thee. Why ask
Thus idly what from me thou shalt not learn?

OEDIPUS
Monster! thy silence would incense a flint.
Will nothing loose thy tongue? Can nothing melt thee,
Or shake thy dogged taciturnity?

TEIRESIAS
Thou blam'st my mood and seest not thine own
Wherewith thou art mated; no, thou taxest me.

OEDIPUS
And who could stay his choler when he heard
How insolently thou dost flout the State?

TEIRESIAS
Well, it will come what will, though I be mute.

OEDIPUS
Since come it must, thy duty is to tell me.

TEIRESIAS
I have no more to say; storm as thou willst,
And give the rein to all thy pent-up rage.

OEDIPUS
Yea, I am wroth, and will not stint my words,
But speak my whole mind. Thou methinks thou art he,
Who planned the crime, aye, and performed it too,
All save the assassination; and if thou
Hadst not been blind, I had been sworn to boot
That thou alone didst do the bloody deed.

TEIRESIAS
Is it so? Then I charge thee to abide
By thine own proclamation; from this day
Speak not to these or me. Thou art the man,
Thou the accursed polluter of this land.

OEDIPUS
Vile slanderer, thou blurtest forth these taunts,
And think'st forsooth as seer to go scot free.

TEIRESIAS
Yea, I am free, strong in the strength of truth.

OEDIPUS
Who was thy teacher? not methinks thy art.

TEIRESIAS
Thou, goading me against my will to speak.

OEDIPUS
What speech? repeat it and resolve my doubt.

TEIRESIAS
Didst miss my sense wouldst thou goad me on?

OEDIPUS
I but half caught thy meaning; say it again.

TEIRESIAS
I say thou art the murderer of the man
Whose murderer thou pursuest.

OEDIPUS
Thou shalt rue it
Twice to repeat so gross a calumny.

TEIRESIAS
Must I say more to aggravate thy rage?

OEDIPUS
Say all thou wilt; it will be but waste of breath.

TEIRESIAS
I say thou livest with thy nearest kin
In infamy, unwitting in thy shame.

OEDIPUS
Think'st thou for aye unscathed to wag thy tongue?

TEIRESIAS
Yea, if the might of truth can aught prevail.

OEDIPUS
With other men, but not with thee, for thou
In ear, wit, eye, in everything art blind.

TEIRESIAS
Poor fool to utter gibes at me which all
Here present will cast back on thee ere long.

OEDIPUS
Offspring of endless Night, thou hast no power
O'er me or any man who sees the sun.

TEIRESIAS
No, for thy weird is not to fall by me.
I leave to Apollo what concerns the god.

OEDIPUS
Is this a plot of Creon, or thine own?

TEIRESIAS
Not Creon, thou thyself art thine own bane.

OEDIPUS
O wealth and empiry and skill by skill
Outwitted in the battlefield of life,
What spite and envy follow in your train!
See, for this crown the State conferred on me.
A gift, a thing I sought not, for this crown
The trusty Creon, my familiar friend,
Hath lain in wait to oust me and suborned
This mountebank, this juggling charlatan,
This tricksy beggar-priest, for gain alone
Keen-eyed, but in his proper art stone-blind.
Say, sirrah, hast thou ever proved thyself
A prophet? When the riddling Sphinx was here

Why hadst thou no deliverance for this folk?
And yet the riddle was not to be solved
By guess-work but required the prophet's art;
Wherein thou wast found lacking; neither birds
Nor sign from heaven helped thee, but I came,
The simple Oedipus; I stopped her mouth
By mother wit, untaught of auguries.
This is the man whom thou wouldst undermine,
In hope to reign with Creon in my stead.
Methinks that thou and thine abettor soon
Will rue your plot to drive the scapegoat out.
Thank thy grey hairs that thou hast still to learn
What chastisement such arrogance deserves.

CHORUS
To us it seems that both the seer and thou,
O Oedipus, have spoken angry words.
This is no time to wrangle but consult
How best we may fulfill the oracle.

TEIRESIAS
King as thou art, free speech at least is mine
To make reply; in this I am thy peer.
I own no lord but Loxias;[2] him I serve
And ne'er can stand enrolled as Creon's man.
Thus then I answer: since thou hast not spared
To twit me with my blindness—thou hast eyes,
Yet see'st not in what misery thou art fallen,
Nor where thou dwellest nor with whom for mate.
Dost know thy lineage? Nay, thou know'st it not,
And all unwitting art a double foe
To thine own kin, the living and the dead;
Aye and the dogging curse of mother and sire
One day shall drive thee, like a two-edged sword,
Beyond our borders, and the eyes that now
See clear shall henceforward endless night.
Ah whither shall thy bitter cry not reach,
What crag in all Cithaeron but shall then
Reverberate thy wail, when thou hast found
With what a hymeneal thou wast borne
Home, but to no fair haven, on the gale!
Aye, and a flood of ills thou guessest not

Shall set thyself and children in one line.
Flout then both Creon and my words, for none
Of mortals shall be striken worse than thou.

OEDIPUS
Must I endure this fellow's insolence?
A murrain on thee! Get thee hence! Begone
Avaunt! and never cross my threshold more.

TEIRESIAS
I ne'er had come hadst thou not bidden me.

OEDIPUS
I know not thou wouldst utter folly, else
Long hadst thou waited to be summoned here.

TEIRESIAS
Such am I—as it seems to thee a fool,
But to the parents who begat thee, wise.

OEDIPUS
What sayest thou—"parents"? Who begat me, speak?

TEIRESIAS
This day shall be thy birthday, and thy grave.

OEDIPUS
Thou lov'st to speak in riddles and dark words.

TEIRESIAS
In reading riddles who so skilled as thou?

OEDIPUS
Twit me with that wherein my greatness lies.

TEIRESIAS
And yet this very greatness proved thy bane.

OEDIPUS
No matter if I saved the commonwealth.

TEIRESIAS
'Tis time I left thee. Come, boy, take me home.

OEDIPUS
Aye, take him quickly, for his presence irks
And lets me; gone, thou canst not plague me more.

TEIRESIAS
I go, but first will tell thee why I came.
Thy frown I dread not, for thou canst not harm me.
Hear then: this man whom thou hast sought to arrest
With threats and warrants this long while, the wretch
Who murdered Laius—that man is here.
He passes for an alien in the land
But soon shall prove a Theban, native born.
And yet his fortune brings him little joy;
For blind of seeing, clad in beggar's weeds,
For purple robes, and leaning on his staff,
To a strange land he soon shall grope his way.
And of the children, inmates of his home,
He shall be proved the brother and the sire,
Of her who bare him son and husband both,
Co-partner, and assassin of his sire.
Go in and ponder this, and if thou find
That I have missed the mark, henceforth declare
I have no wit nor skill in prophecy.

[*Exeunt Teiresias and Oedipus.*]

Translated by F. Storr.

Divine Law vs. Human Law

Sophocles, *Antigone* 376-945

Oedipus' tragedy continues to unfold after his death. His sons Eteocles and Polynices become the kings of Thebes. They agree to alternate their exercise of power. Eteocles is king for one year while Polynices accepts to go into exile. A year later, he returns to Thebes and asks for the throne; Eteocles, however, refuses to relinquish it. The brothers fight and kill each other. Creon, the new king, decides that only Eteocles will be interred and denies Polynices a proper burial, ensuring that his corpse will feed dogs and vultures. The punishment could not be more terrible. Without burial, Polynices will never find repose in the kingdom of death.

Creon's decision may seem surprising; after all, Polynices was only demanding his due. But Creon sees in Eteocles the king who defended his city and in Polynices someone who attacked Thebes and tried to bring about civil war. Antigone does not accept the fate reserved for her brother. She defies Creon's interdiction and provides Polynices the proper funerary rites. She places divine laws (those that command respect for the dead) above human law (Creon's interdiction). She knows that by doing so she will be sentenced to death. In this selection, she is brought before King Creon as a prisoner and found guilty.

Characters

ANTIGONE, Oedipus' daughter
ISMENE, Antigone's sister
CREON, brother of Jocasta and king of Thebes
HAEMON, Creon's son and Antigone's fiancé
CHORUS of elderly men
GUARD

"HAEMON: A State for one man is no State at all.
CREON: The State is his who rules it, so 'tis held.
HAEMON: As monarch of a desert thou wouldst shine."

CHORUS
What strange vision meets my eyes,
Fills me with a wild surprise?
Sure I know her, sure 'tis she,

The maid Antigone.
Hapless child of hapless sire,
Didst thou recklessly conspire,
Madly brave the King's decree?
Therefore are they haling thee?

[*Enter Guard bringing Antigone.*]

GUARD
Here is the culprit taken in the act
Of giving burial. But where's the King?

CHORUS
There from the palace he returns in time.

[*Enter Creon.*]

CREON
Why is my presence timely? What has chanced?

GUARD
No man, my lord, should make a vow, for if
He ever swears he will not do a thing,
His afterthoughts belie his first resolve.
When from the hail-storm of thy threats I fled
I sware thou wouldst not see me here again;
But the wild rapture of a glad surprise
Intoxicates, and so I'm here forsworn.
And here's my prisoner, caught in the very act,
Decking the grave. No lottery this time;
This prize is mine by right of treasure-trove.
So take her, judge her, rack her, if thou wilt.
She's thine, my liege; but I may rightly claim
Hence to depart well quit of all these ills.

CREON
Say, how didst thou arrest the maid, and where?

GUARD
Burying the man. There's nothing more to tell.

CREON
Hast thou thy wits? Or know'st thou what thou say'st?

GUARD
I saw this woman burying the corpse
Against thy orders. Is that clear and plain?

CREON
But how was she surprised and caught in the act?

GUARD
It happened thus. No sooner had we come,
Driven from thy presence by those awful threats,
Than straight we swept away all trace of dust,
And bared the clammy body. Then we sat
High on the ridge to windward of the stench,
While each man kept he fellow alert and rated
Roundly the sluggard if he chanced to nap.
So all night long we watched, until the sun
Stood high in heaven, and his blazing beams
Smote us. A sudden whirlwind then upraised
A cloud of dust that blotted out the sky,
And swept the plain, and stripped the woodlands bare,
And shook the firmament. We closed our eyes
And waited till the heaven-sent plague should pass.
At last it ceased, and lo! there stood this maid.
A piercing cry she uttered, sad and shrill,
As when the mother bird beholds her nest
Robbed of its nestlings; even so the maid
Wailed as she saw the body stripped and bare,
And cursed the ruffians who had done this deed.
Anon she gathered handfuls of dry dust,
Then, holding high a well-wrought brazen urn,
Thrice on the dead she poured a lustral stream.
We at the sight swooped down on her and seized
Our quarry. Undismayed she stood, and when
We taxed her with the former crime and this,
She disowned nothing. I was glad—and grieved;
For 'tis most sweet to 'scape oneself scot-free,
And yet to bring disaster to a friend
Is grievous. Take it all in all, I deem

A man's first duty is to serve himself.

CREON
Speak, girl, with head bent low and downcast eyes,
Does thou plead guilty or deny the deed?

ANTIGONE
Guilty. I did it, I deny it not.

CREON [*to Guard*]
Sirrah, begone whither thou wilt, and thank
Thy luck that thou hast 'scaped a heavy charge.
[*To Antigone*]
Now answer this plain question, yes or no,
Wast thou acquainted with the interdict?

ANTIGONE
I knew, all knew; how should I fail to know?

CREON
And yet wert bold enough to break the law?

ANTIGONE
Yea, for these laws were not ordained of Zeus,
And she who sits enthroned with gods below,
Justice, enacted not these human laws.
Nor did I deem that thou, a mortal man,
Could'st by a breath annul and override
The immutable unwritten laws of Heaven.
They were not born today nor yesterday;
They die not; and none knoweth whence they sprang.
I was not like, who feared no mortal's frown,
To disobey these laws and so provoke
The wrath of Heaven. I knew that I must die,
E'en hadst thou not proclaimed it; and if death
Is thereby hastened, I shall count it gain.
For death is gain to him whose life, like mine,
Is full of misery. Thus my lot appears
Not sad, but blissful; for had I endured
To leave my mother's son unburied there,
I should have grieved with reason, but not now.

And if in this thou judgest me a fool,
Methinks the judge of folly's not acquit.

CHORUS
A stubborn daughter of a stubborn sire,
This ill-starred maiden kicks against the pricks.

CREON
Well, let her know the stubbornest of wills
Are soonest bended, as the hardest iron,
O'er-heated in the fire to brittleness,
Flies soonest into fragments, shivered through.
A snaffle curbs the fieriest steed, and he
Who in subjection lives must needs be meek.
But this proud girl, in insolence well-schooled,
First overstepped the established law, and then—
A second and worse act of insolence—
She boasts and glories in her wickedness.
Now if she thus can flout authority
Unpunished, I am woman, she the man.
But though she be my sister's child or nearer
Of kin than all who worship at my hearth,
Nor she nor yet her sister shall escape
The utmost penalty, for both I hold,
As arch-conspirators, of equal guilt.
Bring forth the older; even now I saw her
Within the palace, frenzied and distraught.
The workings of the mind discover oft
Dark deeds in darkness schemed, before the act.
More hateful still the miscreant who seeks
When caught, to make a virtue of a crime.

ANTIGONE
Would'st thou do more than slay thy prisoner?

CREON
Not I, thy life is mine, and that's enough.

ANTIGONE
Why dally then? To me no word of thine
Is pleasant: God forbid it e'er should please;

Nor am I more acceptable to thee.
And yet how otherwise had I achieved
A name so glorious as by burying
A brother? so my townsmen all would say,
Where they not gagged by terror, Manifold
A king's prerogatives, and not the least
That all his acts and all his words are law.

CREON
Of all these Thebans none so deems but thou.

ANTIGONE
These think as I, but bate their breath to thee.

CREON
Hast thou no shame to differ from all these?

ANTIGONE
To reverence kith and kin can bring no shame.

CREON
Was his dead foeman not thy kinsman too?

ANTIGONE
One mother bare them and the self-same sire.

CREON
Why cast a slur on one by honoring one?

ANTIGONE
The dead man will not bear thee out in this.

CREON
Surely, if good and evil fare alive.

ANTIGONE
The slain man was no villain but a brother.

CREON
The patriot perished by the outlaw's brand.

ANTIGONE
Nathless the realms below these rites require.

CREON
Not that the base should fare as do the brave.

ANTIGONE
Who knows if this world's crimes are virtues there?

CREON
Not even death can make a foe a friend.

ANTIGONE
My nature is for mutual love, not hate.

CREON
Die then, and love the dead if thou must;
No woman shall be the master while I live.

[*Enter Ismene.*]

CHORUS
Lo from out the palace gate,
Weeping o'er her sister's fate,
Comes Ismene; see her brow,
Once serene, beclouded now,
See her beauteous face o'erspread
With a flush of angry red.

CREON
Woman, who like a viper unperceived
Didst harbor in my house and drain my blood,
Two plagues I nurtured blindly, so it proved,
To sap my throne. Say, didst thou too abet
This crime, or dost abjure all privity?

ISMENE
I did the deed, if she will have it so,
And with my sister claim to share the guilt.

ANTIGONE
That were unjust. Thou would'st not act with me
At first, and I refused thy partnership.

ISMENE
But now thy bark is stranded, I am bold
To claim my share as partner in the loss.

ANTIGONE
Who did the deed the under-world knows well:
A friend in word is never friend of mine.

ISMENE
O sister, scorn me not, let me but share
Thy work of piety, and with thee die.

ANTIGONE
Claim not a work in which thou hadst no hand;
One death sufficeth. Wherefore should'st thou die?

ISMENE
What would life profit me bereft of thee?

ANTIGONE
Ask Creon, he's thy kinsman and best friend.

ISMENE
Why taunt me? Find'st thou pleasure in these gibes?

ANTIGONE
'Tis a sad mockery, if indeed I mock.

ISMENE
O say if I can help thee even now.

ANTIGONE
No, save thyself; I grudge not thy escape.

ISMENE
Is e'en this boon denied, to share thy lot?

ANTIGONE
Yea, for thou chosed'st life, and I to die.

ISMENE
Thou canst not say that I did not protest.

ANTIGONE
Well, some approved thy wisdom, others mine.

ISMENE
But now we stand convicted, both alike.

ANTIGONE
Fear not; thou livest, I died long ago
Then when I gave my life to save the dead.

CREON
Both maids, methinks, are crazed. One suddenly
Has lost her wits, the other was born mad.

ISMENE
Yea, so it falls, sire, when misfortune comes,
The wisest even lose their mother wit.

CREON
I' faith thy wit forsook thee when thou mad'st
Thy choice with evil-doers to do ill.

ISMENE
What life for me without my sister here?

CREON
Say not thy sister here: thy sister's dead.

ISMENE
What, wilt thou slay thy own son's plighted bride?

CREON
Aye, let him raise him seed from other fields.

ISMENE
No new espousal can be like the old.

CREON
A plague on trulls who court and woo our sons.

ANTIGONE
O Haemon, how thy sire dishonors thee!

CREON
A plague on thee and thy accursed bride!

CHORUS
What, wilt thou rob thine own son of his bride?

CREON
'Tis death that bars this marriage, not his sire.

CHORUS
So her death-warrant, it would seem, is sealed.

CREON
By you, as first by me; off with them, guards,
And keep them close. Henceforward let them learn
To live as women use, not roam at large.
For e'en the bravest spirits run away
When they perceive death pressing on life's heels.

CHORUS
(Strophe 1)
Thrice blest are they who never tasted pain!
  If once the curse of Heaven attaint a race,
  The infection lingers on and speeds apace,
Age after age, and each the cup must drain.

So when Etesian blasts from Thrace downpour
  Sweep o'er the blackening main and whirl to land
  From Ocean's cavernous depths his ooze and sand,
Billow on billow thunders on the shore.

(Antistrophe 1)
On the Labdacidae[3] I see descending
  Woe upon woe; from days of old some god
  Laid on the race a malison, and his rod
Scourges each age with sorrows never ending.

The light that dawned upon its last born son
  Is vanished, and the bloody axe of Fate
  Has felled the goodly tree that blossomed late.
O Oedipus, by reckless pride undone!

(Strophe 2)
Thy might, O Zeus, what mortal power can quell?
Not sleep that lays all else beneath its spell,
Nor moons that never tier: untouched by Time,
    Throned in the dazzling light
    That crowns Olympus' height,
Thou reignest King, omnipotent, sublime.

    Past, present, and to be,
    All bow to thy decree,
    All that exceeds the mean by Fate
    Is punished, Love or Hate.

(Antistrophe 2)
Hope flits about never-wearying wings;
Profit to some, to some light loves she brings,
But no man knoweth how her gifts may turn,
Till 'neath his feet the treacherous ashes burn.
Sure 'twas a sage inspired that spake this word;
    If evil good appear
    To any, Fate is near;
And brief the respite from her flaming sword.

Hither comes in angry mood
Haemon, latest of thy brood;
Is it for his bride he's grieved,
Or her marriage-bed deceived,
Doth he make his mourn for thee,
Maid forlorn, Antigone?

[*Enter Haemon.*]

CREON
Soon shall we know, better than seer can tell.
Learning may fixed decree anent thy bride,
Thou mean'st not, son, to rave against thy sire?
Know'st not whate'er we do is done in love?

HAEMON
O father, I am thine, and I will take
Thy wisdom as the helm to steer withal.
Therefore no wedlock shall by me be held
More precious than thy loving goverance.

CREON
Well spoken: so right-minded sons should feel,
In all deferring to a father's will.
For 'tis the hope of parents they may rear
A brood of sons submissive, keen to avenge
Their father's wrongs, and count his friends their own.
But who begets unprofitable sons,
He verily breeds trouble for himself,
And for his foes much laughter. Son, be warned
And let no woman fool away thy wits.
Ill fares the husband mated with a shrew,
And her embraces very soon wax cold.
For what can wound so surely to the quick
As a false friend? So spue and cast her off,
Bid her go find a husband with the dead.
For since I caught her openly rebelling,
Of all my subjects the one malcontent,
I will not prove a traitor to the State.
She surely dies. Go, let her, if she will,
Appeal to Zeus the God of Kindred, for
If thus I nurse rebellion in my house,
Shall not I foster mutiny without?
For whoso rules his household worthily,
Will prove in civic matters no less wise.
But he who overbears the laws, or thinks
To overrule his rulers, such as one
I never will allow. Whome'er the State
Appoints must be obeyed in everything,
But small and great, just and unjust alike.

I warrant such a one in either case
Would shine, as King or subject; such a man
Would in the storm of battle stand his ground,
A comrade leal and true; but Anarchy—
What evils are not wrought by Anarchy!
She ruins States, and overthrows the home,
She dissipates and routs the embattled host;
While discipline preserves the ordered ranks.
Therefore we must maintain authority
And yield to title to a woman's will.
Better, if needs be, men should cast us out
Than hear it said, a woman proved his match.

CHORUS
To me, unless old age have dulled wits,
Thy words appear both reasonable and wise.

HAEMON
Father, the gods implant in mortal men
Reason, the choicest gift bestowed by heaven.
'Tis not for me to say thou errest, nor
Would I arraign thy wisdom, if I could;
And yet wise thoughts may come to other men
And, as thy son, it falls to me to mark
The acts, the words, the comments of the crowd.
The commons stand in terror of thy frown,
And dare not utter aught that might offend,
But I can overhear their muttered plaints,
Know how the people mourn this maiden doomed
For noblest deeds to die the worst of deaths.
When her own brother slain in battle lay
Unsepulchered, she suffered not his corse
To lie for carrion birds and dogs to maul:
Should not her name (they cry) be writ in gold?
Such the low murmurings that reach my ear.
O father, nothing is by me more prized
Than thy well-being, for what higher good
Can children covet than their sire's fair fame,
As fathers too take pride in glorious sons?
Therefore, my father, cling not to one mood,
And deemed not thou art right, all others wrong.

For whoso thinks that wisdom dwells with him,
That he alone can speak or think aright,
Such oracles are empty breath when tried.
The wisest man will let himself be swayed
By others' wisdom and relax in time.
See how the trees beside a stream in flood
Save, if they yield to force, each spray unharmed,
But by resisting perish root and branch.
The mariner who keeps his mainsheet taut,
And will not slacken in the gale, is like
To sail with thwarts reversed, keel uppermost.
Relent then and repent thee of thy wrath;
For, if one young in years may claim some sense,
I'll say 'tis best of all to be endowed
With absolute wisdom; but, if that's denied,
(And nature takes not readily that ply)
Next wise is he who lists to sage advice.

CHORUS
If he says aught in season, heed him, King.
[*To Haemon*]
Heed thou thy sire too; both have spoken well.

CREON
What, would you have us at our age be schooled,
Lessoned in prudence by a beardless boy?

HAEMON
I plead for justice, father, nothing more.
Weigh me upon my merit, not my years.

CREON
Strange merit this to sanction lawlessness!

HAEMON
For evil-doers I would urge no plea.

CREON
Is not this maid an arrant law-breaker?

HAEMON
The Theban commons with one voice say, No.

CREON
What, shall the mob dictate my policy?

HAEMON
'Tis thou, methinks, who speakest like a boy.

CREON
Am I to rule for others, or myself?

HAEMON
A State for one man is no State at all.

CREON
The State is his who rules it, so 'tis held.

HAEMON
As monarch of a desert thou wouldst shine.

CREON
This boy, methinks, maintains the woman's cause.

HAEMON
If thou be'st woman, yes. My thought's for thee.

CREON
O reprobate, would'st wrangle with thy sire?

HAEMON
Because I see thee wrongfully perverse.

CREON
And am I wrong, if I maintain my rights?

HAEMON
Talk not of rights; thou spurn'st the due of Heaven.

CREON
O heart corrupt, a woman's minion thou!

HAEMON
Slave to dishonor thou wilt never find me.

CREON
Thy speech at least was all a plea for her.

HAEMON
And thee and me, and for the gods below.

CREON
Living the maid shall never be thy bride.

HAEMON
So she shall die, but one will die with her.

CREON
Hast come to such a pass as threaten me?

HAEMON
What threat is this, vain counsels to reprove?

CREON
Vain fool to instruct thy betters; thou shall rue it.

HAEMON
Wert not my father, I had said thou err'st.

CREON
Play not the spaniel, thou a woman's slave.

HAEMON
When thou dost speak, must no man make reply?

CREON
This passes bounds. By heaven, thou shalt not rate
And jeer and flout me with impunity.
Off with the hateful thing that she may die
At once, beside her bridegroom, in his sight.

HAEMON
Think not that in my sight the maid shall die,

Or by my side; never shalt thou again
Behold my face hereafter. Go, consort
With friends who like a madman for their mate.

[*Exit Haemon.*]

CHORUS
Thy son has gone, my liege, in angry haste.
Fell is the wrath of youth beneath a smart.

CREON
Let him go vent his fury like a fiend:
These sisters twain he shall not save from death.

CHORUS
Surely, thou meanest not to slay them both?

CREON
I stand corrected; only her who touched
The body.

CHORUS
And what death is she to die?

CREON
She shall be taken to some desert place
By man untrod, and in a rock-hewn cave,
With food no more than to avoid the taint
That homicide might bring on all the State,
Buried alive. There let her call in aid
The King of Death, the one god she reveres,
Or learn too late a lesson learnt at last:
'Tis labor lost, to reverence the dead.

CHORUS
(Strophe)
Love resistless in fight, all yield at a glance of thine eye,
Love who pillowed all night on a maiden's cheek dost lie,
Over the upland holds. Shall mortals not yield to thee?

(Antistrophe)
Mad are thy subjects all, and even the wisest heart

Straight to folly will fall, at a touch of thy poisoned dart.
Thou didst kindle the strife, this feud of kinsman with kin,
By the eyes of a winsome wife, and the yearning her heart to win.
For as her consort still, enthroned with Justice above,
Thou bendest man to thy will, O all invincible Love.

Lo I myself am borne aside,
From Justice, as I view this bride.
(O sight an eye in tears to drown)
Antigone, so young, so fair,
Thus hurried down
Death's bower with the dead to share.

ANTIGONE
(Strophe 1)
Friends, countrymen, my last farewell I make;
My journey's done.
One last fond, lingering, longing look I take
At the bright sun.
For Death who puts to sleep both young and old
Hales my young life,
And beckons me to Acheron's dark fold,
An unwed wife.
No youths have sung the marriage song for me,
My bridal bed
No maids have strewn with flowers from the lea,
'Tis Death I wed.

CHORUS
But bethink thee, thou art sped,
Great and glorious, to the dead.
Thou the sword's edge hast not tasted,
No disease thy frame hath wasted.
Freely thou alone shalt go
Living to the dead below.

ANTIGONE
(Antistrophe 1)
Nay, but the piteous tale I've heard men tell
Of Tantalus' doomed child,[4]
Chained upon Siphylus' high rocky fell,

That clung like ivy wild,
Drenched by the pelting rain and whirling snow,
Left there to pine,
While on her frozen breast the tears aye flow—
Her fate is mine.

CHORUS
She was sprung of gods, divine,
Mortals we of mortal line.
Like renown with gods to gain
Recompenses all thy pain.
Take this solace to thy tomb
Hers in life and death thy doom.

ANTIGONE
(Strophe 2)
Alack, alack! Ye mock me. Is it meet
Thus to insult me living, to my face?
Cease, by our country's altars I entreat,
Ye lordly rulers of a lordly race.
O fount of Dirce, wood-embowered plain
Where Theban chariots to victory speed,
Mark ye the cruel laws that now have wrought my bane,
The friends who show no pity in my need!
Was ever fate like mine? O monstrous doom,
Within a rock-built prison sepulchered,
To fade and wither in a living tomb,
And alien midst the living and the dead.

CHORUS
(Strophe 3)
In thy boldness over-rash
Madly thou thy foot didst dash
'Gainst high Justice' altar stair.
Thou a father's guild dost bear.

ANTIGONE
(Antistrophe 2)
At this thou touchest my most poignant pain,
My ill-starred father's piteous disgrace,
The taint of blood, the hereditary stain,

That clings to all of Labdacus' famed race.
Woe worth the monstrous marriage-bed where lay
A mother with the son her womb had borne,
Therein I was conceived, woe worth the day,
Fruit of incestuous sheets, a maid forlorn,
And now I pass, accursed and unwed,
To meet them as an alien there below;
And thee, O brother, in marriage ill-bestead,
'Twas thy dead hand that dealt me this death-blow.

CHORUS
Religion has her chains, 'tis true,
Let rite be paid when rites are due.
Yet is it ill to disobey
The powers who hold by might the sway.
Thou hast withstood authority,
A self-willed rebel, thou must die.

ANTIGONE
Unwept, unwed, unfriended, hence I go,
No longer may I see the day's bright eye;
Not one friend left to share my bitter woe,
And o'er my ashes heave one passing sigh.

CREON
If wail and lamentation aught availed
To stave off death, I trow they'd never end.
Away with her, and having walled her up
In a rock-vaulted tomb, as I ordained,
Leave her alone at liberty to die,
Or, if she choose, to live in solitude,
The tomb her dwelling. We in either case
Are guiltless as concerns this maiden's blood,
Only on earth no lodging shall she find.

ANTIGONE
O grave, O bridal bower, O prison house
Hewn from the rock, my everlasting home,
Whither I go to join the mighty host
Of kinsfolk, Persephassa's guests long dead, [5]
The last of all, of all more miserable,

I pass, my destined span of years cut short.
And yet good hope is mine that I shall find
A welcome from my sire, a welcome too,
From thee, my mother, and my brother dear;
From with these hands, I laved and decked your limbs
In death, and poured libations on your grave.
And last, my Polyneices, unto thee
I paid due rites, and this my recompense!
Yet am I justified in wisdom's eyes.
For even had it been some child of mine,
Or husband mouldering in death's decay,
I had not wrought this deed despite the State.
What is the law I call in aid? 'Tis thus
I argue. Had it been a husband dead
I might have wed another, and have borne
Another child, to take the dead child's place.
But, now my sire and mother both are dead,
No second brother can be born for me.
Thus by the law of conscience I was led
To honor thee, dear brother, and was judged
By Creon guilty of a heinous crime.
And now he drags me like a criminal,
A bride unwed, amerced of marriage-song
And marriage-bed and joys of motherhood,
By friends deserted to a living grave.
What ordinance of heaven have I transgressed?
Hereafter can I look to any god
For succor, call on any man for help?
Alas, my piety is impious deemed.
Well, if such justice is approved of heaven,
I shall be taught by suffering my sin;
But if the sin is theirs, O may they suffer
No worse ills than the wrongs they do to me.

CHORUS
The same ungovernable will
Drives like a gale the maiden still.

CREON
Therefore, my guards who let her stay
Shall smart full sore for their delay.

ANTIGONE
Ah, woe is me! This word I hear
Brings death most near.

CHORUS
I have no comfort. What he saith,
Portends no other thing than death.

ANTIGONE
My fatherland, city of Thebes divine,
Ye gods of Thebes whence sprang my line,
Look, puissant lords of Thebes, on me;
The last of all your royal house ye see.
Martyred by men of sin, undone.
Such meed my piety hath won.

[*Exit Antigone.*]

Translated by F. Storr.

EURIPIDES

c. 485 - *c.* 406 BC

Euripides was born in 485 BC in Salamis. Aristotle would later describe him as the most tragic poet. Contrary to Aeschylus and Sophocles, Euripides chose to live away from city life and dedicated himself to his art. He was not, however, entirely detached from the contemporary political debates of his city, Athens. He praises it a number of times in his tragedies. In his Trojan Women, *he criticizes the war between Athens and Sparta and also alludes to the abuse of power by the League of Delos. He further makes perfectly clear his distrust of demagogues. In the end, on King Archelaus' invitation, Euripides left Athens for Pella in Macedon, where he died about 406 BC.*

Unlike his predecessors, Euripides did not receive recognition worthy of his talents during his lifetime. He became a tragic poet in 455, but would not be awarded first place until 441. Further accolades were accorded him at least three other times. Out of the 92 plays he most likely wrote, only 18 tragedies and one satiric drama, the Cyclops, *survive.*

Posterity would realize and celebrate his impressive contribution. Nurtured on philosophy, sophistry, and rhetoric, Euripides provided a new dimension to theater the public found difficult to accept. He was especially fond of exoticism, and unceasingly questioned the relationships between gods and men to emphasize one's responsibility in the face of one's very own destiny.

Revenge of the Betrayed Woman

Euripides, *Medea* 1002-1376

Medea left her distant native Colchis on the Black Sea to follow the Greek hero Jason to Corinth. But Jason ends up marrying Glauke, the daughter of King Creon. Afraid of reprisals, the king wants to exile Medea and her two sons by Jason. Medea seeks revenge: She kills the new bride by sending her a poisoned dress and golden crown. As Creon grasps his fatally poisoned daughter into his arms, he, too, dies. Medea even murders her own children with the intention of leaving Jason without descendents. She has nothing left to lose. The revenge of this formidable and deeply betrayed woman is horrific, but well expected from a sorceress heralding from a barbaric country.

Characters

MEDEA, formidable witch
JASON, Greek hero
TUTOR to the sons of Medea

"Among human beings no one is happy.
Wealth may flow in to make one man
more lucky than another, but no man
is ever happy, no one."

TUTOR
My lady, your children won't be exiled.
The royal bride was happy to accept,
with own hands, the gifts you sent her.
The boys have now made their peace with her.

[*Medea starts to weep.*]

What's wrong? Why do you stand there in distress?
Things have worked out well. Why turn away again?
Aren't you happy to hear my splendid news?

MEDEA
Alas…

TUTOR
An odd response to the news I bring.

MEDEA
All I can say is I'm so sad…

TUTOR
Have I mistakenly said something bad?
Am I wrong to think my news is good?

MEDEA
You've reported what you had to report.
I'm not blaming you.

TUTOR
Why are you crying?

MEDEA
The gods and I, with my worst intentions,
have brought about this situation.

TUTOR
Be happy. Your children will one day
bring you back home again.

MEDEA
But before that,
I shall bring others to their homes—alas,
how miserable I feel.

TUTOR
You're not the only mother whose children
have been separated from her. We mortals
must bear our bad times patiently.

MEDEA
I'll do so.
But now go in the house. And carry on.
Give the children their usual routine.

[*Tutor exits into the house. The children remain with Medea.*]

Oh children, my children, you still have
a city and a home, where you can live,
once you've left me in wretched suffering.
You can live on here without your mother.
But I'll go to some other country,
an exile, before I've had my joy in you,
before I've seen you happy, or helped
to decorate your marriage beds, your brides,
your bridal chambers, or lifted high
your wedding torches. How miserable
my self-will has made me. I raised you—
and all for nothing. The work I did for you,
the cruel hardships, pains of childbirth—
all for nothing. Once, in my foolishness,
I had many hopes in you—it's true—
that you'd look after me in my old age,
that you'd prepare my corpse with your own hands,
in the proper way, as all people wish.
But now my tender dreams have been destroyed.
For I'll live out my life without you both,
in sorrow. And those loving eyes of yours
will never see your mother any more.
Your life is changing. Oh, my children,
why are you looking at me in that way?
Why smile at me—that last smile of yours?
Alas, what shall I do? You women here,
my heart gives way when I see those eyes,
my children's smiling eyes. I cannot do it.
Good bye to those earlier plans of mine.
I'll take my children from this country.
Why harm them as a way to hurt their father,
and have to suffer twice his pain myself?
No, I won't do that. And so farewell
to what I planned before. But what's going on?
What's wrong with me? Do I really want
my enemies escaping punishment,
while I become someone they ridicule?
I will go through with this. What a coward
I am even to let my heart admit

such sentimental reasons. Children,
you must go into the house.

[*The children move toward the house but remain at the door, looking at Medea.*]

Anyone forbidden
to attend my sacrifice, let such a man
concern himself about these children.
My hand will never lack the strength for this.
And yet... My heart, don't do this murder.
You're made of stone, but leave the boys alone.
Spare my children. If they remain alive,
with me in Athens, they'll make you happy.
No! By those avengers in lower Hell,
I'll never deliver up my children,
hand them over to their enemies,
to be humiliated. They must die—
that's unavoidable, no matter what.
Since that must happen, then their mother,
the one who gave them life, will kill them.
At all events it's settled. There's no way out.
On her head the royal bride already wears
the poisoned crown. That dress is killing her.
But I'm treading an agonizing path,
and send my children on one even worse.
What I want to do now is say farewell.

[*Medea moves to the children near the door, kneels down and hugs them.*]

Give me your right hands, children. Come on.
Let your mother kiss them. Oh, these hands—
how I love them—and how I love these mouths,
faces—the bearing of such noble boys.
I wish you happiness—but somewhere else.
Where you live now your father takes away.
Oh this soft embrace! Their skin's so tender.
My boys' breathing smells so sweet to me.
But you must go inside. Go. I can't stand
to look at you like this any more.
The evil done to me has won the day.
I understand too well the dreadful act
I'm going to commit, but my judgment

can't check my anger, and that incites
the greatest evils human beings do.

[*Medea shepherds the children into the house, leaving the Chorus alone on stage.*]

CHORUS [*chanting*]
Often, before this present time,
I've gone into more complex arguments,
I've struggled with more serious issues,
than my female sex should try to probe.
But we, too, possess an artistic Muse.
She lives with us to teach us wisdom.
Not with all of us—the group of women
able to profit from our muse is small—
among many women you might find one.
And I claim that with human beings
those with no experience of children,
those who have never given birth,
such people have far more happiness
than those who have been parents.
With people who have no children,
because they never come to see
whether their children grow up
to be a blessing or a curse to men,
their failure to have offspring
keeps many troubles from them.
But those who in their own homes
have a sweet race of children growing,
I see them worn out with cares
their whole life long. First,
how they can raise their children well,
next, how they can leave their sons
a means of livelihood. And then,
it's by no means clear that all the work
produces good or useless children.
There's one final problem,
the worst for any mortal human—
I'll tell you: suppose those parents
have found a sufficient way of life,
and seen their children grow
into strong, young, virtuous men,

if fate so wills it, Death comes,
carries off the children's bodies,
away to Hades. What profit, then,
is there for us and our love of sons,
if the gods inflict on mortal men,
in addition to their other troubles,
this most painful extra grief.

[*Enter Medea from the house.*]

MEDEA
My friends, I've long been waiting in suspense
to see what's happening in the royal house.
Now I see one of Jason's servants coming.
His hard rapid breathing indicates to me
he's bringing news of some fresh disaster.

[*Enter the Messenger, coming from the royal palace.*]

MESSENGER
Medea, you must escape—leave this place.
You've done an awful deed, broken every law.
Take ship and go by sea—or go overland
by chariot. But you must go from here.

MEDEA
What's happened that I have to run away?

MESSENGER
The king's daughter has just been destroyed,
her father, too—Creon. You poisoned them.

MEDEA
What really splendid news you bring.
From now on, I'll consider you a friend,
one of my benefactors.

MESSENGER
Are you in your right mind, lady, or insane?
To commit this crime against the royal house,
and then be happy when you hear the news,
without being afraid…

MEDEA
I have some remarks to offer in reply.
But, my friend, don't be in such a hurry.
Tell me of their deaths. If you report
they died in pain, you'll double my rejoicing.

MESSENGER
When your two children came with their father
and went into the bride's home, we servants,
who had shared in your misfortune, were glad,
for a rumour spread at once from ear to ear
that you and your husband's previous quarrel
was now over. Someone kissed the boys' hands,
someone else their golden hair. In my joy,
I went with the children right inside,
into the women's quarters. Our mistress,
whom we now look up to instead of you,
before she caught sight of your two children,
wanted to fix her eyes on Jason only.
But then she veiled her eyes and turned away
her white cheek, disgusted that they'd come.
Your husband tried to change the young bride's mood,
to soften her anger, with these words,
"Don't be so hard-hearted with your family.
Check your anger, and turn your face this way,
look at us again, and count as friends of yours
people your husband considers friends of his.
Now, receive these gifts, and then, for my sake,
beg your father not to exile these two boys."
Once she saw the gifts, she did not hold out,
but agreed with Jason in everything.
And before your children and their father
had gone any distance from the palace,
she took the richly embroidered gown
and put it on, then arranged the golden crown,
fixing it in her hair at a bright mirror,
smiling at her body's lifeless image there.
Then she stood up from her seat and strolled
across the room, moving delicately
on her pale feet, delighted with the gifts,
with a great many glances to inspect
the straightness of the dress against her legs.

But then it happened—a horrific sight.
She changed colour, staggered back and sideways,
trembling, then fell into her chair again,
almost collapsing on the floor. An old woman,
one of her servants, thinking it was a fit
inspired by Pan or some other god,
shouted in festive joy, until she saw
the white spit foaming in her mouth, her eyes
bulging from their sockets, and her pale skin
quite drained of blood. The servant screamed again—
this time, to make up for her former shout,
she cried out in distress. Another slave
ran off at once towards her father's palace,
and another to the girl's new husband
to tell him the grim fate his bride had met.
The whole house rang with people's footsteps,
as they hurried back and forth. By the time
it would take a fast runner to complete
two hundred yards and reach the finish line,
her eyes opened—the poor girl woke up,
breaking her silent fit with a dreadful scream.
She was suffering a double agony—
around her head the golden diadem
shot out amazing molten streams of fire
burning everything, and the fine woven robe,
your children's gift, consumed the poor girl's flesh.
She jumped up from the chair and ran away,
all of her on fire, tossing her head, her hair,
this way and that, trying to shake off
her golden crown—but it was fixed in place,
and when she shook her hair, the fire blazed
twice as high. She fell down on the ground,
overcome by the disaster. No one
could recognize her, except her father.
Her eyes had lost their clear expression,
her face had changed. And there was blood
on top her head, dripping down, mixed with fire.
The flesh was peeling from her bones, chewed off
by the poison's secret jaws, just like resin
oozing from a pine tree. A horrific sight.
Everyone was too scared to touch the corpse—
what we'd seen had warned us. But her father,

poor wretch, didn't know what she's been through.
He came unexpectedly into the house
and stumbled on the corpse. He cried aloud,
embraced his daughter, and kissed her, saying,
"My poor child, what god has been so cruel
to destroy you in this way? Who's taken you
away from me, an old man near my death?
Oh my child, I wish I could die with you."
He ended his lamenting cries. But then,
when he tried to raise his old body up,
he was entangled in that woven dress,
like ivy wrapped around a laurel branch.
He struggled dreadfully, trying to get up
onto his knees, but she held him down.
If he used force, he tore his ancient flesh
clear off his bones. The poor man at last gave up.
His breathing stopped, for he couldn't stand the pain
a moment longer. So the two of them lie dead—
the daughter and her old father, side by side.
It's horrible, something to make one weep.
About you there's nothing I will say.
For you'll know well enough the punishment
that's coming to you. As for human life,
it seems to me, and not for the first time,
nothing but shadows. And I might say,
without feeling any fear, those mortals
who seem wise, who carefully prepare their words,
are guilty of the greatest foolishness.
Among human beings no one is happy.
Wealth may flow in to make one man
more lucky than another, but no man
is ever happy, no one.

[*Exit Messenger.*]

LEADER OF THE CHORUS
This is the day, it seems,
the god tightens trouble around Jason,
and justly so. Oh poor Creon's daughter,
how we pity your misfortune. You're gone,
down in Hades' home—the price you pay
for marrying Jason.

MEDEA
I've made up my mind, my friends.
I'll do it—kill my children now, without delay,
and flee this land. I must not hesitate.
That will hand them over to someone else,
to be slaughtered by a less loving hand.
No matter what, the children have to die.
Since that's the case, then I, who gave them life,
will kill them. Arm yourself for this, my heart.
Why do I put off doing this dreadful act,
since it must be done? Come, pick up the sword,
wretched hand of mine. Pick up the sword,
move to where your life of misery begins.
Don't play the coward. Don't remember now
how much you love them, how you gave them life.
For this short day forget they are your children—
and mourn them later. Although you kill them,
still you loved them. As a woman, I'm so sad.

[*Exit Medea into the house.*]

CHORUS
Hail to Earth,
Hail to the Sun,
whose rays illuminate all things.
Turn your eyes, look down,
see this destroying woman
before she sets her bloody hands,
her instruments of murder,
onto her own children,
those offshoots of your golden race.
It's a dreadful thing for men
to spill the blood of gods.
O light which comes from Zeus,
stop her, take from the house
this blood-thirsty savage Fury
gripped by the spirit of revenge.
The pain you felt in giving birth
was useless, wasted.
Those dear children of yours
you bore them all in vain.

You who left behind you
the inhospitable passage
where the Symplegades dance,[1]
those deadly, dark-blue rocks,
you unhappy woman,
why does your anger
fall so heavily upon your heart,
and one harsh murder
follow so quickly on another?
The polluting moral stain
that taints all mortal men
who shed their family blood
upon the earth—that's is hard to bear.
For the gods send down
onto the houses of the ones who kill
sorrows to match their crimes.

CHILD [*from inside the house*]
Help me… help…

CHORUS
Did you hear that?
Did you hear the children cry?
That wretched, evil woman!

CHILD [*from within*]
What do I do? How can I escape
my mother's hands?

SECOND CHILD
It's over for us…

CHORUS [*shouting in response*]
Should I go in the house?
I'm sure I must prevent this murder.

CHILD
Yes—for the love of gods, stop this! And hurry…

SECOND CHILD
The sword has almost got us—like a snare!

CHORUS
You hard and wretched woman,
just like stone or iron—
to kill your children,
ones you bore yourself,
sealing their fate with your own hands.
Of all women that ever lived before
I know of one, of only one,
who laid hands on her dear children—
and that was Ino.
Driven mad by the gods,
when Hera, Zeus' wife,
sent her wandering in a fit
away from home,
that sad lady leapt into the sea,
because she'd killed her sons
a most unholy murder.
She walked into the surf
at the sea's edge, perishing
so she could join in death
her own two children.
But what horror still remains
after what's happened here?
A woman's marriage bed—
so full of pain—how many evils,
has it brought on mankind?

[*Enter Jason with attendants.*]

JASON
You women standing near the house,
where's Medea, who's done these awful things?
Is she still inside? Or has she left here?
She'll have to hide herself under the earth,
or else fly up to heaven's overarching vault,
if she's going to avoid punishment
from the royal house. Did she really think
she could kill the rulers of this country
and get away unharmed? But at this point
she's no concern of mine. I'm worried
for my children. Those whom she has wronged

will take care of her. I've come for the boys,
to save their lives, in case the next of kin
try to harm me and mine, retribution
for their mother's profane murders.

CHORUS
Unhappy man, you don't know the full extent
of your misfortune, or you would not say this.

JASON
What is it? Is she planning to kill me, too?

CHORUS
Your boys are dead, killed by their mother's hand.

JASON
No. What are you saying? Woman,
you have destroyed me.

CHORUS
The boys are dead.
You must fix your mind on that. They're gone.

JASON
Where did she do this? Inside or outside?

CHORUS
Open the doors and you will see them,
your slaughtered children.

JASON [*shouting into the house, as he shakes the doors*]
You slaves in there,
remove the bar on the door at once,
withdraw the bolts, so I may see two things—
my dead sons and their murderer, that woman
on whom I shall exact revenge.

[*Jason shakes the doors of the house, which remain closed. Medea appears in a winged chariot, rising above the house. The bodies of the two children are visible in the chariot.*]

MEDEA
Why are you rattling the doors like that,
trying to unbar them so you can find
the bodies and me, the one who killed them?
Stop trying. If you want something from me,
then say so, if you want to. But you'll never
have me in your grasp, not in this chariot,
a gift to me from my grandfather Helios,
to protect me from all hostile hands.

JASON
You accursed woman, most hateful
to the gods and me and all mankind.
You dared to take the sword to your own boys,
you—the one who bore them—and to leave me
destroyed and childless. Having done this,
after committing this atrocious crime,
can you still look upon the earth and sun?
May you be destroyed! Now I understand—
I must have lost my mind to bring you here,
from that savage country, to a Greek home.
You were truly evil then—you betrayed
your father and the land that raised you.
But the avenging fury meant for you
the gods have sent to me. You slaughtered
your brother in your home,[2] then came aboard
our fine ship, the Argo. That how you began.
When you married me and bore my children,
in your lust for sex and our marriage bed,
you killed them. No woman from Greece would dare
to do this, but I chose you as my wife
above them all, and that has proved to be
a hateful marriage—it's destroyed me.
You're not a woman. You're a she-lion.
Your nature is more bestial than Scylla,[3]
the Tuscan monster. But my insults,
multiplied a thousand fold, don't hurt you.
Your heart's too hard for that. So be off,
you shameful murderer of your children.
Let me lament my fate. I'll get no delight
from my new bride, nor will I ever speak

to my own living children, the two boys
I bred and raised. They're lost to me.

MEDEA
I would reply to your words at length,
if father Zeus did not already know
what I did for you and what you did to me.
You weren't going to shame my marriage bed
and have a pleasant life ridiculing me.
Nor was that royal bride or Creon,
who gave her to you, going to banish me,
throw me from this place with impunity.
So if you want, call me a lioness
or Scylla, who lives on Tuscan shores.
For I've made contact with your heart at last.

JASON
You have your own share of pain and sorrow.

MEDEA
That's true. But there's relief in knowing
you cannot laugh at me.

JASON
O my children,
you had such an evil mother!

MEDEA
O my children,
victims of your father's evil actions!

JASON
At least it was not my hand that killed them.

MEDEA
No. It was the insult of your new marriage.

JASON
Was it right to murder them for that?

MEDEA
Do you think that insult to a woman
is something insignificant?

JASON
Yes, I do,
to a woman with good sense. But to you
it's completely evil.

MEDEA
Well, your sons are gone.
That should cause you pain.

JASON
I think they'll live
to take out their revenge on you.

MEDEA
The gods are aware who began this fight.

JASON
Yes, they know well your detested heart.

MEDEA
Keep up your hate. How I loathe your voice.

JASON
And I hate yours. It won't be difficult
for the two of us to part.

MEDEA
Tell me how.
What shall I do? For that's what I want, too.

JASON
Let me bury these dead boys and mourn them.

Translated by Ian Johnston.

Recognition of Orestes and Iphigenia

Euripides, *Iphigenia among the Taurians* 456-897

Agamemnon agrees to sacrifice his daughter Iphigenia in return for a favorable wind to sail to Troy. Under the false pretense that she will marry the valiant hero Achilles, he asks her to come to the city (Aulis) where the Greek fleet is at anchor. Agamemnon is about to sacrifice her, when, in the last hour, the goddess Artemis takes pity upon her. Without anybody's knowledge, she replaces the young girl with a doe and carries her to Tauris, a distant barbaric land (today's Crimean Peninsula), where Iphigenia becomes a priestess.

The Greeks obtain a favorable wind and invade Troy. They win the war and return home. Glory is short-lived for Agamemnon, however: His wife Clytemnestra murders him in his palace. His son Orestes avenges him by killing his mother and then goes insane—his punishment by the gods for the murder. After many mishaps, Apollo advises him to travel to Tauris to bring the statue of Artemis back if he wants to rid himself of insanity. At this time, Orestes meets his sister Iphigenia. He fails to recognize her, as he was still an infant when she disappeared. Iphigenia does not recognize him either. Not only that but she prepares to sacrifice him to Artemis, as her function is to offer foreigners who land on shore to the goddess.

The scene is staged in Tauris before the Temple of Artemis. Orestes and his friend Pylades are brought to Iphigenia for sacrifice.

Characters

IPHIGENIA, daughter of Agamemnon
ORESTES, brother of Iphigenia
PYLADES, friend of Orestes
CHORUS of captive Greek women who serve as attendants for Iphigenia

"For to none is given
To know the coming nor the end of woe;
So dark is God, and to great darkness go
His paths, by blind chance mazed from our ken."

LEADER
But lo, the twain whom Thoas sends,
Their arms in bondage grasped sore;

Strange offering this, to lay before
The Goddess! Hold your peace, O friends.

Onward, still onward, to this shrine
They lead the first-fruits of the Greek.
'Twas true, the tale he came to speak,
That watcher of the mountain kine.

O holy one, if it afford
Thee joy, what these men bring to thee,
Take thou their sacrifice, which we,
By law of Hellas, hold abhorred.

[*Enter Orestes and Pylades, bound, and guarded by Taurians. Re-enter Iphigenia.*]

IPHIGENIA
So be it.
My foremost care must be that nothing harms
The temple's holy rule.—Untie their arms.
That which is hallowed may no more be bound.
You, to the shrine within! Let all be found
As the law bids, and as we need this day.

[*Orestes and Pylades are set free; some attendants go into the temple.*]

Ah me!
What mother then was yours, O strangers, say,
And father? And your sister, if you have
A sister: both at once, so young and brave
To leave her brotherless! Who knows when heaven
May send that fortune? For to none is given
To know the coming nor the end of woe;
So dark is God, and to great darkness go
His paths, by blind chance mazed from our ken.
Whence are ye come, O most unhappy men?
From some far home, methinks, ye have found this shore
And far shall stay from home for evermore.

ORESTES
Why weepest thou, woman, to make worse the smart
Of that which needs must be, whoe'er thou art?

I count it not for gentleness, when one
Who means to slay, seeks first to make undone
By pity that sharp dread. Nor praise I him,
With hope long dead, who sheddeth tears to dim
The pain that grips him close. The evil so
Is doubled into twain. He doth but show
His feeble heart, and, as he must have died,
Dies.—Let ill fortune float upon her tide
And weep no more for us. What way this land
Worships its god we know and understand.

IPHIGENIA
Say first... which is it men call Pylades?

ORESTES
Tis this man's name, if that will give thee ease.

IPHIGENIA
From what walled town of Hellas cometh he?

ORESTES
Enough!—How would the knowledge profit thee?

IPHIGENIA
Are ye two brethren of one mother born?

ORESTES
No, not in blood. In love we are brothers sworn.

IPHIGENIA
Thou also hast a name: tell me thereof.

ORESTES
Call me Unfortunate. 'Tis name enough.

IPHIGENIA
I asked not that. Let that with Fortune lie.

ORESTES
Fools cannot laugh at them that nameless die.

IPHIGENIA
Why grudge me this? Hast thou such mighty fame?

ORESTES
My body, if thou wilt, but not my name.

IPHIGENIA
Nor yet the land of Greece where thou wast bred?

ORESTES
What gain to have told it thee, when I am dead?

IPHIGENIA
Nay: why shouldst thou deny so small a grace?

ORESTES
Know then, great Argos was my native place.

IPHIGENIA
Stranger! The truth!… From Argos art thou come?

ORESTES
Mycenae, once a rich land, was my home.

IPHIGENIA
'Tis banishment that brings thee here—or what?

ORESTES
A kind of banishment, half forced, half sought.

IPHIGENIA
Wouldst thou but tell me all I need of thee!

ORESTES
'Twere not much added to my misery.

IPHIGENIA
From Argos!… Oh, how sweet to see thee here!

ORESTES
Enjoy it, then. To me 'tis sorry cheer.

IPHIGENIA
Thou knowest the name of Troy? Far doth it flit.

ORESTES
Would God I had not; nay, nor dreamed of it.

IPHIGENIA
Men fable it is fallen beneath the sword?

ORESTES
Fallen it is. Thou hast heard no idle word.

IPHIGENIA
Fallen! At last!—And Helen taken too?

ORESTES
Aye; on an evil day for one I knew.

IPHIGENIA
Where is she? I too have some anger stored…

ORESTES
In Sparta! Once more happy with her lord!

IPHIGENIA
Oh! hated of all Greece, not only me!

ORESTES
I too have tasted of her wizardry.

IPHIGENIA
And came the armies home, as the tales run?

ORESTES
To answer that were many tales in one.

IPHIGENIA.
Oh, give me this hour full! Thou wilt soon die.

ORESTES
Ask, if such longing holds thee. I will try.

IPHIGENIA
A seer called Calchas! Did he ever come?[4]

ORESTES
Calchas is dead, as the news went at home.

IPHIGENIA
Good news, ye gods!—Odysseus, what of him?

ORESTES
Not home yet, but still living, as men deem.

IPHIGENIA
Curse him! And may he see his home no more.

ORESTES
Why curse him? All his house is stricken sore.

IPHIGENIA
How hath the Nereid's son, Achilles, sped?[5]

ORESTES
Small help his bridal brought him! He is dead.

IPHIGENIA
A fierce bridal, so the sufferers tell!

ORESTES
Who art thou, questioning of Greece so well?

IPHIGENIA
I was Greek. Evil caught me long ago.

ORESTES
Small wonder, then, thou hast such wish to know.

IPHIGENIA
That war-lord, whom they call so high in bliss…

ORESTES
None such is known to me. What name was his?

IPHIGENIA
They called him Agamemnon, Atreus' son.

ORESTES
I know not. Cease.—My questioning is done.

IPHIGENIA
'Twill be such joy to me! How fares he? Tell!

ORESTES
Dead. And hath wrecked another's life as well.

IPHIGENIA
Dead? By what dreadful fortune? Woe is me!

ORESTES
Why sighst thou? Had he any link with thee?

IPHIGENIA
I did but think of his old joy and pride.

ORESTES
His own wife foully stabbed him, and he died.

IPHIGENIA
O God! I pity her that slew… and him that slew.

ORESTES
Now cease thy questions. Add no word thereto.

IPHIGENIA
But one word. Lives she still, that hapless wife?

ORESTES
No. Her own son, her first-born, took her life.

IPHIGENIA
O shipwrecked house! What thought was in his brain?

ORESTES
Justice on her, to avenge his father slain.

IPHIGENIA
Alas! A bad false duty bravely hath he wrought.

ORESTES
Yet God, for all his duty, helps him not.

IPHIGENIA
And not one branch of Atreus' tree lives on?

ORESTES
Electra lives, unmated and alone.

IPHIGENIA
The child they slaughtered… is there word of her?

ORESTES
Why, no, save that she died in Aulis there.

IPHIGENIA
Poor child! Poor father, too, who killed and lied!

ORESTES
For a bad woman's worthless sake she died.

IPHIGENIA
The dead king's son, lives he in Argos still?

ORESTES
He lives, now here, now nowhere, bent with ill.

IPHIGENIA
O dreams, light dreams, farewell! Ye too were lies.

ORESTES
Aye; the gods too, whom mortals deem so wise,
Are nothing clearer than some winged dream;
And all their ways, like man's ways, but a stream
Of turmoil. He who cares to suffer least,
Not blind, as fools are blinded, by a priest,
Goes straight… to what death, those who know him know.

LEADER
We too have kinsmen dear, but, being low,
None heedeth, live they still or live they not.

IPHIGENIA [*with sudden impulse*]
Listen! For I am fallen upon a thought,
Strangers, of some good use to you and me,
Both. And 'tis thus most good things come to be,
When different eyes hold the same for fair.

Stranger, if I can save thee, wilt thou bear
To Argos and the friends who loved my youth
Some word? There is a tablet which, in truth
For me and mine ill works, a prisoner wrote,
Ta'en by the king in war. He knew 'twas not
My will that craved for blood, but One on high
Who holds it righteous her due prey shall die.
And since that day no Greek hath ever come
Whom I could save and send to Argos home
With prayer for help to any friend: but thou,
I think, dost loathe me not; and thou dost know
Mycenae and the names that fill my heart.
Help me! Be saved! Thou also hast thy part,
Thy life for one light letter… [*Orestes looks at Pylades*] For thy friend,
The Law compelleth. He must bear the end
By Artemis ordained, apart from thee.

ORESTES
Strange woman, as thou biddest let it be,
Save one thing. 'Twere for me a heavy weight
Should this man die. 'Tis I and mine own fate
That steer our goings. He but sails with me
Because I suffer much. It must not be
That by his ruin I should 'scape mine own,
And win thy grace withal. 'Tis simply done.
Give him the tablet. He with faithful will
Shall all thy hest in Argolis fulfil.
And I… who cares may kill me. Vile is he
Who leaves a friend in peril and goes free
Himself. And, as it chances, this is one
Right dear to me; his life is as my own.

IPHIGENIA
O royal heart! Surely from some great seed
This branch is born, that can so love indeed.
God grant the one yet living of my race
Be such as thou! For not quite brotherless
Am even I, save that I see him not,
Strangers… Howbeit, thy pleasure shall be wrought.
This man shall bear the message, and thou go
To death. So greatly thou wilt have it so!

ORESTES
Where is the priest who does this cruelty?

IPHIGENIA
'Tis I. This altar's spell is over me.

ORESTES
A grievous office and unblest, O maid.

IPHIGENIA
What dare I do? The law must be obeyed.

ORESTES
A girl to hold a sword and stab men dead!

IPHIGENIA
I shall but sign the water on thy head.

ORESTES
And who shall strike me, if I needs must ask?

IPHIGENIA
There be within these vaults who know their task.

ORESTES
My grave, when they have finished their desire?

IPHIGENIA
A great gulf of the rock, and holy fire.

ORESTES
Woe's me! Would that my sister's hand could close mine eyes!

IPHIGENIA
Alas, she dwelleth under distant skies,
Unhappy one, and vain is all thy prayer.
Yet, Oh, them art from Argos: all of care
That can be, I will give and fail thee not.
Rich raiment to thy burial shall be brought,
And oil to cool thy pyre in golden floods,
And sweet that from a thousand mountain buds
The murmuring bee hath garnered, I will throw
To die with thee in fragrance… I must go
And seek the tablet from the Goddess' room
Within.—Oh, do not hate me for my doom!

Watch them, ye servitors, but leave them free.

It may be, past all hoping, it may be,
My word shall sail to Argos, to his hand
Whom most I love. How joyous will he stand
To know, past hope, that here on the world's rim
His dead are living, and cry out for him!

[*She goes into the Temple.*]

CHORUS
Alas, we pity thee; surely we pity thee:
Who art given over to the holy water,
The drops that fall deadly as drops of blood.

ORESTES
I weep not, ye Greek maidens: but farewell.

CHORUS
Aye, and rejoice with thee; surely rejoice with thee,
Thou happy rover from the place of slaughter;
Thy foot shall stand again where thy father's stood.

PYLADES
While he I love must die? 'Tis miserable.

DIVERSE WOMEN OF THE CHORUS

A. Alas, the deathward faring of the lost!
B. Woe, woe; thou too shalt move to misery.
C. Which one shall suffer most?
D. My heart is torn by two words evenly,
For thee should I most sorrow, or for thee?

ORESTES

By heaven, is thy thought, Pylades, like mine?

PYLADES

O friend, I cannot speak.—But what is thine?

ORESTES

Who can the damsel be? How Greek her tone
Of question, all of Ilion overthrown,
And how the kings came back, the wizard flame
Of Calchas, and Achilles' mighty name,
And ill-starred Agamemnon. With a keen
Pity she spoke, and asked me of his queen
And children... The strange woman comes from there
By race, an Argive maid.—What aileth her
With tablets, else, and questionings as though
Her own heart beat with Argos' joy or woe?

PYLADES

Thy speech is quicker, friend, else I had said
The same; though surely all men visited
By ships have heard the fall of the great kings.
But let that be: I think of other things...

ORESTES

What? If thou hast need of me, let it be said.

PYLADES

I cannot live for shame if thou art dead.
I sailed together with thee; let us die
Together. What a coward slave were I,
Creeping through Argos and from glen to glen
Of wind-torn Phocian hills! And most of men—
For most are bad—will whisper how one day
I left my friend to die and made my way

Home. They will say I watched the sinking breath
Of thy great house and plotted for thy death
To wed thy sister, climb into thy throne...
I dread, I loathe it.—Nay, all ways but one
Are shut. My last breath shall go forth with thine,
Thy bloody sword, thy gulf of fire be mine
Also. I love thee and I dread men's scorn.

ORESTES
Peace from such thoughts! My burden can be borne;
But where one pain sufficeth, double pain
I will not bear. Nay, all that scorn and stain
That fright thee, on mine own head worse would be
If I brought death on him who toiled for me.
It is no bitter thing for such an one
As God will have me be, at last to have done
With living. Thou art happy; thy house lies
At peace with God, unstained in men's eyes;
Mine is all evil fate and evil life...
Nay, thou once safe, my sister for thy wife—[6]
So we agreed:—in sons of hers and thine
My name will live, nor Agamemnon's line
Be blurred for ever like an evil scroll.
Back! Rule thy land! Let life be in thy soul!
And when thou art come to Hellas, and the plain
Of Argos where the horsemen ride, again—
Give me thy hand!—I charge thee, let there be
Some death-mound and a graven stone for me.
My sister will go weep thereat, and shear
A tress or two. Say how I ended here,
Slain by a maid of Argolis, beside
God's altar, in mine own blood purified.

And fare thee well. I have no friend like thee
For truth and love, O boy that played with me,
And hunted on Greek hills, O thou on whom
Hath lain the hardest burden of my doom!
Farewell. The Prophet and the Lord of Lies[7]
Hath done his worst. Far out from Grecian skies
With craft forethought he driveth me, to die
Where none may mark how ends his prophecy!

I trusted in his word. I gave him all
My heart. I slew my mother at his call;
For which things now he casts me here to die.

PYLADES
Thy tomb shall fail thee not. Thy sister I
Will guard for ever. I, O stricken sore,
Who loved thee living and shall love thee more
Dead. But for all thou standest on the brink,
God's promise hath not yet destroyed thee. Think!
How oft, how oft the darkest hour of ill
Breaks brightest into dawn, if Fate but will!

ORESTES
Enough. Nor god nor man can any more
Aid me. The woman standeth at the door.

[*Enter Iphigenia from the Temple.*]

IPHIGENIA
Go ye within; and have all things of need
In order set for them that do the deed.
There wait my word.

[*Attendants go in.*]

Ye strangers, here I hold
The many-lettered tablet, fold on fold.
Yet… one thing still. No man, once unafraid
And safe, remembereth all the vows he made
In fear of death. My heart misgiveth me,
Lest he who bears my tablet, once gone free,
Forget me here and set my charge at naught.

ORESTES
What wouldst thou, then? Thou hast some troubling thought.

IPHIGENIA
His sworn oath let him give, to bear this same
Tablet to Argos, to the friend I name.

ORESTES
And if he give this oath, wilt thou swear too?

IPHIGENIA
What should I swear to do or not to do?

ORESTES
Send him from Tauris safe and free from ill.

IPHIGENIA
I promise. How else could he do my will?

ORESTES
The King will suffer this?

IPHIGENIA
Yes: I can bend
The King, and set upon his ship thy friend.

ORESTES
Choose then what oath is best, and he will swear.

IPHIGENIA [*to Pylades, who has come up to her*]
Say: "To thy friend this tablet I will bear."

PYLADES [*taking the tablet*]
Good. I will bear this tablet to thy friend.

IPHIGENIA
And I save thee beyond this kingdom's end.

PYLADES
What god dost thou invoke to witness this?

IPHIGENIA
Her in whose house I labour, Artemis.

PYLADES
And I the Lord of Heaven, eternal Zeus.

IPHIGENIA
And if thou fail me, or thine oath abuse… ?

PYLADES
May I see home no more. And thou, what then?

IPHIGENIA
May this foot never tread Greek earth again.

PYLADES
But stay: there is one chance we have forgot.

IPHIGENIA
A new oath can be sworn, if this serve not.

PYLADES
In one case set me free. Say I be crossed
With shipwreck, and, with ship and tablet lost
And all I bear, my life be saved alone:
Let not this oath be held a thing undone,
To curse me.

IPHIGENIA
Nay, then, many ways are best
To many ends. The words thou carriest
Enrolled and hid beneath that tablet's rim,
I will repeat to thee, and thou to him
I look for. Safer so. If the scrip sail
Unhurt to Greece, itself will tell my tale
Unaided: if it drown in some wide sea,
Save but thyself, my words are saved with thee.

PYLADES
For thy sake and for mine 'tis fairer so.
Now let me hear his name to whom I go
In Argolis, and how my words should run.

IPHIGENIA [*repeating the words by heart*]
Say: "To Orestes, Agamemnon's son
She that was slain in Aulis, dead to Greece

Yet quick, Iphigenia sendeth peace."

ORESTES
Iphigenia! Where? Back from the dead?

IPHIGENIA
'Tis I. But speak not, lest thou break my thread.—
"Take me to Argos, brother, ere I die,
Back from the Friendless Peoples and the high
Altar of Her whose bloody rites I wreak."

ORESTES [*aside*]
Where am I, Pylades? How shall I speak?

IPHIGENIA
"Else one in grief forsaken shall, like shame,
Haunt thee."

PYLADES [*aside*]
Orestes!

IPHIGENIA [*overhearing him*]
Yes: that is the name.

PYLADES
Ye Gods above!

IPHIGENIA
Why callest thou on God
For words of mine?

PYLADES
'Tis nothing. 'Twas a road
My thoughts had turned. Speak on.—No need for us
To question; we shall hear things marvellous.

IPHIGENIA
Tell him that Artemis my soul did save,
I know not how, and to the altar gave
A fawn instead; the which my father slew,
Not seeing, deeming that the sword he drew
Struck me. But she had borne me far away

And left me in this land.—I charge thee, say
So much. It all is written on the scroll.

PYLADES
An easy charge thou layest on my soul,
A glad oath on thine own. I wait no more,
But here fulfil the service that I swore.
Orestes, take this tablet which I bear
To thine own hand, thy sister's messenger.

ORESTES
I take it, but I reck not of its scrip
Nor message. Too much joy is at my lip.
Sister! Beloved! Wildered though I be,
My arms believe not, yet they crave for thee.
Now, filled with wonder, give me my delight!

[*He goes to embrace her. She stands speechless.*]

LEADER
Stranger, forbear! No living man hath right
To touch that robe. The Goddess were defiled!

ORESTES
O Sister mine, O my dead father's child,
Agamemnon's child; take me and have no fear,
Beyond all dreams 'tis I thy brother here.

IPHIGENIA
My brother? Thou?... Peace! Mock at me no more.
Argos is bright with him and Nauplia's shore.

ORESTES
Unhappy one! Thou hast no brother there.

IPHIGENIA
Orestes... thou? Whom Clytemnestra bare?

ORESTES
To Atreus' firstborn son, thy sire and mine.

IPHIGENIA
Thou sayst it: Oh, give me some proof, some sign!

ORESTES
What sign thou wilt. Ask anything from home.

IPHIGENIA
Nay, thou speak: 'tis from thee the sign should come.

ORESTES
That will I.—First, old tales Electra told.
Thou knowest how Pelops' princes warred of old?[8]

IPHIGENIA
I know: the Golden Lamb that wrought their doom.

ORESTES
Thine own hand wove that story on the loom…

IPHIGENIA
How sweet! Thou movest near old memories.

ORESTES
With a great Sun back beaten in the skies.

IPHIGENIA
Fine linen threads I used. The memories come.

ORESTES
And mother gave thee shrift-water from home
For Aulis…

IPHIGENIA
I remember. Not so fair
A day did drink that water!

ORESTES
And thine hair
They brought us for thy dying gift, and gave
To mother.

IPHIGENIA
Yes: for record on the grave
I sent it, where this head should never lie.

ORESTES
Another token, seen of mine own eye.
The ancient lance that leapt in Pelops' hand,
To win his bride, the virgin of the land,
And smite Oenomaus, in thy chamber hid…

IPHIGENIA [*falling into his arms*]
Beloved! Oh, no other, for indeed
Beloved art thou! In mine arms at last,
Orestes far away.

ORESTES
And thou in mine, the evil dreaming past,
Back from the dead this day!
Yet through the joy tears, tears and sorrow loud
Are o'er mine eyes and thine eyes, like a cloud.

IPHIGENIA
Is this the babe I knew,
The little babe, light lifted like a bird?
O heart of mine, too blest for any word,
What shall I say or do?
Beyond all wonders, beyond stories heard,
This joy is here and true.

ORESTES
Could we but stay thus joined for evermore!

IPHIGENIA
A joy is mine I may not understand,
Friends, and a fear, lest sudden from my hand
This dream will melt and soar
Up to the fiery skies from whence it came.
O Argos land, O hearth and holy flame
That old Cyclopes lit,
I bless ye that he lives, that he is grown,

A light and strength, my brother and mine own;
I bless your name for it.

ORESTES
One blood we are; so much is well. But Fate,
Sister, hath not yet made us fortunate.

IPHIGENIA
O most unfortunate! Did I not feel,
Whose father, misery-hearted, at my bare
Throat held the steel?

ORESTES
Woe's me! Methinks even now I see thee there.

IPHIGENIA
No love-song of Achilles! Crafty arms
Drew me to that cold sleep,
And tears, blind tears amid the altar psalms
And noise of them that weep—
That was my cleansing!

ORESTES
My heart too doth bleed,
To think our father wrought so dire a deed.

IPHIGENIA
My life hath known no father. Any road
To any end may run,
As god's will drives; else…

ORESTES
Else, unhappy one,
Thyself had spilt this day thy brother's blood!

IPHIGENIA
Ah God, my cruel deed!… 'Twas horrible.
'Twas horrible… O brother! Did my heart
Endure it?… And things fell
Right by so frail a chance; and here thou art.
Bloody my hand had been,

My heart heavy with sin.
And now, what end cometh?
Shall Chance yet comfort me,
Finding a way for thee
Back from the Friendless Strand,
Back from the place of death—
Ere yet the slayers come
And thy blood sink in the sand—
Home unto Argos, home?...
Hard heart, so swift to slay,
Is there to life no way?...

No ship!... And how by land?...
A rush of feet
Out to the waste alone.
Nay: 'twere to meet
Death, amid tribes unknown
And trackless ways of the waste...
Surely the sea were best.
Back by the narrow bar
To the Dark Blue Gate!...
Ah God, too far, too far!...
Desolate! Desolate!

What god or man, what unimagined flame,
Can cleave this road where no road is, and bring
To us last wrecks of Agamemnon's name,
Peace from long suffering?

Translated by G. Murray.

HERODOTUS

c. 480 - 420 BC

Herodotus was born about 480 BC in Halicarnassus on the Aegean coast of Asia Minor (modern Bodrum in Turkey). Described by Cicero as the "Father of History", Herodotus traveled extensively in Egypt, Palestine (Gaza), Phoenicia (Tyre), Scythia, and the northern Aegean. He resided at Athens, and, under the authority of Pericles, was among those who founded the city of Thurii (modern Sibari) in South Italy.

Herodotus is best known for his History*; it is also referred to as the* Inquiry, *which is a more accurate translation for the Greek word "historia." The first four books report on the formation of the Persian Empire with a lengthy and celebrated digression about Egypt; the last five volumes discuss the Medic Wars. An arbitrary choice made by Alexandrian scholars is responsible for the work's division into nine books, each of which is given a name of one of the Muses.*

Often criticized for his methodology, his digressions, and his numerous anecdotes (see the True Story *of Lucian in this volume), Herodotus does not exercise as much rational control as does Thucydides. The* Inquiry *is nonetheless invaluable for its ethnographical, geographical, and anthropological information. It also sheds light on the relations between the Barbarians and the Greeks in the fifth century BC.*

Perhaps unfairly referred to by Plutarch as the "King of the Liars," Herodotus intended to preserve the most momentous events of mankind.

Everyday Life in Ancient Egypt: Food, Medicine, Mummification, and More

Herodotus, *History* 2.77-91

Herodotus was fascinated with Egypt, as were Plato and Napoleon later on. He visited the land of the Nile around the middle of the fifth century BC, and devoted an entire book to the description of the country, its geography, its religion, its fauna, and the customs of its inhabitants. For Herodotus, Egyptian civilization preceded that of Greece by several thousand years. In his eyes, Egypt was a "school of wisdom" where the Greeks learned philosophy, the art of naming and venerating the gods, geometry, the measuring of time, and oracular techniques.

"The Egyptians are the most healthy of all men next after the Libyans (in my opinion on account of the seasons, because the seasons do not change, for by the changes of things generally, and especially of the seasons, diseases are most apt to be produced in men)."

Of the Egyptians themselves, those who dwell in the part of Egypt which is sown for crops practice memory more than any other men and are the most learned in history by far of all those of whom I have had experience.

And their manner of life is as follows: for three successive days in each month they purge, hunting after health with emetics and clysters, and they think that all the diseases which exist are produced in men by the food on which they live. For the Egyptians are from other causes also the most healthy of all men next after the Libyans (in my opinion on account of the seasons, because the seasons do not change, for by the changes of things generally, and especially of the seasons, diseases are most apt to be produced in men), and as to their diet, it is as follows: they eat bread, making loaves of maize, which they call "kyllestis", and they use habitually a wine made out of barley, for vines they have not in their land. Of their fish some they dry in the sun and then eat them without cooking, others they eat cured in brine. Of birds they eat quails and ducks and small birds without cooking, after first curing them; and everything else which they have belonging to the class of birds or fishes, except such as have been set apart by them as sacred, they eat roasted or boiled.

In the entertainments of the rich among them, when they have finished eating, a man bears round a wooden figure of a dead body in a coffin, made as like the reality as may be both by painting and carving, and measuring about a cubit or two cubits each way; and this he shows to each of those who are drinking together, saying: "When thou lookest upon this, drink and be merry, for thou shalt be such as this when thou art dead." Thus they do at their carousals.

The customs which they practice are derived from their fathers and they do not acquire others in addition; but besides other customary things among them which are worthy of mention, they have one song, that of Linos, the same who is sung of both in Phoenicia and in Cyprus and elsewhere, having however a name different according to the various nations. This song agrees exactly with that which the Hellenes sing calling on the name of Linos, so that besides many other things about which I wonder among those matters which concern Egypt, I wonder especially about this, namely whence they got the song of Linos. It is evident however that they have sung this song from immemorial time, and in the Egyptian tongue Linos is called Maneros. The Egyptians told me that he was the only son of him who first became king of Egypt, and that he died before his time and was honoured with these lamentations by the Egyptians, and that this was their first and only song.

In another respect the Egyptians are in agreement with some of the Hellenes, namely with the Lacedemonians, but not with the rest, that is to say, the younger of them when they meet the elder give way and move out of the path, and when their elders approach, they rise out of their seat. In this which follows however they are not in agreement with any of the Hellenes,—instead of addressing one another in the roads they do reverence, lowering their hand down to their knee. They wear tunics of linen about their legs with fringes, which they call "calasiris"; above these they have garments of white wool thrown over. Woolen garments however are not taken into the temples, nor are they buried with them, for this is not permitted by religion. In these points they are in agreement with the observances called Orphic and Bacchic (which are really Egyptian), and also with those of the Pythagoreans, for one who takes part in these mysteries is also forbidden by religious rule to be buried in woolen garments; and about this there is a sacred story told.

Besides these things the Egyptians have found out also to what god each month and each day belongs, and what fortunes a man will meet with who is born on any particular day, and how he will die, and what kind of a man he will be: and these inventions were taken up by those of the Hellenes who occupied themselves about poesy. Portents too have been found out by them more than by all other men besides; for when a portent has happened, they observe and write down the event which comes of it, and if ever afterwards anything resembling this happens, they believe that the event which comes of it will be similar. Their divination is ordered thus: the art is assigned not to any man but to certain of the gods, for there are in their land

Oracles of Heracles, of Apollo, of Athene, of Artemis, or Ares, and of Zeus, and moreover that which they hold most in honour of all, namely the Oracle of Leto which is in the city of Buto.[1] The manner of divination however is not established among them according to the same fashion everywhere, but is different in different places. The art of medicine among them is distributed thus: each physician is a physician of one disease and of no more; and the whole country is full of physicians, for some profess themselves to be physicians of the eyes, others of the head, others of the teeth, others of the affections of the stomach, and others of the more obscure ailments.

Their fashions of mourning and of burial are these: Whenever any household has lost a man who is of any regard amongst them, the whole number of women of that house forthwith plaster over their heads or even their faces with mud. Then leaving the corpse within the house they go themselves to and fro about the city and beat themselves, with their garments bound up by a girdle and their breasts exposed, and with them go all the women who are related to the dead man, and on the other side the men beat themselves, they too having their garments bound up by a girdle; and when they have done this, they then convey the body to the embalming.

In this occupation certain persons employ themselves regularly and inherit this as a craft. These, whenever a corpse is conveyed to them, show to those who brought it wooden models of corpses made like reality by painting, and the best of the ways of embalming they say is that of him whose name I think it impiety to mention when speaking of a matter of such a kind;[2] the second which they show is less good than this and also less expensive; and the third is the least expensive of all. Having told them about this, they inquire of them in which way they desire the corpse of their friend to be prepared.

Then they after they have agreed for a certain price depart out of the way, and the others being left behind in the buildings embalm according to the best of these ways thus: First with the crooked iron tool they draw out the brain through the nostrils, extracting it partly thus and partly by pouring in drugs; and after this with a sharp stone of Ethiopia they make a cut along the side and take out the whole contents of the belly, and when they have cleared out the cavity and cleansed it with palm-wine they cleanse it again with spices pounded up; then they fill the belly with pure myrrh pounded up and with cassia and other spices except frankincense, and sew it together again. Having so done they keep it for embalming covered up in natron for seventy days, but for a longer time than this it is not permitted to embalm it; and when the seventy days are past, they wash the corpse and roll its whole body up in fine linen cut into bands, smearing these beneath with gum, which the Egyptians use generally instead of glue. Then the kinsfolk receive it from them and have a wooden figure made in the shape of a man, and when they have had this made they enclose the corpse, and having shut it up within, they store it then in a sepulchral chamber, setting it to stand upright against the wall.

Thus they deal with the corpses which are prepared in the most costly way; but for those who desire the middle way and wish to avoid great cost they prepare the corpse as follows: having filled their syringes with the oil which is got from cedar-wood, with this they forthwith fill the belly of the corpse, and this they do without having either cut it open or taken out the bowels, but they inject the oil by the breech, and having stopped the drench from returning back they keep it then the appointed number of days for embalming, and on the last of the days they let the cedar oil come out from the belly, which they before put in; and it has such power that it brings out with it the bowels and interior organs of the body dissolved; and the natron dissolves the flesh, so that there is left of the corpse only the skin and the bones. When they have done this they give back the corpse at once in that condition without working upon it any more. The third kind of embalming, by which are prepared the bodies of those who have less means, is as follows: they cleanse out the belly with a purge and then keep the body for embalming during the seventy days, and at once after that they give it back to the bringers to carry away.

The wives of men of rank when they die are not given at once to be embalmed, nor such women as are very beautiful or of greater regard than others, but on the third or fourth day after their death (and not before) they are delivered to the embalmers. They do so about this matter in order that the embalmers may not abuse their women, for they say that one of them was taken once doing so to the corpse of a woman lately dead, and his fellow-craftsman gave information.

Whenever any one, either of the Egyptians themselves or of strangers, is found to have been carried off by a crocodile or brought to his death by the river itself, the people of any city by which he may have been cast up on land must embalm him and lay him out in the fairest way they can and bury him in a sacred burial-place, nor may any of his relations or friends besides touch him, but the priests of the Nile themselves handle the corpse and bury it as that of one who was something more than man.

Translated by G.C. Macaulay.

The Battle of Marathon

Herodotus, *History* 6.107-121

The Persians land in 490 BC at Marathon only 42 km (26 miles) northeast of Athens. They threaten to storm the city. The Athenians plead for help from the Lacedemonians, who are in the middle of celebrating their most important religious festival and refuse to go to war before the full moon. Worse still, Hippias, who at one time was a tyrant of Athens and had been expelled from the city years before, sides with the Persian enemy. After heated negotiations, the Athenians and their allies—the Plataeans—decide to fight the battle. Legend has it that nearly 20,000 Greeks defeated twice as many Persians.

"Now the opinions of the generals of the Athenians were divided, and the one party urged that they should not fight a battle, seeing that they were too few to fight with the army of the Medes, while the others, and among them Miltiades, advised that they should do so."

These men were waiting for the full moon; and meanwhile Hippias the son of Peisistratos was guiding the Barbarians in to Marathon, after having seen on the night that was just past a vision in his sleep of this kind: it seemed to Hippias that he lay with his own mother. He conjectured then from the dream that he should return to Athens and recover his rule, and then bring his life to an end in old age in his own land. From the dream, I say, he conjectured this; and after this, as he guided them in, first he disembarked the slaves from Eretria on the island belonging to the Styrians, called Aigleia;[3] and then, as the ships came in to shore at Marathon, he moored them there, and after the Barbarians had come from their ships to land, he was engaged in disposing them in their places. While he was ordering these things, it came upon him to sneeze and cough more violently than was his wont. Then since he was advanced in years, most of his teeth were shaken thereby, and one of these teeth he cast forth by the violence of the cough and the tooth having fallen from him upon the sand, he was very desirous to find it; since however the tooth was not to be found when he searched, he groaned aloud and said to those who were by him: "This land is not ours, nor shall we be able to make it subject to us; but so much part in it as belonged to me the tooth possesses."

Hippias then conjectured that his vision had been thus fulfilled and meanwhile, after the Athenians had been drawn up in the sacred enclosure of Heracles, there joined them the Plataians coming to their help in a body; for the Plataians had given themselves to the Athenians, and the Athenians before this time undertook many toils on behalf of them; and this was the manner in which they gave themselves. Being oppressed by the Thebans, the Plataians at first desired to give themselves to Cleomenes the son of Anaxandrides and to the Lacedemonians, who chanced to come thither; but these did not accept them, and said to them as follows: "We dwell too far off, and such support as ours would be to you but cold comfort; for ye might many times be reduced to slavery before any of us had information of it. But we counsel you rather to give yourselves to the Athenians, who are both neighbours and also not bad helpers."

Thus the Lacedemonians counselled, not so much on account of their goodwill to the Plataians as because they desired that the Athenians should have trouble by being involved in a conflict with the Bœtians. The Lacedemonians, I say, thus counselled the men of Plataia; and they did not fail to follow their counsel, but when the Athenians were doing sacrifice to the twelve gods, they sat down as suppliants at the altar and so gave themselves. Then the Thebans having been informed of these things marched against the Plataians, and the Athenians came to their assistance. And as they were about to join battle, the Corinthians did not permit them to do so, but being by chance there, they reconciled their strife; and both parties having put the matter into their hands, they laid down boundaries for the land, with the condition that the Thebans should leave those of the Bœotians alone who did not desire to be reckoned with the other Boeotians. The Corinthians having given this decision departed; but as the Athenians were going back, the Bœotians attacked them, and having attacked them they were worsted in the fight. Upon that the Athenians passed beyond the boundaries which the Corinthians had set to be for the Plataians, and they made the river Asopos itself to be the boundary of the Thebans towards the land of Plataia and towards the district of Hysiai. The Plataians then had given themselves to the Athenians in the manner which has been said, and at this time they came to Marathon to bring them help.

Now the opinions of the generals of the Athenians were divided, and the one party urged that they should not fight a battle, seeing that they were too few to fight with the army of the Medes,[4] while the others, and among them Miltiades, advised that they should do so: and when they were divided and the worse opinion was like to prevail, then, since he who had been chosen by lot to be polemarch[5] of the Athenians had a vote in addition to the ten (for in old times the Athenians gave the polemarch an equal vote with the generals) and at that time the polemarch was Callimachos of the deme of Aphidnai, to him came Miltiades and said as follows: "With thee now it rests, Callimachos, either to bring Athens under slavery, or by making her free to leave behind thee for all the time that men shall live a memorial such as not even Harmodios and Aristogeiton[6] have left. For now the Athenians have come to a danger the greatest to which they have ever come since they were a people; and on the one hand, if they submit to the Medes, it is determined what they shall suffer, being delivered over to Hippias, while on the other hand, if this city shall gain the victory, it may become the first of the cities of Hellas. How this may happen and how it comes to thee of all men to have the decision of these matters, I am now about to tell. Of us the generals, who are ten in number, the opinions are divided, the one party urging that we fight a battle and the others that we do not fight. Now if we do not, I expect that some great spirit of discord will fall upon the minds of the Athenians and so shake them that they shall go over to the Medes; but if we fight a battle before any unsoundness appear in any part of the Athenian people, then we are able to gain the victory in the fight, if the gods grant equal conditions. These things then all belong to thee and depend on thee; for if thou attach thyself to my opinions, thou hast both a fatherland which is free and a native city which shall be the first among the cities of Hellas; but if thou choose the opinion of those who are earnest against fighting, thou shalt have the opposite of those good things of which I told thee."

Thus speaking Miltiades gained Callimachos to his side; and the opinion of the polemarch being added, it was thus determined to fight a battle. After this, those generals whose opinion was in favour of fighting, as the turn of each one of them to command for the day came round, gave over their command to Miltiades; and he, accepting it, would not however yet bring about a battle, until his own turn to command had come.

And when it came round to him, then the Athenians were drawn up for battle in the order which here follows: on the right wing the polemarch Callimachos was leader (for the custom of the Athenians then was this, that the polemarch should have the right wing); and he leading, next after him came the tribes in order as they were numbered one after another, and last were drawn up the Plataians occupying the left wing: for ever since this battle, when the Athenians offer sacrifices in the solemn assemblies which are made at the four-yearly festivals, the herald of the Athenians prays thus, "that blessings may come to the Athenians and to the Plataians both." On this occasion however, when the Athenians were being drawn up at Marathon something of this kind was done: their army being made equal in length of front to that of the Medes, came to drawn up in the middle with a depth of but few ranks, and here their army was weakest, while each wing was strengthened with numbers.

And when they had been arranged in their places and the sacrifices proved favourable, then the Athenians were let go, and they set forth at a run to attack the Barbarians. Now the space between the armies was not less than eight furlongs; and the Persians seeing them advancing to the attack at a run, made preparations to receive them; and in their minds they charged the Athenians with madness which must be fatal, seeing that they were few and yet were pressing forwards at a run, having neither cavalry nor archers. Such was the thought of the Barbarians; but the Athenians when all in a body they had joined in combat with the Barbarians, fought in a memorable fashion, for they were the first of all the Hellenes about whom we know who went to attack the enemy at a run, and they were the first also who endured to face the Median garments and the men who wore them, whereas up to this time the very name of the Medes was to the Hellenes a terror to hear.

Now while they fought in Marathon, much time passed by; and in the centre of the army, where the Persians themselves and the Sacans were drawn up, the Barbarians were winning, here, I say, the Barbarians had broken the ranks of their opponents and were pursuing them inland, but on both wings the Athenians and the Plataians severally were winning the victory; and being victorious they left that part of the Barbarians which had been routed to fly without molestation, and bringing together the two wings they fought with those who had broken their centre, and the Athenians were victorious. So they followed after the Persians as they fled, slaughtering them, until they came to the sea; and then they called for fire and began to take hold of the ships. In this part of the work was slain the polemarch Callimachos after having proved himself a good man, and also one of the generals, Stesilaos the son of Thrasylaos, was killed; and besides this Kynegeiros the son of Euphorion while taking hold there of the ornament at the stern of a ship had his hand cut off with an axe and fell; and many others also of the Athenians who were men of note were killed.

Seven of the ships the Athenians got possession of in this manner, but with the rest the Barbarians pushed off from land, and after taking the captives from Eretria off the island where they had left them, they sailed round Sunion, purposing to arrive at the city before the Athenians. And an accusation became current among the Athenians to the effect that they formed this design by contrivance of the Alcmaionidai;[7] for these, it was said, having concerted matters with the Persians, displayed to them a shield when they had now embarked in their ships. These then, I say, were sailing round Sunion; and meanwhile the Athenians came to the rescue back to the city as speedily as they could, and they arrived there before the Barbarians came; and having arrived from the temple of Heracles at Marathon they encamped at another temple of Heracles, namely that which is in Kynosarges. The Barbarians however came and lay with their ships in the sea which is off Phaleron, (for this was then the seaport of the Athenians), they anchored their ships, I say, off this place, and then proceeded to sail back to Asia.

In this fight at Marathon there were slain of the Barbarians about six thousand four hundred men, and of the Athenians a hundred and ninety and two. Such was the number which fell on both sides; and it happened also that a marvel occurred there of this kind. An Athenian, Epizelos the son of Cuphagoras, while fighting in the close combat and proving himself a good man, was deprived of the sight of his eyes, neither having received a blow in any part of his body nor having been hit with a missile, and for the rest of his life from this time he continued to be blind, and I was informed that he used to tell about that which had happened to him a tale of this kind, namely that it seemed to him that a tall man in full armour stood against him, whose beard overshadowed his whole shield; and this apparition passed him by, but killed his comrade who stood next to him. Thus, as I was informed, Epizelos told the tale.

Datis, however, as he was going with his army to Asia, when he had come to Myconos saw a vision in his sleep; and of what nature the vision was it is not reported, but as soon as day dawned he caused a search to be made of the ships, and finding in a Phenician ship an image of Apollo overlaid with gold, he inquired from whence it had been carried off. Then having been informed from what temple it came, he sailed in his own ship to Delos, and finding that the Delians had returned then to the island, he deposited the image in the temple and charged the men of Delos to convey it back to Delion in the territory of the Thebans, which is situated by the sea-coast just opposite Chalkis. Datis having given this charge sailed away, the Delians however did not convey the statue back, but after an interval of twenty years the Thebans themselves brought it to Delion by reason of an oracle. Now as to those Eretrians who had been reduced to slavery, Datis and Artaphrenes, when they reached Asia in their voyage, brought them up to Susa; and king Dareios, though he had great anger against the Eretrians before they were made captive, because the Eretrians had done wrong to him unprovoked, yet when he saw that they had been brought up to him and were in his power, he did them no more evil, but established them as settlers in the Kissian land upon one of his own domains, of which the name is Ardericca: and this is distant two hundred and ten furlongs from Susa and forty from the well which produces things of three different kinds; for they draw from it asphalt, salt and oil, in the manner which here follows: the liquid is drawn with a swipe, to which there is fastened half a skin instead of a bucket, and a man strikes this down into it and draws up, and then pours it into a cistern, from which it runs through into another vessel, taking three separate ways. The asphalt and the salt become solid at once, and the oil which is called by the Persians "rhadinake", is black and gives out a disagreeable smell. Here king Dareios established the Eretrians as settlers; and even to my time they continued to occupy this land, keeping still their former language. Thus it happened with regard to the Eretrians.

Of the Lacedemonians there came to Athens two thousand after the full moon, making great haste to be in time, so that they arrived in Attica on the third day after leaving Sparta; and though they had come too late for the battle, yet they desired to behold the Medes; and accordingly they went out to Marathon and looked at the bodies of the slain. Then afterwards they departed home, commending the Athenians and the work which they had done.

Now it is a cause of wonder to me, and I do not accept the report, that the Alcmaionidai could ever have displayed to the Persians a shield by a previous understanding, with the desire that the Athenians should be under the Barbarians and under Hippias; seeing that they are evidently proved to have been haters of despots as much or more than Callias the son of Phainippos and father of Hipponicos, while Callias for his part was the only man of all the Athenians who dared, when Peisistratos was driven out of Athens, to buy his goods offered for sale by the State, and in other ways also he contrived against him everything that was most hostile.

Translated by G.C. Macaulay.

THUCYDIDES

c. 460 - c. 400 BC

Thucydides was born to a prominent Athenian family that owned gold mines in Thrace. The main event of his life was the Peloponnesian War, a conflict in which Athens, Sparta, and their respective allies clashed for nearly 30 years (from 431 to 404 BC). It terminated with the defeat of the metropolis of Attica. This was the end of Athenian supremacy and the age of Pericles, a politician for whom Thucydides held great admiration. It was the close of a century that had begun with the brilliant victory of the Greeks over the Persians at Marathon and at Salamis, and had continued with the construction of the Parthenon and the erection of other celebrated monuments on the Acropolis.

Thucydides was a victim of the plague that spread through Athens at the beginning of the war, between 430 and 427 BC. He managed to survive, however, and in 424 was appointed military commander. Unfortunately, he failed to defend the city of Amphipolis, north of the Aegean, one of the most sensitive points of the Athenian strategy. The price for his failure was exile. Thucydides spent 20 years of his life outside of Athens. He made good use of his forced exile to write the History of the Peloponnesian War. *His work begins with what is called the "archaeology," the history of Greece in times more ancient than Thucydides', and continues with different episodes of the Peloponnesian War. The* History *ends in 411 BC, shortly after the expedition to Sicily that resulted in complete disaster for Athens. Thucydides had intended to cover events through 404 BC but never finished his work.*

Thucydides departed from the methods used by earlier historians, especially Herodotus, who demonstrated a pronounced taste for mythology and genealogy. His project consisted of establishing historical truth by following a strict methodology. He cleared the way for modern historiography, namely scientific writing based on facts and not on fabulous tales.

Greece from Its Origins to the Peloponnesian War

Thucydides, *History of the Peloponnesian War* 1.1-19

Thucydides begins his work with an exposition of historical events in Greece from the most ancient times until the Peloponnesian War. These include the period when Greece had no name, the days of Minos and the pirates, the Trojan War, the colonization of the Aegean, the institution of various tyrannies, the establishment of naval powers throughout the Greek world, and the Persian wars. Thucydides has two objectives: (1) to show that the Peloponnesian War is the most important event in Greek history and (2) to argue that Greek power during his time is the result of the gradual development of navigation and commerce that permitted the accumulation of wealth and the establishment of stable communities.

"Wherever there were tyrants, their habit of providing simply for themselves, of looking solely to their personal comfort and family aggrandizement, made safety the great aim of their policy, and prevented anything great proceeding from them."

Thucydides, an Athenian, wrote the history of the war between the Peloponnesians and the Athenians, beginning at the moment that it broke out, and believing that it would be a great war and more worthy of relation than any that had preceded it. This belief was not without its grounds. The preparations of both the combatants were in every department in the last state of perfection; and he could see the rest of the Hellenic race taking sides in the quarrel; those who delayed doing so at once having it in contemplation. Indeed this was the greatest movement yet known in history, not only of the Hellenes, but of a large part of the barbarian world—I had almost said of mankind. For though the events of remote antiquity, and even those that more immediately preceded the war, could not from lapse of time be clearly ascertained, yet the evidences which an inquiry carried as far back as was practicable leads me to trust, all point to the conclusion that there was nothing on a great scale, either in war or in other matters.

For instance, it is evident that the country now called Hellas had in ancient times no settled population; on the contrary, migrations were of frequent occurrence, the several tribes readily abandoning their homes under the pressure of superior numbers. Without commerce, without freedom of communication either by land or sea, cultivating no more of their territory than the exigencies of life required, destitute of capital, never planting their land (for they could not tell when an invader might not come and take it all away, and when he did come they had no walls to stop him), thinking that the necessities of daily sustenance could be supplied at one place as well as another, they cared little for shifting their habitation, and consequently neither built large cities nor attained to any other form of greatness. The richest soils were always most subject to this change of masters; such as the district now called Thessaly, Boeotia, most of the Peloponnese, Arcadia excepted, and the most fertile parts of the rest of Hellas. The goodness of the land favoured the aggrandizement of particular individuals, and thus created faction which proved a fertile source of ruin. It also invited invasion. Accordingly Attica, from the poverty of its soil enjoying from a very remote period freedom from faction, never changed its inhabitants. And here is no inconsiderable exemplification of my assertion that the migrations were the cause of there being no correspondent growth in other parts. The most powerful victims of war or faction from the rest of Hellas took refuge with the Athenians as a safe retreat; and at an early period, becoming naturalized, swelled the already large population of the city to such a height that Attica became at last too small to hold them, and they had to send out colonies to Ionia.

There is also another circumstance that contributes not a little to my conviction of the weakness of ancient times. Before the Trojan war there is no indication of any common action in Hellas, nor indeed of the universal prevalence of the name; on the contrary, before the time of Hellen, son of Deucalion,[1] no such appellation existed, but the country went by the names of the different tribes, in particular of the Pelasgian.[2] It was not till Hellen and his sons grew strong in Phthiotis, and were invited as allies into the other cities, that one by one they gradually acquired from the connection the name of Hellenes; though a long time elapsed before that name could fasten itself upon all. The best proof of this is furnished by Homer. Born long after the Trojan War, he nowhere calls all of them by that name, nor indeed any of them except the followers of Achilles from Phthiotis, who were the original Hellenes: in his poems they are called Danaans, Argives, and Achaeans. He does not even use the term barbarian, probably because the Hellenes had not yet been marked off from the rest of the world by one distinctive appellation. It appears therefore that the several Hellenic communities, comprising not only those who first acquired the name, city by city, as they came to understand each other, but also those who assumed it afterwards as the name of the whole people, were before the Trojan war prevented by their want of strength and the absence of mutual intercourse from displaying any collective action.

Indeed, they could not unite for this expedition till they had gained increased familiarity with the sea. And the first person known to us by tradition as having established a navy is Minos. He made himself master of what is now called the Hellenic sea, and ruled over the Cyclades, into most of which he sent the first colonies, expelling the Carians and appointing his own sons governors; and thus did his best to put down piracy in those waters, a necessary step to secure the revenues for his own use.

For in early times the Hellenes and the barbarians of the coast and islands, as communication by sea became more common, were tempted to turn pirates, under the conduct of their most powerful men; the motives being to serve their own cupidity and to support the needy. They would fall upon a town unprotected by walls, and consisting of a mere collection of villages, and would plunder it; indeed, this came to be the main source of their livelihood, no disgrace being yet attached to such an achievement, but even some glory. An illustration of this is furnished by the honour with which some of the inhabitants of the continent still regard a successful marauder, and by the question we find the old poets everywhere representing the people as asking of voyagers—"Are they pirates?"—as if those who are asked the question would have no idea of disclaiming the imputation, or their interrogators of reproaching them for it. The same rapine prevailed also by land.

And even at the present day many of Hellas still follow the old fashion, the Ozolian Locrians for instance, the Aetolians, the Acarnanians, and that region of the continent; and the custom of carrying arms is still kept up among these continentals, from the old piratical habits. The whole of Hellas used once to carry arms, their habitations being unprotected and their communication with each other unsafe; indeed, to wear arms was as much a part of everyday life with them as with the barbarians. And the fact that the people in these parts of Hellas are still living in the old way points to a time when the same mode of life was once equally common to all. The Athenians were the first to lay aside their weapons, and to adopt an easier and more luxurious mode of life; indeed, it is only lately that their rich old men left off the luxury of wearing undergarments of linen, and fastening a knot of their hair with a tie of golden grasshoppers, a fashion which spread to their Ionian kindred and long prevailed among the old men there. On the contrary, a modest style of dressing, more in conformity with modern ideas, was first adopted by the Lacedaemonians, the rich doing their best to assimilate their way of life to that of the common people. They also set the example of contending naked, publicly stripping and anointing themselves with oil in their gymnastic exercises. Formerly, even in the Olympic contests, the athletes who contended wore belts across their middles; and it is but a few years since that the practice ceased. To this day among some of the barbarians, especially in Asia, when prizes for boxing and wrestling are offered, belts are worn by the combatants. And there are many other points in which a likeness might be shown between the life of the Hellenic world of old and the barbarian of to-day.

With respect to their towns, later on, at an era of increased facilities of navigation and a greater supply of capital, we find the shores becoming the site of walled towns, and the isthmuses being occupied for the purposes of commerce and defence against a neighbour. But the old towns, on account of the great prevalence of piracy, were built away from the sea, whether on the islands or the continent, and still remain in their old sites. For the pirates used to plunder one another, and indeed all coast populations, whether seafaring or not.

The islanders, too, were great pirates. These islanders were Carians and Phoenicians, by whom most of the islands were colonized, as was proved by the following fact. During the purification of Delos by Athens in this war all the graves in the island were taken up, and it was found that above half their inmates were Carians: they were identified by the fashion of the arms buried with them, and by the method of interment, which was the same as the Carians still follow. But as soon as Minos had formed his navy, communication by sea became easier, as he colonized most of the islands, and thus expelled the malefactors. The coast population now began to apply themselves more closely to the acquisition of wealth, and their life became more settled; some even began to build themselves walls on the strength of their newly acquired riches. For the love of gain would reconcile the weaker to the dominion of the stronger, and the possession of capital enabled the more powerful to reduce the smaller towns to subjection. And it was at a somewhat later stage of this development that they went on the expedition against Troy.

What enabled Agamemnon to raise the armament was more, in my opinion, his superiority in strength, than the oaths of Tyndareus, which bound the suitors to follow him.[3] Indeed, the account given by those Peloponnesians who have been the recipients of the most credible tradition is this. First of all Pelops, arriving among a needy population from Asia with vast wealth, acquired such power that, stranger though he was, the country was called after him; and this power fortune saw fit materially to increase in the hands of his descendants. Eurystheus had been killed in Attica by the Heraclids. Atreus was his mother's brother; and to the hands of his relation, who had left his father on account of the death of Chrysippus, Eurystheus, when he set out on his expedition, had committed Mycenae and the government. As time went on and Eurystheus did not return, Atreus complied with the wishes of the Mycenaeans, who were influenced by fear of the Heraclids—besides, his power seemed considerable, and he had not neglected to court the favour of the populace—and assumed the sceptre of Mycenae and the rest of the dominions of Eurystheus. And so the power of the descendants of Pelops came to be greater than that of the descendants of Perseus. To all this Agamemnon succeeded. He had also a navy far stronger than his contemporaries, so that, in my opinion, fear was quite as strong an element as love in the formation of the confederate expedition. The strength of his navy is shown by the fact that his own was the largest contingent, and that of the Arcadians was furnished by him; this at least is what Homer says, if his testimony is deemed sufficient. Besides, in his account of the transmission of the sceptre, he calls him

Of many an isle, and of all Argos king.

Now Agamemnon's was a continental power; and he could not have been master of any except the adjacent islands (and these would not be many), but through the possession of a fleet.

And from this expedition we may infer the character of earlier enterprises. Now Mycenae may have been a small place, and many of the towns of that age may appear comparatively insignificant, but no exact observer would therefore feel justified in rejecting the estimate given by the poets and by tradition of the magnitude of the armament. For I suppose if Lacedaemon were to become desolate, and the temples and the foundations of the public buildings were left, that as time went on there would be a strong disposition with posterity to refuse to accept her fame as a true exponent of her power. And yet they occupy two-fifths of Peloponnese and lead the whole, not to speak of their numerous allies without. Still, as the city is neither built in a compact form nor adorned with magnificent temples and public edifices, but composed of villages after the old fashion of Hellas, there would be an impression of inadequacy. Whereas, if Athens were to suffer the same misfortune, I suppose that any inference from the appearance presented to the eye would make her power to have been twice as great as it is.

We have therefore no right to be sceptical, nor to content ourselves with an inspection of a town to the exclusion of a consideration of its power; but we may safely conclude that the armament in question surpassed all before it, as it fell short of modern efforts; if we can here also accept the testimony of Homer's poems, in which, without allowing for the exaggeration which a poet would feel himself licensed to employ, we can see that it was far from equalling ours. He has represented it as consisting of twelve hundred vessels; the Boeotian complement of each ship being a hundred and twenty men, that of the ships of Philoctetes[4] fifty. By this, I conceive, he meant to convey the maximum and the minimum complement: at any rate, he does not specify the amount of any others in his catalogue of the ships. That they were all rowers as well as warriors we see from his account of the ships of Philoctetes, in which all the men at the oar are bowmen. Now it is improbable that many supernumeraries sailed, if we except the kings and high officers; especially as they had to cross the open sea with munitions of war, in ships, moreover, that had no decks, but were equipped in the old piratical fashion. So that if we strike the average of the largest and smallest ships, the number of those who sailed will appear inconsiderable, representing, as they did, the whole force of Hellas.

And this was due not so much to scarcity of men as of money. Difficulty of subsistence made the invaders reduce the numbers of the army to a point at which it might live on the country during the prosecution of the war. Even after the victory they obtained on their arrival—and a victory there must have been, or the fortifications of the naval camp could never have been built—there is no indication of their whole force having been employed; on the contrary, they seem to have turned to cultivation of the Chersonese and to piracy from want of supplies. This was what really enabled the Trojans to keep the field for ten years against them; the dispersion of the enemy making them always a match for the detachment left behind. If they had brought plenty of supplies with them, and had persevered in the war without scattering for piracy and agriculture, they would have easily defeated the Trojans in the field, since they could hold their own against them with the division on service. In short, if they had stuck to the siege, the capture of Troy would have cost them less time and less trouble. But as want of money proved the weakness of earlier expeditions, so from the same cause even the one in question, more famous than its predecessors, may be pronounced on the evidence of what it effected to have been inferior to its renown and to the current opinion about it formed under the tuition of the poets.

Even after the Trojan War, Hellas was still engaged in removing and settling, and thus could not attain to the quiet which must precede growth. The late return of the Hellenes from Ilium caused many revolutions, and factions ensued almost everywhere; and it was the citizens thus driven into exile who founded the cities. Sixty years after the capture of Ilium, the modern Boeotians were driven out of Arne by the Thessalians, and settled in the present Boeotia, the former Cadmeis; though there was a division of them there before, some of whom joined the expedition to Ilium. Twenty years later, the Dorians and the Heraclids became masters of Peloponnese; so that much had to be done and many years had to elapse before Hellas could attain to a durable tranquillity undisturbed by removals, and could begin to send out colonies, as Athens did to Ionia and most of the islands, and the Peloponnesians to most of Italy and Sicily and some places in the rest of Hellas. All these places were founded subsequently to the war with Troy.

But as the power of Hellas grew, and the acquisition of wealth became more an object, the revenues of the states increasing, tyrannies were by their means established almost everywhere—the old form of government being hereditary monarchy with definite prerogatives—and Hellas began to fit out fleets and apply herself more closely to the sea. It is said that the Corinthians were the first to approach the modern style of naval architecture, and that Corinth was the first place in Hellas where galleys were built; and we have Ameinocles, a Corinthian shipwright, making four ships for the Samians. Dating from the end of this war, it is nearly three hundred years ago that Ameinocles went to Samos. Again, the earliest sea-fight in history was between the Corinthians and Corcyraeans; this was about two hundred and sixty years ago, dating from the same time. Planted on an isthmus, Corinth had from time out of mind been a commercial emporium; as formerly almost all communication between the Hellenes within and without Peloponnese was carried on overland, and the Corinthian territory was the highway through which it travelled. She had consequently great money resources, as is shown by the epithet "wealthy" bestowed by the old poets on the place, and this enabled her, when traffic by sea became more common, to procure her navy and put down piracy; and as she could offer a mart for both branches of the trade, she acquired for herself all the power which a large revenue affords.

Subsequently the Ionians attained to great naval strength in the reign of Cyrus, the first king of the Persians, and of his son Cambyses, and while they were at war with the former commanded for a while the Ionian sea. Polycrates also, the tyrant of Samos, had a powerful navy in the reign of Cambyses, with which he reduced many of the islands, and among them Rhenea, which he consecrated to the Delian Apollo. About this time also the Phocaeans, while they were founding Marseilles, defeated the Carthaginians in a sea-fight. These were the most powerful navies. And even these, although so many generations had elapsed since the Trojan war, seem to have been principally composed of the old fifty-oars and long-boats, and to have counted few galleys among their ranks. Indeed it was only shortly before the Persian war, and the death of Darius the successor of Cambyses, that the Sicilian tyrants and the Corcyraeans acquired any large number of galleys. For after these there were no navies of any account in Hellas till the expedition of Xerxes; Aegina, Athens, and others may have possessed a few vessels, but they were principally fifty-oars. It was quite at the end of this period that the war with Aegina and the prospect of the barbarian invasion enabled Themistocles to persuade the Athenians to build the fleet with which they fought at Salamis; and even these vessels had not complete decks.

The navies, then, of the Hellenes during the period we have traversed were what I have described. All their insignificance did not prevent their being an element of the greatest power to those who cultivated them, alike in revenue and in dominion. They were the means by which the islands were reached and reduced, those of the smallest area falling the easiest prey. Wars by land there were none, none at least by which power was acquired; we have the usual border contests, but of distant expeditions with conquest for object we hear nothing among the Hellenes. There was no union of subject cities round a great state, no spontaneous combination of equals for confederate expeditions; what fighting there was consisted merely of local warfare between rival neighbours. The nearest approach to a coalition took place in the old war between Chalcis and Eretria; this was a quarrel in which the rest of the Hellenic name did to some extent take sides.

Various, too, were the obstacles which the national growth encountered in various localities. The power of the Ionians was advancing with rapid strides, when it came into collision with Persia, under King Cyrus, who, after having dethroned Croesus and overrun everything between the Halys and the sea, stopped not till he had reduced the cities of the coast; the islands being only left to be subdued by Darius and the Phoenician navy.

Again, wherever there were tyrants, their habit of providing simply for themselves, of looking solely to their personal comfort and family aggrandizement, made safety the great aim of their policy, and prevented anything great proceeding from them; though they would each have their affairs with their immediate neighbours. All this is only true of the mother country, for in Sicily they attained to very great power. Thus for a long time everywhere in Hellas do we find causes which make the states alike incapable of combination for great and national ends, or of any vigorous action of their own.

But at last a time came when the tyrants of Athens and the far older tyrannies of the rest of Hellas were, with the exception of those in Sicily, once and for all put down by Lacedaemon; for this city, though after the settlement of the Dorians, its present inhabitants, it suffered from factions for an unparalleled length of time, still at a very early period obtained good laws, and enjoyed a freedom from tyrants which was unbroken; it has possessed the same form of government for more than four hundred years, reckoning to the end of the late war, and has thus been in a position to arrange the affairs of the other states.

Not many years after the deposition of the tyrants, the battle of Marathon was fought between the Medes and the Athenians. Ten years afterwards, the barbarian returned with the armada for the subjugation of Hellas. In the face of this great danger, the command of the confederate Hellenes was assumed by the Lacedaemonians in virtue of their superior power; and the Athenians, having made up their minds to abandon their city, broke up their homes, threw themselves into their ships, and became a naval people. This coalition, after repulsing the barbarian, soon afterwards split into two sections, which included the Hellenes who had revolted from the King, as well as those who had aided him in the war. At the end of the one stood Athens, at the head of the other Lacedaemon, one the first naval, the other the first military power in Hellas.

For a short time the league held together, till the Lacedaemonians and Athenians quarrelled and made war upon each other with their allies, a duel into which all the

Hellenes sooner or later were drawn, though some might at first remain neutral. So that the whole period from the Median war to this, with some peaceful intervals, was spent by each power in war, either with its rival, or with its own revolted allies, and consequently afforded them constant practice in military matters, and that experience which is learnt in the school of danger.

The policy of Lacedaemon was not to exact tribute from her allies, but merely to secure their subservience to her interests by establishing oligarchies among them; Athens, on the contrary, had by degrees deprived hers of their ships, and imposed instead contributions in money on all except Chios and Lesbos. Both found their resources for this war separately to exceed the sum of their strength when the alliance flourished intact.

Translated by Richard Crawley.

Pericles' Speech for the Dead Soldiers during the First Year of the Peloponnesian War

followed by The Plague of Athens

Thucydides, *History of the Peloponnesian War* 2.34-54

At Athens, it was the tradition to deliver a public eulogy honoring the soldiers who died in combat. In 431-430 BC, Pericles gave the eulogy for the year. Instead of praising the soldiers directly, Pericles exalts the greatness of Athens, the glory of which embraces those who give their lives for her. Thucydides revives for us in this passage a magnificent moment of Athenian patriotism by one of its most brilliant orators, politicians, and strategists.

This famous episode of Athenian history was succeeded by a far more tragic event: an epidemic that, beginning in the second year of the war in 430 BC, ravaged Athens for four years. The scourge would kill more than one third of the population, including Pericles. Thucydides himself fell ill, but he survived and passed down to us a vivid description of its devastation.

"PERICLES: Our constitution does not copy the laws of neighbouring states; we are rather a pattern to others than imitators ourselves. Its administration favours the many instead of the few; this is why it is called a democracy."

Meanwhile these were the first that had fallen, and Pericles, son of Xanthippus, was chosen to pronounce their eulogium. When the proper time arrived, he advanced from the sepulchre to an elevated platform in order to be heard by as many of the crowd as possible, and spoke as follows:

"Most of my predecessors in this place have commended him who made this speech part of the law, telling us that it is well that it should be delivered at the burial of those who fall in battle. For myself, I should have thought that the worth which had displayed itself in deeds would be sufficiently rewarded by honours also shown by deeds; such as you now see in this funeral prepared at the people's cost. And I could have wished that the reputations of many brave men were not to be imperilled in the mouth of a single individual, to stand or fall according as he spoke well or ill. For it is hard to speak properly upon a subject where it is even difficult to convince your hearers that you are speaking the truth. On the one hand, the friend who is familiar with every fact of the story may think that some point has not been set forth with that fullness which he wishes and knows it to deserve; on the other, he who is familiar with every fact of the story may think that some point has not been set forth with that fullness which he wishes and knows it to deserve; on the other, he who is a stranger to the matter may be led by envy to suspect exaggeration if he hears anything above his own nature. For men can endure to hear others praised only so long as they can severally persuade themselves of their own ability to equal the actions recounted: when this point is passed, envy comes in and with it incredulity. However, since our ancestors have stamped this custom with their approval, it becomes my duty to obey the law and to try to satisfy your several wishes and opinions as best I may.

"I shall begin with our ancestors: it is both just and proper that they should have the honour of the first mention on an occasion like the present. They dwelt in the country without break in the succession from generation to generation, and handed it down free to the present time by their valour. And if our more remote ancestors deserve praise, much more do our own fathers, who added to their inheritance the empire which we now possess, and spared no pains to be able to leave their acquisitions to us of the present generation. Lastly, there are few parts of our dominions that have not been augmented by those of us here, who are still more or less in the vigour of life; while the mother country has been furnished by us with everything that can enable her to depend on her own resources whether for war or for peace. That part of our history which tells of the military achievements which gave us our several possessions, or of the ready valour with which either we or our fathers stemmed the tide of Hellenic or foreign aggression, is a theme too familiar to my hearers for me to dilate on, and I shall therefore pass it by. But what was the road by which we reached our position, what the form of government under which our greatness grew, what the national habits out of which it sprang; these are questions which I may try to solve before I proceed to my panegyric upon these men; since I think this to be a subject upon which on the present occasion a speaker may properly dwell, and to which the whole assemblage, whether citizens or foreigners, may listen with advantage.

"Our constitution does not copy the laws of neighbouring states; we are rather a pattern to others than imitators ourselves. Its administration favours the many instead of the few; this is why it is called a democracy. If we look to the laws, they afford equal justice to all in their private differences; if no social standing, advancement in public life falls to reputation for capacity, class considerations not being allowed to interfere with merit; nor again does poverty bar the way, if a man is able to serve the state, he is not hindered by the obscurity of his condition. The freedom which we enjoy in our government extends also to our ordinary life. There, far from exercising a jealous surveillance over each other, we do not feel called upon to be angry with our neighbour for doing what he likes, or even to indulge in those injurious looks which cannot fail to be offensive, although they inflict no positive penalty. But all this ease in our private relations does not make us lawless as citizens. Against this fear is our chief safeguard, teaching us to obey the magistrates and the laws, particularly such as regard the protection of the injured, whether they are actually on the statute book, or belong to that code which, although unwritten, yet cannot be broken without acknowledged disgrace.

"Further, we provide plenty of means for the mind to refresh itself from business. We celebrate games and sacrifices all the year round, and the elegance of our private establishments forms a daily source of pleasure and helps to banish the spleen; while the magnitude of our city draws the produce of the world into our harbour, so that to the Athenian the fruits of other countries are as familiar a luxury as those of his own.

"If we turn to our military policy, there also we differ from our antagonists. We throw open our city to the world, and never by alien acts exclude foreigners from any opportunity of learning or observing, although the eyes of an enemy may occasionally profit by our liberality; trusting less in system and policy than to the native spirit of our citizens; while in education, where our rivals from their very cradles by a painful discipline seek after manliness, at Athens we live exactly as we please, and yet are just as ready to encounter every legitimate danger. In proof of this it may be noticed that the Lacedaemonians do not invade our country alone, but bring with them all their confederates; while we Athenians advance unsupported into the territory of a neighbour, and fighting upon a foreign soil usually vanquish with ease men who are defending their homes. Our united force was never yet encountered by any enemy, because we have at once to attend to our marine and to dispatch our citizens by land upon a hundred different services; so that, wherever they engage with some such fraction of our strength, a success against a detachment is magnified into a victory over the nation, and a defeat into a reverse suffered at the hands of our entire people. And yet if with habits not of labour but of ease, and courage not of art but of nature, we are still willing to encounter danger, we have the double advantage of escaping the experience of hardships in anticipation and of facing them in the hour of need as fearlessly as those who are never free from them.

"Nor are these the only points in which our city is worthy of admiration. We cultivate refinement without extravagance and knowledge without effeminacy; wealth we employ more for use than for show, and place the real disgrace of poverty not in owning to the fact but in declining the struggle against it. Our public men have, besides politics, their private affairs to attend to, and our ordinary citizens, though occupied with the pursuits of industry, are still fair judges of public matters; for, unlike any other nation, regarding him who takes no part in these duties not as unambitious but as useless, we Athenians are able to judge at all events if we cannot originate, and, instead of looking on discussion as a stumbling-block in the way of action, we think it an indispensable preliminary to any wise action at all. Again, in our enterprises we present the singular spectacle of daring and deliberation, each carried to its highest point, and both united in the same persons; although usually decision is the fruit of ignorance, hesitation of reflection. But the palm of courage will surely be adjudged most justly to those, who best know the difference between hardship and pleasure and yet are never tempted to shrink from danger. In generosity we are equally singular, acquiring our friends by conferring, not by receiving, favours. Yet, of course, the doer of the favour is the firmer friend of the two, in order by continued kindness to keep the recipient in his debt; while the debtor feels less keenly from the very consciousness that the return he makes will be a payment, not a free gift. And it is only the Athenians, who, fearless of consequences, confer their benefits not from calculations of expediency, but in the confidence of liberality.

"In short, I say that as a city we are the school of Hellas, while I doubt if the world can produce a man who, where he has only himself to depend upon, is equal to so many emergencies, and graced by so happy a versatility, as the Athenian. And that this is no mere boast thrown out for the occasion, but plain matter of fact, the power of the state acquired by these habits proves. For Athens alone of her contemporaries is found when tested to be greater than her reputation, and alone gives no occasion to her assailants to blush at the antagonist by whom they have been worsted, or to her subjects to question her title by merit to rule. Rather, the admiration of the present and succeeding ages will be ours, since we have not left our power without witness, but have shown it by mighty proofs; and far from needing a Homer for our panegyrist, or other of his craft whose verses might charm for the moment only for the impression which they gave to melt at the touch of fact, we have forced every sea and land to be the highway of our daring, and everywhere, whether for evil or for good, have left imperishable monuments behind us. Such is the Athens for which these men, in the assertion of their resolve not to lose her, nobly fought and died; and well may every one of their survivors be ready to suffer in her cause.

"Indeed if I have dwelt at some length upon the character of our country, it has been to show that our stake in the struggle is not the same as theirs who have no such blessings to lose, and also that the panegyric of the men over whom I am now speaking might be by definite proofs established. That panegyric is now in a great measure complete; for the Athens that I have celebrated is only what the heroism of these and their like have made her, men whose fame, unlike that of most Hellenes, will be found to be only commensurate with their deserts. And if a test of worth be wanted, it is to be found in their closing scene, and this not only in cases in which it set the final seal upon their merit, but also in those in which it gave the first intimation of their having any. For there is justice in the claim that steadfastness in his country's battles should be as a cloak to cover a man's other imperfections; since the good action has blotted out the bad, and his merit as a citizen more than outweighed his demerits as an individual. But none of these allowed either wealth with its prospect of future enjoyment to unnerve his spirit, or poverty with its hope of a day of freedom and riches to tempt him to shrink from danger. No, holding that vengeance upon their enemies was more to be desired than any personal blessings, and reckoning this to be the most glorious of hazards, they joyfully determined to accept the risk, to make sure of their vengeance, and to let their wishes wait; and while committing to hope the uncertainty of final success, in the business before them they thought fit to act boldly and trust in themselves. Thus choosing to die resisting, rather than to live submitting, they fled only from dishonour, but met danger face to face, and after one brief moment, while at the summit of their fortune, escaped, not from their fear, but from their glory.

"So died these men as became Athenians. You, their survivors, must determine to have as unfaltering a resolution in the field, though you may pray that it may have a happier issue. And not contented with ideas derived only from words of the advantages which are bound up with the defence of your country, though these would furnish a valuable text to a speaker even before an audience so alive to them as the present, you must yourselves realize the power of Athens, and feed your eyes upon her from day to day, till love of her fills your hearts; and then, when all her greatness shall break upon you, you must reflect that it was by courage, sense of duty, and a keen feeling of honour in action that men were enabled to win all this, and that no personal failure in an enterprise could make them consent to deprive their country of their valour, but they laid it at her feet as the most glorious contribution that they could offer. For this offering of their lives made in common by them all they each of them individually received that renown which never grows old, and for a sepulchre, not so much that in which their bones have been deposited, but that noblest of shrines wherein their glory is laid up to be eternally remembered upon every occasion on which deed or story shall call for its commemoration. For heroes have the whole earth for their tomb; and in lands far from their own, where the column with its epitaph declares it, there is enshrined in every breast a record unwritten with no tablet to preserve it, except that of the heart. These take as your model and, judging happiness to be the fruit of freedom and freedom of valour, never decline the dangers of war. For it is not the miserable that would most justly be unsparing of their lives; these have nothing to hope for: it is rather they to whom continued life may bring reverses as yet unknown, and to whom a fall, if it came, would be most tremendous in its consequences. And surely, to a man of spirit, the degradation of cowardice must be immeasurably more grievous than the unfelt death which strikes him in the midst of his strength and patriotism!

"Comfort, therefore, not condolence, is what I have to offer to the parents of the dead who may be here. Numberless are the chances to which, as they know, the life of man is subject; but fortunate indeed are they who draw for their lot a death so glorious as that which has caused your mourning, and to whom life has been so exactly measured as to terminate in the happiness in which it has been passed. Still I know that this is a hard saying, especially when those are in question of whom you will constantly be reminded by seeing in the homes of others blessings of which once you also boasted: for grief is felt not so much for the want of what we have never known, as for the loss of that to which we have been long accustomed. Yet you who are still of an age to beget children must bear up in the hope of having others in their stead; not only will they help you to forget those whom you have lost, but will be to the state at once a reinforcement and a security; for never can a fair or just policy be expected of the citizen who does not, like his fellows, bring to the decision the interests and apprehensions of a father. While those of you who have passed your prime must congratulate yourselves with the thought that the best part of your life was fortunate, and that the brief span that remains will be cheered by the fame of the departed. For it is only the love of honour that never grows old; and honour it is, not gain, as some would have it, that rejoices the heart of age and helplessness.

"Turning to the sons or brothers of the dead, I see an arduous struggle before you. When a man is gone, all are wont to praise him, and should your merit be ever so transcendent, you will still find it difficult not merely to overtake, but even to approach their renown. The living have envy to contend with, while those who are no longer in our path are honoured with a goodwill into which rivalry does not enter. On the other hand, if I must say anything on the subject of female excellence to those of you who will now be in widowhood, it will be all comprised in this brief exhortation. Great will be your glory in not falling short of your natural character; and greatest will be hers who is least talked of among the men, whether for good or for bad.

"My task is now finished. I have performed it to the best of my ability, and in word, at least, the requirements of the law are now satisfied. If deeds be in question, those who are here interred have received part of their honours already, and for the rest, their children will be brought up till manhood at the public expense: the state thus offers a valuable prize, as the garland of victory in this race of valour, for the reward both of those who have fallen and their survivors. And where the rewards for merit are greatest, there are found the best citizens.

"And now that you have brought to a close your lamentations for your relatives, you may depart."

The Plague of Athens

Such was the funeral that took place during this winter, with which the first year of the war came to an end. In the first days of summer the Lacedaemonians and their allies, with two-thirds of their forces as before, invaded Attica, under the command of Archidamus, son of Zeuxidamus, King of Lacedaemon, and sat down and laid waste the country. Not many days after their arrival in Attica the plague first began to show itself among the Athenians. It was said that it had broken out in many places previously in the neighbourhood of Lemnos and elsewhere; but a pestilence of such extent and mortality was nowhere remembered. Neither were the physicians at first of any service, ignorant as they were of the proper way to treat it, but they died themselves the most thickly, as they visited the sick most often; nor did any human art succeed any better. Supplications in the temples, divinations, and so forth were found equally futile, till the overwhelming nature of the disaster at last put a stop to them altogether.

It first began, it is said, in the parts of Ethiopia above Egypt, and thence descended into Egypt and Libya and into most of the King's country. Suddenly falling upon Athens, it first attacked the population in Piraeus—which was the occasion of their saying that the Peloponnesians had poisoned the reservoirs, there being as yet no wells there—and afterwards appeared in the upper city, when the deaths became much more frequent. All speculation as to its origin and its causes, if causes can be found adequate to produce so great a disturbance, I leave to other writers, whether lay or professional; for myself, I shall simply set down its nature, and explain the symptoms by which perhaps it may be recognized by the student, if it should ever break out again. This I can the better do, as I had the disease myself, and watched its operation in the case of others.

That year then is admitted to have been otherwise unprecedentedly free from sickness; and such few cases as occurred all determined in this. As a rule, however, there was no ostensible cause; but people in good health were all of a sudden attacked by violent heats in the head, and redness and inflammation in the eyes, the inward parts, such as the throat or tongue, becoming bloody and emitting an unnatural and fetid breath. These symptoms were followed by sneezing and hoarseness, after which the pain soon reached the chest, and produced a hard cough. When it fixed in the stomach, it upset it; and discharges of bile of every kind named by physicians ensued, accompanied by very great distress. In most cases also an ineffectual retching followed, producing violent spasms, which in some cases ceased soon after, in others much later. Externally the body was not very hot to the touch, nor pale in its appearance, but reddish, livid, and breaking out into small pustules and ulcers. But internally it burned so that the patient could not bear to have on him clothing or linen even of the very lightest description; or indeed to be otherwise than stark naked. What they would have liked best would have been to throw themselves into cold water; as indeed was done by some of the neglected sick, who plunged into the rain-tanks in their agonies of unquenchable thirst; though it made no difference whether they drank little or much. Besides this, the miserable feeling of not being able to rest or sleep never ceased to torment them. The body meanwhile did not waste away so long as the distemper was at its height, but held out to a marvel against its ravages; so that when they succumbed, as in most cases, on the seventh or eighth day to the internal inflammation, they had still some strength in them. But if they passed this stage, and the disease descended further into the bowels, inducing a violent ulceration there accompanied by severe diarrhoea, this brought on a weakness which was generally fatal. For the disorder first settled in the head, ran its course from thence through the whole of the body, and, even where it did not prove mortal, it still left its mark on the extremities; for it settled in the privy parts, the fingers and the toes, and many escaped with the loss of these, some too with that of their eyes. Others again were seized with an entire loss of memory on their first recovery, and did not know either themselves or their friends.

But while the nature of the distemper was such as to baffle all description, and its attacks almost too grievous for human nature to endure, it was still in the following circumstance that its difference from all ordinary disorders was most clearly shown. All the birds and beasts that prey upon human bodies, either abstained from touching them (though there were many lying unburied), or died after tasting them. In proof of this, it was noticed that birds of this kind actually disappeared; they were not about the bodies, or indeed to be seen at all. But of course the effects which I have mentioned could best be studied in a domestic animal like the dog.

Such then, if we pass over the varieties of particular cases which were many and peculiar, were the general features of the distemper. Meanwhile the town enjoyed an immunity from all the ordinary disorders; or if any case occurred, it ended in this. Some died in neglect, others in the midst of every attention. No remedy was found that could be used as a specific; for what did good in one case, did harm in another. Strong and weak constitutions proved equally incapable of resistance, all alike being swept away, although dieted with the utmost precaution. By far the most terrible feature in the malady was the dejection which ensued when any one felt himself sickening, for the despair into which they instantly fell took away their power of resistance, and left them a much easier prey to the disorder; besides which, there was the awful spectacle of men dying like sheep, through having caught the infection in nursing each other. This caused the greatest mortality. On the one hand, if they were afraid to visit each other, they perished from neglect; indeed many houses were emptied of their inmates for want of a nurse: on the other, if they ventured to do so, death was the consequence. This was especially the case with such as made any pretensions to goodness: honour made them unsparing of themselves in their attendance in their friends' houses, where even the members of the family were at last worn out by the moans of the dying, and succumbed to the force of the disaster. Yet it was with those who had recovered from the disease that the sick and the dying found most compassion. These knew what it was from experience, and had now no fear for themselves; for the same man was never attacked twice—never at least fatally. And such persons not only received the congratulations of others, but themselves also, in the elation of the moment, half entertained the vain hope that they were for the future safe from any disease whatsoever.

An aggravation of the existing calamity was the influx from the country into the city, and this was especially felt by the new arrivals. As there were no houses to receive them, they had to be lodged at the hot season of the year in stifling cabins, where the mortality raged without restraint. The bodies of dying men lay one upon another, and half-dead creatures reeled about the streets and gathered round all the fountains in their longing for water. The sacred places also in which they had quartered themselves were full of corpses of persons that had died there, just as they were; for as the disaster passed all bounds, men, not knowing what was to become of them, became utterly careless of everything, whether sacred or profane. All the burial rites before in use were entirely upset, and they buried the bodies as best they could. Many from want of the proper appliances, through so many of their friends having died already, had recourse to the most shameless sepultures: sometimes getting the start of those who had raised a pile, they threw their own dead body upon the stranger's pyre and ignited it; sometimes they tossed the corpse which they were carrying on the top of another that was burning, and so went off.

Nor was this the only form of lawless extravagance which owed its origin to the plague. Men now coolly ventured on what they had formerly done in a corner, and not just as they pleased, seeing the rapid transitions produced by persons in prosperity suddenly dying and those who before had nothing succeeding to their property. So they resolved to spend quickly and enjoy themselves, regarding their lives and riches as alike things of a day. Perseverance in what men called honour was popular with none, it was so uncertain whether they would be spared to attain the object; but it was settled that present enjoyment, and all that contributed to it, was both honourable and useful. Fear of gods or law of man there was none to restrain them. As for the first, they judged it to be just the same whether they worshipped them or not, as they saw all alike perishing; and for the last, no one expected to live to be brought to trial for his offences, but each felt that a far severer sentence had been already passed upon them all and hung ever over their heads, and before this fell it was only reasonable to enjoy life a little. Such was the nature of the calamity, and heavily did it weigh on the Athenians; death raging within the city and devastation without. Among other things which they remembered in their distress was, very naturally, the following verse which the old men said had long ago been uttered:

> A Dorian war shall come and with it death.

So a dispute arose as to whether dearth and not death had not been the word in the verse; but at the present juncture, it was of course decided in favour of the latter; for the people made their recollection fit in with their sufferings. I fancy, however, that if another Dorian war should ever afterwards come upon us, and a dearth should happen to accompany it, the verse will probably be read accordingly. The oracle also which had been given to the Lacedaemonians was now remembered by those who knew of it. When the god was asked whether they should go to war, he answered that if they put their might into it, victory would be theirs, and that he would himself be with them. With this oracle events were supposed to tally. For the plague broke out as soon as the Peloponnesians invaded Attica, and never entering Peloponnese (not at least to an extent worth noticing), committed its worst ravages at Athens, and next to Athens, at the most populous of the other towns. Such was the history of the plague.

Translated by Richard Crawley.

Pericles' Speech to Defend Himself from the Accusations of the Athenians

Thucydides, *History of the Peloponnesian War* 2.59-65

It is the second year of the Peloponnesian War. The Spartans and their allies have invaded Attica for the second time, and the plague wreaks havoc. Early enthusiasm for the war gives way to lassitude and doubt. The Athenians are not sure anymore whether Pericles was right in advising them to go to war. He delivers another brilliant speech to justify his politics.

"PERICLES: I am the same man and do not alter, it is you who change, since in fact you took my advice while unhurt, and waited for misfortune to repent of it; and the apparent error of my policy lies in the infirmity of your resolution, since the suffering that it entails is being felt by every one among you, while its advantage is still remote and obscure to all."

After the second invasion of the Peloponnesians a change came over the spirit of the Athenians. Their land had now been twice laid waste; and war and pestilence at once pressed heavy upon them. They began to find fault with Pericles, as the author of the war and the cause of all their misfortunes, and became eager to come to terms with Lacedaemon, and actually sent ambassadors thither, who did not however succeed in their mission. Their despair was now complete and all vented itself upon Pericles. When he saw them exasperated at the present turn of affairs and acting exactly as he had anticipated, he called an assembly, being (it must be remembered) still general, with the double object of restoring confidence and of leading them from these angry feelings to a calmer and more hopeful state of mind. He accordingly came forward and spoke as follows:

"I was not unprepared for the indignation of which I have been the object, as I know its causes; and I have called an assembly for the purpose of reminding you upon certain points, and of protesting against your being unreasonably irritated with me, or cowed by your sufferings. I am of opinion that national greatness is more for the advantage of private citizens, than any individual well-being coupled with public humiliation. A man may be personally ever so well off, and yet if his country be ruined he must be ruined with it; whereas a flourishing commonwealth always affords chances of salvation to unfortunate individuals. Since then a state can support the misfortunes of private citizens, while they cannot support hers, it is surely the duty of every one to be forward in her defence, and not like you to be so confounded with your domestic afflictions as to give up all thoughts of the common safety, and to blame me for having counselled war and yourselves for having voted it. And yet if you are angry with me, it is with one who, as I believe, is second to no man either in knowledge of the proper policy, or in the ability to expound it, and who is moreover not only a patriot but an honest one. A man possessing that knowledge without that faculty of exposition might as well have no idea at all on the matter: if he had both these gifts, but no love for his country, he would be but a cold advocate for her interests; while were his patriotism not proof against bribery, everything would go for a price. So that if you thought that I was even moderately distinguished for these qualities when you took my advice and went to war, there is certainly no reason now why I should be charged with having done wrong.

"For those of course who have a free choice in the matter and whose fortunes are not at stake, war is the greatest of follies. But if the only choice was between submission with loss of independence, and danger with the hope of preserving that independence, in such a case it is he who will not accept the risk that deserves blame, not he who will. I am the same man and do not alter, it is you who change, since in fact you took my advice while unhurt, and waited for misfortune to repent of it; and the apparent error of my policy lies in the infirmity of your resolution, since the suffering that it entails is being felt by every one among you, while its advantage is still remote and obscure to all, and a great and sudden reverse having befallen you, your mind is too much depressed to persevere in your resolves. For before what is sudden, unexpected, and least within calculation, the spirit quails; and putting all else aside, the plague has certainly been an emergency of this kind. Born, however, as you are, citizens of a great state, and brought up, as you have been, with habits equal to your birth, you should be ready to face the greatest disasters and still to keep unimpaired the lustre of your name. For the judgment of mankind is as relentless to the weakness that falls short of a recognized renown, as it is jealous of the arrogance that aspires higher than its due. Cease then to grieve for your private afflictions, and address yourselves instead to the safety of the commonwealth.

"If you shrink before the exertions which the war makes necessary, and fear that after all they may not have a happy result, you know the reasons by which I have often demonstrated to you the groundlessness of your apprehensions. If those are not enough, I will now reveal an advantage arising from the greatness of your dominion, which I think has never yet suggested itself to you, which I never mentioned in my previous speeches, and which has so bold a sound that I should scarce adventure it now, were it not for the unnatural depression which I see around me. You perhaps think that your empire extends only over your allies; I will declare to you the truth. The visible field of action has two parts, land and sea. In the whole of one of these you are completely supreme, not merely as far as you use it at present, but also to what further extent you may think fit: in fine, your naval resources are such that your vessels may go where they please, without the King or any other nation on earth being able to stop them. So that although you may think it a great privation to lose the use of your land and houses, still you must see that this power is something widely different; and instead of fretting on their account, you should really regard them in the light of the gardens and other accessories that embellish a great fortune, and as, in comparison, of little moment. You should know too that liberty preserved by your efforts will easily recover for us what we have lost, while, the knee once bowed, even what you have will pass from you. Your fathers receiving these possessions not from others, but from themselves, did not let slip what their labour had acquired, but delivered them safe to you; and in this respect at least you must prove yourselves their equals, remembering that to lose what one has got is more disgraceful than to be balked in getting, and you must confront your enemies not merely with spirit but with disdain. Confidence indeed a blissful ignorance can impart, ay, even to a coward's breast, but disdain is the privilege of those who, like us, have been assured by reflection of their superiority to their adversary. And where the chances are the same, knowledge fortifies courage by the contempt which is its consequence, its trust being placed, not in hope, which is the prop of the desperate, but in a judgment grounded upon existing resources, whose anticipations are more to be depended upon.

"Again, your country has a right to your services in sustaining the glories of her position. These are a common source of pride to you all, and you cannot decline the burdens of empire and still expect to share its honours. You should remember also that what you are fighting against is not merely slavery as an exchange for independence, but also loss of empire and danger from the animosities incurred in its exercise. Besides, to recede is no longer possible, if indeed any of you in the alarm of the moment has become enamoured of the honesty of such an unambitious part. For what you hold is, to speak somewhat plainly, a tyranny; to take it perhaps was wrong, but to let it go is unsafe. And men of these retiring views, making converts of others, would quickly ruin a state; indeed the result would be the same if they could live independent by themselves; for the retiring and unambitious are never secure without vigorous protectors at their side; in fine, such qualities are useless to an imperial city, though they may help a dependency to an unmolested servitude.

"But you must not be seduced by citizens like these or angry with me—who, if I voted for war, only did as you did yourselves—in spite of the enemy having invaded your country and done what you could be certain that he would do, if you refused to comply with his demands; and although besides what we counted for, the plague has come upon us—the only point indeed at which our calculation has been at fault. It is this, I know, that has had a large share in making me more unpopular than I should otherwise have been—quite undeservedly, unless you are also prepared to give me the credit of any success with which chance may present you. Besides, the hand of heaven must be borne with resignation, that of the enemy with fortitude; this was the old way at Athens, and do not you prevent it being so still. Remember, too, that if your country has the greatest name in all the world, it is because she never bent before disaster; because she has expended more life and effort in war than any other city, and has won for herself a power greater than any hitherto known, the memory of which will descend to the latest posterity; even if now, in obedience to the general law of decay, we should ever be forced to yield, still it will be remembered that we held rule over more Hellenes than any other Hellenic state, that we sustained the greatest wars against their united or separate powers, and inhabited a city unrivalled by any other in resources or magnitude. These glories may incur the censure of the slow and unambitious; but in the breast of energy they will awake emulation, and in those who must remain without them an envious regret. Hatred and unpopularity at the moment have fallen to the lot of all who have aspired to rule others; but where odium must be incurred, true wisdom incurs it for the highest objects. Hatred also is short-lived; but that which makes the splendour of the present and the glory of the future remains for ever unforgotten. Make your decision, therefore, for glory then and honour now, and attain both objects by instant and zealous effort: do not send heralds to Lacedaemon, and do not betray any sign of being oppressed by your present sufferings, since they whose minds are least sensitive to calamity, and whose hands are most quick to meet it, are the greatest men and the greatest communities."

Such were the arguments by which Pericles tried to cure the Athenians of their anger against him and to divert their thoughts from their immediate afflictions.

Translated by Richard Crawley.

ARISTOPHANES

c. 445 - *c.* 386 BC

Aristophanes was the greatest comic poet of Athens. Under an assumed name, he debuted at the Theater of Dionysus in 427 BC. His talent was rapidly acknowledged: In 425 BC, he won first prize in the city's annual contest with the Acharnians, *and again the next year with the* Knights. *In his lifetime, it is likely that he composed 44 plays, only 11 of which have come down to us.*

Because Aristophanes lived during the Peloponnesian War, his comedies mostly evoke the city falling victim to the horrors of the conflict and its quest for salvation. The poet condemns Athenian politics, which he sees as infested with corrupt demagogues. He severely criticizes his fellow citizens for failing to understand the necessity to commit themselves to the well-being of the city. Aristophanes offers several solutions: to transfer the power over to the women (see Lysistrata, *below), to find another city, to transform the savage world into a civilized one, and to restart from the beginning. He further attacks the education bestowed on the populace by the sophists (see* Clouds, *below) and poetry that abandons its didactic purpose. His last comedy,* Plutus, *evokes the volatile political climate of Athens at the beginning of the fourth century BC, when Sparta exercised its hegemony over Greece.*

The premier Greek comic, Aristophanes spares no one: politicians, intellectuals, metoikoi *(foreign residents), and basic citizens fall victim to his pen. His irony and humor are political. Through caricature, vulgarity, puns, and poetry, Aristophanes invites his citizens to reflect and to take action.*

Traditional Education vs. New Education

Aristophanes, *Clouds* 889-1104

Strepsiades, an elderly man threatened with lawsuits, decides to attend Socrates' school, the Thoughtery, with the intention of learning how to deceive his creditors. He is such a lousy student, however, that Socrates sends him back home and advises him instead to send his son, Pheidippides. In through the door comes the son, who by the way is responsible for his father's debts. The very moment the young Pheidippides arrives at the school, two professors quarrel over who will teach him. The first professor is called Just Discourse and advocates the Old Education of modesty and discipline. The second is Unjust Discourse and supports the New Education of pleasure and all the tricks necessary to win a lawsuit. It is no surprise that Unjust Discourse wins the contest and becomes Pheidippides' teacher. Strepsiades' son turns out to be an outstanding student who eventually gets rid of his father's creditors. But Pheidippides also beats up his father, who, in turn, burns down Socrates' school.

Clouds *is a hilarious and darkly humorous comedy. It is a parody on the educational system and on sophist teaching in fifth-century-BC Athens. It caricatures Socrates as a corrupt professor who literally has his head in the clouds, practicing his philosophy in a basket suspended from the ceiling. He considers the Clouds the only authentic gods and the protectors of the philosophers and of the idle rich. This portrait of Socrates is very different from that painted by his admiring disciples, Plato and Xenophon. It is grossly inaccurate from an historical perspective but is wildly entertaining.*

Characters
JUST DISCOURSE
UNJUST DISCOURSE
CHORUS of clouds

"If you happen to commit one of these faults inherent in human weakness, some seduction or adultery, and you are caught in the act, you are lost, if you cannot speak."

JUST DISCOURSE
Come here! Shameless as you may be, will you dare to show your face to the spectators?

UNJUST DISCOURSE
Take me where you will. I seek a throng, so that I may the better annihilate you.

JUST DISCOURSE
Annihilate me! Do you forget who you are?

UNJUST DISCOURSE
I am Reasoning.

JUST DISCOURSE
Yes, the weaker Reasoning.

UNJUST DISCOURSE
But I triumph over you, who claim to be the stronger.

JUST DISCOURSE
By what cunning shifts, pray?

UNJUST DISCOURSE
By the invention of new maxims.

JUST DISCOURSE
... which are received with favour by these fools.

[*He points to the audience.*]

UNJUST DISCOURSE
Say rather, by these wise men.

JUST DISCOURSE
I am going to destroy you mercilessly.

UNJUST DISCOURSE
How pray? Let us see you do it.

JUST DISCOURSE
By saying what is true.

UNJUST DISCOURSE
I shall retort and shall very soon have the better of you. First, maintain that justice has no existence.

JUST DISCOURSE
Has no existence?

UNJUST DISCOURSE
No existence! Why, where is it?

JUST DISCOURSE
With the gods.

UNJUST DISCOURSE
How then, if justice exists, was Zeus not put to death for having put his father in chains?

JUST DISCOURSE
Bah! this is enough to turn my stomach! A basin, quick!

UNJUST DISCOURSE
You are an old driveller and stupid withal.

JUST DISCOURSE
And you a degenerate and shameless fellow.

UNJUST DISCOURSE
Hah! What sweet expressions!

JUST DISCOURSE
An impious buffoon.

UNJUST DISCOURSE
You crown me with roses and with lilies.

JUST DISCOURSE
A parricide.

UNJUST DISCOURSE
Why, you shower gold upon me.

JUST DISCOURSE
Formerly it was a hailstorm of blows.

UNJUST DISCOURSE
I deck myself with your abuse.

JUST DISCOURSE
What impudence!

UNJUST DISCOURSE
What tomfoolery!

JUST DISCOURSE
It is because of you that the youth no longer attends the schools. The Athenians will soon recognize what lessons you teach those who are fools enough to believe you.

UNJUST DISCOURSE
You are overwhelmed with wretchedness.

JUST DISCOURSE
And you, you prosper. Yet you were poor when you said, "I am the Mysian Telephus," and used to stuff your wallet with maxims of Pandeletus to nibble at.[1]

UNJUST DISCOURSE
Oh! the beautiful wisdom, of which you are now boasting!

JUST DISCOURSE
Madman! But yet madder the city that keeps you, you, the corrupter of its youth!

UNJUST DISCOURSE
It is not you who will teach this young man; you are as old and out of date at Cronus.

JUST DISCOURSE
Nay, it will certainly be I, if he does not wish to be lost and to practise verbosity only.

UNJUST DISCOURSE [*to Phidippides*]
Come here and leave him to beat the air.

JUST DISCOURSE
You'll regret it, if you touch him.

CHORUS-LEADER [*stepping between them as they are about to come to blows*]
A truce to your quarrellings and abuse! But you expound what you taught us formerly,

and you, your new doctrine. Thus, after hearing each of you argue, he will be able to choose betwixt the two schools.

JUST DISCOURSE
I am quite agreeable.

UNJUST DISCOURSE
And I too.

LEADER OF THE CHORUS
Who is to speak first?

UNJUST DISCOURSE
Let it be my opponent, he has my full consent; then I shall follow upon the very ground he shall have chosen and shall shatter him with a hail of new ideas and subtle fancies; if after that he dares to breathe another word, I shall sting him in the face and in the eyes with our maxims, which are as keen as the sting of a wasp, and he will die.

CHORUS [*singing*]
Here are two rivals confident in their powers of oratory and in the thoughts over which they have pondered so long. Let us see which will come triumphant out of the contest. This wisdom, for which my friends maintain such a persistent fight, is in great danger.

LEADER OF THE CHORUS
Come then, you, who crowned men of other days with so many virtues, plead the cause dear to you, make yourself known to us.

JUST DISCOURSE
Very well, I will tell you what was the old education, when I used to teach justice with so much success and when modesty was held in veneration. Firstly, it was required of a child, that it should not utter a word. In the street, when they went to the music-school, all the youths of the same district marched lightly clad and ranged in good order, even when the snow was falling in great flakes. At the master's house they had to stand with their legs apart and they were taught to sing either, "Pallas, the Terrible, who overturneth cities," or "A noise resounded from afar" in the solemn tones of the ancient harmony. If anyone indulged in buffoonery or lent his voice any of the soft inflexions, like those which to-day the disciples of Phrynis[2] take so much pains to form, he was treated as an enemy of the Muses and belaboured with blows. In the wrestling school they would sit with outstretched legs and

without display of any indecency to the curious. When they rose, they would smooth over the sand, so as to leave no trace to excite obscene thoughts. Never was a child rubbed with oil below the belt; the rest of their bodies thus retained its fresh bloom and down, like a velvety peach. They were not to be seen approaching a lover and themselves rousing his passion by soft modulation of the voice and lustful gaze. At table, they would not have dared, before those older than themselves, to have taken a radish, an aniseed or a leaf of parsley, and much less eat fish or thrushes or cross their legs.

UNJUST DISCOURSE
What antiquated rubbish! Have we got back to the days of the festivals of Zeus Polieus, to the Buphonia, to the time of the poet Cecides and the golden cicadas?[3]

JUST DISCOURSE
Nevertheless by suchlike teaching I built up the men of Marathon. But you, you teach the children of to-day to bundle themselves quickly into their clothes, and I am enraged when I see them at the Panathenaea[4] forgetting Athene while they dance, and covering their tools with their bucklers. Hence, young man, dare to range yourself beside me, who follow justice and truth; you will then be able to shun the public place, to refrain from the baths, to blush at all that is shameful, to fire up if your virtue is mocked at, to give place to your elders, to honour your parents, in short, to avoid all that is evil. Be modesty itself, and do not run to applaud the dancing girls; if you delight in such scenes, some courtesan will cast you her apple and your reputation will be done for. Do not bandy words with your father, nor treat him as a dotard, nor reproach the old man, who has cherished you, with his age.

UNJUST DISCOURSE
If you listen to him, by Bacchus! you will be the image of the sons of Hippocrates and will be called mother's big ninny.[5]

JUST DISCOURSE
No, but you will pass your days at the gymnasia, glowing with strength and health; you will not go to the public place to cackle and wrangle as is done nowadays; you will not live in fear that you may be dragged before the courts for some trifle exaggerated by quibbling. But you will go down to the Academy to run beneath the sacred olives with some virtuous friend of your own age, your head encircled with the white reed, enjoying your ease and breathing the perfume of the yew and of the fresh sprouts of the poplar, rejoicing in the return of springtide and gladly listening to the gentle rustle of the plane tree and the elm. [*With greater warmth from here on*] If you devote yourself to practising my precepts, your chest will be stout, your colour glowing, your shoulders broad, your tongue short, your hips muscular, but

your tool small. But if you follow the fashions of the day, you will be pallid in hue, have narrow shoulders, a narrow chest, a long tongue, small hips and a big thing; you will know how to spin forth long-winded arguments on law. You will be persuaded also to regard as splendid everything that is shameful and as shameful everything that is honourable; in a word, you will wallow in degeneracy like Antimachus.

CHORUS [*singing*]
How beautiful, high-souled, brilliant is this wisdom that you practise! What a sweet odour of honesty is emitted by your discourse! Happy were those men of other days who lived when you were honoured! And you, seductive talker, come, find some fresh arguments, for your rival has done wonders.

LEADER OF THE CHORUS
You will have to bring out against him all the battery of your wit, it you desire to beat him and not to be laughed out of court.

UNJUST DISCOURSE
At last! I was choking with impatience, I was burning to upset his arguments! If I am called the Weaker Reasoning in the schools, it is just because I was the first to discover the means to confute the laws and the decrees of justice. To invoke solely the weaker arguments and yet triumph is an art worth more than a hundred thousand drachmae. But see how I shall batter down the sort of education of which he is so proud. Firstly, he forbids you to bathe in hot water. What grounds have you for condemning hot baths?

JUST DISCOURSE
Because they are baneful and enervate men.

UNJUST DISCOURSE
Enough said! Oh! you poor wrestler! From the very outset I have seized you and hold you round the middle; you cannot escape me. Tell me, of all the sons of Zeus, who had the stoutest heart, who performed the most doughty deeds?

JUST DISCOURSE
None, in my opinion, surpassed Heracles.

UNJUST DISCOURSE
Where have you ever seen cold baths called 'Bath of Heracles'? And yet who was braver than he?

JUST DISCOURSE
It is because of such quibbles, that the baths are seen crowded with young folk, who chatter there the livelong day while the gymnasia remain empty.

UNJUST DISCOURSE
Next you condemn the habit of frequenting the market-place, while I approve this. If it were wrong Homer would never have made Nestor speak in public as well as all his wise heroes. As for the art of speaking, he tells you, young men should not practise it; I hold the contrary. Furthermore he preaches chastity to them. Both precepts are equally harmful. Have you ever seen chastity of any use to anyone? Answer and try to confute me.

JUST DISCOURSE
To many; for instance, Peleus won a sword thereby.

UNJUST DISCOURSE
A sword! Ah! what a fine present to make him! Poor wretch! Hyperbolus, the lamp-seller, thanks to his villainy, has gained more than... do not know how many talents, but certainly no sword.

JUST DISCOURSE
Peleus owed it to his chastity that he became the husband of Thetis.[6]

UNJUST DISCOURSE
... who left him in the lurch, for he was not the most ardent; in those nocturnal sports between the sheets, which so please women, he possessed but little merit. Get you gone, you are but an old fool. But you, young man, just consider a little what this temperance means and the delights of which it deprives you—young fellows, women, play, dainty dishes, wine, boisterous laughter. And what is life worth without these? Then, if you happen to commit one of these faults inherent in human weakness, some seduction or adultery, and you are caught in the act, you are lost, if you cannot speak. But follow my teaching and you will be able to satisfy your passions, to dance, to laugh, to blush at nothing. Suppose you are caught in the act of adultery. Then up and tell the husband you are not guilty, and recall to him the example of Zeus, who allowed himself to be conquered by love and by women. Being but a mortal, can you be stronger than a god?

JUST DISCOURSE
Suppose your pupil, following your advice, gets the radish rammed up his arse and then is depilated with a hot coal; how are you going to prove to him that he is not a broad-arse?

UNJUST DISCOURSE
What's the matter with being a broad-arse?

JUST DISCOURSE
Is there anything worse than that?

UNJUST DISCOURSE
Now what will you say, if I beat you even on this point?

JUST DISCOURSE
I should certainly have to be silent then.

UNJUST DISCOURSE
Well then, reply! Our advocates, what are they?

JUST DISCOURSE
Sons of broad-arses.

UNJUST DISCOURSE
Nothing is more true. And our tragic poets?

JUST DISCOURSE
Sons of broad-arses.

UNJUST DISCOURSE
Well said again. And our demagogues?

JUST DISCOURSE
Sons of broad-arses.

UNJUST DISCOURSE
You admit that you have spoken nonsense. And the spectators, what are they for the most part? Look at them.

JUST DISCOURSE
I am looking at them.

UNJUST DISCOURSE
Well! What do you see?

JUST DISCOURSE
By the gods, they are nearly all broad-arses. [*pointing*] See, this one I know to be such and that one and that other with the long hair.

UNJUST DISCOURSE
What have you to say, then?

JUST DISCOURSE
I am beaten. Debauchees! in the name of the gods, receive my cloak; I pass over to your ranks.

[*He goes back into the Thoughtery.*]

Anonymous Translator.

Sex Strike

Aristophanes, *Lysistrata* 638-979

Aristophanes wrote this play in 411 BC. The Peloponnesian War had been raging for twenty years and the Athenian fleet had just been destroyed in Sicily. In Lysistrata, *Aristophanes imagines that the women no longer tolerate war. They seize the Acropolis and plan to force their husbands to make peace. They accomplish this bold task through unconventional methods—a sex strike. After a few days, the men cannot take it any longer and beg their wives to return home. The women have their weaknesses, too, and several of them attempt to leave the Acropolis by acting in peculiar ways as they miss their husbands.*

This is a unique comedy whose chief protagonist is a woman—Lysistrata, who conjures up the tactics of the sex strike—and whose principle actors are also women who join together on the Acropolis for a united cause. Despite the seriousness of the subject at hand—the war and its many horrors—its treatment is outrageously comical: the shared misery of men and women denied the sexual pleasures of life.

Characters

LYSISTRATA, Athenian woman
MYRRHINE, Athenian woman
CINESIAS, Myrrhine's husband
CHORUS of women
CHORUS of old men
WOMEN
OLD MAN

"LYSISTRATA: What use calling upon Zeus? The thing is even as I say. I cannot stop them any longer from lusting after the men. They are all for deserting."

CHORUS OF WOMEN [*singing*]
Then, citizens all, hear what I have to say. I have useful counsel to give our city, which deserves it well at my hands for the brilliant distinctions it has lavished on my girlhood. At seven years of age, I carried the sacred vessels; at ten, I pounded barley for the altar of Athene; next, clad in a robe of yellow silk, I played the bear to Artemis at the Brauronia; presently, when I was grown up, a tall, handsome maiden, they put a necklace of dried figs about my neck, and I was one of the Canephori.[7]

LEADER OF CHORUS OF WOMEN
So surely I am bound to give my best advice to Athens. What matters that I was born a woman, if I can cure your misfortunes? I pay my share of tolls and taxes, by giving men to the State. But you, you miserable greybeards, you contribute nothing to the public charges; on the contrary, you have wasted the treasure of our forefathers, as it was called, the treasure amassed in the days of the Persian Wars. You pay nothing at all in return; and into the bargain you endanger our lives and liberties by your mistakes. Have you one word to say for yourselves?... Ah! don't irritate me, you there, or I'll lay my slipper across your jaws; and it's pretty heavy.

CHORUS OF OLD MEN [*singing*]
Outrage upon outrage! things are going from bad to worse. Let us punish the minxes, every one of us that has balls to boast of. Come, off with our tunics, for a man must savour of manhood; come, my friends, let us strip naked from head to foot. Courage, I say, we who in our day garrisoned Lipsydrion;[8] let us be young again, and shake off eld.

LEADER OF CHORUS OF OLD MEN
If we give them the least hold over us, that's the end! Their audacity will know no bounds! We shall see them building ships, and fighting sea-fights, like Artemisia;[9] and, if they want to mount and ride as cavalry, we had best cashier the knights, for indeed women excel in riding, and have a fine firm seat for the gallop. Just think of all those squadrons of Amazons Micon has painted for us engaged in hand-to-hand combat with men. Come then, we must now fit collars to all these willing necks.

CHORUS OF WOMEN [*singing*]
By the blessed goddesses, if you anger me, I will let loose the beast of my evil passions, and a very hailstorm of blows will set you yelling for help. Come, dames, off with your tunics, and quick's the word; women must smell the smell of women in the throes of passion... Now just you dare to measure strength with me, old greybeard, and I warrant you you'll never eat garlic or black beans any more. No, not a word! my anger is at boiling point, and I'll do with you what the beetle did with the eagle's eggs.[10]

LEADER OF CHORUS OF WOMEN
I laugh at your threats, so long as I have on my side Lampito here, and the noble Theban, my dear Ismenia... Pass decree on decree, you can do us no hurt, you wretch abhorred of all your fellows. Why, only yesterday, on occasion of the feast of Hecate, I asked my neighbours of Boeotia for one of their daughters for whom my girls have a lively liking—a fine, fat eel to wit; and if they did not refuse, all along of your silly decrees! We shall never cease to suffer the like, till some one

gives you a neat trip-up and breaks your neck for you!

[*To Lysistrata as she comes out from the Acropolis*]

You, Lysistrata, you who are leader of our glorious enterprise, why do I see you coming towards me with so gloomy an air?

LYSISTRATA
It's the behaviour of these naughty women, it's the female heart and female weakness that so discourage me.

LEADER OF CHORUS OF WOMEN
Tell us, tell us, what is it?

LYSISTRATA
I only tell the simple truth.

LEADER OF CHORUS OF WOMEN
What has happened so disconcerting? Come, tell your friends.

LYSISTRATA
Oh! the thing is so hard to tell—yet so impossible to conceal.

LEADER OF CHORUS OF WOMEN
Never seek to hide any ill that has befallen our cause.

LYSISTRATA
To blurt it out in a word—we want laying!

LEADER OF CHORUS OF WOMEN
Oh! Zeus, oh! Zeus!

LYSISTRATA
What use calling upon Zeus? The thing is even as I say. I cannot stop them any longer from lusting after the men. They are all for deserting. The first I caught was slipping out by the postern gate near the cave of Pan; another was letting herself down by a rope and pulley; a third was busy preparing her escape; while a fourth, perched on a bird's back, was just taking wing for Orsilochus' house, when I seized her by the hair. One and all, they are inventing excuses to be off home. [*Pointing to the gate*] Look! there goes one, trying to get out! Halloa there! whither away so fast?

FIRST WOMAN
I want to go home; I have some Milesian wool in the house, which is getting all eaten up by the worms.

LYSISTRATA
Bah! you and your worms! go back, I say!

FIRST WOMAN
I will return immediately, I swear I will by the two goddesses! I only have just to spread it out on the bed.

LYSISTRATA
You shall not do anything of the kind! I say, you shall not go.

FIRST WOMAN
Must I leave my wool to spoil then?

LYSISTRATA
Yes, if need be.

SECOND WOMAN
Unhappy woman that I am! Alas for my flax! I've left it at home unstript!

LYSISTRATA
So, here's another trying to escape to go home and strip her flax!

SECOND WOMAN
Oh! I swear by the goddess of light, the instant I have put it in condition I will come straight back.

LYSISTRATA
You shall do nothing of the kind! If once you began, others would want to follow suit.

THIRD WOMAN
Oh! goddess divine, Ilithyia, patroness of women in labour, stay, stay the birth, till I have reached a spot less hallowed than Athene's mount!

LYSISTRATA
What mean you by these silly tales?

THIRD WOMAN
I am going to have a child—now, this minute!

LYSISTRATA
But you were not pregnant yesterday!

THIRD WOMAN
Well, I am to-day. Oh! let me go in search of the midwife, Lysistrata, quick, quick!

LYSISTRATA
What is this fable you are telling me? [*Feeling her stomach*] Ah! what have you got there so hard?

THIRD WOMAN
A male child.

LYSISTRATA
No, no, by Aphrodite! nothing of the sort! Why, it feels like something hollow—a pot or a kettle. [*Opening her robe*] Oh! you silly creature, if you have not got the sacred helmet of Pallas—and you said you were with child!

THIRD WOMAN
And so I am, by Zeus, I am!

LYSISTRATA
Then why this helmet, pray?

THIRD WOMAN
For fear my pains should seize me in the Acropolis; I mean to lay my eggs in this helmet, as the doves do.

LYSISTRATA
Excuses and pretences every word! the thing's as clear as daylight. Anyway, you must stay here now till the fifth day, your day of purification.

THIRD WOMAN
I cannot sleep any more in the Acropolis, now I have seen the snake that guards the temple.

FOURTH WOMAN
Ah! and those awful owls with their dismal hooting! I cannot get a wink of rest, and

I'm just dying of fatigue.

LYSISTRATA
You wicked women, have done with your falsehoods! You want your husbands, that's plain enough. But don't you think they want you just as badly? They are spending dreadful nights, oh! I know that well enough. But hold out, my dears, hold out! A little more patience, and the victory will be ours. An oracle promises us success, if only we remain united. Shall I repeat the words?

THIRD WOMAN
Yes, tell us what the oracle declares.

LYSISTRATA
Silence then! Now—"Whenas the swallows, fleeing before the hoopoes, shall have all flocked together in one place, and shall refrain them from all amorous commerce, then will be the end of all the ills of life; yea, and Zeus, who doth thunder in the skies, shall set above what was erst below... "

THIRD WOMAN
What! shall the men be underneath?

LYSISTRATA
"But if dissension do arise among the swallows, and they take wing from the holy temple, it will be said there is never a more wanton bird in all the world."

THIRD WOMAN
Ye gods! the prophecy is clear.

LYSISTRATA
Nay, never let us be cast down by calamity! let us be brave to bear, and go back to our posts. It would be shameful indeed not to trust the promises of the oracle.

[*They all go back into the Acropolis.*]

CHORUS OF OLD MEN [*singing*]
I want to tell you a fable they used to relate to me when I was a little boy. This is it: Once upon a time there was a young man called Melanion, who hated the thought of marriage so sorely that he fled away to the wilds. So he dwelt in the mountains, wove himself nets, and caught hares. He never, never came back, he had such a horror of women. As chaste as Melanion, we loathe the jades just as much as he did.

AN OLD MAN [*beginning a brief duet with one of the women*]
You dear old woman, I would fain kiss you.

WOMAN
I will set you crying without onions.

OLD MAN
And give you a sound kicking.

WOMAN [*pointing*]
Ah, ha! what a dense forest you have there!

OLD MAN
So was Myronides one of the bushiest of men of this side; his backside was all black, and he terrified his enemies as much as Phormio.[11]

CHORUS OF WOMEN [*singing*]
I want to tell you a fable too, to match yours about Melanion. Once there was a certain man called Timon, a tough customer, and a whimsical, a true son of the Furies, with a face that seemed to glare out of a thorn-bush. He withdrew from the world because he couldn't abide bad men, after vomiting a thousand curses at them. He had a holy horror of ill-conditioned fellows, but he was mighty tender towards women.

WOMAN [*beginning another duet*]
Suppose I up and broke your jaw for you!

OLD MAN
I am not a bit afraid of you.

WOMAN
Suppose I let fly a good kick at you?

OLD MAN
I should see your thing then.

WOMAN
You would see that, for all my age, it is very well plucked.

LYSISTRATA [*rushing out of the Acropolis*]
Ho there! come quick, come quick!

ONE OF THE WOMEN
What is it? Why these cries?

LYSISTRATA
A man! a man! I see him approaching all afire with the flames of love. Oh! divine Queen of Cyprus, Paphos and Cythera, I pray you still be propitious to our enterprise.

WOMAN
Where is he, this unknown foe?

LYSISTRATA
Over there—beside the Temple of Demeter.

WOMAN
Yes, indeed, I see him; but who is he?

LYSISTRATA
Look, look! do any of you recognize him?

MYRRHINE [*joyfully*]
I do, I do! it's my husband Cinesias.

LYSISTRATA
To work then! Be it your task to inflame and torture and torment him. Seductions, caresses, provocations, refusals, try every means! Grant every favour, always excepting what is forbidden by our oath on the wine-bowl.

MYRRHINE
Have no fear, I'll do it.

LYSISTRATA
Well, I shall stay here to help you cajole the man and set his passions aflame. The rest of you withdraw.

[*Cinesias enters, in obvious and extreme sexual excitement. A slave follows him carrying an infant.*]

CINESIAS
Alas! alas! how I am tortured by spasm and rigid convulsion! Oh! I am racked on the wheel!

LYSISTRATA
Who is this that dares to pass our lines?

CINESIAS
It is I.

LYSISTRATA
What, a man?

CINESIAS
Very much so!

LYSISTRATA
Get out.

CINESIAS
But who are you that thus repulses me?

LYSISTRATA
The sentinel of the day.

CINESIAS
For the gods' sake, call Myrrhine.

LYSISTRATA
Call Myrrhine, you say? And who are you?

CINESIAS
I am her husband, Cinesias, son of Paeon.

LYSISTRATA
Ah! good day, my dear friend. Your name is not unknown amongst us. Your wife has it forever on her lips; and she never touches an egg or an apple without saying: "This is for Cinesias."

CINESIAS
Really and truly?

LYSISTRATA
Yes, indeed, by Aphrodite! And if we fall to talking of men, quick your wife declares: "Oh! all the rest, they're good for nothing compared with Cinesias."

CINESIAS
Oh! please, please go and call her to me!

LYSISTRATA
And what will you give me for my trouble?

CINESIAS
Anything I've got, if you like. [*Pointing to the evidence of his condition*] I will give you what I have here!

LYSISTRATA
Well, well, I will tell her to come.

[*She enters the Acropolis.*]

CINESIAS
Quick, oh! be quick! Life has no more charms for me since she left my house. I am sad, sad, when I go indoors; it all seems so empty; my victuals have lost their savour. And all because of this erection that I can't get rid of!

MYRRHINE [*to Lysistrata, over her shoulder*]
I love him, oh! I love him; but he won't let himself be loved. No! I shall not come.

CINESIAS
Myrrhine, my little darling Myrrhine, what are you saying? Come down to me quick.

MYRRHINE
No indeed, not I.

CINESIAS
I call you, Myrrhine, Myrrhine; won't you please come?

MYRRHINE
Why should you call me? You do not want me.

CINESIAS
Not want you! Why, here I stand, stiff with desire!

MYRRHINE
Good-bye.

[*She turns, as if to go.*]

CINESIAS
Oh! Myrrhine, Myrrhine, in our child's name, hear me; at any rate hear the child! Little lad, call your mother.

CHILD
Mamma, mamma, mamma!

CINESIAS
There, listen! Don't you pity the poor child? It's six days now you've never washed and never fed the child.

MYRRHINE
Poor darling, your father takes mighty little care of you!

CINESIAS
Come down, dearest, come down for the child's sake.

MYRRHINE
Ah! what a thing it is to be a mother! Well, well, we must come down, I suppose.

CINESIAS [*as Myrrhine approaches*]
Why, how much younger and prettier she looks! And how she looks at me so lovingly! Her cruelty and scorn only redouble my passion.

MYRRHINE [*ignoring him; to the child*]
You are as sweet as your father is provoking! Let me kiss you, my treasure, mother's darling!

CINESIAS
Ah! what a bad thing it is to let yourself be led away by other women! Why give me such pain and suffering, and yourself into the bargain?

MYRRHINE [*as he is about to embrace her*]
Hands off, sir!

CINESIAS
Everything is going to rack and ruin in the house.

MYRRHINE
I don't care.

CINESIAS
But your web that's all being pecked to pieces by the cocks and hens, don't you care for that?

MYRRHINE
Precious little.

CINESIAS
And Aphrodite, whose mysteries you have not celebrated for so long? Oh! won't you please come back home?

MYRRHINE
No, least, not till a sound treaty puts an end to the war.

CINESIAS
Well, if you wish it so much, why, we'll make it, your treaty.

MYRRHINE
Well and good! When that's done, I will come home. Till then, I am bound by an oath.

CINESIAS
At any rate, lie with me for a little while.

MYRRHINE
No, no, no! [*she hesitates*] but just the same I can't say I don't love you.

CINESIAS
You love me? Then why refuse to lie with me, my little girl, my sweet Myrrhine?

MYRRHINE [*pretending to be shocked*]
You must be joking! What, before the child!

CINESIAS [*to the slave*]
Manes, carry the lad home. There, you see, the child is gone; there's nothing to hinder us; won't you lie down now?

MYRRHINE
But, miserable man, where, where?

CINESIAS
In the cave of Pan; nothing could be better.

MYRRHINE
But how shall I purify myself before going back into the citadel?

CINESIAS
Nothing easier! you can wash at the Clepsydra.[12]

MYRRHINE
But my oath? Do you want me to perjure myself?

CINESIAS
I'll take all responsibility; don't worry.

MYRRHINE
Well, I'll be off, then, and find a bed for us.

CINESIAS
There's no point in that; surely we can lie on the ground.

MYRRHINE
No, no! even though you are bad, I don't like your lying on the bare earth.

[*She goes back into the Acropolis.*]

CINESIAS [*enraptured*]
Ah! how the dear girl loves me!

MYRRHINE [*coming back with a cot*]
Come, get to bed quick; I am going to undress. But, oh dear, we must get a mattress.

CINESIAS
A mattress? Oh! no, never mind about that!

MYRRHINE
No, by Artemis! lie on the bare sacking? never! That would be squalid.

CINESIAS
Kiss me!

MYRRHINE
Wait a minute!

[*She leaves him again.*]

CINESIAS
Good god, hurry up!

MYRRHINE [*coming back with a mattress*]
Here is a mattress. Lie down, I am just going to undress. But you've got no pillow.

CINESIAS
I don't want one either!

MYRRHINE
But I do.

[*She leaves him again.*]

CINESIAS
Oh god, oh god, she treats my tool just like Heracles![13]

MYRRHINE [*coming back with a pillow*]
There, lift your head, dear! [Wondering what else to tantalize him with; to herself] Is that all, I wonder?

CINESIAS [*misunderstanding*]
Surely. There's nothing else. Come, my treasure.

MYRRHINE
I am just unfastening my girdle. But remember what you promised me about making peace; mind you keep your word.

CINESIAS
Yes, yes, upon my life I will.

MYRRHINE
Why, you have no blanket!

CINESIAS
My god, what difference does that make? What I want is to make love!

MYRRHINE [*going out again*]
Never fear—directly, directly! I'll be back in no time.

CINESIAS
The woman will kill me with her blankets!

MYRRHINE [*coming back with a blanket*]
Now, get yourself up.

CINESIAS [*pointing*]
I've got this up!

MYRRHINE
Wouldn't you like me to scent you?

CINESIAS
No, by Apollo, no, please don't!

MYRRHINE
Yes, by Aphrodite, but I will, whether you like it or not.

[*She goes out again.*]

CINESIAS
God, I wish she'd hurry up and get through with all this!

MYRRHINE [*coming back with a flask of perfume*]
Hold out your hand; now rub it in.

CINESIAS
Oh! in Apollo's name, I don't much like the smell of it; but perhaps it will improve when it's well rubbed in. It does not somehow smack of the marriage bed!

MYRRHINE
Oh dear! what a scatterbrain I am; if I haven't gone and brought Rhodian perfumes!

CINESIAS
Never mind, dearest, let it go now.

MYRRHINE
You don't really mean that.

[*She goes.*]

CINESIAS
Damn the man who invented perfumes!

MYRRHINE [*coming back with another flask*]
Here, take this bottle.

CINESIAS
I have a better one allready for you, darling. Come, you provoking creature, to bed with you, and don't bring another thing.

MYRRHINE
Coming, coming; I'm just slipping off my shoes. Dear boy, will you vote for peace?

CINESIAS
I'll think about it. [*Myrrhine runs away.*] I'm a dead man, she is killing me! She has gone, and left me in torment! [*in tragic style*] I must have someone to lay, I must! Ah me! the loveliest of women has choused and cheated me. Poor little lad, how am I to give you what you want so badly? Where is Cynalopex?[14] Quick, man, get him a nurse, do!

LEADER OF CHORUS OF OLD MEN
Poor, miserable wretch, baulked in your amorousness! what tortures are yours! Ah! you fill me with pity. Could any man's back and loins stand such a strain. He stands stiff and rigid, and there's never a wench to help him!

CINESIAS
Ye gods in heaven, what pains I suffer!

LEADER OF CHORUS OF OLD MEN
Well, there it is; it's her doing, that abandoned hussy!

CINESIAS
No, no! rather say that sweetest, dearest darling.

[*He departs.*]

LEADER OF CHORUS OF OLD MEN
That dearest darling? no, no, that hussy, say I! Zeus, thou god of the skies, canst not let loose a hurricane, to sweep them all up into the air, and whirl them round, then

drop them down crash! And impale them on the point of this man's tool!

Anonymous translator.

PLATO

c. 427 - 347 BC

Plato was born into one of the great noble families of Athens. By the time he had reached adulthood, the city was about to experience the darkest time in its history. Athens had recently lost the war against Sparta in 404 BC, and faced difficult times when Plato launched his peculiar career. Plato's noble origin, wealth, and education should have shaped him into a politician or sophist. Instead, he chose to become a philosopher, just as his master Socrates whose figure is omnipresent in his work.

In his dialogues, Plato champions a belief that would yield neither to opinion nor image but would reach out for the knowledge of what things and men truly are. The ancients held Plato's works in high esteem. This explains in part the survival of his complete works, as far as we know, and is an extraordinary feat as ancient texts are concerned.

Plato did not focus exclusively on philosophical writing. He also tried his luck with several political undertakings. They bore little fruit. He twice attempted to settle his ideal city in Sicily. His intention was to create a community where the leaders were philosophers who worked on making their citizens better people. But the Sicilian tyrants quickly imprisoned him and then expelled him from the island. At Athens, however, Plato fared far better and succeeded in his more realistic venture of establishing a school called the Academy, where many students came to study under the Master and prominent guest scholars. Plato's most remarkable disciple was none other than Aristotle, the philosopher and scientist who would later become the tutor of Alexander the Great.

Myth of the Androgyne
followed by Praise of Love by Socrates
Plato, *Symposium* 189c-193d

Love ("Eros" in Greek) is the topic of Plato's banquet, the Symposium. *In Plato's time, the symposium was a gathering of society's elites who assembled to eat, drink, and debate. Socrates, Aristophanes, Alcibiades, and the tragic poet Agathon attend the banquet where they express their opinions on the subject of the day and speak in praise of Eros. The speeches of the two most famous participants of the symposium are reproduced below: Aristophanes, the comic poet, explains the power of Eros via the myth of the Androgyne, while Socrates delivers one of the most compelling insights of the dialogue. The latter offers his own definition of Eros and recounts how a woman, Diotima, initiated him to the secrets of love when he was a young man.*

"Mankind, judging by their neglect of him, have never at all understood the power of Love."

Aristophanes professed to open another vein of discourse; he had a mind to praise Love in another way, unlike that either of Pausanias or Eryximachus. Mankind, he said, judging by their neglect of him, have never, as I think, at all understood the power of Love. For if they had understood him they would surely have built noble temples and altars, and offered solemn sacrifices in his honour; but this is not done, and most certainly ought to be done: since of all the gods he is the best friend of men, the helper and the healer of the ills which are the great impediment to the happiness of the race. I will try to describe his power to you, and you shall teach the rest of the world what I am teaching you. In the first place, let me treat of the nature of man and what has happened to it; for the original human nature was not like the present, but different. The sexes were not two as they are now, but originally three in number; there was man, woman, and the union of the two, having a name corresponding to this double nature, which had once a real existence, but is now lost, and the word 'Androgynous' is only preserved as a term of reproach.

In the second place, the primeval man was round, his back and sides forming a circle; and he had four hands and four feet, one head with two faces, looking opposite ways, set on a round neck and precisely alike; also four ears, two privy members, and the remainder to correspond. He could walk upright as men now do, backwards or forwards as he pleased, and he could also roll over and over at a great pace, turning on his four hands and four feet, eight in all, like tumblers going over and over with their legs in the air; this was when he wanted to run fast. Now the sexes were three, and such as I have described them; because the sun, moon, and earth are three; and the man was originally the child of the sun, the woman of the earth, and the man-woman of the moon, which is made up of sun and earth, and they were all round and moved round and round like their parents.

Terrible was their might and strength, and the thoughts of their hearts were great, and they made an attack upon the gods; of them is told the tale of Otys and Ephialtes who, as Homer says, dared to scale heaven, and would have laid hands upon the gods. Doubt reigned in the celestial councils. Should they kill them and annihilate the race with thunderbolts, as they had done the giants, then there would be an end of the sacrifices and worship which men offered to them; but, on the other hand, the gods could not suffer their insolence to be unrestrained. At last, after a good deal of reflection, Zeus discovered a way. He said: 'Methinks I have a plan which will humble their pride and improve their manners; men shall continue to exist, but I will cut them in two and then they will be diminished in strength and increased in numbers; this will have the advantage of making them more profitable to us. They shall walk upright on two legs, and if they continue insolent and will not be quiet, I will split them again and they shall hop about on a single leg.' He spoke and cut men in two, like a sorb-apple which is halved for pickling, or as you might divide an egg with a hair; and as he cut them one after another, he bade Apollo give the face and the half of the neck a turn in order that the man might contemplate the section of himself: he would thus learn a lesson of humility. Apollo was also bidden to heal their wounds and compose their forms. So he gave a turn to the face and pulled the skin from the sides all over that which in our language is called the belly, like the purses which draw in, and he made one mouth at the centre, which he fastened in a knot (the same which is called the navel); he also moulded the breast and took out most of the wrinkles, much as a shoemaker might smooth leather upon a last; he left a few, however, in the region of the belly and navel, as a memorial of the primeval state.

After the division the two parts of man, each desiring his other half, came together, and throwing their arms about one another, entwined in mutual embraces, longing to grow into one, they were on the point of dying from hunger and self-neglect, because they did not like to do anything apart; and when one of the halves died and the other survived, the survivor sought another mate, man or woman as we call them,—being the sections of entire men or women,—and clung to that. They were being destroyed, when Zeus in pity of them invented a new plan: he turned the parts of generation round to the front, for this had not been always their position, and they sowed the seed no longer as hitherto like grasshoppers in the ground, but in one another; and after the transposition the male generated in the female in order that by the mutual embraces of man and woman they might breed, and the race might continue; or if man came to man they might be satisfied, and rest, and go their ways to the business of life: so ancient is the desire of one another which is implanted in us, reuniting our original nature, making one of two, and healing the state of man.

Each of us when separated, having one side only, like a flat fish, is but the indenture of a man, and he is always looking for his other half. Men who are a section of that double nature which was once called Androgynous are lovers of women; adulterers are generally of this breed, and also adulterous women who lust after men: the women who are a section of the woman do not care for men, but have female attachments; the female companions are of this sort. But they who are a section of the male follow the male, and while they are young, being slices of the original man, they hang about men and embrace them, and they are themselves the best of boys and youths, because they have the most manly nature. Some indeed assert that they are shameless, but this is not true; for they do not act thus from any want of shame, but because they are valiant and manly, and have a manly countenance, and they embrace that which is like them. And these when they grow up become our statesmen, and these only, which is a great proof of the truth of what I am saving. When they reach manhood they are lovers of youth, and are not naturally inclined to marry or beget children,—if at all, they do so only in obedience to the law; but they are satisfied if they may be allowed to live with one another unwedded; and such a nature is prone to love and ready to return love, always embracing that which is akin to him.

And when one of them meets with his other half, the actual half of himself, whether he be a lover of youth or a lover of another sort, the pair are lost in an amazement of love and friendship and intimacy, and one will not be out of the other's sight, as I may say, even for a moment: these are the people who pass their whole lives together; yet they could not explain what they desire of one another. For the intense yearning which each of them has towards the other does not appear to be the desire of lover's intercourse, but of something else which the soul of either evidently desires and cannot tell, and of which she has only a dark and doubtful presentiment. Suppose Hephaestus, with his instruments, to come to the pair who are lying side by side and to say to them, 'What do you people want of one another?' they would be unable to explain. And suppose further, that when he saw their perplexity he said: 'Do you desire to be wholly one; always day and night to be in one another's company? for if this is what you desire, I am ready to melt you into one and let you grow together, so that being two you shall become one, and while you live live a common life as if you were a single man, and after your death in the world below still be one departed soul instead of two—I ask whether this is what you lovingly desire, and whether you are satisfied to attain this?'—there is not a man of them who when he heard the proposal would deny or would not acknowledge that this meeting and melting into one another, this becoming one instead of two, was the very expression of his ancient need. And the reason is that human nature was originally one and we were a whole, and the desire and pursuit of the whole is called love.

There was a time, I say, when we were one, but now because of the wickedness of mankind God has dispersed us, as the Arcadians were dispersed into villages by the Lacedaemonians. And if we are not obedient to the gods, there is a danger that we shall be split up again and go about in basso-relievo, like the profile figures having only half a nose which are sculptured on monuments, and that we shall be like tallies. Wherefore let us exhort all men to piety, that we may avoid evil, and obtain the good, of which Love is to us the lord and minister; and let no one oppose him—he is the enemy of the gods who opposes him. For if we are friends of the God and at peace with him we shall find our own true loves, which rarely happens in this world at present. I am serious, and therefore I must beg Eryximachus not to make fun or to find any allusion in what I am saying to Pausanias and Agathon, who, as I suspect, are both of the manly nature, and belong to the class which I have been describing. But my words have a wider application—they include men and women everywhere; and I believe that if our loves were perfectly accomplished, and each one returning to his primeval nature had his original true love, then our race would be happy. And if this would be best of all, the best in the next degree and under present circumstances must be the nearest approach to such an union; and that will be the attainment of a congenial love.

Wherefore, if we would praise him who has given to us the benefit, we must praise the god Love, who is our greatest benefactor, both leading us in this life back to our own nature, and giving us high hopes for the future, for he promises that if we are pious, he will restore us to our original state, and heal us and make us happy and blessed.

Translated by B. Jowett.

Praise of Love by Socrates

Plato, *Symposium* 199c-212c

"No god is a philosopher or seeker after wisdom, for he is wise already."

Aristodemus said that Phaedrus and the company bid Socrates speak in any manner which he thought best. Then, he added, let me have your permission first to ask Agathon a few more questions, in order that I may take his admissions as the premisses of my discourse.

I grant the permission, said Phaedrus: put your questions. Socrates then proceeded as follows:—

In the magnificent oration which you have just uttered, I think that you were right, my dear Agathon, in proposing to speak of the nature of Love first and afterwards of his works—that is a way of beginning which I very much approve. And as you have spoken so eloquently of his nature, may I ask you further, Whether love is the love of something or of nothing? And here I must explain myself: I do not want you to say that love is the love of a father or the love of a mother—that would be ridiculous; but to answer as you would, if I asked is a father a father of something? to which you would find no difficulty in replying, of a son or daughter: and the answer would be right.

Very true, said Agathon.

And you would say the same of a mother?

He assented.

Yet let me ask you one more question in order to illustrate my meaning: Is not a brother to be regarded essentially as a brother of something?

Certainly, he replied.

That is, of a brother or sister?

Yes, he said.

And now, said Socrates, I will ask about Love:—Is Love of something or of nothing?

Of something, surely, he replied.

Keep in mind what this is, and tell me what I want to know—whether Love desires that of which love is.

Yes, surely.

And does he possess, or does he not possess, that which he loves and desires?

Probably not, I should say.

Nay, replied Socrates, I would have you consider whether 'necessarily' is not rather the word. The inference that he who desires something is in want of something, and that he who desires nothing is in want of nothing, is in my judgment, Agathon, absolutely and necessarily true. What do you think?

I agree with you, said Agathon.

Very good. Would he who is great, desire to be great, or he who is strong, desire to be strong?

That would be inconsistent with our previous admissions.

True. For he who is anything cannot want to be that which he is?

Very true.

And yet, added Socrates, if a man being strong desired to be strong, or being swift desired to be swift, or being healthy desired to be healthy, in that case he might be thought to desire something which he already has or is. I give the example in order that we may avoid misconception. For the possessors of these qualities, Agathon, must be supposed to have their respective advantages at the time, whether they choose or not; and who can desire that which he has? Therefore, when a person says, I am well and wish to be well, or I am rich and wish to be rich, and I desire simply to have what I have—to him we shall reply: 'You, my friend, having wealth and health and strength, want to have the continuance of them; for at this moment, whether you choose or no, you have them. And when you say, I desire that which I have and nothing else, is not your meaning that you want to have what you now have in the future?' He must agree with us—must he not?

He must, replied Agathon.

Then, said Socrates, he desires that what he has at present may be preserved to him in the future, which is equivalent to saying that he desires something which is non-existent to him, and which as yet he has not got.

Very true, he said.

Then he and every one who desires, desires that which he has not already, and which is future and not present, and which he has not, and is not, and of which he is in want;—these are the sort of things which love and desire seek?

Very true, he said.

Then now, said Socrates, let us recapitulate the argument. First, is not love of something, and of something too which is wanting to a man?

Yes, he replied.

Remember further what you said in your speech, or if you do not remember I will remind you: you said that the love of the beautiful set in order the empire of the gods, for that of deformed things there is no love—did you not say something of that kind?

Yes, said Agathon.

Yes, my friend, and the remark was a just one. And if this is true, Love is the love of beauty and not of deformity?

He assented.

And the admission has been already made that Love is of something which a man wants and has not?

True, he said.

Then Love wants and has not beauty?

Certainly, he replied.

And would you call that beautiful which wants and does not possess beauty?

Certainly not.

Then would you still say that love is beautiful?

Agathon replied: I fear that I did not understand what I was saying.

You made a very good speech, Agathon, replied Socrates; but there is yet one small question which I would fain ask:—Is not the good also the beautiful?
Yes.

Then in wanting the beautiful, love wants also the good?

I cannot refute you, Socrates, said Agathon:—Let us assume that what you say is true.

Say rather, beloved Agathon, that you cannot refute the truth; for Socrates is easily refuted.

And now, taking my leave of you, I would rehearse a tale of love which I heard from Diotima of Mantineia, a woman wise in this and in many other kinds of knowledge, who in the days of old, when the Athenians offered sacrifice before the coming of the plague, delayed the disease ten years. She was my instructress in the art of love, and I shall repeat to you what she said to me, beginning with the admissions made by Agathon, which are nearly if not quite the same which I made to the wise woman when she questioned me: I think that this will be the easiest way, and I shall take both parts myself as well as I can. As you, Agathon, suggested, I must speak first of the being and nature of Love, and then of his works. First I said to her in nearly the same words which he used to me, that Love was a mighty god, and likewise fair; and she proved to me as I proved to him that, by my own showing, Love was neither fair nor good. 'What do you mean, Diotima,' I said, 'is love then evil and foul?' 'Hush,' she cried; 'must that be foul which is not fair?' 'Certainly,' I said. 'And is that which is not wise, ignorant? do you not see that there is a mean between wisdom and ignorance?' 'And what may that be?' I said. 'Right opinion,' she replied; 'which, as you know, being incapable of giving a reason, is not knowledge (for how can knowledge be devoid of reason? nor again, ignorance, for neither can ignorance attain the truth), but is clearly something which is a mean between ignorance and wisdom.' 'Quite true,' I replied. 'Do not then insist,' she said, 'that what is not fair is of necessity foul, or what is not good evil; or infer that because love is not fair and good he is therefore foul and evil; for he is in a mean between them.' 'Well,' I said, 'Love is surely admitted by all to be a great god.' 'By those who know or by those who do not know?' 'By all.' 'And how, Socrates,' she said with a smile, 'can Love be acknowledged to be a great god by those who say that he is not a god at all?' 'And who are they?' I said. 'You and I are two of them,' she replied. 'How can that be?' I said. 'It is quite intelligible,' she replied; 'for you yourself would acknowledge that the gods are happy and fair—of course you would—would you dare to say that any god was not?' 'Certainly not,' I replied. 'And you mean by the happy, those who are the possessors of things good or fair?' 'Yes.' 'And you admitted that Love, because he was in want, desires those good and fair things of which he is in want?' 'Yes, I did.' 'But how can he be a god who has no portion in what is either good or fair?' 'Impossible.' 'Then you see that you also deny the divinity of Love.'

'What then is Love?' I asked; 'Is he mortal?' 'No.' 'What then?' 'As in the former instance, he is neither mortal nor immortal, but in a mean between the two.' 'What is he, Diotima?' 'He is a great spirit, and like all spirits he is intermediate between the divine and the mortal.' 'And what,' I said, 'is his power?' 'He interprets,' she replied, 'between gods and men, conveying and taking across to the gods the prayers and sacrifices of men, and to men the commands and replies of the gods; he is the mediator who spans the chasm which divides them, and therefore in him all is bound together, and through him the arts of the prophet and the priest, their sacrifices and mysteries and charms, and all prophecy and incantation, find their way. For God mingles not with man; but through Love all the intercourse and converse of God with man, whether awake or asleep, is carried on. The wisdom which understands this is spiritual; all other wisdom, such as that of arts and handicrafts, is mean and vulgar. Now these spirits or intermediate powers are many and diverse, and one of them is Love.' 'And who,' I said, 'was his father, and who his mother?' 'The tale,' she said, 'will take time; nevertheless I will tell you.

On the birthday of Aphrodite there was a feast of the gods, at which the god Poros or Plenty, who is the son of Metis or Discretion, was one of the guests. When the feast was over, Penia or Poverty, as the manner is on such occasions, came about the doors to beg. Now Plenty who was the worse for nectar (there was no wine in those days), went into the garden of Zeus and fell into a heavy sleep, and Poverty considering her own straitened circumstances, plotted to have a child by him, and accordingly she lay down at his side and conceived Love, who partly because he is naturally a lover of the beautiful, and because Aphrodite is herself beautiful, and also because he was born on her birthday, is her follower and attendant. And as his parentage is, so also are his fortunes. In the first place he is always poor, and anything but tender and fair, as the many imagine him; and he is rough and squalid, and has no shoes, nor a house to dwell in; on the bare earth exposed he lies under the open heaven, in the streets, or at the doors of houses, taking his rest; and like his mother he is always in distress. Like his father too, whom he also partly resembles, he is always plotting against the fair and good; he is bold, enterprising, strong, a mighty hunter, always weaving some intrigue or other, keen in the pursuit of wisdom, fertile in resources; a philosopher at all times, terrible as an enchanter, sorcerer, sophist. He is by nature neither mortal nor immortal, but alive and flourishing at one moment when he is in plenty, and dead at another moment, and again alive by reason of his father's nature. But that which is always flowing in is always flowing out, and so he is never in want and never in wealth; and, further, he is in a mean between ignorance and knowledge. The truth of the matter is this: No god is a philosopher or seeker after wisdom, for he is wise already; nor does any man who is wise seek after wisdom. Neither do the ignorant seek after wisdom. For herein is the evil of ignorance, that he who is neither good nor wise is nevertheless satisfied with himself: he has no desire for that of which he feels no want.' 'But who then, Diotima,' I said, 'are the lovers of wisdom, if they are neither the wise nor the foolish?' 'A child may answer that question,' she replied; 'they are those who are in a mean between the two; Love is one of them. For wisdom is a most beautiful thing, and Love is of the beautiful; and therefore Love is also a philosopher or lover of wisdom, and being a lover of wisdom is in a mean between the wise and the ignorant. And of this too his birth is the cause; for his father is wealthy and wise, and his mother poor and foolish. Such, my dear Socrates, is the nature of the spirit Love. The error in your conception of him was very natural, and as I imagine from what you say, has arisen out of a confusion of love and the beloved, which made you think that love was all beautiful. For the beloved is the truly beautiful, and delicate, and perfect, and blessed; but the principle of love is of another nature, and is such as I have described.'

I said, 'O thou stranger woman, thou sayest well; but, assuming Love to be such as you say, what is the use of him to men?' 'That, Socrates,' she replied, 'I will attempt to unfold: of his nature and birth I have already spoken; and you acknowledge that love is of the beautiful. But some one will say: Of the beautiful in what, Socrates and Diotima?—or rather let me put the question more clearly, and ask: When a man loves the beautiful, what does he desire?' I answered her 'That the beautiful may be his.' 'Still,' she said, 'the answer suggests a further question: What is given by the possession of beauty?' 'To what you have asked,' I replied, 'I have no answer ready.' 'Then,' she said, 'let me put the word "good" in the place of the beautiful, and repeat the question once more: If he who loves loves the good, what is it then that he loves?' 'The possession of the good,' I said. 'And what does he gain who possesses the good?' 'Happiness,' I replied; 'there is less difficulty in answering that question.' 'Yes,' she said, 'the happy are made happy by the acquisition of good things. Nor is there any need to ask why a man desires happiness; the answer is already final.' 'You are right.' I said. 'And is this wish and this desire common to all? and do all men always desire their own good, or only some men?—

what say you?' 'All men,' I replied; 'the desire is common to all.' 'Why, then,' she rejoined, 'are not all men, Socrates, said to love, but only some of them? whereas you say that all men are always loving the same things.' 'I myself wonder,' I said, 'why this is.' 'There is nothing to wonder at,' she replied; 'the reason is that one part of love is separated off and receives the name of the whole, but the other parts have other names.' 'Give an illustration,' I said.

She answered me as follows: 'There is poetry, which, as you know, is complex and manifold. All creation or passage of non-being into being is poetry or making, and the processes of all art are creative; and the masters of arts are all poets or makers.' 'Very true.' 'Still,' she said, 'you know that they are not called poets, but have other names; only that portion of the art which is separated off from the rest, and is concerned with music and metre, is termed poetry, and they who possess poetry in this sense of the word are called poets.' 'Very true,' I said. 'And the same holds of love. For you may say generally that all desire of good and happiness is only the great and subtle power of love; but they who are drawn towards him by any other path, whether the path of money-making or gymnastics or philosophy, are not called lovers—the name of the whole is appropriated to those whose affection takes one form only—they alone are said to love, or to be lovers.' 'I dare say,' I replied, 'that you are right.' 'Yes,' she added, 'and you hear people say that lovers are seeking for their other half; but I say that they are seeking neither for the half of themselves, nor for the whole, unless the half or the whole be also a good. And they will cut off their own hands and feet and cast them away, if they are evil; for they love not what is their own, unless perchance there be some one who calls what belongs to him the good, and what belongs to another the evil. For there is nothing which men love but the good. Is there anything?' 'Certainly, I should say, that there is nothing.' 'Then,' she said, 'the simple truth is, that men love the good.' 'Yes,' I said. 'To which must be added that they love the possession of the good?' 'Yes, that must be added.' 'And not only the possession, but the everlasting possession of the good?' 'That must be added too.' 'Then love,' she said, 'may be described generally as the love of the everlasting possession of the good?' 'That is most true.'

'Then if this be the nature of love, can you tell me further,' she said, 'what is the manner of the pursuit? what are they doing who show all this eagerness and heat which is called love? and what is the object which they have in view? Answer me.' 'Nay, Diotima,' I replied, 'if I had known, I should not have wondered at your wisdom, neither should I have come to learn from you about this very matter.' 'Well,' she said, 'I will teach you:—The object which they have in view is birth in beauty, whether of body or soul.' 'I do not understand you,' I said; 'the oracle requires an explanation.' 'I will make my meaning clearer,' she replied. 'I mean to say, that all men are bringing to the birth in their bodies and in their souls. There is a certain age at which human nature is desirous of procreation—procreation which must be in beauty and not in deformity; and this procreation is the union of man and woman, and is a divine thing; for conception and generation are an immortal principle in the mortal creature, and in the inharmonious they can never be. But the deformed is always inharmonious with the divine, and the beautiful harmonious. Beauty, then, is the destiny or goddess of parturition who presides at birth, and therefore, when approaching beauty, the conceiving power is propitious, and diffusive, and benign, and begets and bears fruit: at the sight of ugliness she frowns and contracts and has a sense of pain, and turns away, and shrivels up, and not without a pang refrains from conception. And this is the reason why, when the hour of conception arrives, and the teeming nature is full, there is such a flutter and ecstasy about beauty whose approach is the alleviation of the pain of travail. For love, Socrates, is not, as you imagine, the love of the beautiful only.' 'What then?' 'The love of generation and of birth in beauty.' 'Yes,' I said. 'Yes, indeed,' she replied. 'But why of generation?' 'Because to the mortal creature, generation is a sort of eternity and immortality,' she replied; 'and if, as has been already admitted, love is of the everlasting possession of the good, all men will necessarily desire immortality together with good: Wherefore love is of immortality.'

All this she taught me at various times when she spoke of love. And I remember her once saying to me, 'What is the cause, Socrates, of love, and the attendant desire? See you not how all animals, birds, as well as beasts, in their desire of procreation, are in agony when they take the infection of love, which begins with the desire of union; whereto is added the care of offspring, on whose behalf the weakest are ready to battle against the strongest even to the uttermost, and to die for them, and will let themselves be tormented with hunger or suffer anything in order to maintain their young. Man may be supposed to act thus from reason; but why should animals have these passionate feelings? Can you tell me why?' Again I replied that I did not know. She said to me: 'And do you expect ever to become a master in the art of love, if you do not know this?' 'But I have told you already, Diotima, that my ignorance is the reason why I come to you; for I am conscious that I want a teacher; tell me then the cause of this and of the other mysteries of love.' 'Marvel not,' she said, 'if you believe that love is of the immortal, as we have several times acknowledged; for here again, and on the same principle too, the mortal nature is seeking as far as is possible to be everlasting and immortal: and this is only to be attained by generation, because generation always leaves behind a new existence in the place of the old. Nay even in the life of the same individual there is succession and not absolute unity: a man is called the same, and yet in the short interval which elapses between youth and age, and in which every animal is said to have life and identity, he is undergoing a perpetual process of loss and reparation—hair, flesh, bones, blood, and the whole body are always changing. Which is true not only of the body, but also of the soul, whose habits, tempers, opinions, desires, pleasures, pains, fears, never remain the same in any one of us, but are always coming and going; and equally true of knowledge, and what is still more surprising to us mortals, not only do the sciences in general spring up and decay, so that in respect of them we are never the same; but each of them individually experiences a like change. For what is implied in the word "recollection," but the departure of knowledge, which is ever being forgotten, and is renewed and preserved by recollection, and appears to be the same although in reality new, according to that law of succession by which all mortal things are preserved, not absolutely the same, but by substitution, the old worn-out mortality leaving another new and similar existence behind—unlike the divine, which is always the same and not another? And in this way, Socrates, the mortal body, or mortal anything, partakes of immortality; but the immortal in another way. Marvel not then at the love which all men have of their offspring; for that universal love and interest is for the sake of immortality.'

I was astonished at her words, and said: 'Is this really true, O thou wise Diotima?' And she answered with all the authority of an accomplished sophist: 'Of that, Socrates, you may be assured;—think only of the ambition of men, and you will wonder at the senselessness of their ways, unless you consider how they are stirred by the love of an immortality of fame. They are ready to run all risks greater far than they would have run for their children, and to spend money and undergo any sort of toil, and even to die, for the sake of leaving behind them a name which shall be eternal. Do you imagine that Alcestis would have died to save Admetus, or Achilles to avenge Patroclus, or your own Codrus in order to preserve the kingdom for his sons, if they had not imagined that the memory of their virtues, which still survives among us, would be immortal?[1] Nay,' she said, 'I am persuaded that all men do all things, and the better they are the more they do them, in hope of the glorious fame of immortal virtue; for they desire the immortal.

'Those who are pregnant in the body only, betake themselves to women and beget children—this is the character of their love; their offspring, as they hope, will preserve their memory and giving them the blessedness and immortality which they desire in the future. But souls which are pregnant—for there certainly are men who are more creative in their souls than in their bodies—conceive that which is proper for the soul to conceive or contain. And what are these conceptions?—wisdom and virtue in general. And such creators are poets and all artists who are deserving of the name inventor. But the greatest and fairest sort of wisdom by far is that which is concerned with the ordering of states and families, and which is called temperance and justice. And he who in youth has the seed of these implanted in him and is himself inspired, when he comes to maturity desires to beget and generate. He wanders about seeking beauty that he may beget offspring—for in deformity he will beget nothing—and naturally embraces the beautiful rather than the deformed body; above all when he finds a fair and noble and well-nurtured soul, he embraces the two in one person, and to such an one he is full of speech about virtue and the nature and pursuits of a good man; and he tries to educate him; and at the touch of the beautiful which is ever present to his memory, even when absent, he brings forth that which he had conceived long before, and in company with him tends that which he brings forth; and they are married by a far nearer tie and have a closer friendship than those who beget mortal children, for the children who are their common offspring are fairer and more immortal. Who, when he thinks of Homer and Hesiod and other great poets, would not rather have their children than ordinary human ones? Who would not emulate them in the creation of children such as theirs, which have preserved their memory and given them everlasting glory? Or who would not have such children as Lycurgus left behind him to be the saviours, not only of Lacedaemon, but of Hellas, as one may say? There is Solon,[2] too, who is the revered father of Athenian laws; and many others there are in many other places, both among Hellenes and barbarians, who have given to the world many noble works, and have been the parents of virtue of every kind; and many temples have been raised in their honour for the sake of children such as theirs; which were never raised in honour of any one, for the sake of his mortal children.

'These are the lesser mysteries of love, into which even you, Socrates, may enter; to the greater and more hidden ones which are the crown of these, and to which, if you pursue them in a right spirit, they will lead, I know not whether you will be able to attain. But I will do my utmost to inform you, and do you follow if you can. For he who would proceed aright in this matter should begin in youth to visit beautiful forms; and first, if he be guided by his instructor aright, to love one such form only—out of that he should create fair thoughts; and soon he will of himself perceive that the beauty of one form is akin to the beauty of another; and then if beauty of form in general is his pursuit, how foolish would he be not to recognize that the beauty in every form is and the same! And when he perceives this he will abate his violent love of the one, which he will despise and deem a small thing, and will become a lover of all beautiful forms; in the next stage he will consider that the beauty of the mind is more honourable than the beauty of the outward form. So that if a virtuous soul have but a little comeliness, he will be content to love and tend him, and will search out and bring to the birth thoughts which may improve the young, until he is compelled to contemplate and see the beauty of institutions and laws, and to understand that the beauty of them all is of one family, and that personal beauty is a trifle; and after laws and institutions he will go on to the sciences, that he may see their beauty, being not like a servant in love with the beauty of one youth or man or institution, himself a slave mean and narrow-minded, but drawing towards and contemplating the vast sea of beauty, he will create many fair and noble thoughts and notions in boundless love of wisdom; until on that shore he grows and waxes strong, and at last the vision is revealed to him of a single science, which is the science of beauty everywhere. To this I will proceed; please to give me your very best attention:

'He who has been instructed thus far in the things of love, and who has learned to see the beautiful in due order and succession, when he comes toward the end will suddenly perceive a nature of wondrous beauty (and this, Socrates, is the final cause of all our former toils)—a nature which in the first place is everlasting, not growing and decaying, or waxing and waning; secondly, not fair in one point of view and foul in another, or at one time or in one relation or at one place fair, at another time or in another relation or at another place foul, as if fair to some and foul to others, or in the likeness of a face or hands or any other part of the bodily frame, or in any form of speech or knowledge, or existing in any other being, as for example, in an animal, or in heaven, or in earth, or in any other place; but beauty absolute, separate, simple, and everlasting, which without diminution and without increase, or any change, is imparted to the ever-growing and perishing beauties of all other things. He who from these ascending under the influence of true love, begins to perceive that beauty, is not far from the end. And the true order of going, or being led by another, to the things of love, is to begin from the beauties of earth and mount upwards for the sake of that other beauty, using these as steps only, and from one going on to two, and from two to all fair forms, and from fair forms to fair practices, and from fair practices to fair notions, until from fair notions he arrives at the notion of absolute beauty, and at last knows what the essence of beauty is. This, my dear Socrates,' said the stranger of Mantineia, 'is that life above all others which man should live, in the contemplation of beauty absolute; a beauty which if you once beheld, you would see not to be after the measure of gold, and garments, and fair boys and youths, whose presence now entrances you; and you and many a one would be content to live seeing them only and conversing with them without meat or drink, if that were possible—you only want to look at them and to be with them. But what if man had eyes to see the true beauty—the divine beauty, I mean, pure and clear and unalloyed, not clogged with the pollutions of mortality and all the colours and vanities of human life—thither looking, and holding converse with the true beauty simple and divine? Remember how in that communion only, beholding beauty with the eye of the mind, he will be enabled to bring forth, not images of beauty, but realities (for he has hold not of an image but of a reality), and bringing forth and nourishing true virtue to become the friend of God and be immortal, if mortal man may. Would that be an ignoble life?'

Such, Phaedrus—and I speak not only to you, but to all of you—were the words of Diotima; and I am persuaded of their truth. And being persuaded of them, I try to persuade others, that in the attainment of this end human nature will not easily find a helper better than love: And therefore, also, I say that every man ought to honour him as I myself honour him, and walk in his ways, and exhort others to do the same, and praise the power and spirit of love according to the measure of my ability now and ever.

The words which I have spoken, you, Phaedrus, may call an encomium of love, or anything else which you please.

Translated by B. Jowett.

Philosopher-ruler

Plato, *Republic* 5.471c-480a

The Republic *(a more accurate translation of the title would be the* Constitution*) describes Plato's concept of an ideal state. It addresses politics, philosophy, religion, ethics, and above all education, since, as Plato argues, there cannot be a perfect society as long as leaders are poorly educated. Plato ventures further and earmarks philosophers as the only potentially competent leaders. Thus, the* Republic *is a treatise intended to instruct philosophers on how to become statesmen.*

"Until philosophers are kings, or the kings and princes of this world have the spirit and power of philosophy, and political greatness and wisdom meet in one, cities will never have rest from their evils."

But still I must say, Socrates, that if you are allowed to go on in this way you will entirely forget the other question which at the commencement of this discussion you thrust aside:—Is such an order of things possible, and how, if at all? For I am quite ready to acknowledge that the plan which you propose, if only feasible, would do all sorts of good to the State. I will add, what you have omitted, that your citizens will be the bravest of warriors, and will never leave their ranks, for they will all know one another, and each will call the other father, brother, son; and if you suppose the women to join their armies, whether in the same rank or in the rear, either as a terror to the enemy, or as auxiliaries in case of need, I know that they will then be absolutely invincible; and there are many domestic advantages which might also be mentioned and which I also fully acknowledge: but, as I admit all these advantages and as many more as you please, if only this State of yours were to come into existence, we need say no more about them; assuming then the existence of the State, let us now turn to the question of possibility and ways and means—the rest may be left.

If I loiter for a moment, you instantly make a raid upon me, I said, and have no mercy; I have hardly escaped the first and second waves, and you seem not to be aware that you are now bringing upon me the third, which is the greatest and heaviest. When you have seen and heard the third wave, I think you will be more considerate and will acknowledge that some fear and hesitation was natural respecting a proposal so extraordinary as that which I have now to state and investigate.

The more appeals of this sort which you make, he said, the more determined are we that you shall tell us how such a State is possible: speak out and at once.

Let me begin by reminding you that we found our way hither in the search after justice and injustice.

True, he replied; but what of that?

I was only going to ask whether, if we have discovered them, we are to require that the just man should in nothing fail of absolute justice; or may we be satisfied with an approximation, and the attainment in him of a higher degree of justice than is to be found in other men?

The approximation will be enough.

We were enquiring into the nature of absolute justice and into the character of the perfectly just, and into injustice and the perfectly unjust, that we might have an ideal. We were to look at these in order that we might judge of our own happiness and unhappiness according to the standard which they exhibited and the degree in which we resembled them, but not with any view of showing that they could exist in fact.

True, he said.

Would a painter be any the worse because, after having delineated with consummate art an ideal of a perfectly beautiful man, he was unable to show that any such man could ever have existed?

He would be none the worse.

Well, and were we not creating an ideal of a perfect State?

To be sure.

And is our theory a worse theory because we are unable to prove the possibility of a city being ordered in the manner described?

Surely not, he replied.

That is the truth, I said. But if, at your request, I am to try and show how and under what conditions the possibility is highest, I must ask you, having this in view, to repeat your former admissions.

What admissions?

I want to know whether ideals are ever fully realized in language? Does not the word express more than the fact, and must not the actual, whatever a man may think, always, in the nature of things, fall short of the truth? What do you say?

I agree.

Then you must not insist on my proving that the actual State will in every respect coincide with the ideal: if we are only able to discover how a city may be governed nearly as we proposed, you will admit that we have discovered the possibility which you demand; and will be contented. I am sure that I should be contented—will not you?

Yes, I will.

Let me next endeavour to show what is that fault in States which is the cause of their present maladministration, and what is the least change which will enable a State to pass into the truer form; and let the change, if possible, be of one thing only, or, if not, of two; at any rate, let the changes be as few and slight as possible.

Certainly, he replied.

I think, I said, that there might be a reform of the State if only one change were made, which is not a slight or easy though still a possible one.

What is it? he said.

Now then, I said, I go to meet that which I liken to the greatest of the waves; yet shall the word be spoken, even though the wave break and drown me in laughter and dishonour; and do you mark my words.

Proceed.

I said: 'Until philosophers are kings, or the kings and princes of this world have the spirit and power of philosophy, and political greatness and wisdom meet in one, and those commoner natures who pursue either to the exclusion of the other are compelled to stand aside, cities will never have rest from their evils,—nor the human race, as I believe,—and then only will this our State have a possibility of life and behold the light of day.' Such was the thought, my dear Glaucon, which I would fain have uttered if it had not seemed too extravagant; for to be convinced that in no other State can there be happiness private or public is indeed a hard thing.

Socrates, what do you mean? I would have you consider that the word which you have uttered is one at which numerous persons, and very respectable persons too, in a figure pulling off their coats all in a moment, and seizing any weapon that comes to hand, will run at you might and main, before you know where you are, intending to do heaven knows what; and if you don't prepare an answer, and put yourself in motion, you will be 'pared by their fine wits,' and no mistake.

You got me into the scrape, I said.

And I was quite right; however, I will do all I can to get you out of it; but I can only give you good-will and good advice, and, perhaps, I may be able to fit answers to your questions better than another—that is all. And now, having such an auxiliary, you must do your best to show the unbelievers that you are right.

I ought to try, I said, since you offer me such invaluable assistance. And I think that, if there is to be a chance of our escaping, we must explain to them whom we mean when we say that philosophers are to rule in the State; then we shall be able to defend ourselves: There will be discovered to be some natures who ought to study philosophy and to be leaders in the State; and others who are not born to be philosophers, and are meant to be followers rather than leaders.

Then now for a definition, he said.

Follow me, I said, and I hope that I may in some way or other be able to give you a satisfactory explanation.

Proceed.

I dare say that you remember, and therefore I need not remind you, that a lover, if he is worthy of the name, ought to show his love, not to some one part of that which he loves, but to the whole.

I really do not understand, and therefore beg of you to assist my memory.

Another person, I said, might fairly reply as you do; but a man of pleasure like yourself ought to know that all who are in the flower of youth do somehow or other raise a pang or emotion in a lover's breast, and are thought by him to be worthy of his affectionate regards. Is not this a way which you have with the fair: one has a snub nose, and you praise his charming face; the hook-nose of another has, you say, a royal look; while he who is neither snub nor hooked has the grace of regularity: the dark visage is manly, the fair are children of the gods; and as to the sweet 'honey pale,' as they are called, what is the very name but the invention of a lover who talks in diminutives, and is not averse to paleness if appearing on the cheek of youth? In a word, there is no excuse which you will not make, and nothing which you will not say, in order not to lose a single flower that blooms in the spring-time of youth.

If you make me an authority in matters of love, for the sake of the argument, I assent.

And what do you say of lovers of wine? Do you not see them doing the same? They are glad of any pretext of drinking any wine.

Very good.

And the same is true of ambitious men; if they cannot command an army, they are willing to command a file; and if they cannot be honoured by really great and important persons, they are glad to be honoured by lesser and meaner people,—but honour of some kind they must have.

Exactly.

Once more let me ask: Does he who desires any class of goods, desire the whole class or a part only?

The whole.

And may we not say of the philosopher that he is a lover, not of a part of wisdom only, but of the whole?

Yes, of the whole.

And he who dislikes learning, especially in youth, when he has no power of judging what is good and what is not, such an one we maintain not to be a philosopher or a lover of knowledge, just as he who refuses his food is not hungry, and may be said to have a bad appetite and not a good one?

Very true, he said.

Whereas he who has a taste for every sort of knowledge and who is curious to learn and is never satisfied, may be justly termed a philosopher? Am I not right?

Glaucon said: If curiosity makes a philosopher, you will find many a strange being will have a title to the name. All the lovers of sights have a delight in learning, and must therefore be included. Musical amateurs, too, are a folk strangely out of place among philosophers, for they are the last persons in the world who would come to anything like a philosophical discussion, if they could help, while they run about at the Dionysiac festivals as if they had let out their ears to hear every chorus; whether the performance is in town or country—that makes no difference—they are there. Now are we to maintain that all these and any who have similar tastes, as well as the professors of quite minor arts, are philosophers?

Certainly not, I replied; they are only an imitation.

He said: Who then are the true philosophers?

Those, I said, who are lovers of the vision of truth.

That is also good, he said; but I should like to know what you mean?

To another, I replied, I might have a difficulty in explaining; but I am sure that you will admit a proposition which I am about to make.

What is the proposition?

That since beauty is the opposite of ugliness, they are two?

Certainly.

And inasmuch as they are two, each of them is one?

True again.

And of just and unjust, good and evil, and of every other class, the same remark holds: taken singly, each of them is one; but from the various combinations of them with actions and things and with one another, they are seen in all sorts of lights and appear many?

Very true.

And this is the distinction which I draw between the sight-loving, art-loving, practical class and those of whom I am speaking, and who are alone worthy of the name of philosophers.

How do you distinguish them? he said.

The lovers of sounds and sights, I replied, are, as I conceive, fond of fine tones and colours and forms and all the artificial products that are made out of them, but their mind is incapable of seeing or loving absolute beauty.

True, he replied.

Few are they who are able to attain to the sight of this.

Very true.

And he who, having a sense of beautiful things has no sense of absolute beauty, or who, if another lead him to a knowledge of that beauty is unable to follow—of such an one I ask, Is he awake or in a dream only? Reflect: is not the dreamer, sleeping or waking, one who likens dissimilar things, who puts the copy in the place of the real object?

I should certainly say that such an one was dreaming.

But take the case of the other, who recognises the existence of absolute beauty and is able to distinguish the idea from the objects which participate in the idea, neither putting the objects in the place of the idea nor the idea in the place of the objects—is he a dreamer, or is he awake?

He is wide awake.

And may we not say that the mind of the one who knows has knowledge, and that the mind of the other, who opines only, has opinion?

Certainly.

But suppose that the latter should quarrel with us and dispute our statement, can we administer any soothing cordial or advice to him, without revealing to him that there is sad disorder in his wits?

We must certainly offer him some good advice, he replied.

Come, then, and let us think of something to say to him. Shall we begin by assuring him that he is welcome to any knowledge which he may have, and that we are rejoiced at his having it? But we should like to ask him a question: Does he who has knowledge know something or nothing? You must answer for him.

I answer that he knows something.

Something that is or is not?

Something that is; for how can that which is not ever be known?

And are we assured, after looking at the matter from many points of view, that absolute being is or may be absolutely known, but that the utterly non-existent is utterly unknown?

Nothing can be more certain.

Good. But if there be anything which is of such a nature as to be and not to be, that will have a place intermediate between pure being and the absolute negation of being?

Yes, between them.

And, as knowledge corresponded to being and ignorance of necessity to not-being, for that intermediate between being and not-being there has to be discovered a corresponding intermediate between ignorance and knowledge, if there be such?

Certainly.

Do we admit the existence of opinion?

Undoubtedly.

As being the same with knowledge, or another faculty?

Another faculty.

Then opinion and knowledge have to do with different kinds of matter corresponding to this difference of faculties?

Yes.

And knowledge is relative to being and knows being. But before I proceed further I will make a division.

What division?

I will begin by placing faculties in a class by themselves: they are powers in us, and in all other things, by which we do as we do. Sight and hearing, for example, I should call faculties. Have I clearly explained the class which I mean?

Yes, I quite understand.

Then let me tell you my view about them. I do not see them, and therefore the distinctions of figure, colour, and the like, which enable me to discern the differences of some things, do not apply to them. In speaking of a faculty I think only of its sphere and its result; and that which has the same sphere and the same result I call the same faculty, but that which has another sphere and another result I call different. Would that be your way of speaking?

Yes.

And will you be so very good as to answer one more question? Would you say that knowledge is a faculty, or in what class would you place it?

Certainly knowledge is a faculty, and the mightiest of all faculties.

And is opinion also a faculty?

Certainly, he said; for opinion is that with which we are able to form an opinion.

And yet you were acknowledging a little while ago that knowledge is not the same as opinion?

Why, yes, he said: how can any reasonable being ever identify that which is infallible with that which errs?

An excellent answer, proving, I said, that we are quite conscious of a distinction between them.

Yes.

Then knowledge and opinion having distinct powers have also distinct spheres or subject-matters?

That is certain.

Being is the sphere or subject-matter of knowledge, and knowledge is to know the nature of being?

Yes.

And opinion is to have an opinion?

Yes.

And do we know what we opine? or is the subject-matter of opinion the same as the subject-matter of knowledge?

Nay, he replied, that has been already disproven; if difference in faculty implies difference in the sphere or subject-matter, and if, as we were saying, opinion and knowledge are distinct faculties, then the sphere of knowledge and of opinion cannot be the same.

Then if being is the subject-matter of knowledge, something else must be the subject-matter of opinion?

Yes, something else.

Well then, is not-being the subject-matter of opinion? or, rather, how can there be an opinion at all about not-being? Reflect: when a man has an opinion, has he not an opinion about something? Can he have an opinion which is an opinion about nothing?

Impossible.

He who has an opinion has an opinion about some one thing?

Yes.

And not-being is not one thing but, properly speaking, nothing?

True.

Of not-being, ignorance was assumed to be the necessary correlative; of being, knowledge?

True, he said.
Then opinion is not concerned either with being or with not-being?

Not with either.

And can therefore neither be ignorance nor knowledge?

That seems to be true.

But is opinion to be sought without and beyond either of them, in a greater clearness than knowledge, or in a greater darkness than ignorance?

In neither.

Then I suppose that opinion appears to you to be darker than knowledge, but lighter than ignorance?

Both; and in no small degree.

And also to be within and between them?

Yes.

Then you would infer that opinion is intermediate?

No question.

But were we not saying before, that if anything appeared to be of a sort which is and is not at the same time, that sort of thing would appear also to lie in the interval between pure being and absolute not-being; and that the corresponding faculty is neither knowledge nor ignorance, but will be found in the interval between them?

True.

And in that interval there has now been discovered something which we call opinion?

There has.

Then what remains to be discovered is the object which partakes equally of the nature of being and not-being, and cannot rightly be termed either, pure and simple; this unknown term, when discovered, we may truly call the subject of opinion, and assign each to their proper faculty,—the extremes to the faculties of the extremes and the mean to the faculty of the mean.

True.

This being premised, I would ask the gentleman who is of opinion that there is no absolute or unchangeable idea of beauty—in whose opinion the beautiful is the manifold—he, I say, your lover of beautiful sights, who cannot bear to be told that the beautiful is one, and the just is one, or that anything is one—to him I would appeal, saying, Will you be so very kind, sir, as to tell us whether, of all these beautiful things, there is one which will not be found ugly; or of the just, which will not be found unjust; or of the holy, which will not also be unholy?

No, he replied; the beautiful will in some point of view be found ugly; and the same is true of the rest.

And may not the many which are doubles be also halves?—doubles, that is, of one thing, and halves of another?

Quite true.

And things great and small, heavy and light, as they are termed, will not be denoted by these any more than by the opposite names?

True; both these and the opposite names will always attach to all of them.

And can any one of those many things which are called by particular names be said to be this rather than not to be this?

He replied: They are like the punning riddles which are asked at feasts or the children's puzzle about the eunuch aiming at the bat, with what he hit him, as they say in the puzzle, and upon what the bat was sitting. The individual objects of which I am speaking are also a riddle, and have a double sense: nor can you fix them in your mind, either as being or not-being, or both, or neither.

Then what will you do with them? I said. Can they have a better place than between being and not-being? For they are clearly not in greater darkness or negation than not-being, or more full of light and existence than being.

That is quite true, he said.

Thus then we seem to have discovered that the many ideas which the multitude entertain about the beautiful and about all other things are tossing about in some region which is half-way between pure being and pure not-being?

We have.

Yes; and we had before agreed that anything of this kind which we might find was to be described as matter of opinion, and not as matter of knowledge; being the intermediate flux which is caught and detained by the intermediate faculty.

Quite true.

Then those who see the many beautiful, and who yet neither see absolute beauty, nor can follow any guide who points the way thither; who see the many just, and not absolute justice, and the like,—such persons may be said to have opinion but not knowledge?

That is certain.

But those who see the absolute and eternal and immutable may be said to know, and not to have opinion only?

Neither can that be denied.

The one love and embrace the subjects of knowledge, the other those of opinion? The latter are the same, as I dare say you will remember, who listened to sweet sounds and gazed upon fair colours, but would not tolerate the existence of absolute beauty.

Yes, I remember.

Shall we then be guilty of any impropriety in calling them lovers of opinion rather than lovers of wisdom, and will they be very angry with us for thus describing them?

I shall tell them not to be angry; no man should be angry at what is true.

But those who love the truth in each thing are to be called lovers of wisdom and not lovers of opinion.

Assuredly.

Translated by B. Jowett.

Analogy of the Cave

Plato, *Republic* 7.514a-521b

What does Socrates attempt to explain in the myth of the cave? That philosophers are misunderstood. The ignorant, who perceive themselves as all knowledgeable but are in fact fooled by appearances, reject philosophers who alone understand the true nature of things. Upon attaining knowledge, however, philosophers are required to return among the ignorant to try to teach them, for leaving one's fellow citizens in ignorance is considered a crime.

Socrates tried in vain to bring both the light and the knowledge of truth to his contemporaries. His citizens so badly misunderstood him that they forced him to take his own life in 399 BC.

"The State in which the rulers are most reluctant to govern is always the best and most quietly governed, and the State in which they are most eager, the worst."

And now, I said, let me show in a figure how far our nature is enlightened or unenlightened:—Behold! human beings living in a underground den, which has a mouth open towards the light and reaching all along the den; here they have been from their childhood, and have their legs and necks chained so that they cannot move, and can only see before them, being prevented by the chains from turning round their heads. Above and behind them a fire is blazing at a distance, and between the fire and the prisoners there is a raised way; and you will see, if you look, a low wall built along the way, like the screen which marionette players have in front of them, over which they show the puppets.

I see.

And do you see, I said, men passing along the wall carrying all sorts of vessels, and statues and figures of animals made of wood and stone and various materials, which appear over the wall? Some of them are talking, others silent.

You have shown me a strange image, and they are strange prisoners.

Like ourselves, I replied; and they see only their own shadows, or the shadows of one another, which the fire throws on the opposite wall of the cave?

True, he said; how could they see anything but the shadows if they were never allowed to move their heads?

And of the objects which are being carried in like manner they would only see the shadows?

Yes, he said.

And if they were able to converse with one another, would they not suppose that they were naming what was actually before them?

Very true.

And suppose further that the prison had an echo which came from the other side, would they not be sure to fancy when one of the passers-by spoke that the voice which they heard came from the passing shadow?

No question, he replied.

To them, I said, the truth would be literally nothing but the shadows of the images.

That is certain.

And now look again, and see what will naturally follow if the prisoners are released and disabused of their error. At first, when any of them is liberated and compelled suddenly to stand up and turn his neck round and walk and look towards the light, he will suffer sharp pains; the glare will distress him, and he will be unable to see the realities of which in his former state he had seen the shadows; and then conceive some one saying to him, that what he saw before was an illusion, but that now, when he is approaching nearer to being and his eye is turned towards more real existence, he has a clearer vision,—what will be his reply? And you may further imagine that his instructor is pointing to the objects as they pass and requiring him to name them,—will he not be perplexed? Will he not fancy that the shadows which he formerly saw are truer than the objects which are now shown to him?

Far truer.

And if he is compelled to look straight at the light, will he not have a pain in his eyes which will make him turn away to take refuge in the objects of vision which he can see, and which he will conceive to be in reality clearer than the things which are now being shown to him?

True, he said.

And suppose once more, that he is reluctantly dragged up a steep and rugged ascent, and held fast until he is forced into the presence of the sun himself, is he not likely to be pained and irritated? When he approaches the light his eyes will be dazzled, and he will not be able to see anything at all of what are now called realities.

Not all in a moment, he said.

He will require to grow accustomed to the sight of the upper world. And first he will see the shadows best, next the reflections of men and other objects in the water, and then the objects themselves; then he will gaze upon the light of the moon and the stars and the spangled heaven; and he will see the sky and the stars by night better than the sun or the light of the sun by day?

Certainly.

Last of all he will be able to see the sun, and not mere reflections of him in the water, but he will see him in his own proper place, and not in another; and he will contemplate him as he is.

Certainly.

He will then proceed to argue that this is he who gives the season and the years, and is the guardian of all that is in the visible world, and in a certain way the cause of all things which he and his fellows have been accustomed to behold?

Clearly, he said, he would first see the sun and then reason about him.

And when he remembered his old habitation, and the wisdom of the den and his fellow-prisoners, do you not suppose that he would felicitate himself on the change, and pity them?

Certainly, he would.

And if they were in the habit of conferring honours among themselves on those who were quickest to observe the passing shadows and to remark which of them went before, and which followed after, and which were together; and who were therefore best able to draw conclusions as to the future, do you think that he would care for such honours and glories, or envy the possessors of them? Would he not say with Homer,

> 'Better to be the poor servant of a poor master,'

and to endure anything, rather than think as they do and live after their manner?

Yes, he said, I think that he would rather suffer anything than entertain these false notions and live in this miserable manner.

Imagine once more, I said, such an one coming suddenly out of the sun to be replaced in his old situation; would he not be certain to have his eyes full of darkness?

To be sure, he said.

And if there were a contest, and he had to compete in measuring the shadows with the prisoners who had never moved out of the den, while his sight was still weak, and before his eyes had become steady (and the time which would be needed to acquire this new habit of sight might be very considerable), would he not be ridiculous? Men would say of him that up he went and down he came without his eyes; and that it was better not even to think of ascending; and if any one tried to loose another and lead him up to the light, let them only catch the offender, and they would put him to death.

No question, he said.

This entire allegory, I said, you may now append, dear Glaucon, to the previous argument; the prison-house is the world of sight, the light of the fire is the sun, and you will not misapprehend me if you interpret the journey upwards to be the ascent of the soul into the intellectual world according to my poor belief, which, at your desire, I have expressed—whether rightly or wrongly God knows. But, whether true or false, my opinion is that in the world of knowledge the idea of good appears last of all, and is seen only with an effort; and, when seen, is also inferred to be the universal author of all things beautiful and right, parent of light and of the lord of light in this visible world, and the immediate source of reason and truth in the intellectual; and that this is the power upon which he who would act rationally either in public or private life must have his eye fixed.

I agree, he said, as far as I am able to understand you.

Moreover, I said, you must not wonder that those who attain to this beatific vision are unwilling to descend to human affairs; for their souls are ever hastening into the upper world where they desire to dwell; which desire of theirs is very natural, if our allegory may be trusted.

Yes, very natural.

And is there anything surprising in one who passes from divine contemplations to the evil state of man, misbehaving himself in a ridiculous manner; if, while his eyes are blinking and before he has become accustomed to the surrounding darkness, he is compelled to fight in courts of law, or in other places, about the images or the shadows of images of justice, and is endeavouring to meet the conceptions of those who have never yet seen absolute justice?

Anything but surprising, he replied.

Any one who has common sense will remember that the bewilderments of the eyes are of two kinds, and arise from two causes, either from coming out of the light or from going into the light, which is true of the mind's eye, quite as much as of the bodily eye; and he who remembers this when he sees any one whose vision is perplexed and weak, will not be too ready to laugh; he will first ask whether that soul of man has come out of the brighter life, and is unable to see because unaccustomed to the dark, or having turned from darkness to the day is dazzled by excess of light. And he will count the one happy in his condition and state of being, and he will pity the other; or, if he have a mind to laugh at the soul which comes from below into the light, there will be more reason in this than in the laugh which greets him who returns from above out of the light into the den.

That, he said, is a very just distinction.

But then, if I am right, certain professors of education must be wrong when they say that they can put a knowledge into the soul which was not there before, like sight into blind eyes.

They undoubtedly say this, he replied.

Whereas, our argument shows that the power and capacity of learning exists in the soul already; and that just as the eye was unable to turn from darkness to light without the whole body, so too the instrument of knowledge can only by the movement of the whole soul be turned from the world of becoming into that of being, and learn by degrees to endure the sight of being, and of the brightest and best of being, or in other words, of the good.

Very true.

And must there not be some art which will effect conversion in the easiest and quickest manner; not implanting the faculty of sight, for that exists already, but has been turned in the wrong direction, and is looking away from the truth?

Yes, he said, such an art may be presumed.

And whereas the other so-called virtues of the soul seem to be akin to bodily qualities, for even when they are not originally innate they can be implanted later by habit and exercise, the virtue of wisdom more than anything else contains a divine element which always remains, and by this conversion is rendered useful and profitable; or, on the other hand, hurtful and useless. Did you never observe the narrow intelligence flashing from the keen eye of a clever rogue—how eager he is, how clearly his paltry soul sees the way to his end; he is the reverse of blind, but his keen eye-sight is forced into the service of evil, and he is mischievous in proportion to his cleverness?

Very true, he said.

But what if there had been a circumcision of such natures in the days of their youth; and they had been severed from those sensual pleasures, such as eating and drinking, which, like leaden weights, were attached to them at their birth, and which drag them down and turn the vision of their souls upon the things that are below—if, I say, they had been released from these impediments and turned in the opposite direction, the very same faculty in them would have seen the truth as keenly as they see what their eyes are turned to now.

Very likely.

Yes, I said; and there is another thing which is likely, or rather a necessary inference from what has preceded, that neither the uneducated and uninformed of the truth, nor yet those who never make an end of their education, will be able ministers of State; not the former, because they have no single aim of duty which is the rule of all their actions, private as well as public; nor the latter, because they will not act at all except upon compulsion, fancying that they are already dwelling apart in the islands of the blest.

Very true, he replied.

Then, I said, the business of us who are the founders of the State will be to compel the best minds to attain that knowledge which we have already shown to be the greatest of all—they must continue to ascend until they arrive at the good; but when they have ascended and seen enough we must not allow them to do as they do now.

What do you mean?

I mean that they remain in the upper world: but this must not be allowed; they must be made to descend again among the prisoners in the den, and partake of their labours and honours, whether they are worth having or not.

But is not this unjust? he said; ought we to give them a worse life, when they might have a better?

You have again forgotten, my friend, I said, the intention of the legislator, who did not aim at making any one class in the State happy above the rest; the happiness was to be in the whole State, and he held the citizens together by persuasion and necessity, making them benefactors of the State, and therefore benefactors of one another; to this end he created them, not to please themselves, but to be his instruments in binding up the State.

True, he said, I had forgotten.

Observe, Glaucon, that there will be no injustice in compelling our philosophers to have a care and providence of others; we shall explain to them that in other States, men of their class are not obliged to share in the toils of politics: and this is reasonable, for they grow up at their own sweet will, and the government would rather not have them. Being self-taught, they cannot be expected to show any gratitude for a culture which they have never received. But we have brought you into the world to be rulers of the hive, kings of yourselves and of the other citizens, and have educated you far better and more perfectly than they have been educated, and you are better able to share in the double duty. Wherefore each of you, when his turn comes, must go down to the general underground abode, and get the habit of seeing in the dark. When you have acquired the habit, you will see ten thousand times better than the inhabitants of the den, and you will know what the several images are, and what they represent, because you have seen the beautiful and just and good in their truth. And thus our State, which is also yours, will be a reality, and not a dream only, and will be administered in a spirit unlike that of other States, in which men fight with one another about shadows only and are distracted in the struggle for power, which in their eyes is a great good. Whereas the truth is that the State in which the rulers are most reluctant to govern is always the best and most quietly governed, and the State in which they are most eager, the worst.

Quite true, he replied.

And will our pupils, when they hear this, refuse to take their turn at the toils of State, when they are allowed to spend the greater part of their time with one another in the heavenly light?

Impossible, he answered; for they are just men, and the commands which we impose upon them are just; there can be no doubt that every one of them will take office as a stern necessity, and not after the fashion of our present rulers of State.

Yes, my friend, I said; and there lies the point. You must contrive for your future rulers another and a better life than that of a ruler, and then you may have a well-ordered State; for only in the State which offers this, will they rule who are truly rich, not in silver and gold, but in virtue and wisdom, which are the true blessings of life. Whereas if they go to the administration of public affairs, poor and hungering after their own private advantage, thinking that hence they are to snatch the chief good, order there can never be; for they will be fighting about office, and the civil and domestic broils which thus arise will be the ruin of the rulers themselves and of the whole State.

Most true, he replied.

And the only life which looks down upon the life of political ambition is that of true philosophy. Do you know of any other?

Indeed, I do not, he said.

And those who govern ought not to be lovers of the task? For, if they are, there will be rival lovers, and they will fight.

No question.

Who then are those whom we shall compel to be guardians? Surely they will be the men who are wisest about affairs of State, and by whom the State is best administered, and who at the same time have other honours and another and a better life than that of politics?

They are the men, and I will choose them, he replied.

Translated by B. Jowett.

Atlantis

Plato, *Critias* 113c-121c

According to Plato's dialogue, Critias, *Atlantis was a colossal island that existed more than 11,000 years ago. Its location was well beyond Hercules' columns (or the Strait of Gibraltar) in the Atlantic Ocean. The island was originally known for its wealth and for its unprecedented influence. Most importantly, it was the domain of the god Poseidon. Yet the culture of Atlantis degenerated to the point that it was defeated by the Athenians.*

Atlantis no longer exists. Some argue that it lies at the bottom of the Atlantic Ocean, while others believe that it is entirely the creation of Plato's imagination. The Critias *itself is unfinished and abruptly stops halfway through the narrative. Did Plato's death prevent him from completing his work, or did the philosopher simply take no further pains to finish his fantastic story?*

The person who speaks here is Critias, who has learned of Atlantis from an Athenian sage, Solon, who himself had been instructed by Egyptian priests famous for their ancient wisdom.

"They despised everything but virtue, caring little for their present state of life, and thinking lightly of the possession of gold and other property, which seemed only a burden to them; neither were they intoxicated by luxury; nor did wealth deprive them of their self-control; but they were sober, and saw clearly that all these goods are increased by virtue and friendship with one another, whereas by too great regard and respect for them, they are lost and friendship with them."

I have before remarked in speaking of the allotments of the gods, that they distributed the whole earth into portions differing in extent, and made for themselves temples and instituted sacrifices. And Poseidon, receiving for his lot the island of Atlantis, begat children by a mortal woman, and settled them in a part of the island, which I will describe. Looking towards the sea, but in the centre of the whole island, there was a plain which is said to have been the fairest of all plains and very fertile. Near the plain again, and also in the centre of the island at a distance of about fifty stadia,[3] there was a mountain not very high on any side. In this mountain there dwelt one of the earth-born primeval men of that country, whose name was Evenor, and he had a wife named Leucippe, and they had an only daughter who was called Cleito. The maiden had already reached womanhood, when her father and mother died;

Poseidon fell in love with her and had intercourse with her, and breaking the ground, inclosed the hill in which she dwelt all round, making alternate zones of sea and land larger and smaller, encircling one another; there were two of land and three of water, which he turned as with a lathe, each having its circumference equidistant every way from the centre, so that no man could get to the island, for ships and voyages were not as yet. He himself, being a god, found no difficulty in making special arrangements for the centre island, bringing up two springs of water from beneath the earth, one of warm water and the other of cold, and making every variety of food to spring up abundantly from the soil.

He also begat and brought up five pairs of twin male children; and dividing the island of Atlantis into ten portions, he gave to the first-born of the eldest pair his mother's dwelling and the surrounding allotment, which was the largest and best, and made him king over the rest; the others he made princes, and gave them rule over many men, and a large territory. And he named them all; the eldest, who was the first king, he named Atlas, and after him the whole island and the ocean were called Atlantic. To his twin brother, who was born after him, and obtained as his lot the extremity of the island towards the pillars of Heracles, facing the country which is now called the region of Gades in that part of the world, he gave the name which in the Hellenic language is Eumelus, in the language of the country which is named after him, Gadeirus. Of the second pair of twins he called one Ampheres, and the other Evaemon. To the elder of the third pair of twins he gave the name Mneseus, and Autochthon to the one who followed him. Of the fourth pair of twins he called the elder Elasippus, and the younger Mestor. And of the fifth pair he gave to the elder the name of Azaes, and to the younger that of Diaprepes. All these and their descendants for many generations were the inhabitants and rulers of divers islands in the open sea; and also, as has been already said, they held sway in our direction over the country within the pillars as far as Egypt and Tyrrhenia.[4]

Now Atlas had a numerous and honourable family, and they retained the kingdom, the eldest son handing it on to his eldest for many generations; and they had such an amount of wealth as was never before possessed by kings and potentates, and is not likely ever to be again, and they were furnished with everything which they needed, both in the city and country. For because of the greatness of their empire many things were brought to them from foreign countries, and the island itself provided most of what was required by them for the uses of life. In the first place, they dug out of the earth whatever was to be found there, solid as well as fusile, and that which is now only a name and was then something more than a name, orichalcum, was dug out of the earth in many parts of the island, being more precious in those days than anything except gold. There was an abundance of wood for carpenter's work, and sufficient maintenance for tame and wild animals. Moreover, there were a great number of elephants in the island; for as there was provision for all other sorts of animals, both for those which live in lakes and marshes and rivers, and also for those which live in mountains and on plains, so there was for the animal which is the largest and most voracious of all. Also whatever fragrant things there now are in the earth, whether roots, or herbage, or woods, or essences which distil from fruit and flower, grew and thrived in that land; also the fruit which admits of cultivation, both the dry sort, which is given us for nourishment and any other which we use for food—we call them all by the common name of pulse, and the fruits having a hard rind, affording drinks and meats and ointments, and good store of chestnuts and the like, which furnish pleasure and amusement, and are fruits which spoil with keeping, and the pleasant kinds of dessert, with which we console ourselves after dinner, when we are tired of eating—all these that sacred island which then beheld the light of the sun, brought forth fair and wondrous and in infinite abundance. With such blessings the earth freely furnished them; meanwhile they went on constructing their temples and palaces and harbours and docks. And they arranged the whole country in the following manner:—

First of all they bridged over the zones of sea which surrounded the ancient metropolis, making a road to and from the royal palace. And at the very beginning they built the palace in the habitation of the god and of their ancestors, which they continued to ornament in successive generations, every king surpassing the one who went before him to the utmost of his power, until they made the building a marvel to behold for size and for beauty. And beginning from the sea they bored a canal of three hundred feet in width and one hundred feet in depth and fifty stadia in length, which they carried through to the outermost zone, making a passage from the sea up to this, which became a harbour, and leaving an opening sufficient to enable the largest vessels to find ingress. Moreover, they divided at the bridges the zones of land which parted the zones of sea, leaving room for a single trireme to pass out of one zone into another, and they covered over the channels so as to leave a way underneath for the ships; for the banks were raised considerably above the water. Now the largest of the zones into which a passage was cut from the sea was three stadia in breadth, and the zone of land which came next of equal breadth; but the next two zones, the one of water, the other of land, were two stadia, and the one which surrounded the central island was a stadium only in width. The island in which the palace was situated had a diameter of five stadia. All this including the zones and the bridge, which was the sixth part of a stadium in width, they surrounded by a stone wall on every side, placing towers and gates on the bridges where the sea passed in.

The stone which was used in the work they quarried from underneath the centre island, and from underneath the zones, on the outer as well as the inner side. One kind was white, another black, and a third red, and as they quarried, they at the same time hollowed out double docks, having roofs formed out of the native rock. Some of their buildings were simple, but in others they put together different stones, varying the colour to please the eye, and to be a natural source of delight. The entire circuit of the wall, which went round the outermost zone, they covered with a coating of brass, and the circuit of the next wall they coated with tin, and the third, which encompassed the citadel, flashed with the red light of orichalcum. The palaces in the interior of the citadel were constructed on this wise:—In the centre was a holy temple dedicated to Cleito and Poseidon, which remained inaccessible, and was surrounded by an enclosure of gold; this was the spot where the family of the ten princes first saw the light, and thither the people annually brought the fruits of the earth in their season from all the ten portions, to be an offering to each of the ten.

Here was Poseidon's own temple which was a stadium in length, and half a stadium in width,[5] and of a proportionate height, having a strange barbaric appearance. All the outside of the temple, with the exception of the pinnacles, they covered with silver, and the pinnacles with gold. In the interior of the temple the roof was of ivory, curiously wrought everywhere with gold and silver and orichalcum; and all the other parts, the walls and pillars and floor, they coated with orichalcum. In the temple they placed statues of gold: there was the god himself standing in a chariot—the charioteer of six winged horses—and of such a size that he touched the roof of the building with his head; around him there were a hundred Nereids riding on dolphins, for such was thought to be the number of them by the men of those days. There were also in the interior of the temple other images which had been dedicated by private persons. And around the temple on the outside were placed statues of gold of all the descendants of the ten kings and of their wives, and there were many other great offerings of kings and of private persons, coming both from the city itself and from the foreign cities over which they held sway. There was an altar too, which in size and workmanship corresponded to this magnificence, and the palaces, in like manner, answered to the greatness of the kingdom and the glory of the temple.

In the next place, they had fountains, one of cold and another of hot water, in gracious plenty flowing; and they were wonderfully adapted for use by reason of the pleasantness and excellence of their waters. They constructed buildings about them and planted suitable trees, also they made cisterns, some open to the heaven, others roofed over, to be used in winter as warm baths; there were the kings' baths, and the baths of private persons, which were kept apart; and there were separate baths for women, and for horses and cattle, and to each of them they gave as much adornment as was suitable. Of the water which ran off they carried some to the grove of Poseidon, where were growing all manner of trees of wonderful height and beauty, owing to the excellence of the soil, while the remainder was conveyed by aqueducts along the bridges to the outer circles; and there were many temples built and dedicated to many gods; also gardens and places of exercise, some for men, and others for horses in both of the two islands formed by the zones; and in the centre of the larger of the two there was set apart a race-course of a stadium in width, and in length allowed to extend all round the island, for horses to race in. Also there were guard-houses at intervals for the guards, the more trusted of whom were appointed to keep watch in the lesser zone, which was nearer the Acropolis; while the most trusted of all had houses given them within the citadel, near the persons of the kings. The docks were full of triremes and naval stores, and all things were quite ready for use. Enough of the plan of the royal palace.

Leaving the palace and passing out across the three harbours, you came to a wall which began at the sea and went all round: this was everywhere distant fifty stadia from the largest zone or harbour, and enclosed the whole, the ends meeting at the mouth of the channel which led to the sea. The entire area was densely crowded with habitations; and the canal and the largest of the harbours were full of vessels and merchants coming from all parts, who, from their numbers, kept up a multitudinous sound of human voices, and din and clatter of all sorts night and day.

I have described the city and the environs of the ancient palace nearly in the words of Solon, and now I must endeavour to represent to you the nature and arrangement of the rest of the land. The whole country was said by him to be very lofty and precipitous on the side of the sea, but the country immediately about and surrounding the city was a level plain, itself surrounded by mountains which descended towards the sea; it was smooth and even, and of an oblong shape, extending in one direction three thousand stadia, but across the centre inland it was two thousand stadia. This part of the island looked towards the south, and was sheltered from the north. The surrounding mountains were celebrated for their number and size and beauty, far beyond any which still exist, having in them also many wealthy villages of country folk, and rivers, and lakes, and meadows supplying food enough for every animal, wild or tame, and much wood of various sorts, abundant for each and every kind of work.

I will now describe the plain, as it was fashioned by nature and by the labours of many generations of kings through long ages. It was for the most part rectangular and oblong, and where falling out of the straight line followed the circular ditch. The depth, and width, and length of this ditch were incredible, and gave the impression that a work of such extent, in addition to so many others, could never have been artificial. Nevertheless I must say what I was told. It was excavated to the depth of a hundred feet, and its breadth was a stadium everywhere; it was carried round the whole of the plain, and was ten thousand stadia in length. It received the streams which came down from the mountains, and winding round the plain and meeting at the city, was there let off into the sea. Further inland, likewise, straight canals of a hundred feet in width were cut from it through the plain, and again let off into the ditch leading to the sea: these canals were at intervals of a hundred stadia, and by them they brought down the wood from the mountains to the city, and conveyed the fruits of the earth in ships, cutting transverse passages from one canal into another, and to the city. Twice in the year they gathered the fruits of the earth—in winter having the benefit of the rains of heaven, and in summer the water which the land supplied by introducing streams from the canals.

As to the population, each of the lots in the plain had to find a leader for the men who were fit for military service, and the size of a lot was a square of ten stadia each way, and the total number of all the lots was sixty thousand. And of the inhabitants of the mountains and of the rest of the country there was also a vast multitude, which was distributed among the lots and had leaders assigned to them according to their districts and villages. The leader was required to furnish for the war the sixth portion of a war-chariot, so as to make up a total of ten thousand chariots; also two horses and riders for them, and a pair of chariot-horses without a seat, accompanied by a horseman who could fight on foot carrying a small shield, and having a charioteer who stood behind the man-at-arms to guide the two horses; also, he was bound to furnish two heavy-armed soldiers, two archers, two slingers, three stone-shooters and three javelin-men, who were light-armed, and four sailors to make up the complement of twelve hundred ships. Such was the military order of the royal city—the order of the other nine governments varied, and it would be wearisome to recount their several differences.

As to offices and honours, the following was the arrangement from the first. Each of the ten kings in his own division and in his own city had the absolute control of the citizens, and, in most cases, of the laws, punishing and slaying whomsoever he would. Now the order of precedence among them and their mutual relations were regulated by the commands of Poseidon which the law had handed down. These were inscribed by the first kings on a pillar of orichalcum, which was situated in the middle of the island, at the temple of Poseidon, whither the kings were gathered together every fifth and every sixth year alternately, thus giving equal honour to the odd and to the even number. And when they were gathered together they consulted about their common interests, and enquired if any one had transgressed in anything, and passed judgment, and before they passed judgment they gave their pledges to one another on this wise:—There were bulls who had the range of the temple of Poseidon; and the ten kings, being left alone in the temple, after they had offered prayers to the god that they might capture the victim which was acceptable to him, hunted the bulls, without weapons, but with staves and nooses; and the bull which they caught they led up to the pillar and cut its throat over the top of it so that the blood fell upon the sacred inscription. Now on the pillar, besides the laws, there was inscribed an oath invoking mighty curses on the disobedient. When therefore, after slaying the bull in the accustomed manner, they had burnt its limbs, they filled a bowl of wine and cast in a clot of blood for each of them; the rest of the victim they put in the fire, after having purified the column all round. Then they drew from the bowl in golden cups, and pouring a libation on the fire, they swore that they would judge according to the laws on the pillar, and would punish him who in any point had already transgressed them, and that for the future they would not, if they could help, offend against the writing on the pillar, and would neither command others, nor obey any ruler who commanded them, to act otherwise than according to the laws of their father Poseidon. This was the prayer which each of them offered up for himself and for his descendants, at the same time drinking and dedicating the cup out of which he drank in the temple of the god; and after they had supped and satisfied their needs, when darkness came on, and the fire about the sacrifice was cool, all of them put on most beautiful azure robes, and, sitting on the ground, at night, over the embers of the sacrifices by which they had sworn, and extinguishing all the fire about the temple, they received and gave judgment, if any of them had an accusation to bring against any one; and when they had given judgment, at daybreak they wrote down their sentences on a golden tablet, and dedicated it together with their robes to be a memorial.

There were many special laws affecting the several kings inscribed about the temples, but the most important was the following: They were not to take up arms against one another, and they were all to come to the rescue if any one in any of their cities attempted to overthrow the royal house; like their ancestors, they were to deliberate in common about war and other matters, giving the supremacy to the descendants of Atlas. And the king was not to have the power of life and death over any of his kinsmen unless he had the assent of the majority of the ten.

Such was the vast power which the god settled in the lost island of Atlantis; and this he afterwards directed against our land for the following reasons, as tradition tells. For many generations, as long as the divine nature lasted in them, they were obedient to the laws, and well-affectioned towards the god, whose seed they were; for they possessed true and in every way great spirits, uniting gentleness with wisdom in the various chances of life, and in their intercourse with one another. They despised everything but virtue, caring little for their present state of life, and thinking lightly of the possession of gold and other property, which seemed only a burden to them; neither were they intoxicated by luxury; nor did wealth deprive them of their self-control; but they were sober, and saw clearly that all these goods are increased by virtue and friendship with one another, whereas by too great regard and respect for them, they are lost and friendship with them. By such reflections and by the continuance in them of a divine nature, the qualities which we have described grew and increased among them; but when the divine portion began to fade away, and became diluted too often and too much with the mortal admixture, and the human nature got the upper hand, they then, being unable to bear their fortune, behaved unseemly, and to him who had an eye to see grew visibly debased, for they were losing the fairest of their precious gifts; but to those who had no eye to see the true happiness, they appeared glorious and blessed at the very time when they were full of avarice and unrighteous power. Zeus, the god of gods, who rules according to law, and is able to see into such things, perceiving that an honourable race was in a woeful plight, and wanting to inflict punishment on them, that they might be chastened and improve, collected all the gods into their most holy habitation, which, being placed in the centre of the world, beholds all created things. And when he had called them together, he spake as follows—

Translated by B. Jowett.

Last Moments of Socrates

Plato, *Phaedo* 114d-118a

The Phaedo *is the story of Socrates' last moments in prison at Athens, where he is surrounded by his disciples and friends. In this excerpt, the philosopher is about to drink hemlock and thereby sets an example of a dignified and serene death.*

"Then raising the cup to his lips, quite readily and cheerfully he drank off the poison. And hitherto most of us had been able to control our sorrow; but now when we saw him drinking, and saw too that he had finished the draught, we could no longer forbear, and in spite of myself my own tears were flowing fast; so that I covered my face and wept, not for him, but at the thought of my own calamity in having to part from such a friend."

Wherefore, Simmias, seeing all these things, what ought not we to do that we may obtain virtue and wisdom in this life? Fair is the prize, and the hope great!

A man of sense ought not to say, nor will I be very confident, that the description which I have given of the soul and her mansions is exactly true. But I do say that, inasmuch as the soul is shown to be immortal, he may venture to think, not improperly or unworthily, that something of the kind is true. The venture is a glorious one, and he ought to comfort himself with words like these, which is the reason why I lengthen out the tale. Wherefore, I say, let a man be of good cheer about his soul, who having cast away the pleasures and ornaments of the body as alien to him and working harm rather than good, has sought after the pleasures of knowledge; and has arrayed the soul, not in some foreign attire, but in her own proper jewels, temperance, and justice, and courage, and nobility, and truth—in these adorned she is ready to go on her journey to the world below, when her hour comes. You, Simmias and Cebes, and all other men, will depart at some time or other. Me already, as the tragic poet would say, the voice of fate calls. Soon I must drink the poison; and I think that I had better repair to the bath first, in order that the women may not have the trouble of washing my body after I am dead.

When he had done speaking, Crito said: And have you any commands for us, Socrates—anything to say about your children, or any other matter in which we can serve you?

Nothing particular, Crito, he replied: only, as I have always told you, take care of yourselves; that is a service which you may be ever rendering to me and mine and to all of us, whether you promise to do so or not. But if you have no thought for yourselves, and care not to walk according to the rule which I have prescribed for you, not now for the first time, however much you may profess or promise at the moment, it will be of no avail.

We will do our best, said Crito: And in what way shall we bury you? In any way that you like; but you must get hold of me, and take care that I do not run away from you. Then he turned to us, and added with a smile:—I cannot make Crito believe that I am the same Socrates who have been talking and conducting the argument; he fancies that I am the other Socrates whom he will soon see, a dead body—and he asks, How shall he bury me? And though I have spoken many words in the endeavour to show that when I have drunk the poison I shall leave you and go to the joys of the blessed,— these words of mine, with which I was comforting you and myself, have had, as I perceive, no effect upon Crito. And therefore I want you to be surety for me to him now, as at the trial he was surety to the judges for me: but let the promise be of another sort; for he was surety for me to the judges that I would remain, and you must be my surety to him that I shall not remain, but go away and depart; and then he will suffer less at my death, and not be grieved when he sees my body being burned or buried. I would not have him sorrow at my hard lot, or say at the burial, Thus we lay out Socrates, or, Thus we follow him to the grave or bury him; for false words are not only evil in themselves, but they infect the soul with evil. Be of good cheer, then, my dear Crito, and say that you are burying my body only, and do with that whatever is usual, and what you think best.

When he had spoken these words, he arose and went into a chamber to bathe; Crito followed him and told us to wait. So we remained behind, talking and thinking of the subject of discourse, and also of the greatness of our sorrow; he was like a father of whom we were being bereaved, and we were about to pass the rest of our lives as orphans. When he had taken the bath his children were brought to him—(he had two young sons and an elder one); and the women of his family also came, and he talked to them and gave them a few directions in the presence of Crito; then he dismissed them and returned to us.

Now the hour of sunset was near, for a good deal of time had passed while he was within. When he came out, he sat down with us again after his bath, but not much was said. Soon the jailer, who was the servant of the Eleven,[6] entered and stood by him, saying:—To you, Socrates, whom I know to be the noblest and gentlest and best of all who ever came to this place, I will not impute the angry feelings of other men, who rage and swear at me, when, in obedience to the authorities, I bid them drink the poison—indeed, I am sure that you will not be angry with me; for others, as you are aware, and not I, are to blame. And so fare you well, and try to bear lightly what must needs be—you know my errand. Then bursting into tears he turned away and went out.

Socrates looked at him and said: I return your good wishes, and will do as you bid. Then turning to us, he said, How charming the man is: since I have been in prison he has always been coming to see me, and at times he would talk to me, and was as good to me as could be, and now see how generously he sorrows on my account. We must do as he says, Crito; and therefore let the cup be brought, if the poison is prepared: if not, let the attendant prepare some.

Yet, said Crito, the sun is still upon the hill-tops, and I know that many a one has taken the draught late, and after the announcement has been made to him, he has eaten and drunk, and enjoyed the society of his beloved; do not hurry—there is time enough.

Socrates said: Yes, Crito, and they of whom you speak are right in so acting, for they think that they will be gainers by the delay; but I am right in not following their example, for I do not think that I should gain anything by drinking the poison a little later; I should only be ridiculous in my own eyes for sparing and saving a life which is already forfeit. Please then to do as I say, and not to refuse me.

Crito made a sign to the servant, who was standing by; and he went out, and having been absent for some time, returned with the jailer carrying the cup of poison. Socrates said: You, my good friend, who are experienced in these matters, shall give me directions how I am to proceed. The man answered: You have only to walk about until your legs are heavy, and then to lie down, and the poison will act. At the same time he handed the cup to Socrates, who in the easiest and gentlest manner, without the least fear or change of colour or feature, looking at the man with all his eyes, Echecrates, as his manner was, took the cup and said: What do you say about making a libation out of this cup to any god? May I, or not? The man answered: We only prepare, Socrates, just so much as we deem enough. I understand, he said: but I may and must ask the gods to prosper my journey from this to the other world—even so—and so be it according to my prayer. Then raising the cup to his lips, quite readily and cheerfully he drank off the poison. And hitherto most of us had been able to control our sorrow; but now when we saw him drinking, and saw too that he had finished the draught, we could no longer forbear, and in spite of myself my own tears were flowing fast; so that I covered my face and wept, not for him, but at the thought of my own calamity in having to part from such a friend. Nor was I the first; for Crito, when he found himself unable to restrain his tears, had got up, and I followed; and at that moment, Apollodorus, who had been weeping all the time, broke out in a loud and passionate cry which made cowards of us all. Socrates alone retained his calmness: What is this strange outcry? he said. I sent away the women mainly in order that they might not misbehave in this way, for I have been told that a man should die in peace. Be quiet, then, and have patience. When we heard his words we were ashamed, and refrained our tears; and he walked about until, as he said, his legs began to fail, and then he lay on his back, according to the directions, and the man who gave him the poison now and then looked at his feet and legs; and after a while he pressed his foot hard, and asked him if he could feel; and he said, No; and then his leg, and so upwards and upwards, and showed us that he was cold and stiff. And he felt them himself, and said: When the poison reaches the heart, that will be the end. He was beginning to grow cold about the groin, when he uncovered his face, for he had covered himself up, and said—they were his last words—he said: Crito, I owe a cock to Asclepius; will you remember to pay the debt? The debt shall be paid, said Crito; is there anything else? There was no answer to this question; but in a minute or two a movement was heard, and the attendants uncovered him; his eyes were set, and Crito closed his eyes and mouth.

Such was the end, Echecrates, of our friend; concerning whom I may truly say, that of all the men of his time whom I have known, he was the wisest and justest and best.

Translated by B. Jowett.

XENOPHON

426 - 354 BC

Born in 426 BC near Athens, Xenophon was from an extremely wealthy aristocratic family. He took part in the defense of Athens in the final years of the Peloponnesian War. In 401 BC, he joined the Spartans who were fighting with the Persian prince Cyrus in Asia Minor. After the Campaign of the Ten Thousand was defeated and Cyrus was slain, Xenophon was appointed general. He led the Greek army back to its homeland by journeying across Asia until reaching the shores of the Black Sea. He recounts the expedition in the Anabasis.

His work as a historian also includes the Hellenica*—his principal contribution. Continuing where Thucydides had left off, Xenophon proceeds in the* Hellenica *with an account of the Peloponnesian War from the year 410 BC on. Afterward, he examines the conditions of the Spartan hegemony and concludes his narrative with the destruction of Mantinea in 362 BC. His attachment to Sparta is evident in the* Constitution of the Lacedaemonians *and in* Agesilaus.

Xenophon drew upon his intellectual background with the great philosopher and teacher Socrates to write the Socratic treatises: the Memorabilia, *the* Banquet, *and the* Apology. *He further composed treatises on horsemanship and hunting, an embellished biography of Cyrus, and an essay on tyranny titled* Hieron, *wherein the tyrant Hieron of Sicily has a dialogue with the poet Simonides. When Xenophon returned to Athens after the Campaign of the Ten Thousand, he drafted the* Ways and Means, *a treatise in which he advocates measures to help correct the ailing financial health of Athens.*

Disarray of the Greeks after the Death of Cyrus

Xenophon, *Anabasis* 3.11-45

In the Anabasis, *Xenophon recounts events in which he played a leading role. When Cyrus, who planned to overthrow his brother, the Persian king Artaxerxes, dies at the Battle of Cunaxa near Babylon in 401 BC, the ten thousand Greek mercenaries that fought by his side remain without leadership. They are far from home in the middle of enemy territory, at the heart of the Persian Empire. Xenophon succeeds in the great challenge of bringing them home, leading them through the river valleys of the Tigris and the Euphrates as well as through Armenia to the city of Trebizond on the Black Sea. This is where they screamed their famous shout: "Thalassa, Thalassa—the Sea, the Sea!" The Greeks had not set eyes on seawater in months. One can only imagine their relief at seeing the "Thalassa" after such a long time spent in the deserts of Persia. They would sail until arriving at the Hellespont, would travel onward to Thrace, and would finally reach home. Xenophon, who writes about himself in the third person, explains below his initiative to save his companions from the reprisals of Artaxerxes.*

"For without leaders nothing good or noble, to put it concisely, was ever wrought anywhere."

And now in this season of perplexity, Xenophon too, with the rest, was in sore distress, and could not sleep; but anon, getting a snatch of sleep, he had a dream. It seemed to him in a vision that there was a storm of thunder and lightning, and a bolt fell on his father's house, and thereupon the house was all in a blaze. He sprung up in terror, and pondering the matter, decided that in part the dream was good: in that he had seen a great light from Zeus, whilst in the midst of toil and danger. But partly too he feared it, for evidently it had come from Zeus the king. And the fire kindled all around—what could that mean but that he was hemmed in by various perplexities, and so could not escape from the country of the king? The full meaning, however, is to be discovered from what happened after the dream.

This is what took place. As soon as he was fully awake, the first clear thought which came into his head was, Why am I lying here? The night advances; with the day, it is like enough, the enemy will be upon us. If we are to fall into the hands of the king, what is left us but to face the most horrible of sights, and to suffer the most fearful pains, and then to die, insulted, an ignominious death? To defend ourselves—to ward off that fate—not a hand stirs: no one is preparing, none cares; but here we lie, as though it were time to rest and take our ease. I too! what am I waiting for? a general to undertake the work? and from what city? am I waiting till I am older mysef and of riper age? older I shall never be, if to-day I betray myself to my enemies.

Thereupon he got up, and called together first Proxenus's officers; and when they were met, he said: "Sleep, sirs, I cannot, nor can you, I fancy, nor lie here longer, when I see in what straits we are. Our enemy, we may be sure, did not open war upon us till he felt he had everything amply ready; yet none of us shows a corresponding anxiety to enter the lists of battle in the bravest style.

"And yet, if we yield ourselves and fall into the king's power, need we ask what our fate will be? This man, who, when his own brother, the son of the same parents, was dead, was not content with that, but severed head and hand from the body, and nailed them to a cross. We, then, who have not even the tie of blood in our favour, but who marched against him, meaning to make a slave of him instead of a king—and to slay him if we could: what is likely to be our fate at his hands? Will he not go all lengths so that, by inflicting on us the extreme of ignominy and torture, he may rouse in the rest of mankind a terror of ever marching against him any more? There is no question but that our business is to avoid by all means getting into his clutches.

"For my part, all the while the truce lasted, I never ceased pitying ourselves and congratulating the king and those with him, as, like a helpless spectator, I surveyed the extent and quality of their territory, the plenteousness of their provisions, the multitude of their dependants, their cattle, their gold, and their apparel. And then to turn and ponder the condition of our soldiers, without part or lot in these good things, except we bought it; few, I knew, had any longer the wherewithal to buy, and yet our oath held us down, so that we could not provide ourselves otherwise than by purchase. I say, as I reasoned thus, there were times when I dreaded the truce more than I now dread war.

"Now, however, that they have abruptly ended the truce, there is an end also to their own insolence and to our suspicion. All these good things of theirs are now set as prizes for the combatants. To whichsoever of us shall prove the better men, will they fall as guerdons; and the gods themselves are the judges of the strife. The gods, who full surely will be on our side, seeing it is our enemies who have taken their names falsely; whilst we, with much to lure us, yet for our oath's sake, and the gods who were our witnesses, sternly held aloof. So that, it seems to me, we have a right to enter upon this contest with much more heart than our foes; and further, we are possessed of bodies more capable than theirs of bearing cold and heat and labour;

souls too we have, by the help of heaven, better and braver; nay, the men themselves are more vulnerable, more mortal, than ourselves, if so be the gods vouchsafe to give us victory once again.

"Howbeit, for I doubt not elsewhere similar reflections are being made, whatsoever betide, let us not, in heaven's name, wait for others to come and challenge us to noble deeds; let us rather take the lead in stimulating the rest to valour. Show yourselves to be the bravest of officers, and among generals, the worthiest to command. For myself, if you choose to start forwards on this quest, I will follow; or, if you bid me lead you, my age shall be no excuse to stand between me and your orders. At least I am of full age, I take it, to avert misfortune from my own head."

Such were the speaker's words; and the officers, when they heard, all, with one exception, called upon him to put himself at their head. This was a certain Apollonides there present, who spoke in the Boeotian dialect. This man's opinion was that it was mere nonsense for any one to pretend they could obtain safety otherwise than by an appeal to the king, if he had skill to enforce it; and at the same time he began to dilate on the difficulties. But Xenophon cut him short. "O most marvellous of men! though you have eyes to see, you do not perceive; though you have ears to hear, you do not recollect. You were present with the rest of us now here when, after the death of Cyrus, the king, vaunting himself on that occurrence, sent dictatorially to bid us lay down our arms. But when we, instead of giving up our arms, put them on and went and pitched our camp near him, his manner changed. It is hard to say what he did not do, he was so at his wit's end, sending us embassies and begging for a truce, and furnishing provisions the while, until he had got it. Or to take the contrary instance, when just now, acting precisely on your principles, our generals and captains went, trusting to the truce, unarmed to a conference with them, what came of it? what is happening at this instant? Beaten, goaded with pricks, insulted, poor souls, they cannot even die: though death, I ween, would be very sweet. And you, who know all this, how can you say that it is mere nonsense to talk of self-defence? how can you bid us go again and try the arts of persuasion? In my opinion, sirs, we ought not to admit this fellow to the same rank with ourselves; rather ought we to deprive him of his captaincy, and load him with packs and treat him as such. The man is a disgrace to his own fatherland and the whole of Hellas, that, being a Hellene, he is what he is."

Here Agasias the Stymphalian broke in, exclaiming: "Nay, this fellow has no connection either with Boeotia or with Hellas, none whatever. I have noted both his ears bored like a Lydian's.[1] And so it was. Him then they banished. But the rest visited the ranks, and wherever a general was left, they summoned the general; where he was gone, the lieutenant-general; and where again the captain alone was left, the captain. As soon as they were all met, they seated themselves in front of the place d'armes: the assembled generals and officers, numbering about a hundred. It was nearly midnight when this took place.

Thereupon Hieronymous the Eleian, the eldest of Proxenus's captains, commenced speaking as follows: "Generals and captains, it seemed right to us, in view of the present crisis, ourselves to assemble and to summon you, that we might advise upon some practicable course. Would you, Xenophon, repeat what you said to us?"

Thereupon Xenophon spoke as follows: "We all know only too well, that the king and Tissaphernes have seized as many of us as they could, and it is clear they are plotting to destroy the rest of us if they can. Our business is plain: it is to do all we can to avoid getting into the power of the barbarians; rather, if we can, we will get them into our power. Rely upon this then, all you who are here assembled, now is your great opportunity. The soldiers outside have their eyes fixed upon you; if they think that you are faint-hearted, they will turn cowards; but if you show them that you are making your own preparations to attack the enemy, and setting an example to the rest—follow you, be assured, they will: imitate you they will. May be, it is but right and fair that you should somewhat excel them, for you are generals, you are commanders of brigades or regiments; and if, while it was peace, you had the advantage in wealth and position, so now, when it is war, you are expected to rise superior to the common herd—to think for them, to toil for them, whenever there be need.

"At this very moment you would confer a great boon on the army, if you made it your business to appoint generals and officers to fill the places of those that are lost. For without leaders nothing good or noble, to put it concisely, was ever wrought anywhere; and in military matters this is absolutely true; for if discipline is held to be of saving virtue, the want of it has been the ruin of many ere now. Well, then! when you have appointed all the commanders necessary, it would only be opportune, I take it, if you were to summon the rest of the soldiers and speak some words of encouragement. Even now, I daresay you noticed yourselves the crestfallen air with which they came into camp, the despondency with which they fell to picket duty, so that, unless there is a change for the better, I do not know for what service they will be fit; whether by night, if need were, or even by day. The thing is to get them to turn their thoughts to what they mean to do, instead of to what they are likely to suffer. Do that, and their spirits will soon revive wonderfully. You know, I need hardly remind you, it is not numbers or strength that gives victory in war; but, heaven helping them, to one or other of two combatants it is given to dash with stouter hearts to meet the foe, and such onset, in nine cases out of ten, those others refuse to meet. This observation, also, I have laid to heart, that they, who in matters of war seek in all ways to save their lives, are just they who, as a rule, die dishonourably; whereas they who, recognising that death is the common lot and destiny of all men, strive hard to die nobly: these more frequently, as I observe, do after all attain to old age, or, at any rate, while life lasts, they spend their days more happily. This lesson let all lay to heart this day, for we are just at such a crisis of our fate. Now is the season to be brave ourselves, and to stimulate the rest by our example."

With these words he ceased.

Translated by H.G. Dakyns.

Portrait of Socrates

Xenophon, *Memorabilia* 1.3-1.5

The Memorabilia *is a collection of memoirs about Socrates by his disciple Xenophon. It describes Socrates as a temperate and frugal man who respects the gods and appreciates the company of friends and relatives. Most of all, the* Memorabilia *refutes the accusations made against Socrates in 399 BC that lead to his condemnation. Socrates was neither impious toward the traditional gods nor a danger to the youths, whom he encouraged to practice temperance and piety. The* Memorabilia *is the contribution of a disciple to his master who was unjustly sentenced to death. It is the work of a brilliant mind, certainly one of the most original figures of Athenian society in the second half of the fifth century BC.*

Characters

SOCRATES

XENOPHON

ARISTODEMUS, follower of Socrates

"ARISTODEMUS: My belief is that the Divinity is too grand to need any service which I could render."

It may serve to illustrate the assertion that Socrates benefited his associates partly by the display of his own virtue and partly by verbal discourse and argument, if I set down my various recollections on these heads. And first with regard to religion and the concerns of heaven. In conduct and language his behaviour conformed to the rule laid down by the Pythia in reply to the question, "How shall we act?" as touching a sacrifice or the worship of ancestors, or any similar point. Her answer is: "Act according to the law and custom of your state, and you will act piously." After this pattern Socrates behaved himself, and so he exhorted others to behave, holding them to be but busybodies and vain fellows who acted on any different principle.

His formula or prayer was simple: "Give me that which is best for me," for, said he, the gods know best what good things are—to pray for gold or silver or despotic power were no better than to make some particular throw at dice or stake in battle or any such thing the subject of prayer, of which the future consequences are manifestly uncertain.

If with scant means he offered but small sacrifices he believed that he was in no wise inferior to those who make frequent and large sacrifices from an ampler store. It were ill surely for the very gods themselves, could they take delight in large sacrifices rather than in small, else oftentimes must the offerings of bad men be found acceptable rather than of good; nor from the point of view of men themselves would life be worth living if the offerings of a villain rather than of a righteous man found favour in the sight of Heaven. His belief was that the joy of the gods is greater in proportion to the holiness of the giver, and he was ever an admirer of that line of Hesiod which says,

According to thine ability do sacrifice to the immortal gods.

"Yes," he would say, "in our dealings with friends and strangers alike, and in reference to the demands of life in general, there is no better motto for a man than that: 'let a man do according to his ability.'"

Or to take another point. If it appeared to him that a sign from heaven had been given him, nothing would have induced him to go against heavenly warning: he would as soon have been persuaded to accept the guidance of a blind man ignorant of the path to lead him on a journey in place of one who knew the road and could see; and so he denounced the folly of others who do things contrary to the warnings of God in order to avoid some disrepute among men. For himself he despised all human aids by comparison with counsel from above.

The habit and style of living to which he subjected his soul and body was one which under ordinary circumstances would enable any one adopting it to look existence cheerily in the face and to pass his days serenely: it would certainly entail no difficulties as regards expense. So frugal was it that a man must work little indeed who could not earn the quantum which contented Socrates. Of food he took just enough to make eating a pleasure—the appetite he brought to it was sauce sufficient; while as to drinks, seeing that he only drank when thirsty, any draught refreshed. If he accepted an invitation to dinner, he had no difficulty in avoiding the common snare of over-indulgence, and his advice to people who could not equally control their appetite was to avoid taking what would allure them to eat if not hungry or to drink if not thirsty. Such things are ruinous to the constitution, he said, bad for stomachs, brains, and soul alike; or as he used to put it, with a touch of sarcasm "It must have been by feasting men on so many dainty dishes that Circe produced her pigs; only Odysseus through his continency and the 'promptings of Hermes' abstained from touching them immoderately, and by the same token did not turn into a swine." So much for this topic, which he touched thus lightly and yet seriously.

But as to the concerns of Aphrodite, his advice was to hold strongly aloof from the fascination of fair forms: once lay finger on these and it is not easy to keep a sound head and a sober mind. To take a particular case. It was a mere kiss which, as he had heard, Critobulus had some time given to a fair youth, the son of Alcibiades. Accordingly Critobulus being present, Socrates propounded the question.

Socrates: Tell me, Xenophon, have you not always believed Critobulus to be a man of sound sense, not wild and self-willed? Should you not have said that he was remarkable for his prudence rather than thoughtless or foolhardy?

Xenophon: Certainly that is what I should have said of him.

Socrates: Then you are now to regard him as quite the reverse—a hot-blooded, reckless libertine: this is the sort of man to throw somersaults into knives, or to leap into the jaws of fire.

Xenophon: And what have you seen him doing, that you give him so bad a character?

Socrates: Doing? Why, has not the fellow dared to steal a kiss from the son of Alcibiades, most fair of youths and in the golden prime?

Xenophon: Nay, then, if that is the foolhardy adventure, it is a danger which I could well encounter myself.

Socrates: Pour soul! and what do you expect your fate to be after that kiss? Let me tell you. On the instant you will lose your freedom, the indenture of your bondage will be signed; it will be yours on compulsion to spend large sums on hurtful pleasures; you will have scarcely a moment's leisure left for any noble study; you will be driven to concern yourself most zealously with things which no man, not even a madman, would choose to make an object of concern.

Xenophon: O Heracles! how fell a power to reside in a kiss!

Socrates: Does it surprise you? Do you not know that the tarantula, which is no bigger than a threepenny bit, has only to touch the mouth and it will afflict its victim with pains and drive him out of his senses.

Xenophon: Yes, but then the creature injects something with its bite.

Socrates: Ah, fool! and do you imagine that these lovely creatures infuse nothing with their kiss, simply because you do not see the poison? Do you not know that this wild beast which men call beauty in its bloom is all the more terrible than the tarantula in that the insect must first touch its victim, but this at a mere glance of the beholder, without even contact, will inject something into him—yards away—which will make him man. And may be that is why the Loves are called "archers," because these beauties wound so far off. But my advice to you, Xenophon, is, whenever you catch sight of one of these fair forms, to run helter-skelter for bare life without a glance behind; and to you, Critobulus, I would say, "Go abroad for a year: so long time will it take to heal you of this wound."

Such (he said), in the affairs of Aphrodite, as in meats and drinks, should be the circumspection of all whose footing is insecure. At least they should confine themselves to such diet as the soul would dispense with, save for some necessity of the body; and which even so ought to set up no disturbance. But for himself, it was clear, he was prepared at all points and invulnerable. He found less difficulty in abstaining from beauty's fairest and fullest bloom than many others from weeds and garbage. To sum up: with regard to eating and drinking and these other temptations of the sense, the equipment of his soul made him independent; he could boast honestly that in his moderate fashion his pleasures were no less than theirs who take such trouble to procure them, and his pains far fewer.

A belief is current, in accordance with views maintained concerning Socrates in speech and writing, and in either case conjecturally, that, however powerful he may have been in stimulating men to virtue as a theorist, he was incapable of acting as their guide himself. It would be well for those who adopt this view to weigh carefully not only what Socrates effected "by way of castigation" in cross-questioning whose who conceived themselves to be possessed of all knowledge, but also his everyday conversation with those who spent their time in close intercourse with himself. Having done this, let them decide whether he was incapable of making his companions better.

I will first state what I once heard fall from his lips in a discussion with Aristodemus, "the little," as he was called, on the topic of divinity. Socrates had observed that Aristodemus neither sacrificed nor gave heed to divination, but on the contrary was disposed to ridicule those who did.

So tell me, Aristodemus (he began), are there any human beings who have won your admiration for their wisdom?

Aristodemus: There are.

Socrates: Would you mention to us their names?

Aristodemus: In the writings of epic poetry I have the greatest admiration for Homer. And as a dithyrambic poet for Melanippides. I admire also Sophocles as a tragedian, Polycleitus as a sculptor, and Zeuxis as a painter.

Socrates: Which would you consider the more worthy of admiration, a fashioner of senseless images devoid of motion or one who could fashion living creatures endowed with understanding and activity?

Aristodemus: Decidedly the latter, provided his living creatures owed their birth to design and were not the offspring of some chance.

Socrates: But now if you had two sorts of things, the one of which presents no clue as to what it is for, and the other is obviously for some useful purpose—which would you judge to be the result of chance, which of design?

Aristodemus: Clearly that which is produced for some useful end is the work of design.

Socrates: Does it not strike you then that he who made man from the beginning did for some useful end furnish him with his several senses—giving him eyes to behold the visible word, and ears to catch the intonations of sound? Or again, what good would there be in odours if nostrils had not been bestowed upon us? what perception of sweet things and pungent, and of all the pleasures of the palate, had not a tongue been fashioned in us as an interpreter of the same? And besides all this, do you not think this looks like a matter of foresight, this closing of the delicate orbs of sight with eyelids as with folding doors, which, when there is need to use them for any purpose, can be thrown wide open and firmly closed again in sleep? and, that even the winds of heaven may not visit them too roughly, this planting of the eyelashes as a protecting screen? this coping of the region above the eyes with cornice-work of eyebrow so that no drop of sweat fall from the head and injure them? again this readiness of the ear to catch all sounds and yet not to be surcharged? this capacity of the front teeth of all animals to cut and of the "grinders" to receive the food and reduce it to pulp? the position of the mouth again, close to the eyes and nostrils as a portal of ingress for all the creature's supplies? and lastly, seeing that matter passing out of the body is unpleasant, this hindward direction of the passages, and their removal to a distance from the avenues of sense? I ask you, when you see all these things constructed with such show of foresight can you doubt whether they are products of chance or intelligence?

Aristodemus: To be sure not! Viewed in this light they would seem to be the handiwork of some wise artificer, full of love for all things living.

Socrates: What shall we say of this passion implanted in man to beget offspring, this passion in the mother to rear her babe, and in the creature itself, once born, this deep desire of life and fear of death?

Aristodemus: No doubt these do look like the contrivances of some one deliberately planning the existence of living creatures.

Socrates: Well, and doubtless you feel to have a spark of wisdom yourself?

Aristodemus: Put your questions, and I will answer.

Socrates: And yet you imagine that elsewhere no spark of wisdom is to be found? And that, too, when you know that you have in your body a tiny fragment only of the mighty earth, a little drop of the great waters, and of the other elements, vast in their extent, you got, I presume, a particle of each towards the compacting of your bodily frame? Mind alone, it would seem, which is nowhere to be found, you had the lucky chance to snatch up and make off with, you cannot tell how. And these things around and about us, enormous in size, infinite in number, owe their orderly arrangement, as you suppose, to some vacuity of wit?

Aristodemus: It may be, for my eyes fail to see the master agents of these, as one sees the fabricators of things produced on earth.

Socrates: No more do you see your own soul, which is the master agent of your body; so that, as far as that goes, you may maintain, if you like, that you do nothing with intelligence, but everything by chance.

At this point Aristodemus: I assure you, Socrates, that I do not disdain the Divine power. On the contrary, my belief is that the Divinity is too grand to need any service which I could render.

Socrates: But the grander that power is, which deigns to tend and wait upon you, the more you are called upon to honour it.

Aristodemus: Be well assured, if I could believe the gods take thought for all men, I would not neglect them.

Socrates: How can you suppose that they do not so take thought? Who, in the first place, gave to man alone of living creatures his erect posture, enabling him to see farther in front of him and to contemplate more freely the height above, and to be less subject to distress than other creatures endowed like himself with eyes and ears and mouth. Consider next how they gave to the beast of the field feet as a means of progression only, but to man they gave in addition hands— those hands which have achieved so much to raise us in the scale of happiness above all animals. Did they not make the tongue also? Which belongs indeed alike to man and beast, but in man they fashioned it so as to play on different parts of the mouth at different times, whereby we can produce articulate speech, and have a code of signals to express our every want to one another. Or consider the pleasures of the sexual appetite; limited in the rest of the animal kingdom to certain seasons, but in the case of man a series prolonged unbroken to old age. Nor did it content the Godhead merely to watch over the interests of man's body. What is of far higher import, he implanted in man the noblest and most excellent type of soul. For what other creature, to begin with, has a soul to appreciate the existence of the gods who have arranged this grand and beauteous universe? What other tribe of animals save man can render service to the gods? How apt is the spirit of man to take precautions against hunger and thirst, cold and heat, to alleviate disease and foster strength! how suited to labour with a view to learning! how capable of garnering in the storehouse of his memory all that he has heard or seen or understood! Is it not most evident to you that by the side of other animals men live and move a race of gods—by nature excellent, in beauty of body and of soul supreme? For, mark you, had a creature of man's wit been encased in the body of an ox, he would have been powerless to carry out his wishes, just as the possession of hands divorced from human wit is profitless. And then you come, you who have obtained these two most precious attributes, and give it as your opinion, that the gods take no thought or care for you. Why, what will you have them to do, that you may believe and be persuaded that you too are in their thoughts?

Aristodemus: When they treat me as you tell us they treat you, and send me counsellors to warn me what I am to do and what abstain from doing, I will believe.

Socrates: Send you counsellors! Come now, what when the people of Athens make inquiry by oracle, and the gods' answer comes? Are you not an Athenian? Think you not that to you also the answer is given? What when they send portents to forewarn the states of Hellas? or to all mankind? Are you not a man? a Hellene? Are not these intended for you also? Can it be that you alone are excepted as a signal instance of Divine neglect? Again, do you suppose that the gods could have implanted in the heart of man the belief in their capacity to work him weal or woe had they not the power? Would not men have discovered the imposture in all this lapse of time? Do you not perceive that the wisest and most perdurable of human institutions—be they cities or tribes of men—are ever the most God-fearing; and in the individual man the riper his age and judgment, the deeper his religousness? Ay, my good sir (he broke forth), lay to heart and understand that even as your own mind within you can turn and dispose of your body as it lists, so ought we to think that the wisdom which abides within the universal frame does so dispose of all things as it finds agreeable to itself; for hardly may it be that your eye is able to range over many a league, but that the eye of God is powerless to embrace all things at a glance; or that to your soul it is given to dwell in thought on matters here or far away in Egypt or in Sicily, but that the wisdom and thought of God is not sufficient to include all things at one instant under His care. If only you would copy your own behaviour where human beings are concerned. It is by acts of service and of kindness that you discover which of your fellows are willing to requite you in kind. It is by taking another into your counsel that you arrive at the secret of his wisdom. If, on like principle, you will but make trial of the gods by acts of service, whether they will choose to give you counsel in matters obscure to mortal vision, you shall discover the nature and the greatness of Godhead to be such that they are able at once to see all things and to hear all things and to be present everywhere, nor does the least thing escape their watchful care.

To my mind the effect of words like these was to cause those about him to hold aloof from unholiness, baseness, and injustice, not only whilst they were seen of men, but even in the solitary place, since they must believe that no part of their conduct could escape the eye of Heaven.

I suppose it may be taken as admitted that self-control is a noble acquirement for a man. If so, let us turn and consider whether by language like the following he was likely to lead his listeners onwards to the attainment of this virtue. "Sirs," he would say, "if a war came upon us and we wished to choose a man who would best help us to save ourselves and to subdue our enemy, I suppose we should scarcely select one whom we knew to be a slave to his belly, to wine, or lust, and prone to succumb to toil or sleep. Could we expect such an one to save us or to master our foes? Or if one of us were nearing the end of his days, and he wished to discover some one to whom he might entrust his sons for education, his maiden daughters for protection, and his property in general for preservation, would he deem a libertine worthy of such offices? Why, no one would dream of entrusting his flocks and herds, his storehouses and barns, or the superintendence of his works to the tender mercies of an intemperate slave. If a butler or an errand boy with such a character were offered to us we would not take him as a free gift. And if he would not accept an intemperate slave, what pains should the master himself take to avoid that imputation. For with the incontinent man it is not as with the self-seeker and the covetous. These may at any rate be held to enrich themselves in depriving others. But the intemperate man cannot claim in like fashion to be a blessing to himself if a curse to his neighbours; nay, the mischief which he may cause to others is nothing by comparison with that which redounds against himself, since it is the height of mischief to ruin—I do not say one's own house and property—but one's own body and one's own soul. Or to take an example from social intercourse, no one cares for a guest who evidently takes more pleasure in the wine and the viands than in the friends beside him—who stints his comrades of the affection due to them to dote upon a mistress. Does it not come to this, that every honest man is bound to look upon self-restraint as the very corner-stone of virtue: which he should seek to lay down as the basis and foundation of his soul? Without self-restraint who can lay any good lesson to heart or practise it when learnt in any degree worth speaking of? Or, to put it conversely, what slave of pleasure will not suffer degeneracy of soul and body? By Hera, well may every free man pray to be saved from the service of such a slave; and well too may he who is in bondage to such pleasures supplicate Heaven to send him good masters, seeing that is the one hope of salvation left him."

Well-tempered words: yet his self-restraint shone forth even more in his acts than in his language. Not only was he master over the pleasures which flow from the body, but of those also which are fed by riches, his belief being that he who receives money from this or that chance donor sets up over himself a master, and binds himself to an abominable slavery.

Translated by H.G. Dakyns.

ARISTOTLE

384 - 322 BC

Aristotle was born in 384 BC at Stagira, a Greek town under Macedonian influence located on the coast of Chalcidice (Thrace). His father, Nicomachus, was the personal doctor of Amyntas II, the grandfather of Alexander the Great. Aristotle arrived at Athens and entered Plato's Academy in 366 BC. He studied there until the death of his master, Plato, in c. 347 BC. He then left Athens and journeyed to the Troad, where he taught for three years while examining the marine species of the region. In 345, he traveled to Mytilene on the island of Lesbos (from which the term "lesbian" originates). In 343, at the request of King Philip of Macedon, he became the tutor of Alexander, who was 16 years old at the time. Aristotle held this position until Alexander's succession to the throne in 335; he then returned to Athens and founded his own school of philosophy, the Lyceum. In 323, however, Aristotle was compelled to take refuge at Chalcis in Euboea. Accused of impiety by the anti-Macedonian party at the death of Alexander, he feared for his life. It is after one such trial that Socrates was sentenced to death by drinking hemlock. Aristotle survived for only one year in exile.

It is believed that Aristotle composed roughly 1000 books. The 150 that have survived were not intended for publication but strictly for didactic use at the school. His complete writings were encyclopedic, covering all fields of human knowledge.

Explanation and Function of Tragedy: Mimesis and Katharsis

Aristotle, *Poetics* 1-9 (1447a-1451b)

The Poetics *comprises two books: The first treats tragedy and the second comedy. Only the first book has managed to survive. The second work is lost forever unless it rests in some monastery as Umberto Eco imagines in his novel* The Name of the Rose. *In Eco's novel, the librarian-monk who owns the second book kills any person who dares to read its scandalous content. The monk cannot accept the idea of a highly esteemed philosopher like Aristotle writing on such a frivolous topic as comedy.*

In the first part of the Poetics, *Aristotle uses tragedy to reveal his famous theory of Mimesis and Katharsis. Tragedy, like all poetic forms, is an imitation (Mimesis) of reality, which through the arousal of pity and fear helps the spectator purge himself (Katharsis) from such emotions. It is noteworthy that the* Poetics *was written while the three greatest writers of tragedy—Aeschylus, Sophocles, and Euripides—were already being lauded in the golden age of the genre.*

"It is not the function of the poet to relate what has happened, but what may happen,— what is possible according to the law of probability or necessity. The poet and the historian differ not by writing in verse or in prose. The work of Herodotus might be put into verse, and it would still be a species of history, with metre no less than without it. The true difference is that one relates what has happened, the other what may happen. Poetry, therefore, is a more philosophical and a higher thing than history: for poetry tends to express the universal, history the particular."

I propose to treat of Poetry in itself and of its various kinds, noting the essential quality of each; to inquire into the structure of the plot as requisite to a good poem; into the number and nature of the parts of which a poem is composed; and similarly into whatever else falls within the same inquiry. Following, then, the order of nature, let us begin with the principles which come first.

Epic poetry and Tragedy, Comedy also and Dithyrambic poetry, and the music of the flute and of the lyre in most of their forms, are all in their general conception modes of imitation. They differ, however, from one another in three respects,—the medium, the objects, the manner or mode of imitation, being in each case distinct.

For as there are persons who, by conscious art or mere habit, imitate and represent various objects through the medium of colour and form, or again by the voice; so in the arts above mentioned, taken as a whole, the imitation is produced by rhythm, language, or 'harmony,' either singly or combined.

Thus in the music of the flute and of the lyre, 'harmony' and rhythm alone are employed; also in other arts, such as that of the shepherd's pipe, which are essentially similar to these. In dancing, rhythm alone is used without 'harmony'; for even dancing imitates character, emotion, and action, by rhythmical movement.

There is another art which imitates by means of language alone, and that either in prose or verse—which, verse, again, may either combine different metres or consist of but one kind—but this has hitherto been without a name. For there is no common term we could apply to the mimes of Sophron and Xenarchus and the Socratic dialogues on the one hand; and, on the other, to poetic imitations in iambic, elegiac, or any similar metre. People do, indeed, add the word 'maker' or 'poet' to the name of the metre, and speak of elegiac poets, or epic (that is, hexameter) poets, as if it were not the imitation that makes the poet, but the verse that entitles them all indiscriminately to the name. Even when a treatise on medicine or natural science is brought out in verse, the name of poet is by custom given to the author; and yet Homer and Empedocles[1] have nothing in common but the metre, so that it would be right to call the one poet, the other physicist rather than poet. On the same principle, even if a writer in his poetic imitation were to combine all metres, as Chaeremon[2] did in his *Centaur*, which is a medley composed of metres of all kinds, we should bring him too under the general term poet. So much then for these distinctions.

There are, again, some arts which employ all the means above mentioned, namely, rhythm, tune, and metre. Such are Dithyrambic and Nomic poetry,[3] and also Tragedy and Comedy; but between them the difference is, that in the first two cases these means are all employed in combination, in the latter, now one means is employed, now another.

Such, then, are the differences of the arts with respect to the medium of imitation.

Since the objects of imitation are men in action, and these men must be either of a higher or a lower type (for moral character mainly answers to these divisions, goodness and badness being the distinguishing marks of moral differences), it follows that we must represent men either as better than in real life, or as worse, or as they are. It is the same in painting. Polygnotus depicted men as nobler than they are, Pauson as less noble, Dionysius drew them true to life.

Now it is evident that each of the modes of imitation above mentioned will exhibit these differences, and become a distinct kind in imitating objects that are thus distinct. Such diversities may be found even in dancing, flute-playing, and lyre-playing. So again in language, whether prose or verse unaccompanied by music. Homer, for example, makes men better than they are; Cleophon as they are; Hegemon the Thasian, the inventor of parodies, and Nicochares, the author of the Deiliad, worse than they are. The same thing holds good of Dithyrambs and Nomes; here too one may portray different types, as Timotheus and Philoxenus differed in representing their Cyclopes. The same distinction marks off Tragedy from Comedy; for Comedy aims at representing men as worse, Tragedy as better than in actual life.

There is still a third difference—the manner in which each of these objects may be imitated. For the medium being the same, and the objects the same, the poet may imitate by narration—in which case he can either take another personality as Homer does, or speak in his own person, unchanged—or he may present all his characters as living and moving before us.

These, then, as we said at the beginning, are the three differences which distinguish artistic imitation,—the medium, the objects, and the manner. So that from one point of view, Sophocles is an imitator of the same kind as Homer—for both imitate higher types of character; from another point of view, of the same kind as Aristophanes—for both imitate persons acting and doing. Hence, some say, the name of 'drama' is given to such poems, as representing action. For the same reason the Dorians claim the invention both of Tragedy and Comedy. The claim to Comedy is put forward by the Megarians,—not only by those of Greece proper, who allege that it originated under their democracy, but also by the Megarians of Sicily, for the poet Epicharmus, who is much earlier than Chionides and Magnes, belonged to that country. Tragedy too is claimed by certain Dorians of the Peloponnese. In each case they appeal to the evidence of language. The outlying villages, they say, are by them called "kômai", by the Athenians "dêmoi", and they assume that Comedians were so named not from "kômazein", 'to revel,' but because they wandered 'from village to village', "kata kômas", being excluded contemptuously from the city. They add also that the Dorian word for 'doing' is "drân", and the Athenian, "prattein".

This may suffice as to the number and nature of the various modes of imitation.

Poetry in general seems to have sprung from two causes, each of them lying deep in our nature. First, the instinct of imitation is implanted in man from childhood, one difference between him and other animals being that he is the most imitative of living creatures, and through imitation learns his earliest lessons; and no less universal is the pleasure felt in things imitated. We have evidence of this in the facts of experience. Objects which in themselves we view with pain, we delight to contemplate when reproduced with minute fidelity: such as the forms of the most ignoble animals and of dead bodies. The cause of this again is, that to learn gives the liveliest pleasure, not only to philosophers but to men in general; whose capacity, however, of learning is more limited. Thus the reason why men enjoy seeing a likeness is, that in contemplating it they find themselves learning or inferring, and saying perhaps, 'Ah, that is he.' For if you happen not to have seen the original, the pleasure will be due not to the imitation as such, but to the execution, the colouring, or some such other cause.

Imitation, then, is one instinct of our nature. Next, there is the instinct for 'harmony' and rhythm, metres being manifestly sections of rhythm. Persons, therefore, starting with this natural gift developed by degrees their special aptitudes, till their rude improvisations gave birth to Poetry.

Poetry now diverged in two directions, according to the individual character of the writers. The graver spirits imitated noble actions, and the actions of good men. The more trivial sort imitated the actions of meaner persons, at first composing satires, as the former did hymns to the gods and the praises of famous men. A poem of the satirical kind cannot indeed be put down to any author earlier than Homer; though many such writers probably there were. But from Homer onward, instances can be cited,—his own *Margites*, for example, and other similar compositions. The appropriate metre was also here introduced; hence the measure is still called the iambic or lampooning measure, being that in which people lampooned one another. Thus the older poets were distinguished as writers of heroic or of lampooning verse.

As, in the serious style, Homer is pre-eminent among poets, for he alone combined dramatic form with excellence of imitation, so he too first laid down the main lines of Comedy, by dramatising the ludicrous instead of writing personal satire. His *Margites* bears the same relation to Comedy that the *Iliad* and *Odyssey* do to Tragedy. But when Tragedy and Comedy came to light, the two classes of poets still followed their natural bent: the lampooners became writers of Comedy, and the Epic poets were succeeded by Tragedians, since the drama was a larger and higher form of art. Whether Tragedy has as yet perfected its proper types or not; and whether it is to be judged in itself, or in relation also to the audience,—this raises another question. Be that as it may, Tragedy—as also Comedy—was at first mere improvisation. The one originated with the authors of the Dithyramb, the other with those of the phallic songs, which are still in use in many of our cities. Tragedy advanced by slow degrees; each new element that showed itself was in turn developed. Having passed through many changes, it found its natural form, and there it stopped.

Aeschylus first introduced a second actor; he diminished the importance of the Chorus, and assigned the leading part to the dialogue. Sophocles raised the number of actors to three, and added scene-painting. Moreover, it was not till late that the short plot was discarded for one of greater compass, and the grotesque diction of the earlier satyric form for the stately manner of Tragedy. The iambic measure then replaced the trochaic tetrameter, which was originally employed when the poetry was of the Satyric order, and had greater affinities with dancing. Once dialogue had come in, Nature herself discovered the appropriate measure. For the iambic is, of all measures, the most colloquial: we see it in the fact that conversational speech runs into iambic lines more frequently than into any other kind of verse; rarely into hexameters, and only when we drop the colloquial intonation. The additions to the number of 'episodes' or acts, and the other accessories of which tradition tells, must be taken as already described; for to discuss them in detail would, doubtless, be a large undertaking.

Comedy is, as we have said, an imitation of characters of a lower type, not, however, in the full sense of the word bad, the Ludicrous being merely a subdivision of the ugly. It consists in some defect or ugliness which is not painful or destructive. To take an obvious example, the comic mask is ugly and distorted, but does not imply pain.

The successive changes through which Tragedy passed, and the authors of these changes, are well known, whereas Comedy has had no history, because it was not at first treated seriously. It was late before the Archon granted a comic chorus to a poet; the performers were till then voluntary. Comedy had already taken definite shape when comic poets, distinctively so called, are heard of. Who furnished it with masks, or prologues, or increased the number of actors,—these and other similar details remain unknown. As for the plot, it came originally from Sicily; but of Athenian writers Crates was the first who, abandoning the 'iambic' or lampooning form, generalised his themes and plots.

Epic poetry agrees with Tragedy in so far as it is an imitation in verse of characters of a higher type. They differ, in that Epic poetry admits but one kind of metre, and is narrative in form. They differ, again, in their length: for Tragedy endeavours, as far as possible, to confine itself to a single revolution of the sun, or but slightly to exceed this limit; whereas the Epic action has no limits of time. This, then, is a second point of difference; though at first the same freedom was admitted in Tragedy as in Epic poetry.

Of their constituent parts some are common to both, some peculiar to Tragedy, whoever, therefore, knows what is good or bad Tragedy, knows also about Epic poetry. All the elements of an Epic poem are found in Tragedy, but the elements of a Tragedy are not all found in the Epic poem.

Of the poetry which imitates in hexameter verse, and of Comedy, we will speak hereafter. Let us now discuss Tragedy, resuming its formal definition, as resulting from what has been already said.

Tragedy, then, is an imitation of an action that is serious, complete, and of a certain magnitude; in language embellished with each kind of artistic ornament, the several kinds being found in separate parts of the play; in the form of action, not of narrative; through pity and fear effecting the proper purgation of these emotions. By 'language embellished,' I mean language into which rhythm, 'harmony,' and song enter. By 'the several kinds in separate parts,' I mean, that some parts are rendered through the medium of verse alone, others again with the aid of song.

Now as tragic imitation implies persons acting, it necessarily follows, in the first place, that Spectacular equipment will be a part of Tragedy. Next, Song and Diction, for these are the medium of imitation. By 'Diction' I mean the mere metrical arrangement of the words: as for 'Song,' it is a term whose sense every one understands.

Again, Tragedy is the imitation of an action; and an action implies personal agents, who necessarily possess certain distinctive qualities both of character and thought; for it is by these that we qualify actions themselves, and these—thought and character—are the two natural causes from which actions spring, and on actions again all success or failure depends. Hence, the Plot is the imitation of the action: for by plot I here mean the arrangement of the incidents. By Character I mean that in virtue of which we ascribe certain qualities to the agents. Thought is required wherever a statement is proved, or, it may be, a general truth enunciated. Every Tragedy, therefore, must have six parts, which parts determine its quality—namely, Plot, Character, Diction, Thought, Spectacle, Song. Two of the parts constitute the medium of imitation, one the manner, and three the objects of imitation. And these complete the list. These elements have been employed, we may say, by the poets to a man; in fact, every play contains Spectacular elements as well as Character, Plot, Diction, Song, and Thought.

But most important of all is the structure of the incidents. For Tragedy is an imitation, not of men, but of an action and of life, and life consists in action, and its end is a mode of action, not a quality. Now character determines men's qualities, but it is by their actions that they are happy or the reverse. Dramatic action, therefore, is not with a view to the representation of character: character comes in as subsidiary to the actions. Hence the incidents and the plot are the end of a tragedy; and the end is the chief thing of all. Again, without action there cannot be a tragedy; there may be without character. The tragedies of most of our modern poets fail in the rendering of character; and of poets in general this is often true. It is the same in painting; and here lies the difference between Zeuxis and Polygnotus. Polygnotus delineates character well: the style of Zeuxis is devoid of ethical quality. Again, if you string together a set of speeches expressive of character, and well finished in point of diction and thought, you will not produce the essential tragic effect nearly so well as with a play which, however deficient in these respects, yet has a plot and artistically constructed incidents. Besides which, the most powerful elements of emotional interest in Tragedy—Peripeteia or Reversal of the Situation, and Recognition scenes—are parts of the plot. A further proof is, that novices in the art attain to finish of diction and precision of portraiture before they can construct the plot. It is the same with almost all the early poets.

The Plot, then, is the first principle, and, as it were, the soul of a tragedy: Character holds the second place. A similar fact is seen in painting. The most beautiful colours, laid on confusedly, will not give as much pleasure as the chalk outline of a portrait. Thus Tragedy is the imitation of an action, and of the agents mainly with a view to the action.

Third in order is Thought,—that is, the faculty of saying what is possible and pertinent in given circumstances. In the case of oratory, this is the function of the Political art and of the art of rhetoric: and so indeed the older poets make their characters speak the language of civic life; the poets of our time, the language of the rhetoricians. Character is that which reveals moral purpose, showing what kind of things a man chooses or avoids. Speeches, therefore, which do not make this manifest, or in which the speaker does not choose or avoid anything whatever, are not expressive of character. Thought, on the other hand, is found where something is proved to be or not to be, or a general maxim is enunciated.

Fourth among the elements enumerated comes Diction; by which I mean, as has been already said, the expression of the meaning in words; and its essence is the same both in verse and prose.

Of the remaining elements Song holds the chief place among the embellishments.

The Spectacle has, indeed, an emotional attraction of its own, but, of all the parts, it is the least artistic, and connected least with the art of poetry. For the power of Tragedy, we may be sure, is felt even apart from representation and actors. Besides, the production of spectacular effects depends more on the art of the stage machinist than on that of the poet.

These principles being established, let us now discuss the proper structure of the Plot, since this is the first and most important thing in Tragedy.

Now, according to our definition, Tragedy is an imitation of an action that is complete, and whole, and of a certain magnitude; for there may be a whole that is wanting in magnitude. A whole is that which has a beginning, a middle, and an end. A beginning is that which does not itself follow anything by causal necessity, but after which something naturally is or comes to be. An end, on the contrary, is that which itself naturally follows some other thing, either by necessity, or as a rule, but has nothing following it. A middle is that which follows something as some other thing follows it. A well constructed plot, therefore, must neither begin nor end at haphazard, but conform to these principles.

Again, a beautiful object, whether it be a living organism or any whole composed of parts, must not only have an orderly arrangement of parts, but must also be of a certain magnitude; for beauty depends on magnitude and order. Hence a very small animal organism cannot be beautiful; for the view of it is confused, the object being seen in an almost imperceptible moment of time. Nor, again, can one of vast size be beautiful; for as the eye cannot take it all in at once, the unity and sense of the whole is lost for the spectator; as for instance if there were one a thousand miles long. As, therefore, in the case of animate bodies and organisms a certain magnitude is necessary, and a magnitude which may be easily embraced in one view; so in the plot, a certain length is necessary, and a length which can be easily embraced by the memory. The limit of length in relation to dramatic competition and sensuous presentment, is no part of artistic theory. For had it been the rule for a hundred tragedies to compete together, the performance would have been regulated by the water-clock,—as indeed we are told was formerly done. But the limit as fixed by the nature of the drama itself is this: the greater the length, the more beautiful will the piece be by reason of its size, provided that the whole be perspicuous. And to define the matter roughly, we may say that the proper magnitude is comprised within such limits, that the sequence of events, according to the law of probability or necessity, will admit of a change from bad fortune to good, or from good fortune to bad.

Unity of plot does not, as some persons think, consist in the Unity of the hero. For infinitely various are the incidents in one man's life which cannot be reduced to unity; and so, too, there are many actions of one man out of which we cannot make one action. Hence, the error, as it appears, of all poets who have composed a *Heracleid*, a *Theseid*, or other poems of the kind. They imagine that as Heracles was one man, the story of Heracles must also be a unity. But Homer, as in all else he is of surpassing merit, here too—whether from art or natural genius—seems to have happily discerned the truth. In composing the *Odyssey* he did not include all the adventures of Odysseus—such as his wound on Parnassus, or his feigned madness at the mustering of the host—incidents between which there was no necessary or probable connection; but he made the *Odyssey*, and likewise the *Iliad*, to centre round an action that in our sense of the word is one. As therefore, in the other imitative arts, the imitation is one when the object imitated is one, so the plot, being an imitation of an action, must imitate one action and that a whole, the structural union of the parts being such that, if any one of them is displaced or removed, the whole will be disjointed and disturbed. For a thing whose presence or absence makes no visible difference, is not an organic part of the whole.

It is, moreover, evident from what has been said, that it is not the function of the poet to relate what has happened, but what may happen,—what is possible according to the law of probability or necessity. The poet and the historian differ not by writing in verse or in prose. The work of Herodotus might be put into verse, and it would still be a species of history, with metre no less than without it. The true difference is that one relates what has happened, the other what may happen. Poetry, therefore, is a more philosophical and a higher thing than history: for poetry tends to express the universal, history the particular. By the universal, I mean how a person of a certain type will on occasion speak or act, according to the law of probability or necessity; and it is this universality at which poetry aims in the names she attaches to the personages. The particular is, for example, what Alcibiades did or suffered.

Translated by S.H. Butcher.

DEMOSTHENES

384 - 322 BC

Demosthenes is considered the most important Greek orator. He was born at Athens in 384 BC. As a young orphan, he watched helplessly as his guardians squandered his fortune. Barely an adolescent, he initiated his lifelong search for justice. He realized he would first need to pursue courses in rhetoric and did so under Isaeus, the renowned Athenian instructor of oratory.

Coming of age, and fully skilled in rhetoric, Demosthenes sued his guardians. Although he failed to get all his possessions back, he quickly matured into a speech-writer whose talents were in great demand. Politically driven, he first championed the cause of the pacifist party for which Eubulus was the most outspoken representative. When Philip of Macedon began threatening the interests of Athens in the Aegean, however, Demosthenes took an aggressive political stance against the Macedonians. Following the truce in 346 BC, Demosthenes tirelessly cautioned his citizens against King Philip's threat.

In 324 BC, he was accused of accepting 20 talents from Harpalus, the disloyal secretary of Alexander, and was exiled. He would return to Athens only at the death of Alexander and would actively participate in the uprising against the Macedonians. Forced to flee the Macedonian chief Antipater, he took refuge in the sanctuary of Poseidon on the island of Calauria and poisoned himself.

Imitated and admired throughout antiquity, Demosthenes' works had a strong political impact. The talented orator and patriot is remembered for his persistent efforts to restore Athens to her former glory. Urging his contemporaries to brave the hardships endured by the city during the fourth century, Demosthenes wanted Athens to be considered by all not only as a "School of Greece" but also as the sole polis *capable of promoting the panhellenic* politik *perceived by him as the only salvation.*

Macedonian Threat

Demosthenes, *Philippics* 3

In 341 BC, Philip of Macedon's threat to Athens escalated dramatically. The Macedonian king advanced upon Thrace, challenged Byzantium from afar, and, far more worrisome, installed tyrants in Euboea on the doorstep of Athens.

In the third Philippics, *Demosthenes vehemently warns his citizens against the ambitions of Philip, who wanted to subject all Greeks to his rule. In Demosthenes' eyes, the Athenians must abandon their apathy, which is unworthy of their ancestors and which prevents them from taking action against the Macedonians. Moreover, it is their duty to take the initiative and encourage their fellow Greeks to unite to defend their freedom.*

History would prove Demosthenes right. Philip continued his advance and eventually defeated the Greeks at the Battle of Chaeronea in Boeotia in August 338. Demosthenes' greatest fear was realized: Philip became the uncontested supreme master of Greece.

"Our affairs have declined chiefly owing to the orators, who study to please you rather than advise for the best."

Many speeches, men of Athens, are made in almost every assembly about the hostilities of Philip, hostilities which ever since the treaty of peace he has been committing as well against you as against the rest of the Greeks; and all (I am sure) are ready to avow, though they forbear to do so, that our counsels and our measures should be directed to his humiliation and chastisement: nevertheless, so low have our affairs been brought by inattention and negligence, I fear it is a harsh truth to say, that if all the orators had sought to suggest, and you to pass resolutions for the utter ruining of the commonwealth, we could not methinks be worse off than we are.

A variety of circumstances may have brought us to this state; our affairs have not declined from one or two causes only; but, if you rightly examine, you will find it chiefly owing to the orators, who study to please you rather than advise for the best. Some of whom, Athenians, seeking to maintain the basis of their own power and repute, have no forethought for the future, and therefore think you also ought to have none; others, accusing and calumniating practical statesmen, labor only to make Athens punish Athens, and in such occupations to engage her, that Philip may have liberty to say and do what he pleases. Politics of this kind are common here, but are the causes of your failures and embarrassment.

I beg, Athenians, that you will not resent my plain speaking of the truth. Only consider. You hold liberty of speech in other matters to be the general right of all residents in Athens, insomuch that you allow a measure of it even to foreigners and slaves, and many servants may be seen among you speaking their thoughts more freely than citizens in some other states; and yet you have altogether banished it from your councils. The result has been, that in the assembly you give yourselves airs and are flattered at hearing nothing but compliments, in your measures and proceedings you are brought to the utmost peril. If such be your disposition now, I must be silent: if you will listen to good advice without flattery, I am ready to speak.

For though our affairs are in a deplorable condition, though many sacrifices have been made, still, if you will choose to perform your duty, it is possible to repair it all. A paradox, and yet a truth, am I about to state. That which is the most lamentable in the past is best for the future. How is this? Because you performed no part of your duty, great or small, and therefore you fared ill: had you done all that became you, and your situation were the same, there would be no hope of amendment. Philip has indeed prevailed over your sloth and negligence, but not over the country: you have not been worsted; you have not even bestirred yourselves.

If now we were all agreed that Philip is at war with Athens and infringing the peace, nothing would a speaker need to urge or advise but the safest and easiest way of resisting him. But since, at the very time when Philip is capturing cities and retaining divers of our dominions and assailing all people, there are men so unreasonable as to listen to repeated declarations in the assembly, that some of us are kindling war, one must be cautious and set this matter right: for whoever moves or advises a measure of defense, is in danger of being accused afterward as author of the war.

I will first then examine and determine this point, whether it be in our power to deliberate on peace or war. If the country may be at peace, if it depends on us, (to begin with this,) I say we ought to maintain peace, and I call upon the affirmant to move a resolution, to take some measure, and not to palter with us. But if another, having arms in his hand and a large force around him, amuses you with the name of peace, while he carries on the operations of war, what is left but to defend yourselves? You may profess to be at peace, if you like, as he does; I quarrel not with that. But if any man supposes this to be a peace, which will enable Philip to master all else and attack you last, he is a madman, or he talks of a peace observed toward him by you, not toward you by him. This it is that Philip purchases by all his expenditure, the privilege of assailing you without being assailed in turn.

If we really wait until he avows that he is at war with us, we are the simplest of mortals, for he would not declare that, though he marched even against Attica and Piraeus, at least if we may judge from his conduct to others. For example, to the Olynthians he declared, when he was forty furlongs from their city, that there was no alternative, but either they must quit Olynthus or he Macedonia; though before that time, whenever he was accused of such an intent, he took it ill and sent embassadors to justify himself. Again, he marched towards the Phocions as if they were allies, and there were Phocian envoys who accompanied his march, and many among you contended that his advance would not benefit the Thebans.

And he came into Thessaly of late as a friend and ally, yet he has taken possession of Pherae; and lastly he told these wretched people of Oreus, that he had sent his soldiers out of good-will to visit them, as he heard they were in trouble and dissension, and it was the part of allies and true friends to lend assistance on such occasions. People who would never have harmed him, though they might have adopted measures of defense, he chose to deceive rather than warn them of his attack; and think ye he would declare war against you before he began it, and that while you are willing to be deceived? Impossible. He would be the silliest of mankind, if, while you the injured parties make no complaint against him, but are accusing your own countrymen, he should terminate your intestine strife and jealousies, warn you to turn against him, and remove the pretexts of his hirelings for asserting, to amuse you, that he makes no war upon Athens.

O heavens! would any rational being judge by words rather than by actions, who is at peace with him and who at war? Surely none. Well then; Philip immediately after the peace, before Diopithes was in command or the settlers in the Chersonese had been sent out, took Serrium and Doriscus, and expelled from Serrium and the Sacred Mount the troops whom your general had stationed there. What do you call such conduct? He had sworn the peace. Don't say—what does it signify? how is the state concerned?—Whether it be a trifling matter, or of no concernment to you, is a different question: religion and justice have the same obligation, be the subject of the offense great or small.

Tell me now; when he sends mercenaries into Chersonesus, which the king and all the Greeks have acknowledged to be yours, when he avows himself an auxiliary and writes us word so, what are such proceedings? He says he is not at war; I can not however admit such conduct to be an observance of the peace; far otherwise: I say, by his attempt on Megara, by his setting up despotism in Euboea, by his present advance into Thrace, by his intrigues in Peloponnesus, by the whole course of operations with his army, he has been breaking the peace and making war upon you; unless indeed you will say, that those who establish batteries are not at war, until they apply them to the walls. But that you will not say: for whoever contrives and prepares the means for my conquest, is at war with me, before he darts or draws the bow.

What, if any thing should happen, is the risk you run? The alienation of the Hellespont, the subjection of Megara and Euboea to your enemy, the siding of the Peloponnesians with him. Then can I allow, that one who sets such an engine at work against Athens is at peace with her? Quite the contrary. From the day that he destroyed the Phocians I date his commencement of hostilities. Defend yourselves instantly, and I say you will be wise: delay it, and you may wish in vain to do so hereafter. So much do I dissent from your other counselors, men of Athens, that I deem any discussion about Chersonesus or Byzantium out of place. Succor them—I advise that—watch that no harm befalls them, send all necessary supplies to your troops in that quarter; but let your deliberations be for the safety of all Greece, as being in the utmost peril. I must tell you why I am so alarmed at the state of our affairs: that, if my reasonings are correct, you may share them, and make some provision at least for yourselves, however disinclined to do so for others; but if, in your judgment, I talk nonsense and absurdity, you may treat me as crazed, and not listen to me, either now or in future.

That Philip from a mean and humble origin has grown mighty, that the Greeks are jealous and quarreling among themselves, that it was far more wonderful for him to rise from that insignificance, than it would now be, after so many acquisitions, to conquer what is left; these and similar matters, which I might dwell upon, I pass over. But I observe that all people, beginning with you, have conceded to him a right, which in former times has been the subject of contest in every Grecian war. And what is this? The right of doing what he pleases, openly fleecing and pillaging the Greeks, one after another, attacking and enslaving their cities. You were at the head of the Greeks for seventy-three years,[1] and the Thebans had some power in these latter times after the battle of Leuctra. Yet neither you, my countrymen, nor Thebans nor Lacedaemonians, were ever licensed by the Greeks to act as you pleased; far otherwise.

When you, or rather the Athenians at that time, appeared to be dealing harshly with certain people, all the rest, even such as had no complaint against Athens, thought proper to side with the injured parties in a war against her. So, when the Lacedaemonians became masters and succeeded to your empire, on their attempting to encroach and make oppressive innovations, a general war was declared against them, even by such as had no cause of complaint. But wherefore mention other people? We ourselves and the Lacedaemonians, although at the outset we could not allege any natural injuries, thought proper to make war for the injustice that we saw done to our neighbors.

Yet all the faults committed by the Spartans in those thirty years, and by our ancestors in the seventy, are less, men of Athens, than the wrongs which, in thirteen incomplete years that Philip has been uppermost, he has inflicted on the Greeks: nay they are scarcely a fraction of these, as may easily be shown in a few words. Olynthus and Methone and Apollonia, and thirty-two cities on the borders of Thrace, I pass over; all which he has so cruelly destroyed, that a visitor could hardly tell if they were ever inhabited; and of the Phocians, so considerable a people exterminated, I say nothing. But what is the condition of Thessaly? Has he not taken away her constitutions and her cities, and established tetrarchies, to parcel her out, not only by cities, but also by provinces, for subjection? Are not the Euboean states governed now by despots, and that in an island near to Thebes and Athens? Does he not expressly write in his epistles, "I am at peace with those who are willing to obey me?" Nor does he write so and not act accordingly. He is gone to the Hellespont; he marched formerly against Ambracia; Elis, such an important city in Peloponnesus, he possesses; he plotted lately to get Megara: neither Hellenic nor Barbaric land contains the man's ambition.

And we the Greek community, seeing and hearing this, instead of sending embassies to one another about it and expressing indignation, are in such a miserable state, so intrenched in our miserable towns, that to this day we can attempt nothing that interest or necessity requires; we can not combine, or form any association for succor and alliance; we look unconcernedly on the man's growing power, each resolving (methinks) to enjoy the interval that another is destroyed in, not caring or striving for the salvation of Greece: for none can be ignorant, that Philip, like some course or attack of fever or other disease, is coming even on those that yet seem very far removed. And you must be sensible, that whatever wrong the Greeks sustained from Lacedaemonians or from us, was at least inflicted by genuine people of Greece; and it might be felt in the same manner as if a lawful son, born to a large fortune, committed some fault or error in the management of it; on that ground one would consider him open to censure and reproach, yet it could not be said that he was an alien, and not heir to the property which he so dealt with. But if a slave or a spurious child wasted and spoiled what he had no interest in—Heavens! how much more heinous and hateful would all have pronounced it! And yet in regard to Philip and his conduct they feel not this, although he is not only no Greek and noway akin to Greeks, but not even a barbarian of a place honorable to mention; in fact, a vile fellow of Macedon, from which a respectable slave could not be purchased formerly.

What is wanting to make his insolence complete? Besides his destruction of

Grecian cities, does he not hold the Pythian games, the common festival of Greece, and, if he comes not himself, send his vassals to preside? Is he not master of Thermopylae and the passes into Greece, and holds he not those places by garrisons and mercenaries? Has he not thrust aside Thessalians, ourselves, Dorians, the whole Amphictyonic body, and got preaudience of the oracle, to which even the Greeks do not all pretend? Does he not write to the Thessalians, what form of government to adopt? send mercenaries to Porthmus, to expel the Eretrian commonalty; others to Oreus, to set up Philistides as ruler? Yet the Greeks endure to see all this; methinks they view it as they would a hailstorm, each praying that it may not fall on himself, none trying to prevent it.

And not only are the outrages which he does to Greece submitted to, but even the private wrongs of every people: nothing can go beyond this! Has he not wronged the Corinthians by attacking Ambracia and Leucas? the Achaians, by swearing to give Naupactus to the Aetolians? from the Thebans taken Echinus? Is he not marching against the Byzantines his allies? From us—I omit the rest—but keeps he not Cardia, the greatest city of the Chersonese? Still under these indignities we are all slack and disheartened, and look toward our neighbors, distrusting one another, instead of the common enemy. And how think ye a man, who behaves so insolently to all, how will he act, when he gets each separately under his control?

But what has caused the mischief? There must be some cause, some good reason, why the Greeks were so eager for liberty then, and now are eager for servitude. There was something, men of Athens, something in the hearts of the multitude then, which there is not now, which overcame the wealth of Persia and maintained the freedom of Greece, and quailed not under any battle by land or sea; the loss whereof has ruined all, and thrown the affairs of Greece into confusion. What was this? Nothing subtle or clever: simply that whoever took money from the aspirants for power or the corruptors of Greece were universally detested: it was dreadful to be convicted of bribery; the severest punishment was inflicted on the guilty, and there was no intercession or pardon. The favorable moments for enterprise, which fortune frequently offers to the careless against the vigilant, to them that will do nothing against those that discharge all their duty, could not be bought from orators or generals; no more could mutual concord, nor distrust of tyrants and barbarians, nor any thing of the kind.

But now all such principles have been sold as in open market, and those imported in exchange, by which Greece is ruined and diseased. What are they? Envy where a man gets a bribe; laughter if he confesses it; mercy to the convicted; hatred of those that denounce the crime: all the usual attendants upon corruption. For as to ships and men and revenues and abundance of other materials, all that may be reckoned as constituting national strength—assuredly the Greeks of our day are more fully and perfectly supplied with such advantages than Greeks of the olden time. But they are all rendered useless, unavailable, unprofitable, by the agency of these traffickers.

That such is the present state of things, you must see, without requiring my testimony: that it was different in former times, I will demonstrate, not by speaking my own words, but by showing an inscription of your ancestors, which they graved on a brazen column and deposited in the citadel, not for their own benefit, (they were right-minded enough without such records,) but for a memorial and example to instruct you, how seriously such conduct should be taken up. What says the inscription then? It says: "Let Arthmius, son of Pythonax the Zelite, be declared an outlaw, and an enemy of the Athenian people and their allies, him and his family." Then the cause is written why this was done: because he brought the Median gold into Peloponnesus. That is the inscription.

By the gods! only consider and reflect among yourselves, what must have been the spirit, what the dignity of those Athenians who acted so! One Arthmius a Zelite, subject of the king, (for Zelea is in Asia,) because in his master's service he brought gold into Peloponnesus, not to Athens, they proclaimed an enemy of the Athenians and their allies, him and his family, and outlawed. That is, not the outlawry commonly spoken of: for what would a Zelite care, to be excluded from Athenian franchises? It means not that; but in the statutes of homicide it is written, in cases where a prosecution for murder is not allowed, but killing is sanctioned, "and let him die an outlaw," says the legislator: by which he means, that whoever kills such a person shall be unpolluted. Therefore they considered that the preservation of all Greece was their own concern: but for such opinion, they would not have cared, whether people in Peloponnesus were bought and corrupted. And whomsoever they discovered taking bribes, they chastised and punished so severely as to record their names in brass.

The natural result was, that Greece was formidable to the Barbarian, not the Barbarian to Greece. 'Tis not so now: since neither in this nor in other respects are your sentiments the same. But what are they? You know yourselves: why am I to upbraid you with every thing? The Greeks in general are alike and no better than you. Therefore I say, our present affairs demand earnest attention and wholesome counsel. Shall I say what? Do you bid me, and won't you be angry?

There is a foolish saying of persons who wish to make us easy, that Philip is not yet as powerful as the Lacedaemonians were formerly, who ruled every where by land and sea, and had the king for their ally, and nothing withstood them; yet Athens resisted even that nation, and was not destroyed. I myself believe, that, while every thing has received great improvement, and the present bears no resemblance to the past, nothing has been so changed and improved as the practice of war. For anciently, as I am informed, the Lacedaemonians and all Grecian people would for four or five months, during the season only, invade and ravage the land of their enemies with heavy-armed and national troops, and return home again: and their ideas were so old-fashioned, or rather national, they never purchased an advantage from any; theirs was a legitimate and open warfare.

But now you doubtless perceive, that the majority of disasters have been effected by treason; nothing is done in fair field or combat. You hear of Philip marching where he pleases, not because he commands troops of the line, but because he has attached to him a host of skirmishers, cavalry, archers, mercenaries, and the like. When with these he falls upon a people in civil dissension, and none (for mistrust) will march out to defend the country, he applies engines and besieges them. I need not mention, that he makes no difference between winter and summer, that he has no stated season of repose. You, knowing these things, reflecting on them, must not let the war approach your territories, nor get your necks broken, relying on the simplicity of the old war with the Lacedaemonians, but take the longest time beforehand for defensive measures and preparations, see that he stirs not from home, avoid any decisive engagement. For a war, if we choose, men of Athens, to pursue a right course, we have many natural advantages; such as the position of his kingdom, which we may extensively plunder and ravage, and a thousand more; but for a battle he is better trained than we are.

Nor is it enough to adopt these resolutions and oppose him by warlike measures: you must on calculation and on principle abhor his advocates here, remembering that it is impossible to overcome your enemies abroad, until you have chastised those who are his ministers within the city. Which, by Jupiter and all the gods, you can not and will not do! You have arrived at such a pitch of folly or madness or—I know not what to call it: I am tempted often to think, that some evil genius is driving you to ruin—for the sake of scandal or envy or jest or any other cause, you command hirelings to speak, (some of whom would not deny themselves to be hirelings,) and laugh when they abuse people. And this, bad as it is, is not the worst: you have allowed these persons more liberty for their political conduct than your faithful counselors: and see what evils are caused by listening to such men with indulgence. I will mention facts that you will all remember.

In Olynthus some of the statesmen were in Philip's interest, doing every thing for him; some were on the honest side, aiming to preserve their fellow-citizens from slavery. Which party now destroyed their country? or which betrayed the cavalry, by whose betrayal Olynthus fell? The creatures of Philip; they that, while the city stood, slandered and calumniated the honest counselors so effectually, that the Olynthian people were induced to banish Apollonides.

Nor is it there only, and nowhere else, that such practice has been ruinous. In Eretria, when, after riddance of Plutarch and his mercenaries, the people got possession of their city and of Porthmus, some were for bringing the government over to you, others to Philip. His partisans were generally, rather exclusively, attended to by the wretched and unfortunate Eretrians, who at length were persuaded to expel their faithful advisers. Philip, their ally and friend, sent Hipponicus and a thousand mercenaries, demolished the walls of Porthmus, and established three rulers, Hipparchus, Automedon, Clitarchus. Since that he has driven them out of the country, twice attempting their deliverance: once he sent the troops with Eurylochus, afterward those of Parmenio.

What need of many words? In Oreus Philip's agents were Philistides, Menippus, Socrates, Thoas, and Agapaeus, who now hold the government: that was quite notorious: one Euphraeus, a man that formerly dwelt here among you, was laboring for freedom and independence. How this man was in other respects insulted and trampled on by the people of Oreus, were long to tell: but a year before the capture, discovering what Philistides and his accomplices were about, he laid an information against them for treason. A multitude then combining, having Philip for their paymaster, and acting under his direction, take Euphraeus off to prison as a disturber of the public peace. Seeing which, the people of Oreus, instead of assisting the one and beating the others to death, with them were not angry, but said his punishment was just, and rejoiced at it. So the conspirators, having full liberty of action, laid their schemes and took their measures for the surrender of the city; if any of the people observed it, they were silent and intimidated, remembering the treatment of Euphraeus; and so wretched was their condition, that on the approach of such a calamity none dared to utter a word, until the enemy drew up before the walls: then some were for defense, others for betrayal. Since the city was thus basely and wickedly taken, the traitors have held despotic rule; people who formerly rescued them, and were ready for any maltreatment of Euphraeus, they have either banished or put to death; Euphraeus killed himself, proving by deed, that he had resisted Philip honestly and purely for the good of his countrymen.

What can be the reason—perhaps you wonder—why the Olynthians and Eretrians and Orites were more indulgent to Philip's advocates than to their own? The same which operates with you. They who advise for the best can not always gratify their audience, though they would; for the safety of the state must be attended to: their opponents by the very counsel which is agreeable advance Philip's interest. One party required contribution; the other said there was no necessity: one were for war and mistrust; the other for peace, until they were ensnared. And so on for every thing else; (not to dwell on particulars;) the one made speeches to please for the moment, and gave no annoyance; the other offered salutary counsel, that was offensive. Many rights did the people surrender at last, not from any such motive of indulgence or ignorance, but submitting in the belief that all was lost, Which, by Jupiter and Apollo, I fear will be your case, when on calculation you see that nothing can be done.

I pray, men of Athens, it may never come to this! Better die a thousand deaths than render homage to Philip, or sacrifice any of your faithful counselors. A fine recompense have the people of Oreus got, for trusting themselves to Philip's friends and spurning Euphraeus! Finely are the Eretrian commons rewarded, for having driven away your embassadors and yielded to Clitarchus! Yes; they are slaves, exposed to the lash and the torture. Finally he spared the Olynthians, who appointed Lasthenes to command their horse, and expelled Apollonides! It is folly and cowardice to cherish such hopes, and, while you take evil counsel and shirk every duty, and even listen to those who plead for your enemies, to think you inhabit a city of such magnitude, that you can not suffer any serious misfortune.

Yea, and it is disgraceful to exclaim on any occurrence, when it is too late, "Who would have expected it? However—this or that should have been done, the other left undone." Many things could the Olynthians mention now, which, if foreseen at the time would have prevented their destruction. Many could the Orites mention, many the Phocians, and each of the ruined states. But what would it avail them? As long as the vessel is safe, whether it be great or small, the mariner, the pilot, every man in turn should exert himself, and prevent its being overturned either by accident or design: but when the sea hath rolled over it, their efforts are vain. And we, likewise, O Athenians, while we are safe, with a magnificent city, plentiful resources, lofty reputation—what must we do? Many of you, I dare say, have been longing to ask. Well then, I will tell you; I will move a resolution: pass it, if you please.

First, let us prepare for our own defense; provide ourselves, I mean, with ships, money, and troops—for surely, though all other people consented to be slaves, we at least ought to struggle for freedom. When we have completed our own preparations and made them apparent to the Greeks, then let us invite the rest, and send our embassadors every where with the intelligence, to Peloponnesus, to Rhodes, to Chios, to the king, I say; (for it concerns his interests, not to let Philip make universal conquest;) that, if you prevail, you may have partners of your dangers and expenses, in case of necessity, or at all events that you may delay the operations. For, since the war is against an individual, not against the collected power of a state, even this may be useful; as were the embassies last year to Peloponnesus, and the remonstrances with which I and Polyeuctus, that excellent man, and Hegesippus, and Clitomachus, and Lycurgus, and the other envoys went round, and arrested Philip's progress, so that he neither attacked Ambracia nor started for Peloponnesus.

I say not, however, that you should invite the rest without adopting measures to protect yourselves: it would be folly, while you sacrifice your own interest, to profess a regard for that of strangers, or to alarm others about the future, while for the present you are unconcerned. I advise not this: I bid you send supplies to the troops in Chersonesus, and do what else they require; prepare yourselves and make every effort first, then summon, gather, instruct the rest of the Greeks. That is the duty of a state possessing a dignity such as yours. If you imagine that Chalcidians or Megarians will save Greece, while you run away from the contest, you imagine wrong. Well for any of those people, if they are safe themselves. This work belongs to you: this privilege your ancestors bequeathed to you, the prize of many perilous exertions. But if every one will sit seeking his pleasure, and studying to be idle himself, never will he find others to do his work, and more than this, I fear we shall be under the necessity of doing all that we like not at one time. Were proxies to be had, our inactivity would have found them long ago; but they are not.

Such are the measures which I advise, which I propose: adopt them, and even yet, I believe, our prosperity may be re-established. If any man has better advice to offer, let him communicate it openly. Whatever you determine, I pray to all the gods for a happy result.

Translated by Charles Rann Kennedy.

PLAUTUS

c. 255 - 184 BC

T. Maccius ("big jaw") Plautus ("flat foot") was born in Umbria north of Rome. He came to the city to launch a career in stage production. Before writing comedies, he was first an actor, after which he tried his skills in commercial trade, financially ruined himself, and dabbled in different jobs (including that of a miller's slave). One hundred and thirty plays were attributed to him. However, in the first century BC, the scholar Varro declared only 21 as authentic, and subsequently only these have survived.

Plautus enjoyed imitating the New Comedy of the Greeks. He tried to please the public, which demanded Greek subjects, but was able to accommodate his sketches with Roman "salsa." To grab the public's attention, Plautus liked to begin his plays with a prologue that twisted the play's plot rather than explain it as would have been in line with the common practice at the time. He resorted to parody, the playing on words, the skilful use of music, and vaudeville-like antics. His contemporaries' deceit and roguery fueled his verve.

In modern times, great playwrights have paid respect to Plautus by adapting his works, as did Molière, for example, in his Miser *and* Amphitryon.

When the Cat's Away, the Mice Will Play

Plautus, *The Haunted House*, Act I, Scenes I-III

Theuropides is a wealthy merchant who departs for business in Egypt. He is absent for three years and in the eyes of the members of his household has probably died in a shipwreck somewhere or has been killed by pirates. At any rate, his chances for returning safely are deemed nil. As a result, his son Philolaches has had plenty of time to listen to the sly advice of the slave Tranio. He squanders his father's money on parties and foolish undertakings, such as the purchase of his mistress slave girl's freedom at an exorbitant price.

The problem is that the father is very much alive—and very much on his way back home! Upon learning of the father's return, a wave of panic hits through the prodigal son and his fellow party revelers. Tranio quickly finds a solution: In order to prevent the father from seeing what has transpired in his own house, he suggests pretending that the place is haunted.

Throughout the play, Plautus stages his favorite comic characters: the shifty city slave and his faithful country counterpart, the debauched son, the naïve father, the beautiful but not-too-smart female lover, and her greedy old servant.

Characters

GRUMIO, servant of Theuropides
TRANIO, servant of Philolaches
PHILOLACHES, son of Theuropides
PHILEMATIUM, music-girl and mistress of Philolaches
SCAPHA, Philematium's attendant

"The lover isn't in love with a woman's dress, but with that which stuffs out the dress."

ACT I, SCENE I

[*Enter, from the house of Theuropides, Grumio, pushing out Tranio.*]

GRUMIO
Get out of the kitchen, will you; out of it, you whip-scoundrel, who are giving me your cavilling talk amid the platters; march out of the house, you ruin of your master.

Upon my faith, if Ionly live, I'll be soundly revenged upon you in the country. Get out, I say, you steam of the kitchen. Why are you skulking thus?

TRANIO
Why the plague are you making this noise here before the house? Do you fancy yourself to be in the country? Get out of the house Be off into the country. Go and hang yourself. Get away from the door. [*Striking him*] There now, was it that you wanted?

GRUMIO [*Running away*]
I'm undone! Why are you beating me?

TRANIO
Because you want it.

GRUMIO
I must endure it. Only let the old gentleman return home; only let him come safe home, whom you are devouring in his absence.

TRANIO
You don't say what's either likely or true, you blockhead, as to any one devouring a person in his absence.

GRUMIO
Indeed, you town wit, you minion of the mob, do you throw the country in my teeth? Really, Tranio, I do believe that you feel sure that before long you'll be handed over to the mill.
Within a short period, i' faith, Tranio, you'll full soon be adding to the iron-bound race[1] in the country.
While you choose to, and have the opportunity, drink on, squander his property, corrupt my master's son, a most worthy young man, drink night and day, live like Greeks, make purchase of mistresses, give them their freedom, feed parasites, feast yourselves sumptuously.
Was it thus that the old gentleman enjoined you when he went hence abroad?
Is it after this fashion that he will find his property well husbanded?
Do you suppose that this is the duty of a good servant,
to be ruining both the estate and the son of his master?
For I do consider him as ruined, when he devotes himself to these goings on.
A person, with whom not one of all the young men of Attica
Was before deemed equally frugal or more steady,
the same is now carrying off the palm in the opposite direction.

Through your management and your tutoring has that been done.

TRANIO
What the plague business have you with me or with, what I do?
Prithee, haven't you got your cattle in the country for you to look to?
I choose to drink, to intrigue, to keep my wenches;
this I do at the peril of my own back, and not of yours.

GRUMIO
Then with what assurance he does talk! [*Turning away in disgust*] Faugh!

TRANIO
But may Jupiter and all the Deities confound you; you stink of garlic,
you filth unmistakable, you clod, you he-goat, you pig-sty,
you mixture of dog and she-goat.

GRUMIO
What would you have to be done?
It isn't all that can smell of foreign perfumes,
if you smell of them; or that can take their places at table above their master,
or live on such exquisite dainties as you live upon.
Do you keep to yourself those turtle-doves, that fish, and poultry;
let me enjoy my lot upon garlic diet.
You are fortunate; I unlucky. It must be endured.
Let my good fortune be awaiting me, your bad yourself.

TRANIO
You seem, Grumio, as though you envied me,
because I enjoy myself and you are wretched. It is quite my due.
It's proper for me to make love, and for you to feed the cattle;
for me to fare handsomely, you in a miserable way.

GRUMIO
O riddle for the executioner, as I guess it will turn out;
they'll be so pinking you with goads, as you carry your gibbet along
the streets one day, as soon as ever the old gentleman returns here.

TRANIO
How do you know whether that mayn't happen to yourself sooner than to me?

GRUMIO
Because I have never deserved it; you have deserved it, and you now deserve it.

TRANIO
Do cut short the trouble of your talking,
unless you wish a heavy mischance to befall you.

GRUMIO
Are you going to give me the tares for me to take for the cattle?
If you are not, give me the money. Go on, still persist in the way
In which you've commenced! Drink, live like Greeks,
eat, stuff yourselves, slaughter your fatlings!

TRANIO
Hold your tongue, and be off into the country; I intend to go to the Piraeus
to get me some fish for the evening.
Tomorrow I'll make some one bring you the tares to the farm.
What's the matter? Why now are you staring at me, gallows-bird?

GRUMIO
I' faith, I've an idea that will be your own title before long.

TRANIO
So long as it is as it is, in the meantime I'll put up with that "before long."

GRUMIO
That's the way; and understand this one thing, that that which is
disagreable comes much more speedily than that which you wish for.

TRANIO
Don't you be annoying; now then, away with you into the country, and betake yourself off.
Don't you deceive yourself, henceforth you shan't be causing me any impediment.

[*Exit.*]

GRUMIO [*To himself*]
Is he really gone? Not to care one straw for what I've said!
O immortal Gods, I do implore your aid,
do cause this old gentleman of ours, who has now been three years absent from here,
to return hither as soon as possible, before everything is gone,

both house and land. Unless he does return here,
remnants to last for a few months only are left.
Now I'll be off to the country; but look! I see my master's son,
one who has been corrupted from having been a most excellent young man. [*Exit.*]

SCENE II

[*Enter Philolaches, from the house of Theuropides.*]

PHILOLACHES [*To himself*]
I've often thought and long reflected on it,
and in my breast have held many a debate,
and in my heart (if any heart I have)
have revolved this matter, and long discussed it,
to what thing I'm to consider man as like, and what form he has when he is born?
I've now discovered this likeness.
I think a man is like unto a new house
when he is born. I'll give my proofs of this fact.

[*To the Audience*]
And does not this seem to you like the truth?
But so I'll manage that you shall think it is so.
Beyond a doubt I'll convince you that it is true what I say.
And this yourselves, I'm sure, when you have heard my words,
will say is no otherwise than just as I now affirm that it is.
Listen while I repeat my proofs of this fact;
I want you to be equally knowing with myself upon this matter.

As soon as ever a house is built up, nicely polished off,
carefully erected, and according to rule,
people praise the architect and approve of the house,
they take from it each one a model for himself.
Each one has something similar, quite at his own expense; they do not spare their pains. But when a worthless, lazy, dirty, negligent fellow
Betakes himself thither with an idle family,
then is it imputed as a fault to the house, while a good house is being kept in bad repair.
And this is often the case; a storm comes on
and breaks the tiles and gutters; then
a careless owner takes no heed to put up others.
A shower comes on and streams down the walls;

the rafters admit the rain; the weather rots the labours of the builder;
then the utility of the house becomes diminished;
and yet this is not the fault of the builder. But a great part of mankind
have contracted this habit of delay; if anything can be repaired by means of money,
they are always still putting it off, and don't do it until the walls come
tumbling down; then the whole house has to be built anew.

These instances from buildings I've mentioned; and now I wish
to inform you how you are to suppose that men are like houses.
In the first place then, the parents are the builders-up of the children,
and lay the foundation for the children;
they raise them up, they carefully train them to strength,
and that they may be good both for service and
for view before the public. They spare not either their own pains
or their cost, nor do they deem expense in that to be an expense.
They refine them, teach them literature, the ordinances, the laws;
at their own cost and labour they struggle,
that others may wish for their own children to be like to them.
When they repair to the army, they then find them
some relation of theirs as a protector.
At that moment they pass out of the builder's hands. One year's pay has now been earned; at that period, then, a sample is on view how the building will turn out.

But I was always discreet and virtuous,
just as long as I was under the management of the builder.
After I had left him to follow the bent of my own inclinations,
at once I entirely spoiled the labours of the builders.
Idleness came on; that was my storm;
on its arrival, upon me it brought down hail and showers,
which overthrew my modesty and the bounds of virtue,
and untiled them for me in an instant.
After that I was neglectful to cover in again;
at once passion like a torrent entered my heart;
it flowed down even unto my breast, and soaked through my heart.
Now both property, credit, fair fame, virtue, and honor
have forsaken me; by usage have I become much worse,
and, i' faith (so rotten are these rafters of mine with moisture), I do not seem to myself to be able possibly to patch up my house to prevent it from falling down totally once for all, from perishing from the foundation, and from no one being able to assist me.

My heart pains me, when I reflect how I now am and how I once was,
than whom in youthful age not one there was more active in the arts of exercise,
with the quoit, the javelin, the ball, racing, arms, and horses.
I then lived a joyous life; in frugality and hardihood I was an example to others;
all, even the most deserving, took a lesson from me for themselves.
Now that I'm become worthless, to that, indeed, have I hastened through the bent of my inclinations. [*He stands apart.*]

SCENE III

[*Enter Philematium and Scapha, with all the requisites for a toilet.*]

PHILEMATIUM
On my word, for this long time I've not bathed in cold water with more delight than just now;
nor do I think that I ever was, my dear Scapha, more thoroughly cleansed than now.

SCAPHA
May the upshot of everything be unto you like a plenteous year's harvest.

PHILEMATIUM
What has this harvest got to do with my bathing?

SCAPHA
Not a bit more than your bathing has to do with the harvest.

PHILOLACHES [*apart*]
O beauteous Venus,
this is that storm of mine which stripped off all the modesty
with which I was roofed; through which Desire and Cupid
poured their shower into my breast; and never since have I been able to roof it in.
Now are my walls soaking in my heart; this building is utterly undone.

PHILEMATIUM
Do look, my Scapha, there's a dear, whether this dress quite becomes me.
I wish to please Philolaches my protector, the apple of my eye.

SCAPHA
Nay but, you set yourself off to advantage with pleasing manners, inasmuch as you yourself are pleasing.
The lover isn't in love with a woman's dress, but with that which stuffs out the dress.

PHILOLACHES [*apart*]
So may the Gods bless me, Scapha is waggish; the hussy's quite knowing.
How cleverly she understands all matters, the maxims of lovers too!

PHILEMATIUM
Well now?

SCAPHA
What is it?

PHILEMATIUM
Why look at me and examine, how this becomes me.

SCAPHA
Thanks to your good looks, it happens that whatever you put on becomes you.

PHILOLACHES [*apart*]
Now then, for that expression, Scapha, I'll make you some present or other to-day,
and I won't allow you to have praised her for nothing who is so pleasing to me.

PHILEMATIUM
I don't want you to flatter me.

SCAPHA
Really you are a very simple woman.
Come now, would you rather be censured undeservedly, than be praised with truth?
Upon thy faith, for my own part, even though undeservedly, I'd much rather be praised
Than be found fault with reason, or that other people should laugh at my appearance.

PHILEMATIUM
I love the truth; I wish the truth to be told me; I detest a liar.

SCAPHA
So may you love me, and so may your Philolaches love you, how charming you are.

PHILOLACHES [*apart*]
How say you, you hussy? In what words did you adjure? "So may I love her?"
Why wasn't "So may she love me" added as well? I revoke the present.
What I just now promised you is done for; you have lost the present.

SCAPHA
Troth, for my part I am surprised that you, a person so knowing, so clever, and sowell educated,
are not aware that you are acting foolishly.

PHILEMATIUM
Then give me your advice, I beg, if I have done wrong in anything.

SCAPHA
I' faith, you certainly do wrong, in setting your mind upon him alone, in fact,
and humouring him in particular in this way and slighting other men.
It's the part of a married woman, and not of courtesans, to be devoted to a single lover.

PHILOLACHES [*apart*]
O Jupiter! Why, what pest is this that has befallen my house?
May all the Gods and Goddesses destroy me in the worst of fashions,
if I don't kill this old hag with thirst, and hunger, and cold.

PHILEMATIUM
I don't want you, Scapha, to be giving me bad advice.

SCAPHA
You are clearly a simpleton,
in thinking that he'll for everlasting be your friend and well-wisher.
I warn you of that; he'll forsake you by reason of age and satiety.

PHILEMATIUM
I hope not.

SCAPHA
Things which you don't hope happen more frequently than things which you do hope.
In fine, if you cannot be persuaded by words to believe this to be the truth,
judge of my words from facts; consider this instance, who I now am, and who I once was.
No less than you are now, was I once beloved, and I devoted myself to one,
who, faith, when with age this head changed its hue,
forsook and deserted me. Depend on it, the same will happen to yourself.

PHILOLACHES [*apart*]
I can scarcely withhold myself from flying at the eyes of this mischief-maker.

PHILEMATIUM
I am of opinion that I ought to keep myself alone devoted to him,
since to myself alone has he given freedom for himself alone.

PHILOLACHES [*apart*]
O ye immortal Gods! what a charming woman, and of a disposition how chaste!
By heaven, 'tis excellently done, and I'm rejoiced at it, that it is for her sake I've got nothing left.

SCAPHA
On my word you really are silly.

PHILEMATIUM
For what reason?

SCAPHA
Because you care for this, whether he loves you.

PHILEMATIUM
Prithee, why should I not care for it?

SCAPHA
You now are free.
You've now got what you wanted; if he didn't still love you,
as much money as he gave for your liberty, he'd lose.

PHILOLACHES [*apart*]
Heavens, I'm a dead man if I don't torture her to death after the most shocking fashion.
That evil-persuading enticer to vice is corrupting this damsel.

PHILEMATIUM
Scapha, I can never return him sufficient thanks for what he deserves of me;
don't you be persuading me to esteem him less.

SCAPHA
But take care and reflect upon this one thing, if you devote yourself to him alone,

while now you are at this youthful age, you'll be complaining to no purpose in your aged years.

PHILOLACHES [*apart*]
I could wish myself this instant changed into a quinsy, that I might seize
the throat of that old witch, and put an end to the wicked mischief-maker.

PHILEMATIUM
It befits me now to have the same grateful feelings since I obtained it,
as formerly before I acquired it, when I used to lavish caresses upon him.

PHILOLACHES [*apart*]
May the Gods do towards me what they please, if for that speech
I don't make you free over again, and if I don't torture Scapha to death.

SCAPHA
If you are quite assured that you will have a provision to the end,
and that this lover will be your own for life, I think that you ought to
devote yourself to him alone, and assume the character of a wife.

PHILEMATIUM
Just as a person's character is, he's in the habit of finding means accordingly;
if I keep a good character for myself I shall be rich enough.

PHILOLACHES [*apart*]
By my troth, since selling there must be, my father shall be sold much sooner
than, while I'm alive, I'll ever permit you to be in want or go a-begging.

SCAPHA
What's to become of the rest of those who are in love with you?

PHILEMATIUM
They'll love me the more
when they see me displaying gratitude to one who has done me services.

PHILOLACHES [*apart*]
I do wish that news were brought me now that my father's dead,
that I might disinherit myself of my property, and that she might be my heir.

SCAPHA
This property of his will certainly soon be at an end; day and night there's eating and

drinking, and no one displays thriftiness; 'tis downright cramming.

PHILOLACHES [*apart*]
I' faith, I'm determined to make trial on yourself for the first to be thrifty; for you shall neither eat nor drink anything at my house for the next ten days.

PHILEMATIUM
If you choose to say anything good about him, you shall be at liberty to say it; if you speak otherwise than well, on my word you shall have a beating instantly.

PHILOLACHES [*apart*]
Upon my faith, if I had paid sacrifice to supreme Jove with that money which I gave for her liberty, never could I have so well employed it. Do see, how, from her very heart's core, she loves me! Oh, I'm a fortunate man; I've liberated in her a patron to plead my cause for me.

SCAPHA
I see that, compared with Philolaches, you disregard all other men; now, that on his account I mayn't get a beating, I'll agree with you in preference, if you are quite satisfied that he will always prove a friend to you.

PHILEMATIUM
Give me the mirror, and the casket with my trinkets, directly, Scapha, that I may be quite dressed when Philolaches, my delight, comes here.

SCAPHA
A woman who neglects herself and her youthful age has occasion for a mirror; what need of a mirror have you, who yourself are in especial a mirror for a mirror.

PHILOLACHES [*apart*]
For that expression, Scapha, that you mayn't have said anything so pretty in vain, I'll to-day give something for your savings—to you, my Philematium.

PHILEMATIUM [*while Scapha is dressing her hair*]
Will you see that each hair is nicely arranged in its own place?

SCAPHA
When you yourself are so nice, do believe that your hair must be nice.

PHILOLACHES [*apart*]
Out upon it! what worse thing can possibly be spoken of than this woman? Now the

jade's a flatterer, just now she was all contradictory.

PHILEMATIUM
Hand me the ceruse.

SCAPHA
Why, what need of ceruse have you?

PHILEMATIUM
To paint my cheeks with it.

SCAPHA
On the same principle, you would want to be making ivory white with ink.

PHILOLACHES [*apart*]
Cleverly said that, about the ink and the ivory! Bravo! I applaud you, Scapha.

PHILEMATIUM
Well then, do you give me the rouge.

SCAPHA
I shan't give it. You really are a clever one.
Do you wish to patch up a most clever piece with new daubing?
It's not right that any paint should touch that person, neither ceruse, nor quince-ointment, nor any other wash. Take the mirror, then.

PHILOLACHES [*apart*]
Ah wretched me!—she gave the glass a kiss.
I could much wish for a stone, with which to break the head of that glass.

SCAPHA
Take the towel and wipe your hands.

PHILEMATIUM
Why so, prithee?

SCAPHA
As you've been holding the mirror, I'm afraid that your hands may smell of silver; lest Philolaches should suspect you've been receiving silver somewhere.

PHILOLACHES [*apart*]
I don't think that I ever did see anyone procuress more cunning.
How cleverly and artfully did it occur to the jade's imagination about the mirror!

PHILEMATIUM
Do you think I ought to be perfumed with unguents as well?

SCAPHA
By no means do so.

PHILEMATIUM
For what reason?

SCAPHA
Because, i' faith, a woman smells best when she smells of nothing at all.
For those old women who are in the habit of anointing themselves with unguents, vampt up creatures,
old hags, and toothless, who hide the blemishes of the person with paint, when the sweat has blended itself with the unguents, forthwith they stink just like when a cook has poured together a variety of broths; what they smell of, you don't know, except this only, that you understand that badly they do smell.

PHILOLACHES [*apart*]
How very cleverly she does understand everything! There's nothing more knowing than this knowing woman!
[*To the Audience*] This is the truth, and a very great portion, in fact, of you know it, who have old women for wives at home who purchased you with their portions.

PHILEMATIUM
Come now; examine my golden trinkets and my mantle; does this quite become me, Scapha?

SCAPHA
It befits not me to concern myself about that.

PHILEMATIUM
Whom then, prithee?

SCAPHA
I'll tell you; Philolaches; so that he may not buy anything except that which he fancies will please you.

For a lover buys the favours of a mistress for himself with gold and purple garments.
What need is there for that which he doesn't want as his own, to be shown him still?
Age is to be enveloped in purple; gold ornaments are unsuitable for a woman.
A beautiful woman will be more beautiful naked than drest in purple.
Besides, it's in vain she's well-drest if she's ill-conducted; ill-conduct soils fine ornaments worse than dirt.
But if she's beauteous, she's sufficiently adorned.

PHILOLACHES [*apart*]
Too long have I withheld my hand. [*Coming forward*] What are you about here?

PHILEMATIUM
I'm decking myself out to please you.

PHILOLACHES
You are dressed enough.
[*To Scapha*] Go you hence indoors, and take away this finery.
[*Scapha goes into the house.*] But, my delight, my Philematium, I have a mind to regale together with you.

PHILEMATIUM
And, i' faith, so I have with you; for what you have a mind to, the same have I a mind to, my delight.

PHILOLACHES
Ha! at twenty minae that expression were cheap.

PHILEMATIUM
Give me ten, there's a dear; I wish to let you have that expression bought a bargain.

PHILOLACHES
You've already got ten minae with you; or reckon up the account: thirty minae I gave for your freedom—

PHILEMATIUM
Why reproach me with that?

PHILOLACHES
What, I reproach you with it? Why, I had rather that I myself were reproached with it; no money whatever for this long time have I ever laid out equally well.

PHILEMATIUM
Surely, in loving you, I never could have better employed my pains.

PHILOLACHES
The account, then, of receipts and expenditure fully tallies between ourselves;
you love me, I love you. Each thinks that it is so deservedly.
Those who rejoice at this, may they ever rejoice at the continuance of their own happiness.
Those who envy, let not any one henceforth be ever envious of their blessings.

PHILEMATIUM [*pointing to a couch on the stage*]
Come, take your place, then.
[*At the door, to a servant, who obeys*]
Boy, bring some water for the hands; put a little table here.
See where are the dice. Would you like some perfumes? [*They recline on the couch.*]

PHILOLACHES
What need is there? Along with myrrh I am reclining.
But isn't this my friend who's coming hither with his mistress? 'Tis he; it's
Callidamates; look, he's coming. Capital! my sweet one,
see, our comrades are approaching; they're coming to share the spoil.

Translated by Henri Thomas Riley.

CICERO

106 - 43 BC

Cicero, alias "Chick Pea," was born to an equestrian family at Arpinum on 3 January 106 BC. As a "New Man," he was the first of his family to embark on a political career that would eventually lead him to a consulship. In 91 BC, he journeyed to Rome to complete his education. There, he associated with the greatest rhetors of his time and followed the seminars of the Epicurean philosopher Phaedrus and of the Stoic philosopher Diodotus. A decade passed before he participated in his first court cases. He also traveled to Greece, at first to Athens and then to Rhodes. While at Rhodes, he met the Stoic philosopher Posidonius.

Cicero was a complex man whose existence was split between the failures of his private life—his divorce at the age of 61 and the loss of his beloved daughter, Tullia—and his success as a public lawyer. His genius is further revealed in his rich literary corpus: over 900 letters that are living witness to his many hardships, oratory writings, philosophical works, poems, and short treatises on wide moral values (e.g., On Old Age *and* On Friendship*). He was also a linguist, who, for example, translated Plato's Greek dialogue,* Protagoras, *into Latin.*

Definition of Friendship

Cicero, *On Friendship* 17-35

In the twilight years of his life, Cicero composed numerous philosophical essays. On Friendship *is one of his last works written in 44 BC, shortly after the death of Caesar. Here, he mentions a conversation about friendship that had transpired between Laelius and his sons-in-law, Scaevola and Fannius, more than 80 years earlier in 129 BC. Laelius, a politician admired for his modesty and moderation, was famous for his friendship with Scipio Aemilianus, nicknamed the "African" for destroying Carthage in 146 BC. Through these historic figures, Cicero further desires to discuss his lifetime friendship with the scholar and art collector, Atticus. Moreover, it is Atticus himself who insisted that Cicero write an essay on friendship.*

"What can be more delightful than to have some one to whom you can say everything with the same absolute confidence as to yourself?"

LAELIUS: I should certainly have no objection if I felt confidence in myself. For the theme is a noble one, and we are (as Fannius has said) at leisure. But who am I? and what ability have I? What you propose is all very well for professional philosophers, who are used, particularly if Greeks, to have the subject for discussion proposed to them on the spur of the moment. It is a task of considerable difficulty, and requires no little practice. Therefore for a set discourse on friendship you must go, I think, to professional lecturers. All I can do is to urge on you to regard friendship as the greatest thing in the world; for there is nothing which so fits in with our nature, or is so exactly what we want in prosperity or adversity.

But I must at the very beginning lay down this principle: friendship can only exist between good men. I do not, however, press this too closely, like the philosophers who push their definitions to a superfluous accuracy. They have truth on their side, perhaps, but it is of no practical advantage. Those, I mean, who say that no one but the "wise" is "good." Granted, by all means. But the "wisdom" they mean is one to which no mortal ever yet attained. We must concern ourselves with the facts of everyday life as we find it—not imaginary and ideal perfections. Even Gaius Fannius, Manius Curius, and Tiberius Coruncanius,[1] whom our ancestors decided to be "wise," I could never declare to be so according to their standard. Let them, then, keep this word "wisdom" to themselves. Everybody is irritated by it; no one understands what it means. Let them but grant that the men I mentioned were "good." No, they won't do that either. No one but the "wise" can be allowed that title, say they. Well, then, let us dismiss them and manage as best we may with our own poor mother wit, as the phrase is.

We mean then by the "good" those whose actions and lives leave no question as to their honour, purity, equity, and liberality; who are free from greed, lust, and violence; and who have the courage of their convictions. The men I have just named may serve as examples. Such men as these being generally accounted "good," let us agree to call them so, on the ground that to the best of human ability they follow nature as the most perfect guide to a good life.

Now this truth seems clear to me, that nature has so formed us that a certain tie unites us all, but that this tie becomes stronger from proximity. So it is that fellow-citizens are preferred in our affections to foreigners, relations to strangers; for in their case Nature herself has caused a kind of friendship to exist, though it is one which lacks some of the elements of permanence. Friendship excels relationship in this, that whereas you may eliminate affection from relationship, you cannot do so from friendship. Without it relationship still exists in name, friendship does not. You may best understand this friendship by considering that, whereas the merely natural ties uniting the human race are indefinite, this one is so concentrated, and confined to so narrow a sphere, that affection is ever shared by two persons only or at most by a few.

Now friendship may be thus defined: a complete accord on all subjects human and divine, joined with mutual goodwill and affection. And with the exception of wisdom, I am inclined to think nothing better than this has been given to man by the immortal gods. There are people who give the palm to riches or to good health, or to power and office, many even to sensual pleasures. This last is the ideal of brute beasts; and of the others we may say that they are frail and uncertain, and depend less on our own prudence than on the caprice of fortune. Then there are those who find the "chief good" in virtue. Well, that is a noble doctrine. But the very virtue they talk of is the parent and preserver of friendship, and without it friendship cannot possibly exist.

Let us, I repeat, use the word virtue in the ordinary acceptation and meaning of the term, and do not let us define it in high-flown language. Let us account as good the persons usually considered so, such as Paulus, Cato, Gallus, Scipio, and Philus.[2] Such men as these are good enough for everyday life; and we need not trouble ourselves about those ideal characters which are nowhere to be met with.

Well, between men like these the advantages of friendship are almost more than I can say. To begin with, how can life be worth living, to use the words of Ennius,[3] which lacks that repose which is to be found in the mutual good-will of a friend? What can be more delightful than to have some one to whom you can say everything with the same absolute confidence as to yourself? Is not prosperity robbed of half its value if you have no one to share your joy? On the other hand, misfortunes would be hard to bear if there were not some one to feel them even more acutely than yourself. In a word, other objects of ambition serve for particular ends-riches for use, power for securing homage, office for reputation, pleasure for enjoyment, health for freedom from pain and the full use of the functions of the body. But friendship embraces innumerable advantages. Turn which way you please, you will find it at hand. It is everywhere; and yet never out of place, never unwelcome. Fire and water themselves, to use a common expression, are not of more universal use than friendship. I am not now speaking of the common or modified form of it, though even that is a source of pleasure and profit, but of that true and complete friendship which existed between the select few who are known to fame. Such friendship enhances prosperity, and relieves adversity of its burden by halving and sharing it.

And great and numerous as are the blessings of friendship, this certainly is the sovereign one, that it gives us bright hopes for the future and forbids weakness and despair. In the face of a true friend a man sees as it were a second self. So that where his friend is he is; if his friend be rich, he is not poor; though he be weak, his friend's strength is his; and in his friend's life he enjoys a second life after his own is finished. This last is perhaps the most difficult to conceive. But such is the effect of the respect, the loving remembrance, and the regret of friends which follow us to the grave. While they take the sting out of death, they add a glory to the life of the survivors. Nay, if you eliminate from nature the tie of affection, there will be an end of house and city, nor will so much as the cultivation of the soil be left. If you don't see the virtue of friendship and harmony, you may learn it by observing the effects of quarrels and feuds. Was any family ever so well established, any State so firmly settled, as to be beyond the reach of utter destruction from animosities and factions? This may teach you the immense advantage of friendship.

They say that a certain philosopher of Agrigentum,[4] in a Greek poem, pronounced with the authority of an oracle the doctrine that whatever in nature and the universe was unchangeable was so in virtue of the binding force of friendship; whatever was changeable was so by the solvent power of discord. And indeed this is a truth which everybody understands and practically attests by experience. For if any marked instance of loyal friendship in confronting or sharing danger comes to light, every one applauds it to the echo. What cheers there were, for instance, all over the theatre at a passage in the new play of my friend and guest Pacuvius; where the king, not knowing which of the two was Orestes, Pylades declared himself to be Orestes, that he might die in his stead, while the real Orestes kept on asserting that it was he. The audience rose *en masse* and clapped their hands. And this was at an incident in fiction: what would they have done, must we suppose, if it had been in real life? You can easily see what a natural feeling it is, when men who would not have had the resolution to act thus themselves, shewed how right they thought it in another.

I don't think I have any more to say about friendship. If there is any more, and I have no doubt there is much, you must, if you care to do so, consult those who profess to discuss such matters.

FANNIUS: We would rather apply to you. Yet I have often consulted such persons, and have heard what they had to say with a certain satisfaction. But in your discourse one somehow feels that there is a different strain.

SCAEVOLA: You would have said that still more, Fannius, if you had been present the other day in Scipio's pleasure-grounds when we had the discussion about the State. How splendidly he stood up for justice against Philus's elaborate speech.

FANNIUS: Ah! it was naturally easy for the justest of men to stand up for justice.

SCAEVOLA: Well, then, what about friendship? Who could discourse on it more easily than the man whose chief glory is a friendship maintained with the most absolute fidelity, constancy, and integrity?

LAELIUS: Now you are really using force. It makes no difference what kind of force you use: force it is. For it is neither easy nor right to refuse a wish of my sons-in-law, particularly when the wish is a creditable one in itself.

Well, then, it has very often occurred to me when thinking about friendship, that the chief point to be considered was this: is it weakness and want of means that make friendship desired? I mean, is its object an interchange of good offices, so that each may give that in which he is strong, and receive that in which he is weak? Or is it not rather true that, although this is an advantage naturally belonging to friendship, yet its original cause is quite other, prior in time, more noble in character, and springing more directly from our nature itself? The Latin word for friendship –*amicitia*– is derived from that for love –*amor*–; and love is certainly the prime mover in contracting mutual affection. For as to material advantages, it often happens that those are obtained even by men who are courted by a mere show of friendship and treated with respect from interested motives. But friendship by its nature admits of no feigning, no pretence: as far as it goes it is both genuine and spontaneous. Therefore I gather that friendship springs from a natural impulse rather than a wish for help: from an inclination of the heart, combined with a certain instinctive feeling of love, rather than from a deliberate calculation of the material advantage it was likely to confer. The strength of this feeling you may notice in certain animals. They show such love to their offspring for a certain period, and are so beloved by them, that they clearly have a share in this natural, instinctive affection. But of course it is more evident in the case of man: first, in the natural affection between children and their parents, an affection which only shocking wickedness can sunder; and next, when the passion of love has attained to a like strength-on our finding, that is, some one person with whose character and nature we are in full sympathy, because we think that we perceive in him what I may call the beacon-light of virtue. For nothing inspires love, nothing conciliates affection, like virtue. Why, in a certain sense we may be said to feel affection even for men we have never seen, owing to their honesty and virtue. Who, for instance, fails to dwell on the memory of Gaius Fabricius and Manius Curius[5] with some affection and warmth of feeling, though he has never seen them? Or who but loathes Tarquinius Superbus, Spurius Cassius, Spurius Maelius?[6] We have fought for empire in Italy with two great generals, Pyrrhus and Hannibal.[7] For the former, owing to his probity, we entertain no great feelings of enmity: the latter, owing to his cruelty, our country has detested and always will detest.

Now, if the attraction of probity is so great that we can love it not only in those whom we have never seen, but, what is more, actually in an enemy, we need not be surprised if men's affections are roused when they fancy that they have seen virtue and goodness in those with whom a close intimacy is possible. I do not deny that affection is strengthened by the actual receipt of benefits, as well as by the perception of a wish to render service, combined with a closer intercourse. When these are added to the original impulse of the heart, to which I have alluded, a quite surprising warmth of feeling springs up. And if any one thinks that this comes from a sense of weakness, that each may have some one to help him to his particular need, all I can say is that, when he maintains it to be born of want and poverty, he allows to friendship an origin very base, and a pedigree, if I may be allowed the expression, far from noble. If this had been the case, a man's inclination to friendship would be exactly in proportion to his low opinion of his own resources. Whereas the truth is quite the other way. For when a man's confidence in himself is greatest, when he is so fortified by virtue and wisdom as to want nothing and to feel absolutely self-dependent, it is then that he is most conspicuous for seeking out and keeping up friendships. Did Africanus, for example, want anything of me? Not the least in the world! Neither did I of him. In my case it was an admiration of his virtue, in his an opinion, may be, which he entertained of my character, that caused our affection. Closer intimacy added to the warmth of our feelings. But though many great material advantages did ensue, they were not the source from which our affection proceeded. For as we are not beneficent and liberal with any view of extorting gratitude, and do not regard an act of kindness as an investment, but follow a natural inclination to liberality; so we look on friendship as worth trying for, not because we are attracted to it by the expectation of ulterior gain, but in the conviction that what it has to give us is from first to last included in the feeling itself.

Far different is the view of those who, like brute beasts, refer everything to sensual pleasure. And no wonder. Men who have degraded all their powers of thought to an object so mean and contemptible can of course raise their eyes to nothing lofty, to nothing grand and divine. Such persons indeed let us leave out of the present question. And let us accept the doctrine that the sensation of love and the warmth of inclination have their origin in a spontaneous feeling which arises directly the presence of probity is indicated. When once men have conceived the inclination, they of course try to attach themselves to the object of it, and move themselves nearer and nearer to him. Their aim is that they may be on the same footing and the same level in regard to affection, and be more inclined to do a good service than to ask a return, and that there should be this noble rivalry between them. Thus both truths will be established. We shall get the most important material advantages from friendship; and its origin from a natural impulse rather than from a sense of need will be at once more dignified and more in accordance with fact. For if it were true that its material advantages cemented friendship, it would be equally true that any change in them would dissolve it. But nature being incapable of change, it follows that genuine friendships are eternal.

So much for the origin of friendship. But perhaps you would not care to hear any more.

FANNIUS: Nay, pray go on; let us have the rest, Laelius. I take on myself to speak for my friend here as his senior.

SCAEVOLA: Quite right! Therefore, pray let us hear.

LAELIUS: Well, then, my good friends, listen to some conversations about friendship which very frequently passed between Scipio and myself. I must begin by telling you, however, that be used to say that the most difficult thing in the world was for a friendship to remain unimpaired to the end of life. So many things might intervene: conflicting interests; differences of opinion in politics; frequent changes in character, owing sometimes to misfortunes, sometimes to advancing years. He used to illustrate these facts from the analogy of boyhood, since the warmest affections between boys are often laid aside with the boyish toga; and even if they did manage to keep them up to adolescence, they were sometimes broken by a rivalry in courtship, or for some other advantage to which their mutual claims were not compatible. Even if the friendship was prolonged beyond that time, yet it frequently received a rude shock should the two happen to be competitors for office. For while the most fatal blow to friendship in the majority of cases was the lust of gold, in the case of the best men it was a rivalry for office and reputation, by which it had often happened that the most violent enmity had arisen between the closest friends.

Again, wide breaches and, for the most part, justifiable ones were caused by an immoral request being made of friends, to pander to a man's unholy desires or to assist him in inflicting a wrong. A refusal, though perfectly right, is attacked by those to whom they refuse compliance as a violation of the laws of friendship. Now the people who have no scruples as to the requests they make to their friends, thereby allow that they are ready to have no scruples as to what they will do for their friends; and it is the recriminations of such people which commonly not only quench friendships, but give rise to lasting enmities. "In fact," he used to say, "these fatalities overhang friendship in such numbers that it requires not only wisdom but good luck also to escape them all."

Translated by E.S. Shuckburgh.

CAESAR

100 - 44 BC

C. Iulius Caesar was famous for his laconism. He was also the author of a bellicose collection of works that a Gaul could not evoke without sadness. This soldier-aristocrat heralded from a family with pretensions of Trojan roots (Iulus, son of Aeneas) and even of divine origins (Aeneas being the son of Venus). He embraced a military career in which he would excel. In 47 BC after his victory against Pharnaces at Zela (Black Sea area), Caesar proclaimed "veni, vidi, vici" *("I came, I saw, I conquered"), summarizing well the sobriety of the man and the concision of his style.*

Counted among the "Four Greats" of Roman historians, Caesar was also intermittingly a grammarian. His thought, as well as his method, is well known to us thanks to two collections of notes titled Commentarii, *which Cicero deemed "raw, simple, elegant, and lacking in any oratory ornament." In the* Gallic War, *Caesar retraces the campaign of the Gauls that ended in the crushing defeat of Vercingetorix. He wants the reader to believe that he, the "pacifier," is most of all a liberator. He has not a care for colorful anecdotes and is only interested in geography, military tactics, and bravery. His dry description that claims to be objective is remarkable for its accuracy and technical details. The* Civil War *hints more at the man's ambitions. Caesar pretends that he was forced against his will to take part in the political and military melee of his time, while concurrently maintaining that Pompey and the senate rejected his offering of peace and reconciliation.*

His contemporaries' judgments are contrasted to the image of the man: Cicero admires his writing style, the historian Asinius Pollio believes he is a lousy writer; Tacitus judges his speeches as out of date, and Quintilian admires them. Be that as it may, all agree today that Caesar's works are self-aggrandizing propaganda.

Caesar Besieges Alesia

Caesar, *Gallic War* 7.68-89

In 52 BC, Vercingetorix takes command of the Gauls against Caesar and withdraws to Alesia (modern Alise-Sainte-Reine in Burgundy) after suffering heavy losses. Caesar pursues him and besieges the town using a line of circumvallation. In the meantime, tens of thousands of Gauls band together and come to rescue Vercingetorix. Their intention is to repulse the invader as quickly as possible, but they fail.

The story of the siege is intriguing: It describes the battlefield terrain and the military strategies adopted by each warring party. Caesar writes in the third person. He draws attention to himself by embellishing his own feats and, by doing so, justifies his conquest of Gaul. Caesar held his triumph in 46 BC, after which Vercingetorix was put to death.

"All evils which are distant most powerfully alarm men's minds."

All his cavalry being routed, Vercingetorix led back his troops in the same order as he had arranged them before the camp, and immediately began to march to Alesia, which is a town of the Mandubii; and ordered the baggage to be speedily brought forth from the camp, and follow him closely. Caesar, having conveyed his baggage to the nearest hill, and having left two legions to guard it, pursued as far as the time of day would permit, and after slaying about three thousand of the rear of the enemy, encamped at Alesia on the next day. On reconnoitering the situation of the city, finding that the enemy were panic-stricken, because the cavalry in which they placed their chief reliance were beaten, he encouraged his men to endure the toil, and began to draw a line of circumvallation round Alesia.

The town itself was situated on the top of a hill, in a very lofty position, so that it did not appear likely to be taken, except by a regular siege. Two rivers, on two different sides, washed the foot of the hill. Before the town lay a plain of about three miles in length; on every other side hills at a moderate distance, and of an equal degree of height, surrounded the town. The army of the Gauls had filled all the space under the wall, comprising the part of the hill which looked to the rising sun, and had drawn in front a trench and a stone wall six feet high. The circuit of that fortification, which was commenced by the Romans, comprised eleven miles. The camp was pitched in a strong position, and twenty-three redoubts were raised in it, in which sentinels were placed by day, lest any sally should be made suddenly; and by night the same were occupied by watches and strong guards.

The work having been begun, a cavalry action ensues in that plain, which we have already described as broken by hills, and extending three miles in length. The contest is maintained on both sides with the utmost vigour; Caesar sends the Germans to aid our troops when distressed, and draws up the legions in front of the camp, lest any sally should be suddenly made by the enemy's infantry. The courage of our men is increased by the additional support of the legions; the enemy being put to flight, hinder one another by their numbers, and as only the narrower gates were left open, are crowded together in them; then the Germans pursue them with vigour even to the fortifications. A great slaughter ensues; some leave their horses, and endeavour to cross the ditch and climb the wall. Caesar orders the legions which he had drawn up in front of the rampart to advance a little. The Gauls, who were within the fortifications, were no less panic-stricken, thinking that the enemy were coming that moment against them, and unanimously shout "to arms;" some in their alarm rush into the town; Vercingetorix orders the gates to be shut, lest the camp should be left undefended. The Germans retreat, after slaying many and taking several horses.

Vercingetorix adopts the design of sending away all his cavalry by night, before the fortifications should be completed by the Romans. He charges them when departing "that each of them should go to his respective state, and press for the war all who were old enough to bear arms; he states his own merits, and conjures them to consider his safety, and not surrender him, who had deserved so well of the general freedom, to the enemy for torture; he points out to them that, if they should be remiss, eighty thousand chosen men would perish with him; that, upon making a calculation, he had barely corn for thirty days, but could hold out a little longer by economy." After giving these instructions he silently dismisses the cavalry in the second watch, on that side where our works were not completed; he orders all the corn to be brought to himself; he ordains capital punishment to such as should not obey; he distributes among them, man by man, the cattle, great quantities of which had been driven there by the Mandubii; he began to measure out the corn sparingly, and by little and little; he receives into the town all the forces which he had posted in front of it. In this manner he prepares to await the succours from Gaul, and carry on the war.

Caesar, on learning these proceedings from the deserters and captives, adopted the following system of fortification; he dug a trench twenty feet deep, with perpendicular sides, in such a manner that the base of this trench should extend so far as the edges were apart at the top. He raised all his other works at a distance of four hundred feet from that ditch; he did that with this intention, lest (since he necessarily embraced so extensive an area, and the whole works could not be easily surrounded by a line of soldiers) a large number of the enemy should suddenly, or by night, sally against the fortifications; or lest they should by day cast weapons against our men while occupied with the works. Having left this interval, he drew two trenches fifteen feet broad, and of the same depth; the innermost of them, being in low and level ground, he filled with water conveyed from the river. Behind these he raised a rampart and wall twelve feet high: to this he added a parapet and battlements, with large stakes cut like stags' horns, projecting from the junction of the parapet and battlements, to prevent the enemy from scaling it, and surrounded the entire work with turrets, which were eighty feet distant from one another.

It was necessary, at one and the same time, to procure timber for the rampart, lay in supplies of corn, and raise also extensive fortifications, and the available troops were in consequence of this reduced in number, since they used to advance to some distance from the camp, and sometimes the Gauls endeavoured to attack our works, and to make a sally from the town by several gates and in great force. On which Caesar thought that further additions should be made to these works, in order that the fortifications might be defensible by a small number of soldiers. Having, therefore, cut down the trunks of trees or very thick branches, and having stripped their tops of the bark, and sharpened them into a point, he drew a continued trench everywhere five feet deep. These stakes being sunk into this trench, and fastened firmly at the bottom, to prevent the possibility of their being torn up, had their branches only projecting from the ground. There were five rows in connection with, and intersecting each other; and whoever entered within them were likely to impale themselves on very sharp stakes. The soldiers called these "cippi." Before these, which were arranged in oblique rows in the form of a quincunx, pits three feet deep were dug, which gradually diminished in depth to the bottom. In these pits tapering stakes, of the thickness of a man's thigh, sharpened at the top and hardened in the fire, were sunk in such a manner as to project from the ground not more than four inches; at the same time for the purpose of giving them strength and stability, they were each filled with trampled clay to the height of one foot from the bottom: the rest of the pit was covered over with osiers and twigs, to conceal the deceit. Eight rows of this kind were dug, and were three feet distant from each other. They called this a lily from its resemblance to that flower. Stakes a foot long, with iron hooks attached to them, were entirely sunk in the ground before these, and were planted in every place at small intervals; these they called spurs.

After completing these works, having selected as level ground as he could, considering the nature of the country, and having enclosed an area of fourteen miles, he constructed, against an external enemy, fortifications of the same kind in every respect, and separate from these, so that the guards of the fortifications could not be surrounded even by immense numbers, if such a circumstance should take place owing to the departure of the enemy's cavalry; and in order that the Roman soldiers might not be compelled to go out of the camp with great risk, he orders all to provide forage and corn for thirty days.

Whilst those things are carried on at Alesia, the Gauls, having convened a council of their chief nobility, determine that all who could bear arms should not be called out, which was the opinion of Vercingetorix, but that a fixed number should be levied from each state; lest, when so great a multitude assembled together, they could neither govern nor distinguish their men, nor have the means of supplying them with corn. They demand thirty-five thousand men from the Aedui and their dependents, the Segusiani, Ambivareti, and Aulerci Brannovices; an equal number from the Arverni in conjunction with the Eleuteti Cadurci, Gabali, and Velauni, who were accustomed to be under the command of the Arverni; twelve thousand each from the Senones, Sequani, Bituriges, Santones, Ruteni, and Carnutes; ten thousand from the Bellovaci; the same number from the Lemovici; eight thousand each from the Pictones, and Turoni, and Parisii, and Helvii; five thousand each from the Suessiones, Ambiani, Mediomatrici, Petrocorii, Nervii, Morini, and Nitiobriges; the same number from the Aulerci Cenomani; four thousand from the Atrebates; three thousand each from the Bellocassi, Lexovii, and Aulerci Eburovices; thirty thousand from the Rauraci, and Boii; six thousand, from all the states together which border on the Atlantic, and which in their dialect are called Armoricae (in which number are comprehended the Curisolites, Rhedones, Ambibari, Caltes, Osismii, Lemovices, Veneti, and Unelli). Of these the Bellovaci did not contribute their number, as they said that they would wage war against the Romans on their own account, and at their own discretion, and would not obey the order of any one: however, at the request of Commius, they sent two thousand, in consideration of a tie of hospitality which subsisted between him and them.

Caesar had, as we have previously narrated, availed himself of the faithful and valuable services of this Commius, in Britain, in former years: in consideration of which merits he had exempted from taxes his state, and had conferred on Commius himself the country of the Morini. Yet such was the unanimity of the Gauls in asserting their freedom, and recovering their ancient renown in war, that they were influenced neither by favours, nor by the recollection of private friendship; and all earnestly directed their energies and resources to that war, and collected eight thousand cavalry, and about two hundred and forty thousand infantry. These were reviewed in the country of the Aedui, and a calculation was made of their numbers. Commanders were appointed: the supreme command is entrusted to Commius the

Atrebatian, Viridomarus and Eporedorix the Aeduans, and Vergasillaunus the Arvernian, the cousin-german of Vercingetorix. To them are assigned men selected from each state, by whose advice the war should be conducted. All march to Alesia, sanguine and full of confidence: nor was there a single individual who imagined that the Romans could withstand the sight of such an immense host: especially in an action carried on both in front and rear, when on the inside the besieged would sally from the town and attack the enemy, and on the outside so great forces of cavalry and infantry would be seen.

But those who were blockaded at Alesia, the day being past on which they had expected auxiliaries from their countrymen, and all their corn being consumed, ignorant of what was going on among the Aedui, convened an assembly and deliberated on the exigency of their situation. After various opinions had been expressed among them, some of which proposed a surrender, others a sally, whilst their strength would support it, the speech of Critognatus ought not to be omitted for its singular and detestable cruelty. He sprung from the noblest family among the Arverni, and possessing great influence, says, "I shall pay no attention to the opinion of those who call a most disgraceful surrender by the name of a capitulation; nor do I think that they ought to be considered as citizens, or summoned to the council. My business is with those who approve of a sally: in whose advice the memory of our ancient prowess seems to dwell in the opinion of you all. To be unable to bear privation for a short time is disgraceful cowardice, not true valour. Those who voluntarily offer themselves to death are more easily found than those who would calmly endure distress. And I would approve of this opinion (for honour is a powerful motive with me), could I foresee no other loss, save that of life: but let us, in adopting our design, look back on all Gaul, which we have stirred up to our aid. What courage do you think would our relatives and friends have, if eighty thousand men were butchered in one spot, supposing that they should be forced to come to an action almost over our corpses? Do not utterly deprive them of your aid, for they have spurned all thoughts of personal danger on account of your safety; nor by your folly, rashness, and cowardice, crush all Gaul and doom it to an eternal slavery. Do you doubt their fidelity and firmness because they have not come at the appointed day? What then? Do you suppose that the Romans are employed every day in the outer fortifications for mere amusement? If you cannot be assured by their dispatches, since every avenue is blocked up, take the Romans as evidence that their approach is drawing near; since they, intimidated by alarm at this, labour night and day at their works. What, therefore, is my design? To do as our ancestors did in the war against the Cimbri and Teutones, which was by no means equally momentous; who, when driven into their towns, and oppressed by similar privations, supported life by the corpses of those who appeared useless for war on account of their age, and did not surrender to the enemy: and even if we had not a precedent for such cruel conduct, still I should consider it most glorious that one should be established, and delivered to posterity. For in what was that war like this? The Cimbri, after laying Gaul waste, and inflicting great calamities, at length departed from our country, and sought other lands; they left us our rights, laws, lands, and liberty. But what other motive or wish have the Romans, than, induced by envy, to settle in the lands and states of those whom they have learned by fame to be noble and powerful in war, and impose on them perpetual slavery? For they never have carried on wars on any other terms. But if you know not these things which are going on in distant countries, look to the neighbouring Gaul, which being reduced to the form of a province, stripped of its rights and laws, and subjected to Roman despotism, is oppressed by perpetual slavery."

When different opinions were expressed, they determined that those who, owing to age or ill health, were unserviceable for war, should depart from the town, and that themselves should try every expedient before they had recourse to the advice of Critognatus: however, that they would rather adopt that design, if circumstances should compel them and their allies should delay, than accept any terms of a surrender or peace. The Mandubii, who had admitted them into the town, are compelled to go forth with their wives and children. When these came to the Roman fortifications, weeping, they begged of the soldiers by every entreaty to receive them as slaves and relieve them with food. But Caesar, placing guards on the rampart, forbade them to be admitted.

In the meantime, Commius and the rest of the leaders, to whom the supreme command had been intrusted, came with all their forces to Alesia, and having occupied the entire hill, encamp not more than a mile from our fortifications. The following day, having led forth their cavalry from the camp, they fill all that plain, which, we have related, extended three miles in length, and draw out their infantry a little from that place, and post them on the higher ground. The town Alesia commanded a view of the whole plain. The besieged run together when these auxiliaries were seen; mutual congratulations ensue, and the minds of all are elated with joy. Accordingly, drawing out their troops, they encamp before the town, and cover the nearest trench with hurdles and fill it up with earth, and make ready for a sally and every casualty.

Caesar, having stationed his army on both sides of the fortifications, in order that, if occasion should arise, each should hold and know his own post, orders the cavalry to issue forth from the camp and commence action. There was a commanding view from the entire camp, which occupied a ridge of hills; and the minds of all the soldiers anxiously awaited the issue of the battle. The Gauls had scattered archers and light-armed infantry here and there, among their cavalry, to give relief to their retreating troops, and sustain the impetuosity of our cavalry. Several of our soldiers were unexpectedly wounded by these, and left the battle. When the Gauls were confident that their countrymen were the conquerors in the action, and beheld our men hard pressed by numbers, both those who were hemmed in by the line of circumvallation and those who had come to aid them, supported the spirits of their men by shouts and yells from every quarter. As the action was carried on in sight of all, neither a brave nor cowardly act could be concealed; both the desire of praise and the fear of ignominy, urged on each party to valour. After fighting from noon almost to sunset, without victory inclining in favour of either, the Germans, on one side, made a charge against the enemy in a compact body, and drove them back; and, when they were put to flight, the archers were surrounded and cut to pieces. In other parts, likewise, our men pursued to the camp the retreating enemy, and did not give them an opportunity of rallying. But those who had come forth from Alesia returned into the town dejected and almost despairing of success.

The Gauls, after the interval of a day, and after making, during that time, an immense number of hurdles, scaling ladders, and iron hooks, silently went forth from the camp at midnight and approached the fortifications in the plain. Raising a shout suddenly, that by this intimation those who were besieged in the town might learn their arrival, they began to cast down hurdles and dislodge our men from the rampart by slings, arrows, and stones, and executed the other movements which are requisite in storming. At the same time, Vercingetorix having heard the shout, gives the signal to his troops by a trumpet, and leads them forth from the town. Our troops, as each man's post had been assigned him some days before, man the fortifications; they intimidate the Gauls by slings, large stones, stakes which they had placed along the works, and bullets. All view being prevented by the darkness, many wounds are received on both sides; several missiles are thrown from the engines. But Marcus Antonius, and Caius Trebonius, the lieutenants, to whom the defence of these parts had been allotted, draughted troops from the redoubts which were more remote, and sent them to aid our troops, in whatever direction they understood that they were hard pressed.

Whilst the Gauls were at a distance from the fortification, they did more execution, owing to the immense number of their weapons: after they came nearer, they either unawares empaled themselves on the spurs, or were pierced by the mural darts from the ramparts and towers, and thus perished. After receiving many wounds on all sides, and having forced no part of the works, when day drew nigh, fearing lest they should be surrounded by a sally made from the higher camp on the exposed flank, they retreated to their countrymen. But those within, whilst they bring forward those things which had been prepared by Vercingetorix for a sally, fill up the nearest trenches; having delayed a long time in executing these movements, they learned the retreat of their countrymen before they drew nigh to the fortifications.

Thus they returned to the town without accomplishing their object.

The Gauls, having been twice repulsed with great loss, consult what they should do: they avail themselves of the information of those who were well acquainted with the country; from them they ascertain the position and fortification of the upper camp. There was, on the north side, a hill, which our men could not include in their works, on account of the extent of the circuit, and had necessarily made their camp in ground almost disadvantageous, and pretty steep. Caius Antistius Reginus, and Caius Caninius Rebilus, two of the lieutenants, with two legions, were in possession of this camp. The leaders of the enemy, having reconnoitred the country by their scouts, select from the entire army sixty thousand men; belonging to those states which bear the highest character for courage: they privately arrange among themselves what they wished to be done, and in what manner; they decide that the attack should take place when it should seem to be noon. They appoint over their forces Vergasillaunus, the Arvernian, one of the four generals, and a near relative of Vercingetorix. He, having issued from the camp at the first watch, and having almost completed his march a little before the dawn, hid himself behind the mountain, and ordered his soldiers to refresh themselves after their labour during the night. When noon now seemed to draw nigh, he marched hastily against that camp which we have mentioned before; and, at the same time, the cavalry began to approach the fortifications in the plain, and the rest of the forces to make a demonstration in front of the camp.

Vercingetorix, having beheld his countrymen from the citadel of Alesia, issues forth from the town; he brings forth from the camp long hooks, movable penthouses, mural hooks, and other things, which he had prepared for the purpose of making a sally. They engage on all sides at once, and every expedient is adopted. They flocked to whatever part of the works seemed weakest. The army of the Romans is distributed along their extensive lines, and with difficulty meets the enemy in every quarter. The shouts which were raised by the combatants in their rear, had a great tendency to intimidate our men, because they perceived that their danger rested on the valour of others: for generally all evils which are distant most powerfully alarm men's minds.

Caesar, having selected a commanding situation, sees distinctly whatever is going on in every quarter, and sends assistance to his troops when hard pressed. The idea uppermost in the minds of both parties is, that the present is the time in which they would have the fairest opportunity of making a struggle; the Gauls despairing of all safety, unless they should succeed in forcing the lines: the Romans expecting an end to all their labours if they should gain the day. The principal struggle is at the upper lines, to which, we have said, Vergasillaunus was sent. The least elevation of ground, added to a declivity, exercises a momentous influence. Some are casting missiles, others, forming a testudo, advance to the attack; fresh men by turns relieve the wearied. The earth, heaped up by all against the fortifications, gives the means of ascent to the Gauls, and covers those works which the Romans had concealed in the ground. Our men have no longer arms or strength.

Caesar, on observing these movements, sends Labienus with six cohorts to relieve his distressed soldiers: he orders him, if he should be unable to withstand them, to draw off the cohorts and make a sally; but not to do this except through necessity. He himself goes to the rest, and exhorts them not to succumb to the toil; he shows them that the fruits of all former engagements depend on that day and hour. The Gauls within, despairing of forcing the fortifications in the plains on account of the greatness of the works, attempt the places precipitous in ascent: hither they bring the engines which they had prepared; by the immense number of their missiles they dislodge the defenders from the turrets: they fill the ditches with clay and hurdles, then clear the way; they tear down the rampart and breast-work with hooks.

Caesar sends at first young Brutus, with six cohorts, and afterwards Caius Fabius, his lieutenant, with seven others: finally, as they fought more obstinately, he leads up fresh men to the assistance of his soldiers. After renewing the action, and repulsing the enemy, he marches in the direction in which he had sent Labienus, drafts four cohorts from the nearest redoubt, and orders part of the cavalry to follow him, and part to make the circuit of the external fortifications and attack the enemy in the rear. Labienus, when neither the ramparts or ditches could check the onset of the enemy, informs Caesar by messengers of what he intended to do. Caesar hastens to share in the action.

His arrival being known from the colour of his robe, and the troops of cavalry, and the cohorts which he had ordered to follow him being seen, as these low and sloping grounds were plainly visible from the eminences, the enemy join battle. A shout being raised by both sides, it was succeeded by a general shout along the ramparts and whole line of fortifications. Our troops, laying aside their javelins, carry on the engagement with their swords. The cavalry is suddenly seen in the rear of the Gauls: the other cohorts advance rapidly; the enemy turn their backs; the cavalry intercept them in their flight, and a great slaughter ensues. Sedulius the general and chief of the Lemovices is slain; Vergasillaunus, the Arvernian, is taken alive in the flight, seventy-four military standards are brought to Caesar, and few out of so great a number return safe to their camp. The besieged, beholding from the town the slaughter and flight of their countrymen, despairing of safety, lead back their troops from the fortifications. A flight of the Gauls from their camp immediately ensues on hearing of this disaster, and had not the soldiers been wearied by sending frequent reinforcements, and the labour of the entire day, all the enemy's forces could have been destroyed. Immediately after midnight, the cavalry are sent out and overtake the rear, a great number are taken or cut to pieces, the rest by flight escape in different directions to their respective states.

Vercingetorix, having convened a council the following day, declares, "That he had undertaken that war, not on account of his own exigencies, but on account of the general freedom; and since he must yield to fortune, he offered himself to them for either purpose, whether they should wish to atone to the Romans by his death, or surrender him alive." Ambassadors are sent to Caesar on this subject. He orders their arms to be surrendered, and their chieftains delivered up. He seated himself at the head of the lines in front of the camp, the Gallic chieftains are brought before him. They surrender Vercingetorix, and lay down their arms. Reserving the Aedui and Arverni, to try if he could gain over, through their influence, their respective states, he distributes one of the remaining captives to each soldier, throughout the entire army, as plunder.

Translated by W.A. Macdevitt.

Passage of the Rubicon

Caesar, *Civil War* 1.8-33

Pompey's power increases significantly as Caesar fights the war in Gaul. In 52 BC, Pompey becomes the only consul in Rome while at the same time keeping his office as proconsul to Spain. The situation is extraordinary in three ways: Rome always had two consuls, never just one; a proconsul was normally required to remain in his province; and a proconsul could not be a consul concurrently. In 49 BC, Caesar's command in Gaul ends. He is not permitted to run for the consulship because a candidate must be physically present in Rome when running for office. Caesar is faced with the threat of losing all his power. After trying several times to negotiate with Pompey, Caesar crosses the River Rubicon with his army—an act of war as the river marked the boundary of Italy. Caesar conquers many Italian cities and heads south of Rome to Brindisi, where Pompey has taken refuge. Pompey flees to Greece while Caesar returns to Rome to negotiate with the senate.

Caesar's account is extremely self-justifying. After all, he had just invaded his own country and started a civil war, all of which certainly deserved some sort of explanation.

"In war great events are often brought about by trifling circumstances."

Having made himself acquainted with the disposition of his soldiers, Caesar set off with that legion to Ariminum,[1] and there met the tribunes, who had fled to him for protection; he called his other legions from winter quarters, and ordered them to follow him. Thither came Lucius Caesar, a young man, whose father was a lieutenant general under Caesar. He, after concluding the rest of his speech, and stating for what purpose he had come, told Caesar that he had commands of a private nature for him from Pompey; that Pompey wished to clear himself to Caesar, lest he should impute those actions which he did for the republic, to a design of affronting him; that he had ever preferred the interest of the state to his own private connections; that Caesar, too, for his own honour, ought to sacrifice his desires and resentment to the public good, and not vent his anger so violently against his enemies, lest in his hopes of injuring them, he should injure the republic. He spoke a few words to the same purport from himself, in addition to Pompey's apology. Roscius, the praetor, conferred with Caesar almost in the same words, and on the same subject, and declared that Pompey had empowered him to do so.

Though these things seemed to have no tendency towards redressing his injuries, yet having got proper persons by whom he could communicate his wishes to Pompey; he required of them both, that as they had conveyed Pompey's demands to him, they should not refuse to convey his demands to Pompey; if by so little trouble they could terminate a great dispute, and liberate all Italy from her fears.

"That the honour of the republic had ever been his first object, and dearer to him than life; that he was chagrined, that the favour of the Roman people was wrested from him by the injurious reports of his enemies; that he was deprived of a half-year's command, and dragged back to the city, though the people had ordered that regard should be paid to his suit for the consulate at the next election, though he was not present; that, however, he had patiently submitted to this loss of honour for the sake of the republic; that when he wrote letters to the senate, requiring that all persons should resign the command of their armies, he did not obtain even that request; that levies were made throughout Italy; that the two legions which had been taken from him, under the pretence of the Parthian war, were kept at home, and that the state was in arms. To what did all these things tend, unless to his ruin? But, nevertheless, he was ready to condescend to any terms, and to endure everything for the sake of the republic. Let Pompey go to his own province; let them both disband their armies; let all persons in Italy lay down their arms; let all fears be removed from the city; let free elections, and the whole republic be resigned to the direction of the senate and Roman people. That these things might be the more easily performed, and conditions secured and confirmed by oath, either let Pompey come to Caesar, or allow Caesar to go to him; it might be that all their disputes would be settled by an interview."

Roscius and Lucius Caesar, having received this message, went to Capua, where they met the consuls and Pompey, and declared to them Caesar's terms. Having deliberated on the matter, they replied, and sent written proposals to him by the same persons, the purport of which was, that Caesar should return into Gaul, leave Ariminum, and disband his army: if he complied with this, that Pompey would go to Spain. In the meantime, until security was given that Caesar would perform his promises, that the consuls and Pompey would not give over their levies.

It was not an equitable proposal, to require that Caesar should quit Ariminum and return to his province; but that Pompey should himself retain his province and the legions that belonged to another, and desire that Caesar's army should be disbanded, whilst he himself was making new levies: and that he should merely promise to go to his province, without naming the day on which he would set out; so that if he should not set out till after Caesar's consulate expired, yet he would not appear bound by any religious scruples about asserting a falsehood. But his not granting time for a conference, nor promising to set out to meet him, made the expectation of peace appear very hopeless. Caesar, therefore, sent Marcus Antonius, with five cohorts from Ariminum to Arretium; he himself stayed at Ariminum with two legions, with the intention of raising levies there. He secured Pisaurus, Fanum, and Ancona, with a cohort each.

In the meantime, being informed that Thermus the praetor was in possession of Iguvium, with five cohorts, and was fortifying the town, but that the affections of all the inhabitants were very well inclined towards himself; he detached Curio with three cohorts, which he had at Ariminum and Pisaurus. Upon notice of his approach, Thermus, distrusting the affections of the townsmen, drew his cohorts out of it, and made his escape; his soldiers deserted him on the road, and returned home. Curio recovered Iguvium, with the cheerful concurrence of all the inhabitants. Caesar, having received an account of this, and relying on the affections of the municipal towns, drafted all the cohorts of the thirteenth legion from the garrisons, and set out for Auximum, a town into which Attius had brought his cohorts, and of which he had taken possession, and from which he had sent senators round about the country of Picenum, to raise new levies.

Upon news of Caesar's approach, the senate of Auximum went in a body to Attius Varus; and told him that it was not a subject for them to determine upon: yet neither they, nor the rest of the freemen would suffer Caius Caesar, a general, who had merited so well of the republic, after performing such great achievements, to be excluded from their town and walls; wherefore he ought to pay some regard to the opinion of posterity, and his own danger. Alarmed at this declaration, Attius Varus drew out of the town the garrison which he had introduced, and fled. A few of Caesar's front rank having pursued him, obliged him to halt, and when the battle began, Varus is deserted by his troops: some of them disperse to their homes, the rest come over to Caesar; and along with them, Lucius Pupius, the chief centurion, is taken prisoner and brought to Caesar. He had held the same rank before in Cneius Pompey's army. But Caesar applauded the soldiers of Attius, set Pupius at liberty, returned thanks to the people of Auximum, and promised to be grateful for their conduct.

Intelligence of this being brought to Rome, so great a panic spread on a sudden that when Lentulus, the consul, came to open the treasury, to deliver money to Pompey by the senate's decree, immediately on opening the hallowed door he fled from the city. For it was falsely rumoured that Caesar was approaching, and that his cavalry were already at the gates. Marcellus, his colleague, followed him, and so did most of the magistrates. Cneius Pompey had left the city the day before, and was on his march to those legions which he had received from Caesar, and had disposed in winter quarters in Apulia. The levies were stopped within the city. No place on this side of Capua was thought secure. At Capua they first began to take courage and to rally, and determined to raise levies in the colonies, which had been sent thither by the Julian law:[2] and Lentulus brought into the public market-place the gladiators which Caesar maintained there for the entertainment of the people, and confirmed them in their liberty, and gave them horses and ordered them to attend him; but afterwards, being warned by his friends that this action was censured by the judgment of all, he distributed them among the slaves of the districts of Campania, to keep guard there.

Caesar, having moved forward from Auximum, traversed the whole country of Picenum. All the governors in these countries most cheerfully received him, and aided his army with every necessary. Ambassadors came to him even from Cingulum, a town which Labienus had laid out and built at his own expense, and offered most earnestly to comply with his orders. He demanded soldiers: they sent them. In the meantime, the twelfth legion came to join Caesar; with these two he marched to Asculum, the chief town of Picenum. Lentulus Spinther occupied that town with ten cohorts; but, on being informed of Caesar's approach, he fled from the town, and, in attempting to bring off his cohorts with him, was deserted by a great part of his men. Being left on the road with a small number, he fell in with Vibullius Rufus, who was sent by Pompey into Picenum to confirm the people in their allegiance. Vibullius, being informed by him of the transactions in Picenum, takes his soldiers from him and dismisses him. He collects, likewise, from the neighbouring countries, as many cohorts as he can from Pompey's new levies. Amongst them he meets with Ulcilles Hirrus fleeing from Camerinum, with six cohorts, which he had in the garrison there; by a junction with which he made up thirteen cohorts. With them he marched by hasty journeys to Corfinium, to Domitius Aenobarbus, and informed him that Caesar was advancing with two legions. Domitius had collected about twenty cohorts from Alba, and the Marsians, Pelignians, and neighbouring states.

Caesar, having recovered Asculum and driven out Lentulus, ordered the soldiers that had deserted from him to be sought out and a muster to be made; and, having delayed for one day there to provide corn, he marched to Corfinium. On his approach, five cohorts, sent by Domitius from the town, were breaking down a bridge which was over the river, at three miles' distance from it. An engagement taking place there with Caesar's advanced-guard, Domitius's men were quickly beaten off from the bridge and retreated precipitately into the town. Caesar, having marched his legions over, halted before the town and encamped close by the walls.

Domitius, upon observing this, sent messengers well acquainted with the country, encouraged by a promise of being amply rewarded, with despatches to Pompey to Apulia, to beg and entreat him to come to his assistance. That Caesar could be easily enclosed by the two armies, through the narrowness of the country, and prevented from obtaining supplies: unless he did so, that he and upwards of thirty cohorts, and a great number of senators and Roman knights, would be in extreme danger. In the meantime he encouraged his troops, disposed engines on the walls, and assigned to each man a particular part of the city to defend. In a speech to the soldiers he promised them lands out of his own estate; to every private soldier four acres, and a corresponding share to the centurions and veterans.

In the meantime, word was brought to Caesar that the people of Sulmo, a town about seven miles distant from Corfinium, were ready to obey his orders, but were prevented by Quintus Lucretius, a senator, and Attius, a Pelignian, who were in possession of the town with a garrison of seven cohorts. He sent Marcus Antonius thither, with five cohorts of the eighth legion. The inhabitants, as soon as they saw our standards, threw open their gates, and all the people, both citizens and soldiers, went out to meet and welcome Antonius. Lucretius and Attius leaped off the walls. Attius, being brought before Antonius, begged that he might be sent to Caesar. Antonius returned the same day on which he had set out with the cohorts and Attius. Caesar added these cohorts to his own army, and sent Attius away in safety. The three first days Caesar employed in fortifying his camp with strong works, in bringing in corn from the neighbouring free towns, and waiting for the rest of his forces. Within the three days the eighth legion came to him, and twenty-two cohorts of the new levies in Gaul, and about three hundred horse from the king of Noricum. On their arrival he made a second camp on another part of the town, and gave the command of it to Curio. He determined to surround the town with a rampart and turrets during the remainder of the time. Nearly at the time when the greatest part of the work was completed, all the messengers sent to Pompey returned.

Having read Pompey's letter, Domitius, concealing the truth, gave out in council that Pompey would speedily come to their assistance; and encouraged them not to despond, but to provide everything necessary for the defence of the town. He held private conferences with a few of his most intimate friends, and determined on the design of fleeing. As Domitius's countenance did not agree with his words, and he did everything with more confusion and fear than he had shown on the preceding days, and as he had several private meetings with his friends, contrary to his usual practice, in order to take their advice, and as he avoided all public councils and assemblies of the people, the truth could be no longer hid nor dissembled; for Pompey had written back in answer, "That he would not put matters to the last hazard; that Domitius had retreated into the town of Corfinium, without either his advice or consent. Therefore, if any opportunity should offer, Domitius should come to him with the whole force." But the blockade and works round the town prevented his escape.

Domitius's design being noised abroad, the soldiers in Corfinium early in the evening began to mutiny, and held a conference with each other by their tribunes and centurions, and the most respectable amongst themselves: "that they were besieged by Caesar; that his works and fortifications were almost finished; that their general, Domitius, on whose hopes and expectations they had confided, had thrown them off, and was meditating his own escape; that they ought to provide for their own safety." At first the Marsians differed in opinion, and possessed themselves of that part of the town which they thought the strongest. And so violent a dispute arose between them, that they attempted to fight and decide it by arms. However, in a little time, by messengers sent from one side to the other, they were informed of Domitius's meditated flight, of which they were previously ignorant. Therefore they all with one consent brought Domitius into public view, gathered round him, and guarded him; and sent deputies out of their number to Caesar, to say that they were ready to throw open their gates, to do whatever he should order, and to deliver up Domitius alive into his hands.

Upon intelligence of these matters, though Caesar thought it of great consequence to become master of the town as soon as possible, and to transfer the cohorts to his own camp, lest any change should be wrought on their inclinations by bribes, encouragement, or fictitious messages, because in war great events are often brought about by trifling circumstances; yet, dreading lest the town should be plundered by the soldiers entering into it, and taking advantage of the darkness of the night, he commended the persons who came to him, and sent them back to the town, and ordered the gates and walls to be secured. He disposed his soldiers on the works, which he had begun, not at certain intervals, as was his practice before, but in one continued range of sentinels and stations, so that they touched each other, and formed a circle round the whole fortification; he ordered the tribunes and general officers to ride round; and exhorted them not only to be on their guard against sallies from the town, but also to watch that no single person should get out privately. Nor was any man so negligent or drowsy as to sleep that night. To so great height was their expectation raised, that they were carried away, heart and soul, each to different objects, what would become of the Corfinians, what of Domitius, what of Lentulus, what of the rest; what event would be the consequence of another.

About the fourth watch, Lentulus Spinther said to our sentinels and guards from the walls, that he desired to have an interview with Caesar, if permission were given him. Having obtained it, he was escorted out of town; nor did the soldiers of Domitius leave him till they brought him into Caesar's presence. He pleaded with

Caesar for his life, and entreated him to spare him, and reminded him of their former friendship; and acknowledged that Caesar's favours to him were very great; in that through his interest he had been admitted into the college of priests; in that after his praetorship he had been appointed to the government of Spain; in that he had been assisted by him in his suit for the consulate. Caesar interrupted him in his speech, and told him, "that he had not left his province to do mischief to any man, but to protect himself from the injuries of his enemies; to restore to their dignity the tribunes of the people who had been driven out of the city on his account, and to assert his own liberty, and that of the Roman people, who were oppressed by a few factious men." Encouraged by this address, Lentulus begged leave to return to the town, that the security which he had obtained for himself might be an encouragement to the rest to hope for theirs; saying that some were so terrified that they were induced to make desperate attempts on their own lives. Leave being granted him, he departed.

When day appeared Caesar ordered all the senators and their children, the tribunes of the soldiers, and the Roman knights, to be brought before him. Among the persons of senatorial rank were Lucius Domitius, Publius Lentulus Spinther, Lucius Vibullius Rufus, Sextus Quintilius Varus, the quaestor, and Lucius Rubrius, besides the son of Domitius, and several other young men, and a great number of Roman knights and burgesses, whom Domitius had summoned from the municipal towns. When they were brought before him he protected them from the insolence and taunts of the soldiers; told them in few words that they had not made him a grateful return, on their part, for his very extraordinary kindness to them, and dismissed them all in safety. Sixty sestertia, which Domitius had brought with him and lodged in the public treasury, being brought to Caesar by the magistrates of Corfinium, he gave them back to Domitius, that he might not appear more moderate with respect to the life of men than in money matters, though he knew that it was public money, and had been given by Pompey to pay his army. He ordered Domitius's soldiers to take the oath to himself, and that day decamped and performed the regular march. He stayed only seven days before Corfinium, and marched into Apulia through the country of the Marrucinians, Frentanians, and Larinates.

Pompey, being informed of what had passed at Corfinium, marches from Luceria to Canusium, and thence to Brundusium. He orders all the forces raised everywhere by the new levies to repair to him. He gives arms to the slaves that attended the flocks, and appoints horses for them. Of these he made up about three hundred horses. Lucius, the praetor, fled from Alba, with six cohorts: Rutilus Lupus, the praetor, from Tarracina, with three. These having descried Caesar's cavalry at a distance, which were commanded by Bivius Curius, and having deserted the praetor, carried their colours to Curius and went over to him. In like manner during the rest of his march, several cohorts fell in with the main body of Caesar's army, others with his horse. Cneius Magius, from Cremona, engineer-general to Pompey, was taken prisoner on the road and brought to Caesar, but sent back by him to Pompey with this message: "As hitherto he had not been allowed an interview, and was now on his march to him at Brundusium, that it deeply concerned the commonwealth and general safety that he should have an interview with Pompey; and that the same advantage could not be gained at a great distance when the proposals were conveyed to them by others, as if terms were argued by them both in person."

Having delivered this message he marched to Brundusium with six legions, four of them veterans: the rest those which he had raised in the late levy and completed on his march, for he had sent all Domitius's cohorts immediately from Corfinium to Sicily. He discovered that the consuls were gone to Dyrrachium with a considerable part of the army, and that Pompey remained at Brundusium with twenty cohorts; but could not find out, for a certainty, whether Pompey stayed behind to keep possession of Brundusium, that he might the more easily command the whole Adriatic sea, with the extremities of Italy and the coast of Greece, and be able to conduct the war on either side of it, or whether he remained there for want of shipping; and, being afraid that Pompey would come to the conclusion that he ought not to relinquish Italy, he determined to deprive him of the means of communication afforded by the harbour of Brundusium. The plan of his work was as follows: Where the mouth of the port was narrowest he threw up a mole of earth on either side, because in these places the sea was shallow. Having gone out so far that the mole could not be continued in the deep water, he fixed double floats, thirty feet on either side, before the mole. These he fastened with four anchors at the four corners, that they might not be carried away by the waves. Having completed and secured them, he then joined to them other floats of equal size. These he covered over with earth and mould, that he might not be prevented from access to them to defend them, and in the front and on both sides he protected them with a parapet of wicker work; and on every fourth one raised a turret, two stories high, to secure them the better from being attacked by the shipping and set on fire.

To counteract this, Pompey fitted out large merchant ships, which he found in the harbour of Brundusium: on them he erected turrets three stories high, and, having furnished them with several engines and all sorts of weapons, drove them amongst Caesar's works, to break through the floats and interrupt the works; thus there happened skirmishes every day at a distance with slings, arrows, and other weapons. Caesar conducted matters as if he thought that the hopes of peace were not yet to be given up. And though he was very much surprised that Magius, whom he had sent to Pompey with a message, was not sent back to him; and though his attempting a reconciliation often retarded the vigorous prosecution of his plans, yet he thought that he ought by all means to persevere in the same line of conduct. He therefore sent Caninius Rebilus to have an interview with Scribonius Libo, his intimate friend and relation. He charges him to exhort Libo to effect a peace, but, above all things, requires that he should be admitted to an interview with Pompey. He declared that he had great hopes, if that were allowed him, that the consequence would be that both parties would lay down their arms on equal terms; that a great share of the glory and reputation of that event would redound to Libo, if, through his advice and agency, hostilities should be ended. Libo, having parted from the conference with Caninius, went to Pompey, and, shortly after, returns with answer that, as the consuls were absent, no treaty of compositions could be engaged in without them. Caesar therefore thought it time at length to give over the attempt which he had often made in vain, and act with energy in the war.

When Caesar's works were nearly half finished, and after nine days were spent in them, the ships which had conveyed the first division of the army to Dyrrachium being sent back by the consuls, returned to Brundusium. Pompey, either frightened at Caesar's works or determined from the beginning to quit Italy, began to prepare for his departure on the arrival of the ships; and the more effectually to retard Caesar's attack, lest his soldiers should force their way into the town at the moment of his departure, he stopped up the gates, built walls across the streets and avenues, sunk trenches across the ways, and in them fixed palisadoes and sharp stakes, which he made level with the ground by means of hurdles and clay. But he barricaded with large beams fastened in the ground and sharpened at the ends two passages and roads without the walls, which led to the port. After making these arrangements, he ordered his soldiers to go on board without noise, and disposed here and there, on the wall and turrets, some light-armed veterans, archers and slingers. These he designed to call off by a certain signal, when all the soldiers were embarked, and left row-galleys for them in a secure place.

The people of Brundusium, irritated by the insolence of Pompey's soldiers, and the insults received from Pompey himself, were in favour of Caesar's party. Therefore, as soon as they were aware of Pompey's departure, whilst his men were running up and down, and busied about their voyage, they made signs from the tops of the houses: Caesar, being apprized of the design by them, ordered scaling ladders to be got ready, and his men to take arms, that he might not lose any opportunity of coming to an action. Pompey weighed anchor at nightfall. The soldiers who had been posted on the wall to guard it, were called off by the signal which had been agreed on, and knowing the roads, ran down to the ships. Caesar's soldiers fixed their ladders and scaled the walls: but being cautioned by the people to beware of the hidden stakes and covered trenches, they halted, and being conducted by the inhabitants by a long circuit, they reached the port, and captured with their long boats and small craft two of Pompey's ships, full of soldiers, which had struck against Caesar's moles.

Though Caesar highly approved of collecting a fleet, and crossing the sea, and pursuing Pompey before he could strengthen himself with his transmarine auxiliaries, with the hope of bringing the war to a conclusion, yet he dreaded the delay and length of time necessary to effect it: because Pompey, by collecting all his ships, had deprived him of the means of pursuing him at present. The only resource left to Caesar, was to wait for a fleet from the distant regions of Gaul, Picenum, and the straits of Gibraltar. But this, on account of the season of the year, appeared tedious and troublesome. He was unwilling that, in the meantime, the veteran army, and the two Spains, one of which was bound to Pompey by the strongest obligations, should be confirmed in his interest; that auxiliaries and cavalry should be provided and Gaul and Italy reduced in his absence.

Therefore, for the present, he relinquished all intention of pursuing Pompey, and resolved to march to Spain, and commanded the magistrates of the free towns to procure him ships, and to have them conveyed to Brundusium. He detached Valerius, his lieutenant, with one legion to Sardinia; Curio, the proprietor, to Sicily with three legions; and ordered him, when he had recovered Sicily, to immediately transport his army to Africa. Marcus Cotta was at this time governor of Sardinia: Marcus Cato, of Sicily: and Tubero, by the lots, should have had the government of Africa. The Caralitani, as soon as they heard that Valerius was sent against them, even before he left Italy, of their own accord drove Cotta out of the town; who, terrified because he understood that the whole province was combined against him, fled from Sardinia to Africa. Cato was in Sicily, repairing the old ships of war, and demanding new ones from the states, and these things he performed with great zeal. He was raising levies of Roman citizens, among the Lucani and Brutii, by his lieutenants, and exacting a certain quota of horse and foot from the states of Sicily. When these things were nearly completed, being informed of Curio's approach, he made a complaint that he was abandoned and betrayed by Pompey, who had undertaken an unnecessary war, without making any preparation, and when questioned by him and other members in the senate, had assured them that every thing was ready and provided for the war. After having made these complaints in a public assembly, he fled from his province.

Valerius found Sardinia, and Curio, Sicily, deserted by their governors when they arrived there with their armies. When Tubero arrived in Africa, he found Attius Varus in the government of the province, who, having lost his cohorts, as already related, at Auximum, had straightway fled to Africa, and finding it without a governor, had seized it of his own accord, and making levies, had raised two legions.

From his acquaintance with the people and country, and his knowledge of that province, he found the means of effecting this; because a few years before, at the expiration of his praetorship, he had obtained that province. He, when Tubero came to Utica with his fleet, prevented his entering the port or town, and did not suffer his son, though labouring under sickness, to set foot on shore; but obliged him to weigh anchor and quit the place.

When these affairs were despatched, Caesar, that there might be an intermission from labour for the rest of the season, drew off his soldiers to the nearest municipal towns, and set off in person for Rome. Having assembled the senate, he reminded them of the injustice of his enemies; and told them, "That he aimed at no extraordinary honour, but had waited for the time appointed by law, for standing candidate for the consulate, being contented with what was allowed to every citizen. That a bill had been carried by the ten tribunes of the people (notwithstanding the resistance of his enemies, and a very violent opposition from Cato, who in his usual manner, consumed the day by a tedious harangue) that he should be allowed to stand candidate, though absent, even in the consulship of Pompey; and if the latter disapproved of the bill, why did he allow it to pass? if he approved of it, why should he debar he [Caesar] from the people's favour? He made mention of his own patience, in that he had freely proposed that all armies should be disbanded, by which he himself would suffer the loss both of dignity and honour. He urged the virulence of his enemies, who refused to comply with what they required from others, and had rather that all things should be thrown into confusion, than that they should lose their power and their armies. He expatiated on their injustice, in taking away his legions: their cruelty and insolence in abridging the privileges of the tribunes; the proposals he had made, and his entreaties of an interview, which had been refused him: For which reasons, he begged and desired that they would undertake the management of the republic, and unite with him in the administration of it. But if through fear they declined it, he would not be a burden to them, but take the management of it on himself. That deputies ought to be sent to Pompey, to propose a reconciliation; as he did not regard what Pompey had lately asserted in the senate, that authority was acknowledged to be vested in those persons to whom ambassadors were sent, and fear implied in those that sent them. That these were the sentiments of low, weak minds: that for his part, as he had made it his study to surpass others in glory, so he was desirous of excelling them in justice and equity."

The senate approved of sending deputies, but none could be found fit to execute the commission: for every person, from his own private fears, declined the office. For Pompey, on leaving the city, had declared in the open senate, that he would hold in the same degree of estimation, those who stayed in Rome and those in Caesar's camp. Thus three days were wasted in disputes and excuses. Besides, Lucius

Metellus, one of the tribunes, was suborned by Caesar's enemies, to prevent this, and to embarrass everything else which Caesar should propose. Caesar having discovered his intention, after spending several days to no purpose, left the city, in order that he might not lose any more time, and went to Transalpine Gaul, without effecting what he had intended.

Translated by W.A. Macdevitt.

LUCRETIUS

c. 94 - c. 55

Lucretius is a mystery, as his origins and general life are virtually unknown. Saint Jerome, the translator of the Bible, who for the life of him could never appreciate an Epicurean philosopher, claims that Lucretius lost his mind after ingesting a love potion that his wife had given him. Jerome further insists that Lucretius composed his philosophical work in six books, the De natura rerum, *only in lucid intervals. And not unexpectedly, Jerome practices some "character assassination" late fourth-century-style: he claims that Lucretius committed suicide, a flagrant attack on a man's honor and integrity in the early days of the church. What we do know for certain is that Cicero and his brother had Lucretius' books already in hand in 54 BC and decided to publish them.*

Lucretius begins his poem with an attack on religion: In his eyes, religion is used to justify all barbaric acts, such as, for example, the murder of Iphigenia. As for mankind, it labors to overcome its fear of death and torture beyond the tomb. Lucretius is convinced that a better understanding of the world and of matter will save man such panic and other ridicules. Lucretius is a theoretician of atoms. (Epicureans like himself believe that the world is made up of these particles.) He is also a pastoral poet who is sensitive to the cow that has lost its calf. He further sympathizes with the suffering of men. (See, for example, his description of the plague at Athens in Book VI, largely inspired by Thucydides.)

The Atom

Lucretius, *On the Nature of Things* 1.599-829

Lucretius transmits the most complete account on Epicurism. Its principle is simple: The universe is composed of two elements, matter and void. All matter is made of atoms. They fall into the void, collide by random chance, and then, by multiple combinations, form objects and creatures. Death is nothing more than the separation of atoms. No afterlife exists, no immortality of the soul, but only atoms that start falling again into the void until they form new combinations. Nothing is born from nothing. Nothing returns to nothing. Man must therefore emancipate himself from his fear of dying and live a perfectly happy life, freed from passions and anxieties—a serene life that is very different from that commonly understood as Epicurism. Lucretius reveals here what he means by "atom": It is literally that which is "indivisible," the smallest unit of matter (despite modern scientific discoveries showing that it is composed of smaller units). Lucretius then refutes the rival philosophies of Heraclitus, Empedocles, and Anaxagoras.

"Dolts are ever prone
That to bewonder and adore which hides
Beneath distorted words, holding that true
Which sweetly tickles in their stupid ears,
Or which is rouged in finely finished phrase."

And then again,
Since there is ever an extreme bounding point
Of that first body which our senses now
Cannot perceive, that bounding point indeed
Exists without all parts, a minimum
Of nature, nor was e'er a thing apart,
As of itself, nor shall hereafter be,
Since 'tis itself still parcel of another,
A first and single part, whence other parts
And others similar in order lie
In a packed phalanx, filling to the full
The nature of first body: being thus
Not self-existent, they must cleave to that
From which in nowise they can sundered be.
So primal germs have solid singleness,

Which tightly packed and closely joined cohere
By virtue of their minim particles-
No compound by mere union of the same;
But strong in their eternal singleness,
Nature, reserving them as seeds for things,
Permitteth naught of rupture or decrease.

Moreover, were there not a minimum,
The smallest bodies would have infinites,
Since then a half-of-half could still be halved,
With limitless division less and less.
Then what the difference 'twixt the sum and least?
None: for however infinite the sum,
Yet even the smallest would consist the same
Of infinite parts. But since true reason here
Protests, denying that the mind can think it,
Convinced thou must confess such things there are
As have no parts, the minimums of nature.
And since these are, likewise confess thou must
That primal bodies are solid and eterne.
Again, if Nature, creatress of all things,
Were wont to force all things to be resolved
Unto least parts, then would she not avail
To reproduce from out them anything;
Because whate'er is not endowed with parts
Cannot possess those properties required
Of generative stuff- divers connections,
Weights, blows, encounters, motions, whereby things
Forevermore have being and go on.

And on such grounds it is that those who held
The stuff of things is fire, and out of fire
Alone the cosmic sum is formed, are seen
Mightily from true reason to have lapsed.
Of whom, chief leader to do battle, comes
That Heraclitus, famous for dark speech
Among the silly, not the serious Greeks
Who search for truth. For dolts are ever prone
That to bewonder and adore which hides
Beneath distorted words, holding that true
Which sweetly tickles in their stupid ears,

Or which is rouged in finely finished phrase.
For how, I ask, can things so varied be,
If formed of fire, single and pure? No whit
'Twould help for fire to be condensed or thinned,
If all the parts of fire did still preserve
But fire's own nature, seen before in gross.
The heat were keener with the parts compressed,
Milder, again, when severed or dispersed-
And more than this thou canst conceive of naught
That from such causes could become; much less
Might earth's variety of things be born
From any fires soever, dense or rare.
This too: if they suppose a void in things,
Then fires can be condensed and still left rare;
But since they see such opposites of thought
Rising against them, and are loath to leave
An unmixed void in things, they fear the steep
And lose the road of truth. Nor do they see,
That, if from things we take away the void,
All things are then condensed, and out of all
One body made, which has no power to dart
Swiftly from out itself not anything-
As throws the fire its light and warmth around,
Giving thee proof its parts are not compact.
But if perhaps they think, in other wise,
Fires through their combinations can be quenched
And change their substance, very well: behold,
If fire shall spare to do so in no part,
Then heat will perish utterly and all,
And out of nothing would the world be formed.
For change in anything from out its bounds
Means instant death of that which was before;
And thus a somewhat must persist unharmed
Amid the world, lest all return to naught,
And, born from naught, abundance thrive anew.
Now since indeed there are those surest bodies
Which keep their nature evermore the same,
Upon whose going out and coming in
And changed order things their nature change,
And all corporeal substances transformed,
'Tis thine to know those primal bodies, then,

Are not of fire. For 'twere of no avail
Should some depart and go away, and some
Be added new, and some be changed in order,
If still all kept their nature of old heat:
For whatsoever they created then
Would still in any case be only fire.
The truth, I fancy, this: bodies there are
Whose clashings, motions, order, posture, shapes
Produce the fire and which, by order changed,
Do change the nature of the thing produced,
And are thereafter nothing like to fire
Nor whatso else has power to send its bodies
With impact touching on the senses' touch.

Again, to say that all things are but fire
And no true thing in number of all things
Exists but fire, as this same fellow says,
Seems crazed folly. For the man himself
Against the senses by the senses fights,
And hews at that through which is all belief,
Through which indeed unto himself is known
The thing he calls the fire. For, though he thinks
The senses truly can perceive the fire,
He thinks they cannot as regards all else,
Which still are palpably as clear to sense-
To me a thought inept and crazy too.
For whither shall we make appeal? for what
More certain than our senses can there be
Whereby to mark asunder error and truth?
Besides, why rather do away with all,
And wish to allow heat only, then deny
The fire and still allow all else to be?
Alike the madness either way it seems.
Thus whosoe'er have held the stuff of things
To be but fire, and out of fire the sum,
And whosoever have constituted air[1]
As first beginning of begotten things,
And all whoever have held that of itself
Water alone contrives things, or that earth
Createth all and changes things anew
To divers natures, mightily they seem

A long way to have wandered from the truth.
Add, too, whoever make the primal stuff
Twofold, by joining air to fire, and earth
To water; add who deem that things can grow
Out of the four- fire, earth, and breath, and rain;
As first Empedocles of Acragas,
Whom that three-cornered isle of all the lands
Bore on her coasts, around which flows and flows
In mighty bend and bay the Ionic seas,
Splashing the brine from off their gray-green waves.
Here, billowing onward through the narrow straits,
Swift ocean cuts her boundaries from the shores
Of the Italic mainland. Here the waste
Charybdis; and here Aetna rumbles threats
To gather anew such furies of its flames
As with its force anew to vomit fires,
Belched from its throat, and skyward bear anew
Its lightnings' flash. And though for much she seem
The mighty and the wondrous isle to men,
Most rich in all good things, and fortified
With generous strength of heroes, she hath ne'er
Possessed within her aught of more renown,
Nor aught more holy, wonderful, and dear
Than this true man. Nay, ever so far and pure
The lofty music of his breast divine
Lifts up its voice and tells of glories found,
That scarce he seems of human stock create.

Yet he and those forementioned (known to be
So far beneath him, less than he in all),
Though, as discoverers of much goodly truth,
They gave, as 'twere from out of the heart's own shrine,
Responses holier and soundlier based
Than ever the Pythia pronounced for men
From out the triped and the Delphian laurel,
Have still in matter of first-elements
Made ruin of themselves, and, great men, great
Indeed and heavy there for them the fall:
First, because, banishing the void from things,
They yet assign them motion, and allow
Things soft and loosely textured to exist,

As air, dew, fire, earth, animals, and grains,
Without admixture of void amid their frame.
Next, because, thinking there can be no end
In cutting bodies down to less and less
Nor pause established to their breaking up,
They hold there is no minimum in things;
Albeit we see the boundary point of aught
Is that which to our senses seems its least,
Whereby thou mayst conjecture, that, because
The things thou canst not mark have boundary points,
They surely have their minimums. Then, too,
Since these philosophers ascribe to things
Soft primal germs, which we behold to be
Of birth and body mortal, thus, throughout,
The sum of things must be returned to naught,
And, born from naught, abundance thrive anew-
Thou seest how far each doctrine stands from truth.
And, next, these bodies are among themselves
In many ways poisons and foes to each,
Wherefore their congress will destroy them quite
Or drive asunder as we see in storms
Rains, winds, and lightnings all asunder fly.

Thus too, if all things are create of four,
And all again dissolved into the four,
How can the four be called the primal germs
Of things, more than all things themselves be thought,
By retroversion, primal germs of them?
For ever alternately are both begot,
With interchange of nature and aspect
From immemorial time. But if percase
Thou think'st the frame of fire and earth, the air,
The dew of water can in such wise meet
As not by mingling to resign their nature,
From them for thee no world can be create-
No thing of breath, no stock or stalk of tree:
In the wild congress of this varied heap
Each thing its proper nature will display,
And air will palpably be seen mixed up
With earth together, unquenched heat with water.
But primal germs in bringing things to birth

Must have a latent, unseen quality,
Lest some outstanding alien element
Confuse and minish in the thing create
Its proper being.

But these men begin
From heaven, and from its fires; and first they feign
That fire will turn into the winds of air,
Next, that from air the rain begotten is,
And earth created out of rain, and then
That all, reversely, are returned from earth-
The moisture first, then air thereafter heat-
And that these same ne'er cease in interchange,
To go their ways from heaven to earth, from earth
Unto the stars of the aethereal world-
Which in no wise at all the germs can do.
Since an immutable somewhat still must be,
Lest all things utterly be sped to naught;
For change in anything from out its bounds
Means instant death of that which was before.
Wherefore, since those things, mentioned heretofore,
Suffer a changed state, they must derive
From others ever unconvertible,
Lest an things utterly return to naught.
Then why not rather presuppose there be
Bodies with such a nature furnished forth
That, if perchance they have created fire,
Can still (by virtue of a few withdrawn,
Or added few, and motion and order changed)
Fashion the winds of air, and thus all things
Forevermore be interchanged with all?

"But facts in proof are manifest," thou sayest,
"That all things grow into the winds of air
And forth from earth are nourished, and unless
The season favour at propitious hour
With rains enough to set the trees a-reel
Under the soak of bulking thunderheads,
And sun, for its share, foster and give heat,
No grains, nor trees, nor breathing things can grow."
True- and unless hard food and moisture soft

Recruited man, his frame would waste away,
And life dissolve from out his thews and bones;
For out of doubt recruited and fed are we
By certain things, as other things by others.
Because in many ways the many germs
Common to many things are mixed in things,
No wonder 'tis that therefore divers things
By divers things are nourished. And, again,
Often it matters vastly with what others,
In what positions the primordial germs
Are bound together, and what motions, too,
They give and get among themselves; for these
Same germs do put together sky, sea, lands,
Rivers, and sun, grains, trees, and breathing things,
But yet commixed they are in divers modes
With divers things, forever as they move.
Nay, thou beholdest in our verses here
Elements many, common to many worlds,
Albeit thou must confess each verse, each word
From one another differs both in sense
And ring of sound- so much the elements
Can bring about by change of order alone.
But those which are the primal germs of things
Have power to work more combinations still,
Whence divers things can be produced in turn.

Translated by William Ellery Leonard.

SALLUST

86 - 35 BC

Born in 86 BC at Amiternum northeast of Rome, C. Sallustius Crispus indulged himself in the pleasures of Rome's "Golden Youth." Caesar's favor earned him all the honors: first the quaestorship, and then the plebeian tribunate, during which in 52 he led a heinous campaign against Cicero and Milo. In 50, this scoundrel, whom Cicero loathed, was excluded from the senate for immorality. His penchant for adultery led him to corrupt Milo's wife. But thanks to Caesar's protection, he could return to the stage. His campaigns of pacification and other missions were all failures except for his personal financial enrichment.

What Caesar accomplished, the Ides of March unraveled. Sallust lost all support and was left with only one possibility: retiring to his lavish property on Pincian Hill, the Hill of Gardens in Rome. He devoted himself to writing historic works, such as The Conspiracy of Catiline, The Jugurthine War, *and* The Histories. *In certain respects, Sallust's historic work is clearly inspired by Thucydides. It is written in a very personal style with a taste for dissymmetry and for constructions drawn from Greek phraseology. The portraits are masterful, as are such key speeches as Caesar's in* The Conspiracy of Catiline *(see below) and Cato of Utica's.*

Sallust is a committed historian. Devoted to the cult of the national past, he is not afraid to vent his hatred against the corrupt and venal nobility in order to give Caesar and the democratic party a strong and favorable role. From this prose that struggles to be objective emerges a philosophy of history that favors great men and resolute minds.

A Call to Revolution

Sallust, *The Conspiracy of Catiline* 20-22 and 50-55

Catiline, a patrician inclined to dissipation and homicide, is embittered by his failure to become a consul in 64 BC. His humiliation is further compounded by the appointment of Cicero as one of the two consuls elected that year, a man whom Catiline outright hates and moreover has attempted to assassinate several times. The hatred is mutual, as Cicero's Orations Against Catiline *show. Catiline tries his luck again the following year, but fails once more. As a result, he becomes a revolutionary and gathers a gang of conspirators. Ironically, he is as unsuccessful in conspiracy as he has been in achieving a consulship. His main accomplices—among them Lentulus and Cegethus—are arrested and are put to death. Catiline flees Rome and is killed one year later.*

Sallust, like Cicero, does not like Catiline, whom he describes as a monster of mischievousness. Here, Sallust provides his own version of the conspiracy. Catiline first urges his partisans to support him for the election of 64 BC. Steeped in ranting gibberish, the speech is as much an attempt to be elected as it is a call to revolution. Next, the conspiracy is unveiled, the conspirators are arrested, and the senate deliberates about their fate. Whereas Caesar proposes a lifetime in jail in Italian cities, Cato of Utica pleads with implacable austerity for the death sentence.

"The protection of the gods is not obtained by vows and effeminate supplications; it is by vigilance, activity, and prudent measures, that general welfare is secured."

When Catiline saw those, whom I have just above mentioned, assembled, though he had often discussed many points with them singly, yet thinking it would be to his purpose to address and exhort them in a body, retired with them into a private apartment of his house, where, when all witnesses were withdrawn, he harangued them to the following effect:

"If your courage and fidelity had not been sufficiently proved by me, this favorable opportunity would have occurred to no purpose; mighty hopes, absolute power, would in vain be within our grasp; nor should I, depending on irresolution or ficklemindedness, pursue contingencies instead of certainties. But as I have, on many remarkable occasions, experienced your bravery and attachment to me, I have ventured to engage in a most important and glorious enterprise. I am aware, too, that whatever advantages or evils affect you, the same affect me; and to have the same desires and the same aversions, is assuredly a firm bond of friendship.

"What I have been meditating you have already heard separately. But my ardor for action is daily more and more excited, when I consider what our future condition of life must be, unless we ourselves assert our claims to liberty. For since the government has fallen under the power and jurisdiction of a few, kings and princes have constantly been their tributaries; nations and states have paid them taxes; but all the rest of us, however brave and worthy, whether noble or plebeian, have been regarded as a mere mob, without interest or authority, and subject to those, to whom, if the state were in a sound condition, we should be a terror. Hence, all influence, power, honor, and wealth, are in their hands, or where they dispose of them: to us they have left only insults, dangers, persecutions, and poverty. To such indignities, O bravest of men, how long will you submit? Is it not better to die in a glorious attempt, than, after having been the sport of other men's insolence, to resign a wretched and degraded existence with ignominy?

"But success (I call gods and men to witness!) is in our own hands. Our years are fresh, our spirit is unbroken; among our oppressors, on the contrary, through age and wealth a general debility has been produced. We have therefore only to make a beginning; the course of events will accomplish the rest.

"Who in the world, indeed, that has the feelings of a man, can endure that they should have a superfluity of riches, to squander in building over seas and leveling mountains, and that means should be wanting to us even for the necessaries of life; that they should join together two houses or more, and that we should not have a hearth to call our own? They, though they purchase pictures, statues, and embossed plate; though they pull down now buildings and erect others, and lavish and abuse their wealth in every possible method; yet can not, with the utmost efforts of caprice, exhaust it. But for us there is poverty at home, debts abroad; our present circumstances are bad, our prospects much worse; and what, in a word, have we left, but a miserable existence?

"Will you not, then, awake to action? Behold that liberty, that liberty for which you have so often wished, with wealth, honor, and glory, are set before your eyes. All these prizes fortune offers to the victorious. Let the enterprise itself, then, let the opportunity, let your poverty, your dangers, and the glorious spoils of war, animate you far more than my words. Use me either as your leader or your fellow-soldier; neither my heart nor my hand shall be wanting to you. These objects I hope to effect, in concert with you, in the character of consul; unless, indeed, my expectation deceives me, and you prefer to be slaves rather than masters."

When these men, surrounded with numberless evils, but without any resources or hopes of good, had heard this address, though they thought it much for their advantage to disturb the public tranquillity, yet most of them called on Catiline to state on what terms they were to engage in the contest; what benefits they were to expect from taking up arms; and what support and encouragement they had, and in what quarters. Catiline then promised them the abolition of their debts; a proscription of the wealthy citizens; offices, sacerdotal dignities, plunder, and all other gratifications which war, and the license of conquerors, can afford. He added that Piso was in Hither Spain, and Publius Sittius Nucerinus with an army in Mauritania, both of whom were privy to his plans; that Caius Antonius, whom he hoped to have for a colleague, was canvassing for the consulship, a man with whom he was intimate, and who was involved in all manner of embarrassments; and that, in conjunction with him, he himself, when consul, would commence operations. He, moreover, assailed all the respectable citizens with reproaches, commended each of his associates by name, reminded one of his poverty, another of his ruling passion, several others of their danger or disgrace, and many of the spoils which they had obtained by the victory of Sylla. When he saw their spirits sufficiently elevated, he charged them to attend to his interest at the election of consuls, and dismissed the assembly.

There were some, at the time, who said that Catiline, having ended his speech, and wishing to bind his accomplices in guilt by an oath, handed round among them, in goblets, the blood of a human body mixed with wine; and that when all, after an imprecation, had tasted of it, as is usual in sacred rites, he disclosed his design; and they asserted that he did this, in order that they might be the more closely attached to one another, by being mutually conscious of such an atrocity. But some thought that this report, and many others, were invented by persons who supposed that the odium against Cicero, which afterward arose, might be lessened by imputing an enormity of guilt to the conspirators who had suffered death. The evidence which I have obtained, in support of this charge, is not at all in proportion to its magnitude.

While these occurrences were passing in the senate, and while rewards were being voted, an approbation of their evidence, to the Allobrogian deputies and to Titus Volturcius, the freedmen, and some of the other dependents of Lentulus, were urging the artisans and slaves, in various directions throughout the city, to attempt his rescue;[1] some, too, applied to the ringleaders of the mob, who were always ready to disturb the state for pay. Cethegus, at the same time, was soliciting, through his agents, his slaves and freedmen, men trained to deeds of audacity, to collect themselves into an armed body, and force a way into his place of confinement.

The consul, when he heard that these things were in agitation, having distributed armed bodies of men, as the circumstances and occasion demanded, called a meeting of the senate, and desired to know "what they wished to be done concerning those who had been committed to custody." A full senate, however, had but a short time before declared them traitors to their country. On this occasion, Decimus Junius Silanus, who, as consul elect, was first asked his opinion, moved that capital punishment should be inflicted, not only on those who were in confinement, but also on Lucius Cassius, Publius Furius, Publius Umbrenus, and Quintus Annius, if they should be apprehended; but afterward, being influenced by the speech of Caius Caesar, he said that he would go over to the opinion of Tiberius Nero, who had proposed that the guards should be increased, and that the senate should deliberate further on the matter. Caesar, when it came to his turn, being asked his opinion by the consul, spoke to the following effect:

"It becomes all men, Conscript Fathers, who deliberate on dubious matters, to be influenced neither by hatred, affection, anger, nor pity. The mind, when such feelings obstruct its view, can not easily see what is right; nor has any human being consulted, at the same moment, his passion and his interest. When the mind is freely exerted, its reasoning is sound; but passion, if it gain possession of it, becomes its tyrant, and reason is powerless.

I could easily mention, Conscript Fathers, numerous examples of kings and nations, who, swayed by resentment or compassion, have adopted injudicious courses of conduct; but I had rather speak of these instances in which our ancestors, in opposition, to the impulse of passion, acted with wisdom and sound policy.

In the Macedonian war, which we carried on against king Perses, the great and powerful state of Rhodes, which had risen by the aid of the Roman people, was faithless and hostile to us; yet, when the war was ended, and the conduct of the Rhodians was taken into consideration, our forefathers left them unmolested lest any should say that war was made upon them for the sake of seizing their wealth, rather than of punishing their faithlessness. Throughout the Punic war, too, though the Carthaginians, both during peace and in suspension of arms, were guilty of many acts of injustice, yet our ancestors never took occasion to retaliate, but considered rather what was worthy of themselves, than what might be justly inflicted on their enemies.

Similar caution, Conscript Fathers, is to be observed by yourselves, that the guilt of Lentulus, and the other conspirators, may not have greater weight with you than your own dignity, and that you may not regard your indignation more than your character. If, indeed, a punishment adequate to their crimes be discovered, I consent to extraordinary measures; but if the enormity of their crime exceeds whatever can be devised, I think that we should inflict only such penalties as the laws have provided.

Most of those, who have given their opinions before me, have deplored, in studied and impressive language, the sad fate that threatens the republic; they have recounted the barbarities of war, and the afflictions that would fall on the vanquished; they have told us that maidens would be dishonored, and youths abused; that children would be torn from the embraces of their parents; that matrons would be subjected to the pleasure of the conquerors; that temples and dwelling-houses would be plundered; that massacres and fires would follow; and that every place would be filled with arms, corpses, blood, and lamentation. But to what end, in the name of the eternal gods, was such eloquence directed? Was it intended to render you indignant at the conspiracy? A speech, no doubt, will inflame him whom so frightful and monstrous a reality has not provoked! Far from it: for to no man does evil, directed against himself, appear a light matter; many, on the contrary, have felt it more seriously than was right.

But to different persons, Conscript Fathers, different degrees of license are allowed. If those who pass a life sunk in obscurity, commit any error, through excessive anger, few become aware of it, for their fame is as limited as their fortune; but of those who live invested with extensive power, and in an exalted station, the whole world knows the proceedings. Thus in the highest position there is the least liberty of action; and it becomes us to indulge neither partiality nor aversion, but least of all animosity; for what in others is called resentment, is in the powerful termed violence and cruelty.

I am indeed of opinion, Conscript Fathers, that the utmost degree of torture is inadequate to punish their crime; but the generality of mankind dwell on that which happens last, and, in the case of malefactors, forget their guilt, and talk only of their punishment, should that punishment have been inordinately severe. I feel assured, too, that Decimus Silanus, a man of spirit and resolution, made the suggestions which he offered, from zeal for the state, and that he had no view, in so important a matter, to favor or to enmity; such I know to be his character, and such his discretion. Yet his proposal appears to me, I will not say cruel (for what can be cruel that is directed against such characters?), but foreign to our policy. For assuredly, Silanus, either your fears, or their treason, must have induced you, a consul elect, to propose this new kind of punishment. Of fear it is unnecessary to speak, when by the prompt activity of that distinguished man our consul, such numerous forces are under arms; and as to the punishment, we may say, what is indeed the truth, that in trouble and distress, death is a relief from suffering, and not a torment; that it puts an end to all human woes; and that, beyond it, there is no place either for sorrow or joy.

But why, in the name of the immortal gods, did you not add to your proposal,

Silanus, that, before they were put to death, they should be punished with the scourge? Was it because the Porcian law forbids it? But other laws forbid condemned citizens to be deprived of life, and allow them to go into exile. Or was it because scourging is a severer penalty than death? Yet what can be too severe, or too harsh, toward men convicted of such an offense? But if scourging be a milder punishment than death, how is it consistent to observe the law as to the smaller point, when you disregard it as to the greater?

But who it may be asked, will blame any severity that shall be decreed against these parricides of their country? I answer that time, the course of events, and fortune, whose caprice governs nations, may blame it. Whatever shall fall on the traitors, will fall on them justly; but it is for you, Conscript Fathers, to consider well what you resolve to inflict on others. All precedents productive of evil effects, have had their origin from what was good; but when a government passes into the hands of the ignorant or unprincipled, any new example of severity, inflicted on deserving and suitable objects, is extended to those that are improper and undeserving of it. The Lacedaemonians, when they had conquered the Athenians, appointed thirty men to govern their state. These thirty began their administration by putting to death, even without a trial, all who were notoriously wicked, or publicly detestable; acts at which the people rejoiced, and extolled their justice. But afterward, when their lawless power gradually increased, they proceeded, at their pleasure, to kill the good and the bad indiscriminately, and to strike terror into all; and thus the state, overpowered and enslaved, paid a heavy penalty for its imprudent exultation.

Within our own memory, too, when the victorious Sylla ordered Damasippus,[2] and others of similar character, who had risen by distressing their country, to be put to death, who did not commend the proceeding? All exclaimed that wicked and factious men, who had troubled the state with their seditious practices, had justly forfeited their lives. Yet this proceeding was the commencement of great bloodshed. For whenever anyone coveted the mansion or villa, or even the plate or apparel of another, he exerted his influence to have him numbered among the proscribed. Thus they, to whom the death of Damasippus had been a subject of joy, were soon after dragged to death themselves; nor was there any cessation of slaughter, until Sylla had glutted all his partisans with riches.

Such excesses, indeed, I do not fear from Marcus Tullius,[3] or in these times. But in a large state there arise many men of various dispositions. At some other period, and under another consul, who, like the present, may have an army at his command, some false accusation may be credited as true; and when, with our example for a precedent, the consul shall have drawn the sword on the authority of the senate, who shall stay its progress, or moderate its fury?

Our ancestors, Conscript Fathers, were never deficient in conduct or courage; nor did pride prevent them from imitating the customs of other nations, if they appeared deserving of regard. Their armor, and weapons of war, they borrowed from the Samnites; their ensigns of authority, for the most part, from the Etrurians;[4] and, in short, whatever appeared eligible to them, whether among allies or among enemies, they adopted at home with the greatest readiness, being more inclined to emulate merit than to be jealous of it. But at the same time, adopting a practice from Greece, they punished their citizens with the scourge, and inflicted capital punishment on such as were condemned. When the republic, however, became powerful, and faction grew strong from the vast number of citizens, men began to involve the innocent in condemnation, and other like abuses were practiced; and it was then that the Porcian and other laws were provided, by which condemned citizens were allowed to go into exile. This lenity of our ancestors, Conscript Fathers, I regard as a very strong reason why we should not adopt any new measures of severity. For assuredly there was greater merit and wisdom in those, who raised so mighty an empire from humble means, than in us, who can scarcely preserve what they so honorably acquired. Am I of opinion, then, you will ask, that the conspirators should be set free, and that the army of Catiline should thus be increased? Far from it; my recommendation is, that their property be confiscated, and that they themselves be kept in custody in such of the municipal towns as are best able to bear the expense; that no one hereafter bring their case before the senate, or speak on it to the people; and that the senate now give their opinion, that he who shall act contrary to this, will act against the republic and the general safety."

When Caesar had ended his speech, the rest briefly expressed their assent, some to one speaker, and some to another, in support of their different proposals; but Marcius Porcius Cato, being asked his opinion, made a speech to the following purport:

"My feelings, Conscript Fathers, are extremely different, when I contemplate our circumstances and dangers, and when I revolve in my mind the sentiments of some who have spoken before me. Those speakers, as it seems to me, have considered only how to punish the traitors who have raised war against their country, their parents, their altars, and their homes; but the state of affairs warns us rather to secure ourselves against them, than to take counsel as to what sentence we should pass upon them. Other crimes you may punish after they have been committed; but as to this, unless you prevent its commission, you will, when it has once taken effect, in vain appeal to justice. When the city is taken, no power is left to the vanquished. But, in the name of the immortal gods, I call upon you, who have always valued your mansions and villas, your statues and pictures, at a higher price than the welfare of your country; if you wish to preserve those possessions, of whatever kind they are, to which you are attached; if you wish to secure quiet for the enjoyment of your pleasures, arouse yourselves, and act in defense of your country. We are not now debating on the revenues, or on injuries done to our allies, but our liberty and our life is at stake.

Often, Conscript Fathers, have I spoken at great length in this assembly; often have I complained of the luxury and avarice of our citizens, and, by that very means, have incurred the displeasure of many. I, who never excused to myself, or to my own conscience, the commission of any fault, could not easily pardon the misconduct, or indulge the licentiousness, of others. But though you little regarded my remonstrances, yet the republic remained secure; its own strength was proof against your remissness. The question, however, at present under discussion, is not whether we live in a good or a bad state of morals; nor how great, or how splendid, the empire of the Roman people is; but whether these things around us, of whatever value they are, are to continue our own, or to fall, with ourselves, into the hands of the enemy.

In such a case, does any one talk to me of gentleness and compassion? For some time past, it is true, we have lost the real name of things; for to lavish the property of others is called generosity, and audacity in wickedness is called heroism; and hence the state is reduced to the brink of ruin. But let those, who thus misname things, be liberal, since such is the practice, out of the property of our allies; let them be merciful to the robbers of the treasury; but let them not lavish our blood, and, while they spare a few criminals, bring destruction on all the guiltless.

Caius Caesar, a short time ago, spoke in fair and elegant language, before this assembly, on the subject of life and death; considering as false, I suppose, what is told of the dead; that the bad, going a different way from the good, inhabit places gloomy, desolate, dreary, and full of horror. He accordingly proposed that the property of the conspirators should be confiscated, and themselves kept in custody in the municipal towns; fearing, it seems, that, if they remain at Rome, they may be rescued either by their accomplices in the conspiracy, or by a hired mob; as if, forsooth, the mischievous and profligate were to be found only in the city, and not through the whole of Italy, or as if desperate attempts would not be more likely to succeed where there is less power to resist them. His proposal, therefore, if he fears any danger from them, is absurd; but if, amid such universal terror, he alone is free from alarm, it the more concerns me to fear for you and myself.

Be assured, then, that when you decide on the fate of Lentulus and the other prisoners, you at the same time determine that of the army of Catiline, and of all the conspirators. The more spirit you display in your decision, the more will their confidence be diminished; but if they shall perceive you in the smallest degree irresolute, they will advance upon you with fury.

Do not suppose that our ancestors, from so small a commencement, raised the republic to greatness merely by force of arms. If such had been the case, we should enjoy it in a most excellent condition; for of allies and citizens, as well as arms and horses, we have a much greater abundance than they had. But there were other things which made them great, but which among us have no existence; such as industry at home, equitable government abroad, and minds impartial in council, uninfluenced by any immoral or improper feeling. Instead of such virtues, we have luxury and avarice; public distress, and private superfluity; we extol wealth, and yield to indolence; no distinction is made between good men and bad; and ambition usurps the honors due to virtue. Nor is this wonderful; since you study each his individual interest, and since at home you are slaves to pleasure, and here to money or favor; and hence it happens that an attack is made on the defenseless state.

But on these subjects I shall say no more. Certain citizens, of the highest rank, have conspired to ruin their country; they are engaging the Gauls, the bitterest foes of the Roman name, to join in a war against us; the leader of the enemy is ready to make a descent upon us; and do you hesitate, even in such circumstances, how to treat armed incendiaries arrested within your walls? I advise you to have mercy upon them; they are young men who have been led astray by ambition; send them away, even with arms in their hands. But such mercy, and such clemency, if they turn those arms against you, will end in misery to yourselves. The case is, assuredly, dangerous, but you do not fear it; yes, you fear it greatly, but you hesitate how to act, through weakness and want of spirit, waiting one for another, and trusting to the immortal gods, who have so often preserved your country in the greatest dangers. But the protection of the gods is not obtained by vows and effeminate supplications; it is by vigilance, activity, and prudent measures, that general welfare is secured. When you are once resigned to sloth and indolence, it is in vain that you implore the gods; for they are then indignant and threaten vengeance.

In the days of our forefathers, Titus Manlius Torquatus, during a war with the Gauls, ordered his own son to be put to death, because he had fought with an enemy contrary to orders. That noble youth suffered for excess of bravery; and do you hesitate what sentence to pass on the most inhuman of traitors? Perhaps their former life is at variance with their present crime. Spare, then, the dignity of Lentulus, if he has ever spared his own honor or character, or had any regard for gods or for men. Pardon the youth of Cethegus, unless this be the second time that he has made war upon his country. As to Gabinius, Slatilius, Coeparius, why should I make any remark upon them? Had they ever possessed the smallest share of discretion, they would never have engaged in such a plot against their country.

In conclusion, Conscript Fathers, if there were time to amend an error, I might easily suffer you, since you disregard words, to be corrected by experience of consequences. But we are beset by dangers on all sides; Catiline, with his army, is ready to devour us; while there are other enemies within the walls, and in the heart of the city; nor can any measures be taken, or any plans arranged, without their knowledge. The more necessary is it, therefore, to act with promptitude. What I advise, then, is this: that since the state, by a treasonable combination of abandoned citizens, has been brought into the greatest peril; and since the conspirators have been convicted on the evidence of Titus Volturcius, and the deputies of the Allobroges, and on their own confession, of having concerted massacres, conflagrations, and other horrible and cruel outrages, against their fellow-citizens and their country, punishment be inflicted, according to the usage of our ancestors, on the prisoners who have confessed their guilt, as on men convicted of capital crimes."

When Cato had resumed his seat, all the senators of consular dignity, and a great part of the rest, applauded his opinion, and extolled his firmness of mind to the skies. With mutual reproaches, they accused one another of timidity, while Cato was regarded as the greatest and noblest of men; and a decree of the senate was made as he had advised.

After reading and hearing of the many glorious achievements which the Roman people had performed at home and in the field, by sea as well as by land, I happened to be led to consider what had been the great foundation of such illustrious deeds. I knew that the Romans had frequently, with small bodies of men, encountered vast armies of the enemy; I was aware that they had carried on wars with limited forces against powerful sovereigns; that they had often sustained, too, the violence of adverse fortune; yet that, while the Greeks excelled them in eloquence, the Gauls surpassed them in military glory. After much reflection, I felt convinced that the eminent virtue of a few citizens had been the cause of all these successes; and hence it had happened that poverty had triumphed over riches, and a few over a multitude. And even in later times, when the state had become corrupted by luxury and indolence, the republic still supported itself, by its own strength, under the misconduct of its generals and magistrates; when, as if the parent stock were exhausted, there was certainly not produced at Rome, for many years, a single citizen of eminent ability. Within my recollection, however, there arose two men of remarkable powers, though of very different character, Marcus Cato and Caius Caesar, whom, since the subject has brought them before me, it is not my intention to pass in silence, but to describe, to the best of my ability, the disposition and manners of each.

Their birth, age, and eloquence, were nearly on an equality; their greatness of mind similar, as was also their reputation, though attained by different means. Caesar grew eminent by generosity and munificence; Cato by the integrity of his life. Caesar was esteemed for his humanity and benevolence; austereness had given dignity to Cato. Caesar acquired renown by giving, relieving, and pardoning; Cato by bestowing nothing. In Caesar, there was a refuge for the unfortunate; in Cato, destruction for the bad. In Caesar, his easiness of temper was admired; in Cato, his firmness. Caesar, in fine, had applied himself to a life of energy and activity; intent upon the interest of his friends, he was neglectful of his own; he refused nothing to others that was worthy of acceptance, while for himself he desired great power, the command of an army, and a new war in which his talents might be displayed. But Cato's ambition was that of temperance, discretion, and, above all, of austerity; he did not contend in splendor with the rich, or in faction with the seditious, but with the brave in fortitude, with the modest in simplicity, with the temperate in abstinence; he was more desirous to be, than to appear, virtuous; and thus, the less he courted popularity, the more it pursued him.

When the senate, as I have stated, had gone over to the opinion of Cato, the counsel, thinking it best not to wait till night, which was coming on, lest any new attempts should be made during the interval, ordered the triumvirs to make such preparations as the execution of the conspirators required. He himself, having posted the necessary guards, conducted Lentulus to the prison; and the same office was performed for the rest by the praetors. There is a place in the prison, which is called the Tullian dungeon, and which, after a slight ascent to the left, is sunk about twelve feet under ground. Walls secure it on every side, and over it is a vaulted roof connected with stone arches; but its appearance is disgusting and horrible, by reason of the filth, darkness, and stench. When Lentulus had been let down into this place, certain men, to whom orders had been given, strangled him with a cord. Thus this patrician, who was of the illustrious family of the Cornelii, and who filled the office of consul at Rome, met with an end suited to his character and conduct. On Cethegus, Statilius, Gabinius, and Coeparius, punishment was inflicted in a similar manner.

Translated by the Rev. John Selby Watson.

King Jugurtha Travels to Rome

Sallust, *The Jugurthine War* 30-37

In 111 BC, the consul Bestia lands in Numidia (North Africa) to bring King Jugurtha into line. The latter has seized the town of Cirta, has massacred the Italian residents, and has killed his brother Adherbal. Bestia and his right-hand man, Scaurus, make short work of the situation: they capture towns, take prisoners, and then allow themselves to be bought by Jugurtha. In exchange for an enormous bribe, they accept to open peace negotiations and to conclude a truce that is advantageous to the king. Rome reacts sharply upon learning how the Numidian Jugurtha has corrupted the Roman magistrates. The tribune C. Memmius, known for his eloquence, delivers a speech on the subject before his fellow citizens. It is decided upon to invite the enemy king to Rome to testify against Bestia with the promise of immunity.

"As Jugurtha was going from Rome, he is said, after frequently looking back on it in silence, to have at last exclaimed, "That it was a venal city, and would soon perish, if it could but find a purchaser!"

When rumor had made known the affairs transacted in Africa, and the mode in which they had been brought to pass, the conduct of the consul became a subject of discussion in every place and company at Rome. Among the people there was violent indignation; as to the senators, whether they would ratify so flagitious a proceeding, or annul the act of the consul, was a matter of doubt. The influence of Scaurus, as he was said to be the supporter and accomplice of Bestia, was what chiefly restrained the senate from acting with justice and honor. But Caius Memmius, of whose boldness of spirit, and hatred to the power of the nobility, I have already spoken, excited the people by his harangues, during the perplexity and delay of the senators, to take vengeance on the authors of the treaty; he exhorted them not to abandon the public interest or their own liberty; he set before them the many tyrannical and violent proceedings of the nobles, and omitted no art to inflame the popular passions. But as the eloquence of Memmius, at that period, had great reputation and influence I have thought proper to give in full one out of many of his speeches; and I take, in preference to others, that which he delivered in the assembly of the people, after the return of Bestia, in words to the following effect:

"Were not my zeal for the good of the state, my fellow-citizens, superior to every other feeling, there are many considerations which would deter me from appearing in your cause; I allude to the power of the opposite party, your own tameness of spirit, the absence of all justice, and, above all, the fact that integrity is attended with more danger than honor. Indeed, it grieves me to relate, how, during the last fifteen years, you have been a sport to the arrogance of an oligarchy; how dishonorably, and how utterly unavenged, your defenders have perished; and how your spirit has become degenerate by sloth and indolence; for not even now, when your enemies are in your power, will you rouse yourselves to action, but continue still to stand in awe of those to whom you should be a terror.

Yet, notwithstanding this state of things, I feel prompted to make an attack on the power of that faction. That liberty of speech, therefore, which has been left me by my father, I shall assuredly exert against them; but whether I shall use it in vain, or for your advantage, must, my fellow-citizens, depend upon yourselves. I do not, however, exhort you, as your ancestors have often done, to rise in arms against injustice.

There is at present no need of violence, no need of secession; for your tyrants must work their fall by their own misconduct.

After the murder of Tiberius Gracchus, whom they accused of aspiring to be king, persecutions were instituted against the common people of Rome; and after the slaughter of Caius Gracchus and Marcus Fulvius, many of your order were put to death in prison.[5] But let us leave these proceedings out of the question; let us admit that to restore their rights to the people, was to aspire to sovereignty; let us allow that what can not be avenged without shedding the blood of citizens, was done with justice. You have seen with silent indignation, however, in past years, the treasury pillaged; you have seen kings, and free people, paying tribute to a small party of Patricians, in whose hands were both the highest honors and the greatest wealth; but to have carried on such proceedings with impunity, they now deem but a small matter; and, at last, your laws and your honor, with every civil and religious obligation, have been sacrificed for the benefit of your enemies. Nor do they, who have done these things, show either shame or contrition, but parade proudly before your faces, displaying their sacerdotal dignities, their consulships, and some of them their triumphs, as if they regarded them as marks of honor, and not as fruits of their dishonesty. Slaves, purchased with money, will not submit to unjust commands from their masters; yet you, my fellow-citizens, who are born to empire, tamely endure oppression.

But who are these that have thus taken the government into their hands? Men of the most abandoned character, of blood-stained hands, of insatiable avarice, of enormous guilt, and of matchless pride; men by whom integrity, reputation, public spirit, and indeed every thing, whether honorable or dishonorable, is converted to a means of gain. Some of them make it their defense that they have killed tribunes of the people; others, that they have instituted unjust prosecutions; others, that they have shed your blood; and thus, the more atrocities each has committed, the greater is his security; while your oppressors, whom the same desires, the same aversions, and the same fears, combine in strict union (a union which among good men is friendship, but among the bad confederacy in guilt), have excited in you, through your want of spirit, that terror which they ought to feel for their own crimes.

But if your concern to preserve your liberty were as great as their ardor to increase their power of oppression, the state would not be distracted as it is at present; and the marks of favor which proceed from you, would be conferred, not on the most shameless, but on the most deserving. Your forefathers, in order to assert their rights and establish their authority, twice seceded in arms to Mount Aventine; and will not you exert yourselves, to the utmost of your power, in defense of that liberty which you received from them? Will you not display so much the more spirit in the cause, from the reflection that it is a greater disgrace to lose what has been gained, than not to have gained it at all?

But some will ask me, 'What course of conduct, then, would you advise us to pursue?' I would advise you to inflict punishment on those who have sacrificed the interests of their country to the enemy; not, indeed, by arms, or any violence (which would be more unbecoming, however, for you to inflict than for them to suffer), but by prosecutions, and by the evidence of Jugurtha himself, who, if he has really surrendered, will doubtless obey your summons; whereas, if he shows contempt for it, you will at once judge what sort of a peace or surrender it is, from which springs impunity to Jugurtha for his crimes, immense wealth to a few men in power, and loss and infamy to the republic.

But perhaps you are not yet weary of the tyranny of these men; perhaps these times please you less than those when kingdoms, provinces, laws, rights, the administration of justice, war and peace, and indeed every thing civil and religious, was in the hands of an oligarchy; while you, that is, the people of Rome, though unconquered by foreign enemies, and rulers of all nations around, were content with being allowed to live; for which of you had spirit to throw off your slavery? For myself, indeed, though I think it most disgraceful to receive an injury without resenting it, yet I could easily allow you to pardon these basest of traitors, because they are your fellow-citizens, were it not certain that your indulgence would end in your destruction. For such is their presumption, that to escape punishment for their misdeeds will have but little effect upon them, unless they be deprived, at the same time, of the power of doing mischief; and endless anxiety will remain for you, if you shall have to reflect that you must either be slaves or preserve your liberty by force of arms.

Of mutual trust, or concord, what hope is there? They wish to be lords, you desire to be free; they seek to inflict injury, you to repel it; they treat your allies as enemies, your enemies as allies. With feelings so opposite, can peace or friendship subsist between you? I warn, therefore, and exhort you, not to allow such enormous dishonesty to go unpunished. It is not an embezzlement of the public money that has been committed; nor is it a forcible extortion of money from your allies; offenses which, though great, are now, from their frequency, considered as nothing; but the authority of the senate, and your own power, have been sacrificed to the bitterest of enemies, and the public interest has been betrayed for money, both at home and abroad; and unless these misdeeds be investigated, and punishment be inflicted on the guilty, what remains for us but to live the slaves of those who committed them? For those who do what they will with impunity are undoubtedly kings.

I do not, however, wish to encourage you, O Romans, to be better satisfied at finding your fellow-citizens guilty than innocent, but merely to warn you not to bring ruin on the good, by suffering the bad to escape. It is far better, in any government, to be unmindful of a service than of an injury; for a good man, if neglected, only becomes less active; but a bad man, more daring. Besides, if the crimes of the wicked are suppressed, the state will seldom need extraordinary support from the virtuous."

By repeating these and similar sentiments, Memmius prevailed on the people to send Lucius Cassius, who was then praetor, to Jugurtha, and to bring him, under guarantee of the public faith, to Rome, in order that, by the prince's evidence, the misconduct of Scaurus and the rest, whom they charged with having taken bribes, might more easily be made manifest.

During the course of these proceedings at Rome, those whom Bestia had left in Numidia in command of the army, following the example of their general, had been guilty of many scandalous transactions. Some, seduced by gold, had restored Jugurtha his elephants; others had sold him his deserters; others had ravaged the lands of those at peace with us; so strong a spirit of rapacity, like the contagion of a pestilence, had pervaded the breasts of all.

Cassius, when the measure proposed by Memmius had been carried, and while all the nobility were in consternation, set out on his mission to Jugurtha, whom, alarmed as he was, and despairing of his fortune, from a sense of guilt, he admonished "that since he had surrendered himself to the Romans, he had better make trial of their mercy than their power." He also pledged his own word, which Jugurtha valued not less than that of the public, for his safety. Such, at that period, was the reputation of Cassius.

Jugurtha, accordingly, accompanied Cassius to Rome, but without any mark of royalty, and in the garb, as much as possible, of a suppliant; and, though he felt great confidence on his own part, and was supported by all those through whose power or villainy he had accomplished his projects, he purchased, by a vast bribe, the aid of Caius Baebius, a tribune of the people, by whose audacity he hoped to be protected against the law, and against all harm.

An assembly of the people being convoked, Memmius, although they were violently exasperated against Jugurtha, (some demanding that he should be cast into prison, others that, unless he should name his accomplices in guilt, he should be put to death, according to the usage of their ancestors, as a public enemy), yet, regarding rather their character than their resentment, endeavored to calm their turbulence and mitigate their rage; and assured them that, as far as depended on him, the public faith should not be broken. At length, when silence was obtained, he brought forward Jugurtha, and addressed them. He detailed the misdeeds of Jugurtha at Rome and in Numidia, and set forth his crimes toward his father and brothers; and admonished the prince, "that the Roman people, though they were well aware by whose support and agency he had acted, yet desired further testimony from himself; that, if he disclosed the truth, there was great hope for him in the honor and clemency of the Romans; but if he concealed it, he would certainly not save his accomplices, but ruin himself and his hopes forever."

But when Memmius had concluded his speech, and Jugurtha was expected to give his answer, Caius Baebius, the tribune of the people, whom I have just noticed as having been bribed, enjoined the prince to hold his peace; and though the multitude, who formed the assembly, were desperately enraged, and endeavored to terrify the tribune by outcries, by angry looks, by violent gestures, and by every other act to which anger prompts, his audacity was at last triumphant. The people, mocked and set at naught, withdrew from the place of assembly; and the confidence of Jugurtha, Bestia, and the others, whom this investigation had alarmed, was greatly augmented.

There was at this period in Rome a certain Numidian named Massiva, a son of Gulussa and grandson of Masinissa, who, from having been, in the dissensions among the princes, opposed to Jugurtha, had been obliged, after the surrender of Cirta and the murder of Adherbal, to make his escape out of Africa. Spurius Albinus, who was consul with Quintus Minucius Rufus the year after Bestia, prevailed upon this man, as he was of the family of Masinissa, and as odium and terror hung over

Jugurtha for his crimes, to petition the senate for the kingdom of Numidia. Albinus, being eager for the conduct of a war, was desirous that affairs should be disturbed, rather than sink into tranquillity; especially as, in the division of the provinces, Numidia had fallen to himself, and Macedonia to Minucius.

When Massiva proceeded to carry these suggestions into execution, Jugurtha, finding that he had no sufficient support in his friends, as a sense of guilt deterred some, and evil report or timidity others, from coming forward in his behalf, directed Bomilcar, his most attached and faithful adherent, to procure by the aid of money, by which he had already effected so much, assassins to kill Massiva; and to do it secretly if he could; but, if secrecy should be impossible, to cut him off in any way whatsoever. This commission Bomilcar soon found means to execute; and, by the agency of men versed in such service, ascertained the direction of his journeys, his hours of leaving home, and the times at which he resorted to particular places, and, when all was ready, placed his assassins in ambush. One of their number sprung upon Massiva, though with too little caution, and killed him; but being himself caught, he made, at the instigation of many, and especially of Albinus the consul, a full confession. Bomilcar was accordingly committed for trial, though rather on the principles of reason and justice than in accordance with the law of nations, as he was in the retinue of one who had come to Rome on a pledge of the public faith for his safety. But Jugurtha, though clearly guilty of the crime, did not cease to struggle against the truth, until he perceived that the infamy of the deed was too strong for his interest or his money. For which reason, although, at the commencement of the proceedings, he had given fifty of his friends as bail for Bomilcar, yet, thinking more of his kingdom than of the sureties, he sent him off privately into Numidia; for he feared that if such a man should be executed, his other subjects would be deterred from obeying him. A few days after, he himself departed, having been ordered by the senate to quit Italy. But, as he was going from Rome, he is said, after frequently looking back on it in silence, to have at last exclaimed, "That it was a venal city, and would soon perish, if it could but find a purchaser!"

The war being now renewed, Albinus hastened to transport provisions, money, and other things necessary for the army, into Africa, whither he himself soon followed, with the hope that, before the time of the comitia, which was not far distant, he might be able, by an engagement, by capitulation, or by some other method, to bring the contest to a conclusion.

Jugurtha, on the other hand, tried every means of protracting the war, continually inventing new causes for delay; at one time he promised to surrender, at another he feigned distrust; he retreated when Albinus attacked him, and then, lest his men should lose courage, attacked in return, and thus amused the consul with alternate procrastinations of war and of peace.

There were some, at that time, who thought that Albinus understood Jugurtha's object, and who believed that so ready a protraction of the war, after so much haste at the commencement, was to be attributed less to tardiness than to treachery. However this might be, Albinus, when time passed on, and the day of the comitia approached, left his brother Aulus in the camp as propraetor, and returned to Rome.

The republic, at this time, was grievously distracted by the contentions of the tribunes. Two of them, Publius Lucullus and Lucius Annius, were struggling against the will of their colleagues, to prolong their term of office; and this dispute put off the *comitia* throughout the year. In consequence of this delay, Aulus, who, as I have just said, was left as propraetor in the camp, conceiving hopes either of finishing the war, or of extorting money from Jugurtha by the terror of his army, drew out his troops in the month of January, from their winter-quarters into the field, and by forced marches, during severe weather, made his way to the town of Suthul, where Jugurtha's treasures were deposited. And though this place, both from the inclemency of the season, and from its advantageous situation, could neither be taken nor besieged; for around its walls, which were built on the edge of a steep hill, a marshy plain, flooded by the rains of winter, had been converted into a lake; yet Aulus, either as a feint to strike terror into Jugurtha, or blinded by avarice, began to move forward his mantlets to cast up a rampart, and to hasten all necessary preparations for a siege.

Translated by the Rev. John Selby Watson.

VIRGIL

70 - 19 BC

The "Swan of Mantua" was the poet of the prince (i.e., the future Emperor Augustus) as well as the prince of the poets. Born to a family of modest means, the young Virgil quickly understood that neither rhetoric nor politics was for him. He was interested in Epicurean philosophy and in poetry, especially that of Catullus.

When Octavian confiscated land in northern Italy for his veterans, Virgil was expropriated and then compensated for his loss. Composed during this time, the 10 short pieces about country life—the Bucolics *or* Eclogues*—reveal an esoteric poet who wants to adapt the poetry of Theocritus into Latin and at the same time expose his personal anxieties.*

Maecenas and Augustus were sensitive to Virgil's discreet calls for help. As a result, he was able to dedicate himself to a higher form of poetry to which he aspired. He composed the four books of the Georgics, *all of which glorify work in the field and man's return to the earth—an endeavor the emperor himself would soon find appealing. Virgil had barely finished his work when, eager to sing the glory of Augustus, he began to envision a monumental epic poem. He wanted to create a mythological cloth inspired by Homer to drape over Augustus, and to stir in the heart of his citizens a pride in their past: He would achieve this through the drafting of the* Aeneid, *a scholarly epic centered around the figure of the Trojan hero Aeneas. It is written in a modern and fluid verse that would never find its equal in Latin.*

Unsatisfied with his nearly completed work, the poet demanded on his deathbed that it be tossed into the fire. Defying the will of the dead, Augustus ordered that it be published. From then on, this national epic was considered a true compilation of human knowledge. Both pagans and Christians appropriated it for the benefit of preserving the greatest glory of Rome.

Singing Contest

Virgil, *Eclogues* 3

The Bucolics, *or* Eclogues, *that Virgil composed in his younger years are pastoral poems whose actors include shepherds and herdsmen moving in an idealized country setting. In the third eclogue, the two shepherds Menalcas and Damoetas meet. Menalcas, young and presumptuous, guards the flock of his father who married a second time, and to a woman whom Menalcas dreads. Damoetas, in the meantime, protects the herd of Aegon who is busy flirting with Neaera. Menalcas and Damoetas engage in a singing contest. They ask Palaemon to be arbiter.*

"Naught from the flock I'll venture, for at home
I have a father and a step-dame harsh,
And twice a day both reckon up the flock,
And one withal the kids."

MENALCAS
Who owns the flock, Damoetas? Meliboeus?

DAMOETAS
Nay, they are Aegon's sheep, of late by him
Committed to my care.

MENALCAS
O every way
Unhappy sheep, unhappy flock! while he
Still courts Neaera, fearing lest her choice
Should fall on me, this hireling shepherd here
Wrings hourly twice their udders, from the flock
Filching the life-juice, from the lambs their milk.

DAMOETAS
Hold! not so ready with your jeers at men!
We know who once, and in what shrine with you-
The he-goats looked aside- the light nymphs laughed.

MENALCAS
Ay, then, I warrant, when they saw me slash
Micon's young vines and trees with spiteful hook.

DAMOETAS
Or here by these old beeches, when you broke
The bow and arrows of Damon; for you chafed
When first you saw them given to the boy,
Cross-grained Menalcas, ay, and had you not
Done him some mischief, would have chafed to death.

MENALCAS
With thieves so daring, what can masters do?
Did I not see you, rogue, in ambush lie
For Damon's goat, while loud Lycisca barked?
And when I cried, "Where is he off to now?
Gather your flock together, Tityrus,"
You hid behind the sedges.

DAMOETAS
Well, was he
Whom I had conquered still to keep the goat.
Which in the piping-match my pipe had won!
You may not know it, but the goat was mine.

MENALCAS
You out-pipe him? when had you ever pipe
Wax-welded? in the cross-ways used you not
On grating straw some miserable tune
To mangle?

DAMOETAS
Well, then, shall we try our skill
Each against each in turn? Lest you be loth,
I pledge this heifer; every day she comes
Twice to the milking-pail, and feeds withal
Two young ones at her udder: say you now
What you will stake upon the match with me.

MENALCAS
Naught from the flock I'll venture, for at home
I have a father and a step-dame harsh,
And twice a day both reckon up the flock,
And one withal the kids. But I will stake,
Seeing you are so mad, what you yourself

Will own more priceless far- two beechen cups
By the divine art of Alcimedon
Wrought and embossed, whereon a limber vine,
Wreathed round them by the graver's facile tool,
Twines over clustering ivy-berries pale.
Two figures, one Conon,[1] in the midst he set,
And one- how call you him, who with his wand
Marked out for all men the whole round of heaven,
That they who reap, or stoop behind the plough,
Might know their several seasons? Nor as yet
Have I set lip to them, but lay them by.

DAMOETAS
For me too wrought the same Alcimedon
A pair of cups, and round the handles wreathed
Pliant acanthus, Orpheus in the midst,
The forests following in his wake; nor yet
Have I set lip to them, but lay them by.
Matched with a heifer, who would prate of cups?

MENALCAS
You shall not balk me now; where'er you bid,
I shall be with you; only let us have
For auditor- or see, to serve our turn,
Yonder Palaemon comes! In singing-bouts
I'll see you play the challenger no more.

DAMOETAS
Out then with what you have; I shall not shrink,
Nor budge for any man: only do you,
Neighbour Palaemon, with your whole heart's skill-
For it is no slight matter-play your part.

PALAEMON
Say on then, since on the greensward we sit,
And now is burgeoning both field and tree;
Now is the forest green, and now the year
At fairest. Do you first, Damoetas, sing,
Then you, Menalcas, in alternate strain:
Alternate strains are to the Muses dear.

DAMOETAS
"From Jove the Muse began; Jove filleth all,
Makes the earth fruitful, for my songs hath care."

MENALCAS
"Me Phoebus loves; for Phoebus his own gifts,
Bays and sweet-blushing hyacinths, I keep."

DAMOETAS
"Gay Galatea throws an apple at me,
Then hies to the willows, hoping to be seen."

MENALCAS
"My dear Amyntas comes unasked to me;
Not Delia to my dogs is better known."

DAMOETAS
"Gifts for my love I've found; mine eyes have marked
Where the wood-pigeons build their airy nests."

MENALCAS
"Ten golden apples have I sent my boy,
All that I could, to-morrow as many more."

DAMOETAS
"What words to me, and uttered O how oft,
Hath Galatea spoke! waft some of them,
Ye winds, I pray you, for the gods to hear."

MENALCAS
"It profiteth me naught, Amyntas mine,
That in your very heart you spurn me not,
If, while you hunt the boar, I guard the nets."

DAMOETAS
"Prithee, Iollas, for my birthday guest
Send me your Phyllis; when for the young crops
I slay my heifer, you yourself shall come."

MENALCAS
"I am all hers; she wept to see me go,

And, lingering on the word, 'farewell' she said,
'My beautiful Iollas, fare you well.'"

DAMOETAS
"Fell as the wolf is to the folded flock,
Rain to ripe corn, Sirocco to the trees,
The wrath of Amaryllis is to me."

MENALCAS
"As moisture to the corn, to ewes with young
Lithe willow, as arbute to the yeanling kids,
So sweet Amyntas, and none else, to me."

DAMOETAS
"My Muse, although she be but country-bred,
Is loved by Pollio: O Pierian Maids,
Pray you, a heifer for your reader feed!"

MENALCAS
"Pollio himself too doth new verses make:
Feed ye a bull now ripe to butt with horn,
And scatter with his hooves the flying sand."

DAMOETAS
"Who loves thee, Pollio, may he thither come
Where thee he joys beholding; ay, for him
Let honey flow, the thorn-bush spices bear."

MENALCAS
"Who hates not Bavius, let him also love
Thy songs, O Maevius, ay, and therewithal
Yoke foxes to his car, and he-goats milk."

DAMOETAS
"You, picking flowers and strawberries that grow
So near the ground, fly hence, boys, get you gone!
There's a cold adder lurking in the grass."

MENALCAS
"Forbear, my sheep, to tread too near the brink;
Yon bank is ill to trust to; even now

The ram himself, see, dries his dripping fleece!"

DAMOETAS
"Back with the she-goats, Tityrus, grazing there
So near the river! I, when time shall serve,
Will take them all, and wash them in the pool."

MENALCAS
"Boys, get your sheep together; if the heat,
As late it did, forestall us with the milk,
Vainly the dried-up udders shall we wring."

DAMOETAS
"How lean my bull amid the fattening vetch!
Alack! alack! for herdsman and for herd!
It is the self-same love that wastes us both."

MENALCAS
"These truly -nor is even love the cause-
Scarce have the flesh to keep their bones together
Some evil eye my lambkins hath bewitched."

DAMOETAS
"Say in what clime -and you shall be withal
My great Apollo- the whole breadth of heaven
Opens no wider than three ells to view."

MENALCAS
"Say in what country grow such flowers as bear
The names of kings upon their petals writ,
And you shall have fair Phyllis for your own."

PALAEMON
Not mine betwixt such rivals to decide:
You well deserve the heifer, so does he,
With all who either fear the sweets of love,
Or taste its bitterness. Now, boys, shut off
The sluices, for the fields have drunk their fill.

Anonymous translator.

Creation of the World and of Humankind

Virgil, *Eclogues* 6

The Roman public reserved an enthusiastic reception at the theater for this sixth eclogue. The tone is successively pastoral and epic. In his drunken stupor, Silenus is surprised to find himself placed into chains of garlands. In exchange for his liberation, he agrees to sing. In this manner, he evokes the creation of the world, the great heroes of mythology, and, finally, a contemporary for whom Virgil had a grand admiration: the poet Gallus. The sixth eclogue is an erudite poem that condenses a multitude of subjects into a few lines. It is dedicated to Varus, who replaces Pollio as Virgil's patron.

"He sang
How through the mighty void the seeds were driven
Of earth, air, ocean, and of liquid fire,
How all that is from these beginnings grew,
And the young world itself took solid shape."

First my Thalia[2] stooped in sportive mood
To Syracusan strains, nor blushed within
The woods to house her. When I sought to tell
Of battles and of kings, the Cynthian god
Plucked at mine ear and warned me: "Tityrus,
Beseems a shepherd-wight to feed fat sheep,
But sing a slender song." Now, Varus, I-
For lack there will not who would laud thy deeds,
And treat of dolorous wars- will rather tune
To the slim oaten reed my silvan lay.
I sing but as vouchsafed me; yet even this
If, if but one with ravished eyes should read,
Of thee, O Varus, shall our tamarisks
And all the woodland ring; nor can there be
A page more dear to Phoebus, than the page
Where, foremost writ, the name of Varus stands.

Speed ye, Pierian Maids! Within a cave
Young Chromis and Mnasyllos chanced to see
Silenus sleeping, flushed, as was his wont,

With wine of yesterday. Not far aloof,
Slipped from his head, the garlands lay, and there
By its worn handle hung a ponderous cup.
Approaching-for the old man many a time
Had balked them both of a long hoped-for song-
Garlands to fetters turned, they bind him fast.
Then Aegle, fairest of the Naiad-band,
Aegle came up to the half-frightened boys,
Came, and, as now with open eyes he lay,
With juice of blood-red mulberries smeared him o'er,
Both brow and temples. Laughing at their guile,
And crying, "Why tie the fetters? loose me, boys;
Enough for you to think you had the power;
Now list the songs you wish for -songs for you,
Another meed for her" -forthwith began.
Then might you see the wild things of the wood,
With Fauns in sportive frolic beat the time,
And stubborn oaks their branchy summits bow.
Not Phoebus doth the rude Parnassian crag
So ravish, nor Orpheus so entrance the heights
Of Rhodope or Ismarus: for he sang
How through the mighty void the seeds were driven
Of earth, air, ocean, and of liquid fire,
How all that is from these beginnings grew,
And the young world itself took solid shape,
Then 'gan its crust to harden, and in the deep
Shut Nereus off, and mould the forms of things
Little by little; and how the earth amazed
Beheld the new sun shining, and the showers
Fall, as the clouds soared higher, what time the woods
'Gan first to rise, and living things to roam
Scattered among the hills that knew them not.
Then sang he of the stones by Pyrrha cast,[3]
Of Saturn's reign, and of Prometheus' theft,[4]
And the Caucasian birds, and told withal
Nigh to what fountain by his comrades left
The mariners cried on Hylas till the shore
"Then Re-echoed "Hylas, Hylas!;[5] soothed
Pasiphae with the love of her white bull-[6]
Happy if cattle-kind had never been!-
O ill-starred maid, what frenzy caught thy soul

The daughters too of Proetus[7] filled the fields
With their feigned lowings, yet no one of them
Of such unhallowed union e'er was fain
As with a beast to mate, though many a time
On her smooth forehead she had sought for horns,
And for her neck had feared the galling plough.
O ill-starred maid! thou roamest now the hills,
While on soft hyacinths he, his snowy side
Reposing, under some dark ilex now
Chews the pale herbage, or some heifer tracks
Amid the crowding herd. Now close, ye Nymphs,
Ye Nymphs of Dicte, close the forest-glades,
If haply there may chance upon mine eyes
The white bull's wandering foot-prints: him belike
Following the herd, or by green pasture lured,
Some kine may guide to the Gortynian stalls.
Then sings he of the maid so wonder-struck
With the apples of the Hesperids,[8] and then
With moss-bound, bitter bark rings round the forms
Of Phaethon's fair sisters, from the ground
Up-towering into poplars.[9] Next he sings
Of Gallus wandering by Permessus' stream,
And by a sister of the Muses led
To the Aonian mountains, and how all
The choir of Phoebus rose to greet him;[10] how
The shepherd Linus, singer of songs divine,
Brow-bound with flowers and bitter parsley, spake:
"These reeds the Muses give thee, take them thou,
Erst to the aged bard of Ascra[11] given,
Wherewith in singing he was wont to draw
Time-rooted ash-trees from the mountain heights.
With these the birth of the Grynean grove[12]
Be voiced by thee, that of no grove beside
Apollo more may boast him." Wherefore speak
Of Scylla, child of Nisus, who, 'tis said,
Her fair white loins with barking monsters girt
Vexed the Dulichian ships,[13] and, in the deep
Swift-eddying whirlpool, with her sea-dogs tore
The trembling mariners? or how he told
Of the changed limbs of Tereus-what a feast,

What gifts, to him by Philomel were given;[14]
How swift she sought the desert, with what wings
Hovered in anguish o'er her ancient home?
All that, of old, Eurotas, happy stream,
Heard, as Apollo mused upon the lyre,
And bade his laurels learn, Silenus sang;
Till from Olympus, loth at his approach,
Vesper, advancing, bade the shepherds tell
Their tale of sheep, and pen them in the fold.

Anonymous translator.

Expropriation

Virgil, *Eclogues* 9

The ninth eclogue is one of Virgil's most personal. It treats the confiscation of land that took place in northern Italy near Mantua and Cremona. During the summer of 40 BC, Virgil was nearly stripped of his patrimony. He imagines here the encounter of Moeris and Lycidas. Moeris' master, Menalcas, is deprived of his estate, and his slave leaves for town to offer kids to the new proprietor. Moeris and Lycidas stroll a moment together while singing verses composed by Menalcas.

"Time carries all things, even our wits, away."

LYCIDAS
Say whither, Moeris? Make you for the town,
Or on what errand bent?

MOERIS
O Lycidas,
We have lived to see, what never yet we feared,
An interloper own our little farm,
And say, "Be off, you former husbandmen!
These fields are mine." Now, cowed and out of heart,
Since Fortune turns the whole world upside down,
We are taking him- ill luck go with the same!-
These kids you see.

LYCIDAS
But surely I had heard
That where the hills first draw from off the plain,
And the high ridge with gentle slope descends,
Down to the brook-side and the broken crests
Of yonder veteran beeches, all the land
Was by the songs of your Menalcas saved.

MOERIS
Heard it you had, and so the rumour ran,
But 'mid the clash of arms, my Lycidas,
Our songs avail no more than, as 'tis said,
Doves of Dodona when an eagle comes.

Nay, had I not, from hollow ilex-bole
Warned by a raven on the left, cut short
The rising feud, nor I, your Moeris here,
No, nor Menalcas, were alive to-day.

LYCIDAS
Alack! could any of so foul a crime
Be guilty? Ah! how nearly, thyself,
Reft was the solace that we had in thee,
Menalcas! Who then of the Nymphs had sung,
Or who with flowering herbs bestrewn the ground,
And o'er the fountains drawn a leafy veil?-
Who sung the stave I filched from you that day
To Amaryllis wending, our hearts' joy?-
"While I am gone, 'tis but a little way,
Feed, Tityrus, my goats, and, having fed,
Drive to the drinking-pool, and, as you drive,
Beware the he-goat; with his horn he butts."

MOERIS
Ay, or to Varus[15] that half-finished lay,
"Varus, thy name, so still our Mantua live-
Mantua to poor Cremona all too near-
Shall singing swans bear upward to the stars."

LYCIDAS
So may your swarms Cyrnean yew-trees shun,
Your kine with cytisus their udders swell,
Begin, if aught you have. The Muses made
Me too a singer; I too have sung; the swains
Call me a poet, but I believe them not:
For naught of mine, or worthy Varius yet
Or Cinna deem I,[16] but account myself
A cackling goose among melodious swans.

MOERIS
'Twas in my thought to do so, Lycidas;
Even now was I revolving silently
If this I could recall- no paltry song:
"Come, Galatea,[17] what pleasure is 't to play
Amid the waves? Here glows the Spring, here earth

Beside the streams pours forth a thousand flowers;
Here the white poplar bends above the cave,
And the lithe vine weaves shadowy covert: come,
Leave the mad waves to beat upon the shore."

LYCIDAS
What of the strain I heard you singing once
On a clear night alone? the notes I still
Remember, could I but recall the words.

MOERIS
"Why, Daphnis, upward gazing, do you mark
The ancient risings of the Signs? for look
Where Dionean Caesar's star comes forth[18]
In heaven, to gladden all the fields with corn,
And to the grape upon the sunny slopes
Her colour bring! Now, the pears;
So shall your children's children pluck their fruit.
Time carries all things, even our wits, away.
Oft, as a boy, I sang the sun to rest,
But all those songs are from my memory fled,
And even his voice is failing Moeris now;
The wolves eyed Moeris first: but at your wish
Menalcas will repeat them oft enow.

LYCIDAS
Your pleas but linger out my heart's desire:
Now all the deep is into silence hushed,
And all the murmuring breezes sunk to sleep.
We are half-way thither, for Bianor's tomb
Begins to show: here, Moeris, where the hinds
Are lopping the thick leafage, let us sing.
Set down the kids, yet shall we reach the town;
Or, if we fear the night may gather rain
Ere we arrive, then singing let us go,
Our way to lighten; and, that we may thus
Go singing, I will case you of this load.

MOERIS
Cease, boy, and get we to the work in hand:
We shall sing better when himself is come.

Anonymous translator.

Dido's Death

Virgil, *Aeneid* 4.408-705

After the war against Troy, Aeneas leaves the city and undertakes a long sea voyage. He eventually reaches the Latium in Italy, where his descendants will later found Rome. In the long term this would result in the revenge of the Trojans over the Greeks: Although the Greeks won the Trojan War, the defeated Trojans would establish Rome, the empire of which would, in turn, conquer Greece.

During their journey, Aeneas and his compatriots anchor at Carthage (modern Tunisia) where the queen of the country, Dido, welcomes them. She left her homeland, Tyre in Phoenicia (her Phoenician name is Eliza), in traumatic circumstances and founded Carthage. She lives by herself (her husband Sychaeus died in Tyre) and falls madly in love with Aeneas. He abandons her, though, and continues his journey to Sicily. In this passage, we learn Dido's reaction when she realizes that Aeneas left her without even saying goodbye. She speaks to her sister, Anna.

"'T was dead of night, when weary bodies close
Their eyes in balmy sleep and soft repose:
Unhappy Dido was alone awake.
Nor sleep nor ease the furious queen can find;
Sleep fled her eyes, as quiet fled her mind.
Despair, and rage, and love divide her heart;
Despair and rage had some, but love the greater part."

What pangs the tender breast of Dido tore,
When, from the tow'r, she saw the cover'd shore,
And heard the shouts of sailors from afar,
Mix'd with the murmurs of the wat'ry war!
All-pow'rful Love! what changes canst thou cause
In human hearts, subjected to thy laws!
Once more her haughty soul the tyrant bends:
To pray'rs and mean submissions she descends.
No female arts or aids she left untried,
Nor counsels unexplor'd, before she died.
"Look, Anna! look! the Trojans crowd to sea;
They spread their canvas, and their anchors weigh.
The shouting crew their ships with garlands bind,

Invoke the sea gods, and invite the wind.
Could I have thought this threat'ning blow so near,
My tender soul had been forewarn'd to bear.
But do not you my last request deny;
With yon perfidious man your int'rest try,
And bring me news, if I must live or die.
You are his fav'rite; you alone can find
The dark recesses of his inmost mind:
In all his trusted secrets you have part,
And know the soft approaches to his heart.
Haste then, and humbly seek my haughty foe;
Tell him, I did not with the Grecians go,
Nor did my fleet against his friends employ,
Nor swore the ruin of unhappy Troy,
Nor mov'd with hands profane his father's dust:
Why should he then reject a just!
Whom does he shun, and whither would he fly!
Can he this last, this only pray'r deny!
Let him at least his dang'rous flight delay,
Wait better winds, and hope a calmer sea.
The nuptials he disclaims I urge no more:
Let him pursue the promis'd Latian shore.
A short delay is all I ask him now;
A pause of grief, an interval from woe,
Till my soft soul be temper'd to sustain
Accustom'd sorrows, and inur'd to pain.
If you in pity grant this one request,
My death shall glut the hatred of his breast."
This mournful message pious Anna bears,
And seconds with her own her sister's tears:
But all her arts are still employ'd in vain;
Again she comes, and is refus'd again.
His harden'd heart nor pray'rs nor threat'nings move;
Fate, and the god, had stopp'd his ears to love.

As, when the winds their airy quarrel try,
Justling from ev'ry quarter of the sky,
This way and that the mountain oak they bend,
His boughs they shatter, and his branches rend;
With leaves and falling mast they spread the ground;
The hollow valleys echo to the sound:

Unmov'd, the royal plant their fury mocks,
Or, shaken, clings more closely to the rocks;
Far as he shoots his tow'ring head on high,
So deep in earth his fix'd foundations lie.
No less a storm the Trojan hero bears;
Thick messages and loud complaints he hears,
And bandied words, still beating on his ears.
Sighs, groans, and tears proclaim his inward pains;
But the firm purpose of his heart remains.

The wretched queen, pursued by cruel fate,
Begins at length the light of heav'n to hate,
And loathes to live. Then dire portents she sees,
To hasten on the death her soul decrees:
Strange to relate! for when, before the shrine,
She pours in sacrifice the purple wine,
The purple wine is turn'd to putrid blood,
And the white offer'd milk converts to mud.
This dire presage, to her alone reveal'd,
From all, and ev'n her sister, she conceal'd.
A marble temple stood within the grove,
Sacred to death, and to her murther'd love;
That honor'd chapel she had hung around
With snowy fleeces, and with garlands crown'd:
Oft, when she visited this lonely dome,
Strange voices issued from her husband's tomb;
She thought she heard him summon her away,
Invite her to his grave, and chide her stay.
Hourly 't is heard, when with a boding note
The solitary screech owl strains her throat,
And, on a chimney's top, or turret's height,
With songs obscene disturbs the silence of the night.
Besides, old prophecies augment her fears;
And stern Aeneas in her dreams appears,
Disdainful as by day: she seems, alone,
To wander in her sleep, thro' ways unknown,
Guideless and dark; or, in a desart plain,
To seek her subjects, and to seek in vain:
Like Pentheus, when, distracted with his fear,
He saw two suns, and double Thebes, appear;
Or mad Orestes, when his mother's ghost

Full in his face infernal torches toss'd,
And shook her snaky locks: he shuns the sight,
Flies o'er the stage, surpris'd with mortal fright;
The Furies guard the door and intercept his flight.[19]

Now, sinking underneath a load of grief,
From death alone she seeks her last relief;
The time and means resolv'd within her breast,
She to her mournful sister thus address'd
(Dissembling hope, her cloudy front she clears,
And a false vigor in her eyes appears):
"Rejoice!" she said. "Instructed from above,
My lover I shall gain, or lose my love.
Nigh rising Atlas, next the falling sun,
Long tracts of Ethiopian climates run:
There a Massylian priestess I have found,
Honor'd for age, for magic arts renown'd:
Th' Hesperian temple was her trusted care;
'T was she supplied the wakeful dragon's fare.
She poppy seeds in honey taught to steep,
Reclaim'd his rage, and sooth'd him into sleep.
She watch'd the golden fruit; her charms unbind
The chains of love, or fix them on the mind:
She stops the torrents, leaves the channel dry,
Repels the stars, and backward bears the sky.
The yawning earth rebellows to her call,
Pale ghosts ascend, and mountain ashes fall.
Witness, ye gods, and thou my better part,
How loth I am to try this impious art!
Within the secret court, with silent care,
Erect a lofty pile, expos'd in air:
Hang on the topmost part the Trojan vest,
Spoils, arms, and presents, of my faithless guest.
Next, under these, the bridal bed be plac'd,
Where I my ruin in his arms embrac'd:
All relics of the wretch are doom'd to fire;
For so the priestess and her charms require."

Thus far she said, and farther speech forbears;
A mortal paleness in her face appears:
Yet the mistrustless Anna could not find

The secret fun'ral in these rites design'd;
Nor thought so dire a rage possess'd her mind.
Unknowing of a train conceal'd so well,
She fear'd no worse than when Sichaeus fell;
Therefore obeys. The fatal pile they rear,
Within the secret court, expos'd in air.
The cloven holms and pines are heap'd on high,
And garlands on the hollow spaces lie.
Sad cypress, vervain, yew, compose the wreath,
And ev'ry baleful green denoting death.
The queen, determin'd to the fatal deed,
The spoils and sword he left, in order spread,
And the man's image on the nuptial bed.
And now (the sacred altars plac'd around)
The priestess enters, with her hair unbound,
And thrice invokes the pow'rs below the ground.
Night, Erebus, and Chaos she proclaims,
And threefold Hecate, with her hundred names,
And three Dianas: next, she sprinkles round
With feign'd Avernian drops the hallow'd ground;
Culls hoary simples, found by Phoebe's light,
With brazen sickles reap'd at noon of night;
Then mixes baleful juices in the bowl,
And cuts the forehead of a newborn foal,
Robbing the mother's love. The destin'd queen
Observes, assisting at the rites obscene;
A leaven'd cake in her devoted hands
She holds, and next the highest altar stands:
One tender foot was shod, her other bare;
Girt was her gather'd gown, and loose her hair.
Thus dress'd, she summon'd, with her dying breath,
The heav'ns and planets conscious of her death,
And ev'ry pow'r, if any rules above,
Who minds, or who revenges, injur'd love.

'T was dead of night, when weary bodies close
Their eyes in balmy sleep and soft repose:
The winds no longer whisper thro' the woods,
Nor murm'ring tides disturb the gentle floods.
The stars in silent order mov'd around;
And Peace, with downy wings, was brooding on the ground

The flocks and herds, and party-color'd fowl,
Which haunt the woods, or swim the weedy pool,
Stretch'd on the quiet earth, securely lay,
Forgetting the past labors of the day.
All else of nature's common gift partake:
Unhappy Dido was alone awake. Nor sleep nor ease the furious queen can find;
Sleep fled her eyes, as quiet fled her mind.
Despair, and rage, and love divide her heart;
Despair and rage had some, but love the greater part.

Then thus she said within her secret mind:
"What shall I do? what succor can I find?
Become a suppliant to Hyarba's pride,
And take my turn, to court and be denied?
Shall I with this ungrateful Trojan go,
Forsake an empire, and attend a foe?
Himself I refug'd, and his train reliev'd-
'T is true- but am I sure to be receiv'd?
Can gratitude in Trojan souls have place!
Laomedon still lives in all his race![20]
Then, shall I seek alone the churlish crew,
Or with my fleet their flying sails pursue?
What force have I but those whom scarce before
I drew reluctant from their native shore?
Will they again embark at my desire,
Once more sustain the seas, and quit their second Tyre?
Rather with steel thy guilty breast invade,
And take the fortune thou thyself hast made.
Your pity, sister, first seduc'd my mind,
Or seconded too well what I design'd.
These dear-bought pleasures had I never known,
Had I continued free, and still my own;
Avoiding love, I had not found despair,
But shar'd with salvage beasts the common air.
Like them, a lonely life I might have led,
Not mourn'd the living, nor disturb'd the dead."
These thoughts she brooded in her anxious breast.
On board, the Trojan found more easy rest.
Resolv'd to sail, in sleep he pass'd the night;
And order'd all things for his early flight.
To whom once more the winged god appears;

His former youthful mien and shape he wears,
And with this new alarm invades his ears:
"Sleep'st thou, O goddess-born![21] and canst thou drown
Thy needful cares, so near a hostile town,
Beset with foes; nor hear'st the western gales
Invite thy passage, and inspire thy sails?
She harbors in her heart a furious hate,
And thou shalt find the dire effects too late;
Fix'd on revenge, and obstinate to die.
Haste swiftly hence, while thou hast pow'r to fly.
The sea with ships will soon be cover'd o'er,
And blazing firebrands kindle all the shore.
Prevent her rage, while night obscures the skies,
And sail before the purple morn arise.
Who knows what hazards thy delay may bring?
Woman's a various and a changeful thing."
Thus Hermes in the dream; then took his flight
Aloft in air unseen, and mix'd with night.

Twice warn'd by the celestial messenger,
The pious prince arose with hasty fear;
Then rous'd his drowsy train without delay:
"Haste to your banks; your crooked anchors weigh,
And spread your flying sails, and stand to sea.
A god commands: he stood before my sight,
And urg'd us once again to speedy flight.
O sacred pow'r, what pow'r soe'er thou art,
To thy blest orders I resign my heart.
Lead thou the way; protect thy Trojan bands,
And prosper the design thy will commands."
He said: and, drawing forth his flaming sword,
His thund'ring arm divides the many-twisted cord.
An emulating zeal inspires his train:
They run; they snatch; they rush into the main.
With headlong haste they leave the desert shores,
And brush the liquid seas with lab'ring oars.

Aurora now had left her saffron bed,
And beams of early light the heav'ns o'erspread,
When, from a tow'r, the queen, with wakeful eyes,
Saw day point upward from the rosy skies.

She look'd to seaward; but the sea was void,
And scarce in ken the sailing ships descried.
Stung with despite, and furious with despair,
She struck her trembling breast, and tore her hair.
"And shall th' ungrateful traitor go," she said,
"My land forsaken, and my love betray'd?
Shall we not arm? not rush from ev'ry street,
To follow, sink, and burn his perjur'd fleet?
Haste, haul my galleys out! pursue the foe!
Bring flaming brands! set sail, and swiftly row!
What have I said? where am I? Fury turns
My brain; and my distemper'd bosom burns.
Then, when I gave my person and my throne,
This hate, this rage, had been more timely shown.
See now the promis'd faith, the vaunted name,
The pious man, who, rushing thro' the flame,
Preserv'd his gods, and to the Phrygian shore[22]
The burthen of his feeble father bore!
I should have torn him piecemeal; strow'd in floods
His scatter'd limbs, or left expos'd in woods;
Destroy'd his friends and son; and, from the fire,
Have set the reeking boy before the sire.
Events are doubtful, which on battles wait:
Yet where's the doubt, to souls secure of fate?
My Tyrians, at their injur'd queen's command,
Had toss'd their fires amid the Trojan band;
At once extinguish'd all the faithless name;
And I myself, in vengeance of my shame,
Had fall'n upon the pile, to mend the fun'ral flame.
Thou Sun, who view'st at once the world below;
Thou Juno, guardian of the nuptial vow;
Thou Hecate hearken from thy dark abodes!
Ye Furies, fiends, and violated gods,
All pow'rs invok'd with Dido's dying breath,
Attend her curses and avenge her death!
If so the Fates ordain, Jove commands,
Th' ungrateful wretch should find the Latian lands,
Yet let a race untam'd, and haughty foes,
His peaceful entrance with dire arms oppose:
Oppress'd with numbers in th' unequal field,
His men discourag'd, and himself expell'd,

Let him for succor sue from place to place,
Torn from his subjects, and his son's embrace.
First, let him see his friends in battle slain,
And their untimely fate lament in vain;
And when, at length, the cruel war shall cease,
On hard conditions may he buy his peace:
Nor let him then enjoy supreme command;
But fall, untimely, by some hostile hand,
And lie unburied on the barren sand!
These are my pray'rs, and this my dying will;
And you, my Tyrians, ev'ry curse fulfil.
Perpetual hate and mortal wars proclaim,
Against the prince, the people, and the name.
These grateful off'rings on my grave bestow;
Nor league, nor love, the hostile nations know!
Now, and from hence, in ev'ry future age,
When rage excites your arms, and strength supplies the rage
Rise some avenger of our Libyan blood,
With fire and sword pursue the perjur'd brood;
Our arms, our seas, our shores, oppos'd to theirs;
And the same hate descend on all our heirs!"
This said, within her anxious mind she weighs
The means of cutting short her odious days.
Then to Sichaeus' nurse she briefly said
(For, when she left her country, hers was dead):
"Go, Barce, call my sister. Let her care
The solemn rites of sacrifice prepare;
The sheep, and all th' atoning off'rings bring,
Sprinkling her body from the crystal spring
With living drops; then let her come, and thou
With sacred fillets bind thy hoary brow.
Thus will I pay my vows to Stygian Jove,[23]
And end the cares of my disastrous love;
Then cast the Trojan image on the fire,
And, as that burns, my passions shall expire."

The nurse moves onward, with officious care,
And all the speed her aged limbs can bear.
But furious Dido, with dark thoughts involv'd,
Shook at the mighty mischief she resolv'd.
With livid spots distinguish'd was her face;

Red were her rolling eyes, and discompos'd her pace;
Ghastly she gaz'd, with pain she drew her breath,
And nature shiver'd at approaching death.

Then swiftly to the fatal place she pass'd,
And mounts the fun'ral pile with furious haste;
Unsheathes the sword the Trojan left behind
(Not for so dire an enterprise design'd).
But when she view'd the garments loosely spread,
Which once he wore, and saw the conscious bed,
She paus'd, and with a sigh the robes embrac'd;
Then on the couch her trembling body cast,
Repress'd the ready tears, and spoke her last:
"Dear pledges of my love, while Heav'n so pleas'd,
Receive a soul, of mortal anguish eas'd:
My fatal course is finish'd; and I go,
A glorious name, among the ghosts below.
A lofty city by my hands is rais'd,
Pygmalion punish'd, and my lord appeas'd.[24]
What could my fortune have afforded more,
Had the false Trojan never touch'd my shore!"
Then kiss'd the couch; and, "Must I die," she said,
"And unreveng'd? 'T is doubly to be dead!
Yet ev'n this death with pleasure I receive:
On any terms, 't is better than to live.
These flames, from far, may the false Trojan view;
These boding omens his base flight pursue!"

She said, and struck; deep enter'd in her side
The piercing steel, with reeking purple dyed:
Clogg'd in the wound the cruel weapon stands;
The spouting blood came streaming on her hands.
Her sad attendants saw the deadly stroke,
And with loud cries the sounding palace shook.
Distracted, from the fatal sight they fled,
And thro' the town the dismal rumor spread.
First from the frighted court the yell began;
Redoubled, thence from house to house it ran:
The groans of men, with shrieks, laments, and cries
Of mixing women, mount the vaulted skies.
Not less the clamor, than if-ancient Tyre,

Or the new Carthage, set by foes on fire-
The rolling ruin, with their lov'd abodes,
Involv'd the blazing temples of their gods.

Her sister hears; and, furious with despair,
She beats her breast, and rends her yellow hair,
And, calling on Eliza's name aloud,
Runs breathless to the place, and breaks the crowd.
"Was all that pomp of woe for this prepar'd;
These fires, this fun'ral pile, these altars rear'd?
Was all this train of plots contriv'd," said she,
"All only to deceive unhappy me?
Which is the worst? Didst thou in death pretend
To scorn thy sister, or delude thy friend?
Thy summon'd sister, and thy friend, had come;
One sword had serv'd us both, one common tomb:
Was I to raise the pile, the pow'rs invoke,
Not to be present at the fatal stroke?
At once thou hast destroy'd thyself and me,
Thy town, thy senate, and thy colony!
Bring water; bathe the wound; while I in death
Lay close my lips to hers, and catch the flying breath."
This said, she mounts the pile with eager haste,
And in her arms the gasping queen embrac'd;
Her temples chaf'd; and her own garments tore,
To stanch the streaming blood, and cleanse the gore.
Thrice Dido tried to raise her drooping head,
And, fainting thrice, fell grov'ling on the bed;
Thrice op'd her heavy eyes, and sought the light,
But, having found it, sicken'd at the sight,
And clos'd her lids at last in endless night.

Then Juno, grieving that she should sustain
A death so ling'ring, and so full of pain,
Sent Iris down, to free her from the strife
Of lab'ring nature, and dissolve her life.
For since she died, not doom'd by Heav'n's decree,
Or her own crime, but human casualty,
And rage of love, that plung'd her in despair,
The Sisters had not cut the topmost hair,
Which Proserpine and they can only know;

Nor made her sacred to the shades below.[25]
Downward the various goddess took her flight,
And drew a thousand colors from the light;
Then stood above the dying lover's head,
And said: "I thus devote thee to the dead.
This off'ring to th' infernal gods I bear."
Thus while she spoke, she cut the fatal hair:
The struggling soul was loos'd, and life dissolv'd in air.

Translated by John Dryden.

Descent into the Underworld

Virgil, *Aeneid* 6.268-535

After leaving Carthage, Aeneas resumes his sea voyage and lands at Cumae in South Italy. There he meets the Sibyl, a prophetess with whom he descends into the underworld to meet one last time his father, Anchises, who died during the journey from Troy. Aeneas enters the subterranean world alive and returns safe and sound—a feat only Theseus and Heracles accomplished before him. He crosses the Acheron and Cocytus rivers on the barge of the guardian Charon. He catches sight of Cerberus, the dog with three heads, and the damned phantoms of both monsters and heroes. He also meets Dido who has just killed herself.

More than a thousand years later, the Aeneid *would inspire* The Divine Comedy, *in which Virgil leads Dante through the dangers and obstacles of Hell and Purgatory.*

"Minos, the strict inquisitor, appears;
And lives and crimes, with his assessors, hears.
Round in his urn the blended balls he rolls,
Absolves the just, and dooms the guilty souls."

Obscure they went thro' dreary shades, that led
Along the waste dominions of the dead.
Thus wander travelers in woods by night,
By the moon's doubtful and malignant light,
When Jove in dusky clouds involves the skies,
And the faint crescent shoots by fits before their eyes.

Just in the gate and in the jaws of hell,
Revengeful Cares and sullen Sorrows dwell,
And pale Diseases, and repining Age,
Want, Fear, and Famine's unresisted rage;
Here Toils, and Death, and Death's half-brother, Sleep,
Forms terrible to view, their sentry keep;
With anxious Pleasures of a guilty mind,
Deep Frauds before, and open Force behind;
The Furies' iron beds; and Strife, that shakes
Her hissing tresses and unfolds her snakes.

Full in the midst of this infernal road,
An elm displays her dusky arms abroad:
The God of Sleep there hides his heavy head,
And empty dreams on ev'ry leaf are spread.
Of various forms unnumber'd specters more,
Centaurs, and double shapes, besiege the door.
Before the passage, horrid Hydra stands,
And Briareus with all his hundred hands;
Gorgons, Geryon with his triple frame;
And vain Chimaera vomits empty flame.
The chief unsheath'd his shining steel, prepar'd,
Tho' seiz'd with sudden fear, to force the guard,
Off'ring his brandish'd weapon at their face;
Had not the Sibyl stopp'd his eager pace,
And told him what those empty phantoms were:
Forms without bodies, and impassive air.
Hence to deep Acheron they take their way,
Whose troubled eddies, thick with ooze and clay,
Are whirl'd aloft, and in Cocytus lost.
There Charon stands, who rules the dreary coast-
A sordid god: down from his hoary chin
A length of beard descends, uncomb'd, unclean;
His eyes, like hollow furnaces on fire;
A girdle, foul with grease, binds his obscene attire.
He spreads his canvas; with his pole he steers;
The freights of flitting ghosts in his thin bottom bears.
He look'd in years; yet in his years were seen
A youthful vigor and autumnal green.
An airy crowd came rushing where he stood,
Which fill'd the margin of the fatal flood:
Husbands and wives, boys and unmarried maids,
And mighty heroes' more majestic shades,
And youths, intomb'd before their fathers' eyes,
With hollow groans, and shrieks, and feeble cries.
Thick as the leaves in autumn strow the woods,
Or fowls, by winter forc'd, forsake the floods,
And wing their hasty flight to happier lands;
Such, and so thick, the shiv'ring army stands,
And press for passage with extended hands.
Now these, now those, the surly boatman bore:
The rest he drove to distance from the shore.

The hero, who beheld with wond'ring eyes
The tumult mix'd with shrieks, laments, and cries,
Ask'd of his guide, what the rude concourse meant;
Why to the shore the thronging people bent;
What forms of law among the ghosts were us'd;
Why some were ferried o'er, and some refus'd.

"Son of Anchises, offspring of the gods,"
The Sibyl said, "you see the Stygian floods,
The sacred stream which heav'n's imperial state
Attests in oaths, and fears to violate.
The ghosts rejected are th' unhappy crew
Depriv'd of sepulchers and fun'ral due:
The boatman, Charon; those, the buried host,
He ferries over to the farther coast;
Nor dares his transport vessel cross the waves
With such whose bones are not compos'd in graves.
A hundred years they wander on the shore;
At length, their penance done, are wafted o'er."
The Trojan chief his forward pace repress'd,
Revolving anxious thoughts within his breast,
He saw his friends, who, whelm'd beneath the waves,
Their fun'ral honors claim'd, and ask'd their quiet graves.
The lost Leucaspis in the crowd he knew,
And the brave leader of the Lycian crew,
Whom, on the Tyrrhene seas, the tempests met;
The sailors master'd, and the ship o'erset.

Amidst the spirits, Palinurus press'd,
Yet fresh from life, a new-admitted guest,
Who, while he steering view'd the stars, and bore
His course from Afric to the Latian shore,
Fell headlong down. The Trojan fix'd his view,
And scarcely thro' the gloom the sullen shadow knew.
Then thus the prince: "What envious pow'r, O friend,
Brought your lov'd life to this disastrous end?
For Phoebus, ever true in all he said,
Has in your fate alone my faith betray'd.
The god foretold you should not die, before
You reach'd, secure from seas, th' Italian shore.
Is this th' unerring pow'r?" The ghost replied;

"Nor Phoebus flatter'd, nor his answers lied;
Nor envious gods have sent me to the deep:
But, while the stars and course of heav'n I keep,
My wearied eyes were seiz'd with fatal sleep.
I fell; and, with my weight, the helm constrain'd
Was drawn along, which yet my gripe retain'd.
Now by the winds and raging waves I swear,
Your safety, more than mine, was then my care;
Lest, of the guide bereft, the rudder lost,
Your ship should run against the rocky coast.
Three blust'ring nights, borne by the southern blast,
I floated, and discover'd land at last:
High on a mounting wave my head I bore,
Forcing my strength, and gath'ring to the shore.
Panting, but past the danger, now I seiz'd
The craggy cliffs, and my tir'd members eas'd.
While, cumber'd with my dropping clothes, I lay,
The cruel nation, covetous of prey,
Stain'd with my blood th' unhospitable coast;
And now, by winds and waves, my lifeless limbs are toss'd:
Which O avert, by yon ethereal light,
Which I have lost for this eternal night!
Or, if by dearer ties you may be won,
By your dead sire, and by your living son,
Redeem from this reproach my wand'ring ghost;
Or with your navy seek the Velin coast,
And in a peaceful grave my corpse compose;
Or, if a nearer way your mother shows,
Without whose aid you durst not undertake
This frightful passage o'er the Stygian lake,
Lend to this wretch your hand, and waft him o'er
To the sweet banks of yon forbidden shore."
Scarce had he said, the prophetess began:
"What hopes delude thee, miserable man?
Think'st thou, thus unintomb'd, to cross the floods,
To view the Furies and infernal gods,
And visit, without leave, the dark abodes?
Attend the term of long revolving years;
Fate, and the dooming gods, are deaf to tears.
This comfort of thy dire misfortune take:
The wrath of Heav'n, inflicted for thy sake,

With vengeance shall pursue th' inhuman coast,
Till they propitiate thy offended ghost,
And raise a tomb, with vows and solemn pray'r;
And Palinurus' name the place shall bear."
This calm'd his cares; sooth'd with his future fame,
And pleas'd to hear his propagated name.

Now nearer to the Stygian lake they draw:
Whom, from the shore, the surly boatman saw;
Observ'd their passage thro' the shady wood,
And mark'd their near approaches to the flood.
Then thus he call'd aloud, inflam'd with wrath:
"Mortal, whate'er, who this forbidden path
In arms presum'st to tread, I charge thee, stand,
And tell thy name, and bus'ness in the land.
Know this, the realm of night- the Stygian shore:
My boat conveys no living bodies o'er;
Nor was I pleas'd great Theseus once to bear,
Who forc'd a passage with his pointed spear,
Nor strong Alcides- men of mighty fame,
And from th' immortal gods their lineage came.[26]
In fetters one the barking porter tied,
And took him trembling from his sov'reign's side:
Two sought by force to seize his beauteous bride."
To whom the Sibyl thus: "Compose thy mind;
Nor frauds are here contriv'd, nor force design'd.
Still may the dog the wand'ring troops constrain
Of airy ghosts, and vex the guilty train,
And with her grisly lord his lovely queen remain.
The Trojan chief, whose lineage is from Jove,
Much fam'd for arms, and more for filial love,
Is sent to seek his sire in your Elysian grove.
If neither piety, nor Heav'n's command,
Can gain his passage to the Stygian strand,
This fatal present shall prevail at least."
Then shew'd the shining bough, conceal'd within her vest.
No more was needful: for the gloomy god
Stood mute with awe, to see the golden rod;
Admir'd the destin'd off'ring to his queen-
A venerable gift, so rarely seen.
His fury thus appeas'd, he puts to land;

The ghosts forsake their seats at his command:
He clears the deck, receives the mighty freight;
The leaky vessel groans beneath the weight.
Slowly she sails, and scarcely stems the tides;
The pressing water pours within her sides.
His passengers at length are wafted o'er,
Expos'd, in muddy weeds, upon the miry shore.

No sooner landed, in his den they found
The triple porter of the Stygian sound,
Grim Cerberus, who soon began to rear
His crested snakes, and arm'd his bristling hair.
The prudent Sibyl had before prepar'd
A sop, in honey steep'd, to charm the guard;
Which, mix'd with pow'rful drugs, she cast before
His greedy grinning jaws, just op'd to roar.
With three enormous mouths he gapes; and straight,
With hunger press'd, devours the pleasing bait.
Long draughts of sleep his monstrous limbs enslave;
He reels, and, falling, fills the spacious cave.
The keeper charm'd, the chief without delay
Pass'd on, and took th' irremeable way.
Before the gates, the cries of babes new born,
Whom fate had from their tender mothers torn,
Assault his ears; then those, whom form of laws
Condemn'd to die, when traitors judg'd their cause.
Nor want they lots, nor judges to review
The wrongful sentence, and award a new.
Minos, the strict inquisitor, appears;
And lives and crimes, with his assessors, hears.
Round in his urn the blended balls he rolls,
Absolves the just, and dooms the guilty souls.
The next, in place and punishment, are they
Who prodigally throw their souls away;
Fools, who, repining at their wretched state,
And loathing anxious life, suborn'd their fate.
With late repentance now they would retrieve
The bodies they forsook, and wish to live;
Their pains and poverty desire to bear,
To view the light of heav'n, and breathe the vital air:
But fate forbids; the Stygian floods oppose,

And with circling streams the captive souls inclose.
Not far from thence, the Mournful Fields appear
So call'd from lovers that inhabit there.
The souls whom that unhappy flame invades,
In secret solitude and myrtle shades
Make endless moans, and, pining with desire,
Lament too late their unextinguish'd fire.
Here Procris, Eriphyle here he found,
Baring her breast, yet bleeding with the wound
Made by her son. He saw Pasiphae there,
With Phaedra's ghost, a foul incestuous pair.
There Laodamia, with Evadne, moves,
Unhappy both, but loyal in their loves:
Caeneus, a woman once, and once a man,
But ending in the sex she first began.
Not far from these Phoenician Dido stood,
Fresh from her wound, her bosom bath'd in blood;
Whom when the Trojan hero hardly knew,
Obscure in shades, and with a doubtful view,
(Doubtful as he who sees, thro' dusky night,
Or thinks he sees, the moon's uncertain light,)
With tears he first approach'd the sullen shade;
And, as his love inspir'd him, thus he said:
"Unhappy queen! then is the common breath
Of rumor true, in your reported death,
And I, alas! the cause? By Heav'n, I vow,
And all the pow'rs that rule the realms below,
Unwilling I forsook your friendly state,
Commanded by the gods, and forc'd by fate-
Those gods, that fate, whose unresisted might
Have sent me to these regions void of light,
Thro' the vast empire of eternal night.
Nor dar'd I to presume, that, press'd with grief,
My flight should urge you to this dire relief.
Stay, stay your steps, and listen to my vows:
'T is the last interview that fate allows!"
In vain he thus attempts her mind to move
With tears, and pray'rs, and late-repenting love.
Disdainfully she look'd; then turning round,
But fix'd her eyes unmov'd upon the ground,
And what he says and swears, regards no more

Than the deaf rocks, when the loud billows roar;
But whirl'd away, to shun his hateful sight,
Hid in the forest and the shades of night;
Then sought Sichaeus thro' the shady grove,
Who answer'd all her cares, and equal'd all her love.

Some pious tears the pitying hero paid,
And follow'd with his eyes the flitting shade,
Then took the forward way, by fate ordain'd,
And, with his guide, the farther fields attain'd,
Where, sever'd from the rest, the warrior souls remain'd.
Tydeus he met, with Meleager's race,
The pride of armies, and the soldiers' grace;
And pale Adrastus with his ghastly face.
Of Trojan chiefs he view'd a num'rous train,
All much lamented, all in battle slain;
Glaucus and Medon, high above the rest,
Antenor's sons, and Ceres' sacred priest.
And proud Idaeus, Priam's charioteer,
Who shakes his empty reins, and aims his airy spear.
The gladsome ghosts, in circling troops, attend
And with unwearied eyes behold their friend;
Delight to hover near, and long to know
What bus'ness brought him to the realms below.
But Argive chiefs, and Agamemnon's train,
When his refulgent arms flash'd thro' the shady plain,
Fled from his well-known face, with wonted fear,
As when his thund'ring sword and pointed spear
Drove headlong to their ships, and glean'd the routed rear.
They rais'd a feeble cry, with trembling notes;
But the weak voice deceiv'd their gasping throats.

Here Priam's son, Deiphobus, he found,
Whose face and limbs were one continued wound:
Dishonest, with lopp'd arms, the youth appears,
Spoil'd of his nose, and shorten'd of his ears.
He scarcely knew him, striving to disown
His blotted form, and blushing to be known;
And therefore first began: "O Teucer's race,
Who durst thy faultless figure thus deface?
What heart could wish, what hand inflict, this dire disgrace?

'Twas fam'd, that in our last and fatal night
Your single prowess long sustain'd the fight,
Till tir'd, not forc'd, a glorious fate you chose,
And fell upon a heap of slaughter'd foes.
But, in remembrance of so brave a deed,
A tomb and fun'ral honors I decreed;
Thrice call'd your manes on the Trojan plains:
The place your armor and your name retains.
Your body too I sought, and, had I found,
Design'd for burial in your native ground."

The ghost replied: "Your piety has paid
All needful rites, to rest my wand'ring shade;
But cruel fate, and my more cruel wife,
To Grecian swords betray'd my sleeping life.
These are the monuments of Helen's love:
The shame I bear below, the marks I bore above.
You know in what deluding joys we pass'd
The night that was by Heav'n decreed our last:
For, when the fatal horse, descending down,
Pregnant with arms, o'erwhelm'd th' unhappy town
She feign'd nocturnal orgies; left my bed,
And, mix'd with Trojan dames, the dances led
Then, waving high her torch, the signal made,
Which rous'd the Grecians from their ambuscade.
With watching overworn, with cares oppress'd,
Unhappy I had laid me down to rest,
And heavy sleep my weary limbs possess'd.
Meantime my worthy wife our arms mislaid,
And from beneath my head my sword convey'd;
The door unlatch'd, and, with repeated calls,
Invites her former lord within my walls.
Thus in her crime her confidence she plac'd,
And with new treasons would redeem the past.
What need I more? Into the room they ran,
And meanly murther'd a defenseless man.
Ulysses, basely born, first led the way.
Avenging pow'rs! with justice if I pray,
That fortune be their own another day!
But answer you; and in your turn relate,
What brought you, living, to the Stygian state:

Driv'n by the winds and errors of the sea,
Or did you Heav'n's superior doom obey?
Or tell what other chance conducts your way,
To view with mortal eyes our dark retreats,
Tumults and torments of th' infernal seats."

Translated by John Dryden.

HORACE

65 - 8 BC

Born in Venusia in southern Italy, Quintus Horatius Flaccus was probably the son of a public slave who later became a freedman. After an unpleasant sojourn in Rome, Horace left for Athens around 45 BC and followed the lessons of Greek philosophers. It was not long thereafter that he was convinced of Greece's intellectual superiority. After Caesar's violent death, Horace returned to Italy where he enrolled in the army of Brutus, one of Caesar's murderers. After several setbacks, amnesty eventually permitted him to return to Rome. The following year, he met the famous Maecenas who protected him and, like Virgil, soon secured the trust of Emperor Augustus. From then on, he divided his time between Rome and his villa in the northern countryside.

Around 35 or 34 BC, Horace published his first Satires, *in which he settles old scores with his enemies and takes pleasure in emphasizing the shortcomings of his contemporaries. The first* Epodes *are contemporaneous, although he was prudent enough not to publish them. (They contained explicit language.) The second book of the* Satires *was published around 30 or 29 BC. Ten years later, he published the* Odes, *which express a new lyricism. Horace also continued to produce epistles with a free and liberating tone, in which one senses his urge to repudiate poetry in favor of philosophy.*

Horace inspired two 17th-century French writers: Jean de La Fontaine, who proclaims, "I instruct myself in Horace," and Boileau, whose Poetic Art *is influenced by Horace's "Letter to the Pisos."*

Grass Is Always Greener on the Other Side

Horace, *Satires* 1.1

In his Satires, Horace enjoys taking an ironic perspective on people's flaws. In this first satire, he treats one of his favorite subjects: the perpetual dissatisfaction with one's destiny that manifests itself through the coveting of the fortune of others and the insatiable appetite to accumulate more wealth.

"But to go mad with watching, nights and days
To stand in dread of thieves, fires, runaways
Who filch and fly,—in these if wealth consist,
Let me rank lowest on the paupers' list."

How comes it, say, Maecenas, if you can,
That none will live like a contented man
Where choice or chance directs, but each must praise
The folk who pass through life by other ways?
"Those lucky merchants!" cries the soldier stout,
When years of toil have well-nigh worn him out:
What says the merchant, tossing o'er the brine?
"Yon soldier's lot is happier, sure, than mine:
One short, sharp shock, and presto! all is done:
Death in an instant comes, or victory's won."
The lawyer lauds the farmer, when a knock
Disturbs his sleep at crowing of the cock:
The farmer, dragged to town on business, swears
That only citizens are free from cares.
I need not run through all: so long the list,
Fabius himself would weary and desist:[1]
So take in brief my meaning: just suppose
Some God should come, and with their wishes close:
"See, here am I, come down of my mere grace
To right you: soldier, take the merchant's place!
You, counsellor, the farmer's! go your way,
One here, one there! None stirring? all say nay?
How now? you won't be happy when you may."
Now, after this, would Jove be aught to blame
If with both cheeks he burst into a flame,

And vowed, when next they pray, they shall not find
His temper easy, or his ear inclined?

Well, not to treat things lightly (though, for me,
Why truth may not be gay, I cannot see:
Just as, we know, judicious teachers coax
With sugar-plum or cake their little folks
To learn their alphabet, still we will try
A graver tone, and lay our joking by.
The man that with his plough subdues the land,
The soldier stout, the vintner sly and bland,
The venturous sons of ocean, all declare
That with one view the toils of life they bear,
When age has come, and labour has amassed
Enough to live on, to retire at last:
E'en so the ant (for no bad pattern she),
That tiny type of giant industry,
Drags grain by grain, and adds it to the sum
Of her full heap, foreseeing cold to come:
Yet she, when winter turns the year to chill,
Stirs not an inch beyond her mounded hill,
But lives upon her savings: you, more bold,
Ne'er quit your gain for fiercest heat or cold:
Fire, ocean, sword, defying all, you strive
To make yourself the richest man alive.
Yet where's the profit, if you hide by stealth
In pit or cavern your enormous wealth?
"Why, once break in upon it, friend, you know,
And, dwindling piece by piece, the whole will go."
But, if 'tis still unbroken, what delight
Can all that treasure give to mortal wight?
Say, you've a million quarters on your floor;
Your stomach is like mine, it holds no more:
Just as the slave who 'neath the bread-bag sweats
No larger ration than his fellows gets.
What matters it to reasonable men
Whether they plough a hundred fields or ten?
"But there's a pleasure, spite of all you say,
In a large heap from which to take away."
If both contain the modicum we lack,
Why should your barn be better than my sack?

You want a draught of water: a mere urn,
Perchance a goblet, well would serve your turn.
You say, "The stream looks scanty at its head;
I'll take my quantum where 'tis broad instead."
But what befalls the wight who yearns for more
Than Nature bids him? Down the waters pour,
And whelm him, bank and all; while he whose greed
Is kept in check, proportioned to his need,
He neither draws his water mixed with mud,
Nor leaves his life behind him in the flood.

But there's a class of persons, led astray
By false desires, and this is what they say:
"You cannot have enough: what you possess,
That makes your value, be it more or less."
What answer would you make to such as these?
Why, let them hug their misery if they please,
Like the Athenian miser, who was wont
To meet men's curses with a hero's front:
"Folks hiss me," said he, "but myself I clap
When I tell o'er my treasures on my lap."
So Tantalus catches at the waves that fly
His thirsty palate—Laughing, are you? why?
Change but the name, of you the tale is told:
You sleep, mouth open, on your hoarded gold;
Gold that you treat as sacred, dare not use,
In fact, that charms you as a picture does.
Come, will you hear what wealth can fairly do?
'Twill buy you bread, and vegetables too,
And wine, a good pint measure; add to this
Such needful things as flesh and blood would miss.
But to go mad with watching, nights and days
To stand in dread of thieves, fires, runaways
Who filch and fly,—in these if wealth consist,
Let me rank lowest on the paupers' list.

"But if you suffer from a chill attack,
Or other chance should lay you on your back,
You then have one who'll sit by your bed-side,
Will see the needful remedies applied,
And call in a physician, to restore

Your health, and give you to your friends once more."
Nor wife nor son desires your welfare: all
Detest you, neighbours, gossips, great and small.
What marvel if, when wealth's your one concern,
None offers you the love you never earn?
Nay, would you win the kinsmen Nature sends
Made ready to your hand, and keep them friends,
'Twere but lost labour, as if one should train
A donkey for the course by bit and rein.

Make then an end of getting: know, the more
Your wealth, the less the risk of being poor;
And, having gained the object of your quest,
Begin to slack your efforts and take rest;
Nor act like one Ummidius (never fear,
The tale is short, and 'tis the last you'll hear),
So rich, his gold he by the peck would tell,
So mean, the slave that served him dressed as well;
E'en to his dying day he went in dread
Of perishing for simple want of bread,
Till a brave damsel, of Tyndarid line
The true descendant, clove him down the chine.[2]

"What? would you have me live like some we know,
Maenius or Nomentanus?" There you go!
Still in extremes! in bidding you forsake
A miser's ways, I say not, Be a rake.
'Twixt Tanais and Visellius' sire-in-law
A step there is, and broader than a straw.
Yes, there's a mean in morals: life has lines,
To north or south of which all virtue pines.

Now to resume our subject: why, I say,
Should each man act the miser in his way,
Still discontented with his natural lot,
Still praising those who have what he has not?
Why should he waste with very spite, to see
His neighbour has a milkier cow than he,
Ne'er think how much he's richer than the mass,
But always strive this man or that to pass?
In such a contest, speed we as we may,

There's some one wealthier ever in the way.
So from their base when vying chariots pour,
Each driver presses on the car before,
Wastes not a thought on rivals overpast,
But leaves them to lag on among the last.
Hence comes it that the man is rarely seen
Who owns that his a happy life has been,
And, thankful for past blessings, with good will
Retires, like one who has enjoyed his fill.
Enough: you'll think I've rifled the scrutore
Of blind Crispinus, if I prose on more.

Translated by John Conington.

The Bore

Horace, *Satires* 1.9

Horace strolls one morning on the Sacred Way when a stranger approaches him. The stranger continues to follow Horace's every step, talking endlessly and refusing to leave the poet alone. Horace finally understands that this utter bore is actually trying to be introduced to the poet's powerful protector, Maecenas.

"Down go my ears, in donkey-fashion, straight;
You've seen them do it, when their load's too great."

Long the Sacred Road I strolled one day,
Deep in some bagatelle (you know my way),
When up comes one whose name I scarcely knew—
"The dearest of dear fellows! how d'ye do?"
He grasped my hand—"Well, thanks: the same to you."
Then, as he still kept walking by my side,
To cut things short, "You've no commands?" I cried.
"Nay, you should know me: I'm a man of lore."
"Sir, I'm your humble servant all the more."
All in a fret to make him let me go,
I now walk fast, now loiter and walk slow,
Now whisper to my servant, while the sweat
Ran down so fast, my very feet were wet.
"O had I but a temper worth the name,
Like yours, Bolanus!" inly I exclaim,
While he keeps running on at a hand-trot,
About the town, the streets, I know not what.
Finding I made no answer, "Ah! I see,
You 're at a strait to rid yourself of me;
But 'tis no use: I'm a tenacious friend,
And mean to hold you till your journey's end,"
"No need to take you such a round: I go
To visit an acquaintance you don't know:
Poor man! he's ailing at his lodging, far
Beyond the bridge, where Caesar's gardens are."
"O, never mind: I've nothing else to do,
And want a walk, so I'll step on with you."

Down go my ears, in donkey-fashion, straight;
You've seen them do it, when their load's too great.
"If I mistake not," he begins, "you'll find
Viscus not more, nor Varius, to your mind:
There's not a man can turn a verse so soon,
Or dance so nimbly when he hears a tune.
While, as for singing—ah! my forte is there:
Tigellius' self might envy me, I'll swear."

He paused for breath: I falteringly strike in:
"Have you a mother? have you kith or kin
To whom your life is precious?" "Not a soul:
My line's extinct, I have interred the whole."
O happy they! (so into thought I fell)
After life's endless babble they sleep well.
My turn is next: dispatch me, for the weird
Has come to pass which I so long have feared,
The fatal weird a Sabine beldame sung,
All in my nursery days, when life was young:
"No sword nor poison e'er shall take him off,
Nor gout, nor pleurisy, nor racking cough.
A babbling tongue shall kill him, let him fly
All talkers, as he wishes not to die."

We got to Vesta's temple, and the sun
Told us a quarter of the day was done.
It chanced he had a suit, and was bound fast
Either to make appearance or be cast.
"Step here a moment, if you love me." "Nay;
I know no law; 'twould hurt my health to stay,
And then, my call." "I'm doubting what to do,
Whether to give my lawsuit up or you.
"Me, pray!" "I will not." On he strides again:
I follow, unresisting, in his train.

"How stand you with Maecenas?" he began:
"He picks his friends with care; a shrewd wise man.
In fact, I take it, one could hardly name
A head so cool in life's exciting game.
'Twould be a good deed done, if you could throw
Your servant in his way; I mean, you know,

Just to play second; in a month, I'll swear,
You'd make an end of every rival there."
"O, you mistake. We don't live there in league.
I know no house more sacred from intrigue.
I'm never distanced in my friend's good grace
By wealth or talent: each man finds his place."
"A miracle! if 'twere not told by you,
I scarce should credit it." "And yet 'tis true."
"Ah, well, you double my desire to rise
To special favour with a man so wise."
"You've but to wish it: 'twill be your own fault,
If, with your nerve, you win not by assault.
He can be won: that puts him on his guard,
And so the first approach is always hard."
"No fear of me, sir: a judicious bribe
Will work a wonder with the menial tribe.
Say, I'm refused admittance for to-day;
I'll watch my time; I'll meet him in the way,
Escort him, dog him. In this world of ours
The path to what we want ne'er runs on flowers."

'Mid all this prate there met us, as it fell,
Aristius, my good friend, who knew him well.
We stop. Inquiries and replies go round:
"Where do you hail from?" "Whither are you bound?"
There as he stood, impassive as a clod,
I pull at his limp arms, frown, wink, and nod,
To urge him to release me. With a smile
He feigns stupidity. I burn with bile.
"Something there was you said you wished to tell
To me in private." "Ay, I mind it well;
But not just now: 'tis a Jews' fast to-day;
Affront a sect so touchy! nay, friend, nay."
"Faith, I've no scruples." "Ah! but I've a few.
I'm weak, you know, and do as others do.
Some other time: excuse me." Wretched me!
That ever man so black a sun should see!
Off goes the rogue, and leaves me in despair,
Tied to the altar, with the knife in air,
When, by rare chance, the plaintiff in the suit
Knocks up against us: "Whither now, you brute?"

He roars like thunder, then to me: "You'll stand
My witness, sir?" "My ear's at your command."
Off to the court he drags him, shouts succeed,
A mob collects: thank Phoebus, I am freed.

Translated by John Conington.

City Mouse, Country Mouse

Horace, *Satires* 2.6

This satire was written sometime after Maecenas furnished Horace with a villa in the charming Sabine countryside north of Rome. Here, the poet celebrates the pleasures of rural life, a rugged existence far from the agitation of the city where he must endlessly respond to the solicitations of strangers who imagine that, because he is a close friend of Maecenas, he can acquire anything he desires.

"Come now, go home with me: remember, all
Who live on earth are mortal, great and small.
Then take, good sir, your pleasure while you may.
With life so short, 'twere wrong to lose a day."

This used to be my wish: a bit of land,
A house and garden with a spring at hand,
And just a little wood. The gods have crowned
My humble vows; I prosper and abound.
Nor ask I more, kind Mercury, save that thou
Wouldst give me still the goods thou giv'st me now:
If crime has ne'er increased them, nor excess
And want of thrift are like to make them less;
If I ne'er pray like this, "O might that nook
Which spoils my field be mine by hook or crook!
O for a stroke of luck like his, who found
A crock of silver, turning up the ground,
And, thanks to good Alcides, farmed as buyer
The very land where he had slaved for hire!"
If what I have contents me, hear my prayer:
Still let me feel thy tutelary care,
And let my sheep, my pastures, this and that,
My all, in fact, (except my brains,) be fat.

Now, lodged in my hill-castle, can I choose
Companion fitter than my homely Muse?
Here no town duties vex, no plague-winds blow,
Nor Autumn, friend to graveyards, works me woe.
Sire of the morning (do I call thee right,

Or hear'st thou Janus' name with more delight?)
Who introducest, so the gods ordain,
Life's various tasks, inaugurate my strain.
At Rome to bail I'm summoned. "Do your part,"
Thou bidd'st me; "quick, lest others get the start."
So, whether Boreas roars, or winter's snow
Clips short the day, to court I needs must go.
I give the fatal pledge, distinct and loud,
Then pushing, struggling, battle with the crowd.
"Now, madman!" clamours some one, not without
A threat or two, "just mind what you're about:
What? you must knock down all that's in your way,
Because you're posting to Maecenas, eh?"
This pleases me, I own; but when I get
To black Esquiliae, trouble waits me yet:
For other people's matters in a swarm
Buzz round my head and take my ears by storm.
"Sir, Roscius would be glad if you'd arrange
By eight a. m. to be with him on 'Change."
"Quintus, the scribes entreat you to attend
A meeting of importance, as their friend."
"Just get Maecenas' seal attached to these."
"I'll try." "O, you can do it, if you please."
Seven years, or rather eight, have well-nigh passed
Since with Maecenas' friends I first was classed,
To this extent, that, driving through the street,
He'd stop his car and offer me a seat,
Or make such chance remarks as "What's o'clock?"
"Will Syria's champion beat the Thracian cock?"
"These morning frosts are apt to be severe;"
Just chit-chat, suited to a leaky ear.
Since that auspicious date, each day and hour
Has placed me more and more in envy's power:
"He joined his play, sat next him at the games:
A child of Fortune!" all the world exclaims.
From the high rostra a report comes down,
And like a chilly fog, pervades the town:
Each man I meet accosts me "Is it so?
You live so near the gods, you're sure to know:
That news about the Dacians?[3] have you heard
No secret tidings?" "Not a single word."

"O yes! you love to banter us poor folk."
"Nay, if I've heard a tittle, may I choke!"
"Will Caesar grant his veterans their estates
In Italy, or t'other side of the straits?"
I swear that I know nothing, and am dumb:
They think me deep, miraculously mum.
And so my day between my fingers slips,
While fond regrets keep rising to my lips.
O my dear homestead in the country! when
Shall I behold your pleasant face again;
And, studying now, now dozing and at ease,
Imbibe forgetfulness of all this tease?
O when, Pythagoras, shall thy brother bean,[4]
With pork and cabbage, on my board be seen?
O happy nights and suppers half divine,
When, at the home-gods' altar, I and mine
Enjoy a frugal meal, and leave the treat
Unfinished for my merry slaves to eat!
Not bound by mad-cap rules, but free to choose
Big cups or small, each follows his own views:
You toss your wine off boldly, if you please,
Or gently sip, and mellow by degrees.
We talk of—not our neighbour's house or field,
Nor the last feat of Lepos, the light-heeled—
But matters which to know concerns us more,
Which none but at his peril can ignore;
Whether 'tis wealth or virtue makes men blest,
What leads to friendship, worth or interest,
In what the good consists, and what the end
And chief of goods, on which the rest depend:
While neighbour Cervius, with his rustic wit,
Tells old wives' tales, this case or that to hit.
Should some one be unwise enough to praise
Arellius' toilsome wealth, he straightway says:
"One day a country mouse in his poor home
Received an ancient friend, a mouse from Rome.
The host, though close and careful, to a guest
Could open still; so now he did his best.
He spares not oats or vetches: in his chaps
Raisins he brings and nibbled bacon-scraps,
Hoping by varied dainties to entice

His town-bred guest, so delicate and nice,
Who condescended graciously to touch
Thing after thing, but never would take much,
While he, the owner of the mansion, sate
On threshed-out straw, and spelt and darnels ate.
At length the townsman cries: "I wonder how
You can live here, friend, on this hill's rough brow.
Take my advice, and leave these ups and downs,
This hill and dale, for humankind and towns.
Come now, go home with me: remember, all
Who live on earth are mortal, great and small.
Then take, good sir, your pleasure while you may.
With life so short, 'twere wrong to lose a day."
This reasoning made the rustic's head turn round;
Forth from his hole he issues with a bound,
And they two make together for their mark,
In hopes to reach the city during dark.
The midnight sky was bending over all,
When they set foot within a stately hall,
Where couches of wrought ivory had been spread
With gorgeous coverlets of Tyrian red,
And viands piled up high in baskets lay,
The relics of a feast of yesterday.
The townsman does the honours, lays his guest
At ease upon a couch with crimson dressed,
Then nimbly moves in character of host,
And offers in succession boiled and roast;
Nay, like a well-trained slave, each wish prevents,
And tastes before the tit-bits he presents.
The guest, rejoicing in his altered fare,
Assumes in turn a genial diner's air,
When hark! a sudden banging of the door.
Each from his couch is tumbled on the floor.
Half dead, they scurry round the room, poor things,
While the whole house with barking mastiffs rings.
Then says the rustic: "It may do for you,
This life, but I don't like it; so adieu:
Give me my hole, secure from all alarms,
I'll prove that tares and vetches still have charms."

Translated by John Conington.

The Nouveau Riche

Horace, *Satires* 2.8

In this passage, Horace asks his friend, the comic poet Fundanius, to describe an exuberant dinner that took place at the residence of the upstart Nasidenius Rufus. Horace's caricature of Nasidenius personifies the nouveau riche: Nasidenius tries exhaustively to impress his guests with the most expensive dishes and imported wines from the Greek islands and all regions of Italy. The banquet resembles a comedy, and Fundanius is a particularly appropriate narrator.

A few years later, Petronius deals with the same issue in his Satyricon, *where guests attending the ostentatious banquet of a nouveau riche freedman are exposed to their host's extravagancies in grandiloquence and bad taste.*

"Because, you know, hot wines do double wrong;
They dull the palate, and they edge the tongue."

HORACE
That rich Nasidienus—let me hear
How yesterday you relished his good cheer:
For when I tried to get you, I was told
You'd been there since the day was six hours old.

FUNDANIUS
O, 'twas the finest treat.

HORACE
Inform me, pray,
What first was served your hunger to allay.

FUNDANIUS
First a Lucanian boar; 'twas captured wild
(So the host told us) when the wind was mild;
Around it, turnips, lettuce, radishes,
By way of whet, with brine and Coan lees.
Then, when the board, a maple one, was cleared,
A high-girt slave with purple cloth appeared
And rubbed and wiped it clean; another boy

Removed the scraps, and all that might annoy:
"While dark Hydaspes, like an Attic maid
Who carries Ceres' basket, grave and staid,
Came in with Caecuban, and, close behind,
Alcon with Chian, which had ne'er been brined.
Then said our host: "If Alban you'd prefer,
Maecenas, or Falern, we have them, Sir."[5]

HORACE
What sorry riches! but I fail to glean
Who else was present at so rare a scene.

FUNDANIUS
Myself at top, then Viscus, and below
Was Varius; after us came Balatro,
Vibidius also, present at the treat
Unasked, as members of Maecenas' suite.
Porcius and Nomentanus last, and he,
Our host, who lay betwixt them, made the three;
Porcius the undermost, a witty droll,
Who makes you laugh by swallowing cheesecakes whole;
While Nomentanus' specialty was this,
To point things out that vulgar eyes might miss;
For fish and fowl, in fact whate'er was placed
Before us, had, we found, a novel taste,
As one experiment sufficed to show,
Made on a flounder and a turbot's roe.
Then, turning the discourse to fruit, he treats
Of the right time for gathering honey-sweets;
Plucked when the moon's on wane, it seems they're red;
For further details see the fountain-head.
When thus to Balatro Vibidius: "Fie!
Let's drink him out, or unrevenged we die;
Here, bigger cups." Our entertainer's cheek
Turned deadly white, as thus he heard him speak;
For of the nuisances that can befall
A man like him, your toper's worst of all,
Because, you know, hot wines do double wrong;
They dull the palate, and they edge the tongue.
On go Vibidius and his mate, and tilt
Whole flagons into cups Allifae-built;[6]

We follow suit: the host's two friends alone
Forbore to treat the wine-flask as their own.

A lamprey now appears, a sprawling fish,
With shrimps about it swimming in the dish.
Whereon our host remarks: "This fish was caught
While pregnant: after spawning it is naught.
We make our sauce with oil, of the best strain
Venafrum[7] yields, and caviare from Spain,
Pour in Italian wine, five years in tun,
While yet 'tis boiling; when the boiling's done,
Chian suits best of all; white pepper add,
And vinegar, from Lesbian wine turned bad.
Rockets and elecampanes with this mess
To boil, is my invention, I profess:
To put sea-urchins in, unwashed as caught,
'Stead of made pickle, was Curtillus' thought."

Meantime the curtains o'er the table spread
Came tumbling in a heap from overhead,
Dragging withal black dust in whirlwinds, more
Than Boreas raises on Campania's floor.
We, when the shock is over, smile to see
The danger less than we had feared 'twould be,
And breathe again. Poor Rufus drooped his head
And wept so sore, you'd think his son was dead;
And things seemed hastening to a tragic end,
But Nomentanus thus consoled his friend:
"O Fortune, cruellest of heavenly powers,
Why make such game of this poor life of ours?"
Varius his napkin to his mouth applied,
A laugh to stifle, or at least to hide:
But Balatro, with his perpetual sneer,
Cries, "Such is life, capricious and severe,
And hence it comes that merit never gains
A meed of praise proportioned to its pains.
What gross injustice! just that I may get
A handsome dinner, you must fume and fret,
See that the bread's not burned, the sauce not spoiled,
The servants in their places, curled and oiled.
Then too the risks; the tapestry, as of late,

May fall; a stumbling groom may break a plate.
But gifts, concealed by sunshine, are displayed
In hosts, as in commanders, by the shade."
Rufus returned, "Heaven speed things to your mind!
Sure ne'er was guest so friendly and so kind;"
Then takes his slippers. Head to head draws near,
And each man's lips are at his neighbour's ear.

HORACE
'Tis better than a play: but please report
What further things occurred to make you sport.

FUNDANIUS
Well, while Vibidius takes the slaves to task,
Enquiring if the tumble broke the flask,
And Balatro keeps starting some pretence
For mirth, that we may laugh without offence,
With altered brow returns our sumptuous friend,
Resolved, what chance has damaged, art shall mend.
More servants follow, staggering 'neath the load
Of a huge dish where limbs of crane were stowed,
Salted and floured; a goose's liver, crammed
To twice its bulk, so close the figs were jammed;
And wings of hares dressed separate, better so
Than eaten with the back, as gourmands know.
Then blackbirds with their breasts all burnt to coal,
And pigeons without rumps, not served up whole,
Dainties, no doubt, but then there came a speech
About the laws and properties of each;
At last the feeder and the food we quit,
Taking revenge by tasting ne'er a bit,
As if Canidia's mouth had breathed an air
Of viperous poison on the whole affair.

Translated by John Conington.

The Poet's Outlook

Horace, *Odes* 1.1

Horace has absolutely no interest in the joys of athletic victories, agriculture, maritime commerce, and hunting. Only poetry matters to him. He invokes the Muses to provide him with inspiration that will make him touch the stars and does not forget to thank Maecenas, his protector and patron of the arts.

"To me the artist's meed, the ivy wreath
Is very heaven: me the sweet cool of woods,
Where Satyrs frolic with the Nymphs, secludes
From rabble rout, so but Euterpe's breath
Fail not the flute, nor Polyhymnia fly
Averse from stringing new the Lesbian lyre.
O, write my name among that minstrel choir,
And my proud head shall strike upon the sky!"

Maecenas, born of monarch ancestors,[8]
The shield at once and glory of my life!
There are who joy them in the Olympic strife
And love the dust they gather in the course;
The goal by hot wheels shunn'd, the famous prize,
Exalt them to the gods that rule mankind;
This joys, if rabbles fickle as the wind
Through triple grade of honours bid him rise,
That, if his granary has stored away
Of Libya's thousand floors the yield entire;[9]
The man who digs his field as did his sire,
With honest pride, no Attalus may sway
By proffer'd wealth to tempt Myrtoan seas,
The timorous captain of a Cyprian bark.[10]
The winds that make Icarian billows dark
The merchant fears, and hugs the rural ease
Of his own village home; but soon, ashamed
Of penury, he refits his batter'd craft.
There is, who thinks no scorn of Massic draught,[11]
Who robs the daylight of an hour unblamed,
Now stretch'd beneath the arbute on the sward,

Now by some gentle river's sacred spring;
Some love the camp, the clarion's joyous ring,
And battle, by the mother's soul abhorr'd.
See, patient waiting in the clear keen air,
The hunter, thoughtless of his delicate bride,
Whether the trusty hounds a stag have eyed,
Or the fierce Marsian boar has burst the snare.
To me the artist's meed, the ivy wreath
Is very heaven: me the sweet cool of woods,
Where Satyrs frolic with the Nymphs, secludes
From rabble rout, so but Euterpe's breath
Fail not the flute, nor Polyhymnia fly
Averse from stringing new the Lesbian lyre.
O, write my name among that minstrel choir,
And my proud head shall strike upon the sky!

Translated by John Conington.

The Golden Mean
Horace, *Odes* 2.10

Horace relishes the pleasures of life—but in moderation. His famous saying "aurea mediocritas" *("The Golden Mean"), which sometimes is understood with irony nowadays (in the sense of a mediocrity that is satisfied with itself), held a completely different meaning for the poet. For Horace, subscribing to a just measure is the wisest way of living one's life. It enables one—including the poet—to avoid excesses in success as well as in adversity, and at best, to make the most of one's life that is all too short.*

"Be brave in trouble; meet distress
With dauntless front; but when the gale
Too prosperous blows, be wise no less,
And shorten sail."

Licinius, trust a seaman's lore:
Steer not too boldly to the deep,
Nor, fearing storms, by treacherous shore
Too closely creep.
Who makes the golden mean his guide,
Shuns miser's cabin, foul and dark,
Shuns gilded roofs, where pomp and pride
Are envy's mark.
With fiercer blasts the pine's dim height
Is rock'd; proud towers with heavier fall
Crash to the ground; and thunders smite
The mountains tall.
In sadness hope, in gladness fear
'Gainst coming change will fortify
Your breast. The storms that Jupiter
Sweeps o'er the sky
He chases. Why should rain to-day
Bring rain to-morrow? Python's foe
Is pleased sometimes his lyre to play,
Nor bends his bow. [12]
Be brave in trouble; meet distress
With dauntless front; but when the gale

Too prosperous blows, be wise no less,
And shorten sail.

Translated by John Conington.

Invitation to the Countryside

Horace, *Odes* 3.29

Maecenas provides Horace a villa in the tranquil Italian countryside. In turn, Horace invites his benefactor to leave Rome—and all its congestion, agitation, dust, and heat—to bask in the temperate rustic life for a few days. It is also an invitation to grasp the pleasures of the day—a variation on the theme of "Carpe diem" *("Seize the day") that made Horace famous.*

"Control the present: all beside
Flows like a river seaward borne,
Now rolling on its placid tide,
Now whirling massy trunks uptorn."

Heir of Tyrrhenian kings, for you
A mellow cask, unbroach'd as yet,
Maecenas mine, and roses new,
And fresh-drawn oil your locks to wet,
Are waiting here. Delay not still,
Nor gaze on Tibur, never dried,
And sloping Aesule, and the hill
Of Telegon the parricide.[13]
O leave that pomp that can but tire,
Those piles, among the clouds at home;
Cease for a moment to admire
The smoke, the wealth, the noise of Rome!
In change e'en luxury finds a zest:
The poor man's supper, neat, but spare,
With no gay couch to seat the guest,
Has smooth'd the rugged brow of care.
Now glows the Ethiop maiden's sire;
Now Procyon rages all ablaze;
The Lion maddens in his ire,
As suns bring back the sultry days:[14]
The shepherd with his weary sheep
Seeks out the streamlet and the trees,
Silvanus' lair; the still banks sleep

Untroubled by the wandering breeze.
You ponder on imperial schemes,
And o'er the city's danger brood:
Bactrian and Serian haunt your dreams,
And Tanais, toss'd by inward feud.[15]
The issue of the time to be
Heaven wisely hides in blackest night,
And laughs, should man's anxiety
Transgress the bounds of man's short sight.
Control the present: all beside
Flows like a river seaward borne,
Now rolling on its placid tide,
Now whirling massy trunks uptorn,
And waveworn crags, and farms, and stock,
In chaos blent, while hill and wood
Reverberate to the enormous shock,
When savage rains the tranquil flood
Have stirr'd to madness. Happy he,
Self-centred, who each night can say,
"My life is lived: the morn may see
A clouded or a sunny day:
That rests with Jove: but what is gone,
He will not, cannot turn to nought;
Nor cancel, as a thing undone,
What once the flying hour has brought."
Fortune, who loves her cruel game,
Still bent upon some heartless whim,
Shifts her caresses, fickle dame,
Now kind to me, and now to him:
She stays; 'tis well: but let her shake
Those wings, her presents I resign,
Cloak me in native worth, and take
Chaste Poverty undower'd for mine.
Though storms around my vessel rave,
I will not fall to craven prayers,
Nor bargain by my vows to save
My Cyprian and Sidonian wares,
Else added to the insatiate main.
Then through the wild Aegean roar

The breezes and the Brethren Twain
Shall waft my little boat ashore.

Translated by John Conington.

LIVY

59 BC - AD 17

Born at Padua into a family of local dignitaries, Livy dedicated his life to study and research. According to Seneca, he wrote philosophical treatises and dialogues early on that were as much about philosophy as they were about history. The great achievement of his life, however, was the Ab Urbe condita libri, *in which he attempted to account for all of Roman history in 142 books, beginning with the landing of Aeneas on Italy's shores. Death prevented him from completing his work, which got only as far as 9 BC with the murder of Drusus, the brother of Emperor Tiberius.*

From this immense corpus, only 36 complete books and additional fragments have been preserved. Pessimism mixed with Stoicism emanates from the first books. It seems that Livy began writing at the time of the war between Octavian and Mark Antony, as his tone is shaped by the recent conflict that tore apart Rome. When Octavian triumphed, Livy joined his camp and later advised the young Claudius.

As a historian, Livy used compilations of ancient chroniclers but also depended heavily on his intuition. His work suffers from his extreme nationalistic feelings and also from his condescending attitude toward various peoples, such as the Carthaginians. Faithful to the classical historiography of his times, he peppered his works with eloquent yet unauthentic speeches. Nonetheless, his success in posterity—from Velleius Paterculus to Lucan, from Plutarch to Cassius Dio, and from Dante to Machiavelli—pays homage to the richness of his narrative.

The Origins of Rome

Livy, *History of Rome* 1.1-10

Only two Trojans escaped the war safe and sound, at least according to Livy: Antenor, who founded Padua in Venetia (the city where Livy was born), and Aeneas, who landed in Latium on the Tyrrhenian shore of Italy and established the city of Lavinium. There, Aeneas married an indigenous woman and fathered a line of kings. The most famous of them, Romulus, would one day found Rome with his twin brother Remus. First inhabited by shepherds and brigands married to women kidnapped from the nearby Sabine people, the city would acquire power nearly equal to that of the gods. So follows the legend of the foundation of Rome in the year 753 BC.

"Anger unaccompanied by strength is fruitless."

To begin with, it is generally admitted that, after the taking of Troy, while all the other Trojans were treated with severity, in the case of two, Æneas and Antenor, the Greeks forbore to exercise the full rights of war, both on account of an ancient tie of hospitality, and because they had persistently recommended peace and the restoration of Helen; and then Antenor, after various vicissitudes, reached the inmost bay of the Adriatic Sea, accompanied by a body of the Eneti, who had been driven from Paphlagonia[1] by civil disturbance, and were in search both of a place of settlement and a leader, their chief Pylæmenes having perished at Troy; and that the Eneti and Trojans, having driven out the Euganei, who dwelt between the sea and the Alps, occupied these districts. In fact, the place where they first landed is called Troy, and from this it is named the Trojan canton. The nation as a whole is called Veneti.

It is also agreed that Æneas, an exile from home owing to a like misfortune, but conducted by the fates to the founding of a greater empire, came first to Macedonia, that he was then driven ashore at Sicily in his quest for a settlement, and sailing thence directed his course to the territory of Laurentum. This spot also bears the name of Troy. When the Trojans, having disembarked there, were driving off booty from the country, as was only natural, seeing that they had nothing left but their arms and ships after their almost boundless wandering, Latinus the king and the Aborigines, who then occupied these districts, assembled in arms from the city and country to repel the violence of the new-comers. In regard to what followed there is a twofold tradition. Some say that Latinus, having been defeated in battle, first made peace and then concluded an alliance with Æneas; others, that when the armies had taken up their position in order of battle, before the trumpets sounded, Latinus advanced to the front, and invited the leader of the strangers to a conference. He then inquired what manner of men they were, whence they had come, for what reasons they had left their home, and in quest of what they had landed on Laurentine territory. After he heard that the host were Trojans, their chief Æneas, the son of Anchises and Venus, and that, exiled from home, their country having been destroyed by fire, they were seeking a settlement and a site for building a city, struck with admiration both at the noble character of the nation and the hero, and at their spirit, ready alike for peace or war, he ratified the pledge of future friendship by clasping hands. Thereupon a treaty was concluded between the chiefs, and mutual greetings passed between the armies. Æneas was hospitably entertained at the house of Latinus; there Latinus, in the presence of his household gods, cemented the public league by a family one, by giving Æneas his daughter in marriage. This event fully confirmed the Trojans in the hope of at length terminating their wanderings by a lasting and permanent settlement. They built a town, which Æneas called Lavinium after the name of his wife. Shortly afterward also, a son was the issue of the recently concluded marriage, to whom his parents gave the name of Ascanius.

Aborigines and Trojans were soon afterward the joint objects of a hostile attack. Turnus, king of the Rutulians, to whom Lavinia had been affianced before the arrival of Æneas, indignant that a stranger had been preferred to himself, had made war on Æneas and Latinus together. Neither army came out of the struggle with satisfaction. The Rutulians were vanquished: the victorious Aborigines and Trojans lost their leader Latinus. Thereupon Turnus and the Rutulians, mistrustful of their strength, had recourse to the prosperous and powerful Etruscans, and their king Mezentius, whose seat of government was at Cære, at that time a flourishing town. Even from the outset he had viewed with dissatisfaction the founding of a new city, and, as at that time he considered that the Trojan power was increasing far more than was altogether consistent with the safety of the neighbouring peoples, he readily joined his forces in alliance with the Rutulians. Æneas, to gain the good-will of the Aborigines in face of a war so serious and alarming, and in order that they might all be not only under the same laws but might also bear the same name, called both nations Latins. In fact, subsequently, the Aborigines were not behind the Trojans in zeal and loyalty toward their king Æneas. Accordingly, in full reliance on this state of mind of the two nations, who were daily becoming more and more united, and in spite of the fact that Etruria was so powerful, that at this time it had filled with the fame of its renown not only the land but the sea also, throughout the whole length of Italy from the Alps to the Sicilian Strait, Æneas led out his forces into the field, although he might have repelled their attack by means of his fortifications. Thereupon a battle was fought, in which victory rested with the Latins, but for Æneas it was even the last of his acts on earth. He, by whatever name laws human and divine demand he should be called, was buried on the banks of the river Numicus: they call him Jupiter Indiges.

Ascanius, the son of Æneas, was not yet old enough to rule; the government, however, remained unassailed for him till he reached the age of maturity. In the interim, under the regency of a woman—so great was Lavinia's capacity—the Latin state and the boy's kingdom, inherited from his father and grandfather, was secured for him. I will not discuss the question—for who can state as certain a matter of such antiquity?—whether it was this Ascanius, or one older than he, born of Creusa, before the fall of Troy, and subsequently the companion of his father's flight, the same whom, under the name of Iulus, the Julian family represents to be the founder of its name. Be that as it may, this Ascanius, wherever born and of whatever mother—it is at any rate agreed that his father was Æneas—seeing that Lavinium was over-populated, left that city, now a flourishing and wealthy one, considering those times, to his mother or stepmother, and built himself a new one at the foot of the Alban mount, which, from its situation, being built all along the ridge of a hill, was called Alba Longa.

There was an interval of about thirty years between the founding of Lavinium and the transplanting of the colony to Alba Longa. Yet its power had increased to such a degree, especially owing to the defeat of the Etruscans, that not even on the death of Æneas, nor subsequently between the period of the regency of Lavinia, and the first beginnings of the young prince's reign, did either Mezentius, the Etruscans, or any other neighbouring peoples venture to take up arms against it. Peace had been concluded on the following terms, that the river Albula, which is now called Tiber, should be the boundary of Latin and Etruscan territory. After him Silvius, son of Ascanius, born by some accident in the woods, became king. He was the father of Æneas Silvius, who afterward begot Latinus Silvius. By him several colonies were transplanted, which were called Prisci Latini. From this time all the princes, who ruled at Alba, bore the surname of Silvius. From Latinus sprung Alba; from Alba, Atys; from Atys, Capys; from Capys, Capetus; from Capetus, Tiberinus, who, having been drowned while crossing the river Albula, gave it the name by which it was generally known among those of later times. He was succeeded by Agrippa, son of Tiberinus; after Agrippa, Romulus Silvius, having received the government from his father, became king. He was killed by a thunderbolt, and handed on the kingdom to Aventinus, who, owing to his being buried on that hill, which now forms part of the city of Rome, gave it its name. After him reigned Proca, who begot Numitor and Amulius. To Numitor, who was the eldest son, he bequeathed the ancient kingdom of the Silvian family. Force, however, prevailed more than a father's wish or the respect due to seniority. Amulius drove out his brother and seized the kingdom: he added crime to crime, murdered his brother's male issue, and, under pretence of doing honour to his brother's daughter, Rea Silvia, having chosen her a Vestal Virgin, deprived her of all hopes of issue by the obligation of perpetual virginity.

My opinion, however, is that the origin of so great a city and an empire next in power to that of the gods was due to the fates. The Vestal Rea was ravished by force, and having brought forth twins, declared Mars to be the father of her illegitimate offspring, either because she really imagined it to be the case, or because it was less discreditable to have committed such an offence with a god. But neither gods nor men protected either her or her offspring from the king's cruelty. The priestess was bound and cast into prison; the king ordered the children to be thrown into the flowing river. By some chance which Providence seemed to direct, the Tiber, having over flown its banks, thereby forming stagnant pools, could not be approached at the regular course of its channel; notwithstanding it gave the bearers of the children hope that they could be drowned in its water however calm. Accordingly, as if they had executed the king's orders, they exposed the boys in the nearest land-pool, where now stands the *ficus Ruminalis*, which they say was called *Romularis*. At that time the country in those parts was a desolate wilderness. The story goes, that when the shallow water, subsiding, had left the floating trough, in which the children had been exposed, on dry ground, a thirsty she-wolf from the mountains around directed her course toward the cries of the infants, and held down her teats to them with such gentleness, that the keeper of the king's herd found her licking the boys with her tongue. They say that his name was Faustulus; and that they were carried by him to his homestead and given to his wife Larentia to be brought up. Some are of the opinion that Larentia was called Lupa among the shepherds from her being a common prostitute, and hence an opening was afforded for the marvellous story. The children, thus born and thus brought up, as soon as they reached the age of youth, did not lead a life of inactivity at home or amid the flocks, but, in the chase, scoured the forests. Having thus gained strength, both in body and spirit, they now were not only able to withstand wild beasts, but attacked robbers laden with booty, and divided the spoils with the shepherds, in whose company, as the number of their young associates increased daily, they carried on business and pleasure.

Even in these early times it is said that the festival of the Lupercal, as now celebrated, was solemnized on the Palatine Hill, which was first called Pallantium, from Pallanteum, a city of Arcadia, and afterward Mount Palatius. There Evander, who, belonging to the above tribe of the Arcadians, had for many years before occupied these districts, is said to have appointed the observance of a solemn festival, introduced from Arcadia, in which naked youths ran about doing honour in wanton sport to Pan Lycæus, who was afterward called Inuus[2] by the Romans. When they were engaged in this festival, as its periodical solemnization was well known, a band of robbers, enraged at the loss of some booty, lay in wait for them, and took Remus prisoner, Romulus having vigorously defended himself: the captive Remus they delivered up to King Amulius, and even went so far as to bring accusations against him. They made it the principal charge that having made incursions into Numitor's lands, and, having assembled a band of young men, they had driven off their booty after the manner of enemies. Accordingly, Remus was delivered up to Numitor for punishment. Now from the very first Faustulus had entertained hopes that the boys who were being brought up by him, were of royal blood: for he both knew that the children had been exposed by the king's orders, and that the time, at which he had taken them up, coincided exactly with that period. But he had been unwilling to disclose the matter, as yet not ripe for discovery, till either a fitting opportunity or the necessity for it should arise. Necessity came first. Accordingly, urged by fear, he disclosed the whole affair to Romulus. By accident also, Numitor, while he had Remus in custody, having heard that the brothers were twins, by comparing their age and their natural disposition entirely free from servility, felt his mind struck by the recollection of his grandchildren, and by frequent inquiries came to the conclusion he had already formed, so that he was not far from openly acknowledging Remus. Accordingly a plot was concerted against the king on all sides. Romulus, not accompanied by a body of young men—for he was not equal to open violence—but having commanded the shepherds to come to the palace by different roads at a fixed time, made an attack upon the king, while Remus, having got together another party from Numitor's house, came to his assistance; and so they slew the king.

Numitor, at the beginning of the fray, giving out that enemies had invaded the city and attacked the palace, after he had drawn off the Alban youth to the citadel to secure it with an armed garrison, when he saw the young men, after they had compassed the king's death, advancing toward him to offer congratulations, immediately summoned a meeting of the people, and recounted his brother's unnatural behaviour toward him, the extraction of his grandchildren, the manner of their birth, bringing up, and recognition, and went on to inform them of the king's death, and that he was responsible for it. The young princes advanced through the midst of the assembly with their band in orderly array, and, after they had saluted their grandfather as king, a succeeding shout of approbation, issuing from the whole multitude, ratified for him the name and authority of sovereign. The government of Alba being thus intrusted to Numitor, Romulus and Remus were seized with the desire of building a city on the spot where they had been exposed and brought up. Indeed, the number of Alban and Latin inhabitants was too great for the city; the shepherds also were included among that population, and all these readily inspired hopes that Alba and Lavinium would be insignificant in comparison with that city, which was intended to be built. But desire of rule, the bane of their grandfather, interrupted these designs, and thence arose a shameful quarrel from a sufficiently amicable beginning. For as they were twins, and consequently the respect for seniority could not settle the point, they agreed to leave it to the gods, under whose protection the place was, to choose by augury which of them should give a name to the new city, and govern it when built. Romulus chose the Palatine and Remus the Aventine, as points of observation for taking the auguries.

It is said that an omen came to Remus first, six vultures; and when, after the omen had been declared, twice that number presented themselves to Romulus, each was hailed king by his own party, the former claiming sovereign power on the ground of priority of time, the latter on account of the number of birds. Thereupon, having met and exchanged angry words, from the strife of angry feelings they turned to bloodshed: there Remus fell from a blow received in the crowd. A more common account is that Remus, in derision of his brother, leaped over the newly-erected walls, and was thereupon slain by Romulus in a fit of passion, who, mocking him, added words to this effect:" So perish every one hereafter, who shall leap over my walls." Thus Romulus obtained possession of supreme power for himself alone. The city, when built, was called after the name of its founder. He first proceeded to fortify the Palatine Hill, on which he himself had been brought up. He offered sacrifices to Hercules, according to the Grecian rite, as they had been instituted by Evander; to the other gods, according to the Alban rite.

There is a tradition that Hercules, having slain Geryon, drove off his oxen, which were of surpassing beauty, to that spot: and that he lay down in a grassy spot on the banks of the river Tiber, where he had swam across, driving the cattle before him, to refresh them with rest and luxuriant pasture, being also himself fatigued with journeying. There, when sleep had overpowered him, heavy as he was with food and wine, a shepherd who dwelt in the neighbourhood, by name Cacus, priding himself on his strength, and charmed with the beauty of the cattle, desired to carry them off as booty; but because, if he had driven the herd in front of him to the cave, their tracks must have conducted their owner thither in his search, he dragged the most beautiful of them by their tails backward into a cave. Hercules, aroused from sleep at dawn, having looked over his herd and observed that some of their number were missing, went straight to the nearest cave, to see whether perchance their tracks led thither. When he saw that they were all turned away from it and led in no other direction, troubled and not knowing what to make up his mind to do, he commenced to drive off his herd from so dangerous a spot. Thereupon some of the cows that were driven away, lowed, as they usually do, when they missed those that were left; and the lowings of those that were shut in being heard in answer from the cave, caused Hercules to turn round. And when Cacus attempted to prevent him by force as he was advancing toward the cave, he was struck with a club and slain, while vainly calling upon the shepherds to assist him.

At that time Evander, who was an exile from the Peloponnesus, governed the country more by his personal ascendancy than by absolute sway. He was a man held in reverence on account of the wonderful art of writing, an entirely new discovery to men ignorant of accomplishments, and still more revered on account of the supposed divinity of his mother Carmenta, whom those peoples had marvelled at as a prophetess before the arrival of the Sybil in Italy. This Evander, roused by the assembling of the shepherds as they hastily crowded round the stranger, who was charged with open murder, after he heard an account of the deed and the cause of it, gazing upon the personal appearance and mien of the hero, considerably more dignified and majestic than that of a man, asked who he was. As soon as he heard the name of the hero, and that of his father and native country, "Hail!" said he, "Hercules, son of Jupiter! my mother, truthful interpreter of the will of the gods, has declared to me that thou art destined to increase the number of the heavenly beings, and that on this spot an altar shall be dedicated to thee, which in after ages a people most mighty on earth shall call Greatest, and honour in accordance with rites instituted by thee." Hercules, having given him his right hand, declared that he accepted the prophetic intimation, and would fulfil the predictions of the fates, by building and dedicating an altar.

Thereon then for the first time sacrifice was offered to Hercules with a choice heifer taken from the herd, the Potitii and Pinarii, the most distinguished families who then inhabited those parts, being invited to serve at the feast. It so happened that the Potitii presented themselves in due time and the entrails were set before them: but the Pinarii did not arrive until the entrails had been eaten up, to share the remainder of the feast. From that time it became a settled institution, that, as long as the Pinarian family existed, they should not eat of the entrails of the sacrificial victims. The Potitii, fully instructed by Evander, discharged the duties of chief priests of this sacred function for many generations, until their whole race became extinct, in consequence of this office, the solemn prerogative of their family, being delegated to public slaves. These were the only religious rites that Romulus at that time adopted from those of foreign countries, being even then an advocate of immortality won by merit, to which the destiny marked out for him was conducting him.

The duties of religion having been thus duly completed, the people were summoned to a public meeting. And, as they could not be united and incorporated into one body by any other means save legal ordinances, Romulus gave them a code of laws: and, judging that these would only be respected by a nation of rustics, if he dignified himself with the insignia of royalty, he clothed himself with greater majesty—above all, by taking twelve lictors to attend him, but also in regard to his other appointments. Some are of opinion that he was influenced in his choice of that number by that of the birds which had foretold that sovereign power should be his when the auguries were taken. I myself am not indisposed to follow the opinion of those, who are inclined to believe that it was from the neighbouring Etruscans—from whom the curule chair and purple-bordered toga were borrowed—that the apparitors of this class, as well as the number itself, were introduced; and that the Etruscans employed such a number because, as their king was elected from twelve states in common, each state assigned him one lictor.

In the meantime, the city was enlarged by taking in various plots of ground for the erection of buildings, while they built rather in the hope of an increased population in the future, than in view of the actual number of the inhabitants of the city at that time. Next, that the size of the city might not be without efficiency, in order to increase the population, following the ancient policy of founders of cities, who, by bringing together to their side a mean and ignoble multitude, were in the habit of falsely asserting that an offspring was born to them from the earth, he opened as a sanctuary the place which, now inclosed, is known as the "two groves," and which people come upon when descending from the Capitol. Thither, a crowd of all classes from the neighbouring peoples, without distinction, whether freemen or slaves, eager for change, flocked for refuge, and therein lay the foundation of the city's strength, corresponding to the commencement of its enlargement. Having now no reason to be dissatisfied with his strength, he next instituted a standing council to direct that strength. He created one hundred senators, either because that number was sufficient, or because there were only one hundred who could be so elected. Anyhow they were called fathers, by way of respect, and their descendants patricians.

By this time the Roman state was so powerful, that it was a match for any of the neighbouring states in war. But owing to the scarcity of women its greatness was not likely to outlast the existing generation, seeing that the Romans had no hope of issue at home, and they did not intermarry with their neighbours. So then, by the advice of the senators, Romulus sent around ambassadors to the neighbouring states, to solicit an alliance and the right of intermarriage for his new subjects, saying that cities, like everything else, rose from the humblest beginnings; next, that those which the gods and their own merits assisted, gained for themselves great power and high renown; that he knew full well that the gods had aided the first beginnings of Rome and that merit on their part would not be wanting; therefore, as men, let them not be reluctant to mix their blood and stock with men. The embassy nowhere obtained a favourable hearing. But, although the neighbouring peoples treated it with such contempt, yet at the same time they dreaded the growth of such a mighty power in their midst to the danger of themselves and of their posterity. In most cases when they were dismissed they were asked the question, whether they had opened a sanctuary for women also: for that in that way only could they obtain suitable matches.

The Roman youths were bitterly indignant at this, and the matter began unmistakably to point to open violence. Romulus in order to provide a fitting opportunity and place for this, dissembling his resentment, with this purpose in view, instituted games to be solemnized every year in honour of Neptunus Equester, which he called Consualia. He then ordered the show to be proclaimed among the neighbouring peoples; and the Romans prepared to solemnize it with all the pomp with which they were then acquainted or were able to exhibit, in order to make the spectacle famous, and an object of expectation. Great numbers assembled, being also desirous of seeing the new city, especially all the nearest peoples, the Caeninenses, Crustumini, and Antemnates. The entire Sabine population attended with their wives and children. They were hospitably invited to the different houses; and, when they saw the position of the city, its fortified walls, and how crowded with houses it was, they were astonished that the power of Rome had increased so rapidly.

When the time of the show arrived, and their eyes and minds alike were intent upon it, then, according to preconcerted arrangement, a disturbance was made, and, at a given signal, the Roman youths rushed in different directions to carry off the unmarried women. A great number were carried off at hap-hazard, by those into whose hands they severally fell. Some of the common people, to whom the task had been assigned, conveyed to their homes certain women of surpassing beauty, who were destined for the leading senators. They say that one, far distinguished beyond the rest in form and beauty, was carried off by the party of a certain Talassius, and that, when several people wanted to know to whom they were carrying her, a cry was raised from time to time, to prevent her being molested, that she was being carried to Talassius, and that from this the word was used in connection with marriages. The festival being disturbed by the alarm thus caused, the sorrowing parents of the maidens retired, complaining of the violated compact of hospitality, and invoking the god, to whose solemn festival and games they had come, having been deceived by the pretence of religion and good faith.

Nor did the maidens entertain better hopes for themselves, or feel less indignation. Romulus, however, went about in person and pointed out that what had happened was due to the pride of their fathers, in that they had refused the privilege of intermarriage to their neighbours; but that, notwithstanding, they would be lawfully wedded, and enjoy a share of all their possessions and civil rights, and—a thing dearer than all else to the human race—the society of their common children: only let them calm their angry feelings, and bestow their affections on those on whom fortune had bestowed their bodies. Esteem (said he) often arose subsequent to wrong: and they would find them better husbands for the reason that each of them would endeavour, to the utmost of his power, after having discharged, as far as his part was concerned, the duty of a husband, to quiet the longing for country and parents. To this the blandishments of the husbands were added, who excused what had been done on the plea of passion and love, a form of entreaty that works most successfully upon the feelings of women.

By this time the minds of the maidens were considerably soothed, but their parents, especially by putting on the garb of mourning, and by their tears and complaints, stirred up the neighbouring states. Nor did they confine their feelings of indignation to their own home only, but they flocked from all quarters to Titus Tatius, king of the Sabines, and embassies crowded thither, because the name of Tatius was held in the greatest esteem in those quarters. The Caeninenses, Crustumini, and Antemnates were the people who were chiefly affected by the outrage. As Tatius and the Sabines appeared to them to be acting in too dilatory a manner, these three peoples by mutual agreement among themselves made preparations for war unaided. However, not even the Crustumini and Antemnates bestirred themselves with sufficient activity to satisfy the hot-headedness and anger of the Caeninenses: accordingly the people of Caenina, unaided, themselves attacked the Roman territory. But Romulus with his army met them while they were ravaging the country in straggling parties, and in a trifling engagement convinced them that anger unaccompanied by strength is fruitless. He routed their army and put it to flight, followed in pursuit of it when routed, cut down their king in battle and stripped him of his armour, and, having slain the enemy's leader, took the city at the first assault.

Then, having led back his victorious army, being a man both distinguished for his achievements, and one equally skilful at putting them in the most favourable light, he ascended the Capitol, carrying suspended on a portable frame, cleverly contrived for that purpose, the spoils of the enemy's general, whom he had slain. There, having laid them down at the foot of an oak held sacred by the shepherds, at the same time that he presented the offering, he marked out the boundaries for a temple of Jupiter, and bestowed a surname on the god. "Jupiter Feretrius," said he, "I, King Romulus, victorious over my foes, offer to thee these royal arms, and dedicate to thee a temple within those quarters, which I have just now marked out in my mind, to be a resting-place for the *spolia opima*, which posterity, following my example, shall bring hither on slaying the kings or generals of the enemy." This is the origin of that temple, the first that was ever consecrated at Rome. It was afterward the will of the gods that neither the utterances of the founder of the temple, in which he solemnly declared that his posterity would bring such spoils thither, should be spoken in vain, and that the honour of the offering should not be rendered common owing to the number of those who enjoyed it. In the course of so many years and so many wars the *spolia opima* were only twice gained: so rare has been the successful attainment of this honour.

Translated by D. Spillan and Cyrus Edmonds.

Hannibal Crosses the Alps

Livy, *History of Rome* 11.32-38

The Carthaginian general Hamilcar demanded that his son Hannibal swear an oath never to befriend the Romans. Hannibal would not disappoint: He matured into a formidable enemy of Rome, against which he launched the Second Punic War. His plan was to invade Italy from the north. He left from Carthago Nova (Carthagena) in Spain, crossed the Pyrenees, and traveled through southern France until reaching the foothills of the Alps. Awestruck by the daunting mountain peaks and seemingly endless drifts of snow, the soldiers' anguish was palpable. After all, they mostly originated from the arid desert lands of North Africa and Spain. But the indigenous peoples had their own anxieties to contend with too, such as the terrific sight of Hannibal's advancing army with never-before-seen gigantic monsters leading the charge—the conqueror's imposing elephants. It is 218 BC.

"Though the elephants were driven through steep and narrow roads with great loss of time, yet wherever they went they rendered the army safe from the enemy, because men unacquainted with such animals were afraid of approaching too nearly."

From the Druentia,[3] by a road that lay principally through plains, Hannibal arrived at the Alps without molestation from the Gauls that inhabit those regions. Then, though the scene had been previously anticipated from report, (by which uncertainties are wont to be exaggerated,) yet the height of the mountains when viewed so near, and the snows almost mingling with the sky, the shapeless huts situated on the cliffs, the cattle and beasts of burden withered by the cold, the men unshorn and wildly dressed, all things, animate and inanimate, stiffened with frost, and other objects more terrible to be seen than described, renewed their alarm.

To them, marching up the first acclivities, the mountaineers appeared occupying the heights over head; who, if they had occupied the more concealed valleys, might, by rushing out suddenly to the attack, have occasioned great flight and havoc. Hannibal orders them to halt, and having sent forward Gauls to view the ground, when he found there was no passage that way, he pitches his camp in the widest valley he could find, among places all rugged and precipitous. Then, having learned from the same Gauls, when they had mixed in conversation with the mountaineers, from whom they differed little in language and manners, that the pass was only beset during the day, and that at night each withdrew to his own dwelling, he advanced at the dawn to the heights, as if designing openly and by day to force his way through the defile. The day then being passed in feigning a different attempt from that which was in preparation, when they had fortified the camp in the same place where they had halted, as soon as he perceived that the mountaineers had descended from the heights, and that the guards were withdrawn, having lighted for show a greater number of fires than was proportioned to the number that remained, and having left the baggage in the camp, with the cavalry and the principal part of the infantry, he himself with a party of light-armed, consisting of all the most courageous of his troops, rapidly cleared the defile, and took post on those very heights which the enemy had occupied.

At dawn of light the next day the camp broke up, and the rest of the army began to move forward. The mountaineers, on a signal being given, were now assembling from their forts to their usual station, when they suddenly behold part of the enemy overhanging them from above, in possession of their former position, and the others passing along the road. Both these objects, presented at the same time to the eye and the mind, made them stand motionless for a little while; but when they afterwards saw the confusion in the pass, and that the marching body was thrown into disorder by the tumult which itself created, principally from the horses being terrified, thinking that whatever terror they added would suffice for the destruction of the enemy, they scramble along the dangerous rocks, as being accustomed alike to pathless and circuitous ways. Then indeed the Carthaginians were opposed at once by the enemy and by the difficulties of the ground; and each striving to escape first from the danger, there was more fighting among themselves than with their opponents. The horses in particular created danger in the lines, which, being terrified by the discordant clamours which the groves and re-echoing valleys augmented, fell into confusion; and if by chance struck or wounded, they were so dismayed that they occasioned a great loss both of men and baggage of every description; and as the pass on both sides was broken and precipitous, this tumult threw many down to an immense depth, some even of the armed men; but the beasts of burden, with their loads, were rolled down like the fall of some vast fabric.

Though these disasters were shocking to view, Hannibal however kept his place for a little, and kept his men together, lest he might augment the tumult and disorder; but afterwards, when he saw the line broken, and that there was danger that he should bring over his army, preserved to no purpose if deprived of their baggage, he hastened down from the higher ground; and though he had routed the enemy by the first onset alone, he at the same time increased the disorder in his own army. But that tumult was composed in a moment, after the roads were cleared by the flight of the mountaineers; and presently the whole army was conducted through, not only without being disturbed, but almost in silence. He then took a fortified place, which was the capital of that district, and the little villages that lay around it, and fed his army for three days with the corn and cattle he had taken; and during these three days, as the soldiers were neither obstructed by the mountaineers, who had been daunted by the first engagement, nor yet much by the ground, he made considerable way.

He then came to another state, abounding, for a mountainous country, with inhabitants; where he was nearly overcome, not by open war, but by his own arts of treachery and ambuscade. Some old men, governors of forts, came as deputies to the Carthaginian, professing, "that having been warned by the useful example of the calamities of others, they wished rather to experience the friendship than the hostilities of the Carthaginians: they would, therefore, obediently execute his commands, and begged that he would accept of a supply of provisions, guides of his march, and hostages for the sincerity of their promises." Hannibal, when he had answered them in a friendly manner, thinking that they should neither be rashly trusted nor yet rejected, lest if repulsed they might openly become enemies, having received the hostages whom they proffered, and made use of the provisions which they of their own accord brought down to the road, follows their guides, by no means as among a people with whom he was at peace, but with his line of march in close order. The elephants and cavalry formed the van of the marching body; he himself, examining every thing around, and intent on every circumstance, followed with the choicest of the infantry.

When they came into a narrower pass, lying on one side beneath an overhanging eminence, the barbarians, rising at once on all sides from their ambush, assail them in front and rear, both at close quarters and from a distance, and roll down huge stones on the army. The most numerous body of men pressed on the rear; against whom the infantry, facing about and directing their attack, made it very obvious, that had not the rear of the army been well supported, a great loss must have been sustained in that pass. Even as it was they came to the extremity of danger, and almost to destruction: for while Hannibal hesitates to lead down his division into the defile, because, though he himself was a protection to the cavalry, lie had not in the same way left any aid to the infantry in the rear; the mountaineers, charging obliquely, and on having broken through the middle of the army, took possession of the road; and one night was spent by Hannibal without his cavalry and baggage.

Next day, the barbarians running in to the attack between the two divisions less vigorously, the forces were re-united, and the defile passed, not without loss, but yet with a greater destruction of beasts of burden than of men. From that time the mountaineers fell upon them in smaller parties, more like an attack of robbers than war, sometimes on the van, sometimes on the rear, according as the ground afforded them advantage, or stragglers advancing or loitering gave them an opportunity. Though the elephants were driven through steep and narrow roads with great loss of time, yet wherever they went they rendered the army safe from the enemy, because men unacquainted with such animals were afraid of approaching too nearly. On the ninth day they came to a summit of the Alps, chiefly through places trackless; and after many mistakes of their way, which were caused either by the treachery of the guides, or, when they were not trusted, by entering valleys at random, on their own conjectures of the route. For two days they remained encamped on the summit; and rest was given to the soldiers, exhausted with toil and fighting: and several beasts of burden, which had fallen down among the rocks, by following the track of the army arrived at the camp.

A fall of snow, it being now the season of the setting of the constellation of the Pleiades, caused great fear to the soldiers, already worn out with weariness of so many hardships. On the standards being moved forward at daybreak, when the army proceeded slowly over all places entirely blocked up with snow, and languor and despair strongly appeared in the countenances of all, Hannibal, having advanced before the standards, and ordered the soldiers to halt on a certain eminence, whence there was a prospect far and wide, points out to them Italy and the plains of the Po, extending themselves beneath the Alpine mountains; and said "that they were now surmounting not only the ramparts of Italy, but also of the city of Rome; that the rest of the journey would be smooth and down-hill; that after one, or, at most, a second battle, they would have the citadel and capital of Italy in their power and possession." The army then began to advance, the enemy now making no attempts beyond petty thefts, as opportunity offered. But the journey proved much more difficult than it had been in the ascent, as the declivity of the Alps being generally shorter on the side of Italy is consequently steeper; for nearly all the road was precipitous, narrow, and slippery, so that neither those who made the least stumble could prevent themselves from falling, nor, when fallen, remain in the same place, but rolled, both men and beasts of burden, one upon another.

They then came to a rock much more narrow, and formed of such perpendicular ledges, that a light-armed soldier, carefully making the attempt, and clinging with his hands to the bushes and roots around, could with difficulty lower himself down. The ground, even before very steep by nature, had been broken by a recent falling away of the earth into a precipice of nearly a thousand feet in depth. Here when the cavalry had halted, as if at the end of their journey, it is announced to Hannibal, wondering what obstructed the march that the rock was impassable. Having then gone himself to view the place, it seemed clear to him that he must lead his army round it, by however great a circuit, through the pathless and untrodden regions around. But this route also proved impracticable; for while the new snow of a moderate depth remained on the old, which had not been removed, their footsteps were planted with ease as they walked upon the new snow, which was soft and not too deep; but when it was dissolved by the trampling of so many men and beasts of burden, they then walked on the bare ice below, and through the dirty fluid formed by the melting snow. Here there was a wretched struggle, both on account of the slippery ice not affording any hold to the step, and giving way beneath the foot more readily by reason of the slope; and whether they assisted themselves in rising by their hands or their knees, their supports themselves giving way, they would stumble again; nor were there any stumps or roots near; by pressing against which, one might with hand or foot support himself; so that they only floundered on the smooth ice and amid the melted snow. The beasts of burden sometimes also went into this lower ice by merely treading upon it, at others they broke it completely through, by the violence with which they struck in their hoofs in their struggling, so that most of them, as if taken in a trap, stuck in the hardened and deeply frozen ice.

At length, after the men and beasts of burden had been fatigued to no purpose, the camp was pitched on the summit, the ground being cleared for that purpose with great difficulty, so much snow was there to be dug out and carried away. The soldiers being then set to make a way down the cliff by which alone a passage could be effected, and it being necessary that they should cut through the rocks, having felled and lopped a number of large trees which grew around, they make a huge pile of timber; and as soon as a strong wind fit for exciting the flames arose, they set fire to it, and, pouring vinegar on the heated stones, they render them soft and crumbling. They then open a way with iron instruments through the rock thus heated by the fire, and soften its declivities by gentle windings, so that not only the beasts of burden, but also the elephants could be led down it. Four days were spent about this rock, the beasts nearly perishing through hunger: for the summits of the mountains are for the most part bare, and if there is any pasture the snows bury it. The lower parts contain valleys, and some sunny hills, and rivulets flowing beside woods, and scenes more worthy of the abode of man. There the beasts of burden were sent out to pasture, and rest given for three days to the men, fatigued with forming the passage. They then descended into the plains, the country and the dispositions of the inhabitants being now less rugged.

In this manner chiefly they came to Italy in the fifth month (as some authors relate) after leaving New Carthage, having crossed the Alps in fifteen days. What number of forces Hannibal had when he had passed into Italy is by no means agreed upon by authors. Those who state them at the highest, make mention of a hundred thousand foot and twenty thousand horse; those who state them at the lowest, of twenty thousand foot and six thousand horse. Lucius Cincius Alimentus, who relates that he was made prisoner by Hannibal, would influence me most as an authority, did he not confound the number by adding the Gauls and Ligurians. Including these, (who, it is more probable, flocked to him afterwards, and so some authors assert,) he says, that eighty thousand foot and ten thousand horse were brought into Italy; and that he had heard from Hannibal himself, that after crossing the Rhone he had lost thirty-six thousand men, and an immense number of horses, and other beasts of burden, among the Taurini, the next nation to the Gauls, as he descended into Italy.

Translated by D. Spillan and Cyrus Edmonds.

TIBULLUS

c. 55 - 19 BC

Albius Tibullus was a country gentleman born at Gabii near Rome. He counted among his friends Valerius Messala Corvinus, an earlier student peer of Horace. Messala is best known for his pacification of Aquitany (in modern France) and Syria. Playing the guardian of letters, Messala had surrounded himself with a few poets—such as Lygdamus (the brother of Ovid), the woman poet Sulpicia, and, of course, Tibullus, whose works today are found in the Corpus Tibullianum.

Tibullus followed his mentor Messala in the East, where he fell ill, and then in Gaul, where he acquired an extreme distaste for weapons. He then dedicated himself entirely to his passions (and lovers) with an intention to "make love, not war."

He created a new perspective on love in the Western world: He sang about his affair first with Delia, which was thwarted by her marriage to another man; then with Glycera; and next with Nemesis, a courtesan who was thoroughly unimpressed with his talent. He also experienced homosexual love with a certain Marathus, a handsome young man who was otherwise drawn to the seductive Pholoe. Tibullus further wrote about more chaste and melancholic kinds of love: the love for rural life (his own) and for conjugal happiness (of others).

Tibullus ranks with Virgil and Horace among the pioneers of pastoral poetry, but without the moral underpinning of the latter poets. Even as he celebrates the quietude and charm of rustic life, Cupid's arrows continue to strike him.

The Simple Life
Tibullus 1.1

In this elegy, the first poem of his collection, Tibullus champions the role of a poet leading a simple and tranquil life in the country, far from wealth that stirs envy, and far from war and its tragedies. After all, what worth is gold compared to a life of moderate work and abundant food in the company of one's beloved wife? Tibullus' outlook reminds one of Horace's later proclamation: "Carpe diem" *("Seize the day"). The poem is dedicated to Delia with whom Tibullus had a passionate but tormented affair.*

"If I might hold my Delia to my side,
The bare ground were a happier bed
Than theirs who, on a couch of silken pride,
Must mourn for love long dead."

Give, if thou wilt, for gold a life of toil!
Let endless acres claim thy care!
While sounds of war thy fearful slumbers spoil,
And far-off trumpets scare!

To me my poverty brings tranquil hours;
My lowly hearth-stone cheerly shines;
My modest garden bears me fruit and flowers,
And plenteous native wines.

I set my tender vines with timely skill,
Or pluck large apples from the bough;
Or goad my lazy steers to work my will,
Or guide my own rude plough.

Full tenderly upon my breast I bear
A lamb or small kid gone astray;
And yearly worship with my swains prepare,
The shepherd's ancient way.

I love those rude shrines in a lonely field
Where rustic faith the god reveres,

Or flower-crowned cross-road mile-stones, half concealed
  By gifts of travellers.

Whatever fruit the kindly seasons show,
  Due tribute to our gods I pour;
O'er Ceres' brows the tasseled wheat I throw,
  Or wreathe her temple door.

My plenteous orchards fear no pelf or harm,
  By red Priapus sentinelled;
By his huge sickle's formidable charm
  The bird thieves are dispelled.

With offerings at my hearth, and faithful fires,
  My Lares I revere: not now
As when with greater gifts my wealthier sires
  Performed the hallowing vow.

No herds have I like theirs: I only bring
  One white lamb from my little fold,
While my few bondmen at the altar sing
  Our harvest anthems old.
Gods of my hearth! ye never learned to slight
  A poor man's gift. My bowls of clay
To ye are hallowed by the cleansing rite,
  The best, most ancient way.

If from my sheep the thief, the wolf, be driven,
  If fatter flocks allure them more,
To me the riches to my fathers given
  Kind Heaven need not restore.

My small, sure crop contents me; and the storm
  That pelts my thatch breaks not my rest,
While to my heart I clasp the beauteous form
  Of her it loves the best.

My simple cot brings such secure repose,
  When so companioned I can lie,
That winds of winter and the whirling snows
  Sing me soft lullaby.

This lot be mine! I envy not their gold
  Who rove the furious ocean foam:
A frugal life will all my pleasures hold,
  If love be mine, and home.

Enough I travel, if I steal away
  To sleep at noon-tide by the flow
Of some cool stream. Could India's jewels pay
  For longer absence? No!

Let great Messala vanquish land and sea,
  And deck with spoils his golden hall!
I am myself a conquest, and must be
  My Delia's captive thrall.

Be Delia mine, and Fame may flout and scorn,
  Or brand me with the sluggard's name!
With cheerful hands I'll plant my upland corn,
  And live to laugh at Fame.

If I might hold my Delia to my side,
  The bare ground were a happier bed
Than theirs who, on a couch of silken pride,
  Must mourn for love long dead.
Gilt couch, soft down, slow fountains murmuring song—
  These bring no peace. Befooled by words
Was he who, when in love a victor strong,
  Left it for spoils and swords.

For such let sad Cilicia's captives bleed,
  Her citadels his legions hold!
And let him stride his swift, triumphal steed,
  In silvered robes or gold!

These eyes of mine would look on only thee
  In that last hour when light shall fail.
Embrace me, dear, in death! Let thy hand be
  In my cold fingers pale!

With thine own arms my lifeless body lay
  On that cold couch so soon on fire!

Give thy last kisses to my grateful clay,
  And weep beside my pyre!

And weep! Ah, me! Thy heart will wear no steel
  Nor be stone-cold that rueful day:
Thy faithful grief may all true lovers feel
  Nor tearless turn away!

Yet ask I not that thou shouldst vex my shade
  With cheek all wan and blighted brow:
But, O, to-day be love's full tribute paid,
  While the swift Fates allow.

Soon Death, with shadow-mantled head, will come,
  Soon palsied age will creep our way,
Bidding love's flatteries at last be dumb,
  Unfit for old and gray.

But light-winged Venus still is smiling fair:
  By night or noon we heed her call;
To pound on midnight doors I still may dare,
  Or brave for love a brawl.

I am a soldier and a captain good
  In love's campaign, and calmly yield
To all who hunger after wounds and blood,
  War's trumpet-echoing field.
Ye toils and triumphs unto glory dear!
  Ye riches home from conquest borne!
If my small fields their wonted harvest bear,
  Both wealth and want I scorn!

Translated by Theodore C. Williams.

War is a Crime
Tibullus 1.10

The message in this passage is vintage Tibullus: One must enjoy life day by day, because death can strike at any time. The poet deplores the murderous war and invokes peace with all his poetic genius. Tibullus was not the only Roman to hold this view after years of civil wars that ravaged Italy. The causes of the conflicts? Cupidity. Gold. Luxury. There was no war when people appreciated a simple and hardy life in a countryside that provides in abundance fruits of the fields and pleasures of the vine.

"Gold makes our crime. No need for plundering war,
When bowls of beech-wood held the frugal feast."

Whoe'er first forged the terror-striking sword,
His own fierce heart had tempered like its blade.
What slaughter followed! Ah! what conflict wild!
What swifter journeys unto darksome death!
But blame not him! Ourselves have madly turned
On one another's breasts that cunning edge
Wherewith he meant mere blood of beast to spill.

Gold makes our crime. No need for plundering war,
When bowls of beech-wood held the frugal feast.
No citadel was seen nor moated wall;
The shepherd chief led home his motley flock,
And slumbered free from care. Would I had lived
In that good, golden time; nor e'er had known
A mob in arms arrayed; nor felt my heart
Throb to the trumpet's call! Now to the wars
I must away, where haply some chance foe
Bears now the blade my naked side shall feel.
Save me, dear Lares of my hearth and home!
Ye oft my childish steps did guard and bless,
As timidly beneath your seat they strayed.
Deem it no shame that hewn of ancient oak
Your simple emblems in my dwelling stand!
For so the pious generations gone

Revered your powers, and with offerings rude
To rough-hewn gods in narrow-built abodes,
Lived beautiful and honorable lives.
Did they not bring to crown your hallowed brows
Garlands of ripest corn, or pour new wine
In pure libation on the thirsty ground?
Oft on some votive day the father brought
The consecrated loaf, and close behind
His little daughter in her virgin palm
Bore honey bright as gold. O powers benign!
To ye once more a faithful servant prays
For safety! Let the deadly brazen spear
Pass harmless o'er my head! and I will slay
For sacrifice, with many a thankful song,
A swine and all her brood, while I, the priest,
Bearing the votive basket myrtle-bound,
Walk clothed in white, with myrtle in my hair.

Grant me but this! and he who can may prove
Mighty in arms and by the grace of Mars
Lay chieftains low; and let him tell the tale
To me who drink his health, while on the board
His wine-dipped finger draws, line after line,
Just how his trenches ranged! What madness dire
Bids men go foraging for death in war?
Our death is always near, and hour by hour,
With soundless step a little nearer draws.

What harvest down below, or vineyard green?
There Cerberus howls, and o'er the Stygian flood
The dark ship goes; while on the clouded shore
With hollow cheek and tresses lustreless,
Wanders the ghostly throng. O happier far
Some white-haired sire, among his children dear,
Beneath a lowly thatch! His sturdy son
Shepherds the young rams; he, his gentle ewes;
And oft at eve, his willing labor done,
His careful wife his weary limbs will bathe
From a full, steaming bowl. Such lot be mine!
So let this head grow gray, while I shall tell,
Repeating oft, the deeds of long ago!

Then may long Peace my country's harvests bless!
Till then, let Peace on all our fields abide!
Bright-vestured Peace, who first beneath their yoke
Led oxen in the plough, who first the vine
Did nourish tenderly, and chose good grapes,
That rare old wine may pass from sire to son!
Peace! who doth keep the plow and harrow bright,
While rust on some forgotten shelf devours
The cruel soldier's useless sword and shield.
From peaceful holiday with mirth and wine
The rustic, not half sober, driveth home
With wife and weans upon the lumbering wain.

But wars by Venus kindled ne'er have done;
The vanquished lass, with tresses rudely torn,
Of doors broke down, and smitten cheek complains;
And he, her victor-lover, weeps to see
How strong were his wild hands. But mocking Love
Teaches more angry words, and while they rave,
Sits with a smile between! O heart of stone!
O iron heart! that could thy sweetheart strike!
Ye gods avenge her! Is it not enough
To tear her soft robe from her limbs away,
And loose her knotted hair?—Enough, indeed,
To move her tears! Thrice happy is the wight
Whose frown some lovely mistress weeps to see!
But he who gives her blows!—Go, let him bear
A sword and spear! In exile let him be
From Venus' mild domain! Come blessed Peace!
Come, holding forth thy blade of ripened corn!
Fill thy large lap with mellow fruits and fair!

Translated by Theodore C. Williams.

Riches Are Useless
Tibullus 3.3

Tibullus addresses Neaera in this ode. She has left him, and he implores her to return—Tibullus' love affairs were rarely happy. He implores Juno, the goddess of marriage, and Venus to help him regain Neaera's love. His despair would otherwise lead him to death.

"With thee, Neaera, poverty looks fair,
And lacking thee, a kingdom were in vain."

'Tis vain to plague the skies with eager prayer,
And offer incense with thy votive song,
If only thou dost ask for marbles fair,
To deck thy palace for the gazing throng.

Not wider fields my oxen to employ,
Nor flowing harvests and abundant land,
I ask of heaven; but for a long life's joy
With thee, and in old age to clasp thy hand.

If when my season of sweet light is o'er,
I, carrying nothing, unto Charon yield,[1]
What profits me a ponderous golden store,
Or that a thousand yoke must plough my field?

What if proud Phrygian columns fill my halls,
Taenarian, Carystian, and the rest,[2]
Or branching groves adorn my spacious walls,
Or golden roof, or floor with marbles dressed?

What pleasure in rare Erythraean dyes,
Or purple pride of Sidon and of Tyre,
Or all that can solicit envious eyes,
And which the mob of fools so well admire?

Wealth has no power to lift life's load of care,
Or free man's lot from Fortune's fatal chain;

With thee, Neaera, poverty looks fair,
  And lacking thee, a kingdom were in vain.
O golden day that shall at last restore
  My lost love to my arms! O blest indeed,
And worthy to be hallowed evermore!
  May some kind god my long petition heed!

No! not dominion, nor Pactolian stream,
  Nor all the riches the wide world can give!
These other men may ask. My fondest dream
  Is, poor but free, with my true wife to live.

Saturnian Juno, to all nuptials kind,
  Receive with grace my ever-anxious vow!
Come, Venus, wafted by the Cyprian wind,
  And from thy car of shell smile on me now!

But if the mournful sisters, by whose hands
  Our threads of life are spun, refuse me all—
May Pluto bid me to his dreary lands,
  Where those wide rivers through the darkness fall!

Translated by Theodore C. Williams.

A Dream from Phoebus
Tibullus 3.4

The plea of Tibullus to Neaera in the previous elegy fails. In this passage, Apollo appears in the poet's dream to announce that she is leaving him for another man. Good fortune to any poet or god who crosses the path of such a whimsical woman!

"The gods tell truth."

Be kinder, gods! Let not the dreams come true
Which last night's cruel slumber bade believe!
Begone! your vain, delusive spells undo,
Nor ask me to receive!

The gods tell truth. With truth the Tuscan seer
In entrails dark a book of fate may find;
But dreams are folly and with fruitless fear
Address the trembling mind.

Although mankind, against night's dark surprise
With sprinkled meal or salt ward off the ill,
And often turn deaf ear to prophets wise,
While dreams deceive them still;—

May bright Lucina[3] my foreboding mind
From such vain terrors of the night redeem,
For in my soul no deed of guilt I find,
Nor do my lips blaspheme.

Now had the Night upon her ebon wain
Passed o'er the upper sky, and dipped a wheel
In the blue sea: but Sleep, the friend of pain,
Refused my sense to seal.

Sleep stands defeated at the house of care:
And only when from purpled orient skies
Peered Phoebus forth, did tardy slumber bear
Down on my weary eyes.

Then seemed a youth with holy laurel crowned
 To fill my door: a wight so wondrous rare
Was not in all the vanished ages found.
 No marble half so fair!

Adown his neck, with myrtle-buds inwove
 And Syrian dews, his unshorn tresses flow:
White is he as the moon in heaven above,
 But rose is blent with snow.

Like that soft blush on face of virgin fair
 Led to her husband; or as maidens twine
Lilies in amaranth; or Autumn's air
 Tinges the apples fine.

A long, loose mantle to his ankles played,—
 Such vesture did his lucent shape enfold:
His left hand bore the vocal lyre, all made
 Of gleaming shell and gold.

He smote its strings with ivory instrument,
 And words auspicious tuned his heavenly tongue;
Then, while his hands and voice concording blent,
 These sad, sweet words he sung:

"Hail, blest of Heaven! For a poet divine
 Phoebus and Bacchus and the Muses bless.
But Bacchus and the skilful Sisters nine
 No prophecies possess.

"But of what Fate ordains for times to be
 Jove gave me vision. Therefore, minstrel dear!
Receive what my unerring lips decree!
 The Cynthian wisdom hear![4]

"She whom thy love holds dearer than sweet child
 Is to a mother's breast, or virgin soft
To longing lover, she for whom thy wild
 Prayers vex high Heaven so oft,

"Who worries thee each day, and vainly fills

Dark-mantled sleep with visions that beguile,
Lovely Neaera, theme of all thy quills,
Now elsewhere gives her smile.

"For sighs not thine her fickle passions flame:
For thy chaste house Neaera has no care.
O cruel tribe! O woman, faithless name!
Curse on the false and fair!

"But woo her still! For mutability
Is woman's soul. Fond vows may yet prevail,
Fierce love bears well a woman's cruelty,
Nor at the lash will quail.

"That I did feed Admetus' heifers white
Is no light tale. Upon the lyric string
Nor more could I my joyful notes indite,
Nor with sweet concord sing.

"On oaten pipe I sued the woodland Muse—
I, of Latona and the Thunderer son!
Thou knowst not what love is, if thou refuse
T'endure a cruel one.

"Go, then, and ply her with persuasive woe!
Soft supplications the hard heart subdue.
Then, if my oracles the future know,
Give her this message true:

"'The God whose seat is Delos' marble isle,
Declares this marriage happy and secure.
It has Apollo's own auspicious smile.
Cast off that rival wooer!'"

He spoke: dull slumber from my body fell.
Can I believe such perils round me fold?
That such discordant vows thy tongue can tell?
Thy heart in guilt so bold?
Thou wert not gendered by the Pontic Sea,
Nor where Chimaera's lips fierce flame out-pour,
Nor of that dog with tongues and foreheads three,

His back all snakes and gore;

Nor out of Scylla's whelp-engirdled womb;
Nor wert thou of fell lioness the child;
Nor was thy cradle Scythia's forest-gloom,
Nor Syrtis' sandy wild.[5]
No, but thy home was human! round its fire
Sate creatures lovable: of all her kind
Thy mother was the mildest, and thy sire
Showed a most friendly mind.

May Heaven in these bad dreams good omen show,
And bid warm south-winds to oblivion blow!

Translated by Theodore C. Williams.

A Farewell Toast
Tibullus 3.6

Tibullus proclaimed earlier that he would rather die than lose Neaera. In the end, he prefers drowning his misery in wine! He tries to be a good sport and wishes his mistress the best; in truth, however, he is furious about her perjury, infidelity, and treachery. Tibullus decidedly needs a lot, a whole lot of wine, to forget her.

"Come radiant Bacchus!... Let love in wine be drowned!"

Come radiant Bacchus! With the hallowed leaf
  Of grape and ivy be thy forehead crowned!
For thou canst chase away or cure my grief—
  Let love in wine be drowned!

Dear bearer of my cup, come, brim it o'er!
  Pour forth unstinted our Falernian wine!
Care's cruel brood is gone; I toil no more,
  If Phoebus o'er me shine.

Dear, jovial friends, let not a lip be dry!
  Drink as I drink, and every toast obey!
And him who will not with my wine-cup vie,
  May some false lass betray!

This god makes all men rich. He tames proud souls,
  And bids them by a woman's hand be chained;
Armenian tigresses his power controls,
  And lions tawny-maned.

That love-god is as strong; but I delight
  In Bacchus rather. Fill our cups once more!
Just and benign is he, if mortal wight
  Him and his vines adore!

But, O! he rages, if his gift ye spurn.
  Drink, if ye dare not a god's anger brave!
How fierce his stroke, let temperate fellows learn

Of Pentheus' gory grave.[6]

Away such fear! Rather may some fierce stroke
On that false beauty fall!—O frightful prayer!
O, I am mad! O may my curse be broke,
And melt in misty air!

For, O Neaera, though I am forgot,
I ask all gods to bless thee, every one.
Back to my cups I go. This wine has brought
After long storms, the sun.

Alas! How hard to masque dull grief in joy!
A sad heart's jest—what bitter mockery!
With vain deceit my laughing lips employ
Loud mirth that is a lie.

But why complain and moan? O wretched me!
When will my lagging sorrows haste and go?
Delightful Bacchus at his mystery
Forbids these words of woe.

Once, by the wave, lone Ariadne pale,
Abandoned of false Theseus, weeping stood:—
Our wise Catullus tells the doleful tale
Of love's ingratitude.[7]

Take warning friends! How fortunate is he,
Who learns of others' loss his own to shun!
Trust not caressing arms and sighs, nor be
By flatteries undone!

Though by her own sweet eyes her oath she swear,
By solemn Juno, or by Venus gay,
At oaths of love Jove laughs, and bids the air
Waft the light things away.

It is but folly, then, to fume and fret,
If one light lass that old deception wrought;
O that I too might evermore forget
To speak my heart's true thought!

O that my long, long nights brought peace and thee!
  That nought but thee my waking eyes did fill!
Thou wert most false and cruel, woe is me!
  False! But I love thee still.
How well fresh water mixes with old wine!
  Bacchus loves water-nymphs. Bring water, boy!
What care I where she sleeps? This night of mine
  Shall I in sighs employ?

Make the cup strong, I tell you! Stronger there!
  Wine only! While the Syrian balm o'er-flows!
Long would I revel with anointed hair,
  And wear this wreath of rose.

Translated by Theodore C. Williams.

OVID
43 BC - AD 17

Montaigne reflects: "The first taste I had for books came from the pleasure of reading the fables of Ovid's Metamorphoses." *Chaucer also paid tribute to Ovid, whom he refers to as the "Venus' Clerk." Born at Sulmo in the Abruzzi (a mountainous region in central Italy) on 20 March 43 BC, Publius Ovidius Naso was the youngest Augustan poet and knew only peace. He quickly lost interest in political existence to benefit from a high life devoted to eroticism and poetry. For obscure reasons, he was exiled in AD 8 to Romania where he died in sorrow.*

His work is imposing both in breadth and in diversity and is divided into three main groups. The first group gathers the Heroines, *which he began writing at 18 years of age; these are letters composed by mythological heroines to their lovers or husbands. The group also contains the* Loves, *in which, in a playful tone, Ovid celebrates Venus. The second group includes the* Fasti*—a calendar of pagan festivals— and the* Metamorphoses, *which fills 14 books devoted to the origins of the world and to the fables about the transformation of human beings into animals, plants, or rocks. The third group opens with his exile. Except for the heinous attack* Against Ibis, *the poet then devoted himself to elegy: He composed the* Sorrows *and the* Epistles from Pontus *(the Pontus Euxinus or Black Sea), each written as letters of exile addressed to his wife and friends.*

Echo and Narcissus

Ovid, *Metamorphoses* 3.340-511

"In truth," says Jupiter to his wife Juno, "the sense of pleasure in the male is far more dull and dead than what you females share." Juno disagrees. So they decide to confer with Tiresias, who, born a man, had become a woman for seven years before returning to his first gender. Tiresias agrees with Jupiter. Juno, a poor loser, blinds him. Jupiter gives Tiresias the knowledge of the future to compensate for the loss of his eyesight. From then on, followers would come from afar to consult the seer Tiresias. Thus, the Naiad Liriope, mother of Narcissus, pays him a visit.

"Ah wretched me! I now begin too late
To find out all the long-perplex'd deceit;
It is my self I love, my self I see;
The gay delusion is a part of me.
I kindle up the fires by which I burn,
And my own beauties from the well return."

Fam'd far and near for knowing things to come,
From him th' enquiring nations sought their doom;
The fair Liriope his answers try'd,
And first th' unerring prophet justify'd.
This nymph the God Cephisus had abus'd,
With all his winding waters circumfus'd,
And on the Nereid got a lovely boy,
Whom the soft maids ev'n then beheld with joy.

The tender dame, sollicitous to know
Whether her child should reach old age or no,
Consults the sage Tiresias, who replies,
"If e'er he knows himself he surely dies."
Long liv'd the dubious mother in suspence,
'Till time unriddled all the prophet's sense.

Narcissus now his sixteenth year began,
Just turn'd of boy, and on the verge of man;
Many a friend the blooming youth caress'd,
Many a love-sick maid her flame confess'd:

Such was his pride, in vain the friend caress'd,
The love-sick maid in vain her flame confess'd.

Once, in the woods, as he pursu'd the chace,
The babbling Echo had descry'd his face;
She, who in others' words her silence breaks,
Nor speaks her self but when another speaks.
Echo was then a maid, of speech bereft,
Of wonted speech; for tho' her voice was left,
Juno a curse did on her tongue impose,
To sport with ev'ry sentence in the close.
Full often when the Goddess might have caught
Jove and her rivals in the very fault,
This nymph with subtle stories would delay
Her coming, 'till the lovers slip'd away.
The Goddess found out the deceit in time,
And then she cry'd, "That tongue, for this thy crime,
Which could so many subtle tales produce,
Shall be hereafter but of little use."
Hence 'tis she prattles in a fainter tone,
With mimick sounds, and accents not her own.
This love-sick virgin, over-joy'd to find
The boy alone, still follow'd him behind.
When glowing warmly at her near approach,
As sulphur blazes at the taper's touch,
She long'd her hidden passion to reveal,
And tell her pains, but had not words to tell.
She can't begin, but waits for the rebound,
To catch his voice, and to return the sound.

The boy, from his companions parted, said
Is any nigh? I, Echo answer made.
He round about him gazed, (much appall'd)
And cry'd out, come. She him, who called, called.
Then looking back, and seeing none appear'd,
Why shunst thou me? The self-same voice he heard
Deceived by the image of his words;
Then let us joyn, said he: No sound accords
More to her wish: her faculties combine
In dear consent; who answer'd, Let us joyn!
Flattering herself, out of the woods she sprung;

And would about his struggling neck have hung.
Thrust back, he said, life shall this breast forsake,
Ere thou, light nymph, on me thy pleasure take.
On me thy pleasure take, the nymph replyes
To that disdainfull boy, who from her flyes.

The nymph, when nothing could Narcissus move,
Still dash'd with blushes for her slighted love,
Liv'd in the shady covert of the woods,
In solitary caves and dark abodes;
Where pining wander'd the rejected fair,
'Till harrass'd out, and worn away with care,
The sounding skeleton, of blood bereft,
Besides her bones and voice had nothing left.
Her bones are petrify'd, her voice is found
In vaults, where still it doubles ev'ry sound.

Thus did the nymphs in vain caress the boy,
He still was lovely, but he still was coy;
When one fair virgin of the slighted train
Thus pray'd the Gods, provok'd by his disdain,
"Oh may he love like me, and love like me in vain!"
Rhamnusia pity'd the neglected fair,[1]
And with just vengeance answer'd to her pray'r.
There stands a fountain in a darksom wood,
Nor stain'd with falling leaves nor rising mud;
Untroubled by the breath of winds it rests,
Unsully'd by the touch of men or beasts;
High bow'rs of shady trees above it grow,
And rising grass and chearful greens below.
Pleas'd with the form and coolness of the place,
And over-heated by the morning chace,
Narcissus on the grassie verdure lyes.
But whilst within the chrystal fount he tries
To quench his heat, he feels new heats arise.
For as his own bright image he survey'd,
He fell in love with the fantastic shade;
And o'er the fair resemblance hung unmov'd,
Nor knew, fond youth! it was himself he lov'd.
The well-turn'd neck and shoulders he descries,
The spacious forehead, and the sparkling eyes;

The hands that Bacchus might not scorn to show,
And hair that round Apollo's head might flow;
With all the purple youthfulness of face,
That gently blushes in the wat'ry glass.
By his own flames consum'd the lover lyes,
And gives himself the wound by which he dies.
To the cold water oft he joins his lips,
Oft catching at the beauteous shade he dips
His arms, as often from himself he slips.
Nor knows he who it is his arms pursue
With eager clasps, but loves he knows not who.

What could, fond youth, this helpless passion move?
What kindled in thee this unpity'd love?
Thy own warm blush within the water glows,
With thee the colour'd shadow comes and goes,
Its empty being on thy self relies;
Step thou aside, and the frail charmer dies.

Still o'er the fountain's wat'ry gleam he stood,
Mindless of sleep, and negligent of food;
Still view'd his face, and languish'd as he view'd.
At length he rais'd his head, and thus began
To vent his griefs, and tell the woods his pain.
"You trees," says he, "and thou surrounding grove,
Who oft have been the kindly scenes of love,
Tell me, if e'er within your shades did lye
A youth so tortur'd, so perplex'd as I?
I, who before me see the charming fair,
Whilst there he stands, and yet he stands not there.
In such a maze of love my thoughts are lost,
And yet no bulwark'd town, nor distant coast,
Preserves the beauteous youth from being seen,
No mountains rise, nor oceans flow between.
A shallow water hinders my embrace;
And yet the lovely mimick wears a face
That kindly smiles, and when I bend to join
My lips to his, he fondly bends to mine.
Hear, gentle youth, and pity my complaint,
Come from thy well, thou fair inhabitant.
My charms an easy conquest have obtain'd

O'er other hearts, by thee alone disdain'd.
But why should I despair? I'm sure he burns
With equal flames, and languishes by turns.
When-e'er I stoop, he offers at a kiss,
And when my arms I stretch, he stretches his.
His eye with pleasure on my face he keeps,
He smiles my smiles, and when I weep he weeps.
When e'er I speak, his moving lips appear
To utter something, which I cannot hear.

"Ah wretched me! I now begin too late
To find out all the long-perplex'd deceit;
It is my self I love, my self I see;
The gay delusion is a part of me.
I kindle up the fires by which I burn,
And my own beauties from the well return.
Whom should I court? how utter my complaint?
Enjoyment but produces my restraint,
And too much plenty makes me die for want.
How gladly would I from my self remove!
And at a distance set the thing I love.
My breast is warm'd with such unusual fire,
I wish him absent whom I most desire.
And now I faint with grief; my fate draws nigh;
In all the pride of blooming youth I die.
Death will the sorrows of my heart relieve.
Oh might the visionary youth survive,
I should with joy my latest breath resign!
But oh! I see his fate involv'd in mine."

This said, the weeping youth again return'd
To the clear fountain, where again he burn'd;
His tears defac'd the surface of the well,
With circle after circle, as they fell:
And now the lovely face but half appears,
O'er-run with wrinkles, and deform'd with tears.
"Ah whither," cries Narcissus, "dost thou fly?
Let me still feed the flame by which I die;
Let me still see, tho' I'm no further blest."
Then rends his garment off, and beats his breast:
His naked bosom redden'd with the blow,

In such a blush as purple clusters show,
Ere yet the sun's autumnal heats refine
Their sprightly juice, and mellow it to wine.
The glowing beauties of his breast he spies,
And with a new redoubled passion dies.
As wax dissolves, as ice begins to run,
And trickle into drops before the sun;
So melts the youth, and languishes away,
His beauty withers, and his limbs decay;
And none of those attractive charms remain,
To which the slighted Echo su'd in vain.

She saw him in his present misery,
Whom, spight of all her wrongs, she griev'd to see.
She answer'd sadly to the lover's moan,
Sigh'd back his sighs, and groan'd to ev'ry groan:
"Ah youth! belov'd in vain," Narcissus cries;
"Ah youth! belov'd in vain," the nymph replies.
"Farewel," says he; the parting sound scarce fell
From his faint lips, but she reply'd, "farewel."
Then on th' wholsome earth he gasping lyes,
'Till death shuts up those self-admiring eyes.
To the cold shades his flitting ghost retires,
And in the Stygian waves it self admires.
For him the Naiads and the Dryads mourn,[2]
Whom the sad Echo answers in her turn;
And now the sister-nymphs prepare his urn:
When, looking for his corps, they only found
A rising stalk, with yellow blossoms crown'd.

Translated by Sir Samuel Garth, John Dryden, et al.

Philemon and Baucis

Ovid, *Metamorphoses* 8.612-724

The river-god Achelous has just given his guests Theseus, Pirithous, and Lelex an account of how Perimele, with whom he was in love, was turned into an island, which ensured her immortality. Pirithous refuses to believe such nonsense. Lelex then decides to illustrate the power of the gods by telling the story of Philemon and Baucis. This is a tale in which the just are saved and the unjust are annihilated, in essence evoking the biblical story of Sodom and Gomorrah.

"Heav'n's pow'r is infinite: Earth, Air, and Sea,
The manufacture mass, the making Pow'r obey."

Thus Achelous ends: his audience hear
With admiration, and admiring, fear
The Pow'rs of Heav'n; except Ixion's Son,
Who laugh'd at all the Gods, believ'd in none.
He shook his impious head, and thus replies:
These legends are no more than pious lies;
You attribute too much to heav'nly sway,
To think they give us forms, and take away.

The rest of better minds, their sense declar'd
Against this doctrine, and with horror heard.
Then Lelex rose, an old experienc'd man,
And thus with sober gravity began;
Heav'n's pow'r is infinite: Earth, Air, and Sea,
The manufacture mass, the making Pow'r obey.
By proof to clear your doubt; in Phrygian ground
Two neighb'ring trees, with walls encompass'd round,
Stand on a mod'rate rise, with wonder shown,
One a hard oak, a softer linden one.
I saw the place, and them, by Pittheus sent
To Phrygian realms, my grandsire's government.[3]
Not far from thence is seen a lake, the haunt
Of coots, and of the fishing cormorant.
Here Jove with Hermes came; but in disguise
Of mortal men conceal'd their deities;

One laid aside his thunder, one his rod;
And many toilsome steps together trod.
For harbour at a thousand doors they knock'd,
Not one of all the thousand but was lock'd.
At last an hospitable house they found,
A homely shed; the roof, not far from ground,
Was thatch'd with reeds, and straw, together bound.
There Baucis and Philemon liv'd, and there
Had liv'd long marry'd, and a happy pair;
Now old in love, though little was their store,
Inur'd to want, their poverty they bore,
Nor aim'd at wealth, professing to be poor.
For master, or for servant here to call,
Was all alike, where only two were all.
Command was none, where equal love was paid,
Or rather both commanded, both obey'd.

From lofty roofs the Gods repuls'd before,
Now stooping, enter'd through the little door.
The man (their hearty welcome first express'd)
A common settle drew for either guest,
Inviting each his weary limbs to rest.
But ere they sate, officious Baucis lays
Two cushions stuff'd with straw, the seat to raise;
Coarse, but the best she had; then rakes the load
Of ashes from the hearth, and spreads abroad
The living coals; and, lest they should expire,
With leaves, and bark she feeds her infant fire:
It smoaks; and then with trembling breath she blows,
'Till in a chearful blaze the flames arose.
With brush-wood, and with chips she strengthens these,
And adds at last the boughs of rotten trees.
The fire thus form'd, she sets the kettle on
(Like burnish'd gold the little seether shone),
Next took the coleworts which her husband got
From his own ground (a small well-water'd spot);
She stripp'd the stalks of all their leaves; the best
She cull'd, and them with handy care she drest.
High o'er the hearth a chine of bacon hung;
Good old Philemon seiz'd it with a prong,
And from the sooty rafter drew it down,

Then cut a slice, but scarce enough for one;
Yet a large portion of a little store,
Which for their sakes alone he wish'd were more.
This in the pot he plung'd without delay,
To tame the flesh, and drain the salt away.
The time beween, before the fire they sat,
And shorten'd the delay by pleasing chat.
A beam there was, on which a beechen pail
Hung by the handle, on a driven nail:
This fill'd with water, gently warm'd, they set
Before their guests; in this they bath'd their feet,
And after with clean towels dry'd their sweat.
This done, the host produc'd the genial bed,
Sallow the feet, the borders, and the sted,
Which with no costly coverlet they spread,
But coarse old garments; yet such robes as these
They laid alone, at feasts, on holidays.
The good old housewife, tucking up her gown,
The table sets; th' invited Gods lie down.
The trivet-table of a foot was lame,
A blot which prudent Baucis overcame,
Who thrusts beneath the limping leg a sherd,
So was the mended board exactly rear'd:
Then rubb'd it o'er with newly gather'd mint,
A wholsom herb, that breath'd a grateful scent.
Pallas began the feast, where first was seen
The party-colour'd olive, black, and green:
Autumnal cornels next in order serv'd,
In lees of wine well pickled, and preserv'd.
A garden-sallad was the third supply,
Of endive, radishes, and succory;
Then curds, and cream, the flow'r of country fare,
And new-laid eggs, which Baucis' busie care
Turn'd by a gentle fire, and roasted rare.
All these in earthen ware were serv'd to board;
And next in place, an earthen pitcher stor'd,
With liquor of the best the cottage could afford.
This was the table's ornament and pride,
With figures wrought: like pages at his side
Stood beechen bowls; and these were shining clean,
Varnish'd with wax without, and lin'd within.

By this the boiling kettle had prepar'd,
And to the table sent the smoaking lard;
On which with eager appetite they dine,
A sav'ry bit, that serv'd to relish wine:
The wine itself was suiting to the rest,
Still working in the must, and lately press'd.
The second course succeeds like that before,
Plums, apples, nuts, and of their wintry store
Dry figs, and grapes, and wrinkled dates were set
In canisters, t' enlarge the little treat.
All these a milk-white honey-comb surround,
Which in the midst the country-banquet crown'd.
But the kind hosts their entertainment grace
With hearty welcome, and an open face:
In all they did, you might discern with ease,
A willing mind, and a desire to please.

Mean-time the beechen bowls went round, and still,
Though often empty'd, were observ'd to fill;
Fill'd without hands, and of their own accord
Ran without feet, and danc'd about the board.
Devotion seiz'd the pair, to see the feast
With wine, and of no common grape, increas'd;
And up they held their hands, and fell to pray'r,
Excusing, as they could, their country fare.

One goose they had ('twas all they could allow),
A wakeful centry, and on duty now,
Whom to the Gods for sacrifice they vow.
Her with malicious zeal the couple view'd;
She ran for life, and limping they pursu'd;
Full well the fowl perceiv'd their bad intent,
And would not make her master's compliment;
But persecuted, to the Pow'rs she flies,
And close between the legs of Jove she lies.
He with a gracious ear the suppliant heard,
And sav'd her life; then what he has declar'd,
And own'd the God. The neighbourhood, said he,
Shall justly perish for impiety.
You stand alone exempted; but obey
With speed, and follow where we lead the way:

Leave these accurs'd; and to the mountain's height
Ascend; nor once look backward in your flight.

They haste, and what their tardy feet deny'd,
The trusty staff (their better leg) supply'd.
An arrow's flight they wanted to the top,
And there secure, but spent with travel, stop;
Then turn their now no more forbidden eyes;
Lost in a lake the floated level lies:
A watry desart covers all the plains,
Their cot alone, as in an isle, remains.
Wondring, with weeping eyes, while they deplore
Their neighbours' fate, and country now no more,
Their little shed, scarce large enough for two,
Seems, from the ground increas'd, in height and bulk to grow.
A stately temple shoots within the skies,
The crotches of their cot in columns rise:
The pavement polish'd marble they behold,
The gates with sculpture grac'd, the spires and tiles of gold.

Then thus the sire of Gods, with looks serene,
Speak thy desire, thou only just of men;
And thou, o woman, only worthy found
To be with such a man in marriage bound.

A-while they whisper; then, to Jove address'd,
Philemon thus prefers their joint request:
We crave to serve before your sacred shrine,
And offer at your altars rites divine.
And since not any action of our life
Has been polluted with domestic strife;
We beg one hour of death, that neither she
With widow's tears may live to bury me,
Nor weeping I, with wither'd arms may bear
My breathless Baucis to the sepulcher.

The Godheads sign their suit. They run their race
In the same tenour all th' appointed space:
Then, when their hour was come, while they relate
These past adventures at the temple gate,
Old Baucis is by old Philemon seen

Sprouting with sudden leaves of spritely green:
Old Baucis look'd where old Philemon stood,
And saw his lengthen'd arms a sprouting wood.
New roots their fasten'd feet begin to bind,
Their bodies stiffen in a rising rind.
Then, ere the bark above their shoulders grew,
They give, and take at once their last adieu.
At once, Farewell, o faithful spouse, they said;
At once th' incroaching rinds their closing lips invade.
Ev'n yet, an ancient Tyanaean[4] shows
A spreading oak, that near a linden grows;
The neighbourhood confirm the prodigy,
Grave men, not vain of tongue, or like to lie.
I saw my self the garlands on their boughs,
And tablets hung for gifts of granted vows;
And off'ring fresher up, with pious pray'r,
The good, said I, are God's peculiar care,
And such as honour Heav'n, shall heav'nly honour share.

Translated by Sir Samuel Garth, John Dryden, et al.

LUCAN

AD 39 - 65

Marcus Annaeus Lucanus was the son of Mela, the younger brother of Seneca. Born in Cordoba in AD 39, he was less than a year old when he first arrived in Rome. He was nursed on Stoicism as much as on his mother's milk. The fellow student of Persius, he demonstrated precocious talent and, pleasing to the prince, obtained a quaestorship (one of the four main magistracies in Rome) well before his time. (Typically, a citizen had to be at least 27 years of age for such an honor.) The protégé of Nero, Lucan wrote a poem in praise of the emperor that earned him the victory palm at the Neronian games in 60.

Jealousy, however, quickly brought disgrace upon him: Implicated, as was his uncle Seneca, in the conspiracy of Piso in 65, Lucan had no other choice but to commit suicide. Since calumny revels in tarnishing the dead, people asserted that, because Lucan had denounced his mother, he was as much a coward in death as he was a vile flatterer in life. His wife, Polla Argentaria, nonetheless continued to celebrate his memory and his honor.

Lucan left behind an abundance of diverse works: a Descent into the Underworld*; an* Iliacon*; an* Orpheus*; and* Epigrams, *of which only fragments survive. His greatest work is the* Civil War *(also referred to as* Pharsalia*), which consists of ten volumes and covers the same subject as Julius Caesar's* Civil War *(*Bellum Civile*): from the crossing of the Rubicon to the passionate love affairs of Cleopatra (49-48 BC).*

With this epic poet, the Latin language grew more expressive, the tone more tragic, and the philosophy Stoic. His method is that of a historian (even if Lucan does not mind making up facts) and of an astute observer. Lucan's works would inspire great writers and philosophers, including Agrippa d'Aubigné, Corneille, and Goethe.

Caesar and Cleopatra. The Source of the Nile.

Lucan, *Pharsalia* 10.53-398

Pompey, nicknamed "the Great" ("Magnus" in Latin) in imitation of Alexander, takes refuge in Egypt after Caesar defeats him at the battle of Pharsalus. On the order of King Ptolemy, Pompey is assassinated as soon as he arrives on 28 September 48 BC. His decapitated body is abandoned on the shore. Sometime later, Caesar lands at Alexandria where Pompey's head is presented to him. He visits the tomb of the founder of the city, Alexander, and then receives King Ptolemy who relinquishes himself. Caesar establishes Cleopatra on the throne and resides with her in an intense love affair out of which a son is born—Caesarion.

"Give me certain hope
To see the fount of Nile—and civil war
Then shall I leave."

Now from the stream Pelusian of the Nile,
Was come the boyish king,[1] taming the rage
Of his effeminate people: pledge of peace;
And Caesar safely trod Pellaean halls;[2]
When Cleopatra bribed her guard to break
The harbour chains, and borne in little boat
Within the Macedonian palace gates,
Caesar unknowing, entered: Egypt's shame;
Fury of Latium; to the bane of Rome
Unchaste. For as the Spartan queen of yore[3]
By fatal beauty Argos urged to strife
And Ilium's homes, so Cleopatra roused
Italia's frenzy. By her drum she called
Down on the Capitol terror (if to speak
Such word be lawful); mixed with Roman arms
Coward Canopus, hoping she might lead
A Pharian triumph, Caesar in her train;[4]
And 'twas in doubt upon Leucadian waves
Whether a woman, not of Roman blood,
Should hold the world in awe.[5] Such lofty thoughts
Seized on her soul upon that night in which
The wanton daughter of Pellaean kings

First shared our leaders' couches. Who shall blame
Antonius for the madness of his love,
When Caesar's haughty breast drew in the flame?
Who red with carnage, 'mid the clash of arms,
In palace haunted by Pompeius' shade,
Gave place to love; and in adulterous bed,
Magnus forgotten, from the Queen impure,
To Julia gave a brother.[6] On the bounds
Of furthest Libya permitting thus
His foe to gather: he in dalliance base
Waited upon his mistress, and to her
Pharos would give, for her would conquer all.

Then Cleopatra, trusting to her charms,
Tearless approached him, though in form of grief;
Her tresses loose as though in sorrow torn,
So best becoming her; and thus began:
"If, mighty Caesar, aught to noble birth
Be due, give ear. Of Lagian race[7] am I
Offspring illustrious; from my father's throne
Cast forth to banishment; unless thy hand
Restore to me the sceptre: then a Queen
Falls at thy feet embracing. To our race
Bright star of justice thou! Nor first shall I
As woman rule the cities of the Nile;
For, neither sex preferring, Pharos bows
To queenly governance. Of my parted sire
Read the last words, by which 'tis mine to share
With equal rights the kingdom and the bed.
And loves the boy his sister, were he free;
But his affections and his sword alike
Pothinus orders.[8] Nor wish I myself
To wield my father's power; but this my prayer:
Save from this foul disgrace our royal house,
Bid that the king shall reign, and from the court
Remove this hateful varlet, and his arms.
How swells his bosom for that his the hand
That shore Pompeius' head! And now he threats
Thee, Caesar, also; which the Fates avert!
'Twas shame enough upon the earth and thee
That of Pothinus Magnus should have been

The guilt or merit."

Caesar's ears in vain
Had she implored, but aided by her charms
The wanton's prayers prevailed, and by a night
Of shame ineffable, passed with her judge,
She won his favour.

When between the pair
Caesar had made a peace, by costliest gifts
Purchased, a banquet of such glad event
Made fit memorial; and with pomp the Queen
Displayed her luxuries, as yet unknown
To Roman fashions. First uprose the hall
Like to a fane which this corrupted age
Could scarcely rear: the lofty ceiling shone
With richest tracery, the beams were bound
In golden coverings; no scant veneer
Lay on its walls, but built in solid blocks
Of marble, gleamed the palace. Agate stood
In sturdy columns, bearing up the roof;
Onyx and porphyry on the spacious floor
Were trodden 'neath the foot; the mighty gates
Of Maroe's throughout were formed,
He mere adornment; ivory clothed the hall,
And fixed upon the doors with labour rare
Shells of the tortoise gleamed, from Indian seas,
With frequent emeralds studded. Gems of price
And yellow jasper on the couches shone.
Lustrous the coverlets; the major part
Dipped more than once within the vats of Tyre
Had drunk their juice: part feathered as with gold;
Part crimson dyed, in manner as are passed
Through Pharian leash the threads. There waited slaves
In number as a people, some in ranks
By different blood distinguished, some by age;
This band with Libyan, that with auburn hair
Red so that Caesar on the banks of Rhine
None such had witnessed; some with features scorched
By torrid suns, their locks in twisted coils
Drawn from their foreheads. Eunuchs too were there,

Unhappy race; and on the other side
Men of full age whose cheeks with growth of hair
Were hardly darkened.

Upon either hand
Lay kings, and Caesar in the midst supreme.
There in her fatal beauty lay the Queen
Thick daubed with unguents, nor with throne content
Nor with her brother spouse; laden she lay
On neck and hair with all the Red Sea spoils,
And faint beneath the weight of gems and gold.
Her snowy breast shone through Sidonian lawn
Which woven close by shuttles of the east
The art of Nile had loosened. Ivory feet
Bore citron tables brought from woods that wave
On Atlas, such as Caesar never saw
When Juba was his captive.[9] Blind in soul
By madness of ambition, thus to fire
By such profusion of her wealth, the mind
Of Caesar armed, her guest in civil war!
Not though he aimed with pitiless hand to grasp
The riches of a world; not though were here
Those ancient leaders of the simple age,
Fabricius or Curius stern of soul,
Or he who, Consul, left in sordid garb
His Tuscan plough, could all their several hopes
Have risen to such spoil.[10] On plates of gold
They piled the banquet sought in earth and air
And from the deepest seas and Nilus' waves,
Through all the world; in craving for display,
No hunger urging. Frequent birds and beasts,
Egypt's high gods, they placed upon the board:
In crystal goblets water of the Nile
They handed, and in massive cups of price
Was poured the wine; no juice of Mareot grape
But noble vintage of Falernian growth
Which in few years in Meroe's vats had foamed,
(For such the clime) to ripeness. On their brows
Chaplets were placed of roses ever young
With glistening nard entwined; and in their locks
Was cinnamon infused, not yet in air

Its fragrance perished, nor in foreign climes;
And rich amomum from the neighbouring fields.
Thus Caesar learned the booty of a world
To lavish, and his breast was shamed of war
Waged with his son-in-law for meagre spoil,
And with the Pharian realm he longed to find
A cause of battle.

When of wine and feast
They wearied and their pleasure found an end,
Caesar drew out in colloquy the night
Thus with Achoreus, on the highest couch
With linen ephod as a priest begirt:
"O thou devoted to all sacred rites,
Loved by the gods, as proves thy length of days,
Tell, if thou wilt, whence sprang the Pharian race;
How lie their lands, the manners of their tribes,
The form and worship of their deities.
Expound the sculptures on your ancient fanes:
Reveal your gods if willing to be known:
If to th' Athenian sage your fathers taught
Their mysteries, who worthier than I
To bear in trust the secrets of the world?
True, by the rumour of my kinsman's flight
Here was I drawn; yet also by your fame:
And even in the midst of war's alarms
The stars and heavenly spaces have I conned;
Nor shall Eudoxus' year excel mine own.[11]
But though such ardour burns within my breast,
Such zeal to know the truth, yet my chief wish
To learn the source of your mysterious flood
Through ages hidden: give me certain hope
To see the fount of Nile—and civil war
Then shall I leave."

He spake, and then the priest:
"The secrets, Caesar, of our mighty sires
Kept from the common people until now
I hold it right to utter. Some may deem
That silence on these wonders of the earth
Were greater piety. But to the gods

I hold it grateful that their handiwork
And sacred edicts should be known to men.

"A different power by the primal law,
Each star possesses. These alone control
The movement of the sky, with adverse force
Opposing: while the sun divides the year,
And day from night, and by his potent rays
Forbids the stars to pass their stated course.
The moon by her alternate phases sets
The varying limits of the sea and shore.
'Neath Saturn's sway the zone of ice and snow
Has passed; while Mars in lightning's fitful flames
And winds abounds' beneath high Jupiter
Unvexed by storms abides a temperate air;
And fruitful Venus' star contains the seeds
Of all things. Ruler of the boundless deep
The god Cyllenian:[12] whene'er he holds
That part of heaven where the Lion dwells
With neighbouring Cancer joined, and Sirius star
Flames in its fury; where the circular path
(Which marks the changes of the varying year)
Gives to hot Cancer and to Capricorn
Their several stations, under which doth lie
The fount of Nile, he, master of the waves,
Strikes with his beam the waters. Forth the stream
Brims from his fount, as Ocean when the moon
Commands an increase; nor shall curb his flow
Till night wins back her losses from the sun.

"Vain is the ancient faith that Ethiop snows
Send Nile abundant forth upon the lands.
Those mountains know nor northern wind nor star.
Of this are proof the breezes of the South,
Fraught with warm vapours, and the people's hue
Burned dark by suns: and 'tis in time of spring,
When first are thawed the snows, that ice-fed streams
In swollen torrents tumble; but the Nile
Nor lifts his wave before the Dog star burns;
Nor seeks again his banks, until the sun
In equal balance measures night and day.

Nor are the laws that govern other streams
Obeyed by Nile. For in the wintry year
Were he in flood, when distant far the sun,
His waters lacked their office; but he leaves
His channel when the summer is at height,
Tempering the torrid heat of Egypt's clime.
Such is the task of Nile; thus in the world
He finds his purpose, lest exceeding heat
Consume the lands: and rising thus to meet
Enkindled Lion, to Syene's prayers
By Cancer burnt gives ear; nor curbs his wave
Till the slant sun and Meroe's lengthening shades
Proclaim the autumn. Who shall give the cause?
'Twas Parent Nature's self which gave command
Thus for the needs of earth should flow the Nile.

"Vain too the fable that the western winds
Control his current, in continuous course
At stated seasons governing the air;
Or hurrying from Occident to South
Clouds without number which in misty folds
Press on the waters; or by constant blast,
Forcing his current back whose several mouths
Burst on the sea;—so, forced by seas and wind,
Men say, his billows pour upon the land.
Some speak of hollow caverns, breathing holes
Deep in the earth, within whose mighty jaws
Waters in noiseless current underneath
From northern cold to southern climes are drawn:
And when hot Meroe pants beneath the sun,
Then, say they, Ganges through the silent depths
And Padus pass: and from a single fount
The Nile arising not in single streams
Pours all the rivers forth. And rumour says
That when the sea which girdles in the world
O'erflows, thence rushes Nile, by lengthy course,
Softening his saltness. More, if it be true
That ocean feeds the sun and heavenly fires,
Then Phoebus journeying by the burning Crab
Sucks from its waters more than air can hold

Upon his passage—this the cool of night
Pours on the Nile.

"If, Caesar, 'tis my part
To judge such difference, 'twould seem that since
Creation's age has passed, earth's veins by chance
Some waters hold, and shaken cast them forth:
But others took when first the globe was formed
A sure abode; by Him who framed the world
Fixed with the Universe.

"And, Roman, thou,
In thirsting thus to know the source of Nile
Dost as the Pharian and Persian kings
And those of Macedon; nor any age
Refused the secret, but the place prevailed
Remote by nature. Greatest of the kings
By Memphis worshipped, Alexander grudged
To Nile its mystery, and to furthest earth
Sent chosen Ethiops whom the crimson zone
Stayed in their further march, while flowed his stream
Warm at their feet. Sesostris[13] westward far
Reached, to the ends of earth; and necks of kings
Bent 'neath his chariot yoke: but of the springs
Which fill your rivers, Rhone and Po, he drank.
Not of the fount of Nile. Cambyses king
In madman quest led forth his host to where
The long-lived races dwell: then famine struck,
Ate of his dead and, Nile unknown, returned.
No lying rumour of thy hidden source
Has e'er made mention; wheresoe'er thou art
Yet art thou sought, nor yet has nation claimed
In pride of place thy river as its own.
Yet shall I tell, so far as has the god,
Who veils thy fountain, given me to know.
Thy progress. Daring to upraise thy banks
'Gainst fiery Cancer's heat, thou tak'st thy rise
Beneath the zenith: straight towards the north
And mid Bootes flowing; to the couch
Bending, or to the risings, of the sun
In sinuous bends alternate; just alike

To Araby's peoples and to Libyan sands.
By Seres first beheld, yet know they not
Whence art thou come; and with no native stream
Strik'st thou the Ethiop fields. Nor knows the world
To whom it owes thee. Nature ne'er revealed
Thy secret origin, removed afar.
Nor did she wish thee to be seen of men
While still a tiny rivulet, but preferred
Their wonder to their knowledge. Where the sun
Stays at his limit, dost thou rise in flood
Untimely; such try right: to other lands
Bearing try winter: and by both the poles
Thou only wanderest. Here men ask thy rise
And there thine ending. Meroe rich in soil
And tilled by swarthy husbandmen divides
Thy broad expanse, rejoicing in the leaves
Of groves of ebony, which though spreading far
Their branching foliage, by no breadth of shade
Soften the summer sun—whose rays direct
Pass from the Lion to the fervid earth.
Next dost thou journey onwards past the realm
Of burning Phoebus, and the sterile sands,
With equal volume; now with all thy strength
Gathered in one, and now in devious streams
Parting the bank that crumbles at thy touch.
Then by our kingdom's gates, where Philae parts
Arabian peoples from Egyptian fields
The sluggish bosom of thy flood recalls
Try wandering currents, which through desert wastes
Flow gently on to where the merchant track
Divides the Red Sea waters from our own.
Who, gazing, Nile, upon thy tranquil flow,
Could picture how in wild array of foam
(Where shelves the earth) thy billows shall be plunged
Down the steep cataracts, in fuming wrath
That rocks should bar the passage of thy stream
Free from its source? For whirled on high the spray
Aims at the stars, and trembles all the air
With rush of waters; and with sounding roar
The foaming mass down from the summit pours
In hoary waves victorious. Next an isle

In all our ancient lore "untrodden" named
Stems firm thy torrent; and the rocks we call
Springs of the river, for that here are marked
The earliest tokens of the coming flood.
With mountain shores now nature hems thee in
And shuts thy waves from Libya; in the midst
Hence do thy waters run, till Memphis first
Forbids the barrier placed upon thy stream
And gives thee access to the open fields."

Thus did they pass, as though in peace profound,
The nightly watches. But Pothinus' mind,
Once with accursed butchery imbued,
Was frenzied still; since great Pompeius fell
No deed to him was crime; his rabid soul
Th' avenging goddesses and Magnus' shade
Stirred to fresh horrors; and a Pharian hand
No less was worthy, as he deemed, to shed
That blood which Fortune purposed should bedew
The conquered fathers; and the fell revenge
Due to the senate for the civil war
This hireling almost snatched. Avert, ye fates,
Far hence the shame that not by Brutus' hand
This blow be struck![14] Shall thus the tyrant's fall
Just at our hands, become a Pharian crime,
Reft of example? To prepare a plan
(Fated to fail) he dares; nor veils in fraud
A plot for murder, but with open war
Attacks th' unconquered chieftain: from his crimes
He gained such courage as to send command
To lop the head of Caesar, and to join
In death the kinsmen chiefs. These words by night
His faithful servants to Achillas bear,
His foul associate, whom the boy had made
Chief of his armies, and who ruled alone
O'er Egypt's land and o'er himself her king:
"Now lay thy limbs upon the sumptuous couch
And sleep in luxury, for the Queen hath seized
The palace; nor alone by her betrayed,
But Caesar's gift, is Pharos. Dost delay
Nor hasten to the chamber of thy Queen?

Thou only? Married to the Latian chief,
The impious sister now her brother weds
And hurrying from rival spouse to spouse
Hath Egypt won, and plays the bawd for Rome.
By amorous potions she has won the man:
Then trust the boy! Yet give him but a night
In her enfondling arms, and drunk with love
Thy life and mine he'll barter for a kiss.
We for his sister's charms by cross and flame
Shall pay the penalty: nor hope of aid;
Here stands adulterous Caesar, here the King
Her spouse: how hope we from so stern a judge
To gain acquittal? Shall she not condemn
Those who ne'er sought her favours? By the deed
We dared together and lost, by Magnus' blood
Which wrought the bond between us, be thou swift
With hasty tumult to arouse the war.
Dash in with nightly band, and mar with death
Their shameless nuptials: on the very bed
With either lover smite the ruthless Queen.
Nor let the fortunes of the Western chief
Make pause our enterprise. We share with him
The glory of his empire o'er the world.
Pompeius fallen makes us too sublime.
There lies the shore that bids us hope success:
Ask of our power from the polluted wave,
And gaze upon the scanty tomb which holds
Not all Pompeius' ashes.[15] Peer to him
Was he whom now thou fearest. Noble blood
True, is not ours: what boots it? Nor are realms
Nor wealth of peoples given to our command.
Yet have we risen to a height of power
For deeds of blood, and Fortune to our hands
Attracts her victims. Lo! a nobler now
Lies in our compass, and a second death
Hesperia shall appease; for Caesar's blood,
Shed by these hands, shall give us this, that Rome
Shall love us, guilty of Pompeius' fall.
Why fear these titles, why this chieftain's strength?
For shorn of these, before your swords he lies
A common soldier. To the civil war

This night shall bring completion, and shall give
To peoples slain fit offerings, and send
That life the world demands beneath the shades.
Rise then in all your hardihood and smite
This Caesar down, and let the Roman youths
Strike for themselves, and Lagos for its King.
Nor do thou tarry: full of wine and feast
Thou'lt fall upon him in the lists of love;
Then dare the venture, and the heavenly gods
Shall grant of Cato's and of Brutus' prayers
To thee fulfilment."

Translated by Sir Edward Ridley.

PETRONIUS

Died AD 66

Nobody knows for sure who Petronius was. He is generally identified as the Petronius mentioned by Tacitus. The Annals *do indeed mention a certain Petronius, a carefree and refined hedonist who attained the good graces of Nero and was accepted as the "Arbiter of Elegance." The victim of slander, Petronius lost favor with the emperor and was forced to take his own life. Before killing himself, he wrote a pamphlet about the debauchery of the prince and had it delivered to him. A realistic yet airy and caustic novel by Petronius has survived. It is titled the* Satyricon *(but is alternately referred to as the* Satiricon*) because it is as much about satirical stories as about tales on satyrs. "Satiricon" also means "mixture," and the narration consists of prose "mixed" with poems.*

The novel acutely examines society. In the company of his friend Ascyltus and his slave Giton, the narrator Encolpius heads from one adventure to the next in a coastal city in southern Italy. Joined by the poet Eumolpus, they embark on a voyage and are wrecked near Croton. Three events pace the narration: the banquet at the villa of the freedman Trimalchio; the tale of the widow of Ephesus; and the men's stay at Croton, a paradise for spry old men and legacy hunters. The sleazy inns, brothels, and baths, where the dregs of the world hang out, reflect the shamelessness and licentiousness of high imperial society. The narrative is rich in bonhomie and is often expressed with false ingenuity, parody, and mockery. For the first time, a "vulgar" spoken Latin language ascends to the status of a written language.

Magnificence of the Nouveau Riche

Petronius, *Satyricon* 32-41

The actors of the Satyricon *do not project the image of the virtuous protagonists of the love novels or of the fearless warriors of the epics. Far from it. Encolpius, a former gladiator and murderer on the run, only cares for his young minion Giton. The unscrupulous Ascyltos accompanies them. He is also a fleeing slave. Although a fearful coward, his hands are nonetheless covered with various crimes. In their wanderings, the three heroes search endlessly for good luck. They reach Trimalchio's splendid residence in a city in southern Italy. The host is immensely wealthy, woefully ignorant, and somewhat arrogant. Further, he is a former slave who made quite a fortune—basically the caricature of an upstart. Thus, here are our three antiheroes who enjoy Trimalchio's magnificence and provide us with a description of a feast where everything is excessive and grotesque—a banquet that is very different from Plato's.*

"A day's nothing at all: it's night before you can turn around, so you can't do better than to go right to the dining-room from your bed."

We were in the midst of these delicacies when, to the sound of music, Trimalchio himself was carried in and bolstered up in a nest of small cushions, which forced a snicker from the less wary. A shaven poll protruded from a scarlet mantle, and around his neck, already muffled with heavy clothing, he had tucked a napkin having a broad purple stripe and a fringe that hung down all around. On the little finger of his left hand he wore a massive gilt ring, and on the first joint of the next finger, a smaller one which seemed to me to be of pure gold, but as a matter of fact it had iron stars soldered on all around it. And then, for fear all of his finery would not be displayed, he bared his right arm, adorned with a golden arm-band and an ivory circlet clasped with a plate of shining metal.

Picking his teeth with a silver quill, "Friends," said he, "it was not convenient for me to come into the dining-room just yet, but for fear my absence should cause you any inconvenience, I gave over my own pleasure. Permit me, however, to finish my game." A slave followed with a terebinth table and crystal dice, and I noted one piece of luxury that was superlative; for instead of black and white pieces, he used gold and silver coins. He kept up a continual flow of various coarse expressions. We were still dallying with the relishes when a tray was brought in, on which was a basket containing a wooden hen with her wings rounded and spread out as if she were brooding. Two slaves instantly approached, and to the accompaniment of music, commenced to feel around in the straw. They pulled out some pea-hen's eggs, which they distributed among the diners. Turning his head, Trimalchio saw what was going on. "Friends," he remarked. "I ordered pea-hen's eggs set under the hen, but I'm afraid they're addled, by Hercules, I am; let's try them anyhow, and see if they're still fit to suck." We picked up our spoons, each of which weighed not less than half a pound, and punctured the shells, which were made of flour and dough, and as a matter of fact, I very nearly threw mine away for it seemed to me that a chick had formed already, but upon hearing an old experienced guest vow, "There must be something good here," I broke open the shell with my hand and discovered a fine fat fig-pecker, imbedded in a yolk seasoned with pepper.

Having finished his game, Trimalchio was served with a helping of everything and was announcing in a loud voice his willingness to join anyone in a second cup of honied wine, when, to a flourish of music, the relishes were suddenly whisked away by a singing chorus, but a small dish happened to fall to the floor, in the scurry, and a slave picked it up. Seeing this, Trimalchio ordered that the boy be punished by a box on the ear, and made him throw it down again; a janitor followed with his broom and swept the silver dish away among the litter. Next followed two long-haired Ethiopians, carrying small leather bottles, such as are commonly seen in the hands of those who sprinkle sand in the arena, and poured wine upon our hands, for no one offered us water. When complimented upon these elegant extras, the host cried out, "Mars loves a fair fight: and so I ordered each one a separate table: that way these stinking slaves won't make us so hot with their crowding." Some glass bottles carefully sealed with gypsum were brought in at that instant; a label bearing this inscription was fastened to the neck of each one:

OPIMIAN FALERNIAN ONE HUNDRED YEARS OLD.[1]

While we were studying the labels, Trimalchio clapped his hands and cried, "Ah me! To think that wine lives longer than poor little man. Let's fill 'em up! There's life in wine and this is the real Opimian, you can take my word for that. I offered no such vintage yesterday, though my guests were far more respectable." We were tippling away and extolling all these elegant devices, when a slave brought in a silver skeleton, so contrived that the joints and movable vertebra could be turned in any direction. He threw it down upon the table a time or two, and its mobile articulation caused it to assume grotesque attitudes, whereupon Trimalchio chimed in:

"Poor man is nothing in the scheme of things
And Orcus grips us and to Hades flings
Our bones! This skeleton before us here

Is as important as we ever were!
Let's live then while we may and life is dear."

The applause was followed by a course which, by its oddity, drew every eye, but it did not come up to our expectations. There was a circular tray around which were displayed the signs of the zodiac, and upon each sign the caterer had placed the food best in keeping with it. Ram's vetches on Aries, a piece of beef on Taurus, kidneys and lamb's fry on Gemini, a crown on Cancer, the womb of an unfarrowed sow on Virgo, an African fig on Leo, on Libra a balance, one pan of which held a tart and the other a cake, a small seafish on Scorpio, a bull's eye on Sagittarius, a sea lobster on Capricornus, a goose on Aquarius and two mullets on Pisces. In the middle lay a piece of cut sod upon which rested a honeycomb with the grass arranged around it. An Egyptian slave passed bread around from a silver oven and in a most discordant voice twisted out a song in the manner of the mime in the musical farce called Laserpitium. Seeing that we were rather depressed at the prospect of busying ourselves with such vile fare, Trimalchio urged us to fall to: "Let us fall to, gentlemen, I beg of you, this is only the sauce!"

While he was speaking, four dancers ran in to the time of the music, and removed the upper part of the tray. Beneath, on what seemed to be another tray, we caught sight of stuffed capons and sows' bellies, and in the middle, a hare equipped with wings to resemble Pegasus. At the corners of the tray we also noted four figures of Marsyas and from their bladders spouted a highly spiced sauce upon fish which were swimming about as if in a tide-race. All of us echoed the applause which was started by the servants, and fell to upon these exquisite delicacies, with a laugh. "Carver," cried Trimalchio, no less delighted with the artifice practised upon us, and the carver appeared immediately. Timing his strokes to the beat of the music he cut up the meat in such a fashion as to lead you to think that a gladiator was fighting from a chariot to the accompaniment of a water-organ. Every now and then Trimalchio would repeat "Carver, Carver," in a low voice, until I finally came to the conclusion that some joke was meant in repeating a word so frequently, so I did not scruple to question him who reclined above me. As he had often experienced byplay of this sort he explained, "You see that fellow who is carving the meat, don't you? Well, his name is Carver. Whenever Trimalchio says Carver, carve her, by the same word, he both calls and commands!"

I could eat no more, so I turned to my whilom informant to learn as much as I could and sought to draw him out with far-fetched gossip. I inquired who that woman could be who was scurrying about hither and yon in such a fashion. "She's called Fortunata," he replied. "She's the wife of Trimalchio, and she measures her money by the peck. And only a little while ago, what was she! May your genius pardon me, but you would not have been willing to take a crust of bread from her hand. Now, without rhyme or reason, she's in the seventh heaven and is Trimalchio's factotum, so much so that he would believe her if she told him it was dark when it was broad daylight! As for him, he don't know how rich he is, but this harlot keeps an eye on everything and where you least expect to find her, you're sure to run into her. She's temperate, sober, full of good advice, and has many good qualities, but she has a scolding tongue, a very magpie on a sofa, those she likes, she likes, but those she dislikes, she dislikes! Trimalchio himself has estates as broad as the flight of a kite is long, and piles of money. There's more silver plate lying in his steward's office than other men have in their whole fortunes! And as for slaves, damn me if I believe a tenth of them knows the master by sight. The truth is, that these stand-a-gapes are so much in awe of him that any one of them would step into a fresh dunghill without ever knowing it, at a mere nod from him!"

"And don't you get the idea that he buys anything; everything is produced at home, wool, pitch, pepper, if you asked for hen's milk you would get it. Because he wanted his wool to rival other things in quality, he bought rams at Tarentum and sent 'em into his flocks with a slap on the arse. He had bees brought from Attica, so he could produce Attic honey at home, and, as a side issue, so he could improve the native bees by crossing with the Greek. He even wrote to India for mushroom seed one day, and he hasn't a single mule that wasn't sired by a wild ass. Do you see all those cushions? Not a single one but what is stuffed with either purple or scarlet wool! He hasn't anything to worry about! Look out how you criticize those other fellow-freedmen-friends of his, they're all well heeled. See the fellow reclining at the bottom of the end couch? He's worth his 800,000 any day, and lie rose from nothing. Only a short while ago he had to carry faggots on his own back. I don't know how true it is, but they say that he snatched off an Incubo's hat and found a treasure![2] For my part, I don't envy any man anything that was given him by a god. He still carries the marks of his box on the ear, and he isn't wishing himself any bad luck! He posted this notice, only the other day:

> CAIUS POMPONIUS DIOGENES HAS PURCHASED A HOUSE. THIS GARNET FOR RENT AFTER THE KALENDS OF JULY.

"What do you think of the fellow in the freedman's place? He has a good front, too, hasn't he? And he has a right to. He saw his fortune multiplied tenfold, but he lost heavily through speculation at the last. I don't think he can call his very hair his own, and it is no fault of his either, by Hercules, it isn't. There's no better fellow anywhere his rascally freedmen cheated him out of everything. You know very well how it is; everybody's business is nobody's business, and once let business affairs start to go wrong, your friends will stand from under! Look at the fix he's in, and think what a fine trade he had! He used to be an undertaker. He dined like a king, boars roasted whole in their shaggy hides, bakers' pastries, birds, cooks and bakers! More wine was spilled under his table than another has in his wine cellar. His life was like a pipe dream, not like an ordinary mortal's. When his affairs commenced to go wrong, and he was afraid his creditors would guess that he was bankrupt, he advertised an auction and this was his placard:

> JULIUS PROCULUS WILL SELL AT AUCTION HIS SUPERFLUOUS FURNITURE.

Trimalchio broke in upon this entertaining gossip, for the course had been removed and the guests, happy with wine, had started a general conversation. Lying back upon his couch, "You ought to make this wine go down pleasantly," he said, "the fish must have something to swim in. But I say, you didn't think I'd be satisfied with any such dinner as you saw on the top of that tray? 'Is Ulysses no better known?' Well, well, we shouldn't forget our culture, even at dinner. May the bones of my patron rest in peace, he wanted me to become a man among men. No one can show me anything new, and that little tray has proved it. This heaven where the gods live, turns into as many different signs, and sometimes into the Ram: therefore, whoever is born under that sign will own many flocks and much wool, a hard head, a shameless brow, and a sharp horn. A great many school-teachers and rambunctious butters-in are born under that sign." We applauded the wonderful penetration of our astrologer and he ran on, "Then the whole heaven turns into a bull-calf and the kickers and herdsmen and those who see to it that their own bellies are full, come into the world. Teams of horses and oxen are born under the Twins, and well-hung wenchers and those who bedung both sides of the wall. I was born under the Crab and therefore stand on many legs and own much property on land and sea, for the crab is as much at home on one as he is in the other. For that reason, I put nothing on that sign for fear of weighing down my own destiny. Bulldozers and gluttons are born under the Lion, and women and fugitives and chain-gangs are born under the Virgin. Butchers and perfumers are born under the Balance, and all who think that it is their business to straighten things out. Poisoners and assassins are born under the Scorpion. Cross-eyed people who look at the vegetables and sneak away with the bacon, are born under the Archer. Horny-handed sons of toil are born under Capricorn. Bartenders and pumpkin-heads are born under the Water-Carrier. Caterers and rhetoricians are born under the Fishes: and so the world turns round, just like a mill, and something bad always comes to the top, and men are either being born or else they're dying. As to the sod and the honeycomb in the middle, for I never do anything without a reason, Mother Earth is in the centre, round as an egg, and all that is good is found in her, just like it is in a honeycomb."

"Bravo!" we yelled, and, with hands uplifted to the ceiling, we swore that such fellows as Hipparchus and Aratus were not to be compared with him.[3] At length some slaves came in who spread upon the couches some coverlets upon which were embroidered nets and hunters stalking their game with boar-spears, and all the paraphernalia of the chase. We knew not what to look for next, until a hideous uproar commenced, just outside the dining-room door, and some Spartan hounds commenced to run around the table all of a sudden. A tray followed them, upon which was served a wild boar of immense size, wearing a liberty cap upon its head, and from its tusks hung two little baskets of woven palm fibre, one of which contained Syrian dates, the other, Theban. Around it hung little suckling pigs made from pastry, signifying that this was a brood-sow with her pigs at suck. It turned out that these were souvenirs intended to be taken home. When it came to carving the boar, our old friend Carver, who had carved the capons, did not appear, but in his place a great bearded giant, with bands around his legs, and wearing a short hunting cape in which a design was woven. Drawing his hunting-knife, he plunged it fiercely into the boar's side, and some thrushes flew out of the gash. Fowlers, ready with their rods, caught them in a moment, as they fluttered around the room and Trimalchio ordered one to each guest, remarking, "Notice what fine acorns this forest-bred boar fed on," and as he spoke, some slaves removed the little baskets from the tusks and divided the Syrian and Theban dates equally among the diners.

Getting a moment to myself, in the meantime, I began to speculate as to why the boar had come with a liberty cap upon his head. After exhausting my invention with a thousand foolish guesses, I made bold to put the riddle which teased me to my old informant. "Why, sure," he replied, "even your slave could explain that; there's no riddle, everything's as plain as day! This boar made his first bow as the last course of yesterday's dinner and was dismissed by the guests, so today he comes back as a freedman!" I damned my stupidity and refrained from asking any more questions for fear I might leave the impression that I had never dined among decent people before. While we were speaking, a handsome boy, crowned with vine leaves and ivy, passed grapes around, in a little basket, and impersonated Bacchus-happy, Bacchus-drunk, and Bacchus-dreaming, reciting, in the meantime, his master's verses, in a shrill voice. Trimalchio turned to him and said, "Dionisus, be thou Liber," whereupon the boy immediately snatched the cap from the boar's head, and put it upon his own.[4] At that Trimalchio added, "You can't deny that my father's middle name was Liber!" We applauded Trimalchio's conceit heartily, and kissed the boy as he went around. Trimalchio retired to the close-stool, after this course, and we, having freedom of action with the tyrant away, began to draw the other guests out. After calling for a bowl of wine, Dama spoke up, "A day's nothing at all: it's night before you can turn around, so you can't do better than to go right to the dining-room from your bed. It's been so cold that I can hardly get warm in a bath, but a hot drink's as good as an overcoat: I've had some long pegs, and between you and me, I'm a bit groggy; the booze has gone to my head."

Translated by W.C. Firebaugh.

PLUTARCH

c. AD 45 - 125

Born at Chaeronea in Boeotia, Plutarch was from a family of local dignitaries. In his youth, he went to Athens to study philosophy, rhetoric, and science. Shortly thereafter, he obtained Athenian citizenship and next visited Egypt, Asia Minor, and, finally, Rome. In Rome, he taught philosophy and rhetoric. He befriended government officials and familiars of the emperor and was granted Roman citizenship. He then returned to his native region and served as a priest of Delphi during the last 30 years of his life. In this capacity, he took part in the revival of the sanctuary under Trajan and later Hadrian.

Plutarch left us an important oeuvre in which philosophy and biography occupy privileged positions. As a moralist, he was interested in the lives of famous men. He drafted a significant number of biographies in which he analyzes the virtues and the vices of those depicted in order to propose models for future generations. Today, we can still read 23 pairs of his Parallel Lives of Famous Men *in which he compares famous Greeks with famous Romans, such as Alexander with Julius Caesar and Demosthenes with Cicero.*

We further possess many of Plutarch's treatises on moral philosophy, which are collected under the title Moralia. *His works are of great diversity, ranging from an essay titled* On the Sign of Socrates *to a collection of reflections grouped under the heading* Advice to Married Couples. *Another work by Plutarch, the* Greek and Roman Questions, *is mainly concerned with religious and literary themes and reveals the author's curiosity regarding antiquarian problems.*

Plutarch's influence was already considerable in antiquity. Shakespeare borrowed extensively from the Parallel Lives *when he composed his* Julius Caesar, Anthony and Cleopatra, Timon of Athens, *and* Coriolanus. *Nowadays, Plutarch's works are invaluable for all who are interested in Greco-Roman civilization.*

Making of a Conqueror
Plutarch, *Alexander* 1-8

Alexander the Great possessed strong character traits that equipped him to conquer peoples from the Danube River to the Nile and the Indus: intelligence, a fiery temperament, ambition, military genius, and an extraordinary nature enhanced by a brilliant education entrusted to the great philosopher Aristotle.

"Then Alexander went to Delphi, to consult Apollo concerning the success of the war he had undertaken, and happening to come on one of the forbidden days, when it was esteemed improper to give any answers from the oracle, he sent messengers to desire the priestess to do her office; and when she refused, on the plea of a law to the contrary, he went up himself, and began to draw her by force into the temple, until tired and overcome with his importunity, "My son," said she, "thou art invincible." Alexander taking hold of what she spoke, declared he had received such an answer as he wished for, and that it was needless to consult the god any further."

It being my purpose to write the lives of Alexander the king, and of Caesar, by whom Pompey was destroyed, the multitude of their great actions affords so large a field that I were to blame if I should not by way of apology forewarn my reader that I have chosen rather to epitomize the most celebrated parts of their story, than to insist at large on every particular circumstance of it. It must be borne in mind that my design is not to write histories, but lives. And the most glorious exploits do not always furnish us with the clearest discoveries of virtue or vice in men; sometimes a matter of less moment, an expression or a jest, informs us better of their characters and inclinations, than the most famous sieges, the greatest armaments, or the bloodiest battles whatsoever. Therefore as portrait-painters are more exact in the lines and features of the face in which the character is seen, than in the other parts of the body, so I must be allowed to give my more particular attention to the marks and indications of the souls of men, and while I endeavor by these to portray their lives, may be free to leave more weighty matters and great battles to be treated of by others.

It is agreed on by all hands, that on the father's side, Alexander descended from Hercules by Caranus, and from Aeacus by Neoptolemus on the mother's side.[1] His father Philip, being in Samothrace, when he was quite young, fell in love there with Olympias, in company with whom he was initiated in the religious ceremonies of the country, and her father and mother being both dead, soon after, with the consent of her brother Arymbas, he married her. The night before the consummation of their marriage, she dreamed that a thunderbolt fell upon her body, which kindled a great fire, whose divided flames dispersed themselves all about, and then were extinguished. And Philip some time after he was married, dreamt that he sealed up his wife's body with a seal, whose impression, as he fancied, was the figure of a lion. Some of the diviners interpreted this as a warning to Philip to look narrowly to his wife; but Aristander of Telmessus, considering how unusual it was to seal up anything that was empty, assured him the meaning of his dream was, that the queen was with child of a boy, who would one day prove as stout and courageous as a lion.

Once, moreover, a serpent was found lying by Olympias as she slept, which more than anything else, it is said, abated Philip's passion for her; and whether he feared her as an enchantress, or thought she had commerce with some god, and so looked on himself as excluded, he was ever after less fond of her conversation. Others say, that the women of this country having always been extremely addicted to the enthusiastic Orphic rites, and the wild worship of Bacchus, (upon which account they were called Clodones, and Mimallones,) imitated in many things the practices of the Edonian and Thracian women about Mount Haemus, from whom the word "threskeuein", seems to have been derived, as a special term for superfluous and over-curious forms of adoration; and that Olympias, zealously affecting these fanatical and enthusiastic inspirations, to perform them with more barbaric dread, was wont in the dances proper to these ceremonies to have great tame serpents about her, which sometimes creeping out of the ivy and the mystic fans, sometimes winding themselves about the sacred spears, and the women's chaplets, made a spectacle which the men could not look upon without terror.

Philip, after this vision, sent Chaeron of Megalopolis to consult the oracle of Apollo at Delphi, by which he was commanded to perform sacrifice, and henceforth pay particular honor, above all other gods, to Ammon; and was told he should one day lose that eye with which he presumed to peep through the chink of the door, when he saw the god, under the form of a serpent, in the company of his wife. Eratosthenes says that Olympias, when she attended Alexander on his way to the army in his first expedition, told him the secret of his birth, and bade him behave himself with courage suitable to his divine extraction. Others again affirm that she wholly disclaimed any pretensions of the kind, and was wont to say, "When will Alexander leave off slandering me to Juno?"[2]

Alexander was born the sixth of Hecatombaeon, which month the Macedonians call Lous, the same day that the temple of Diana at Ephesus was burnt; which Hegesias of Magnesia makes the occasion of a conceit, frigid enough to have stopped the conflagration. The temple, he says, took fire and was burnt while its mistress was absent, assisting at the birth of Alexander. And all the Eastern soothsayers who happened to be then at Ephesus, looking upon the ruin of this temple to be the forerunner of some other calamity, ran about the town, beating their faces, and crying, that this day had brought forth something that would prove fatal and destructive to all Asia.

Just after Philip had taken Potidaea, he received these three messages at one time, that Parmenio had overthrown the Illyrians in a great battle, that his race-horse had won the course at the Olympic games, and that his wife had given birth to Alexander; with which being naturally well pleased, as an addition to his satisfaction, he was assured by the diviners that a son, whose birth was accompanied with three such successes, could not fail of being invincible.

The statues that gave the best representation of Alexander's person, were those of Lysippus, (by whom alone he would suffer his image to be made,) those peculiarities which many of his successors afterwards and his friends used to affect to imitate, the inclination of his head a little on one side towards his left shoulder, and his melting eye, having been expressed by this artist with great exactness. But Apelles, who drew him with thunderbolts in his hand, made his complexion browner and darker than it was naturally; for he was fair and of a light color, passing into ruddiness in his face and upon his breast. Aristoxenus in his *Memoirs* tells us that a most agreeable odor exhaled from his skin, and that his breath and body all over was so fragrant as to perfume the clothes which he wore next him; the cause of which might probably be the hot and adjust temperament of his body. For sweet smells, Theophrastus conceives, are produced by the concoction of moist humors by heat, which is the reason that those parts of the world which are driest and most burnt up, afford spices of the best kind, and in the greatest quantity; for the heat of the sun exhausts all the superfluous moisture which lies in the surface of bodies, ready to generate putrefaction. And this hot constitution, it may be, rendered Alexander so addicted to drinking, and so choleric.

His temperance, as to the pleasures of the body, was apparent in him in his very childhood, as he was with much difficulty incited to them, and always used them with great moderation; though in other things he was extremely eager and vehement, and in his love of glory, and the pursuit of it, he showed a solidity of high spirit and magnanimity far above his age. For he neither sought nor valued it upon every occasion, as his father Philip did, (who affected to show his eloquence almost to a degree of pedantry, and took care to have the victories of his racing chariots at the Olympic games engraved on his coin,) but when he was asked by some about him, whether he would run a race in the Olympic games, as he was very swift-footed, he answered, he would, if he might have kings to run with him. Indeed, he seems in general to have looked with indifference, if not with dislike, upon the professed athletes. He often appointed prizes, for which not only tragedians and musicians, pipers and harpers, but rhapsodists also, strove to outvie one another; and delighted in all manner of hunting and cudgel-playing, but never gave any encouragement to contests either of boxing or of the pancratium.

While he was yet very young, he entertained the ambassadors from the king of Persia, in the absence of his father, and entering much into conversation with them, gained so much upon them by his affability, and the questions he asked them, which were far from being childish or trifling, (for he inquired of them the length of the ways, the nature of the road into inner Asia, the character of their king, how he carried himself to his enemies, and what forces he was able to bring into the field,) that they were struck with admiration of him, and looked upon the ability so much famed of Philip, to be nothing in comparison with the forwardness and high purpose that appeared thus early in his son. Whenever he heard Philip had taken any town of importance, or won any signal victory, instead of rejoicing at it altogether, he would tell his companions that his father would anticipate everything, and leave him and them no opportunities of performing great and illustrious actions. For being more bent upon action and glory than either upon pleasure or riches, he esteemed all that he should receive from his father as a diminution and prevention of his own future achievements; and would have chosen rather to succeed to a kingdom involved in troubles and wars, which would have afforded him frequent exercise of his courage, and a large field of honor, than to one already flourishing and settled, where his inheritance would be an inactive life, and the mere enjoyment of wealth and luxury.

The care of his education, as it might be presumed, was committed to a great many attendants, preceptors, and teachers, over the whole of whom Leonidas, a near kinsman of Olympias, a man of an austere temper, presided, who did not indeed himself decline the name of what in reality is a noble and honorable office, but in general his dignity, and his near relationship, obtained him from other people the title of Alexander's foster father and governor. But he who took upon him the actual place and style of his pedagogue, was Lysimachus the Acarnanian, who, though he had nothing specially to recommend him, but his lucky fancy of calling himself Phoenix, Alexander Achilles, and Philip Peleus,[3] was therefore well enough esteemed, and ranked in the next degree after Leonidas.

Philonicus the Thessalian brought the horse Bucephalas to Philip, offering to sell him for thirteen talents;[4] but when they went into the field to try him, they found him so very vicious and unmanageable, that he reared up when they endeavored to mount him, and would not so much as endure the voice of any of Philip's attendants.

Upon which, as they were leading him away as wholly useless and untractable, Alexander, who stood by, said, "What an excellent horse do they lose, for want of address and boldness to manage him!" Philip at first took no notice of what he said; but when he heard him repeat the same thing several times, and saw he was much vexed to see the horse sent away, "Do you reproach," said he to him, "those who are older than yourself, as if you knew more, and were better able to manage him than they?" "I could manage this horse," replied he, "better than others do." "And if you do not," said Philip, "what will you forfeit for your rashness?" "I will pay," answered Alexander, "the whole price of the horse." At this the whole company fell a laughing; and as soon as the wager was settled amongst them, he immediately ran to the horse, and taking hold of the bridle, turned him directly towards the sun, having, it seems, observed that he was disturbed at and afraid of the motion of his own shadow; then letting him go forward a little, still keeping the reins in his hand, and stroking him gently when he found him begin to grow eager and fiery, he let fall his upper garment softly, and with one nimble leap securely mounted him, and when he was seated, by little and little drew in the bridle, and curbed him without either striking or spurring him. Presently, when he found him free from all rebelliousness, and on]y impatient for the course, he let him go at full speed, inciting him now with a commanding voice, and urging him also with his heel. Philip and his friends looked on at first in silence and anxiety for the result, till seeing him turn at the end of his career, and come back rejoicing and triumphing for what he had performed, they all burst out into acclamations of applause; and his father, shedding tears, it is said, for joy, kissed him as he came down from his horse, and in his transport, said, "O my son, look thee out a kingdom equal to and worthy of thyself, for Macedonia is too little for thee."

After this, considering him to be of a temper easy to be led to his duty by reason, but by no means to be compelled, he always endeavored to persuade rather than to command or force him to anything; and now looking upon the instruction and tuition of his youth to be of greater difficulty and importance, than to be wholly trusted to the ordinary masters in music and poetry, and the common school subjects, and to require, as Sophocles says,

The bridle and the rudder too,

he sent for Aristotle, the most learned and most cerebrated philosopher of his time, and rewarded him with a magnificence worthy of him. For he repeopled his native city Stagira, which he had caused to be demolished a little before, and restored all the citizens who were in exile or slavery, to their habitations. As a place for the pursuit of their studies and exercises, he assigned the temple of the Nymphs, near Mieza, where, to this very day, they show you Aristotle's stone seats, and the shady walks which he was wont to frequent. It would appear that Alexander received from him not only his doctrines of Morals, and of Politics, but also something of those more abstruse and profound theories which these philosophers, by the very names they gave them, professed to reserve for oral communication to the initiated, and did not allow many to become acquainted with. For when he was in Asia, and heard Aristotle had published some treatises of that kind, he wrote to him, using very plain language to him in behalf of philosophy, the following letter. "Alexander to Aristotle greeting. You have not done well to publish your books of oral doctrine; for what is there now that we excel others in, if those things which we have been particularly instructed in be laid open to all? For my part, I assure you, I had rather excel others in the knowledge of what is excellent, than in the extent of my power and dominion. Farewell." And Aristotle, soothing this passion for preeminence, speaks, in his excuse for himself, of these doctrines, as in fact both published and not published: as indeed, to say the truth, his books on metaphysics are written in a style which makes them useless for ordinary teaching, and instructive only, in the way of memoranda, for those who have been already conversant in that sort of learning.

Doubtless also it was to Aristotle, that he owed the inclination he had, not to the theory only, but likewise to the practice of the art of medicine. For when any of his friends were sick, he would often prescribe them their course of diet, and medicines proper to their disease, as we may find in his epistles. He was naturally a great lover of all kinds of learning and reading; and Onesicritus[5] informs us, that he constantly laid Homer's *Iliad*, according to the copy corrected by Aristotle, called the casket copy, with his dagger under his pillow, declaring that he esteemed it a perfect portable treasure of all military virtue and knowledge. When he was in the upper Asia, being destitute of other books, he ordered Harpalus to send him some; who furnished him with Philistus's History, a great many of the plays of Euripides, Sophocles, and Aeschylus, and some dithyrambic odes, composed by Telestes and Philoxenus. For awhile he loved and cherished Aristotle no less, as he was wont to say himself, than if he had been his father, giving this reason for it, that as he had received life from the one, so the other had taught him to live well. But afterwards, upon some mistrust of him, yet not so great as to make him do him any hurt, his familiarity and friendly kindness to him abated so much of its former force and affectionateness, as to make it evident he was alienated from him. However, his violent thirst after and passion for learning, which were once implanted, still grew up with him, and never decayed; as appears by his veneration of Anaxarchus, by the present of fifty talents which he sent to Xenocrates, and his particular care and esteem of Dandamis and Calanus.

Translated by A.H. Clough.

Portrait of Pericles. His Domestic Politics. Construction of the Acropolis.

Plutarch, *Pericles* 7-16

Who was Pericles, the bold leader of Athenian democracy and the builder of the Acropolis? He was an aristocrat. His timid personality as a young man would mature into strength and confidence. As a political and military leader, he was a ruthless rival for his political enemies and a master in the art of persuasion.

"He was able generally to lead the people along, with their own wills and consents, by persuading and showing them what was to be done; and sometimes, too, urging and pressing them forward extremely against their will, he made them, whether they would or no, yield submission to what was for their advantage."

Pericles, while yet but a young man, stood in considerable apprehension of the people, as he was thought in face and figure to be very like the tyrant Pisistratus, and those of great age remarked upon the sweetness of his voice, and his volubility and rapidity in speaking, and were struck with amazement at the resemblance. Reflecting, too, that he had a considerable estate, and was descended of a noble family, and had friends of great influence, he was fearful all this might bring him to be banished as a dangerous person; and for this reason meddled not at all with state affairs, but in military service showed himself of a brave and intrepid nature. But when Aristides was now dead, and Themistocles driven out, and Cimon[6] was for the most part kept abroad by the expeditions he made in parts out of Greece, Pericles, seeing things in this posture, now advanced and took his side, not with the rich and few, but with the many and poor, contrary to his natural bent, which was far from democratical; but, most likely, fearing he might fall under suspicion of aiming at arbitrary power, and seeing Cimon on the side of the aristocracy, and much beloved by the better and more distinguished people, he joined the party of the people, with a view at once both to secure himself and procure means against Cimon.

He immediately entered, also, on quite a new course of life and management of his time. For he was never seen to walk in any street but that which led to the marketplace and the council-hall, and he avoided invitations of friends to supper, and all friendly visiting and intercourse whatever; in all the time he had to do with the public, which was not a little, he was never known to have gone to any of his friends to a supper, except that once when his near kinsman Euryptolemus married, he remained present till the ceremony of the drink-offering, and then immediately rose from table and went his way. For these friendly meetings are very quick to defeat any assumed superiority, and in intimate familiarity an exterior of gravity is hard to maintain. Real excellence, indeed, is most recognized when most openly looked into; and in really good men, nothing which meets the eyes of external observers so truly deserves their admiration, as their daily common life does that of their nearer friends. Pericles, however, to avoid any feeling of commonness, or any satiety on the part of the people, presented himself at intervals only, not speaking to every business, nor at all times coming into the assembly, but, as Critolaus says, reserving himself, like the Salaminian galley, for great occasions,[7] while matters of lesser importance were dispatched by friends or other speakers under his direction. And of this number we are told Ephialtes[8] made one, who broke the power of the council of Areopagus, giving the people, according to Plato's expression, so copious and so strong a draught of liberty, that, growing wild and unruly, like an unmanageable horse, it, as the comic poets say, —

> " — *got beyond all keeping in,*
> *Champing at Euboea, and among the islands leaping in.*"

The style of speaking most consonant to his form of life and the dignity of his views he found, so to say, in the tones of that instrument with which Anaxagoras had furnished him; of his teaching he continually availed himself, and deepened the colors of rhetoric with the dye of natural science. For having, in addition to his great natural genius, attained, by the study of nature, to use the words of the divine Plato, this height of intelligence, and this universal consummating power, and drawing hence whatever might be of advantage to him in the art of speaking, he showed himself far superior to all others. Upon which account, they say, he had his nickname given him, though some are of opinion he was named the Olympian from the public buildings with which he adorned the city; and others again, from his great power in public affairs, whether of war or peace. Nor is it unlikely that the confluence of many attributes may have conferred it on him. However, the comedies represented at the time, which, both in good earnest and in merriment, let fly many hard words at him, plainly show that he got that appellation especially from his speaking; they speak of his "thundering and lightning" when he harangued the people, and of his wielding a dreadful thunderbolt in his tongue.

A saying also of Thucydides, the son of Melesias, stands on record, spoken by him by way of pleasantry upon Pericles's dexterity. Thucydides was one of the noble and distinguished citizens, and had been his greatest opponent; and, when Archidamus, the king of the Lacedaemonians, asked him whether he or Pericles were the better wrestler, he made this answer: "When I," said he, "have thrown him and given him a fair fall, by persisting that he had no fall, he gets the better of me, and makes the bystanders, in spite of their own eyes, believe him." The truth, however, is, that Pericles himself was very careful what and how he was to speak, insomuch that, whenever he went up to the hustings, he prayed the gods that no one word might unawares slip from him unsuitable to the matter and the occasion.

He has left nothing in writing behind him, except some decrees; and there are but very few of his sayings recorded; one, for example, is, that he said Aegina must, like a gathering in a man's eye, be removed from Piraeus; and another, that he said he saw already war moving on its way towards them out of Peloponnesus. Again, when on a time Sophocles, who was his fellow-commissioner in the generalship, was going on board with him, and praised the beauty of a youth they met with in the way to the ship, "Sophocles," said he, "a general ought not only to have clean hands, but also clean eyes." And Stesimbrotus tells us, that, in his encomium on those who fell in battle at Samos, he said they were become immortal, as the gods were. "For," said he, "we do not see them themselves, but only by the honors we pay them, and by the benefits they do us, attribute to them immortality; and the like attributes belong also to those that die in the service of their country."

Since Thucydides describes the rule of Pericles as an aristocratical government, that went by the name of a democracy, but was, indeed, the supremacy of a single great man, while many others say, on the contrary, that by him the common people were first encouraged and led on to such evils as appropriations of subject territory; allowances for attending theaters, payments for performing public duties, and by these bad habits were, under the influence of his public measures, changed from a sober, thrifty people, that maintained themselves by their own labors, to lovers of expense, intemperance, and license, let us examine the cause of this change by the actual matters of fact.

At the first, as has been said, when he set himself against Cimon's great authority, he did caress the people. Finding himself come short of his competitor in wealth and money, by which advantages the other was enabled to take care of the poor, inviting every day some one or other of the citizens that was in want to supper, and bestowing clothes on the aged people, and breaking down the hedges and enclosures of his grounds, that all that would might freely gather what fruit they pleased, Pericles, thus outdone in popular arts, by the advice of one Damonides of Oea, as Aristotle states, turned to the distribution of the public moneys; and in a short time having bought the people over, what with moneys allowed for shows and for service on juries, and what with other forms of pay and largess, he made use of them against the council of Areopagus, of which he himself was no member, as having never been appointed by lot either chief archon, or lawgiver, or king, or captain. For from of old these offices were conferred on persons by lot, and they who had acquitted themselves duly in the discharge of them were advanced to the court of Areopagus. And so Pericles, having secured his power and interest with the populace, directed the exertions of his party against this council with such success, that most of those causes and matters which had been used to be tried there, were, by the agency of Ephialtes, removed from its cognizance, Cimon, also, was banished by ostracism as a favorer of the Lacedaemonians and a hater of the people, though in wealth and noble birth he was among the first, and had won several most glorious victories over the barbarians, and had filled the city with money and spoils of war; as is recorded in the history of his life. So vast an authority had Pericles obtained among the people.

The ostracism was limited by law to ten years; but the Lacedaemonians, in the mean time, entering with a great army into the territory of Tanagra, and the Athenians going out against them, Cimon, coming from his banishment before his time was out, put himself in arms and array with those of his fellow-citizens that were of his own tribe, and desired by his deeds to wipe off the suspicion of his favoring the Lacedaemonians, by venturing his own person along with his countrymen. But Pericles's friends, gathering in a body, forced him to retire as a banished man. For which cause also Pericles seems to have exerted himself more in that than in any battle, and to have been conspicuous above all for his exposure of himself to danger. All Cimon's friends, also, to a man, fell together side by side, whom Pericles had accused with him of taking part with the Lacedaemonians. Defeated in this battle on their own frontiers, and expecting a new and perilous attack with return of spring, the Athenians now felt regret and sorrow for the loss of Cimon, and repentance for their expulsion of him. Pericles, being sensible of their feelings, did not hesitate or delay to gratify it, and himself made the motion for recalling him home. He, upon his return, concluded a peace betwixt the two cities; for the Lacedaemonians entertained as kindly feelings towards him as they did the reverse towards Pericles and the other popular leaders.

Yet some there are who say that Pericles did not propose the order for Cimon's return till some private articles of agreement had been made between them, and this by means of Elpinice, Cimon's sister; that Cimon, namely, should go out to sea with a fleet of two hundred ships, and be commander-in-chief abroad, with a design to reduce the king of Persia's territories, and that Pericles should have the power at home.

This Elpinice, it was thought, had before this time procured some favor for her brother Cimon at Pericles's hands, and induced him to be more remiss and gentle in urging the charge when Cimon was tried for his life; for Pericles was one of the committee appointed by the commons to plead against him. And when Elpinice came and besought him in her brother's behalf, he answered, with a smile, "O Elpinice, you are too old a woman to undertake such business as this." But, when he appeared to impeach him, he stood up but once to speak, merely to acquit himself of his commission, and went out of court, having done Cimon the least prejudice of any of his accusers.

How, then, can one believe Idomeneus, who charges Pericles as if he had by treachery procured the murder of Ephialtes, the popular statesman, one who was his friend, and of his own party in all his political course, out of jealousy, forsooth, and envy of his great reputation? This historian, it seems, having raked up these stories, I know not whence, has befouled with them a man who, perchance, was not altogether free from fault or blame, but yet had a noble spirit, and a soul that was bent on honor; and where such qualities are, there can no such cruel and brutal passion find harbor or gain admittance. As to Ephialtes, the truth of the story, as Aristotle has told it, is this: that having made himself formidable to the oligarchical party, by being an uncompromising asserter of the people's rights in calling to account and prosecuting those who any way wronged them, his enemies, lying in wait for him, by the means of Aristodicus the Tanagraean, privately dispatched him.

Cimon, while he was admiral, ended his days in the Isle of Cyprus. And the aristocratical party, seeing that Pericles was already before this grown to be the greatest and foremost man of all the city, but nevertheless wishing there should be somebody set up against him, to blunt and turn the edge of his power, that it might not altogether prove a monarchy, put forward Thucydides of Alopece, a discreet person, and a near kinsman of Cimon's, to conduct the opposition against him; who, indeed, though less skilled in warlike affairs than Cimon was, yet was better versed in speaking and political business, and keeping close guard in the city, and engaging with Pericles on the hustings, in a short time brought the government to an equality of parties. For he would not suffer those who were called the honest and good (persons of worth and distinction) to be scattered up and down and mix themselves and be lost among the populace, as formerly, diminishing and obscuring their superiority amongst the masses; but taking them apart by themselves and uniting them in one body, by their combined weight he was able, as it were upon the balance, to make a counter-poise to the other party.

For, indeed, there was from the beginning a sort of concealed split, or seam, as it might be in a piece of iron, marking the different popular and aristocratical tendencies; but the open rivalry and contention of these two opponents made the gash deep, and severed the city into the two parties of the people and the few. And so Pericles, at that time more than at any other, let loose the reins to the people, and made his policy subservient to their pleasure, contriving continually to have some great public show or solemnity, some banquet, or some procession or other in the town to please them, coaxing his countrymen like children, with such delights and pleasures as were not, however, unedifying. Besides that every year he sent out threescore galleys, on board of which there went numbers of the citizens, who were in pay eight months,[9] learning at the same time and practicing the art of seamanship.

He sent, moreover, a thousand of them into the Chersonese as planters, to share the land among them by lot, and five hundred more into the isle of Naxos, and half that number to Andros, a thousand into Thrace to dwell among the Bisaltae, and others into Italy, when the city Sybaris, which now was called Thurii, was to be repeopled. And this he did to ease and discharge the city of an idle, and, by reason of their idleness, a busy, meddling crowd of people; and at the same time to meet the necessities and restore the fortunes of the poor townsmen, and to intimidate, also, and check their allies from attempting any change, by posting such garrisons, as it were, in the midst of them.

That which gave most pleasure and ornament to the city of Athens, and the greatest admiration and even astonishment to all strangers, and that which now is Greece's only evidence that the power she boasts of and her ancient wealth are no romance or idle story, was his construction of the public and sacred buildings. Yet this was that of all his actions in the government which his enemies most looked askance upon and caviled at in the popular assemblies, crying out how that the commonwealth of Athens had lost its reputation and was ill-spoken of abroad for removing the common treasure of the Greeks from the isle of Delos into their own custody; and how that their fairest excuse for so doing, namely, that they took it away for fear the barbarians should seize it, and on purpose to secure it in a safe place, this Pericles had made unavailable, and how that "Greece cannot but resent it as an insufferable affront, and consider herself to be tyrannized over openly, when she sees the treasure, which was contributed by her upon a necessity for the war, wantonly lavished out by us upon our city, to gild her all over, and to adorn and set her forth, as it were some vain woman, hung round with precious stones and figures and temples, which cost a world of money."

Pericles, on the other hand, informed the people, that they were in no way obliged to give any account of those moneys to their allies, so long as they maintained their defense, and kept off the barbarians from attacking them; while in the meantime they did not so much as supply one horse or man or ship, but only found money for the service; "which money," said he, "is not theirs that give it, but theirs that receive it, if so be they perform the conditions upon which they receive it." And that it was good reason, that, now the city was sufficiently provided and stored with all things necessary for the war, they should convert the overplus of its wealth to such undertakings, as would hereafter, when completed, give them eternal honor, and, for the present, while in process, freely supply all the inhabitants with plenty. With their variety of workmanship and of occasions for service, which summon all arts and trades and require all hands to be employed about them, they do actually put the whole city, in a manner, into state-pay; while at the same time she is both beautified and maintained by herself. For as those who are of age and strength for war are provided for and maintained in the armaments abroad by their pay out of the public stock, so, it being his desire and design that the undisciplined mechanic multitude that stayed at home should not go without their share of public salaries, and yet should not have them given them for sitting still and doing nothing, to that end he thought fit to bring in among them, with the approbation of the people, these vast projects of buildings and designs of works, that would be of some continuance before they were finished, and would give employment to numerous arts, so that the part of the people that stayed at home might, no less than those that were at sea or in garrisons or on expeditions, have a fair and just occasion of receiving the benefit and having their share of the public moneys.

The materials were stone, brass, ivory, gold, ebony cypress-wood; and the arts or trades that wrought and fashioned them were smiths and carpenters, molders, founders and braziers, stone-cutters, dyers, goldsmiths, ivory-workers, painters, embroiderers, turners; those again that conveyed them to the town for use, merchants and mariners and ship-masters by sea, and by land, cartwrights, cattle-breeders, waggoners, rope-makers, flax-workers, shoe-makers and leather-dressers, roadmakers, miners. And every trade in the same nature, as a captain in an army has his particular company of soldiers under him, had its own hired company of journeymen and laborers belonging to it banded together as in array, to be as it were the instrument and body for the performance of the service. Thus, to say all in a word, the occasions and services of these public works distributed plenty through every age and condition.

As then grew the works up, no less stately in size than exquisite in form, the workmen striving to outvie the material and the design with the beauty of their workmanship, yet the most wonderful thing of all was the rapidity of their execution. Undertakings, any one of which singly might have required, they thought, for their completion, several successions and ages of men, were every one of them accomplished in the height and prime of one man's political service. Although they say, too, that Zeuxis once, having heard Agatharchus the painter boast of dispatching his work with speed and ease, replied, "I take a long time." For ease and speed in doing a thing do not give the work lasting solidity or exactness of beauty; the expenditure of time allowed to a man's pains beforehand for the production of a thing is repaid by way of interest with a vital force for its preservation when once produced.

For which reason Pericles's works are especially admired, as having been made quickly, to last long. For every particular piece of his work was immediately, even at that time, for its beauty and elegance, antique; and yet in its vigor and freshness looks to this day as if it were just executed.[10] There is a sort of bloom of newness upon those works of his, preserving them from the touch of time, as if they had some perennial spirit and undying vitality mingled in the composition of them.

Phidias had the oversight of all the works, and was surveyor-general, though upon the various portions other great masters and workmen were employed. For Callicrates and Ictinus built the Parthenon; the chapel at Eleusis, where the mysteries were celebrated, was begun by Coroebus, who erected the pillars that stand upon the floor or pavement, and joined them to the architraves; and after his death Metagenes of Xypete added the frieze and the upper line of columns; Xenocles of Cholargus roofed or arched the lantern on the top of the temple of Castor and Pollux; and the long wall, which Socrates says he himself heard Pericles propose to the people, was undertaken by Callicrates.[11] This work Cratinus ridicules, as long in finishing,—

'Tis long since Pericles, if words would do it,
Talk'd up the wall; yet adds not one mite to it.

The Odeum, or music-room, which in its interior was full of seats and ranges of pillars, and outside had its roof made to slope and descend from one single point at the top, was constructed, we are told, in imitation of the king of Persia's Pavilion; this likewise by Pericles's order; which Cratinus again, in his comedy called The Thracian Women, made an occasion of raillery,—

So, we see here,
Jupiter Long-pate Pericles appear,
Since ostracism time, he's laid aside his head,
And wears the new Odeum in its stead.

Pericles, also, eager for distinction, then first obtained the decree for a contest in musical skill to be held yearly at the Panathenaea, and he himself, being chosen judge, arranged the order and method in which the competitors should sing and play on the flute and on the harp. And both at that time, and at other times also, they sat in this music-room to see and hear all such trials of skill.

The propylaea, or entrances to the Acropolis, were finished in five years' time, Mnesicles being the principal architect. A strange accident happened in the course of building, which showed that the goddess was not averse to the work, but was aiding and cooperating to bring it to perfection. One of the artificers, the quickest and the handiest workman among them all, with a slip of his foot fell down from a great height, and lay in a miserable condition, the physicians having no hopes of his recovery. When Pericles was in distress about this, Minerva appeared to him at night in a dream, and ordered a course of treatment, which he applied, and in a short time and with great ease cured the man. And upon this occasion it was that he set up a brass statue of Minerva, surnamed Health, in the citadel near the altar, which they say was there before. But it was Phidias who wrought the goddess's image in gold, and he has his name inscribed on the pedestal as the workman of it; and indeed the whole work in a manner was under his charge, and he had, as we have said already, the oversight over all the artists and workmen, through Pericles's friendship for him; and this, indeed, made him much envied, and his patron shamefully slandered with stories, as if Phidias were in the habit of receiving, for Pericles's use, freeborn women that came to see the works. The comic writers of the town, when they had got hold of this story, made much of it, and bespattered him with all the ribaldry they could invent, charging him falsely with the wife of Menippus, one who was his friend and served as lieutenant under him in the wars; and with the birds kept by Pyrilampes, an acquaintance of Pericles, who, they pretended, used to give presents of peacocks to Pericles's female friends. And how can one wonder at any number of strange assertions from men whose whole lives were devoted to mockery, and who were ready at any time to sacrifice the reputation of their superiors to vulgar envy and spite, as to some evil genius, when even Stesimbrotus the Thasian has dared to lay to the charge of Pericles a monstrous and fabulous piece of criminality with his son's wife? So very difficult a matter is it to trace and find out the truth of anything by history, when, on the one hand, those who afterwards write it find long periods of time intercepting their view, and, on the other hand, the contemporary records of any actions and lives, partly through envy and ill-will, partly through favor and flattery, pervert and distort truth.

When the orators, who sided with Thucydides and his party, were at one time crying out, as their custom was, against Pericles, as one who squandered away the public money, and made havoc of the state revenues, he rose in the open assembly and put the question to the people, whether they thought that he had laid out much; and they saying, "Too much, a great deal." "Then," said he, "since it is so, let the cost not go to your account, but to mine; and let the inscription upon the buildings stand in my name." When they heard him say thus, whether it were out of a surprise to see the greatness of his spirit, or out of emulation of the glory of the works, they cried aloud, bidding him to spend on, and lay out what he thought fit from the public purse, and to spare no cost, till all were finished.

At length, coming to a final contest with Thucydides, which of the two should ostracize the other out of the country, and having gone through this peril, he threw his antagonist out, and broke up the confederacy that had been organized against him. So that now all schism and division being at an end, and the city brought to evenness and unity, he got all Athens and all affairs that pertained to the Athenians into his own hands, their tributes, their armies, and their galleys, the islands, the sea, and their wide-extended power, partly over other Greeks and partly over barbarians, and all that empire, which they possessed, founded and fortified upon subject nations and royal friendships and alliances.

After this he was no longer the same man he had been before, nor as tame and gentle and familiar as formerly with the populace, so as readily to yield to their pleasures and to comply with the desires of the multitude, as a steersman shifts with the winds. Quitting that loose, remiss, and, in some cases, licentious court of the popular will, he turned those soft and flowery modulations to the austerity of aristocratical and regal rule; and employing this uprightly and undeviatingly for the country's best interests, he was able generally to lead the people along, with their own wills and consents, by persuading and showing them what was to be done; and sometimes, too, urging and pressing them forward extremely against their will, he made them, whether they would or no, yield submission to what was for their advantage. In which, to say the truth, he did but like a skillful physician, who, in a complicated and chronic disease, as he sees occasion, at one while allows his patient the moderate use of such things as please him, at another while gives him keen pains and drugs to work the cure. For there arising and growing up, as was natural, all manner of distempered feelings among a people which had so vast a command and dominion, he alone, as a great master, knowing how to handle and deal fitly with each one of them, and, in an especial manner, making that use of hopes and fears, as his two chief rudders, with the one to check the career of their confidence at any time, with the other to raise them up and cheer them when under any discouragement, plainly showed by this, that rhetoric, or the art of speaking, is, in Plato's language, the government of the souls of men, and that her chief business is to address the affections and passions, which are as it were the strings and keys to the soul, and require a skillful and careful touch to be played on as they should be. The source of this predominance was not barely his power of language, but, as Thucydides assures us, the reputation of his life, and the confidence felt in his character; his manifest freedom from every kind of corruption, and superiority to all considerations of money. Notwithstanding he had made the city Athens, which was great of itself, as great and rich as can be imagined, and though he were himself in power and interest more than equal to many kings and absolute rulers, who some of them also bequeathed by will their power to their children, he, for his part, did not make the patrimony his father left him greater than it was by one drachma.

Thucydides, indeed, gives a plain statement of the greatness of his power; and the comic poets, in their spiteful manner, more than hint at it, styling his companions and friends the new Pisistratidae,[12] and calling on him to abjure any intention of usurpation, as one whose eminence was too great to be any longer proportionable to and compatible with a democracy or popular government. And Teleclides says the Athenians had surrendered up to him —

The tribute of the cities, and with them, the cities too,
to do withthem as he pleases, and undo;
To build up, if he likes, stone walls around a town;
and again, if so helikes, to pull them down;
Their treaties and alliances, power, empire, peace, and war,
theirwealth and their success forevermore.

Nor was all this the luck of some happy occasion; nor was it the mere bloom and grace of a policy that flourished for a season; but having for forty years together maintained the first place among statesmen such as Ephialtes and Leocrates and Myronides and Cimon and Tolmides[13] and Thucydides were, after the defeat and banishment of Thucydides, for no less than fifteen years longer, in the exercise of one continuous unintermitted command in the office, to which he was annually reelected, of General, he preserved his integrity unspotted; though otherwise he was not altogether idle or careless in looking after his pecuniary advantage; his paternal estate, which of right belonged to him, he so ordered that it might neither through negligence be wasted or lessened, nor yet, being so full of business as he was, cost him any great trouble or time with taking care of it; and put it into such a way of management as he thought to be the most easy for himself, and the most exact. All his yearly products and profits he sold together in a lump, and supplied his household needs afterward by buying everything that he or his family wanted out of the market. Upon which account, his children, when they grew to age, were not well pleased with his management, and the women that lived with him were treated with little cost, and complained of this way of housekeeping, where everything was ordered and set down from day to day, and reduced to the greatest exactness; since there was not there, as is usual in a great family and a plentiful estate, any thing to spare, or over and above; but all that went out or came in, all disbursements and all receipts, proceeded as it were by number and measure. His manager in all this was a single servant, Evangelus by name, a man either naturally gifted or instructed by Pericles so as to excel every one in this art of domestic economy.

All this, in truth, was very little in harmony with Anaxagoras's wisdom; if, indeed, it be true that he, by a kind of divine impulse and greatness of spirit, voluntarily quitted his house, and left his land to lie fallow and to be grazed by sheep like a common. But the life of a contemplative philosopher and that of an active statesman are, I presume, not the same thing; for the one merely employs, upon great and good objects of thought, an intelligence that requires no aid of instruments nor supply of any external materials; whereas the other, who tempers and applies his virtue to human uses, may have occasion for affluence, not as a matter of mere necessity, but as a noble thing; which was Pericles's case, who relieved numerous poor citizens.

However, there is a story, that Anaxagoras himself, while Pericles was taken up with public affairs, lay neglected, and that, now being grown old, he wrapped himself up with a resolution to die for want of food; which being by chance brought to Pericles's ear, he was horror-struck, and instantly ran thither, and used all the arguments and entreaties he could to him, lamenting not so much Anaxagoras's condition as his own, should he lose such a counselor as he had found him to be; and that, upon this, Anaxagoras unfolded his robe, and showing himself, made answer: "Pericles," said he, "even those who have occasion for a lamp supply it with oil."

Translated by A.H. Clough.

EPICTETUS

c. AD 50 - 130

Epictetus was born at Hierapolis in Phrygia (western Turkey). He became the slave of a freedman of Nero in Rome. Once granted his freedom, he founded a school of philosophy. Emperor Domitian's decree against philosophers, however, forced him to flee Rome. He escaped to Nikopolis in northwestern Greece, where he taught until his death.

Epictetus never put ink to paper. Fortunately, one of his most faithful auditors—the future Roman historian and statesman Arrian—transcribed Epictetus' oral teachings. From the Discourses, *only four of eight books survive. The complete collection was comprised in part of a technical section today lost, in which ancient Stoicism was explained, interpreted, and commented on. A less formal part included liberal discussions about the practice of Stoicism through spiritual exercise and asceticism. As for the* Manual, *it summarizes Epictetus' most poignant teachings.*

Epictetus' influence on Emperor Marcus Aurelius was enormous, as was his impact on late Neoplatonism, which integrated the Manual *into its program of study. Epictetus' teachings would be further adopted by Byzantine monasticism and followers of Christian spirituality. Hints of his teachings also occur in later works, such as Montaigne's* Essays *and Descartes'* Letter to Princess Elizabeth. *Finally, the influence of Epictetus on the writings of Pascal is evident. The latter alternates between praising the* Manual *and criticizing the* Discourses.

In What Manner We Ought to Bear Sickness

Epictetus, *Discourses* 3.10

"What is philosophizing? Is it not a preparation against events which may happen?"

When the need of each opinion comes, we ought to have it in readiness: on the occasion of breakfast, such opinions as relate to breakfast; in the bath, those that concern the bath; in bed, those that concern bed.

Let sleep not come upon thy languid eyes
Before each daily action thou hast scann'd;
What's done amiss, what done, what left undone;
From first to last examine all, and then
Blame what is wrong, in what is right rejoice.

And we ought to retain these verses in such way that we may use them, not that we may utter them aloud, as when we exclaim, "Paean Apollo." Again in fever we should have ready such opinions as concern a fever; and we ought not, as soon as the fever begins, to lose and forget all. A man who has a fever may say: If I philosophize any longer, may I be hanged; wherever I go, I must take care of the poor body, that a fever may not come. But what is philosophizing? Is it not a preparation against events which may happen? Do you not understand that you are saying something of this kind? "If I shall still prepare myself to bear with patience what happens, may I be hanged." But this is just as if a man after receiving blows should give up the Pancratium. In the Pancratium it is in our power to desist and not to receive blows.

But in the other matter if we give up philosophy, what shall we gain? What then should a man say on the occasion of each painful thing? It was for this that I exercised myself, for this I disciplined myself. God says to you: Give me a proof that you have duly practised athletics, that you have eaten what you ought, that you have been exercised, that you have obeyed the aliptes (the oiler and rubber). Then do you show yourself weak when the time for action comes? Now is the time for the fever. Let it be borne well. Now is the time for thirst, bear it well. Now is the time for hunger, bear it well. Is it not in your power? Who shall hinder you? The physician will hinder you from drinking; but he cannot prevent you from bearing thirst well: and he will hinder you from eating; but he cannot prevent you from bearing hunger well.

But I cannot attend to my philosophical studies. And for what purpose do you follow them? Slave, is it not that you may be happy, that you may be constant, is it not that you may be in a state conformable to nature and live so? What hinders you when you have a fever from having your ruling faculty conformable to nature? Here is the proof of the thing, here is the test of the philosopher. For this also is a part of life, like walking, like sailing, like journeying by land, so also is fever. Do you read when you are walking? No. Nor do you when you have a fever. But if you walk about well, you have all that belongs to a man who walks. If you bear a fever well, you have all that belongs to a man in a fever. What is it to bear a fever well? Not to blame God or man; not to be afflicted at that which happens, to expect death well and nobly, to do what must be done: when the physician comes in, not to be frightened at what he says; nor if he says you are doing well, to be overjoyed. For what good has he told you? and when you were in health, what good was that to you? And even if he says you are in a bad way, do not despond.

For what is it to be ill? is it that you are near the severance of the soul and the body? what harm is there in this? If you are not near now, will you not afterwards be near? Is the world going to be turned upside down when you are dead? Why then do you flatter the physician? Why do you say if you please, master, I shall be well? Why do you give him an opportunity of raising his eyebrows (being proud; or showing his importance)? Do you not value a physician, as you do a shoemaker when he is measuring your foot, or a carpenter when he is building your house, and so treat the physician as to the body which is not yours, but by nature dead? He who has a fever has an opportunity of doing this: if he does these things, he has what belongs to him.

For it is not the business of a philosopher to look after these externals, neither his wine nor his oil nor his poor body, but his own ruling power. But as to externals how must he act? so far as not to be careless about them. Where then is there reason for fear? where is there then still reason for anger, and of fear about what belongs to others, about things which are of no value? For we ought to have these two principles in readiness, that except the will nothing is good nor bad; and that we ought not to lead events, but to follow them. My brother ought not to have behaved thus to me. No, but he will see to that; and, however he may behave, I will conduct myself towards him as I ought. For this is my own business; that belongs to another: no man can prevent this, the other thing can be hindered.

What Solitude Is, and What Kind of Person a Solitary Man Is

Epictetus, *Discourses* 3.13

"Every great power is dangerous to beginners."

Solitude is a certain condition of a helpless man. For because a man is alone, he is not for that reason also solitary; just as though a man is among numbers, he is not therefore not solitary. When then we have lost either a brother, or a son, or a friend on whom we were accustomed to repose, we say that we are left solitary, though we are often in Rome, though such a crowd meet us, though so many live in the same place, and sometimes we have a great number of slaves. For the man who is solitary, as it is conceived, is considered to be a helpless person and exposed to those who wish to harm him. For this reason when we travel, then especially do we say that we are lonely when we fall among robbers, for it is not the sight of a human creature which removes us from solitude, but the sight of one who is faithful and modest and helpful to us. For if being alone is enough to make solitude, you may say that even Zeus is solitary in the conflagration[1] and bewails himself saying, Unhappy that I am who have neither Hera, nor Athena, nor Apollo, nor brother, nor son, nor descendant, nor kinsman. This is what some say that he does when he is alone at the conflagration. For they do not understand how a man passes his life when he is alone, because they set out from a certain natural principle, from the natural desire of community and mutual love and from the pleasure of conversation among men. But none the less a man ought to be prepared in a manner for this also (being alone), to be able to be sufficient for himself and to be his own companion. For as Zeus dwells with himself, and is tranquil by himself, and thinks of his own administration and of its nature, and is employed in thoughts suitable to himself; so ought we also to be able to talk with ourselves, not to feel the want of others also, not to be unprovided with the means of passing our time; to observe the divine administration, and the relation of ourselves to everything else; to consider how we formerly were affected towards things that happened and how at present; what are still the things which give us pain; how these also can be cured and how removed; if any things require improvement, to improve them according to reason.

For you see that Caesar appears to furnish us with great peace, that there are no longer enemies nor battles nor great associations of robbers nor of pirates, but we can travel at every hour and sail from east to west. But can Caesar give us security from fever also, can he from shipwreck, from fire, from earthquake or from lightning? Well, I will say, can he give us security against love? He cannot. From sorrow?

He cannot. From envy? He cannot. In a word then he cannot protect us from any of these things. But the doctrine of philosophers promises to give us security even against these things. And what does it say? "Men, if you will attend to me, wherever you are, whatever you are doing, you will not feel sorrow, nor anger, nor compulsion, nor hindrance, but you will pass your time without perturbations and free from everything." When a man has this peace, not proclaimed by Caesar (for how should he be able to proclaim it?), but by God through reason, is he not content when he is alone? when he sees and reflects, "Now no evil can happen to me; for me there is no robber, no earthquake, everything is full of peace, full of tranquillity: every way, every city, every meeting, neighbor, companion is harmless. One person whose business it is, supplies me with food; another with raiment; another with perceptions, and preconceptions. And if he does not supply what is necessary, He gives the signal for retreat, opens the door, and says to you, 'Go.' Go whither? To nothing terrible, but to the place from which you came, to your friends and kinsmen, to the elements: what there was in you of fire goes to fire; of earth, to earth; of air, to air; of water to water: no Hades, nor Acheron, nor Cocytus, nor Pyriphlegethon, but all is full of Gods and Demons."

When a man has such things to think on, and sees the sun, the moon and stars, and enjoys earth and sea, he is not solitary nor even helpless. Well then, if some man should come upon me when I am alone and murder me? Fool, not murder You, but your poor body. What kind of solitude then remains? what want? why do we make ourselves worse than children; and what do children do when they are left alone? They take up shells and ashes, and they build something, then pull it down, and build something else, and so they never want the means of passing the time. Shall I then, if you sail away, sit down and weep, because I have been left alone and solitary? Shall I then have no shells, no ashes? But children do what they do through want of thought (or deficiency in knowledge), and we through knowledge.

Every great power is dangerous to beginners. You must then bear such things as you are able, but conformably to nature. Practice sometimes a way of living like a man in health. Abstain from food, drink water, abstain sometimes altogether from desire, in order that you may some time desire consistently with reason; and if consistently with reason, when you have anything good in you, you will desire well. "Not so; but we wish to live like wise men immediately and to be useful to men." Useful how? what are you doing? have you been useful to yourself? "But, I suppose, you wish to exhort them." You exhort them! You wish to be useful to them. Show to them in your own example what kind of men philosophy makes, and don't trifle. When you are eating, do good to those who eat with you; when you are drinking, to those who are drinking with you; by yielding to all, giving way, bearing with them, thus do them good, and do not spit on them your phlegm.

Against Those Who Lament over Being Pitied

Epictetus, *Discourses* 4.6

"It is a royal thing, O Cyrus, to do right and to be ill-spoken of."

"I am grieved," a man says, "at being pitied." Whether, then, is the fact of your being pitied a thing which concerns you or those who pity you? Well, is it in your power to stop this pity? "It is in my power, if I show them that I do not require pity." And whether, then, are you in the condition of not deserving pity, or are you not in that condition? "I think I am not: but these persons do not pity me for the things for which, if they ought to pity me, it would be proper, I mean, for my faults; but they pity me for my poverty, for not possessing honourable offices, for diseases and deaths and other such things." Whether, then, are you prepared to convince the many that not one of these things is an evil, but that it is possible for a man who is poor and has no office and enjoys no honour to be happy; or to show yourself to them as rich and in power? For the second of these things belong, to a man who is boastful, silly and good for nothing. And consider by what means the pretense must be supported. It will be necessary for you to hire slaves and to possess a few silver vessels, and to exhibit them in public, if it is possible, though they are often the same, and to attempt to conceal the fact that they are the same, and to have splendid garments, and all other things for display, and to show that you are a man honoured by the great, and to try to sup at their houses, or to be supposed to sup there, and as to your person to employ some mean arts, that you may appear to be more handsome and nobler than you are. These things you must contrive, if you choose to go by the second path in order not to be pitied.

But the first way is both impracticable and long, to attempt the very thing which Zeus has not been able to do, to convince all men what things are good and bad. Is this power given to you? This only is given to you, to convince yourself; and you have not convinced yourself. Then I ask you, do you attempt to persuade other men? and who has lived so long with you as you with yourself? and who has so much power of convincing you as you have of convincing yourself; and who is better disposed and nearer to you than you are to yourself? How, then, have you not convinced yourself in order to learn? At present are not things upside down? Is this what you have been earnest about doing, to learn to be free from grief and free from disturbance, and not to be humbled, and to be free? Have you not heard, then, that there is only one way which leads to this end, to give up the things which do not depend on the will, to withdraw from them, and to admit that they belong to others?

For another man, then, to have an opinion about you, of what kind is it? "It is a thing independent of the will." Then is it nothing to you? "It is nothing." When, then, you are still vexed at this and disturbed, do you think that you are convinced about good and evil?

Will you not, then, letting others alone, be to yourself both scholar and teacher? "The rest of mankind will look after this, whether it is to their interest to be and to pass their lives in a state contrary to nature: but to me no man is nearer than myself. What, then, is the meaning of this, that I have listened to the words of the philosophers and I assent to them, but in fact I am no way made easier? Am I so stupid? And yet, in all other things such as I have chosen, I have not been found very stupid; but I learned letters quickly, and to wrestle, and geometry, and to resolve syllogisms. Has not, then, reason convinced me? and indeed no other things have I from the beginning so approved and chosen: and now I read about these things, hear about them, write about them; I have so far discovered no reason stronger than this. In what, then, am I deficient? Have the contrary opinions not been eradicated from me? Have the notions themselves not been exercised nor used to be applied to action, but as armour are laid aside and rusted and cannot fit me? And yet neither in the exercises of the palaestra, nor in writing or reading am I satisfied with learning, but I turn up and down the syllogisms which are proposed, and I make others, and sophistical syllogisms also. But the necessary theorems, by proceeding from which a man can become free from grief, fear, passions, hindrance, and a free man, these I do not exercise myself in nor do I practice in these the proper practice. Then I care about what others will say of me, whether I shall appear to them worth notice, whether I shall appear happy."

Wretched man, will you not see what you are saying about yourself? What do you appear to yourself to be? in your opinions, in your desires, in your aversions from things, in your movements, in your preparation, in your designs, and in other acts suitable to a man? But do you trouble yourself about this, whether others pity you? "Yes, but I am pitied not as I ought to be." Are you then pained at this? and is he who is pained, an object of pity? "Yes." How, then, are you pitied not as you ought to be? For by the very act that you feel about being pitied, you make yourself deserving of pity. What then says Antisthenes? Have you not heard? "It is a royal thing, O Cyrus, to do right and to be ill-spoken of."[2] My head is sound, and all think that I have the headache. What do I care for that? I am free from fever, and people sympathize with me as if I had a fever: "Poor man, for so long a time you have not ceased to have fever." I also say with a sorrowful countenance: "In truth it is now a long time that I have been ill." "What will happen then?" "As God may please": and at the same time I secretly laugh at those who are pitying me. What, then, hinders the same being done in this case also? I am poor, but I have a right opinion about poverty. Why, then, do I care if they pity me for my poverty? I am not in power; but others are: and I have the opinion which I ought to have about having and not having power. Let them look to it who pity me; but I am neither hungry nor thirsty nor do I suffer cold; but because they are hungry or thirsty they think that I too am. What, then, shall I do for them? Shall I go about and proclaim and say: "Be not mistaken, men, I am very well, I do not trouble myself about poverty, nor want of power, nor in a word about anything else than right opinions. These I have free from restraint, I care for nothing at all." What foolish talk is this? How do I possess right opinions when I am not content with being what I am, but am uneasy about what I am supposed to be?

"But," you say, "others will get more and be preferred to me." What, then, is more reasonable than for those who have laboured about anything to have more in that thing in which they have laboured? They have laboured for power, you have laboured about opinions; and they have laboured for wealth, you for the proper use of appearances. See if they have more than you in this about which you have laboured, and which they neglect; if they assent better than you with respect to the natural rules of things; if they are less disappointed than you in their desires; if they fall less into things which they would avoid than you do; if in their intentions, if in the things which they propose to themselves, if in their purposes, if in their motions toward an object they take a better aim; if they better observe a proper behavior, as men, as sons, as parents, and so on as to the other names by which we express the relations of life. But if they exercise power, and you do not, will you not choose to tell yourself the truth, that you do nothing for the sake of this, and they do all? But it is most unreasonable that he who looks after anything should obtain less than he who does not look after it.

"Not so: but since I care about right opinions, it is more reasonable for me to have power." Yes in the matter about which you do care, in opinions. But in a matter in which they have cared more than you, give way to them. The case is just the same as if, because you have right opinions, you thought that in using the bow you should hit the mark better than an archer, and in working in metal you should succeed better than a smith. Give up, then, your earnestness about opinions and employ yourself about the things which you wish to acquire; and then lament, if you do not succeed; for you deserve to lament. But now you say that you are occupied with other things, that you are looking after other things; but the many say this truly, that one act has no community with another. He who has risen in the morning seeks whom he shall salute, to whom he shall say something agreeable, to whom he shall send a present, how he shall please the dancing man, how by bad behavior to one he may please another. When he prays, he prays about these things; when he sacrifices, he sacrifices for these things: the saying of Pythagoras

Let sleep not come upon thy languid eyes

he transfers to these things. "Where have I failed in the matters pertaining to flattery?" "What have I done?" Anything like a free man, anything like a noble-minded man? And if he finds anything of the kind, he blames and accuses himself: "Why did you say this? Was it not in your power to lie? Even the philosophers say that nothing hinders us from telling a lie." But do you, if indeed you have cared about nothing else except the proper use of appearances, as soon as you have risen in the morning reflect, "What do I want in order to be free from passion, and free from perturbation? What am I? Am I a poor body, a piece of property, a thing of which something is said? I am none of these. But what am I? I am a rational animal. What then is required of me?" Reflect on your acts. "Where have I omitted the things which conduce to happiness? What have I done which is either unfriendly or unsocial? what have I not done as to these things which I ought to have done?"

So great, then, being, the difference in desires, actions, wishes, would you still have the same share with others in those things about which you have not laboured, and they have laboured? Then are you surprised if they pity you, and are you vexed? But they are not vexed if you pity them. Why? Because they are convinced that they have that which is good, and you are not convinced. For this reason you are not satisfied with your own, but you desire that which they have: but they are satisfied with their own, and do not desire what you have: since, if you were really convinced that with respect to what is good, it is you who are the possessor of it and that they have missed it, you would not even have thought of what they say about you.

What Things We Ought to Despise, And What Things We Ought to Value

Epictetus, *Discourses* 4.10

"If you wish to be a consul, you must keep awake, run about, kiss hands, waste yourself with exhaustion at other men's doors, say and do many things unworthy of a free man, send gifts to many, daily presents to some. And what is the thing that is got? Twelve bundles of rods, to sit three or four times on the tribunal, to exhibit the games in the Circus and to give suppers in small baskets."

The difficulties of all men are about external things, their helplessness is about externals. "What shall I do, how will it be, how will it turn out, will this happen, will that?" All these are the words of those who are turning themselves to things which are not within the power of the will. For who says, "How shall I not assent to that which is false? how shall I not turn away from the truth?" If a man be of such a good disposition as to be anxious about these things, I will remind him of this: "Why are you anxious? The thing is in your own power. Be assured; do not be precipitate in assenting before you apply the natural rule." On the other side, if a man is anxious about desire, lest it fail in its purpose and miss its end, and with respect to the avoidance of things, lest he should fall into that which he would avoid, I will first kiss him, because he throws away the things about which others are in a flutter, and their fears, and employs his thoughts about his own affairs and his own condition. Then I shall say to him: "If you do not choose to desire that which you will fall to obtain nor to attempt to avoid that into which you will fall, desire nothing which belongs to others, nor try to avoid any of the things which are not in your power. If you do not observe this rule, you must of necessity fall in your desires and fall into that which you would avoid. What is the difficulty here? where is there room for the words, 'How will it be?' and 'How will it turn out?' and, 'Will this happen or that?'

Now is not that which will happen independent of the will? "Yes." And the nature of good and of evil, is it not in the things which are within the power of the will? "Yes." Is it in your power, then, to treat according to nature everything which happens? Can any person hinder you? "No man." No longer then say to me, "How will it be?" For however it may be, you will dispose of it well, and the result to you will be a fortunate one. What would Hercules have been if he had said, "How shall a great lion not appear to me, or a great boar, or savage men?" And what do you care for that? If a great boar appear, you will fight a greater fight: if bad men appear, you relieve the earth of the bad. "Suppose, then, that I may lose my life in this way." You will die a good man, doing a noble act. For since we must certainly die, of necessity a man must be found doing something, either following the employment of a husbandman, or digging, or trading, or serving in a consulship or suffering from indigestion or from diarrhea. What then do you wish to be doing, when you are found by death? I for my part would wish to be found doing something which belongs to a man, beneficent, suitable to the general interest, noble. But if I cannot be found doing things so great, I would be found doing at least that which I cannot be hindered from doing, that which is permitted me to do, correcting, myself, cultivating the faculty which makes use of appearances, labouring at freedom from the affects, rendering to the relations of life their due; if I succeed so far, also touching on the third topic, safety in the forming judgements about things. If death surprises me when I am busy about these things, it is enough for me if I can stretch out my hands to God and say:

"The means which I have received from Thee for seeing Thy administration and following it, I have not neglected: I have not dishonoured Thee by my acts: see how I have used my perceptions, see how I have used my preconceptions: have I ever blamed Thee? have I been discontented with anything that happens, or wished it to be otherwise? have I wished to transgress the relations? That Thou hast given me life, I thank Thee for what Thou has given me: so long as I have used the things which are Thine, I am content; take them back and place them wherever Thou mayest choose; for Thine were all things, Thou gavest them to me." Is it not enough to depart in this state of mind, and what life is better and more becoming than that of a man who is in this state of mind? and what end is more happy?

But that this may be done, a man must receive no small things, nor are the things small which he must lose. You cannot both wish to be a consul and to have these things, and to be eager to have lands and these things also; and to be solicitous about slaves and about yourself. But if you wish for anything which belongs to another, that which is your own is lost. This is the nature of the thing: nothing is given or had for nothing. And where is the wonder? If you wish to be a consul, you must keep awake, run about, kiss hands, waste yourself with exhaustion at other men's doors, say and do many things unworthy of a free man, send gifts to many, daily presents to some. And what is the thing that is got? Twelve bundles of rods, to sit three or four times on the tribunal, to exhibit the games in the Circus and to give suppers in small baskets.

Or, if you do not agree about this, let some one show me what there is besides these things. In order, then, to secure freedom from passions, tranquillity, to sleep well when you do sleep, to be really awake when you are awake, to fear nothing, to be anxious about nothing, will you spend nothing and give no labour? But if anything belonging to you be lost while you are thus busied, or be wasted badly, or another obtains what you ought to have obtained, will you immediately be vexed at what has happened? Will you not take into the account on the other side what you receive and for what, how much for how much? Do you expect to have for nothing things so great? And how can you? One work has no community with another. You cannot have both external things after bestowing care on them and your own ruling faculty: but if you would have those, give up this. If you do not, you will have neither this nor that, while you are drawn in different ways to both. The oil will be spilled, the household vessels will perish: but I shall be free from passions. There will be a fire when I am not present, and the books will be destroyed: but I shall treat appearances according to nature.

"Well; but I shall have nothing to eat." If I am so unlucky, death is a harbour; and death is the harbour for all; this is the place of refuge; and for this reason not one of the things in life is difficult: as soon as you choose, you are out of the house, and are smoked no more. Why, then, are you anxious, why do you lose your sleep, why do you not straightway, after considering wherein your good is and your evil, say, "Both of them are in my power? Neither can any man deprive me of the good, nor involve me in the bad against my will. Why do I not throw myself down and snore? for all that I have is safe. As to the things which belong to others, he will look to them who gets them, as they may be given by Him who has the power. Who am I who wish to have them in this way or in that? is a power of selecting them given to me? has any person made me the dispenser of them? Those things are enough for me over which I have power: I ought to manage them as well as I can: and all the rest, as the Master of them may choose."

When a man has these things before his eyes, does he keep awake and turn hither and thither? What would he have, or what does he regret, Patroclus or Antilochus or Menelaus?[3] For when did he suppose that any of his friends was immortal, and when had he not before his eyes that on the morrow or the day after he or his friend must die? "Yes," he says, "but I thought that he would survive me and bring up my son." You were a fool for that reason, and you were thinking of what was uncertain. Why, then, do you not blame yourself, and sit crying like girls? "But he used to set my food before me." Because he was alive, you fool, but now he cannot: but Automedon will set it before you, and if Automedon also dies, you will find another. But if the pot, in which your meat was cooked, should be broken, must you die of hunger, because you have not the pot which you are accustomed to? Do you not send and buy a new pot? He says:

"No greater ill could fall on me."

Why is this your ill? Do you, then, instead of removing it, blame your mother for not foretelling it to you that you might continue grieving from that time? What do you think? do you not suppose that Homer wrote this that we may learn that those of noblest birth, the strongest and the richest, the most handsome, when they have not the opinions which they ought to have, are not prevented from being most wretched and unfortunate?

Against or to Those Who Readily Tell Their Own Affairs

Epictetus, *Discourses* 4.13

"We have this opinion that we can safely trust him who has already told us his own affairs; for the notion rises in our mind that this man could never divulge our affairs because he would be cautious that we also should not divulge his. In this way also the incautious are caught by the soldiers at Rome."

When a man has seemed to us to have talked with simplicity about his own affairs, how is it that at last we are ourselves also induced to discover to him our own secrets and we think this to be candid behavior? In the first place, because it seems unfair for a man to have listened to the affairs of his neighbour, and not to communicate to him also in turn our own affairs; next, because we think that we shall not present to them the appearance of candid men when we are silent about our own affairs. Indeed men are often accustomed to say, "I have told you all my affairs, will you tell me nothing of your own? where is this done?" Besides, we have also this opinion that we can safely trust him who has already told us his own affairs; for the notion rises in our mind that this man could never divulge our affairs because he would be cautious that we also should not divulge his. In this way also the incautious are caught by the soldiers at Rome. A soldier sits by you in a common dress and begins to speak ill of Caesar; then you, as if you had received a pledge of his fidelity by his having begun the abuse, utter yourself also what you think, and then you are carried off in chains.

Something of this kind happens to us generally. Now as this man has confidently intrusted his affairs to me, shall I also do so to any man whom I meet? For when I have heard, I keep silence, if I am of such a disposition; but he goes forth and tells all men what he has heard. Then if I hear what has been done, if I be a man like him, I resolve to be revenged, I divulge what he has told me; I both disturb others and am disturbed myself. But if I remember that one man does not injure another, and that every man's acts injure and profit him, I secure this, that I do not anything like him, but still I suffer what I do suffer through my own silly talk.

"True: but it is unfair when you have heard the secrets of your neighbour for you in turn to communicate nothing to him." Did I ask you for your secrets, my man? did you communicate your affairs on certain terms, that you should in return hear mine also? If you are a babbler and think that all who meet you are friends, do you wish me also to be like you? But why, if you did well in entrusting your affairs to me, and it is not well for me to intrust mine to you, do you wish me to be so rash? It is just the same as if I had a cask which is water-tight, and you one with a hole in it, and you should come and deposit with me your wine that I might put it into my cask, and then should complain that I also did not intrust my wine to you, for you have a cask with a hole in it. How then is there any equality here? You intrusted your affairs to a man who is faithful and modest, to a man who thinks that his own actions alone are injurious and useful, and that nothing external is. Would you have me intrust mine to you, a man who has dishonoured his own faculty of will, and who wishes to gain some small bit of money or some office or promotion in the court, even if you should be going to murder your own children, like Medea? Where is this equality? But show yourself to me to be faithful, modest, and steady; show me that you have friendly opinions; show that your cask has no hole in it; and you will see how I shall not wait for you to trust me with your affairs, but I myself shall come to you and ask you to hear mine. For who does not choose to make use of a good vessel? Who does not value a benevolent and faithful adviser? who will not willingly receive a man who is ready to bear a share, as we may say, of the difficulty of his circumstances, and by this very act to ease the burden, by taking a part of it.

"True: but I trust you; you do not trust me." In the first place, not even do you trust me, but you are a babbler, and for this reason you cannot hold anything; for indeed, if it is true that you trust me, trust your affairs to me only; but now, whenever you see a man at leisure, you seat yourself by him and say: "Brother, I have no friend more benevolent than you nor dearer; I request you to listen to my affairs." And you do this even to those who are not known to you at all. But if you really trust me, it is plain that you trust me because I am faithful and modest, not because I have told my affairs to you. Allow me, then, to have the same opinion about you. Show me that, if one man tells his affairs to another, he who tells them is faithful and modest. For if this were so, I would go about and tell my affairs to every man, if that would make me faithful and modest. But the thing is not so, and it requires no common opinions. If, then, you see a man who is busy about things not dependent on his will and subjecting his will to them, you must know that this man has ten thousand persons to compel and hinder him. He has no need of pitch or the wheel to compel him to declare what he knows: but a little girl's nod, if it should so happen, will move him, the blandishment of one who belongs to Caesar's court, desire of a magistracy or of an inheritance, and things without end of that sort. You must remember, then, among general principles that secret discourses require fidelity and corresponding opinions. But where can we now find these easily? Or if you cannot answer that question, let some one point out to me a man who can say: "I care only about the things which are my own, the things which are not subject to hindrance, the things which are by nature free." This I hold to be the nature of the good: but let all other things be as they are allowed; I do not concern myself.

Translated by George Long.

TACITUS

c. AD 56 - 116

Tacitus was first and foremost a politician served by his brilliant talents as an orator, his friendship with Pliny the Younger, and his marrying well to Agricola's daughter. (Agricola was the commander who under Emperor Vespasian conquered Britain.) He was a consul in AD 97 and later a proconsul in Asia Minor. As a lawyer, Tacitus was first interested in rhetoric and would only turn to history after his consulship.

His debut in literature was a critical essay titled Dialogue on Orators, *in which he takes the position that the ancients are superior to his contemporaries and ponders the causes of decadence in the art of oratory. Two short monographs would follow: an apology (in this sense, a defense) of his father-in-law, Agricola, and an ethnographic essay about the "German threat." It is only after these works that he began to write history, first with the* Histories *retracing the destiny of Rome from the reign of Galba to that of Domitian, and second with the* Annals *stretching further into the past, from Tiberius to Nero.*

Tacitus used firsthand documentation and struggled for impartiality. He tried to penetrate the secret of the soul to better explain what makes history "tick" and to recreate the atmosphere of the times he evokes.

Customs and Institutions of the Germans

Tacitus, *Germania* 1-27

The Germania *is an ethnographic study of the German people. It discusses their customs, their character, their beliefs, their institutions, and even the geography of their land. At the time Tacitus composed the work in AD 98, eight Roman legions were stationed along the Rhine frontier. The Romans understood full well the potential danger this remote northern region posed for the empire. Who possibly could forget this formidable enemy that in AD 9, less than a century before Tacitus wrote his* Germania, *had annihilated three Roman legions totaling 20,000 men, inflicting upon Rome one of its most crushing defeats? The Germanic conqueror was named Arminius, and Germans today continue to preserve the memory of their first great national hero: His name survives in the form of "Hermann," and is widely popular in Germany.*

"They even think it base and spiritless to earn by sweat what they might purchase with blood."

Germany is separated from Gaul, Rhaetia, and Pannonia, by the rivers Rhine and Danube; from Sarmatia and Dacia, by mountains and mutual dread. The rest is surrounded by an ocean, embracing broad promontories and vast insular tracts, in which our military expeditions have lately discovered various nations and kingdoms. The Rhine, issuing from the inaccessible and precipitous summit of the Rhaetic Alps, bends gently to the west, and falls into the Northern Ocean. The Danube, poured from the easy and gently raised ridge of Mount Abnoba, visits several nations in its course, till at length it bursts out by six channels into the Pontic sea; a seventh is lost in marshes.

The people of Germany appear to me indigenous, and free from intermixture with foreigners, either as settlers or casual visitants. For the emigrants of former ages performed their expeditions not by land, but by water; and that immense, and, if I may so call it, hostile ocean, is rarely navigated by ships from our world. Then, besides the danger of a boisterous and unknown sea, who would relinquish Asia, Africa, or Italy, for Germany, a land rude in its surface, rigorous in its climate, cheerless to every beholder and cultivator, except a native?

In their ancient songs, which are their only records or annals, they celebrate the god Tuisto, sprung from the earth, and his son Mannus, as the fathers and founders of their race. To Mannus they ascribe three sons, from whose names the people bordering on the ocean are called Ingaevones; those inhabiting the central parts, Herminones; the rest, Istaevones. Some, however, assuming the licence of antiquity, affirm that there were more descendants of the god, from whom more appellations were derived; as those of the Marsi, Gambrivii, Suevi, and Vandali; and that these are the genuine and original names. That of Germany, on the other hand, they assert to be a modern addition; for that the people who first crossed the Rhine, and expelled the Gauls, and are now called Tungri, were then named Germans; which appellation of a particular tribe, not of a whole people, gradually prevailed; so that the title of Germans, first assumed by the victors in order to excite terror, was afterwards adopted by the nation in general. They have likewise the tradition of a Hercules of their country, whose praises they sing before those of all other heroes as they advance to battle.

A peculiar kind of verses is also current among them, by the recital of which, termed "barding," they stimulate their courage; while the sound itself serves as an augury of the event of the impending combat. For, according to the nature of the cry proceeding from the line, terror is inspired or felt: nor does it seem so much an articulate song, as the wild chorus of valor. A harsh, piercing note, and a broken roar, are the favorite tones; which they render more full and sonorous by applying their mouths to their shields. Some conjecture that Ulysses, in the course of his long and fabulous wanderings, was driven into this ocean, and landed in Germany; and that Asciburgium, a place situated on the Rhine, and at this day inhabited, was founded by him, and named Askipurgion.[1] They pretend that an altar was formerly discovered here, consecrated to Ulysses, with the name of his father Laertes subjoined; and that certain monuments and tombs, inscribed with Greek characters, are still extant upon the confines of Germany and Rhaetia. These allegations I shall neither attempt to confirm nor to refute: let every one believe concerning them as he is disposed.

I concur in opinion with those who deem the Germans never to have intermarried with other nations; but to be a race, pure, unmixed, and stamped with a distinct character. Hence a family likeness pervades the whole, though their numbers are so great: eyes stern and blue; ruddy hair; large bodies, powerful in sudden exertions, but impatient of toil and labor, least of all capable of sustaining thirst and heat. Cold and hunger they are accustomed by their climate and soil to endure.

The land, though varied to a considerable extent in its aspect, is yet universally shagged with forests, or deformed by marshes: moister on the side of Gaul, more bleak on the side of Noricum and Pannonia. It is productive of grain, but unkindly to fruit-trees. It abounds in flocks and herds, but in general of a small breed. Even the beeve kind are destitute of their usual stateliness and dignity of head: they are, however, numerous, and form the most esteemed, and, indeed, the only species of wealth. Silver and gold the gods, I know not whether in their favor or anger, have denied to this country. Not that I would assert that no veins of these metals are generated in Germany; for who has made the search? The possession of them is not coveted by these people as it is by us. Vessels of silver are indeed to be seen among them, which have been presented to their ambassadors and chiefs; but they are held in no higher estimation than earthenware. The borderers, however, set a value on gold and silver for the purpose of commerce, and have learned to distinguish several kinds of our coin, some of which they prefer to others: the remoter inhabitants continue the more simple and ancient usage of bartering commodities. The money preferred by the Germans is the old and well-known species, such as the Serrati and Bigati. They are also better pleased with silver than gold; not on account of any fondness for that metal, but because the smaller money is more convenient in their common and petty merchandise.

Even iron is not plentiful among them; as may be inferred from the nature of their weapons. Swords or broad lances are seldom used; but they generally carry a spear, (called in their language "framea",) which has an iron blade, short and narrow, but so sharp and manageable, that, as occasion requires, they employ it either in close or distant fighting. This spear and a shield are all the armor of the cavalry. The foot have, besides, missile weapons, several to each man, which they hurl to an immense distance. They are either naked, or lightly covered with a small mantle; and have no pride in equipage: their shields only are ornamented with the choicest colors. Few are provided with a coat of mail; and scarcely here and there one with a casque or helmet. Their horses are neither remarkable for beauty nor swiftness, nor are they taught the various evolutions practised with us. The cavalry either bear down straight forwards, or wheel once to the right, in so compact a body that none is left behind the rest. Their principal strength, on the whole, consists in their infantry: hence in an engagement these are intermixed with the cavalry; so Well accordant with the nature of equestrian combats is the agility of those foot soldiers, whom they select from the whole body of their youth, and place in the front of the line. Their number, too, is determined; a hundred from each canton: and they are distinguished at home by a name expressive of this circumstance; so that what at first was only an appellation of number, becomes thenceforth a title of honor. Their line of battle is disposed in wedges. To give ground, provided they rally again, is considered rather as a prudent strategem, than cowardice. They carry off their slain even while the battle remains undecided. The greatest disgrace that can befall them is to have abandoned their shields. A person branded with this ignominy is not permitted to join in their religious rites, or enter their assemblies; so that many, after escaping from battle, have put an end to their infamy by the halter.

In the election of kings they have regard to birth; in that of generals, to valor. Their kings have not an absolute or unlimited power; and their generals command less through the force of authority, than of example. If they are daring, adventurous, and conspicuous in action, they procure obedience from the admiration they inspire. None, however, but the priests are permitted to judge offenders, to inflict bonds or stripes; so that chastisement appears not as an act of military discipline, but as the instigation of the god whom they suppose present with warriors. They also carry with them to battle certain images and standards taken from the sacred groves. It is a principal incentive to their courage, that their squadrons and battalions are not formed by men fortuitously collected, but by the assemblage of families and clans. Their pledges also are near at hand; they have within hearing the yells of their women, and the cries of their children. These, too, are the most revered witnesses of each man's conduct, these his most liberal applauders. To their mothers and their wives they bring their wounds for relief, nor do these dread to count or to search out the gashes. The women also administer food and encouragement to those who are fighting.

Tradition relates, that armies beginning to give way have been rallied by the females, through the earnestness of their supplications, the interposition of their bodies, and the pictures they have drawn of impending slavery, a calamity which these people bear with more impatience for their women than themselves; so that those states who have been obliged to give among their hostages the daughters of noble families, are the most effectually bound to fidelity. They even suppose somewhat of sanctity and prescience to be inherent in the female sex; and therefore neither despise their counsels, nor disregard their responses. We have beheld, in the reign of Vespasian, Veleda, long reverenced by many as a deity. Aurima, moreover, and several others, were formerly held in equal veneration, but not with a servile flattery, nor as though they made them goddesses.

Of the gods, Mercury is the principal object of their adoration; whom, on certain days, they think it lawful to propitiate even with human victims. To Hercules and Mars they offer the animals usually allotted for sacrifice. Some of the Suevi also perform sacred rites to Isis. What was the cause and origin of this foreign worship, I have not been able to discover; further than that her being represented with the symbol of a galley, seems to indicate an imported religion. They conceive it unworthy the grandeur of celestial beings to confine their deities within walls, or to represent them under a human similitude: woods and groves are their temples; and they affix names of divinity to that secret power, which they behold with the eye of adoration alone.

No people are more addicted to divination by omens and lots. The latter is performed in the following simple manner. They cut a twig from a fruit-tree, and divide it into small pieces, which, distinguished by certain marks, are thrown promiscuously upon a white garment. Then, the priest of the canton, if the occasion be public; if private, the master of the family; after an invocation of the gods, with his eyes lifted up to heaven, thrice takes out each piece, and, as they come up, interprets their signification according to the marks fixed upon them. If the result prove unfavorable, there is no more consultation on the same affair that day; if propitious, a confirmation by omens is still required. In common with other nations, the Germans are acquainted with the practice of auguring from the notes and flight of birds; but it is peculiar to them to derive admonitions and presages from horses also. Certain of these animals, milk-white, and untouched by earthly labor, are pastured at the public expense in the sacred woods and groves. These, yoked to a consecrated chariot, are accompanied by the priest, and king, or chief person of the community, who attentively observe their manner of neighing and snorting; and no kind of augury is more credited, not only among the populace, but among the nobles and priests. For the latter consider themselves as the ministers of the gods, and the horses, as privy to the divine will. Another kind of divination, by which they explore the event of momentous wars, is to oblige a prisoner, taken by any means whatsoever from the nation with whom they are at variance, to fight with a picked man of their own, each with his own country's arms; and, according as the victory falls, they presage success to the one or to the other party.

On affairs of smaller moment, the chiefs consult; on those of greater importance, the whole community; yet with this circumstance, that what is referred to the decision of the people, is first maturely discussed by the chiefs. They assemble, unless upon some sudden emergency, on stated days, either at the new or full moon, which they account the most auspicious season for beginning any enterprise. Nor do they, in their computation of time, reckon, like us, by the number of days, but of nights. In this way they arrange their business; in this way they fix their appointments; so that, with them, the night seems to lead the day. An inconvenience produced by their liberty is, that they do not all assemble at a stated time, as if it were in obedience to a command; but two or three days are lost in the delays of convening. When they all think fit, they sit down armed. Silence is proclaimed by the priests, who have on this occasion a coercive power. Then the king, or chief, and such others as are conspicuous for age, birth, military renown, or eloquence, are heard; and gain attention rather from their ability to persuade, than their authority to command. If a proposal displease, the assembly reject it by an inarticulate murmur; if it prove agreeable, they clash their javelins; for the most honorable expression of assent among them is the sound of arms.

Before this council, it is likewise allowed to exhibit accusations, and to prosecute capital offences. Punishments are varied according to the nature of the crime. Traitors and deserters are hung upon trees: cowards, dastards, and those guilty of unnatural practices, are suffocated in mud under a hurdle. This difference of punishment has in view the principle, that villainy should he exposed while it is punished, but turpitude concealed. The penalties annexed to slighter offences are also proportioned to the delinquency. The convicts are fined in horses and cattle: part of the mulct goes to the king or state; part to the injured person, or his relations. In the same assemblies chiefs are also elected, to administer justice through the cantons and districts. A hundred companions, chosen from the people, attended upon each of them, to assist them as well with their advice as their authority.

The Germans transact no business, public or private, without being armed: but it is not customary for any person to assume arms till the state has approved his ability to use them. Then, in the midst of the assembly, either one of the chiefs, or the father, or a relation, equips the youth with a shield and javelin. These are to them the manly gown; this is the first honor conferred on youth: before this they are considered as part of a household; afterwards, of the state. The dignity of chieftain is bestowed even on mere lads, whose descent is eminently illustrious, or whose fathers have performed signal services to the public; they are associated, however, with those of mature strength, who have already been declared capable of service; nor do they blush to be seen in the rank of companions. For the state of companionship itself has its several degrees, determined by the judgment of him whom they follow; and there is a great emulation among the companions, which shall possess the highest place in the favor of their chief; and among the chiefs, which shall excel in the number and valor of his companions. It is their dignity, their strength, to be always surrounded with a large body of select youth, an ornament in peace, a bulwark in war. And not in his own country alone, but among the neighboring states, the fame and glory of each chief consists in being distinguished for the number and bravery of his companions. Such chiefs are courted by embassies; distinguished by presents; and often by their reputation alone decide a war.

In the field of battle, it is disgraceful for the chief to be surpassed in valor; it is disgraceful for the companions not to equal their chief; but it is reproach and infamy during a whole succeeding life to retreat from the field surviving him. To aid, to protect him; to place their own gallant actions to the account of his glory, is their first and most sacred engagement. The chiefs fight for victory; the companions for their chief. If their native country be long sunk in peace and inaction, many of the young nobles repair to some other state then engaged in war. For, besides that repose is unwelcome to their race, and toils and perils afford them a better opportunity of distinguishing themselves; they are unable, without war and violence, to maintain a large train of followers. The companion requires from the liberality of his chief, the warlike steed, the bloody and conquering spear: and in place of pay, he expects to be supplied with a table, homely indeed, but plentiful. The funds for this munificence must be found in war and rapine; nor are they so easily persuaded to cultivate the earth, and await the produce of the seasons, as to challenge the foe, and expose themselves to wounds; nay, they even think it base and spiritless to earn by sweat what they might purchase with blood.

During the intervals of war, they pass their time less in hunting than in a sluggish repose, divided between sleep and the table. All the bravest of the warriors, committing the care of the house, the family affairs, and the lands, to the women, old men, and weaker part of the domestics, stupefy themselves in inaction: so wonderful is the contrast presented by nature, that the same persons love indolence, and hate tranquillity! It is customary for the several states to present, by voluntary and individual contributions, cattle or grain to their chiefs; which are accepted as honorary gifts, while they serve as necessary supplies. They are peculiarly pleased with presents from neighboring nations, offered not only by individuals, but by the community at large; such as fine horses, heavy armor, rich housings, and gold chains. We have now taught them also to accept of money.

It is well known that none of the German nations inhabit cities; or even admit of contiguous settlements. They dwell scattered and separate, as a spring, a meadow, or a grove may chance to invite them. Their villages are laid out, not like ours in rows of adjoining buildings; but every one surrounds his house with a vacant space, either by way of security against fire, or through ignorance of the art of building. For, indeed, they are unacquainted with the use of mortar and tiles; and for every purpose employ rude unshapen timber, fashioned with no regard to pleasing the eye. They bestow more than ordinary pains in coating certain parts of their buildings with a kind of earth, so pure and shining that it gives the appearance of painting. They also dig subterraneous caves, and cover them over with a great quantity of dung. These they use as winter-retreats, and granaries; for they preserve a moderate temperature; and upon an invasion, when the open country is plundered, these recesses remain unviolated, either because the enemy is ignorant of them, or because he will not trouble himself with the search.

The clothing common to all is a sagum fastened by a clasp, or, in want of that, a thorn. With no other covering, they pass whole days on the hearth, before the fire. The more wealthy are distinguished by a vest, not flowing loose, like those of the Sarmatians and Parthians, but girt close, and exhibiting the shape of every limb. They also wear the skins of beasts, which the people near the borders are less curious in selecting or preparing than the more remote inhabitants, who cannot by commerce procure other clothing. These make choice of particular skins, which they variegate with spots, and strips of the furs of marine animals, the produce of the exterior ocean, and seas to us unknown. The dress of the women does not differ from that of the men; except that they more frequently wear linen, which they stain with purple; and do not lengthen their upper garment into sleeves, but leave exposed the whole arm, and part of the breast.

The matrimonial bond is, nevertheless, strict and severe among them; nor is there anything in their manners more commendable than this. Almost singly among the barbarians, they content themselves with one wife; a very few of them excepted, who, not through incontinence, but because their alliance is solicited on account of their rank, practise polygamy. The wife does not bring a dowry to her husband, but receives one from him. The parents and relations assemble, and pass their approbation on the presents—presents not adapted to please a female taste, or decorate the bride; but oxen, a caparisoned steed, a shield, spear, and sword. By virtue of these, the wife is espoused; and she in her turn makes a present of some arms to her husband. This they consider as the firmest bond of union; these, the sacred mysteries, the conjugal deities. That the woman may not think herself excused from exertions of fortitude, or exempt from the casualties of war, she is admonished by the very ceremonial of her marriage, that she comes to her husband as a partner in toils and dangers; to suffer and to dare equally with him, in peace and in war: this is indicated by the yoked oxen, the harnessed steed, the offered arms. Thus she is to live; thus to die. She receives what she is to return inviolate and honored to her children; what her daughters-in-law are to receive, and again transmit to her grandchildren.

They live, therefore, fenced around with chastity; corrupted by no seductive spectacles, no convivial incitements. Men and women are alike unacquainted with clandestine correspondence. Adultery is extremely rare among so numerous a people. Its punishment is instant, and at the pleasure of the husband. He cuts off the hair of the offender, strips her, and in presence of her relations expels her from his house, and pursues her with stripes through the whole village. Nor is any indulgence shown to a prostitute. Neither beauty, youth, nor riches can procure her a husband: for none there looks on vice with a smile, or calls mutual seduction the way of the world. Still more exemplary is the practice of those states in which none but virgins marry, and the expectations and wishes of a wife are at once brought to a period. Thus, they take one husband as one body and one life; that no thought, no desire, may extend beyond him; and he may be loved not only as their husband, but as their marriage. To limit the increase of children, or put to death any of the later progeny is accounted infamous: and good habits have there more influence than good laws elsewhere.

In every house the children grow up, thinly and meanly clad, to that bulk of body and limb which we behold with wonder. Every mother suckles her own children, and does not deliver them into the hands of servants and nurses. No indulgence distinguishes the young master from the slave. They lie together amidst the same cattle, upon the same ground, till age separates, and valor marks out, the free-born. The youths partake late of the pleasures of love, and hence pass the age of puberty unexhausted: nor are the virgins hurried into marriage; the same maturity, the same full growth is required: the sexes unite equally matched and robust; and the children inherit the vigor of their parents. Children are regarded with equal affection by their maternal uncles as by their fathers: some even consider this as the more sacred bond of consanguinity, and prefer it in the requisition of hostages, as if it held the mind by a firmer tie, and the family by a more extensive obligation. A person's own children, however, are his heirs and successors; and no wills are made. If there be no children, the next in order of inheritance are brothers, paternal and maternal uncles. The more numerous are a man's relations and kinsmen, the more comfortable is his old age; nor is it here any advantage to be childless.

It is an indispensable duty to adopt the enmities of a father or relation, as well as their friendships: these, however, are not irreconcilable or perpetual. Even homicide is atoned by a certain fine in cattle and sheep; and the whole family accepts the satisfaction, to the advantage of the public weal, since quarrels are most dangerous in a free state. No people are more addicted to social entertainments, or more liberal in the exercise of hospitality. To refuse any person whatever admittance under their roof, is accounted flagitious. Every one according to his ability feasts his guest: when his provisions are exhausted, he who was late the host, is now the guide and companion to another hospitable board. They enter the next house uninvited, and are received with equal cordiality. No one makes a distinction with respect to the rights of hospitality, between a stranger and an acquaintance. The departing guest is presented with whatever he may ask for; and with the same freedom a boon is desired in return. They are pleased with presents; but think no obligation incurred either when they give or receive.

As soon as they arise from sleep, which they generally protract till late in the day, they bathe, usually in warm water, as cold weather chiefly prevails there. After bathing they take their meal, each on a distinct seat and a separate table. Then they proceed, armed, to business, and not less frequently to convivial parties, in which it is no disgrace to pass days and nights, without intermission, in drinking. The frequent quarrels that arise amongst them, when intoxicated, seldom terminate in abusive language, but more frequently in blood. In their feasts, they generally deliberate on the reconcilement of enemies, on family alliances, on the appointment of chiefs, and finally on peace and war; conceiving that at no time the soul is more opened to sincerity, or warmed to heroism. These people, naturally void of artifice or disguise, disclose the most secret emotions of their hearts in the freedom of festivity. The minds of all being thus displayed without reserve, the subjects of their deliberation are again canvassed the next day; and each time has its advantages. They consult when unable to dissemble; they determine when not liable to mistake.

Their drink is a liquor prepared from barley or wheat brought by fermentation to a certain resemblance of wine. Those who border on the Rhine also purchase wine. Their food is simple; wild fruits, fresh venison, or coagulated milk. They satisfy hunger without seeking the elegances and delicacies of the table. Their thirst for liquor is not quenched with equal moderation. If their propensity to drunkenness be gratified to the extent of their wishes, intemperance proves as effectual in subduing them as the force of arms.

They have only one kind of public spectacle, which is exhibited in every company. Young men, who make it their diversion, dance naked amidst drawn swords and presented spears. Practice has conferred skill at this exercise; and skill has given grace; but they do not exhibit for hire or gain: the only reward of this pastime, though a hazardous one, is the pleasure of the spectators. What is extraordinary, they play at dice, when sober, as a serious business: and that with such a desperate venture of gain or loss, that, when everything else is gone, they set their liberties and persons on the last throw. The loser goes into voluntary servitude; and, though the youngest and strongest, patiently suffers himself to be bound and sold. Such is their obstinacy in a bad practice—they themselves call it honor. The slaves thus acquired are exchanged away in commerce, that the winner may get rid of the scandal of his victory.

The rest of their slaves have not, like ours, particular employments in the family allotted them. Each is the master of a habitation and household of his own. The lord requires from him a certain quantity of grain, cattle, or cloth, as from a tenant; and so far only the subjection of the slave extends. His domestic offices are performed by his own wife and children. It is usual to scourge a slave, or punish him with chains or hard labor. They are sometimes killed by their masters; not through severity of chastisement, but in the heat of passion, like an enemy; with this difference, that it is done with impunity. Freedmen are little superior to slaves; seldom filling any important office in the family; never in the state, except in those tribes which are under regal government. There, they rise above the free-born, and even the nobles: in the rest, the subordinate condition of the freedmen is a proof of freedom.

Lending money upon interest, and increasing it by usury, is unknown amongst them: and this ignorance more effectually prevents the practice than a prohibition would do. The lands are occupied by townships, in allotments proportional to the number of cultivators; and are afterwards parcelled out among the individuals of the district, in shares according to the rank and condition of each person. The wide extent of plain facilitates this partition. The arable lands are annually changed, and a part left fallow; nor do they attempt to make the most of the fertility and plenty of the soil, by their own industry in planting orchards, inclosing meadows, and watering gardens. Corn is the only product required from the earth: hence their year is not divided into so many seasons as ours; for, while they know and distinguish by name Winter, Spring, and Summer, they are unacquainted equally with the appellation and bounty of Autumn.

Their funerals are without parade. The only circumstance to which they attend, is to burn the bodies of eminent persons with some particular kinds of wood. Neither vestments nor perfumes are heaped upon the pile: the arms of the deceased, and sometimes his horse, are given to the flames. The tomb is a mound of turf. They contemn the elaborate and costly honours of monumental structures, as mere burthens to the dead. They soon dismiss tears and lamentations; slowly, sorrow and regret. They think it the women's part to bewail their friends, the men's to remember them.

Translated by Edward Brooks.

SUETONIUS

c. AD 70 - 130

Gaius Suetonius Tranquillus was born to an equestrian family. We know him through the letters of Pliny the Younger, who was both his friend and advocate. Shortly before his death, Pliny entrusted his protégé Suetonius to a certain Septicius, whom Emperor Hadrian had elevated to the prefecture of the praetorian guards in AD 119. Suetonius then became the chief of imperial correspondence, a position that lasted until he fell into disfavor with his protector in 122.

Throughout his career, and despite his reluctance to publish books, Suetonius was as prolific a writer as Varro. He wrote numerous treatises on diverse subjects, sometimes in Greek; these included, for example, Roman customs, grammar, celebrated courtesans, and Greek games. It is possible, too, that Suetonius compiled an encyclopedia of natural history, as did Pliny the Elder. Moreover, we know that he wrote the partially preserved About Grammarians and Rhetoricians *and biographical sketches like the one he did of Terence.*

Suetonius likely took advantage of his position at the imperial court by nosing around the archives, collecting small details and anecdotes for use in his Lives of the Twelve Caesars. *Many modern scholars view Suetonius' portraits as nothing but voyeurism and attention-getting, not fully understanding that his intention was to be a witness of his times while simultaneously offering lessons to future princes.*

Caesar at War. His Courage, Severity, and Clemency.

Suetonius, *Caesar* 57-75

What portrait does Suetonius paint of Caesar? He describes his political and military ascension; his liaisons with several queens, including Cleopatra; his talent as an orator and as a writer; and his extraordinary skills as a warrior, the subject of the passage excerpted below. So great were Caesar's military qualities that the later Plutarch would place him on equal ground with Alexander. The end of the story is common knowledge: Caesar's power takes on an increasingly monarchal flavor mixed with arrogance. This leads his citizens to fear that his ambitions are to become king. The Romans, who loathe kings, assassinate him, hoping that the Republic would return. Instead, the adoptive son and successor of Caesar, the future Emperor Augustus, forges the Roman Empire.

"When the issue of a battle was doubtful, he sent away all the horses, and his own first, that having no means of flight, they might be under the greater necessity of standing their ground."

Caesar was perfect in the use of arms, an accomplished rider, and able to endure fatigue beyond all belief. On a march, he used to go at the head of his troops, sometimes on horseback, but oftener on foot, with his head bare in all kinds of weather. He would travel post in a light carriage without baggage, at the rate of a hundred miles a day; and if he was stopped by floods in the rivers, he swam across, or floated on skins inflated with wind, so that he often anticipated intelligence of his movements.

In his expeditions, it is difficult to say whether his caution or his daring was most conspicuous. He never marched his army by roads which were exposed to ambuscades, without having previously examined the nature of the ground by his scouts. Nor did he cross over to Britain, before he had carefully examined, in person, the navigation, the harbours, and the most convenient point of landing in the island. When intelligence was brought to him of the siege of his camp in Germany, he made his way to his troops, through the enemy's stations, in a Gaulish dress. He crossed the sea from Brundisium and Dyrrachium, in the winter, through the midst of the enemy's fleets; and the troops, under orders to join him, being slow in their movements, notwithstanding repeated messages to hurry them, but to no purpose, he at last went privately, and alone, aboard a small vessel in the night time, with his head muffled up; nor did he make himself known, or suffer the master to put about, although the wind blew strong against them, until they were ready to sink.

He was never deterred from any enterprise, nor retarded in the prosecution of it, by superstition. When a victim, which he was about to offer in sacrifice, made its escape, he did not therefore defer his expedition against Scipio and Juba.[1] And happening to fall, upon stepping out of the ship, he gave a lucky turn to the omen, by exclaiming, "I hold thee fast, Africa." To chide the prophecies which were spread abroad, that the name of the Scipios was, by the decrees of fate, fortunate and invincible in that province, he retained in the camp a profligate wretch, of the family of the Cornelii, who, on account of his scandalous life, was surnamed Salutio.

He not only fought pitched battles, but made sudden attacks when an opportunity offered; often at the end of a march, and sometimes during the most violent storms, when nobody could imagine he would stir. Nor was he ever backward in fighting, until towards the end of his life. He then was of opinion, that the oftener he had been crowned with success, the less he ought to expose himself to new hazards; and that nothing he could gain by a victory would compensate for what he might lose by a miscarriage. He never defeated the enemy without driving them from their camp; and giving them no time to rally their forces. When the issue of a battle was doubtful, he sent away all the horses, and his own first, that having no means of flight, they might be under the greater necessity of standing their ground.

He rode a very remarkable horse, with feet almost like those of a man, the hoofs being divided in such a manner as to have some resemblance to toes. This horse he had bred himself, and the soothsayers having interpreted these circumstances into an omen that its owner would be master of the world, he brought him up with particular care, and broke him in himself, as the horse would suffer no one else to mount him. A statue of this horse was afterwards erected by Caesar's order before the temple of Venus Genitrix.

He often rallied his troops, when they were giving way, by his personal efforts; stopping those who fled, keeping others in their ranks, and seizing them by their throat turned them towards the enemy; although numbers were so terrified, that an eagle-bearer, thus stopped, made a thrust at him with the spear-head; and another, upon a similar occasion, left the standard in his hand.

The following instances of his resolution are equally, and even more remarkable. After the battle of Pharsalia,[2] having sent his troops before him into Asia, as he was passing the straits of the Hellespont in a ferry-boat, he met with Lucius Cassius, one of the opposite party, with ten ships of war; and so far from endeavouring to escape, he went alongside his ship, and calling upon him to surrender, Cassius humbly gave him his submission.

At Alexandria, in the attack of a bridge, being forced by a sudden sally of the enemy into a boat, and several others hurrying in with him, he leaped into the sea, and saved himself by swimming to the next ship, which lay at the distance of two hundred paces; holding up his left hand out of the water, for fear of wetting some papers which he held in it; and pulling his general's cloak after him with his teeth, lest it should fall into the hands of the enemy.

He never valued a soldier for his moral conduct or his means, but for his courage only; and treated his troops with a mixture of severity and indulgence; for he did not always keep a strict hand over them, but only when the enemy was near. Then indeed he was so strict a disciplinarian, that he would give no notice of a march or a battle until the moment of action, in order that the troops might hold themselves in readiness for any sudden movement; and he would frequently draw them out of the camp without any necessity for it, especially in rainy weather, and upon holy-days. Sometimes, giving them orders not to lose sight of him, he would suddenly depart by day or by night, and lengthen the marches in order to tire them out, as they followed him at a distance.

When at any time his troops were dispirited by reports of the great force of the enemy, he rallied their courage; not by denying the truth of what was said, or by diminishing the facts, but, on the contrary, by exaggerating every particular. Accordingly, when his troops were in great alarm at the expected arrival of king Juba, he called them together, and said, "I have to inform you that in a very few days the king will be here, with ten legions, thirty thousand horse, a hundred thousand light-armed foot, and three hundred elephants. Let none of you, therefore, presume to make further enquiry, or indulge in conjectures, but take my word for what I tell you, which I have from undoubted intelligence; otherwise I shall put them aboard an old crazy vessel, and leave them exposed to the mercy of the winds, to be transported to some other country."

He neither noticed all their transgressions, nor punished them according to strict rule. But for deserters and mutineers he made the most diligent enquiry, and their punishment was most severe; other delinquencies he would connive at. Sometimes, after a great battle ending in victory, he would grant them a relaxation from all kinds of duty, and leave them to revel at pleasure; being used to boast, "that his soldiers fought nothing the worse for being well oiled." In his speeches, he never addressed them by the title of "Soldiers," but by the kinder phrase of "Fellow-soldiers;" and kept them in such splendid order, that their arms were ornamented with silver and gold, not merely for parade, but to render the soldiers more resolute to save them in battle, and fearful of losing them. He loved his troops to such a degree, that when he heard of the defeat of those under Titurius,[3] he neither cut his hair nor shaved his beard, until he had revenged it upon the enemy; by which means he engaged their devoted affection, and raised their valour to the highest pitch.

Upon his entering on the civil war, the centurions of every legion offered, each of them, to maintain a horseman at his own expense, and the whole army agreed to serve gratis, without either corn or pay; those amongst them who were rich, charging themselves with the maintenance of the poor. No one of them, during the whole course of the war, deserted to the enemy; and many of those who were made prisoners, though they were offered their lives, upon condition of bearing arms against him, refused to accept the terms. They endured want, and other hardships, not only when they were besieged themselves, but when they besieged others, to such a degree, that Pompey, when blocked up in the neighbourhood of Dyrrachium, upon seeing a sort of bread made of an herb, which they lived upon, said, "I have to do with wild beasts," and ordered it immediately to be taken away; because, if his troops should see it, their spirit might be broken by perceiving the endurance and determined resolution of the enemy. With what bravery they fought, one instance affords sufficient proof; which is, that after an unsuccessful engagement at Dyrrachium, they called for punishment; insomuch that their general found it more necessary to comfort than to punish them. In other battles, in different quarters, they defeated with ease immense armies of the enemy, although they were much inferior to them in number. In short, one cohort of the sixth legion held out a fort against four legions belonging to Pompey, during several hours; being almost every one of them wounded by the vast number of arrows discharged against them, and of which there were found within the ramparts a hundred and thirty thousand. This is no way surprising, when we consider the conduct of some individuals amongst them; such as that of Cassius Scaeva, a centurion, or Caius Acilius, a common soldier, not to speak of others. Scaeva, after having an eye struck out, being run through the thigh and the shoulder, and having his shield pierced in an hundred and twenty places, maintained obstinately the guard of the gate of a fort, with the command of which he was intrusted. Acilius, in the sea-fight at Marseilles, having seized a ship of the enemy's with his right hand, and that being cut off, in imitation of that memorable instance of resolution in Cynaegirus amongst the Greeks,[4] boarded the enemy's ship, bearing down all before him with the boss of his shield.

They never once mutinied during all the ten years of the Gallic war, but were sometimes refractory in the course of the civil war. However, they always returned quickly to their duty, and that not through the indulgence, but in submission to the authority, of their general; for he never yielded to them when they were insubordinate, but constantly resisted their demands. He disbanded the whole ninth legion with ignominy at Placentia, although Pompey was still in arms, and would not receive them again into his service, until they had not only made repeated and humble entreaties, but until the ringleaders in the mutiny were punished.

When the soldiers of the tenth legion at Rome demanded their discharge and rewards for their service, with violent threats and no small danger to the city, although the war was then raging in Africa, he did not hesitate, contrary to the advice of his friends, to meet the legion, and disband it. But addressing them by the title of "Quirites," instead of "Soldiers," he by this single word so thoroughly brought them round and changed their determination, that they immediately cried out, they were his "soldiers," and followed him to Africa, although he had refused their service. He nevertheless punished the most mutinous among them, with the loss of a third of their share in the plunder, and the land destined for them.

In the service of his clients, while yet a young man, he evinced great zeal and fidelity. He defended the cause of a noble youth, Masintha, against king Hiempsal,[5] so strenuously, that in a scuffle which took place upon the occasion, he seized by the beard the son of king Juba; and upon Masintha's being declared tributary to Hiempsal, while the friends of the adverse party were violently carrying him off, he immediately rescued him by force, kept him concealed in his house a long time, and when, at the expiration of his praetorship, he went to Spain, he took him away in his litter, in the midst of his lictors bearing the fasces, and others who had come to attend and take leave of him.

He always treated his friends with such kindness and good-nature, that when Caius Oppius, in travelling with him through a forest, was suddenly taken ill, he resigned to him the only place there was to shelter them at night, and lay upon the ground in the open air. When he had placed himself at the head of affairs, he advanced some of his faithful adherents, though of mean extraction, to the highest offices; and when he was censured for this partiality, he openly said, "Had I been assisted by robbers and cut-throats in the defence of my honour, I should have made them the same recompense."

The resentment he entertained against any one was never so implacable that he did not very willingly renounce it when opportunity offered. Although Caius Memmius had published some extremely virulent speeches against him, and he had answered him with equal acrimony, yet he afterwards assisted him with his vote and interest, when he stood candidate for the consulship. When C. Calvus, after publishing some scandalous epigrams upon him, endeavoured to effect a reconciliation by the intercession of friends, he wrote to him, of his own accord, the first letter. And when Valerius Catullus, who had, as he himself observed, fixed such a stain upon his character in his verses upon Mamurra[6] as never could be obliterated, he begged his pardon, invited him to supper the same day; and continued to take up his lodging with his father occasionally, as he had been accustomed to do.

His temper was also naturally averse to severity in retaliation. After he had captured the pirates, by whom he had been taken, having sworn that he would crucify them, he did so indeed; but he first ordered their throats to be cut. He could never bear the thought of doing any harm to Cornelius Phagitas, who had dogged him in the night when he was sick and a fugitive, with the design of carrying him to Sylla, and from whose hands he had escaped with some difficulty by giving him a bribe. Philemon, his amanuensis, who had promised his enemies to poison him, he put to death without torture. When he was summoned as a witness against Publius Clodius, his wife Pompeia's gallant, who was prosecuted for the profanation of religious ceremonies, he declared he knew nothing of the affair, although his mother Aurelia, and his sister Julia, gave the court an exact and full account of the circumstances. And being asked why then he had divorced his wife? "Because," he said, "my family should not only be free from guilt, but even from the suspicion of it."

Both in his administration and his conduct towards the vanquished party in the civil war, he showed a wonderful moderation and clemency. For while Pompey declared that he would consider those as enemies who did not take arms in defence of the republic, he desired it to be understood, that he should regard those who remained neuter as his friends. With regard to all those to whom he had, on Pompey's recommendation, given any command in the army, he left them at perfect liberty to go over to him, if they pleased. When some proposals were made at Ilerda for a surrender,[7] which gave rise to a free communication between the two camps, and Afranius and Petreius, upon a sudden change of resolution, had put to the sword all Caesar's men who were found in the camp, he scorned to imitate the base treachery which they had practised against himself. On the field of Pharsalia, he called out to the soldiers "to spare their fellow-citizens," and afterwards gave permission to every man in his army to save an enemy. None of them, so far as appears, lost their lives but in battle, excepting only Afranius, Faustus, and young Lucius Caesar; and it is thought that even they were put to death without his consent. Afranius and Faustus had borne arms against him, after obtaining their pardon; and Lucius Caesar had not only in the most cruel manner destroyed with fire and sword his freed-men and slaves, but cut to pieces the wild beasts which he had prepared for the entertainment of the people. And finally, a little before his death, he permitted all whom he had not before pardoned, to return into Italy, and to bear offices both civil and military. He even replaced the statues of Sylla and Pompey, which had been thrown down by the populace. And after this, whatever was devised or uttered, he chose rather to check than to punish it. Accordingly, having detected certain conspiracies and nocturnal assemblies, he went no farther than to intimate by a proclamation that he knew of them; and as to those who indulged themselves in the liberty of reflecting severely upon him, he only warned them in a public speech not to persist in their offence. He bore with great moderation a virulent libel written against him by Aulus Caecinna, and the abusive lampoons of Pitholaus, most highly reflecting on his reputation.

Translated by Alexander Thomson and T. Forester.

Nero's Debauchery. Murder of His Mother and Other Assassinations. Great Fire of Rome

Suetonius, *Nero* 26-38

Nero was born on 15 December AD 37 under ominous auspices that led his father to say that "Nothing but what was detestable and pernicious to the public could ever be produced of himself and Agrippina." Nero was adopted at the age of ten by Emperor Claudius and the philosopher Seneca tutored him. The child would grow in accordance with his birth, exhibiting signs of innate cruelty and leading the emperor to believe that his son Britannicus was illegitimate. Nero also testified against his aunt, Domitia Lepida, who had taken some care of him as an infant. This is at least the profile Suetonius provides us.

Nero became emperor at 17 years of age after Claudius died in circumstances not at all mysterious to the young leader. The new sovereign quickly demonstrated a healthy appetite for all kinds of games (e.g., chariot races, gladiatorial fights, and theatrical presentations) and a limited interest in the affairs of state. The worst was yet to come.

"He thought there was no other use of riches and money than to squander them away profusely; regarding all those as sordid wretches who kept their expenses within due bounds; and extolling those as truly noble and generous souls, who lavished away and wasted all they possessed."

Petulancy, lewdness, luxury, avarice, and cruelty, Nero practised at first with reserve and in private, as if prompted to them only by the folly of youth; but, even then, the world was of opinion that they were the faults of his nature, and not of his age. After it was dark, he used to enter the taverns disguised in a cap or a wig, and ramble about the streets in sport, which was not void of mischief. He used to beat those he met coming home from supper; and, if they made any resistance, would wound them, and throw them into the common sewer. He broke open and robbed shops; establishing an auction at home for selling his booty. In the scuffles which took place on those occasions, he often ran the hazard of losing his eyes, and even his life; being beaten almost to death by a senator, for handling his wife indecently. After this adventure, he never again ventured abroad at that time of night, without some tribunes following him at a little distance. In the day-time he would be carried to the theatre incognito in a litter, placing himself upon the upper part of the proscenium, where he not only witnessed the quarrels which arose on account of the performances, but also encouraged them. When they came to blows, and stones and pieces of broken benches began to fly about, he threw them plentifully amongst the people, and once even broke a praetor's head.

His vices gaining strength by degrees, he laid aside his jocular amusements, and all disguise; breaking out into enormous crimes, without the least attempt to conceal them. His revels were prolonged from mid-day to midnight, while he was frequently refreshed by warm baths, and, in the summer time, by such as were cooled with snow. He often supped in public, in the Naumachia, with the sluices shut, or in the Campus Martius, or the Circus Maximus, being waited upon at table by common prostitutes of the town, and Syrian strumpets and glee-girls. As often as he went down the Tiber to Ostia, or coasted through the gulf of Baiae, booths furnished as brothels and eating-houses, were erected along the shore and river banks; before which stood matrons, who, like bawds and hostesses, allured him to land. It was also his custom to invite himself to supper with his friends; at one of which was expended no less than four millions of sesterces in chaplets, and at another something more in roses.

Besides the abuse of free-born lads, and the debauch of married women, he committed a rape upon Rubria, a Vestal Virgin. He was upon the point of marrying Acte, his freedwoman, having suborned some men of consular rank to swear that she was of royal descent. He gelded the boy Sporus, and endeavoured to transform him into a woman. He even went so far as to marry him, with all the usual formalities of a marriage settlement, the rose-coloured nuptial veil, and a numerous company at the wedding. When the ceremony was over, he had him conducted like a bride to his own house, and treated him as his wife. It was jocularly observed by some person, "that it would have been well for mankind, had such a wife fallen to the lot of his father Domitius." This Sporus he carried about with him in a litter round the solemn assemblies and fairs of Greece, and afterwards at Rome through the Sigillaria,[8] dressed in the rich attire of an empress; kissing him from time to time as they rode together. That he entertained an incestuous passion for his mother, but was deterred by her enemies, for fear that this haughty and overbearing woman should, by her compliance, get him entirely into her power, and govern in every thing, was universally believed; especially after he had introduced amongst his concubines a strumpet, who was reported to have a strong resemblance to Agrippina.

He prostituted his own chastity to such a degree, that after he had defiled every part of his person with some unnatural pollution, he at last invented an extraordinary kind of diversion; which was, to be let out of a den in the arena, covered with the skin of a wild beast, and then assail with violence the private parts both of men and women, while they were bound to stakes. After he had vented his furious passion upon them, he finished the play in the embraces of his freedman Doryphorus, to whom he was married in the same way that Sporus had been married to himself; imitating the cries and shrieks of young virgins, when they are ravished. I have been informed from numerous sources, that he firmly believed, no man in the world to be chaste, or any part of his person undefiled; but that most men concealed that vice, and were cunning enough to keep it secret. To those, therefore, who frankly owned their unnatural lewdness, he forgave all other crimes.

He thought there was no other use of riches and money than to squander them away profusely; regarding all those as sordid wretches who kept their expenses within due bounds; and extolling those as truly noble and generous souls, who lavished away and wasted all they possessed. He praised and admired his uncle Caius,[9] upon no account more, than for squandering in a short time the vast treasure left him by Tiberius. Accordingly, he was himself extravagant and profuse, beyond all bounds. He spent upon Tiridates eight hundred thousand sesterces a day, a sum almost incredible; and at his departure, presented him with upwards of a million.[10] He likewise bestowed upon Menecrates the harper, and Spicillus a gladiator, the estates and houses of men who had received the honour of a triumph. He enriched the usurer Cercopithecus Panerotes with estates both in town and country; and gave him a funeral, in pomp and magnificence little inferior to that of princes. He never wore the same garment twice. He has been known to stake four hundred thousand sesterces on a throw of the dice. It was his custom to fish with a golden net, drawn by silken cords of purple and scarlet. It is said, that he never travelled with less than a thousand baggage-carts; the mules being all shod with silver, and the drivers dressed in scarlet jackets of the finest Canusian cloth,[11] with a numerous train of footmen, and troops of Mazacans,[12] with bracelets on their arms, and mounted upon horses in splendid trappings.

In nothing was he more prodigal than in his buildings. He completed his palace by continuing it from the Palatine to the Esquiline hill, calling the building at first only "The Passage," but, after it was burnt down and rebuilt, "The Golden House." Of its dimensions and furniture, it may be sufficient to say thus much: the porch was so high that there stood in it a colossal statue of himself a hundred and twenty feet in height; and the space included in it was so ample, that it had triple porticos a mile in length, and a lake like a sea, surrounded with buildings which had the appearance of a city. Within its area were corn fields, vineyards, pastures, and woods, containing a vast number of animals of various kinds, both wild and tame. In other parts it was entirely over-laid with gold, and adorned with jewels and mother of pearl. The supper rooms were vaulted, and compartments of the ceilings, inlaid with ivory, were made to revolve, and scatter flowers; while they contained pipes which shed unguents upon the guests. The chief banqueting room was circular, and revolved perpetually, night and day, in imitation of the motion of the celestial bodies. The baths were supplied with water from the sea and the Albula. Upon the dedication of this magnificent house after it was finished, all he said in approval of it was, "that he had now a dwelling fit for a man."

He commenced making a pond for the reception of all the hot streams from Baiae, which he designed to have continued from Misenum to the Avernian lake, in a conduit, enclosed in galleries; and also a canal from Avernum to Ostia, that ships might pass from one to the other, without a sea voyage. The length of the proposed canal was one hundred and sixty miles; and it was intended to be of breadth sufficient to permit ships with five banks of oars to pass each other. For the execution of these designs, he ordered all prisoners, in every part of the empire, to be brought to Italy; and that even those who were convicted of the most heinous crimes, in lieu of any other sentence, should be condemned to work at them. He was encouraged to all this wild and enormous profusion, not only by the great revenue of the empire, but by the sudden hopes given him of an immense hidden treasure, which queen Dido, upon her flight from Tyre, had brought with her to Africa. This, a Roman knight pretended to assure him, upon good grounds, was still hid there in some deep caverns, and might with a little labour be recovered.

But being disappointed in his expectations of this resource, and reduced to such difficulties, for want of money, that he was obliged to defer paying his troops, and the rewards due to the veterans, he resolved upon supplying his necessities by means of false accusations and plunder. In the first place, he ordered, that if any freedman, without sufficient reason, bore the name of the family to which he belonged, the half, instead of three fourths, of his estate should be brought into the exchequer at his decease; also that the estates of all such persons as had not in their wills been mindful of their prince, should be confiscated; and that the lawyers who had drawn or dictated such wills, should be liable to a fine. He ordained likewise, that all words and actions, upon which any informer could ground a prosecution, should be deemed treason. He demanded an equivalent for the crowns which the cities of Greece had at any time offered him in the solemn games. Having forbad any one to use the colours of amethyst and Tyrian purple, he privately sent a person to sell a few ounces of them upon the day of the Nundinae, and then shut up all the merchants' shops, on the pretext that his edict had been violated.[13] It is said, that, as he was playing and singing in the theatre, observing a married lady dressed in the purple which he had prohibited, he pointed her out to his procurators; upon which she was immediately dragged out of her seat, and not only stripped of her clothes, but her property. He never nominated a person to any office without saying to him, "You know what I want; and let us take care that nobody has any thing he can call his own." At last he rifled many temples of the rich offerings with which they were stored, and melted down all the gold and silver statues, and amongst them those of the penates, which Galba afterwards restored.

He began the practice of parricide and murder with Claudius himself; for although he was not the contriver of his death, he was privy to the plot. Nor did he make any secret of it; but used afterwards to commend, in a Greek proverb, mushrooms as food fit for the gods, because Claudius had been poisoned with them.[14] He traduced his memory both by word and deed in the grossest manner; one while charging him with folly, another while with cruelty. For he used to say by way of jest, that he had ceased "morari" amongst men, pronouncing the first syllable long;[15] and treated as null many of his decrees and ordinances, as made by a doting old blockhead. He enclosed the place where his body was burnt with only a low wall of rough masonry. He attempted to poison Britannicus, as much out of envy because he had a sweeter voice, as from apprehension of what might ensue from the respect which the people entertained for his father's memory.[16] He employed for this purpose a woman named Locusta, who had been a witness against some persons guilty of like practices. But the poison she gave him, working more slowly than he expected, and only causing a purge, he sent for the woman, and beat her with his own hand, charging her with administering an antidote instead of poison; and upon her alleging in excuse, that she had given Britannicus but a gentle mixture in order to prevent suspicion, "Think you," said he, "that I am afraid of the Julian law;"[17] and obliged her to prepare, in his own chamber and before his eyes, as quick and strong a dose as possible. This he tried upon a kid: but the animal lingering for five hours before it expired, he ordered her to go to work again; and when she had done, he gave the poison to a pig, which dying immediately, he commanded the potion to be brought into the eating-room and given to Britannicus, while he was at supper with him. The prince had no sooner tasted it than he sunk on the floor, Nero meanwhile, pretending to the guests, that it was only a fit of the falling sickness, to which, he said, he was subject. He buried him the following day, in a mean and hurried way, during violent storms of rain. He gave Locusta a pardon, and rewarded her with a great estate in land, placing some disciples with her, to be instructed in her trade.

His mother being used to make strict inquiry into what he said or did, and to reprimand him with the freedom of a parent, he was so much offended, that he endeavoured to expose her to public resentment, by frequently pretending a resolution to quit the government, and retire to Rhodes. Soon afterwards, he deprived her of all honour and power, took from her the guard of Roman and German soldiers, banished her from the palace and from his society, and persecuted her in every way he could contrive; employing persons to harass her when at Rome with law-suits, and to disturb her in her retirement from town with the most scurrilous and abusive language, following her about by land and sea. But being terrified with her menaces and violent spirit, he resolved upon her destruction, and thrice attempted it by poison. Finding, however, that she had previously secured herself by antidotes, he contrived machinery, by which the floor over her bed-chamber might be made to fall upon her while she was asleep in the night. This design miscarrying likewise, through the little caution used by those who were in the secret, his next stratagem was to construct a ship which could be easily shivered, in hopes of destroying her either by drowning, or by the deck above her cabin crushing her in its fall. Accordingly, under colour of a pretended reconciliation, he wrote her an extremely affectionate letter, inviting her to Baiae, to celebrate with him the festival of Minerva. He had given private orders to the captains of the galleys which were to attend her, to shatter to pieces the ship in which she had come, by falling foul of it, but in such manner that it might appear to be done accidentally. He prolonged the entertainment, for the more convenient opportunity of executing the plot in the night; and at her return for Bauli, instead of the old ship which had conveyed her to Baiae, he offered that which he had contrived for her destruction. He attended her to the vessel in a very cheerful mood, and, at parting with her, kissed her breasts; after which he sat up very late in the night, waiting with great anxiety to learn the issue of his project. But receiving information that every thing had fallen out contrary to his wish, and that she had saved herself by swimming,—not knowing what course to take, upon her freedman, Lucius Agerinus bringing word, with great joy, that she was safe and well, he privately dropped a poniard by him. He then commanded the freedman to be seized and put in chains, under pretence of his having been employed by his mother to assassinate him; at the same time ordering her to be put to death, and giving out, that, to avoid punishment for her intended crime, she had laid violent hands upon herself. Other circumstances, still more horrible, are related on good authority; as that he went to view her corpse, and handling her limbs, pointed out some blemishes, and commended other points; and that, growing thirsty during the survey, he called for drink.

Yet he was never afterwards able to bear the stings of his own conscience for this atrocious act, although encouraged by the congratulatory addresses of the army, the senate, and people. He frequently affirmed that he was haunted by his mother's ghost, and persecuted with the whips and burning torches of the Furies. Nay, he attempted by magical rites to bring up her ghost from below, and soften her rage against him. When he was in Greece, he durst not attend the celebration of the Eleusinian mysteries, at the initiation of which, impious and wicked persons are warned by the voice of the herald from approaching the rites. Besides the murder of his mother, he had been guilty of that of his aunt; for, being obliged to keep her bed in consequence of a complaint in her bowels, he paid her a visit, and she, being then advanced in years, stroking his downy chin, in the tenderness of affection, said to him: "May I but live to see the day when this is shaved for the first time, and I shall then die contented." He turned, however, to those about him, made a jest of it, saying, that he would have his beard immediately taken off, and ordered the physicians to give her more violent purgatives. He seized upon her estate before she had expired; suppressing her will, that he might enjoy the whole himself.

He had, besides Octavia, two other wives: Poppaea Sabina, whose father had borne the office of quaestor, and who had been married before to a Roman knight: and, after her, Statilia Messalina, great-grand-daughter of Taurus who was twice consul, and received the honour of a triumph. To obtain possession of her, he put to death her husband, Atticus Vestinus, who was then consul. He soon became disgusted with Octavia, and ceased from having any intercourse with her; and being censured by his friends for it, he replied, "She ought to be satisfied with having the rank and appendages of his wife." Soon afterwards, he made several attempts, but in vain, to strangle her, and then divorced her for barrenness. But the people, disapproving of the divorce, and making severe comments upon it, he also banished her. At last he put her to death, upon a charge of adultery, so impudent and false, that, when all those who were put to the torture positively denied their knowledge of it, he suborned his pedagogue, Anicetus, to affirm, that he had secretly intrigued with and debauched her.

He married Poppaea twelve days after the divorce of Octavia, and entertained a great affection for her; but, nevertheless, killed her with a kick which he gave her when she was big with child, and in bad health, only because she found fault with him for returning late from driving his chariot. He had by her a daughter, Claudia Augusta, who died an infant. There was no person at all connected with him who escaped his deadly and unjust cruelty. Under pretence of her being engaged in a plot against him, he put to death Antonia, Claudius's daughter, who refused to marry him after the death of Poppaea. In the same way, he destroyed all who were allied to him either by blood or marriage; amongst whom was young Aulus Plautinus. He first compelled him to submit to his unnatural lust, and then ordered him to be executed, crying out, "Let my mother bestow her kisses on my successor thus defiled;" pretending that he had been his mothers paramour, and by her encouraged to aspire to the empire. His step-son, Rufinus Crispinus, Poppaea's son, though a minor, he ordered to be drowned in the sea, while he was fishing, by his own slaves, because he was reported to act frequently amongst his play-fellows the part of a general or an emperor. He banished Tuscus, his nurse's son, for presuming, when he was procurator of Egypt, to wash in the baths which had been constructed in expectation of his own coming. Seneca, his preceptor, he forced to kill himself, though, upon his desiring leave to retire, and offering to surrender his estate, he solemnly swore, "that there was no foundation for his suspicions, and that he would perish himself sooner than hurt him." Having promised Burrhus, the pretorian prefect, a remedy for a swelling in his throat, he sent him poison. Some old rich freedmen of Claudius, who had formerly not only promoted his adoption, but were also instrumental to his advancement to the empire, and had been his governors, he took off by poison given them in their meat or drink.

Nor did he proceed with less cruelty against those who were not of his family. A blazing star, which is vulgarly supposed to portend destruction to kings and princes, appeared above the horizon several nights successively. He felt great anxiety on account of this phenomenon, and being informed by one Babilus, an astrologer, that princes were used to expiate such omens by the sacrifice of illustrious persons, and so avert the danger foreboded to their own persons, by bringing it on the heads of their chief men, he resolved on the destruction of the principal nobility in Rome. He was the more encouraged to this, because he had some plausible pretence for carrying it into execution, from the discovery of two conspiracies against him; the former and more dangerous of which was that formed by Piso, and discovered at Rome; the other was that of Vinicius, at Beneventum. The conspirators were brought to their trials loaded with triple fetters. Some ingenuously confessed the charge; others avowed that they thought the design against his life an act of favour for which he was obliged to them, as it was impossible in any other way than by death to relieve a person rendered infamous by crimes of the greatest enormity. The children of those who had been condemned, were banished the city, and afterwards either poisoned or starved to death. It is asserted that some of them, with their tutors, and the slaves who carried their satchels, were all poisoned together at one dinner; and others not suffered to seek their daily bread.

From this period he butchered, without distinction or quarter, all whom his caprice suggested as objects for his cruelty; and upon the most frivolous pretences. To mention only a few: Salvidienus Orfitus was accused of letting out three taverns attached to his house in the Forum to some cities for the use of their deputies at Rome. The charge against Cassius Longinus, a lawyer who had lost his sight, was, that he kept amongst the busts of his ancestors that of Caius Cassius, who was concerned in the death of Julius Caesar. The only charge objected against Paetus Thrasea was, that he had a melancholy cast of features, and looked like a school-master. He allowed but one hour to those whom he obliged to kill themselves; and, to prevent delay, he sent them physicians "to cure them immediately, if they lingered beyond that time;" for so he called bleeding them to death. There was at that time an Egyptian of a most voracious appetite, who would digest raw flesh, or any thing else that was given him. It was credibly reported, that the emperor was extremely desirous of furnishing him with living men to tear and devour. Being elated with his great success in the perpetration of crimes, he declared, "that no prince before himself ever knew the extent of his power." He threw out strong intimations that he would not even spare the senators who survived, but would entirely extirpate that order, and put the provinces and armies into the hands of the Roman knights and his own freedmen. It is certain that he never gave or vouchsafed to allow any one the customary kiss, either on entering or departing, or even returned a salute. And at the inauguration of a work, the cut through the Isthmus,[18] he, with a loud voice, amidst the assembled multitude, uttered a prayer, that "the undertaking might prove fortunate for himself and the Roman people," without taking the smallest notice of the senate.

He spared, moreover, neither the people of Rome, nor the capital of his country. Somebody in conversation saying—

When I am dead let fire devour the world—

"Nay," said he, "let it be while I am living". And he acted accordingly: for, pretending to be disgusted with the old buildings, and the narrow and winding streets, he set the city on fire so openly, that many of consular rank caught his own household servants on their property with tow, and torches in their hands, but durst not meddle with them. There being near his Golden House some granaries, the site of which he exceedingly coveted, they were battered as if with machines of war, and set on fire, the walls being built of stone. During six days and seven nights this terrible devastation continued, the people being obliged to fly to the tombs and monuments for lodging and shelter. Meanwhile, a vast number of stately buildings, the houses of generals celebrated in former times, and even then still decorated with the spoils of war, were laid in ashes; as well as the temples of the gods, which had been vowed and dedicated by the kings of Rome, and afterwards in the Punic and Gallic wars: in short, everything that was remarkable and worthy to be seen which time had spared. This fire he beheld from a tower in the house of Mecaenas, and "being greatly delighted," as he said, "with the beautiful effects of the conflagration," he sung a poem on the ruin of Troy, in the tragic dress he used on the stage. To turn this calamity to his own advantage by plunder and rapine, he promised to remove the bodies of those who had perished in the fire, and clear the rubbish at his own expense; suffering no one to meddle with the remains of their property. But he not only received, but exacted contributions on account of the loss, until he had exhausted the means both of the provinces and private persons.

Translated by Alexander Thomson and T. Forester.

LUCIAN

c. AD 120 - 180

Probably born at Samosata in Syria, Lucian is one of the most brilliant minds in antiquity. After studying rhetoric and philosophy, he employed his talents as a litigant, teacher, and lecturer. He traveled often in Asia Minor, Italy, Greece, and Gaul. He eventually settled in Egypt, where he obtained a post in the Roman administration. He probably died there around AD 180.

Lucian was a prolific writer: The ancients attributed no less than 86 works to him. He practiced all literary genres, often writing them as parodies. His experience as a rhetor and sophist induced him to compose stylistic exercises, encomiums (as, for example, his well-known praises for the fly and for astrology), polemics, and letters (an especially popular activity in this period). His work closely reflects earlier Hellenistic sensibilities and in addition is strongly influenced by the novel, new comedy, and mime. His True Story *is a parody of the epic adventure novel. Profoundly shaped by cynic philosophy, he threw himself into the satire of religious ideas, mythological tales, and, above all, human vanity. He introduced a new type of dialogue that broke with the serious tone of platonic discourse.*

Lucian was a rationalist and a cynic, who mocked those beliefs of his times riddled with superstition and ignorance. His work exposes that which his contemporary intellectuals considered humorous, and it remains a powerful remedy against self-importance.

Voyage to the Moon

Lucian, *True Story* 1-26

Lucian's True Story *is a story in which nothing is true. It is a brazen caricature of the adventure novels popular at the time. Further, it is an exuberant parody of the great classical works of Greek literature. In this fantastic tale of a trip to the moon and of a war between the Moon and the Sun, one recognizes Lucian's tunnel-vision treatment of the heroic adventures of Homer's Ulysses, Herodotus' descriptions of fabulous peoples and animals, and the glorious battle tales of Thucydides and Xenophon.*

"For I now make the only true statement you are to expect—that I am a liar. This confession is, I consider, a full defence against all imputations. My subject is, then, what I have neither seen, experienced, nor been told, what neither exists nor could conceivably do so. I humbly solicit my readers' incredulity."

Athletes and physical trainers do not limit their attention to the questions of perfect condition and exercise; they say there is a time for relaxation also—which indeed they represent as the most important element in training. I hold it equally true for literary men that after severe study they should unbend the intellect, if it is to come perfectly efficient to its next task.

The rest they want will best be found in a course of literature which does not offer entertainment pure and simple, depending on mere wit or felicity, but is also capable of stirring an educated curiosity—in a way which I hope will be exemplified in the following pages. They are intended to have an attraction independent of any originality of subject, any happiness of general design, any verisimilitude in the piling up of fictions. This attraction is in the veiled reference underlying all the details of my narrative; they parody the cock-and-bull stories of ancient poets, historians, and philosophers; I have only refrained from adding a key because I could rely upon you to recognize as you read.

Ctesias, son of Ctesiochus of Cnidus, in his work on India and its characteristics, gives details for which he had neither the evidence of his eyes nor of hearsay. Iambulus's *Oceanica* is full of marvels; the whole thing is a manifest fiction, but at the same time pleasant reading. Many other writers have adopted the same plan, professing to relate their own travels, and describing monstrous beasts, savages, and strange ways of life. The fount and inspiration of their humour is the Homeric

Odysseus, entertaining Alcinous's court with his prisoned winds, his men one-eyed or wild or cannibal, his beasts with many heads, and his metamorphosed comrades; the Phaeacians were simple folk, and he fooled them to the top of their bent.

When I come across a writer of this sort, I do not much mind his lying; the practice is much too well established for that, even with professed philosophers; I am only surprised at his expecting to escape detection. Now I am myself vain enough to cherish the hope of bequeathing something to posterity; I see no reason for resigning my right to that inventive freedom which others enjoy; and, as I have no truth to put on record, having lived a very humdrum life, I fall back on falsehood—but falsehood of a more consistent variety; for I now make the only true statement you are to expect—that I am a liar. This confession is, I consider, a full defence against all imputations. My subject is, then, what I have neither seen, experienced, nor been told, what neither exists nor could conceivably do so. I humbly solicit my readers' incredulity.

Starting on a certain date from the Pillars of Heracles, I sailed with a fair wind into the Atlantic. The motives of my voyage were a certain intellectual restlessness, a passion for novelty, a curiosity about the limits of the ocean and the peoples who might dwell beyond it. This being my design, I provisioned and watered my ship on a generous scale. My crew amounted to fifty, all men whose interests, as well as their years, corresponded with my own. I had further provided a good supply of arms, secured the best navigator to be had for money, and had the ship—a sloop—specially strengthened for a long and arduous voyage.

For a day and a night we were carried quietly along by the breeze, with land still in sight. But with the next day's dawn the wind rose to a gale, with a heavy sea and a dark sky; we found ourselves unable to take in sail. We surrendered ourselves to the elements, let her run, and were storm-driven for more than eleven weeks. On the eightieth day the sun came out quite suddenly, and we found ourselves close to a lofty wooded island, round which the waves were murmuring gently, the sea having almost fallen by this time. We brought her to land, disembarked, and after our long tossing lay a considerable time idle on shore; we at last made a start, however, and leaving thirty of our number to guard the ship I took the other twenty on a tour of inspection.

We had advanced half a mile inland through woods, when we came upon a brazen pillar, inscribed in Greek characters—which however were worn and dim—'Heracles and Dionysus reached this point.' Not far off were two footprints on rock; one might have been an acre in area, the other being smaller; and I conjecture that the latter was Dionysus's, and the other Heracles's; we did obeisance, and proceeded. Before we had gone far, we found ourselves on a river which ran wine; it was very like Chian;[1] the stream full and copious, even navigable in parts. This evidence of Dionysus's sojourn was enough to convince us that the inscription on the pillar was authentic. Resolving to find the source, I followed the river up, and discovered, instead of a fountain, a number of huge vines covered with grapes; from the root of each there issued a trickle of perfectly clear wine, the joining of which made the river. It was well stocked with great fish, resembling wine both in colour and taste; catching and eating some, we at once found ourselves intoxicated; and indeed when opened the fish were full of wine-lees; presently it occurred to us to mix them with ordinary water fish, thus diluting the strength of our spirituous food.

We now crossed the river by a ford, and came to some vines of a most extraordinary kind. Out of the ground came a thick well-grown stem; but the upper part was a woman, complete from the loins upward. They were like our painters' representations of Daphne in the act of turning into a tree just as Apollo overtakes her. From the finger-tips sprang vine twigs, all loaded with grapes; the hair of their heads was tendrils, leaves, and grape-clusters. They greeted us and welcomed our approach, talking Lydian, Indian, and Greek, most of them the last. They went so far as to kiss us on the mouth; and whoever was kissed staggered like a drunken man. But they would not permit us to pluck their fruit, meeting the attempt with cries of pain. Some of them made further amorous advances; and two of my comrades who yielded to these solicitations found it impossible to extricate themselves again from their embraces; the man became one plant with the vine, striking root beside it; his fingers turned to vine twigs, the tendrils were all round him, and embryo grape-clusters were already visible on him.

We left them there and hurried back to the ship, where we told our tale, including our friends' experiment in viticulture. Then after taking some casks ashore and filling them with wine and water we bivouacked near the beach, and next morning set sail before a gentle breeze. But about midday, when we were out of sight of the island, a waterspout suddenly came upon us, which swept the ship round and up to a height of some three hundred and fifty miles above the earth. She did not fall back into the sea, but was suspended aloft, and at the same time carried along by a wind which struck and filled the sails.

For a whole week we pursued our airy course, and on the eighth day descried land; it was an island with air for sea, glistening, spherical, and bathed in light. We reached it, cast anchor, and landed; inspection soon showed that it was inhabited and cultivated. In the daytime nothing could be discerned outside of it; but night revealed many neighbouring islands, some larger and some smaller than ours; there was also another land below us containing cities, rivers, seas, forests, and mountains; and this we concluded to be our Earth.

We were intending to continue our voyage, when we were discovered and detained by the Horse-vultures, as they are called. These are men mounted on huge vultures, which they ride like horses; the great birds have ordinarily three heads. It will give you some idea of their size if I state that each of their quill-feathers is longer and thicker than the mast of a large merchantman. This corps is charged with the duty of patrolling the land, and bringing any strangers it may find to the king; this was what was now done with us. The king surveyed us, and, forming his conclusions from our dress, 'Strangers,' said he, 'you are Greeks, are you not?' we assented. 'And how did you traverse this vast space of air?' In answer we gave a full account of ourselves, to which he at once replied with his own history. It seemed he too was a mortal, named Endymion, who had been conveyed up from our Earth in his sleep, and after his arrival had become king of the country;[2] this was, he told us, what we knew on our Earth as the moon. He bade us be of good cheer and entertain no apprehensions; all our needs should be supplied.

'And if I am victorious,' he added, 'in the campaign which I am now commencing against the inhabitants of the Sun, I promise you an extremely pleasant life at my court.' We asked about the enemy, and the quarrel. 'Phaethon,' he replied, 'king of the Sun (which is inhabited, like the Moon), has long been at war with us.[3] The occasion was this: I wished at one time to collect the poorest of my subjects and send them as a colony to Lucifer,[4] which is uninhabited. Phaethon took umbrage at this, met the emigrants half way with a troop of Horse-ants, and forbade them to proceed. On that occasion, being in inferior force, we were worsted and had to retreat; but I now intend to take the offensive and send my colony. I shall be glad if you will participate; I will provide your equipment and mount you on vultures from the royal coops; the expedition starts to-morrow.' I expressed our readiness to do his pleasure.

That day we were entertained by the king; in the morning we took our place in the ranks as soon as we were up, our scouts having announced the approach of the enemy. Our army numbered 100,000 (exclusive of camp-followers, engineers, infantry, and allies), the Horse-vultures amounting to 80,000, and the remaining 20,000 being mounted on Salad-wings. These latter are also enormous birds, fledged with various herbs, and with quill-feathers resembling lettuce leaves. Next these were the Millet- throwers and the Garlic-men. Endymion had also a contingent from the North of 30,000 Flea-archers and 50,000 Wind-coursers. The former have their name from the great fleas, each of the bulk of a dozen elephants, which they ride. The Wind-coursers are infantry, moving through the air without wings; they effect this by so girding their shirts, which reach to the ankle, that they hold the wind like a sail and propel their wearers ship-fashion. These troops are usually employed as skirmishers. 70,000 Ostrich-slingers and 50,000 Horse-cranes were said to be on their way from the stars over Cappadocia. But as they failed to arrive I did not actually see them; and a description from hearsay I am not prepared to give, as the marvels related of them put some strain on belief.

Such was Endymion's force. They were all armed alike; their helmets were made of beans, which grow there of great size and hardness; the breastplates were of overlapping lupine-husks sewn together, these husks being as tough as horn; as to shields and swords, they were of the Greek type.

When the time came, the array was as follows: on the right were the Horse-vultures, and the King with the elite of his forces, including ourselves. The Salad-wings held the left, and in the center were the various allies. The infantry were in round numbers 60,000,000; they were enabled to fall in thus: there are in the Moon great numbers of gigantic spiders, considerably larger than an average Aegean island; these were instructed to stretch webs across from the Moon to Lucifer; as soon as the work was done, the King drew up his infantry on this artificial plain, entrusting the command to Nightbat, son of Fairweather, with two lieutenants.

On the enemy's side, Phaethon occupied the left with his Horse-ants; they are great winged animals resembling our ants except in size; but the largest of them would measure a couple of acres. The fighting was done not only by their riders; they used their horns also; their numbers were stated at 50,000. On their right was about an equal force of Sky-gnats—archers mounted on great gnats; and next them the Sky-pirouetters, light-armed infantry only, but of some military value; they slung monstrous radishes at long range, a wound from which was almost immediately fatal, turning to gangrene at once; they were supposed to anoint their missiles with mallow juice. Next came the Stalk-fungi, 10,000 heavy-armed troops for close quarters; the explanation of their name is that their shields are mushrooms, and their spears asparagus stalks. Their neighbours were the Dog-acorns, Phaethon's contingent from Sirius. These were 5,000 in number, dog-faced men fighting on winged acorns. It was reported that Phaethon too was disappointed of the slingers whom he had summoned from the Milky Way, and of the Cloud-centaurs. These latter, however, arrived, most unfortunately for us, after the battle was decided; the slingers failed altogether, and are said to have felt the resentment of Phaethon, who wasted their territory with fire. Such was the force brought by the enemy.

As soon as the standards were raised and the asses on both sides (their trumpeters) had brayed, the engagement commenced. The Sunite left at once broke without awaiting the onset of the Horse-vultures, and we pursued, slaying them. On the other hand, their right had the better of our left, the Sky-gnats pressing on right up to our infantry. When these joined in, however, they turned and fled, chiefly owing to the moral effect of our success on the other flank. The rout became decisive, great numbers were taken and slain, and blood flowed in great quantities on to the clouds, staining them as red as we see them at sunset; much of it also dropped earthwards, and suggested to me that it was possibly some ancient event of the same kind which persuaded Homer that Zeus had rained blood at the death of Sarpedon.[5]

Relinquishing the pursuit, we set up two trophies, one for the infantry engagement on the spiders' webs, and one on the clouds for the air- battle. It was while we were thus engaged that our scouts announced the approach of the Cloud-centaurs, whom Phaethon had expected in time for the battle. They were indeed close upon us, and a strange sight, being compounded of winged horses and men; the human part, from the middle upwards, was as tall as the Colossus of Rhodes, and the equine the size of a large merchantman. Their number I cannot bring myself to write down, for fear of exciting incredulity. They were commanded by Sagittarius. Finding their friends defeated, they sent a messenger after Phaethon to bring him back, and, themselves in perfect order, charged the disarrayed Moonites, who had left their ranks and were scattered in pursuit or pillage; they routed the whole of them, chased the King home, and killed the greater part of his birds; they tore up the trophies, and overran the woven plain; I myself was taken, with two of my comrades. Phaethon now arrived, and trophies were erected on the enemy's part. We were taken off to the Sun the same day, our hands tied behind with a piece of the cobweb.

They decided not to lay siege to the city; but after their return they constructed a wall across the intervening space, cutting off the Sun's rays from the Moon. This wall was double, and built of clouds; the consequence was total eclipse of the Moon, which experienced a continuous night. This severity forced Endymion to negotiate. He entreated that the wall might be taken down, and his kingdom released from this life of darkness; he offered to pay tribute, conclude an alliance, abstain from hostilities in future, and give hostages for these engagements. The Sunites held two assemblies on the question, in the first of which they refused all concessions; on the second day, however, they relented, and peace was concluded on the following terms.

Articles of peace between the Sunites and their allies of the one part, and the Moonites and their allies of the other part.

1. The Sunites shall demolish the party-wall, shall make no further incursion into the

Moon, and shall hold their captives to ransom at a fixed rate.

2. The Moonites shall restore to the other stars their autonomy, shall not bear arms against the Sunites, and shall conclude with them a mutual defensive alliance.

3. The King of the Moonites shall pay to the King of the Sunites, annually, a tribute of ten thousand jars of dew, and give ten thousand hostages of his subjects.

4. The high contracting parties shall found the colony of Lucifer in common, and shall permit persons of any other nationality to join the same.

5. These articles shall be engraved on a pillar of electrum, which shall be set up on the border in mid-air.

Sworn to on behalf of the Sun by Firebrace, Heaton, and Flashman; and on behalf of the Moon by Nightwell, Monday, and Shimmer.

Peace concluded, the removal of the wall and restoration of captives at once followed. As we reached the Moon, we were met and welcomed by our comrades and King Endymion, all weeping for joy. The King wished us to remain and take part in founding the colony, and, women not existing in the Moon, offered me his son in marriage. I refused, asking that we might be sent down to the sea again; and finding that he could not prevail, he entertained us for a week, and then sent us on our way.

I am now to put on record the novelties and singularities which attracted my notice during our stay in the Moon. When a man becomes old, he does not die, but dissolves in smoke into the air. There is one universal diet; they light a fire, and in the embers roast frogs, great numbers of which are always flying in the air; they then sit round as at table, snuffing up the fumes which rise and serve them for food; their drink is air compressed in a cup till it gives off a moisture resembling dew. Beauty with them consists in a bald head and hairless body; a good crop of hair is an abomination. On the comets, as I was told by some of their inhabitants who were there on a visit, this is reversed. They have beards, however, just above the knee; no toe-nails, and but one toe on each foot. They are all tailed, the tail being a large cabbage of an evergreen kind, which does not break if they fall upon it.

Their mucus is a pungent honey; and after hard work or exercise they sweat milk all over, which a drop or two of the honey curdles into cheese. The oil which they make from onions is very rich, and as fragrant as balsam. They have an abundance of water-producing vines, the stones of which resemble hailstones; and my own belief is that it is the shaking of these vines by hurricanes, and the consequent bursting of the grapes, that results in our hailstorms. They use the belly as a pouch in which to keep necessaries, being able to open and shut it. It contains no intestines or liver, only a soft hairy lining; their young, indeed, creep into it for protection from cold. The clothing of the wealthy is soft glass, and of the poor, woven brass; the land is very rich in brass, which they work like wool after steeping it in water. It is with some hesitation that I describe their eyes, the thing being incredible enough to bring doubt upon my veracity. But the fact is that these organs are removable; any one can take out his eyes and do without till he wants them; then he has merely to put them in; I have known many cases of people losing their own and borrowing at need; and some—the rich, naturally—keep a large stock. Their ears are plane-leaves, except with the breed raised from acorns; theirs being of wood.

Another marvel I saw in the palace. There is a large mirror suspended over a well of no great depth; any one going down the well can hear every word spoken on our Earth; and if he looks at the mirror, he sees every city and nation as plainly as though he were standing close above each. The time I was there, I surveyed my own people and the whole of my native country; whether they saw me also, I cannot say for certain. Any one who doubts the truth of this statement has only to go there himself, to be assured of my veracity.

Translated by H. W. Fowler and F. G. Fowler.

MARCUS AURELIUS

AD 121 - 180

Marcus Aurelius was born at Rome in AD 121. He benefited from Emperor Hadrian's protection after the death of his father. On Hadrian's order in AD 138, the young Marcus was adopted by the successor of Hadrian, Antoninus Pius. He married Antoninus' daughter in AD 145, became emperor in 161, and immediately shared power with his adoptive half-brother, Lucius Aurelius Verus. His reign suffered all kinds of hardships—military, political, and personal. He succeeded, however, in strengthening the imperial authority and in maintaining a sound financial and judiciary administration. He died in AD 180 at Vindobona (Vienna) during a military campaign on the Danube and bequeathed the throne to his son Commodus.

This emperor was also a scholar and a philosopher. He studied Greek and Latin rhetoric. He read the Discourses *of Epictetus. In the twilight of his life (172-173), he drafted notes for his personal use that became known as the* Meditations *(also titled* To Myself*). They follow the maxim of the freedman Epictetus: Meditate and write each day on the distinction between that which is one's and that which is not one's; between that which is possible for oneself and that which is not possible for oneself. The* Meditations *is not an intimate journal but an effort to put into practice the spiritual exercises codified by the Stoics. It is a reflection on how one should live in accordance with nature (that is to say, with a universal, human, and individual purpose).*

As Hume adroitly observes, Marcus Aurelius, the last great representative of imperial Stoicism, was "a man of action and virtue." Montesquieu remarks on the emperor's sense of obligation and duty, his lack of complaisance vis-à-vis himself, and his resolve: "When one watches the spectacle of one's own life, one has a better opinion of oneself because one has a better opinion of men."

Autobiography of a Stoic

Marcus Aurelius, *Meditations* 1

In the first book of the Meditations, *Marcus Aurelius reflects on the many gifts that he received from his parents, professors, masters, friends, and the gods. In one respect, it is an autobiography, a collection of reflections that Marcus Aurelius, following the Stoic precept, made strictly for himself without any intention of publishing them. In all likelihood, a friend or family member saved his corpus of philosophical exercises at his death. It survived. In the* Meditations, *one discovers the great simplicity and spiritual strength of an emperor and the Stoic philosophy that helped him lead an empire heavily steeped in military campaigns—among others, against the Germans—and challenged by natural disasters.*

"From my mother, I learned piety and beneficence, and abstinence, not only from evil deeds, but even from evil thoughts."

From my grandfather Verus I learned good morals and the government of my temper.

From the reputation and remembrance of my father, modesty and a manly character.

From my mother, piety and beneficence, and abstinence, not only from evil deeds, but even from evil thoughts; and further, simplicity in my way of living, far removed from the habits of the rich.

From my great-grandfather, not to have frequented public schools, and to have had good teachers at home, and to know that on such things a man should spend liberally.

From my governor, to be neither of the green nor of the blue party at the games in the Circus, nor a partisan either of the Parmularius or the Scutarius at the gladiators' fights; from him too I learned endurance of labor, and to want little, and to work with my own hands, and not to meddle with other people's affairs, and not to be ready to listen to slander.

From Diognetus, not to busy myself about trifling things, and not to give credit to what was said by miracle-workers and jugglers about incantations and the driving away of daemons and such things; and not to breed quails for fighting, nor to give myself up passionately to such things; and to endure freedom of speech; and to have become intimate with philosophy; and to have been a hearer, first of Bacchius, then of Tandasis and Marcianus; and to have written dialogues in my youth; and to have desired a plank bed and skin, and whatever else of the kind belongs to the Grecian discipline.

From Rusticus I received the impression that my character required improvement and discipline; and from him I learned not to be led astray to sophistic emulation, nor to writing on speculative matters, nor to delivering little hortatory orations, nor to showing myself off as a man who practices much discipline, or does benevolent acts in order to make a display; and to abstain from rhetoric, and poetry, and fine writing; and not to walk about in the house in my outdoor dress, nor to do other things of the kind; and to write my letters with simplicity, like the letter which Rusticus wrote from Sinuessa to my mother; and with respect to those who have offended me by words, or done me wrong, to be easily disposed to be pacified and reconciled, as soon as they have shown a readiness to be reconciled; and to read carefully, and not to be satisfied with a superficial understanding of a book; nor hastily to give my assent to those who talk overmuch; and I am indebted to him for being acquainted with the discourses of Epictetus, which he communicated to me out of his own collection.

From Apollonius I learned freedom of will and undeviating steadiness of purpose; and to look to nothing else, not even for a moment, except to reason; and to be always the same, in sharp pains, on the occasion of the loss of a child, and in long illness; and to see clearly in a living example that the same man can be both most resolute and yielding, and not peevish in giving his instruction; and to have had before my eyes a man who clearly considered his experience and his skill in expounding philosophical principles as the smallest of his merits; and from him I learned how to receive from friends what are esteemed favors, without being either humbled by them or letting them pass unnoticed.

From Sextus, a benevolent disposition, and the example of a family governed in a fatherly manner, and the idea of living conformably to nature; and gravity without affectation, and to look carefully after the interests of friends, and to tolerate ignorant persons, and those who form opinions without consideration. He had the power of readily accommodating himself to all, so that intercourse with him was more agreeable than any flattery; and at the same time he was most highly venerated by those who associated with him; and he had the faculty both of discovering and ordering, in an intelligent and methodical way, the principles necessary for life; and he never showed anger or any other passion, but was entirely free from passion, and also most affectionate; and he could express approbation without noisy display, and he possessed much knowledge without ostentation.

From Alexander the grammarian, to refrain from fault-finding, and not in a reproachful way to chide those who uttered any barbarous or solecistic or strange-sounding expression; but dexterously to introduce the very expression which ought to have been used, and in the way of answer or giving confirmation, or joining in an inquiry about the thing itself, not about the word, or by some other fit suggestion.

From Fronto I learned to observe what envy and duplicity and hypocrisy are in a tyrant, and that generally those among us who are called Patricians are rather deficient in paternal affection.

From Alexander the Platonic, not frequently nor without necessity to say to any one, or to write in a letter, that I have no leisure; nor continually to excuse the neglect of duties required by our relation to those with whom we live, by alleging urgent occupations.

From Catulus, not to be indifferent when a friend finds fault, even if he should find fault without reason, but to try to restore him to his usual disposition; and to be ready to speak well of teachers, as it is reported of Domitius and Athenodotus; and to love my children truly.

From my brother Severus, to love my kin, and to love truth, and to love justice; and through him I learned to know Thrasea, Helvidius, Cato, Dion, Brutus;[1] and from him I received the idea of a polity in which there is the same law for all, a polity administered with regard to equal rights and equal freedom of speech, and the idea of a kingly government which respects most of all the freedom of the governed; I learned from him also consistency and undeviating steadiness in my regard for philosophy; and a disposition to do good, and to give to others readily, and to cherish good hopes, and to believe that I am loved by my friends; and in him I observed no concealment of his opinions with respect to those whom he condemned, and that his friends had no need to conjecture what he wished or did not wish, but it was quite plain.

From Maximus I learned self-government, and not to be led aside by anything; and cheerfulness in all circumstances, as well as in illness; and a just admixture in the moral character of sweetness and dignity, and to do what was set before me without complaining. I observed that everybody believed that he thought as he spoke, and that in all that he did he never had any bad intention; and he never showed amazement and surprise, and was never in a hurry, and never put off doing a thing, nor was perplexed nor dejected, nor did he ever laugh to disguise his vexation, nor, on the other hand, was he ever passionate or suspicious. He was accustomed to do acts of beneficence, and was ready to forgive, and was free from all falsehood; and he presented the appearance of a man who could not be diverted from right, rather than of a man who had been improved. I observed, too, that no man could ever think that he was despised by Maximus, or ever venture to think himself a better man. He had also the art of being humorous in an agreeable way.

In my father I observed mildness of temper, and unchangeable resolution in the things which he had determined after due deliberation; and no vain-glory in those things which men call honors; and a love of labor and perseverance; and a readiness to listen to those who had anything to propose for the common weal; and undeviating firmness in giving to every man according to his deserts; and a knowledge derived from experience of the occasions for vigorous action and for remission. And I observed that he had overcome all passion for boys; and he considered himself no more than any other citizen; and he released his friends from all obligation to sup with him or to attend him of necessity when he went abroad, and those who had failed to accompany him, by reason of any urgent circumstances, always found him the same. I observed, too, his habit of careful inquiry in all matters of deliberation, and his persistency, and that he never stopped his investigation through being satisfied with appearances which first present themselves; and that his disposition was to keep his friends, and not to be soon tired of them, nor yet to be extravagant in his affection; and to be satisfied on all occasions, and cheerful; and to foresee things a long way off, and to provide for the smallest without display; and to check immediately popular applause and all flattery; and to be ever watchful over the things which were necessary for the administration of the empire, and to be a good manager of the expenditure, and patiently to endure the blame which he got for such conduct; and he was neither superstitious with respect to the gods, nor did he court men by gifts or by trying to please them, or by flattering the populace; but he showed sobriety in all things and firmness, and never any mean thoughts or action, nor love of novelty. And the things which conduce in any way to the commodity of life, and of which fortune gives an abundant supply, he used without arrogance and without excusing himself; so that when he had them, he enjoyed them without affectation, and when he had them not, he did not want them. No one could ever say of him that he was either a sophist or a [home-bred] flippant slave or a pedant; but every one acknowledged him to be a man ripe, perfect, above flattery, able to manage his own and other men's affairs. Besides this, he honored those who were true philosophers, and he did not reproach those who pretended to be philosophers, nor yet was he easily led by them. He was also easy in conversation, and he made himself agreeable without any offensive affectation. He took a reasonable care of his body's health, not as one who was greatly attached to life, nor out of regard to personal appearance, nor yet in a careless way, but so that through his own attention he very seldom stood in need of the physician's art or of medicine or external applications. He was most ready to give without envy to those who possessed any particular faculty, such as that of eloquence or knowledge of the law or of morals, or of anything else; and he gave them his help, that each might enjoy reputation according to his deserts; and he always acted conformably to the institutions of his country, without showing any affectation of doing so. Further, he was not fond of change nor unsteady, but he loved to stay in the same places, and to employ himself about the same things; and after his paroxysms of headache he came immediately fresh and vigorous to his usual occupations. His secrets were not many, but very few and very rare, and these only about public matters; and he showed prudence and economy in the exhibition of the public spectacles and the construction of public buildings, his donations to the people, and in such things, for he was a man who looked to what ought to be done, not to the reputation which is got by a man's acts. He did not take the bath at unseasonable hours; he was not fond of building houses, nor curious about what he ate, nor about the texture and color of his clothes, nor about the beauty of his slaves. His dress came from Lorium, his villa on the coast, and from Lanuvium generally. We know how he behaved to the toll-collector at Tusculum who asked his pardon; and such was all his behavior. There was in him nothing harsh, nor implacable, nor violent, nor, as one may say, anything carried to the sweating point; but he examined all things severally, as if he had abundance of time, and without confusion, in an orderly way, vigorously and consistently. And that might be applied to him which is recorded of Socrates, that he was able both to abstain from, and to enjoy, those things which many are too weak to abstain from, and cannot enjoy without excess. But to be strong enough both to bear the one and to be sober in the other is the mark of a man who has a perfect and invincible soul, such as he showed in the illness of Maximus.

To the gods I am indebted for having good grandfathers, good parents, a good sister, good teachers, good associates, good kinsmen and friends, nearly everything good. Further, I owe it to the gods that I was not hurried into any offence against any of them, though I had a disposition which, if opportunity had offered, might have led me to do something of this kind; but, through their favor, there never was such a concurrence of circumstances as put me to the trial. Further, I am thankful to the gods that I was not longer brought up with my grandfather's concubine, and that I preserved the flower of my youth, and that I did not make proof of my virility before the proper season, but even deferred the time; that I was subjected to a ruler and a father who was able to take away all pride from me, and to bring me to the knowledge that it is possible for a man to live in a palace without wanting either guards or embroidered dresses, or torches and statues, and such-like show; but that it is in such a man's power to bring himself very near to the fashion of a private person, without being for this reason either meaner in thought, or more remiss in action, with respect to the things which must be done for the public interest in a manner that befits a ruler. I thank the gods for giving me such a brother, who was able by his moral character to rouse me to vigilance over myself, and who at the same time pleased me by his respect and affection; that my children have not been stupid nor deformed in body; that I did not make more proficiency in rhetoric, poetry, and the other studies, in which I should perhaps have been completely engaged, if I had seen that I was making progress in them; that I made haste to place those who brought me up in the station of honor, which they seemed to desire, without putting them off with hope of my doing it some other time after, because they were then still young; that I knew Apollonius, Rusticus, Maximus; that I received clear and frequent impressions about living according to nature, and what kind of a life that is, so that, so far as depended on the gods, and their gifts, and help, and inspirations, nothing hindered me from forthwith living according to nature, though I still fall short of it through my own fault, and through not observing the admonitions of the gods, and, I may almost say, their direct instructions; that my body has held out so long in such a kind of life; that I never touched either Benedicta or Theodotus, and that, after having fallen into amatory passions, I was cured, and though I was often out of humor with Rusticus, I never did anything of which I had occasion to repent; that, though it was my mother's fate to die young, she spent the last years of her life with me; that, whenever I wished to help any man in his need, or on any other occasion, I was never told that I had not the means of doing it; and that to myself the same necessity never happened, to receive anything from another; that I have such a wife, so obedient, and so affectionate, and so simple; that I had abundance of good masters for my children; and that remedies have been shown to me by dreams against blood-spitting and giddiness, and by the oracle at Caieta;[2] and that, when I had an inclination to philosophy, I did not fall into the hands of any sophist, and that I did not waste my time on writers [of histories], or in the resolution of syllogisms, or occupy myself about the investigation of appearances in the heavens; for all these things require the help of the gods and fortune.

Translated by George Long.

Notes

Homer

1 The Myrmidons were a people inhabiting Thessaly in northern Greece.
2 That is, an enormous amount of gold, approximately 182 kg (400 lb).
3 Echetus was a legendary king of Epirus, a region in northern Greece. He was the classic example of a cruel tyrant who tortures and kills.

Hesiod

1 It was common for the poets to invoke the Muses for inspiration. The Muses were born in Pieria, near Mount Olympus in northern Greece, where their father Zeus resides.

Aeschylus

1 Typhon—a monster and the son of Earth and Tartarus—had one hundred dragons' heads instead of fingers. He wounded Zeus and took him to a cave in Cilicia (South Turkey). Zeus eventually defeated him and buried him under Mount Etna in Italy.

Pindar

1 In this context, Pisa is the district in Greece (not the city in Italy) where Olympia was located.
2 Amphiaraus was one of the seven Argive chiefs who besieged Thebes. The earth swallowed him with his chariot, horses, and charioteer.
3 Phyntis was Agesias' charioteer.
4 That is, Diagoras won the games of Olympia (the Alpheus, the largest river of the Peloponnesus, flows past Olympia) and of Delphi (Castalia is a spring on Mount Parnassus that dominates Delphi).
5 The goddess Athena.
6 Lachesis is one of the three Moirai or goddesses of Destiny. It is up to her to intervene when lots are drawn.
7 The highest mountain on the island of Rhodes, where Zeus had a temple.
8 The daughter of Epaphus is Libya who gave her name to the land where Cyrene would be founded.
9 Battus, the son of Polymnestus, asked the priestess of Delphi how to cure his stuttering.
10 The Amphictyons were responsible for the sanctuary of Delphi. Mynian is another name for Argonaut. Aeolus was the great-grandfather of Jason, the leader of the Argonauts.
11 The Centaur Cheiron.

12 Phrixus and Helle were the children of Athamas who was the brother of Cretheus and of Salmoneus. Their mother was Nephele. Their persecutor was their mother-in-law Ino.
13 That is, Heracles, the son of Zeus and Alcmene, and Castor and Pollux, the sons of Zeus and Leto. Heracles, Castor, and Pollux participated in the expedition of the Argonauts.
14 The Lemnian women massacred their husbands who deserted them because of their vile smell. Euphemus seduced one of them, Malache, and fathered a son who would become the ancestor of Battus.
15 The island of Thera (modern Santorini), the southernmost of the Cycladic group.

Sophocles

1 Oedipus is the son of Labdacus, who is the son of Polydorus. Cadmus, who founded Thebes and was the son of the Phoenician Agenor, was Polydorus' father.
2 Loxias is another name for Apollo, the god of divination.
3 The Labdacidae are the descendents of Labdacus: Laius (murdered by his own son Oedipus), Oedipus, Polynices (killed by his brother Eteocles), and Antigone (sentenced to death for burying her brother Polynices).
4 Prometheus was enchained for giving fire to mankind. See Hesiod's *Works and Days* and *Prometheus Bound* in this volume.
5 Persephassa, or Persephone, is the queen of the underworld.

Euripides

1 The Symplegades are the "Clashing Rocks" on the Bosphorus that Medea had to pass while sailing with Jason from Chalcis on the Black Sea to Greece.
2 Medea killed her brother Absyrtus at their father's home before embarking on the Argo ship.
3 Scylla is a monster—part woman and part dog—ambushed in the straight of Messina south of the Tyrrhenian (or Tuscan) Sea. She devours anything that passes within her reach.
4 Calchas, the seer who foretold that the Greek fleet would not be able to sail to Troy unless Iphigenia was sacrificed to the goddess Artemis.
5 Achilles, Iphigenia's fiancé, was the son of the Nereid Thetis.
6 Pylades was engaged to Orestes' sister, Electra.
7 Apollo.
8 To ensure they recognize one another, Iphigenia and Orestes retrace their family history. Atreus, the son of Pelops and the grandfather of both Iphigenia and of Orestes, owned a ram with a golden fleece that was to designate him as the king of Mycenae. However, his wife Aerope stole the ram and gave it to her brother-in-law, Thyestes, who became king. Displeased, Zeus decided that another

portent would decide upon the king: the sun was to turn away from its course, which it did, definitively securing the throne for Atreus. Atreus had a son, Agamemnon, who married Clytemnestra, the daughter of Tyndarus, and fathered Iphigenia, Orestes, and Electra.

Herodotus

1 Town in the eastern part of the Nile Delta.
2 Osiris was the god of embalming.
3 Small island near Eretria. Hippias helps the Persians in the battle against Athens.
4 Another name for the Persians.
5 Commander of the army.
6 The Athenians Harmodius and Aristogeiton were considered heroes because they tried to put an end to Hippias' tyranny. They were honored with bronze statues.
7 Noble Athenian family suspected of conspiring with the Persian invaders.

Thucydides

1 Hellen is the son of the "Greek Noah," Deucalion. Deucalion and his wife Pyrrha were the only survivors of the universal flood, thanks to an ark that he built following Prometheus' advice.
2 The Pelasgians are a mythical people who settled in Greece long before the Greeks arrived.
3 In this passage, Thucydides provides us a quick lesson on the circumstances that led up to the Trojan War. The suitors of the beautiful Helen had promised her father, Tyndarus, to help him in case she were ever in danger. When the Trojan Paris raped her, the suitors chose Agamemnon as their chief and embarked on an expedition to get her back. So began the Trojan War and Agamemnon's epic adventures. According to Thucydides, however, Agamemnon's power preceded the War. He was the grandson of a wealthy immigrant from Asia Minor, Pelops, who secured power in the "Peloponnesus." Agamemnon inherited power after several members of his family died, including Chrysippus, Eurysteus, and Atreus.
4 Philoctetes was one of Helen's suitors. This is the reason he joined the expedition against Troy.

Aristophanes

1 The Unjust Discourse survives either by begging or by winning trials with sophisms. Telephus was Hercules' son. Achilles wounded him in the thigh and the injury would not heal. Following the advice of an oracle, he departed Mysia (not far from Troy in Asia Minor) and traveled to Greece dressed in rags as a beggar. He offered to show the Greeks the road to Troy, but only if they would heal him. Achilles healed the wound and Telephus guided the Greeks to Troy. Pandeletus was a professional informer who was always trying to win trials in order to make money.

2 Phrynis of Mytilene was a player of cithara (cf. today's "guitar") and won the prize at the Panathenaic festival in 456/5 BC.

3 The Buphonia was a very ancient festival celebrated at Athens in honor of Zeus "Polieus," the "Protector of the City"; bulls were sacrificed, thus the name Buphonia. Until Medic times high-ranking Athenians put their hair up and secured it with a hairpin in the shape of a cicada. Cecides was an ancient dithyrambic poet. In the time of Aristophanes, the Medic Wars had already been over for more than 50 years.

4 The Panathenaea was a festival celebrated every year to honor Athena. Every four years it was celebrated with special pomp: the Great Panathenaea. Religious processions, athletic competitions, and horse races were all part of the event.

5 Hippocrates, Pericles' nephew, had three sons whom the comic playwrights ridiculed for their stupidity.

6 Peleus resisted Hippolyte's advances. She was angered by his behavior and, for revenge, accused him of trying to seduce her. The gods nonetheless awarded Peleus for his chastity by marrying him off to the goddess Thetis. He would father Achilles with her.

7 That is, the chorus women have followed the complete curriculum of any respectable Athenian. The Arrephoroi are the four girls chosen to weave Athena's dress, or *peplos*. The Bears are the girls consecrated to Artemis at the festival of the Brauronia celebrated every five years at Brauron in Attica. During the processions the Canephoroi carried the baskets in which the ritual objects were hidden.

8 In 513 BC, the partisans of the tyrants and their opponents waged war at Lipsydrion in Attica. The opponents of the tyranny were defeated. The siege took place 100 years before Aristophanes himself writes: the chorus elders could not possibly have attended the battle and brag for no reason.

9 Queen of Caria (Turkey). She built a fleet and went to the aid of Xerxes during his expedition against the Greeks in 480 BC.

10 Allusion to the fable of Aesop, *The Eagle and the Beetle*. In order to take revenge on the eagle that ate its offspring, the beetle breaks its eggs. The moral is: even the weak can find a way to take revenge upon the strong.

11 Myronides and Phormio were two valiant Athenian warriors who fought in the Peloponnesian War.

12 Spring located above the Cave of Pan where the statue of Aphrodite was bathed every year. After the seduction, all one needed to do was to bathe in the spring to be purified.

13 Heracles was famous for his gluttony. The comic poets often represent him starving and exasperated by his host's inability to provide him with food quickly enough.

14 Nickname of the keeper of a brothel.

Plato

1 Three famous examples of devotion: toward a spouse, a friend, and one's native country. Admetus obtained permission from the gods not to die on the day fixed by Destiny if he could find somebody to die in his place; his wife Alcestis accepted to give her life for him. Achilles knew he would die if he returned to the battlefield in order to avenge his friend Patroclus. The mythical king of Athens, Codrus, from whom Plato's family claimed to herald, sacrificed his life for the victory of the city.

2 Lycurgus is the father of the laws in Sparta, just as Solon is in Athens. Plato had a great admiration for Solon, one of his ancestors.

3 Fifty stadiums are approximately 9 km (5.5 miles).

4 Tyrrhenia refers to Etruria (or Tuscany) in Italy.

5 The temple was colossal: 177 meters (582 ft) by 86.5 (281 ft). It was far larger than the temple of Artemis at Ephesus, one of the seven wonders of the ancient world, that measured 115 meters by 55. Legend has it that the temple of Artemis at Ephesus was destroyed by fire on Alexander's day of birth, on 20 July 356 BC.

6 The Eleven were in charge of the prisons and executions in Athens.

Xenophon

1 The Lydians had pierced ears.

Aristotle

1 Philosopher from Acragas, in Sicily, in the 5th century BC.

2 Tragic poet active about the middle of the 4th or 5th century BC.

3 Nomic and Dithyrambic poetry were performed at religious festivals, the latter specifically at events honoring the god Dionysus.

Demosthenes

1 Athens led the Greeks from the end of the Persian Wars through the close of the Peloponnesian War in 404 BC.

Plautus

1 The slaves who work in chains in the countryside.

Cicero

1 Gaius Fannius, Manius Curius, and Tiberius Coruncanius were great men and friends living in the first quarter of the 3rd century BC. Fannius and Curius fought against Pyrrhus, while Coruncanius struggled against the Etruscans.

2 Aemilius Paulus won the Third Macedonian War at Pydna in 168 BC by defeating King Perseus. The ancients considered Cato the Censor (first half of

the 2nd century BC) as a model of integrity and incorruptibility. Gallus was a military tribune in the war against Perseus. Scipio Aemilianus, the son of Aemilius Paulus, won the third Punic War and destroyed Carthage in 146 BC. Philus was a philhellene, a well-read orator, and a fan of astronomy.

3 The Romans considered Ennius (239-169 BC) the father of Latin poetry. He wrote tragedies, comedies, epigrams, and a versified history of Rome, the *Annals*.

4 Empedocles, born c. 485 BC.

5 Gaius Fabricius, a consul in 282 and 278 BC, refused the gifts offered by Pyrrhus, the king of Epirus in northern Greece. Manius Curius Dentatus was a friend of Fabricius. He was a consul in 290 BC and defeated Pyrrhus and the Italic people of the Samnites.

6 Three examples of tyrannical power the Romans despised and dreaded. The Romans favored the Republic where power is split between magistracies. Tarquinius was the last king of Rome; Brutus expelled him in 509 BC and installed the Republic. Spurius Cassius and Spurius Maelius were both suspected of aspiring to tyranny; they were murdered in 486 and 439 BC, respectively.

7 The Romans waged war with Pyrrhus, the king of Epirus, from 282 to 272 BC, and with the Carthaginian general Hannibal from 219 to 201 BC.

Caesar

1 The first town one reaches after crossing the border of Cisalpine Gaul. Thus, Caesar is in Italy with his army.

2 An agrarian law passed by Caesar in 59 BC for Pompey's veterans. Caesar's complete name is Gaius Julius Caesar, thus the term "Julian" law.

Lucretius

1 According to Lucretius all matter is composed of atoms. He criticizes the philosophers who differ in opinion: Heraclitus hypothesizes that everything is made of fire, Anaximenes of air, Thales of water, Pherecydes of earth, Oenopides of Chios of air and fire, and Xenophanes of Colophon of earth and water. Lucretius then refutes Empedocles of Acragas, whose genius he still greatly admires. Acragas (modern Agrigento) is located in Sicily, hence the allusions to the triangular-shaped island, to the Etna, and to Charybdis, a sea-monster lurking along the Sicilian side of the Strait of Messina.

Sallust

1 The Allobroges are a Gallic tribe whose deputies helped Cicero gather evidence against Catiline.

2 Allusion to the Civil War between Marius and Sylla that ended in the latter's victory in 82 BC. Sylla executed many of his opponents, including Damasippus, one of Marius' most violent supporters.

3 Marcus Tullius Cicero.

4 The Samnites were a war-like people of Central Italy that the Romans defeated only at the end of three long and costly wars (343-290 BC). The Etrurians (or Etruscans) were the most powerful inhabitants of Italy before the Roman expansion.

5 The two Gracchi brothers, Tiberius and Caius, attempted to implement agrarian reform in Rome but were both brutally murdered. Marcus Fulvius was a supporter of Tiberius Sempronius Gracchus, who also shared his fate.

Virgil

1 Conon of Samos, a mathematician and astronomer of the 3rd century BC.

2 Thalia, the Muse of comedy and of pastoral poetry. Virgil means that he renounced epic poetry and devoted himself to pastoral poetry following Apollo's advice.

3 After the flood, the two sole survivors landed on Mount Parnassus. In order to repopulate the earth, they picked up stones (the "bones of their mother"), and threw them over their shoulders. The stones tossed by Pyrrha turned into women, and those thrown by her husband, Deucalion, turned into men.

4 Saturn's reign refers to the Golden Age. Prometheus stole fire for mankind. To punish him, Zeus had his liver devoured by an eagle in the Caucasus.

5 Hylas accompanied Heracles on the expedition of the Argonauts. When they anchored in Mysia, he went to draw water, but the Nymphs of the place fell in love with him and kept him. Heracles called for Hylas, but in vain. Since then, the Mysians continue to search for Hylas every year by ritually calling his name.

6 Pasiphae, the wife of Minos, fell in love with a white bull, seduced it, and gave birth to the Minotaur (a monster that is half man and half bull and is locked inside the Labyrinth). The Dicte is a mountain and Gortyn a city in Crete.

7 The daughters of Proetus, whom Hera made insane, believed that they had been changed to heifers. They escaped into the countryside and wandered to and fro.

8 Atalanta, defeated at the race because she stopped to pick up the apples of the Hesperides.

9 The Heliades changed into poplars at the death of their brother, Phaethon.

10 Permessus is a river in Boeotia, the source of which is Mount Helicon, the sojourn of the Muses. Aonia is an ancient name for Boeotia.

11 Hesiod, born at Ascra in Boeotia.

12 Grynium was located on the west coast of Asia Minor and had a sacred grove, which served as the sanctuary of Apollo.

13 Dulichium is an island near Ithaca, Ulysses' homeland. According to the *Odyssey*, Ulysses' ship battles Scylla, a marine monster lurking in the Strait of Messina.

14 Tereus married Procne, but fell in love with her sister, Philomela. He raped her

and cut her tongue out to prevent her from speaking. The two sisters got their revenge and escaped Tereus' reprisal by turning into birds—the former into a nightingale and the latter into a swallow. Tereus was changed into a hoopoe.

15 Varus was one of those responsible for confiscating land in North Italy and redistributing it to war veterans. It seems as though Varus helped Virgil keep his land or obtain compensation for it.

16 Varius, a friend of Virgil, was considered the master of epic poetry in Rome until the appearance of the *Aeneid*. After Virgil's death, Augustus requested him and Tucca to edit the *Aeneid*. Cinna was an epic poet famous for his *Zmyrna*, a miniature epic.

17 Galatea, the sea-goddess loved by the Cyclops.

18 A comet shot across the sky shortly after the assassination of Julius Caesar who claimed to descend from Dione's daughter, Venus.

19 Two examples of hallucinatory delirium provoked by the Eumenides (also called the Furies), the goddesses of vengeance. Pentheus was punished for refusing to acknowledge the cult of Dionysus (see the *Bacchae* of Euripides), and Orestes for killing his adulterous mother, Clytemnestra, to avenge his father, Agamemnon (see *Iphigenia among the Taurians* in this volume).

20 Laomedon was one of the first kings of Troy and was infamous for his perjuries. He refused to pay Apollo and Poseidon their promised salary for building the walls of the city. He also declined to give Hercules the divine horses guaranteed him if he freed Troy from the threatening sea-monster.

21 Aeneas was thought to be the son of Venus.

22 Allusion to a famous episode of the legend of the pious Aeneas that is often represented in art. After the fall of Troy, Aeneas fled carrying his elderly father on his back and his young son Ascanius in his arms. He also transported the Penates and the statue of Athena, the most sacred gods of Troy.

23 The Styx is one of the rivers of the underworld.

24 The king of Tyre, Pygmalion, ordered the assassination of Dido's husband to seize his treasures.

25 The three sisters Parcae personify Destiny and preside over the duration of every person's life. They are represented as spinners: while one sister spins a thread, another winds it, and the third cuts it when the corresponding life is terminated.

26 Theseus and his friend Pirithous descended into the underworld to conquer Persephone. They became prisoners and were tied to the Chair of Oblivion. Heracles managed to free Theseus, but Pirithous remained an eternal prisoner.

Horace

1 Fabius, just as Crispinus at the end of the satire, was a talkative Stoic philosopher and a bore.

2 Allusion to Clytemnestra, the daughter of Tyndarus, who killed her husband,

Agamemnon, when he returned from Troy.

3 Rumor had it that the Dacians, who settled the left bank of the Danube, were about to invade Italy.

4 The philosopher Pythagoras and his disciples did not eat beans.

5 The slaves bring the best wines from all over Italy and from the Greek island of Cos. Such wines are still much appreciated nowadays.

6 Allifae is a town in Samnium (Central Italy), where large earthenware mugs were manufactured.

7 Venafrum in Campania, where some of the finest olive oil was produced.

8 The ancestors of Maecenas, the patron and friend of Horace, had been the chiefs (referred to as "Lucumons") of the Etruscan city of Arretium.

9 The province of Africa (Libya) was one of the main suppliers of wheat for Rome and Italy.

10 In this passage, Horace's poetry is extremely erudite and is rich in historical and mythological allusions. Attalus III, the king of Pergamum in Turkey, bequeathed his kingdom and wealth to the Roman people in 133 BC. The Cypriotes conducted a lot of trade by sea. Their forests further provided wood for the construction of ships. Myrtos is an island surrounded by a reef south of Euboea in the Aegean Sea. The idea expressed here is that a wise man would rather plow his field than sail dangerous seas to acquire riches.

11 Icaros is an island in the Aegean Sea. Mount Massicus in northern Campania (northeast of Rome) was renowned for its superb wine.

12 Pythons' enemy is Apollo, a benevolent god when he plays the lyre or a formidable one when he draws his bow to spread illness and death.

13 Horace invites Maecenas to visit the Roman countryside. Tibur (modern Tivoli), Aesule, and Tusculum (founded by Ulysses' son, Telegonus, who accidentally killed his father) are three towns in the countryside surrounding Rome.

14 By referring to the constellations, Horace indicates the onset of the summer heat. The Ethiopian maiden is Andromeda whose father, Cepheus, became a constellation that rose on the 9th of July. Procyon, the smaller Dog Star, rose on the 25th of July, and the Lion on the 20th.

15 The names refer to the eastern extremities of Asia. The Bactrians represent the most remote parts of the kingdom of the Parthians in Iran. The Seres is an ancient name referring to the Chinese. The Tanais, today referred to as the Don, is a river in southern Russia.

Livy

1 Paphlagonia is a region of northern Asia Minor.

2 God of the livestock associated with Faunus or Pan.

3 The Druentia (or modern Durance) is one of the principal rivers descending from the southern slope of the French Alps in the direction of the Mediterranean.

Tibullus

1 Charon, the ferryman in the underworld for the dead.
2 The marble from Synnas in Phrygia was white; that of Taenarum, a promontory in Laconia, was black; and that of Carystus in Euboea, was green with undulations.
3 Juno Lucina, the patroness of marriage and childbirth.
4 Mountain on the Cycladic island of Delos where Apollo was born.
5 The Chimaera was a beast. It was part-lion,-snake, and -goat. Scylla was a sea-monster whose body was girded with dogs that guarded the Strait of Messina. Scythia was considered the barbaric country *par excellence*. The Syrtis were dangerous waters off the coast of North Africa.
6 Pentheus had refused to welcome the cult of Dionysus in Thebes (in central Greece). The god turned his mother insane and she tore him into pieces.
7 Catullus, the famous Roman lyric poet (84-54 BC).

Ovid

1 Nemesis had a famous temple at Rhamnus, a borough in Attica. She was asked to punish excesses and injustice.
2 The Naiads are the nymphs of the springs and the rivers, while the Dryads are the nymphs of the forests.
3 Pelops, the father of Pittheus, reigned in Phrygia (Western Asia Minor) before becoming the sovereign of the "Peloponnesus."
4 Thynos, a hero of Bithynia in Phrygia.

Lucan

1 The 13-year-old King Ptolemy XIII ordered the deportation of his sister, Cleopatra, from Egypt. He was supposed to share power with her. Cleopatra, who was about 20 years old at the time, took refuge in Syria. Caesar arranged for her to return to Egypt in secret: she hid in a sack used to transport mattresses and managed to be loaded onto a small boat to Alexandria.
2 The term Pellaean refers to Alexandria: Pella is the capital of Macedonia that is the home of Alexander the Great who founded the magnificent city of Alexandria, Egypt.
3 Helen of Sparta, the reason behind the Trojan War.
4 Canopus was a city located 19 km (12 miles) east of Alexandria. Pharus, originally an island, was joined to the Egyptian mainland by a mole constructed on the order of Alexander the Great. On Pharus stood the celebrated lighthouse that was one of the seven wonders of the ancient world. Here, "Caesar" refers to Augustus.
5 Allusion to the Battle of Actium in 31 BC, where Octavian defeated Mark Antony and became the master of Rome.

6 Caesar remained in Egypt for nine months in the middle of the Civil War. He had a son with Cleopatra, Caesarion, who became Ptolemy XV. Caesar already had a daughter, Julia, who married Pompey and died in childbirth in 54 BC.

7 The dynasty of the Lagidae, to which Cleopatra and her brother belonged, reigned in Egypt from 305 BC until its conquest by Octavian (Augustus) in 30 BC. The Roman statesman and general Mark Antony also had a long affair with Cleopatra, from which three children were born. Mark Antony and Cleopatra would marry in 37 BC.

8 Achilles was King Ptolemy's powerful general. Pothinus, the eunuch, was his tutor. They both conspired to kill Pompey. Caesar exposed the plot. Pothinus was put to death and Achillas escaped.

9 Juba, the king of the Numidians in North Africa, helped Cato and Scipio after the Battle of Pharsalus and was defeated by Caesar.

10 Fabricius, Curius, and Quinctius Cincinnatus were three Roman heroes always cited for their honesty, austerity, and modesty. Fabricius refused to be corrupted by Pyrrhus while negotiating the release of Roman prisoners. Pyrrhus was so impressed that he freed the prisoners without ransom. Curius Dentatus, in addition to definitively defeating Pyrrhus, rejected being bought by the Samnites, a neighboring people and an enemy of Rome. Quinctius Cincinnatus was a simple farmer, but of such moral virtue that the Romans asked him to accept power and save them from their enemy, the Aequians. Cincinnatus agreed to leave his plow, was victorious in battle, and returned to his farm.

11 A disciple of Plato and a Greek astronomer of the 4th century BC who improved the annual calendar; unfortunately it was not adopted by his contemporaries. It was Caesar who would install the new calendar in 45 BC. With Caesar discussing the subject in 48 BC, Lucan intends to represent the general as already caring for his future reforms early on.

12 Mercury.

13 The Pharaoh Sesostris, a half historical and half legendary figure, was believed to have sailed up the Nile until the Third Cataract and to have conquered vast lands on the three continents—Africa, Asia, and Europe—almost 2000 years before Lucan.

14 Brutus, one of the assassins of Caesar.

15 When he arrived in Egypt, Pompey was executed and his head later presented to Caesar. The rest of his corpse was burned on a pyre on the beach of Pelusium (to the east of the Nile Delta) where a tomb was constructed.

Petronius

1 Trimalchio boasts about nothing and exposes his ignorance. Opimius was a consul in 121 BC, a year that produced wines of exceptional quality. Since Trimachio's banquet happened well after 21 BC, it is impossible that the "century-old" wine he serves belongs to the 21 BC vintage.

2 Incubi are demons believed to emerge at night, land on the chests of people while they sleep, and give them horrible dreams. They wore a conical hat that they sometimes lost. Any person fortunate enough to find one of the hats acquired the power of discovering hidden treasures.

3 Aratus (3rd century BC) wrote books on astronomy that earned him immediate fame and had a significant impact on the discipline. His *Phaenomena*, originally written in Greek verses, was translated into Latin by Cicero and Germanicus, and later into Arabic. Hipparchus (2nd century BC) founded scientific astronomy and invented the plane astrolabe. He also wrote a commentary on Aratus. By comparison, Trimalchion is a far cry from Hipparchus or Aratus: his guests laud his "many" accomplishments tongue-in-cheek.

4 Here, the play on words involves the term "*liber*." In Latin, it means "free" while at the same time corresponding to Liber, the Roman counterpart of the Greek god Dionysus-Bacchus.

Plutarch

1 This is literary *topos*: the illustrious origins, whether divine or heroic, of the great leaders of the earth. Alexander counts among his ancestors Hercules, Aeacus (son of Zeus and judge in the underworld), and Achilles (Neoptolemus' father). Alexander himself was thought to be the son of Zeus.

2 Juno/Hera was the jealous spouse of Jupiter/Zeus who cheated on his wife with Olympias and fathered Alexander.

3 Phoenix and Peleus were the older mentor and father of Achilles, respectively.

4 That is, for an enormous amount of gold: 13 talents are the equivalent of about 340 kg (740 lb).

5 Onesicritus accompanied Alexander's admiral Nearchus on his exploration of the Indian Ocean and the Persian Gulf. He later wrote a fictional biography of Alexander.

6 Aristides, Themistocles, and Cimon: three of the greatest Athenian politicians of the 5th century BC.

7 The *Salaminia* was a ship used for official state business.

8 Ephialtes was an Athenian politician and leading opponent of Cimon.

9 The ancient Greeks did not travel by sea during the four months of winter.

10 The Parthenon was dedicated in 438 BC more than 500 years before Plutarch's time.

11 The Long Walls connected Athens to its harbor, the Piraeus.

12 This refers to the Athenian tyrant Pisistratus and his sons Hippias and Hipparchus.

13 Leocrates, Myronides, and Tolmides are famous generals.

Epictetus

1 Theory of the philosopher Heraclitus according to which everything is borne out of fire and everything returns to it.

2 Words of Antisthenes, the founder of the Cynic tradition and the friend of Socrates, to Cyrus who was the king of Persia in the 6th century BC.

3 The idea is that one must do everything to preserve one's serenity and peace of mind no matter what transpires, including the death of a friend. To illustrate this concept, Epictetus provides the example of the Homeric heroes Patroclus, Menelaus, Antilochus, and Automedon. Patroclus was tied to Achilles through a legendary friendship. When the Greeks found themselves in a critical situation, Patroclus wore Achilles' armor and massacred a significant number of Trojans. Menelaus fought by his side. Patroclus eventually was felled, and Antilochus—Achilles' best friend second only to Patroclus—was put in charge of informing Achilles about the death of Patroclus. After Achilles' death, his charioteer and companion in battle, Automedon, continued to serve his son, Pyrrhus-Neoptolemus.

Tacitus

1 It was believed that Asciburgum (modern Asberg, Germany) owed its name to the goatskin bottle (*askos* in Greek) containing the winds that Aeolus gave to Ulysses. Ulysses' companions opened the bottle and allowed the furious winds to escape, preventing the hero from returning to Ithaca. The town was likely an important trade center for amber in antiquity.

Suetonius

1 Juba I, the king of Numidia, sided with Scipio and the Pompeians against Caesar. Caesar defeated them at Thapsus on 6 April 46 BC.

2 Pharsalus is a city in Thessaly where Caesar defeated Pompey in 48 BC.

3 Q. Titurius Sabinus, a lieutenant of Caesar, was killed with most of his soldiers in an ambush set by Ambiorix.

4 Cynaegyrus, the brother of the tragic poet Aeschylus, was killed at the Battle of Marathon while trying to seize a Persian ship at the stern.

5 Hiempsal wanted to force Masintha to pay him ransom. Masintha came to Rome and pleaded his cause before the Senate. The Senate, however, agreed that Juba, Hiempsal's son, was right.

6 Marmurra was Caesar's minion showered with princely gifts.

7 Ilerda, a city in Catalonia, Spain. Afranius and Petreius were generals of Pompey.

8 The festival of the Sigillaria owes its name to the fact that statuettes (*sigilla*) were presented as gifts. It was held on the last day of the Saturnalia, a Roman-like carnival where the world functioned upside down. For example, the slaves generally did whatever they pleased, enjoyed some freedom, and dined before their masters.

9 Emperor Caligula.
10 Tiridates, the king of Armenia, whom Nero received lavishly in Rome in AD 66.
11 Canossa, a city in Apulia (South Italy), was renowned for its wool.
12 Inhabitants of Mauretania in Africa whose horses were greatly prized.
13 The Nundinae were the market days.
14 Emperor Claudius was Nero's adopted father.
15 Latin *morari* means "to sojourn" but, by lengthening the first syllable of the word, Nero formed a new word inspired by the Greek "*moros*" ("dull," "stupid," cf. English "moron").
16 Britannicus, the son of Emperor Claudius, should have succeeded him on the throne.
17 *Lex Iulia de sicariis*, a law passed by Julius Caesar that included an article about murder by poisoning.
18 The Isthmus of Corinth. Emperor Nero was the first to attempt an excavation of a canal through the Isthmus. Nero himself began the digging with a little golden pickaxe and put to work 6,000 Jewish prisoners sent from Judaea. Three months later, however, he died and the project was abandoned. It would not be until 1893 that the actual canal would be completed.

Lucian

1 That is, the wine of Chios, a Greek island in the northeastern Aegean, and one of the most appreciated wines in antiquity.
2 Legend has it that Endymion was a young shepherd of rare beauty with whom the Moon fell in love. At his request, the gods granted him eternal sleep and thereby his youth was preserved forever. Lucian imagines that Endymion was brought to the moon in his sleep and became its king.
3 Phaethon was the son of the Sun. His father permitted him to drive his chariot, but he drove too low and nearly set the earth ablaze. Next, he ventured too high in the sky and the stars complained. Zeus struck him down. Lucian turns Phaethon into the king of the sun.
4 Venus or the Morning Star.
5 Mockery directed at Homer. In the *Iliad,* when the gods decide that Sarpedon must die at Troy, his father Zeus sheds a rain of blood as a sign of mourning.

Marcus Aurelius

1 Thrasea and Helvidius are two "martyrs" to Stoicism: the former was forced by Nero to commit suicide in AD 66, while the latter was assassinated under Vespasian. Cato of Utica is the Stoic who committed suicide after being defeated by Caesar in 46 BC. Thrasea mentioned above wrote a biography of Cato. Dio is probably Dio of Syracuse whom Plutarch places in parallel with Brutus, Caesar's murderer.
2 Seaport in Campania that was probably the vacation residence of the imperial family.

Chronological Chart of the Greco-Roman World

Dates are approximate.

3000-1100 BC	Minoan civilization in Crete
1600-1100 BC	Mycenaean civilization in Greece
1450 BC	The Mycenaeans take over Crete
1184 BC	The Greeks conquer Troy
1100 BC	The Greeks begin settling the Aegean Islands and the coast of Asia Minor
814 BC	Founding of Carthage
800-480 BC	Archaic Period in Greece
776 BC	First Olympic Games
775-580 BC	The Greeks found colonies in Southern Italy and Sicily and on the Black Sea
753 BC	Founding of Rome
753-509 BC	Monarchy at Rome (seven kings)
600 BC	Coinage is invented in Lydia (Asia Minor)
509-27 BC	Roman Republic
490 BC	The Greeks defeat the Persians at Marathon
480 BC	The Persians sack Athens; the Greeks defeat the Persians at Salamis
480-323 BC	Classical Period in Greece
470-456 BC	Construction of the Temple of Zeus at Olympia

462-429 BC	Pericles leads Athens
461-446 BC	First Peloponnesian War between Athens and Corinth, ending in the Thirty Years Peace
447-432 BC	Construction of the Parthenon at Athens
431-404 BC	Second Peloponnesian War between Athens and Sparta, in which Athens is defeated
401 BC	Ten thousand Greek mercenaries support Cyrus against King Artaxerxes of Persia
399 BC	Socrates is sentenced to death
390 BC	The Gauls sack Rome
387 BC	Plato founds the Academy at Athens
359-338 BC	Philip of Macedon conquers Greece
336-323 BC	Alexander conquers the Persian Empire and founds Alexandria in Egypt
335 BC	Aristotle founds the Lyceum at Athens
334-264 BC	Rome conquers all of Italy south of the Po River
323-146 BC	Hellenistic Period in Greece
313 BC	Zeno of Citium founds the Stoic school at Athens
307 BC	Epicurus founds the Garden at Athens
290 BC	Founding of the Library at Alexandria
280-275 BC	King Pyrrhus of Epirus at war with the Romans; Pyrrhus is defeated
279 BC	The Gauls invade Greece

270 BC	Aristarchus of Samos proposes the heliocentric theory
265-211 BC	Archimedes active
264-241 BC	First Punic War between Rome and Carthage; Hamilcar is defeated
260-211 BC	Eratosthenes active; calculates the circumference of the earth
220-167 BC	The Romans conquer most of the inhabited world
218-201 BC	Second Punic War: Hannibal invades Italy and then is defeated near Zama in Africa
167 BC	The Romans put an end to the Macedonian kingdom
149-146 BC	Third Punic War, ending in the destruction of Carthage
146 BC	Rome destroys Corinth and achieves its conquest of Greece
112-105 BC	Rome at war with King Jugurtha of Numidia
88-31 BC	Civil Wars in Italy
73-71 BC	Slave revolt led by Spartacus
44 BC	Assassination of Caesar
30 BC	Egypt becomes a Roman province
27 BC-AD 476	Roman Empire
27 BC-AD 14	Principate of August, the first Roman emperor
AD 70	Destruction of the Temple of Jerusalem
AD 79	The eruption of Vesuvius destroys Pompeii and Herculaneum

AD 80	Inauguration of the Colosseum at Rome
AD 98-117	Greatest extent of the Roman Empire under Trajan
AD 212	Roman citizenship is granted to all inhabitants of the Empire
AD 293	Diocletian establishes the Tetrarchy: two emperors (each named "*Augustus*" and assisted by a "*Caesar*") rule the Roman Empire
AD 312	Christianity becomes the official religion of the Roman Empire
AD 324	Founding of Constantinople
AD 395	The Roman Empire is divided into western and eastern parts
AD 410	Alaric, king of the Visigoths, sacks Rome
AD 455	The Vandals sack Rome
AD 476	Romulus Augustulus is removed from the throne: end of the Western Roman Empire
AD 529	Emperor Justinian orders the closure of the Academy at Athens
AD 1453	Constantinople falls to the Turks: end of the Eastern Roman Empire

Select Greek Gods and Their Roman Equivalents

Greek/Latin Name	Domain	Attributes
Aphrodite/Venus	love, sex	doves, chariot drawn by doves
Apollo/Apollo	music, poetry, prophecy, medicine, sun	bow, lyre, laurel
Ares/Mars	violent and bloodstained war	weapons, armor
Artemis/Diana	hunting, childbirth, moon	bow, quiver, doe, crescent moon
Asclepius/Aesculapius	medicine	snake, snake(s) coiled around a staff
Athena/Minerva	intellect, education, scence, handicrafts, inteligent war	owl, helmet, spear, aegis, olive tree
Demeter/Ceres	earth, agriculture, corn	wheat, torches, snake
Dionysus/Bacchus	wine, theater, tragedy	panther, thyrsus, grapevine, ivy
Hades/Pluto	underworld, the dead	horn of plenty, scepter
Hephaistus/Vulcan	metalworking	cap, blacksmith's tools

Greek/Latin Name	Domain	Attributes
Hera/Juno	marriage, queen of the gods	scepter, diadem, peacock
Hermes/Mercury	trade, market, thieves, travelers, messenger of the gods	winged sandals and hat, caduceus
Poseidon/Neptune	sea, ocean, storms, springs, earthquakes	fish, trident, chariot drawn by sea-creatures
Zeus/Jupiter (or Jove)	sky, light, rain, king of the gods	scepter, thunderbolt, oak tree, eagle

Further Reading

Beard, Mary. *A Very Short Introduction to the Classics*. Oxford: Oxford University Press, 1995.

Boatwright, Mary Taliaferro, et al. *The Romans: From Village to Empire*. Oxford: Oxford University Press, 2004.

Collection des Universités de France ("*Budé Collection*"). Paris: Les Belles Lettres, 1920-present.

Conte, Gian Biagio. *Latin Literature: A History*. Transl. Joseph B. Solodow. Baltimore: Johns Hopkins University Press, 1999.

Hornblower, Simon, and Spawforth, Antony, eds. *The Oxford Classical Dictionary*, 3rd ed. Oxford: Oxford University Press, 2003.

Loeb Classical Library. Cambridge: Harvard University Press, 1911-present.

Pomeroy, Sarah, et al. *Ancient Greece: A Political, Social, and Cultural History*. Oxford: Oxford University Press, 1999.

Richard, Carl J. *The Founders and the Classics. Greece, Rome, and the American Enlightenment*. Cambridge: Harvard University Press, 1994.

Saïd, Suzanne. *A Short History of Greek Literature*. New York: Routledge, 1999.

Talbert, Richard J.A., ed. *Barrington Atlas of the Greek and Roman World*. Princeton: Princeton University Press, 2000.

www.ingramcontent.com/pod-product-compliance
Lightning Source LLC
Chambersburg PA
CBHW030523310726
48979CB00010B/1780/J
* 9 7 8 0 9 8 6 1 0 8 4 7 1 *